Contents

Table of statutes

vi

Table of cases

Preface

This is a book about people and the way in which they organise themselves to produce and distribute wealth. Its central focus is therefore upon business organisations, that is to say combinations of individuals whose common aim is to make profit. It is also concerned with the environment in which such organisations operate, and it seeks to show how far the business organisation adapts to economic, social and legal change, either through choice or force. In doing so the interrelationship between economic and social factors, and the creation of rules of law, becomes readily apparent. In the context of trade and commerce, legal development and growth as a consequence of economic expansion has been particularly marked. It can be seen for example in the developments that have taken place over the last three hundred years in company law. In much more recent times the influence of social policy as an economic factor has become increasingly significant. For example by legislating to achieve the aim of sexual equality in relation to the terms and conditions of employment for men and women, an economic cost has been imposed, which like any other, has been passed on to the ultimate consumer.

The functioning of an economy is not the product of a set of random forces combining to create a workable system. Nor does the existence of a body of rules of law derive from the inheritance of a perfect code based upon a set of ultimate truths. The existence of an identifiable economic system is owed to administrative machinery through which resources can be controlled and allocated, and a legal system can only come into being if there are institutions, such as a courts structure, to support it. Economic and legal systems are two of the characteristics which distinguish one state from another. In the governance of a state the existence of a strong economy is a prime requirement, for it guarantees political and social stability. By means of legislation in relation to economic policy a government can strive to ensure that such stability is maintained. Hence in considering the business organisation as an economic entity one is also led to considering the nature and role of government as a law maker and thus as an economic manipulator and catalyst. This is the story of a particular state, the United Kingdom, and of the relationships within that state between the state itself, the organisation and the individual.

Since this book is about people and the business organisations they have created to trade by, it is useful to outline the historical development of these organisations, for mere descriptions of modern business organisations do not explain why they possess their particular characteristics, or indeed why there are different forms of organisation at all. Furthermore an historical outline demonstrates how far the law has played an indispensable role in the development of commercial activity in this country.

The story really begins in early medieval times, when commercial activity, both export and domestic, was beginning to expand rapidly, particularly in the wool trade and the cloth industry.

In early medieval times a number of different types of associations were legally recognised. Among them were the merchant and craft guilds. These were organisations designed for the mutual protection of their members, which fixed wages and prices, and matters such as the relationship between the master and his apprentices. By obtaining a Royal Charter these guilds could obtain a monopoly over their trade or product. Their members were however one-man businesses, contributing their own capital, personally responsible for their own debts, and bound only to observe the rules of their own guild.

In contrast two types of organisation existed in which trading was carried out on a joint basis. The advantage of a joint trading venture is the pooling of resources and a sharing of profits, whereas the disadvantage is the liability of each trading partner for the actions of the co-partners, and unlimited liability for the debts of the organisation. In fact two variants of what is now the modern partnership were recognised. In one, the open partnership, each partner contributed money, goods or services to the organisation, was recognised by the courts as being an agent for co-traders, and was personally liable for partnership debts. In the other, the commenda, a financier or group of financiers would contribute capital to a trader, and would share in the profits made, although taking no part in the management of the business, or being responsible for any debts beyond their capital contribution. These early forms of trading illustrate a principal feature of all joint trading activity; a combination of the elements of financial risk, capital contribution and profit sharing balanced among the participating members.

As a response to the needs of merchants for speedy and simple procedures by which they could resolve disputes amongst themselves, courts, known as piepowder courts, began to appear at the fairs and markets which were the venues at which most mercantile transactions took place. The authority for holding such courts derived from Royal Charter. The law administered in them gave effect to the customs of trade upon which they based their dealings, and although in time these courts became obsolescent, by that time the law of the merchants (lex mercatoria) had become absorbed into the common law of England.

As overseas trade developed from the fourteenth century onwards a new type of organisation, the charter company, began to appear. These companies were an extension of the guild principle, and their main advantage to members was the trade monopoly which, like the merchants guilds, was granted to them under Royal Charter. Indeed the early charter companies were simply a modification of the merchants guilds. Members traded using their own stock and on their own account, under a common set of rules which governed their trade, hence they were 'regulated companies'.

The first joint stock company, in which the members traded using stock they contributed jointly, was the Muscovy Company, which received its charter in 1555. Many such companies followed. Originally trading consisted of a single venture, but gradually trading within these organisations became continuous. Because the stock was jointly contributed profits were shared in accordance with individual contributions. The charter company was recognised as a separate legal entity having full capacity and being obliged to act by deed under seal. The charter would often provide that the company could call upon its members to make contributions ('leviations') in order to meet its liabilities. The great advantage of obtaining a Royal Charter for a trading organisation lay in the monopoly of trade which the charter could grant, and the powers granted to the members over the territory in which they carried out their trade, powers for example to make by-laws.

These corporate bodies enjoyed certain advantages over other non-incorporated organisations such as partnerships. Not all these advantages were originally fully appreciated by members. A corporation, as a legal entity in its own right, enjoyed perpetual succession, could sue both outsiders and its own members, and conferred upon its members the benefit of limited liability, a development that was legally recognised long before the true commercial advantage to members became apparent.

During the seventeenth century the great monopolistic trading companies were in decline. Their monopolies were being seen as a restraint upon trade, their powers excessive and a usurpation of the role of the state in the government of overseas territories. As they declined so domestic trading companies began to expand, both corporate and non corporate. At the beginning of the eighteenth century a particularly dramatic increase in speculation and company flotations occured, culminating in the collapse of the South Sea Company (the 'South Sea Bubble'), a company which had attempted to acquire most of the National Debt, as a means of being able to raise very large sums upon which it could expand its trade. The theory of the company was that speculators would have confidence in contributing to a company which owned such an enormous interest-bearing loan, however the scheme collapsed, resulting in the passing of the Bubble Act of 1719. This prohibited trafficking in the charters of defunct companies, and prohibited unincorporated trading associations from creating transferable shares. The 1719 Act was repealed in 1825, by which time, as a consequence of it, unincorporated associations had expanded in considerable numbers. Although the passage of the Act of 1719 had the immediate effect of ensuring that such organisations restricted the transfer of shares, this gradual transfer of shares became more and more common.

During the nineteenth century modern English company law began to emerge as a result of legislative changes. The main developments that took place were:

Joint Stock Companies Registration and Regulation Act 1844, which introduced incorporation by registration in substitution for incorporation by Royal Charter or letters patent, and created the office of Registrar of Companies. In the case of companies inviting the public to subscribe for shares a prospectus had to be registered and the company's audited accounts filed with the Registrar for public inspection.

The Limited Liability Act 1855, which introduced the principle of limited liability for all registered companies.

The Joint Stock Companies Act 1856 introduced the requirement of a 'Memorandum of Association' and 'Articles of Association' as the documents regulating the company's affairs.

The Companies Act 1907, which introduced the private limited company.

The principal statutory rules regulating companies are now found in the provisions of the Companies Acts 1948 – 81. Companies registered under the Companies Act 1948 represent the most important form of business organisation in the United Kingdom. *An examination of the environment in which they operate, their objectives and the means available to achieve them is the fundamental task of this book.*

Acknowledgements

The Publishers wish to thank the following for permission to reproduce copyright material:

The Bank of England; The British Petroleum Company PLC; The Boots Company PLC; Cambridge University Press for a figure from S J Prais: *The Evolution of Giant Firms in Britain*; Central Statistical Office; Halifax Building Society; the Controller of Her Majesty's Stationery Office for Crown copyright material; Lloyds Bank PLC Limited; Macmillan, London and Basingstoke for L Hannah and J Kay: *Concentration in Modern Industry*; Oyez the Solicitors' Law Stationery Society Limited; Securicor Limited and the Society of Motor Manufacturers and Traders.

Foreword

This book has been written as a response to the need for a multi-disciplinary test to cover such BTEC Higher National level modules as the Business Environment. In providing a coverage of this module we hope that the text may be of value to students studying on professional courses and at foundation level on degree courses where it will give a detailed introduction to the economic, legal and governmental context within which the modern organisation operates.

Our aim in writing the text was to try and show how the environment which contains and regulates the functioning of all organisations is drawn from areas which have traditionally been regarded as discrete subject disciplines, but which in practice demonstrate a considerable measure of interrelationship. We have tried to present and explain the subject matter of the text as clearly and simply as possible, and as an aid to the understanding of principles and concepts, we have provided case studies at the end of a number of chapters, showing theoretical rules at work in a practical environment. These case studies provide stimulus material which may be used as a basis for integrated assignments. Additionally a glossary of terms is included to aid students in grasping the meaning of basic terminology.

PC
JE
TH
SW

1 The market

There are fools in every market; one asks too little, one asks too much.

Russian proverb

Introduction

The United Kingdom is a complex society which requires the interaction of millions of individuals and hundreds of thousands of organisations to provide it with the products and services which it needs to exist. The environment in which these individuals and organisations work has to be suitable to ensure that the nation makes the most efficient use of its resources – both natural and manufactured. It is in the interests of us all that society is able to create as much income and wealth as possible. This is clearly subject to certain constraints that exist within it such as the need for social justice, equality, and freedom of the individual.

The production and consumption of goods and services by and for society could be undertaken in an environment which was unrestricted by any government restraints. There have always been those who have promoted the idea of a completely free market as a desirable economic and political objective. For them, the freedom of individuals and organisations to enter into freely negotiated and agreed bargains is also sacrosanct. However, the society in which we live is not sufficiently ordered for us to be confident that the community, people or businesses within it will not become victims of those among us who are either unscrupulous or selfish enough to take advantage of the weak or the unwary. Increasingly, the State has become aware of the dangers which exist and so, through legislation passed by Parliament and the common law, it has sought over the centuries to establish a set of rules which attempt to regulate the workings of the business world. This regulatory trend has become more marked as the twentieth century has progressed. The business environment in the United Kingdom has evolved into an intricate and dynamic entity, involving the independent actions of a multiplicity of people undertaking a host of tasks.

1

The business environment

The three participant groups within the business environment are:

1 *Individuals* – acting as consumers of goods and services, as factors in the production of these through their labour and as the providers of capital to finance production.
2 *Business organisations* – primarily as suppliers of goods and services either at the manufacturing stage or in an intermediate role in the supply process such as distributors or retailers. Organisations are also consumers, not just of labour but also of a variety of goods required for production.
3 *The State* – with a variety of roles – as consumer of many goods and services, as employer of an increasing proportion of the workforce, as producer of many products and services required by society and finally as a regulator, through its law-making and law enforcement function, of the actions of private individuals and businesses.

It is necessary to attempt to assess what each of these participants seeks from the business environment and analyse how each influences its workings.

The individual

There are over fifty five million individuals in the United Kingdom. Each one has different needs, different abilities and different aspirations. Despite this wide diversity, they all have one thing in common – they are all consumers. They all need food to eat, clothes to wear and somewhere to live. These varying demands must be met by some form of production. If an individual has a unique type of need then perhaps it could be met by one single supplier. However, most individuals require goods and services which are relatively common with many other consumers and so a variety of producers may compete to meet their demands. This combination of many individual demands for a product subsumed into one overall demand is called *aggregate demand*, either for one product or in a wider sense for all goods and services required by society in general.

Individuals all try to maximise their own welfare. For some this may mean increasing their income and wealth so improving their standard of living. Others may prefer to raise the quality of their life by having greater leisure, living in a preferred part of the country or gaining satisfaction from helping others and yet receiving no material benefit for themselves. Whatever each person wishes as an individual, almost all would like the right to determine for themselves how they live, for whom they work and on what they spend their money – *the freedom of the individual*. But, if everyone could have all they desired and do anything they wished there would be inevitable conflicts. Unfortunately there are insufficient goods and services produced or which could be produced to meet everyone's wants. If society were to allow all to do whatever they wished, there would certainly be disputes between individuals. Also the acts of many of these individuals may not be beneficial to society as a whole. So, although the United Kingdom is considered to be one of the freest countries in the world, there are many limitations placed on economic, social and legal freedoms.

UK citizens are able to vote for whoever they wish and yet, if they live in a safe constituency dominated by a single political party, a vote for an opposing candidate is as good as a wasted vote. They have freedom of speech and yet this is regulated by the laws relating to obscenity and defamation. They can work for whoever they wish but only if the economic climate provides a wide variety of job opportunities. They can buy anything they desire, subject to limitations such as restrictions on the purchase of alcoholic drinks outside licencing hours, dangerous drugs prohibited by the law, or cigarettes if under sixteen years old. They have the freedom to earn as much as they can but the State will take tax from their earnings. Thus, in most aspects of individual behaviour the State places restrictions on freedom of action.

In reality, the measure of an individual's freedom is gauged by reference to the limitations on behaviour. To protect these residual freedoms and also carry out other functions the State maintains a legal system comprising such institutions as a court structure to administer the law. Individuals are allowed to own private goods which generally may not be taken from them either by other individuals or by the State. They are protected in their transactions for purchases of goods from other individuals or organisations. In most cases they cannot be dismissed from employment without good reason. These and many other individual freedoms are protected under the law. So the State has, through the law, introduced a series of checks and balances to restrict and also protect the freedom of the individual.

As well as acting as consumers, individuals have an important role to play in the business environment as part of the workforce. Most people work for one major reason – in order to earn sufficient income to be able to pay for the goods and services they desire. Few are in such an enviable position that they can work without monetary reward. An increasing proportion of the population are unable to find employment. For the majority of the adult population it is essential to find a job which combines sufficient income with some level of job satisfaction and also matches their talents and abilities. If an individual has particular skills which are in great demand he or she can expect to earn a higher reward than someone without such a talent. However, there are inequalities in the labour market – some individuals receive an income which is much greater than the benefit which their employer or society gains from their work. This may be due to their own shrewdness or because they have formed themselves into an association with others which has managed to force up the price of its members' labour, by restricting entry into that trade or profession, or by establishing such a powerful position that it can dictate wage rates. So the individual, at

3

least in the present state of technology, is an essential element in the productive process and it may be argued that the workforce is the country's most vital resource.

People working as individuals would only be capable of producing a limited range of goods or services. Much that modern society requires must be manufactured using a variety of skills that can rarely be found in one person. So people must work with one another in a co-ordinated manner if they are to increase their own welfare and that of society. This has led to the growth of organisations in which individual workers combine their talents in order to improve their mutual positions.

The business organisation

Business organisations are formed by producers in response to the demands of consumers. It has already been stated that consumers have a wide range of needs and this has led to the establishment of an extensive variety of producers of both goods and services. The consumers' main objective is to maximise their own welfare and satisfaction and it is assumed that business organisations have as their chief aim a *maximisation of their profit*. This is achieved by the production of goods and services as cheaply and efficiently as possible and by selling them for as high a return as the market allows. Business organisations seek to expand in order to raise potential profit levels. The assumption that all business organisations have as their sole objective the maximisation of profit is sometimes misconceived. There are many different types of organisations with a complex variety of objectives. Some organisations will seek maximum profit, others may be satisfied if the level of return is sufficient to allow them to survive in business. There are many businesses which will unscrupulously attempt to exploit the consumer to the utmost and yet there are also some producers who do have the consumers' interests at heart and act altruistically.

This complexity of organisational objectives and the behaviour which results from them will be considered in more detail in Chapters 3 and 4. However, it is sufficient to say that all types of business organisation include some element of risk either in their initial establishment or in their operation. This element of capital venture and the profits which could possibly accrue is the usual motive for the formation of any business. The entrepreneur is the person who recognises a business opportunity and either provides the initial capital input personally or persuades others to put up the money. The entrepreneur has also the responsibility of ensuring that the organisation functions efficiently and successfully. This is where the risk is involved. If the business is unsuccessful the individual's investment and also that of others may be lost. In order to achieve this required level of success, an organisation must attempt to take the greatest advantage of the opportunities which are available to it. The danger lies in the fact that it may take unfair advantage of consumers or other organisations in achieving its aim. It could also act in a manner which is detrimental to society.

The government does not wish to shackle the enterprise of organisations which, if fruitful, can benefit not only the organisation and its employees but also society as a whole. However, it is mindful of the need to regulate those practices which are undesirable and so it has established a body of law and an array of economic constraints by which it can control business organisations and encourage those activities which it regards as favourable. The government acts not just as watchdog, police officer and judge, but also as catalyst, supplier and financer of industry and commerce.

The State

Since the Norman Conquest, a central administrative body has been in existence which may be said to comprise the State. Over the centuries State institutions have developed, undertaking a law-making function (*Parliament*), an executive or administrative function (*the Government*), and a judicial or conflict-resolving function (*the Courts*). Initially however, the State saw its main task as the protection of society both from external and internal threat. This has now become just one facet of the modern-day State. The legal system which has evolved protects individuals and organisations both under the *criminal law* and also under the *civil law*, from commercial and economic threat and abuse. The fine balance between ensuring the freedom of individuals and promoting the greatest welfare for the rest of the community must be met.

As society and the economy has developed and become more complex and sophisticated, a legal system has evolved capable of reacting to changing demands. A legal framework has grown up in response to the actions of the business environment. Legislation is passed to regulate business practices seen by the government of the time as being unsatisfactory. People's inventiveness may permit them to evade the legal traps which the law has placed in their path and so the legislature and the judiciary must be sufficiently flexible to adapt to society's needs by improving and refining the law. Many practices which in the past were regarded as being unsatisfactory, may now be acceptable and other actions which had previously not ever been considered nor attempted may require legislation or judicial intervention to control them. Thus, economic development acts as a stimulant for the evolution of a sophisticated legal system and the corollary is also true in that changes in the law facilitate economic development. Such issues face all governments and the decisions reached are essentially *value judgements* based on the elected government's perceptions of how society should be structured.

The business environment forms the most diverse and most complex section of the economy and yet its basic fundamental aims are relatively

5

straightforward. It seeks to meet the varying requirements of individuals as consumers and also as members of society. However, the State is clearly much more than a controller of economic and business practice through a legal framework. It has grown to be the single biggest employer in the country, the biggest spender and one of the most important producers. These differing roles have come about for a variety of reasons which it would be beyond the scope of this book to consider in detail, but it is obvious that conflicts can and do arise between the various facets of the State's activities. State enterprise must be controlled by the law in the same way as private enterprise. The State as a supplier of goods and services is subject to the same contractual rules as private enterprise.

In attempting to improve the economic welfare of the population, the State has also intervened through economic means to stimulate the economy and to ensure a fair distribution of employment, income and wealth. It attempts to co-ordinate the dynamic and fluid economic situation that exists within the country and may adopt a variety of different means, both tried and untried, to achieve its objectives.

A major institution of the State is the *Government*, comprising the majority party in Parliament. The significance of this fact is that there is no guarantee of consistent State policies over time. The electoral see-saw will periodically change the political party in power which forms the Government and so radically alter not only the methods it uses to ensure its aims but also those aims themselves. One government's conception of freedom of the individual may differ considerably from that of another. For instance, a government may believe that the implementation of a rigid incomes policy is in the national interest although the consequence for an individual may be to limit the freedom to negotiate an equitable reward for his or her labours. Alternatively a different government may discard such a policy in favour of free collective bargaining.

The economic problem

The UK has economic resources or factors of production which it uses to produce the goods and services demanded by its consumers. These resources include all things which are available to produce goods and services, and are usually classified into *Land*, *Labour* and *Capital*. Land includes all natural resources, ie not only industrial and agricultural land but also minerals, forests, climate, etc. Labour resources encompass all human resources – people, their availability, skills and talents. Capital may be regarded as manufactured physical assets which are used in the production process. Examples would include plant, machinery, etc. Since land, labour and capital must be combined in the production process, a fourth factor, a system of *Organisation*, is necessary. This system is determined by the type of economic system existing in the country, ie private or State enterprise economies.

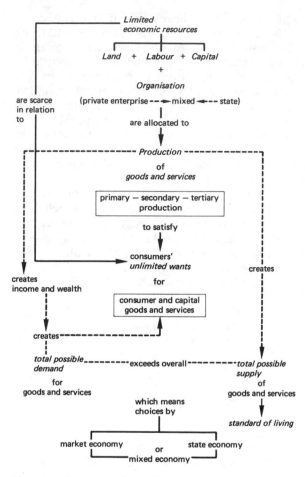

Fig 1.1   The economic problem

The economic resources described facilitate the production of goods and services for use or consumption by individuals in society. The consumer purchases a product or service because it satisfies a want or need. The consumer's objective is to maximise and increase satisfaction and it is this which produces the basic economic problem facing both individuals and societies. In reality, the wants of consumers for goods and services are unlimited, whereas the available resources to produce the goods and services are limited. Although production expands over time, consumers' demands also increase in response to the growing variety of goods and services available, so that no society however wealthy can satisfy its every requirement. This imbalance between scarce resources and unlimited wants means that a choice has to be made both by individuals and societies as to the goods and services to be produced, and whose wants will be satisfied or unsatisfied.

7

The problem of limited resources means that if one product is produced it is not possible to use the same resources for the production of something else. The cost to an individual or society of using resources to produce and consume one product is the opportunity foregone of producing and consuming the other. In practice it is usually a decision about more of one and less of the other rather than complete alternatives. This *opportunity cost* is one of the most fundamental concepts in society since it expresses the basic economic problem.

Arising from this economic problem, it is necessary for society to have evolved some system or mechanism to determine how these choices are to be made, and having made a choice to develop a framework of law by which the system is regulated.

Whatever economic system has evolved, one of its main policy objectives is the satisfaction of its consumers' wants. The level to which these wants are satisfied may be said to determine an individual's *standard of living*. A rising standard of living, as measured by the increasing level of consumption of goods and services, is probably a common objective of all individuals and governments worldwide. How far from this objective our world is at present is demonstrated in Table 1.1.

United States	£4600	Hungary	£2200
Canada	4200	Soviet Union	2150
Sweden	4000	Brazil	1500
West Germany	3900	Portugal	1500
France	3800	Mexico	1200
Switzerland	3750	South Korea	1050
Japan	3200	Egypt	450
United Kingdom	2900	India	300
East Germany	2400	China	290
Italy	2250	Kenya	250

Sources: World bank; up-dated to 1980 figures and converted to sterling by the authors.

Table 1.1   Per Capita GNPs 1980

The wide differences between countries can be explained in terms of income and wealth. The production process creates income for consumers in return for their contribution of labour or capital. This income is received in money by the individual, but actually represents a level of consumption over which the consumer has control. Income is in fact merely the return to the individual from a flow of goods and services produced by the economy over time. Current income to both an individual and the economy can be used for satisfying current wants by consumption of goods and services. Alternatively, some of current income may be converted into assets such as capital machinery, factories, etc. This allocation of production or income will reduce current consumption by individuals and depress their standard of living. But this capital

8

accumulation will enable more goods and services to be produced and consumed in the future. This is the economic choice in another guise — maximum current consumption or higher consumption in the future.

The continued activity of the economic system is one of accumulation of wealth represented by an increase in the physical stock of assets from past production. Western economies have a vast stock of wealth of many different kinds, eg industrial, social and individual. It is this combination of income and wealth which determines the standard of living achieved in the society, whatever economic system is adopted.

The allocation of resources — alternative systems

Basically there are two alternative economic systems which allocate the limited resources in the economy and provide answers to the questions of:

What goods and services shall be produced?
How shall the goods and services be produced?
For whom shall they be produced?

These decisions may be undertaken by a planning authority of the State as in the *Planned* or *Command* economies of the Communist Bloc. The Planning Authority allocates the economic resources to production and also determines how they are to be distributed. This extreme form of economic system is most apparent in the USSR and China. However, both these countries have sectors in which the market system plays some part, eg agriculture. The major defects in such an economy are mainly the result of having a large administrative bureaucracy making decisions about complex and changing economic factors. The relative insensitivity to consumer preferences in such economies, and the rigidities of planning have led the Communist economies to introduce a limited degree of private enterprise into their system in recent years.

The Western economies have generally adopted the *Market* or *Private/Free Enterprise* systems in which economic decisions are the result of the actions of individual consumers and producers acting through the process of demand and supply. Individual consumers seek to maximise their satisfaction by demanding that combination of goods and services which is best for them. These decisions are signalled by variations in price to the producers, who in seeking to maximise profits, produce those goods and services demanded by the consumers. In this way the decisions about production and distribution are the result of the aggregation of millions of individual decisions. The market economy is a simple but highly efficient means of solving the basic economic problem.

However, as with the planned economy, the market economy is subject to several defects which can result in inefficiencies and misallocation of resources. Broadly the defects may be categorised under three headings:

1 Failure to provide for the satisfaction of collective wants

The market system, in responding to individual wants, produces private goods/services very efficiently. But where wants are not individual but collective, the market is either not likely to provide the need at all, or at best, to make inadequate provision. These are *public goods* which, because they cannot be withheld from one individual without excluding them from all, must be supplied to the entire community. Unless it is possible to exclude individuals from consumption of such goods, a private producer will not supply them since the community overall cannot be forced to pay. Neither can the private producer exclude those who do not pay from consumption of that good or service. Another important characteristic of public goods is that consumption by one individual does not reduce the amount available for consumption by others. Public goods are characterised by two factors − *non-exclusion* and *non-competitive consumption* − although strictly this definition relates only to pure public goods. An example of this is the provision of external defence and internal law and order. Once one individual is protected, then all are protected. One person cannot choose to opt out because it is not possible to defend only those who are willing to pay. If provision of public goods is to be made it must come from the State, financed via collective taxation which is chargeable on all eligible under the law. In many Western economies this State provision has been taken further to cover areas such as health and education. Although these could be market supplied, such provision may result in economic or social inefficiencies. These public goods which are supplied by government mainly because of their collective consumption are classified as *social goods* while the second group − education, etc − are called *merit goods*.

2 Failure due to market structure

The perfect working of the market requires the existence of a competitive situation otherwise it is likely that the free working of the market will not produce the most efficient allocation of resources. A non-competitive situation may result, for example, in exploitation of the consumer in several ways. The behaviour of dominant organisations is examined in the next chapter, but obvious exploitation may exist in higher prices or unfair contractual terms dictated to the consumer by the supplier.

3 Failures inherent in the market mechanism

The most important failure results from the fact that the price system only takes account of *private costs* and *private benefits*. When private producers make a product and private consumers buy it, then the costs and benefits incurred by both relate only to them. There may be other costs or benefits to society which will not be taken into account by the free market. All or most economic activities create these social costs and benefits (*externalities*) but it is when divergence between private and social costs and benefits is significant that problems can result, eg the private costs to a producer of chemicals will not include the social costs which result from possible damage to the environment. Similarly, the private benefits to an individual consumer may be less than the overall social benefits, as with education and some aspects of health treatment. Where the private costs of an economic activity are less than the social costs, then the working of the market is likely to lead to either over production or over consumption. Conversely, activities which result in private benefits being less than social benefits will probably be under consumed in a market economy. Either way the best allocation of resources will not be achieved by the price mechanism alone.

A further problem inherent in a market economy is that the pattern of demand depends to a great extent upon the distribution of income and wealth. An unequal distribution of income and wealth within society will naturally produce a demand structure which does not necessarily reflect most of society's wants. Although this is a criticism of the income distribution rather than the price mechanism it is a powerful argument against a market economy in such circumstances, especially when a market economy may tend to reinforce such inequalities of income. Other criticisms which can be aimed at the market economy are that it can be unstable in terms of unemployment, inflation, etc. It is these criticisms of both planned and market systems which have resulted in the hybrid or *mixed economies* of the UK and Western Europe. Historically the UK developed as a market economy based upon the laissez-faire principles supported by the classical economists such as Adam Smith and others. (Although even Smith recognised and accepted the 'collective wants' failure.) The pattern of development was generally one of gradual State intervention in the economy to correct or remedy deficiencies which became apparent in the free market system. The position today is broadly one where the public sector accounts for an increasing proportion of production, the private sector providing the remaining balance.

The free market economy

The Western economies generally operate a free market system to solve the economic problem described earlier. It is through the interaction of demand and supply upon market prices that resource allocation is determined. The price of a product or service is simply the rate at which it can be exchanged for anything else or its value in terms of other things.

For example, in a barter economy with three goods, x, y and z, there are two basic problems to solve. First, the double coincidence of wants,

11

that is, each party to the exchange must want what the other has. (One has x and the other has y.) Secondly, a problem arises as to the respective values of x and y. This is easily solved by valuing x, y and z in terms of a common denominator 'p' or 'money', ie

$$x = 100p \qquad y = 50p \qquad z = 10p$$

Therefore the value or price of x is 100p or 2y, etc. Its price is its value or exchange rate in terms of y and z. This is the role of money acting as a *unit of account*. The first problem was solved by using money as a *medium of exchange* between x and y in place of direct barter. If x is to have a price, however, two conditions must be fulfilled. There must be a demand for it and it must be scarce in relation to that demand. In other words, a priced good can only exist if there is scarcity in relation to demand. The absence of these conditions results in 'free' goods which have no price.

Prices are determined in the market, which is simply the aggregate of all buyers and sellers of that good. Markets take many different forms. The layperson's notion of a market is a physical location where goods or services are bought or sold. Examples include Billingsgate, the Stock Exchange or a street market. However, an economist would use the term in a wider sense, namely the sum of all transactions in either a particular product (*a product market*) or in all products or services (*the aggregate market*). The importance of markets is such that economists have developed the idea of perfect and imperfect markets.

The perfect market

A perfectly competitive market is one where the following assumptions apply:

a) There are large numbers of buyers and sellers, each of whom only buys or sells a small proportion of total market demand or supply. Variations in their own demand or supply cannot influence market demand or supply and hence leave price unaffected. Price is determined by combined market forces, ie the cumulative action of all buyers and sellers.

b) All goods sold in the market are identical in every respect and are divisible. This means that they can be sold in various amounts at the same price per unit. For example, it is almost impossible to differentiate between the four-star petrol produced by one petrol company and another.

c) Both buyers and sellers are fully aware of prevailing market prices and conditions, ie they are said to have perfect knowledge of the market.

d) The product is portable from one part of the market to another. This means that the price prevailing in one part of the market will be the same as in another. For example, the price of petrol in Edinburgh will be the same as that in Exeter.

e) There is perfect mobility of the factors of production in the market and no barriers exist to prevent new sellers from entering the market. Perfect mobility means, for instance, an employee is free to choose an employer. A barrier to entry into a market could exist where the massive capital investment required to establish a petrol company effectively prevents most new competitors from entering that market.

f) Buyers and sellers both act rationally, ie sellers attempt to maximise their profits and buyers their satisfaction.

If all these factors exist a consequence is that a price emerges at which all parties within the market willing to transact can find a respective buyer or seller. This price is known as the *market equilibrium price*. Since in the real world the conditions of perfect competition taken together are never totally fulfilled, it follows that market equilibrium is simply a notional point around which the market moves. In practice all markets tend towards *disequilibrium*. The world market for oil fluctuates between positions of surplus and shortage. In so doing at some stage in the shift from one position to another the market achieves an equilibrium balance.

Having stated that in practice there are no perfect markets, it may appear irrelevant to pay attention to this concept. However, it is useful as it acts as a yardstick against which the level of competitiveness existing in other markets can be judged. Perfect competition is an example of how economists develop theoretical models in an attempt to help them explain observed behaviour in the real world. The explanation suggested by the model can be tested against reality and then either accepted, rejected or modified.

The imperfect market

The merit of such a model is that it describes a situation in which the free market economy will produce the optimum allocation of resources. It therefore provides a measure against which to judge real world markets and assess their efficiency. It has already been noted that in the real world conditions of perfect competition are unlikely to be fully met. Where this is so an imperfectly competitive market is said to exist. Forms of this market include monopolistic competition, oligopoly and monopoly.

The extreme form of imperfect competition is *monopoly*, where only one seller of the product exists. In practice, however, less rigorous definitions are applied, eg an organisation can be referred to the Monopolies Commission if it accounts for over 25% of market sales. *Monopolistic competition* is, in a sense, a mixture of elements of both monopoly and perfect competition. The market consists of large numbers of sellers producing very similar, although not identical goods or services. They are not perfect substitutes for each other because the sellers attempt *product differentiation*, ie they practice branding in an effort to convince the consumer that x and y are really different in some respect. With extensive advertising they are attempting to create a 'monopoly' for x in what is a very competitive market.

Alternatively, geographical barriers may create a monopolistic competitive market structure. Between the market forms of monopoly and monopolistic competition is the most significant market form which is known as *oligopoly*. It will be explained in the following chapter that the real economy exhibits a high degree of concentration whereby a relatively few organisations dominate the market between them. Oligopolies are perhaps the most characteristic market form in the modern economy, being found in a wide range of different industrial sectors. Therefore in practice it is the oligopoly market which merits most attention with reference to its behaviour.

Having examined the meaning of the term 'market' and the basic different forms of market structure, it is now possible to examine the market functions. The basic economic problem was how to solve the allocation of resources, which expressed itself via market forces of demand and supply. How demand and supply interact in the competitive market to determine price, and in so doing the allocation of resources, is now examined.

Market demand

Demand is a consumer's want or desire for a product plus the money or ability to purchase it. At this stage only market or aggregate demand is considered rather than the demand from a single consumer, so demand is defined as the quantity of a product consumers are prepared to buy at various prices in a specified time period. Since demand is a 'flow' concept and varies with time, the period under consideration must always be stated. The variables which influence demand are complex and differ in importance with alternative goods or services. It is possible to identify the major variables which influence the demand for x as follows:

a) *variables causing an extension or contraction in demand.*
b) *variables causing an increase or decrease in demand.*

a) The variable causing an extension/contraction in demand – price of x

First considered is the relationship between the demand for x and the price of x, while assuming *ceteris paribus*, ie all other things remaining unchanged. Normally, for most goods or services, a fall in price will mean that more is demanded and vice-versa. This is called an extension or contraction in demand because although more or less is demanded it is only because price is lower or higher. The reasons for this relationship are examined in a later chapter, but the basic explanation can be given in terms of the income and substitution effects of a price change.

14

(i) *Income effect* – if the price of x falls, the purchasing power of consumers' money income has effectively risen and so they can afford to purchase more of x. A rise in the price of x has the opposite effect. It reduces real incomes and the quantity purchased.

(ii) *Substitution effect* – if the price of x falls then it becomes cheaper relative to its substitutes, thereby persuading consumers to substitute x in place of y so expanding the demand for x and vice-versa.

Therefore both income and substitution effects work to produce an expansion in demand as price falls and vice-versa.

To illustrate this price-demand relationship, imaginary data is used showing the demand for milk in a market. The schedule is given below.

Price of milk in pence per pint	Quantity of milk demanded in pints per week (millions)
15	20
14	40
13	60
12	80
11	100
10	120

Table 1.2 Demand for milk per week in a market

This demand schedule is plotted on a graph with price on the vertical axis and demand on the horizontal axis. A smooth curve is drawn through these points to produce the demand curve of Fig 1.2 downward sloping from left to right.

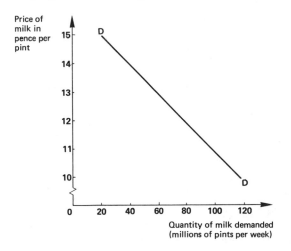

Fig 1.2 A demand curve

15

(NB Although *demand* is the dependant variable it is still plotted on the horizontal axis because when a supply curve is added, then *price* becomes the dependant variable and is correctly plotted on the vertical axis.)

The shape of the demand curve is determined by the relationship between price and demand, but it is drawn on the assumption that all other variables are constant. As price varies it produces extensions or contractions in demand which are movements from one point to another on the curve.

b) Variables causing an increase/decrease in demand

All the variables discussed below have one thing in common. Any variation will produce either an increase or decrease in the quantity of x demanded, ie an increase in demand means that more is being demanded at every price. A decrease in demand means that less is demanded at every price. An increase in demand is shown in Table 1.3 and the effect is to move the demand curve to the right. D to D_1 shown in Fig 1.3. A decrease in demand will move the demand curve to the left D_1 to D.

Price of milk in pence per pint	Quantity of milk demanded in pints per week (millions)	
	Period 1	Period 2
15	20	40
14	40	60
13	60	80
12	80	100
11	100	120
10	120	140

Table 1.3 An increase in the demand for milk

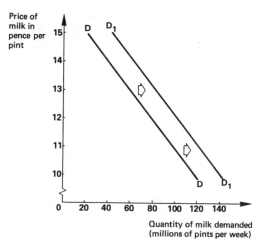

Fig 1.3 An increase in demand

16

Many variables may increase or decrease demand, but the more important are as follows:

(i) *Price of y* Changes in the prices of another product, y, can produce increases or decreases in the demand for x. The relationship between changes in the price of y and changes in the demand for x depend upon whether y is a *substitute* or *complementary product* for x. For example, if x and y are substitutes or competitive products as with BP and Shell petrol, then if the price of Shell (y) falls relative to BP (x) then it initially produces an extension in the demand for Shell. The substitution effect means that most motorists now substitute the cheaper Shell petrol in place of the dearer BP thereby causing a decrease in the demand for BP. A rise in the price of y (Shell) will have the opposite effect of increasing the demand for BP petrol. The demand for x (BP) varies directly with the price of its substitute y (Shell). How close this relationship is between x and y depends upon how close x and y are as substitutes. Sellers of the respective petrols will attempt to reduce the degree of substitutability between their products in the opinion of the consumer by various methods such as advertising claims regarding their brand.

If x and y are complementary such as video cassette recorders (y) and video cassettes (x), then as the price of vcr's falls (causing an extension in demand) it will produce an increase in the demand for the cassettes which consumers will purchase to use on their vcr's. The demand for x (cassettes) varies inversely with the price of y (vcr's), its complementary product. Again, the strength of this relationship depends upon the degree to which x and y are complementary. For example, a rise in the price of petrol will probably produce a decrease in the demand for all cars. But more marked will be the decrease in the demand for large cars since the complementary link between the two is closer than with cars in general. Finally it must be remembered that to some extent the demand for x is influenced by changes in the prices of all other goods since all goods purchased are competing for the finite expenditure of consumers. A rise in the price of food or petrol may tend to decrease the demand for holidays abroad if consumers can no longer afford them. These relationships between x and y do assume that no other variables change − ceteris paribus.

(ii) *Market income* Normally a rise in market income will result in an increase in the demand for x and vice-versa. There are however two possible exceptions to this usual rule. First, x may be an *inferior* product, ie one that is replaced by a *superior* product preferred by the consumer when market income rises. In this case a rise in market income will produce a decrease in demand for x. An example might be black and white TV's

17

which gradually were replaced with colour sets as consumers' incomes rose. The second exception is with a product where market demand already has reached its maximum and any further increase in income simply has no effect on demand. These products with 'satiated' demand might be such things as bread, newspapers, etc. It is possible for one product, such as black and white TV's, to pass through all three relationships – normal, satiated and inferior – during its life cycle. Each good or service has its own income-demand relationship. In addition to changes in the level of market income, changes in the distribution of income and wealth will also produce changes in demand. For example, a redistribution in favour of the poorer consumers would probably increase total demand since they would spend a higher proportion of income than the rich, as well as altering the structure of demand between goods and services.

(iii) *Consumer preferences* Changes in consumer preferences are one of the most powerful influences on demand and, unlike market income, changes can be influenced by the seller via advertising and promotion campaigns. Indeed a consumer's total perception of a particular product will take account of all relevant terms in the contractual bargain. Such would include express terms such as price and implied terms such as quality, reliability, etc. Certainly advertising can produce increases in demand for products and even change the consumer's 'image' of x, altering its income-demand relationship or the substitutability between x and y.

(iv) *Other variables* In addition to the variables discussed, other factors may influence demand. Changes in the size and structure of the population will influence demand. Temporary changes may be produced by transient factors such as expectations of future inflation or shortages. Non-economic variables such as political or social unrest may influence demand in specific cases, eg a threat of war increasing the demand for certain raw materials.

In conclusion, the demand for x is influenced by all these variables, and any change will cause demand to vary (in most cases) leading to increases/decreases in demand as the case may be.

These determinants of market demand are illustrated in Fig 1.4.

Having considered demand variables and the relationships which exist, it is now possible to examine the other side of the economic problem, that is, the market supply and the variables which influence it.

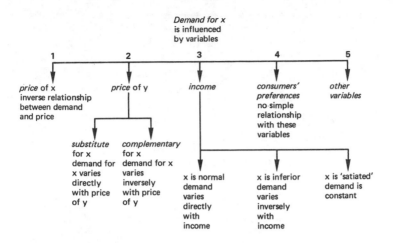

Fig 1.4   Market demand

Market supply

Supply refers to the quantity of a product or service which producers will offer for sale at various prices in a specific time period. As with demand the factors which influence supply may be divided into two groups:

a) *variables which cause an extension or contraction in supply;*
b) *variables which cause either an increase or decrease in supply.*

a) The variable causing an extension/contraction in supply –
price of x

The supply of x will be influenced by its price and usually the higher the price the greater the quantity supplied and vice-versa, and usually the higher the price the more profitable it will be for the supplier. Since the supplier's objective is to maximise profit, the higher price encourages more to be produced. This direct relationship is shown in Table 1.4 which relates the supply of milk to its price in a market. The schedule is shown plotted on the graph in Fig 1.5 with price on the vertical axis and quantity supplied on the horizontal axis.

Price of milk in pence per pint	Quantity of milk supplied in pints per week (millions)
15	100
14	80
13	60
12	40
11	20
10	0

Table 1.4   Supply of milk per week in a market

19

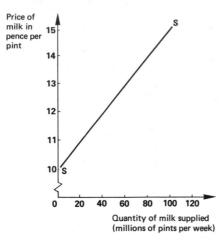

Fig 1.5   A supply curve

This supply curve which slopes downwards from right to left shows that as price rises there is an extension in supply or a contraction in supply for a fall in price, ie more or less is supplied because the price is higher or lower. As with demand, the supply curve is drawn on the assumption that all other supply factors are constant and that changes in price cause movements along the curve, but do not move the curve's position.

b) Variables causing either an increase or decrease in supply
As previously discussed with demand, all the next group of variables similarly cause either an increase or a decrease in supply, ie more or less will be supplied at all existing prices. An increase in supply is illustrated in Table 1.5, and the result shown in Fig 1.6 is to move the supply curve to the right S to S_1. A decrease in supply has the opposite effect of moving the supply curve to the left S_1 to S. Several variables may result in an increase or decrease in supply of which the following are the most relevant.

(i) *Changes in the price of y*   Economic resources can often be allocated to produce competing goods, x or y for example. The supply of x will be influenced not only by its own price, but the price of y, its alternative in the utilisation of the same economic resources. Since x and y use the same economic resources, their costs of production will be similar and therefore the respective profitability of x and y will be determined by their relative prices. An example might be milk and beef which utilise similar resources. A rise in the price of beef (y), for whatever reason, relative to milk, makes beef production more profitable and attractive to the farmer. This could result in farmers shifting resources from milk to beef production, eg sending dairy herds

20

for meat and by building up beef stock in preference to dairy herds. The result would be a decrease in the supply of milk, the supply curve shifts to the left. A fall in the price and profitability of beef relative to milk would produce the opposite effect of an increase in the supply of milk. It may be concluded therefore that generally the supply of x will vary inversely with the price of its resource competitors.

(ii) *Changes in the prices (costs) of the factors of production* · Any change in the price or cost of an economic input or factor of production utilised, will invariably affect the quantity of x supplied by the producer the various prices or costs of supplying that quantity. If the cost of a factor rises, eg the cost of dairy feedstuff, then the same quantity of milk (Q_1) can only be supplied at a higher price (P_2). Alternatively, at the old price of milk (P_1), less can now be supplied (Q_2). The supply curve moves to the left as the result of a decrease in supply as in Fig 1.7. If the costs of any factor fall this results in an increase in supply so that more can be supplied at the original prices (ie $Q_2 - Q_1$) or the same quantity may be supplied at a lower price. The supply curve shifts to the right.

Price of milk in pence per pint	Quantity of milk supplied in pints per week (millions)	
	Period 1	Period 2
15	100	140
14	80	120
13	60	100
12	40	80
11	20	60
10	0	40

Table 1.5 An increase in the supply of milk

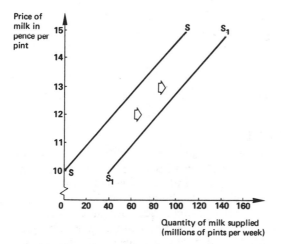

Fig 1.6 An increase in supply

(iii) *Technological developments* Supply of many products is clearly influenced by scientific or technical developments. Many developments may result in increased production levels without changes in costs, causing an increase in supply to occur. At any time what is produced, and for what cost, is very much influenced by the state of technology in the economy.

(iv) *Other factors* Supply may be influenced by other variables, depending on the product concerned. For example, milk and most agricultural products are influenced by climatic factors. Political and social changes such as wars or strikes will influence supply. Government policies in the form of taxes imposed or subsidies given also affect supply, although these policies strictly work by changing the costs of production for the producer.

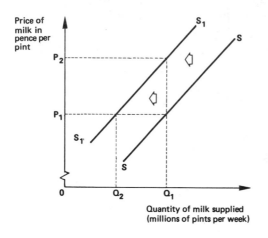

Fig 1.7   An increase in costs of production causing a decrease in supply

The determination of market price

Having examined market demand and supply individually, it is possible to combine demand and supply together to determine the equilibrium of the market price for x. The demand and supply schedules of Tables 1.2 and 1.4 are combined and plotted in the graph shown in Fig 1.8.

Three situations with different market prices are now examined. First, suppose market price is at 11p, then consumers would be prepared to demand 100 million pints. But at this price the producers will supply only 20 million pints. In this situation clearly demand exceeds

22

supply, ie excess demand of 80 million pints. In the market, when demand exceeds supply, the result will be a rise in price for two reasons. Producers will tend to raise prices as they see that they can sell more than they are currently producing. Similarly consumers will be prepared to pay higher prices in order to obtain supplies. As price rises in the market this will tend to both contract demand from consumers and expand supply from producers.

In the second situation, market price is at 14p, resulting in a demand from consumers of 40 million pints faced with producers willing to supply 80 million pints. Clearly this situation represents excess supply of 40 million and market price would tend to fall, because producers would find themselves with excess stocks. In an attempt to sell surplus stocks, the producers will reduce prices which will result in both a contraction in supply and an expansion in demand. In the third case, price is at 13p, then demand and supply of milk are both at 60 million pints. Consumers and producers are both demanding and supplying the same quantity and therefore there would be no pressure on price to change. This price which balances demand and supply in a market is called the *equilibrium price*.

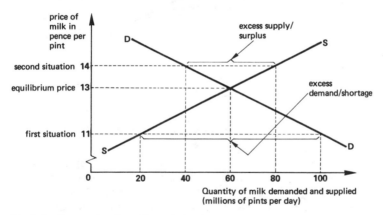

Fig 1.8   Determination of market price

In a free market situation the price will not necessarily always be at this equilibrium price, but at any other price there will be a situation of either *excess demand* or *excess supply*. These two situations will set up market forces which will tend to increase or decrease market price leading to a movement of price towards equilibrium.

Together demand and supply interacting determine the equilibrium price and it is this price which results in the market for milk or any other product being balanced between consumers' demand and producers' supply. So, when the market is in equilibrium, supply meets demand at a price which satisfies both consumer and producer. This is called the *equilibrium position*. In theory, all markets move towards an equilibrium price where the amount demanded per period is the same as the amount supplied per period. Thus, there are no sellers who do not find a buyer, and no buyers who do not find a seller.

Changes in demand and supply and equilibrium price

Equilibrium price balances demand and supply but any change in either demand or supply variables will change market equilibrium price. Using the example of supply and demand for milk, suppose our equilibrium price is 13p, but as a result of a successful promotion campaign the demand for milk increases, shifting the demand curve from D to D_1 as before (see Fig 1.9).

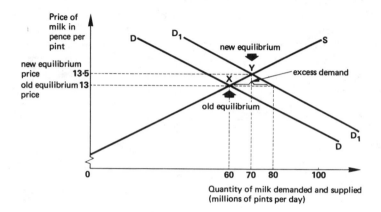

Fig 1.9   Increase in demand shifting equilibrium from X to Y

At the original price of 13p, demand now exceeds supply by 20 million pints. As already explained, market price would be forced upwards thereby contracting demand but expanding supply until a new equilibrium price is established at 13.5p, where demand and supply are equal. A decrease in demand, as illustrated by the demand curve moving from D_1 to D (caused perhaps by a fall in market incomes), will produce the opposite effect of excess supply at the new equilibrium price of 13.5p, thereby causing prices to fall back to 13p. However if market demand moves from D to D_1 and price accordingly rises this may encourage the supply side to similarly move (as a result of existing suppliers producing more, or new suppliers entering the market). A shift of supply from S to S_1 together with the original increase in demand will mean an equilibrium between new supply S_1 and new demand D_1 at $12\frac{1}{2}$p, and 90 million pints will be sold. This cobweb effect of changing supply and demand is illustrated in Fig 1.10.

But in the real world most markets are not in equilibrium. There are constantly 'cut price offers' advertised (indicating excess supply) or

24

queues for goods and services (indicating excess demand) or stock piling of products (indicating insufficient demand). There is no one unique market price at any one time. For instance in a house sale, the seller may have taken less for the house than the final agreed price and the buyer may have been willing to pay more. But there is a certain price below which the seller is not willing to sell and another price above which the buyer is not willing to buy. The actual selling price falls somewhere between the two and is the result of negotiation and bargaining between buyer and seller. Therefore in most situations there is no 'fixed price'. A shopkeeper will offer to sell a product at a certain price but is most probably willing to lower the price if he or she gets no buyers. The negotiation in this case is non verbal but is demonstrated by the consumers' willingness or unwillingness to buy at the price offered.

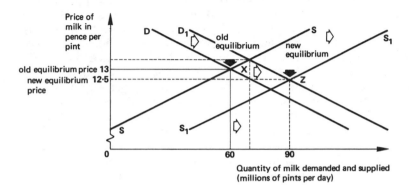

Fig 1.10 Increase in demand followed by increase in supply shifting equilibrium from X to Z.

The transaction: making the agreement to transact

If the consumer decides that the price offered by the seller is acceptable the goods or services are bought at that price. The consumer must enter into a transaction which will result in their acquisition. All consumers wishing to purchase goods or services in a commercial market, whether they be commercial undertakings, public corporations, local authorities or private individuals, effect their purchase in the same way; they enter into a *contract*.

The freedom of the individual to secure provision of a choice of goods and services by contract is fundamental to the market economy. Effective market demand at a given price (ie the total quantity sold at that price) for a product is represented by the sum of individual contracts made by the consumers for that product. In a perfect market where there are many buyers and sellers, all with similar products, and everyone has a perfect knowledge of the market, the self-interested consumer will, by his or her contracts, favour those business organisations which produce the goods/services at the lowest price. If an organisation produces too much, or sets too high a price, then these goods will not be the object of contracts and the organisation will go out of business unless the price is reduced, or production is switched to goods which consumers want and will contract to purchase.

By aggregating the quantities of a product sold via all contracts which could be formed at each price level, the demand curve for the product is created. This formation of a valid contract is obviously of great importance in the understanding of the working of the market.

The idea of contract

The idea of transactions under which goods are bought and sold is as old as civilisation. Indeed the growth of transacting has contributed to the economic advancement of those societies for whom trade has been a major feature of social activity. Trading is of course the means by which a market is created and whenever buying and selling takes place and goods or services are exchanged demands are created and fulfilled. Having already considered the market from an economic standpoint, it is now proposed to examine the legal mechanisms which are involved in the operation of markets. If persons are to have the courage to take financial risk, and trade, there must be a readily recognisable code by which they do business; a set of rules that provides a framework of conduct by which the parties must abide. Without such rules trading would be a chance affair in which trading anarchy would prevail. This would certainly not be an adequate basis for promoting the confidence suppliers generally look for if they are intending to employ skills, labour and money in operating a business.

If trading is to flourish those participating require the reassurance of knowing that should a transaction fail to meet their expectations there is some formal means available for resolving the conflict if informal means have failed. This formal means is available through the process of *litigation* which enables an aggrieved party to bring legal proceedings against another. Such proceedings are brought before a civil court, which has the *jurisdiction* to make a judgment in favour of one of the parties. In actions brought before the courts where the dispute concerns an agreement allegedly made between the parties, the action is founded upon the Law of Contract.

The contract

The contract is the legal mechanism which enables the market to function effectively and is described below.

If a trading agreement is analysed it will be noticed that in every case the parties who have negotiated their deal will have entered into mutual undertakings. In the simplest type of transaction, a seller will agree to sell identified goods to a purchaser for a stated sum. The seller is thereby promising the purchaser that ownership of the goods will be transfered to the purchaser. The purchaser is similarly making a promise – to pay the agreed price. The majority of contracts that are made consist of exchanged promises. Sometimes each party will make a single promise to the other. On other occasions in more complex transactions such as large-scale building contracts and international trade deals, detailed and multiple groups of promises are exchanged. One of the tasks faced by the courts when they are called upon to resolve disputes arising from agreements, is whether the promises that have been made are legally binding. If they are, the parties have made a contract to which the law of contract will apply. There may however be reasons why a court will declare that the agreement is not legally binding, and therefore not a contract. It is the task of the courts to determine whether an agreement has satisfied the legal formalities which enable it to be treated as a contract. They do so not only by reference to legal rules, but also the express or implied intention of the parties.

In all economic systems a contract is simply an agreement concerning an economic transaction which the law will enforce. Under English law it has been defined as an agreement intended by the parties to it to have legal consequences and to be legally enforceable. Every contract therefore must involve an agreement but of course not all agreements are contracts. Purely social or domestic agreements are generally not classified as contracts mainly because the parties to such agreements do not intend legal consequences to result. The task of determining the presence of this legal intention is basically one of interpreting the agreement and also considering the surrounding circumstances. These include the respective economic values transferred by the parties under the contract. Certainly, the courts have in the past inferred that a family arrangement is presumed not to be intended to be legally binding. In a *commercial* agreement however, such an intention to create legal consequences is inferred. These presumptions may nevertheless be rebutted (refuted) depending on the individual circumstances of each case.

In *Rose and Frank Co* v. *Crompton (J R) and Bros Ltd* (1925) in a commercial agreement it was expressly provided that 'this arrangement is not entered into as a formal or legal agreement and shall not be subject to the legal jurisdiction in the Law Courts'. The House of Lords held that the agreement could not be enforced as a contract because this clause expressly negated any intention to be legally bound. Similarly in *Merritt* v. *Merritt* (1970) the Court of Appeal considered whether a husband's written promises to pay his wife £40 a month in return for her paying off the mortgage and an undertaking to transfer the house to her, was intended to have legal consequences. The Court decided that such promises amounted to a legal contract. The crucial circumstance relied on by Lord Denning in his judgment was the fact that the husband

and wife were separated. This was sufficient to ensure that the presumption of fact against intention to create a contract in a family agreement did not operate.

In every contract it is usual for a party to bind himself or herself personally to the performance of obligations and also to confer rights on the other party, eg the supplier of goods agrees to sell them to a consumer; a builder agrees to build a householder an extension; an investor purchases shares in a company; a tour operator agrees to provide a holiday-maker with a package tour; an employee agrees to work for an organisation; a landlord agrees to lease premises to a tenant. These examples illustrate that most transactions within the business environment, for the purchase or hire of goods or services, the employment of workers, etc are all contractual agreements. These are all examples of *simple* contracts.

The term simple contract is used to distinguish this type of contract from contracts of *record* and *specialty* contracts. Briefly, contracts of record are obligations recorded by a court of law in its official records and specialty contracts, also called *deeds*, are formal contracts signed, sealed and delivered. Simple contracts however comprise the vast majority of contracts entered into and it is therefore important to consider in some detail their essential requirements. Firstly, it may be useful to determine whether the law attaches any formalities to the making of contractual bargains.

Formalities

It is a general rule of the common law that valid contracts may be made orally. Oral evidence may be given of the terms of a contract and despite the fact that a written contract is easier to prove, an oral contract may be just as effective. Statute has provided exceptions to this general rule however so that certain contracts may be void or unenforceable unless they are in a special form. A *void* contract is one which has no legal effect. It is a non existent contract. An *unenforceable* contract is one which is valid in all respects except it is unenforceable in a court of law. This means that should one of the parties seek to enforce the contract by legal action that person will be unable to do so because the court will not entertain the action. In addition, certain contracts may be described as *voidable*. This means that the contract suffers from a defect which entitles one of the parties to set it aside at his or her option. Until this option is exercised, however, the contract remains valid and enforceable. Certain contracts are still required to be made by deed, eg under the Law of Property Act 1925, s. 52 in the case of a lease for more than three years. Certain contracts are void unless they are in written form, like a consumer credit agreements (eg a hire-purchase agreement) (Consumer Credit Act 1974), contracts of marine insurance (Marine Insurance Act 1906), certain negotiable instruments, eg cheques, agreements between employer and employee for certain deductions of wages (Truck Acts, 1831 and 1896), and an acknowledgement of a debt which has become statute-barred under the Limitation Act 1939. Certain contracts although not void are unenforceable if not evidenced in writing, eg contracts of guarantee whereby a person promises to answer for the debt of another (Statute of Frauds 1677, s. 4), and contracts for the sale or other disposition of land or any interest in land (Law of Property Act 1925, s. 40).

In the previous two cases the absence of sufficient written evidence does not render the contract invalid. It simply means that the contract is unenforceable by court action. Briefly the written evidence required must include the main terms of the contract and be signed by the person agreeing to sell or to guarantee.

Having dealt with the main formalities attaching to the making of contracts it is now possible to consider some of the main features of a valid simple contract.

Formation of the contractual bargain

The substance of a contractual bargain is the mutual agreement of the parties arrived at through a process of economic bargaining. It must be shown therefore that one party to the contract has made an offer (the *offeror*) which in turn has been accepted by the other party (the *offeree*). It is only when there is acceptance of a valid offer that a contractual bargain is concluded. Therefore the need to determine when a valid offer has been made can be a crucial and difficult question, particularly when the parties have been involved in drawn-out contractual negotiations. And yet it must be remembered that many contractual bargains (eg sale of goods) are concluded following only one offer from the consumer which is accepted by the retailer, no negotiations taking place between the parties at all, save the actual offer and acceptance.

Characteristics of a valid offer

The offer must be:

1 Certain

The terms of a contractual offer must be certain or capable of being made certain. It is only if the details of the bargain are certain that the parties can be expected to reach any real agreement.

> In *Scammell* v. *Ouston* (1941) the Court held that an offer to sell a van 'on hire purchase terms over a period of two years' was too vague to create a contract as there were a wide variety of hire purchase terms available and the offeror had failed to specify such terms in detail.

Similarly an offer may be uncertain if a vital term is not included and remains to be settled by further negotiation. In most contracts price is the most important term and so to omit it may mean a valid offer has not been made.

> In *Courtney and Fairbairn Ltd* v. *Tolaini Brothers (Hotels) Ltd* (1975) an agreement was concluded for the development of certain land. The agreement purported to deal with the cost of the work by including a clause 'to negotiate fair and reasonable contract sums'. The Court held such a clause to be too vague in the absence of any precise method of calculating the cost in the future. On the other hand, the reference of disputes over price to arbitration was held to be a sufficiently precise method in *Foley* v. *Classique Coaches Ltd* (1934) despite the obvious failure to agree a price in the contract.

Certainly in the past the courts have been willing to render vague terms certain. They have done this by reference to relevant trade practices or a previous course of dealings between the parties and under the Sale of Goods Act 1979, by reference to the prevailing market price at the time the contract was made. They may even imply a term into a contract to give it 'business efficacy', that is, achieve the presumed intention of the parties.

2 Communicated
To be valid and effective the offer must be communicated to the offeree. It is not possible in law to accept an offer of which you are unaware. Therefore if an offer of reward for the completion of an act is made, such completion if made in ignorance of the offer would not amount to a valid acceptance. The offer may be communicated to a specific person, a specific group and following the famous decision in *Carlill* v. *Carbolic Smoke Ball Co Ltd* (1893) to the world at large.

> In *Carlill* v. *Carbolic Smoke Ball Co Ltd* (1893) the defendants, the Carbolic Smoke Ball Co sellers of a medicinal preparation, the carbolic smoke ball, had placed an advertisement in a London newspaper offering £100 reward to anyone who contracted cold or influenza after using their product in a prescribed manner. The advertisement also stated that '£1000 is deposited with the Alliance Bank, Regent Street, showing our sincerity in the matter'. The plaintiff, Mrs. Carlill, having used the product in the prescribed manner and having contracted influenza, sued the company in contract for the £100 reward. One of the main factors raised in its defence by the company was that the offer lacked sufficient certainty as it had been made to no one in particular. Unfortunately for the company the Court saw nothing amiss with a general offer made to the whole world which contractually

bound the company to those offerees who had accepted its terms. The argument that the company had not intended to create legal relations by the offer was also rejected by the Court. Considering the objective view of the ordinary person to the advertisement the Court regarded as crucial the claim of the company that it had placed £1000 on bank deposit. This, it was decided, demonstrated a clear intention on behalf of the company to be legally bound.

3 Distinguished from an invitation to treat

An offer must be distinguished from an *invitation to treat*, ie an invitation from a seller to a potential customer to make an offer. A purported acceptance of an invitation to treat therefore will only be regarded as an act amounting to an offer. There are well-known situations recognised by the common law and statute as constituting invitations to treat, eg

a) *Display of goods* a display of goods in a shop-window does not constitute an offer, merely an invitation to the public to enter the shop and make an offer to buy. Therefore there is no contractual duty on a shopkeeper to sell goods which have been wrongly priced. The price tag is not an offer by the shopkeeper to sell, merely an invitation to customers to make an offer at that price. It is the customer who makes the offer to purchase the goods and such an offer may be accepted or rejected as the shopkeeper pleases. Obviously if no offers are forthcoming from consumers the shopkeeper may vary the invitation to treat by lowering the price in the hope of creating effective demand. The shopkeeper thus hopes to stimulate contractual offers from the consumer. Any supplier with a surplus may lower the price in order to sell excess stock. Similarly if demand exceeds supply, the price at which the shopkeeper is inviting consumers to make an offer will increase. An offer at a lower price will be rejected. The principle that a display of goods in a shop-window is merely an invitation to treat was upheld by the Court in *Fisher* v. *Bell* (1961).

> *Fisher* v. *Bell* (1961) involved a criminal prosecution brought against a shopkeeper for contravening the Restriction of Offensive Weapons Act, 1959, which made it an offence to 'offer for sale or hire' a flick knife. The accused had displayed a flick knife in his shop-window with a ticket which stated 'Ejector knife − 4/-'. The Divisional Court of the Queen's Bench Division held that no offence had been committed since no offer for sale had been made. Lord Chief Justice Parker confirmed the legal position by stating 'the display of an article with a price on it in a shop-window is merely an invitation to treat. It is in no sense an offer for sale, the acceptance of which constitutes a contract'.
>
> The question as to the contractual position in a self-service store arose in *Pharmaceutical Soc of Gt Britain* v. *Boots Cash Chemists (Southern) Ltd* (1953). Here a prosecution had been brought alleging a contravention of the Pharmacy and Poisons Act 1933 in that the sale of some medicines was not under the supervision of a qualified pharmacist. The defendants employed a pharmacist to supervise the cash till but not the shelves in the self-service store. The Court of Appeal was clear that the contract of sale took place at the cash till so that the Act had been complied with. Lord Justice Somervell regarded the self-service store as 'a convenient method

of enabling customers to see what there is for sale, to choose, and' possibly, to put back and substitute articles which they wish to have, and then go to the cashier and offer to buy what they have chosen'.

b) *Advertisements* generally, advertisements containing goods or services for sale in newspapers, magazines, or catalogues do not constitute offers but are simply declarations of an intention on the part of the seller to contract if consumers wish to make offers.

The case of *Partridge* v. *Crittenden* (1968) illustrates the legal position. Here an advertisement in a magazine referred to certain wild birds for sale at a specific price. The question before the Court was whether such an advertisement amounted to the offence of offering for sale a wild bird contrary to the Protection of Birds Act, 1954. The Court held that the advertisement constituted an invitation to treat and not an offer for sale and the offence was not therefore established.

As previously stated however it is possible to include a general offer in an advertisement – *Carlill* v. *Carbolic Smoke Ball Co Ltd*. The reward of £100 constituted an offer to the world at large capable of acceptance by any offeree who complied with its terms.

As far as auction sales are concerned the law is largely settled. The decision in *Payne* v. *Cave* (1789) was given statutory force in the Sale of Goods Act 1979, s. 57(2), which provides: 'A sale by auction is concluded when the auctioneer announces its completion by the fall of the hammer'. The request for bids by the auctioneer is the invitation to treat and the bids constitute the offer. A freely operated auction sale is one of the clearest examples of a market system operating. Consumers will bid against each other if effective demand exists. If it does not the auctioneer may have to accept a very low price (however there may be a reserved price on goods below which a seller is not willing to go).

The Queen's Bench Divisional Court confirmed the position relating to auction sales in *British Car Auctions Ltd* v. *Wright* (1972). Here a prosecution had been brought for the auction sale of an unroadworthy car contrary to the Road Traffic Act, 1972. The Court decided that the magistrates court conviction of 'offering to sell' such a vehicle should be quashed. Lord Chief Justice Widgery stated: 'the auctioneer when he stands on his rostrum does not make an offer to sell the goods on behalf of the vendor; he stands there making an invitation to those present at the auction themselves to make offers to buy'.

c) *Tenders*   it is common in the business environment when organisations require goods or services to be supplied, to invite suppliers to
submit competitive tenders. Clearly in most cases a potential buyer
will invite several possible suppliers to submit tenders with the likely
acceptance of only the most competitive. Also it is usual practice for
the tender to describe the goods or services to be supplied and their
cost. Submission of a tender will constitute an offer in law and
acceptance of the tender a binding contract. It should be pointed out
however that an invitation to tender that suggests that the buyer *may*
require the goods or services will only result in a contract for the sale
of such goods or services as and when required by the buyer. Failure
by the buyer to order any, or only a small amount of the goods or
services, will not result in a breach of contract. The supplier of
course has similar freedom to revoke the standing offer prior to
orders being made.

The recent Court of Appeal decision in *Gibson* v. *Manchester City
Council* (1979) has cast some doubt on the traditional legal approach of
distinguishing between an offer and an invitation to treat where
protracted correspondence has taken place.

> The *Gibson* v. *Manchester City Council* (1979) case involved the
> prospective sale of a council house. The plaintiff council tenant,
> having completed a request for information, received a letter from
> the council saying it might be prepared to sell the house to him for
> £2180 freehold and that if he wished to make a formal application
> to purchase he should return an application form. This the tenant
> did, however he left the purchase price blank requesting that the
> price should take into account defects in the path of the property.
> A further letter from the council stated that defects in the path had
> been taken into account in fixing the price. In interpreting the
> above correspondence a majority of the Court of Appeal held that
> a contract of sale had indeed been entered into. Lord Denning put
> forward the view that in such circumstances there was no need to
> look for a strict offer and acceptance. Rather, 'you should look at
> the correspondence as a whole and at the conduct of the parties
> and see therefrom whether the parties have come to an agreement
> on everything that was material'. This decision was later reversed
> however following a further appeal to the House of Lords in 1979.
> The Law Lords adopted the more traditional approach by
> analysing each piece of correspondence and held that no firm offer
> had been made or accepted by the council. The words the council
> 'may be prepared to sell' only amounted to an invitation to treat
> and thus no contract of sale had resulted.

d) Must terminate or be terminated
An offer may terminate by *lapse*; obviously if the offeror specifies that

34

the offer is to remain open for a specified period of time and there has been no acceptance within that period then the offer will lapse and be extinguished. The promise of the offeror to keep the offer open for a specified period will only be legally binding if it is embodied within a separate contract. It shall be seen later that such a contract will only arise if the offeree provides some *consideration* (value) in return for the promise.

If no time period is stipulated by the offeror then the offer will lapse after a reasonable period of time. What constitutes a reasonable period will depend mainly on the subject matter of the offer.

> In *Ramsgate Victoria Hotel Ltd* v. *Montefiore* (1866) the defendant applied for shares in the plaintiff company on 8 June. The company purported to accept the offer on 23 November. The Court held that as no time limit had in fact been specified the allotment of shares (the acceptance) should have been made within a reasonable period. In the circumstances five months was not a reasonable period particularly as the shares were subject to a fluctuating market value.

It is obvious that in times of rapid inflation, a reasonable period of time for the offer to remain open will be shorter. This is a fact that the courts will have regard to.

An offer may be terminated by the revocation of the offeror; generally, unless the offeror has contracted to keep the offer open for a specified period, the rule is that it may be withdrawn at any time prior to acceptance. It is lawful therefore for a bidder at an auction sale to withdraw their bid prior to acceptance. For revocation to be effective it must be communicated, though it need not necessarily be communicated by the offeror.

> In *Dickinson* v. *Dodds* (1876) an offer to sell certain houses was expressed to be open until Friday at 9.00 am. On the Thursday afternoon the offeree learned from a third party that the offeror had been negotiating a sale of one of the properties to another buyer, a Mr. Allen. The Court held that the information communicated by the third party to the offeror amounted to an effective communication of a revocation of the original offer, for it indicated that the offeror no longer intended to sell him the property.

For the purposes of revocation, communication means *actual* communication rather than the mere posting of a letter which may, as shall be seen later, in certain circumstances constitute an acceptance.

> A good illustration is provided by the case of *Byrne & Co* v. *Leon Van Tienhoven & Co* (1880). Here an offer for the sale of tin plate

was posted on 1 October by the offeror in Cardiff to the offeree in New York. The offer was received by the offeree on 11 October and immediately an acceptance was telegraphed and confirmed by letter on 15 October. Previously, on 8 October, the offeror had sent a letter of revocation which the offeree received on 20 October. On the question as to whether a valid contract had been entered into the Court held that there had been no effective revocation as the offer had been accepted on 11 October. The rule that acceptance may be complete on posting applied here, but for an effective revocation actual communication is required.

The rule that an offeror can revoke prior to acceptance could provide a problem in a contract where acceptance is to be performance of an act by the offeree, eg an offer of £1000 to be paid to the first footballer to score thirty league goals in a season. The question is, could the offer be withdrawn when the Newcastle United striker has scored 29 goals by Easter? (At the time of writing this is unfortunately most unlikely!) It is suggested that such an offer would carry with it an implied promise on the part of the offeror that the offer will remain open for the football season and therefore cannot be revoked during that period.

An offer may be terminated by the rejection or acceptance of the offeree. The express rejection of the offeree will terminate an offer. Rejection may also be implied if the offeree simply ignores the offer. The law imposes no obligation on the offeree even to give the offer any consideration. Similarly an implied rejection will occur where there has been a counter offer and this will extinguish the original offer which cannot then be revived.

In *Hyde* v. *Wrench* (1840) the defendant's offer to sell a farm for £1000 was met by the plaintiff's counter offer to buy for £950. The plaintiff later accepted the defendant's original offer. The Court held that the counter offer to buy for £950 had destroyed the original offer which was no longer capable of acceptance. It must be stressed that there is no counter offer where the offeree is merely requesting further information or attempting to get the offeror to modify his offer. Such occurred in *Stevenson* v. *McLean* (1880) where in response to an offer of a quantity of iron at a specified price the offeree requested information over the minimum delivery time. Receiving no reply to this request, the offeree went ahead and accepted. In determining whether a contract had been formed the Court held that the offeree's request was not a counter offer so as to imply rejection but rather a mere enquiry which did not destroy the original offer. A contract had therefore been entered into. The recent case of *Butler Machine Tool Co* v. *Ex-Cell-O Corporation (England) Ltd* (1978) demonstrates that the rules relating to counter offer may be of crucial importance in determining the applicable terms in a contract. Here the plaintiff sellers offered to deliver a machine tool subject to their own terms which included a price variation clause (one under which price alters with the level of inflation). The defendant buyers purported to accept the offer with an order containing some different terms and no price variation clause. The order contained a tear-off acknowledgement slip which was signed and returned by the sellers. In determining whether the price variation clause was indeed part of the contract the Court held that the buyers' reply constituted a counter offer which the sellers had accepted by their acknowledgement. The buyers' terms were those therefore applicable and there was no price variation clause in the contract.

Characteristics of a valid acceptance

Some of the rules relating to a valid acceptance have already been referred to above. The following points apply to an acceptance. It should be:

1 *Unconditional* Acceptance is the unconditional agreement by the offeree to the exact terms of the offer. If the offeree attaches conditions to that acceptance this will amount to a counter offer, eg *Hyde* v. *Wrench* (1840).

2 *Communicated* An acceptance must be actually communicated to the offeror by words, writing or conduct. The general rule is that if the offeror stipulates a mode of acceptance then to accept the offeree must comply with the method specified. However if the offeror merely directs the offeree to a possible mode of acceptance, any other mode used which is no less advantageous to the offeror will be binding.

> Thus in *Yates Building Co* v. *R J Pulleyn* (1976) the Court of Appeal held that an acceptance by ordinary post by the offeree was no less advantageous to the offeror than registered post or recorded delivery which he had directed. Silence however cannot amount to acceptance, even if the offeror indicates willingness to it as a mode of acceptance. In *Felthouse* v. *Bindley* (1862) the plaintiff wrote to his nephew offering to buy his horse and stating 'If I hear no more about him I shall consider the horse mine at £30.15s.'. Receiving no reply the plaintiff claimed a binding contract but the Court held that the offer had not been accepted as there had been no communication of such an intention.

The rule relating to silence of course goes some way to prevent the practice of *inertia selling* although additional statutory protection is given by the Unsolicited Goods and Services Act 1971. If the post is used as the mode of acceptance between the parties then acceptance is completed at the moment the letter, properly addressed and prepaid, is posted. This rule applies provided:

a) The post is a means of communication within the contemplation of the parties, eg either the offeror states in the offer that acceptance may be by post, or the offer is made by post and acceptance by post can therefore be implied; and
b) There is no contrary intention, ie requiring actual communication. The postal rule can of course be disadvantageous to the offeror particularly if the letter of acceptance is delayed or lost in the post.

> In *Household Fire Insurance Co* v. *Grant* (1879) the defendant's offer to buy shares was accepted and the letter of allotment was posted to him, but he did not receive it. The Court decided that there was a contract for the sale of shares on delivery of the letter of acceptance to the common agent of the parties, the Post Office. The Lord Chamberlain, Lord Herschell, in *Henthorn* v. *Fraser* (1892) stated the position thus: 'Where the circumstances are such that it must have been within the contemplation of the parties that, according to the ordinary usages of mankind, the post might be used as a means of communicating the acceptance of the offer, the acceptance is complete as soon as it is posted'.

The case of *Byrne & Co* v. *Leon Van Tienhoven & Co* (1880) provides a comparison with the rules relating to revocation. As far as instantaneous communications are concerned, by telephone or telex, it is settled that actual communication of acceptance is required.

> In *Entores* v. *Miles Far East Corporation* (1955) the Court of Appeal was faced with the problem of determining when the contract was entered into where there was a telex communication. Lord Denning expressed the view of the court when he said, 'The contract is only complete when the acceptance is received by the offeror; and the contract is made at the place where the acceptance is received'.

In *Holwell Securities Ltd* v. *Hughes* (1974) it was confirmed that the postal rules may be expressly excluded by agreement.

The foregoing rules on offer and acceptance relate to the reaching of mutual agreement which is essential to the contractual bargain. English contract law however demands that the parties to a contractual bargain provide one further element. It is termed the *consideration*.

Consideration

Consideration refers to the value that is transferred under a contract to buy a promise. It may consist in the words of Lush.J in *Currie* v. *Misa* (1875) 'either in some right, interest, profit or benefit accruing to the one party, or some forbearance, detriment, loss or responsibility given, suffered or undertaken by the other'. Both parties to a simple contract must have furnished consideration in some form for the contract to be binding. This is not the case for a specialty contract (deed) however, where a gratuitous promise from one party may be enforceable if embodied in such a contract, eg the promise of an individual to make a gift of property to another individual. As previously stated consideration need not be present to support a specialty contract.

In simple contracts the consideration may take various forms. It is most easily recognisable when it takes the form of money and goods being transferred under a contract of sale, eg the transfer of £1.00 in return for twenty cigarettes. Consideration is said to be *executory* when the parties to a contract transfer promises, as in the usual business contract, eg in return for a promise of payment A agrees to transfer goods or services to B. Where executory promises are made the obligations that they embody are to be performed at some time in the future. Consideration is said to be *executed* where in return for a promise the offeree performs requested consideration which also amounts to acceptance of the offer, eg in response to an offer of £5 for return of a dog, the offeree finds and returns the dog to its owner.

Characteristics of valid consideration

1 *Adequacy of consideration*   The first characteristic of valid consideration is that although it must be real and be of some value it need not necessarily be of adequate value. In the absence of factors such as fraud, duress or misrepresentation the courts will not value the respective consideration transferred under the contract. The parties to a contract are thus free to negotiate their own bargain and if it turns out that a purchaser agrees a price well in excess of a realistic market price this alone will not be a ground for relief.

> In *Chappell and Co Ltd* v. *Nestlé Co Ltd* (1960) the defendants, hoping to promote the sale of their products, had offered a particular record (Rocking Shoes) for sale at the reduced price of 1/6d plus three chocolate bar wrappers. A dispute arose as to the assessment of royalties payable by the defendants to the plaintiffs who owned the copyright of the record. The plaintiffs argued that the royalties payable should take into account not only the money consideration exchanged for the record but also the value of the chocolate wrappers, despite the fact that they were simply disposed of by the defendants. The Court held that the subsequent disposal of the wrappers was immaterial, that each wrapper represented a sale of a chocolate bar and that it therefore formed part of the consideration transferred.

Provided a promise is supported therefore by something of value the courts are willing to enforce it.

The case of *Haigh* v. *Brooks* (1839) illustrates a most important feature of consideration, namely that it is for the parties to satisfy themselves that the consideration they have agreed is of value to them. It is not the task of the courts to make good what turn out to be bad, ie uneconomic agreements.

> In *Haigh* v. *Brooks* (1839) the defendant had provided the plaintiffs with a written document which guaranteed a debt of £10 000 owed by a firm to the plaintiffs. Sometime later the plaintiffs agreed to return the guarantee to the defendant and release him from liability, if in consideration he would pay certain debts owed by them. The guarantee was duly returned but the defendant refused to pay the debts. His defence was that the guarantee was a legally invalid document and therefore unenforceable. This was because it failed to satisfy certain statutory requirements. The Court held that the agreement was binding, even if the guarantee was legally invalid, since the defendant had received what he bargained for — his release from his supposed liability. In the words of Lord Chief Justice Denman, 'The plaintiffs were induced by the defendant's promise to part with something which they might have kept, and the defendant obtained what he desired by means of that promise'.

2 *Sufficiency of consideration* Consideration is said to be insufficient and therefore not capable of supporting a contract where it involves a promise to do what the promisor is already legally bound to do. Performance of a public duty will not be sufficient consideration to support a contractual promise.

> In *Collins* v. *Godefroy* (1831) the plaintiff having been served with a subpoena (order or writ to attend court) agreed with the defendant that in return for the plaintiff's attendance at court the defendant should pay his expenses. In determining the validity of the agreement the Court held that the promise of payment was not supported by sufficient consideration as the plaintiff was merely fulfilling a public duty which he was obliged to perform.

If it can be shown that a party performs an act which exceeds their public duty however then this may be sufficient to support a contract.

> In *Glasbrook Brothers* v. *Glamorgan County Council* (1925) the promise of the police authority to provide a special force billetted at a pit colliery to keep order during a strike was held to be in excess of their statutory duty. The Court was thus willing to enforce the colliery owners' promise of payment for police protection.

A party may alternatively be under an existing contractual duty, the performance of which would not be sufficient to support a contractual promise.

In *Stilk* v. *Myrick* (1809) after two sailors had deserted a ship, the remainder, in return for a promise of extra wages agreed to work the ship home. The Court held that since the sailors were bound by their existing contracts to work the ship home, there was no consideration to support the promise of extra wages which was therefore unenforceable.

The position is different, of course, if because of the change in circumstances the parties could be said to have negotiated fresh contractual terms.

In *Hartley* v. *Ponsonby* (1857) a ship's crew became so depleted that continuance of the voyage was inherently dangerous. Continuing in service in these circumstances, the Court held, was sufficient to support the promise of extra wages which constituted a fresh contractual bargain.

There is a well-known common law rule that the payment of a smaller amount to a creditor cannot alone be sufficient consideration to support the creditor's promise not to sue for the full debt. If however it is at the creditor's request and benefit that a smaller amount is paid at an earlier date than due, a different place than agreed, or in a different form, then this may be sufficient consideration for the creditor's promise to take it in full settlement. The courts have recognised that it would be unfair to bind a creditor to a promise extracted by the debtor's economic pressure, ie take this in full settlement or get nothing.

A good example of this situation is the case of *D & C Builders Ltd* v. *Rees* (1965). Here the defendant, knowing that the plaintiff builders were in financial difficulties, offered a £300 cheque to them as full satisfaction of a contractual debt of £482 for work done. The plaintiff builders accepted the cheque in full settlement and then sued for the balance. The Court held that there was no true agreement by the builders to accept the cheque in full satisfaction as they had merely submitted to economic pressure. The argument that the cheque was an altered mode of payment and sufficient to discharge the debt was rejected on the ground that it was not done at the builders' request.

The concept of economic duress is not limited to duress surrounding contractual payment but may also be constituted by a threatened breach of contract.

In the recent case of *North Ocean Shipping Co* v. *Hyundai Construction Co* (1978) the High Court considered the effect of such pressure and decided that it rendered the contract voidable, at the instance of the innocent party. The case involved a ship-building contract, the builders agreeing to build a tanker for the owners, the price payable by instalments. The contract stipulated that security was to be provided by the builders opening a letter of credit in the owners' favour. However there was no provision for any subsequent adjustment of the price. Following devaluation of the US dollar in 1973 the builders demanded an increase in the price under a threat to break the contract and agreeing to a corresponding increase in the letter of credit. The owners agreed to such increase which they paid and eventually the tanker was transferred. The owners then by court action attempted to reclaim the excess price for which they allege no sufficient consideration was provided and that it was paid under economic duress. The Court held that:

a) The rule in *Stilk* v. *Myrick* still applies – that performance of an existing contractual duty is not sufficient to support a fresh promise of payment. Here however the increase in the letter of credit was sufficient consideration to support the promise of extra payment, and

b) The effect of economic duress was to render the contract voidable, however in this case the owners had by their action affirmed the contract.

3 *Past consideration* It is an established common law rule that past consideration is no consideration and is not sufficient to support a contract. Consideration would be in the past where a service is rendered which was not requested and no promise of payment has been made.

> In *Re McArdle* (1951) a house was left by will to the deceased's wife for life and thereafter in equal shares to the five children. The wife of one of the children executed repairs and improvements to the house and later the five children agreed, in writing, to reimburse her for the cost on their mother's death. The Court held that no valid contract had been entered into on the ground that the wife's work was a past act which could not support the promise of future payment.

Of course the position would have been different had the work been done at the express or implied request of the children in circumstances which raised an implication of a promise to pay.

> This was the case in *Re Casey's Patents, Stewart* v. *Casey* (1892). Here the joint owners of a valuable patent had entered into an

arrangement with Casey under which Casey agreed to manage and publicise their invention. Two years later the joint owners promised Casey a third share of the patent 'in consideration of your services as manager'. The Court held such a promise to be legally binding rejecting the argument of past consideration. Here the request to render a service carried with it an implied promise to pay and the subsequent promise of a third share was merely the fixing of the value of the services rendered.

It is accepted therefore that in the business environment, if a service is rendered on request, the request will carry with it an implied promise of payment, eg if a car is left at a garage for repair and no price is expressly agreed, then it is implied that the owner will pay a reasonable sum for the repair. Under s. 8 Sale of Goods Act 1979, it is provided that where in a contract for the sale of goods the price has not been determined by the parties, a reasonable sum shall be payable for the goods.

4 *Privity of contract* The rights and obligations that are created under a contract are consequences of contractual liability which can only bind the contracting parties themselves. Any person who is outside the contract because he or she has provided no consideration to support the agreement is said to be a *stranger to the contract*. That person cannot be held legally accountable under the agreement, nor enforce rights which have been granted under it, for that person is not privy, or party to it.

An application of this principle can be clearly seen in *Beswick* v. *Beswick* (1967). Peter Beswick owned a coal merchants business which, on his retirement, he agreed to sell to his nephew. In return the nephew promised to keep his uncle on as a 'consultant' for the rest of the uncle's life, and promised to pay a weekly annuity of £5 after the uncle's death to his widow. When the uncle died the nephew refused to make the agreed payments, and the widow brought proceedings against him to compel him to perform his obligations under the agreement. She brought her action in two capacities, firstly in her personal capacity simply as a third party beneficiary under the agreement, and secondly in her capacity as administratrix of her husband's estate, ie his personal representative. The House of Lords held that although her action must fail where it was based upon her status merely as a third party beneficiary, her action in her representative capacity succeeded, and she could obtain specific performance of the contract, the Court ordering the nephew to make the agreed payments. She was 'standing in the shoes' of her husband.

It is important to point out that there are a number of exceptions to the privity of contract rule. To take one example under the Restrictive Trade Practices Act 1956, individual price maintenance agreements may be enforced against a person who was not a party to the sale but who subsequently acquired the goods with notice of the condition (s. 25(1)).

Discharge of contract

Having considered the essential elements of a valid contract it is now possible to show how a contract is discharged. The term 'discharge of contract' simply refers to the ways in which a contract may be brought to an end. The parties to a contract will have secured certain rights and be subject to certain obligations under it, eg

a) In a contract for the sale of goods, the seller has the right to payment of the price and the obligation to transfer the goods; the buyer is obliged to pay the price and has the right to obtain the goods. Similarly,

b) In a contract for the sale of a service, the seller has the right of payment of the price and the obligation to perform the service and the buyer is obliged to pay the price and has the right to obtain the benefit of the service.

The usual method of discharge of a contract is therefore by the parties performing their respective obligations under it.

1 *Discharge by performance* The general rule is that complete performance, complying precisely to the contractual terms, is necessary to discharge the contract.

An illustration of this common law rule is the case of *Sumpter* v. *Hedges* (1898). Here the plaintiff builder agreed to erect some houses for a lump sum of £565. Having carried out half the work to the value of £333 the builder was unable to complete because of financial difficulties. In an action by the builder to recover compensation for the value of work done the Court of Appeal confirmed that he was not entitled to payment. The legal position was expressed by Lord Justice Smith who stated 'The law is that where there is a contract to do work for a lump sum, until the work is completed, the price of it cannot be recovered'.

On the face of it the decision of the court appears to be harsh in its effect upon the builder. In fact the difficulty for the court is an obvious one, namely that a single sum has been agreed in consideration of the completion of specified works. If these works are not completed in their entirety the court would be varying the clearly expressed intentions of the parties if it was to award the builder payment of a proportionate part of the lump sum. In other words, by agreeing a lump sum the parties have impliedly excluded the possibility of part payment for partially fulfilled building work.

As far as sale of goods contracts are concerned the Sale of Goods Act

1979, s. 30, provides that where a seller delivers less or even more goods than were contracted to be sold, or goods complying with the contract mixed with other goods, the buyer has the right of rejection of the goods.

In *Re Moore and Co and Landauer and Co*, (1921), a contract had been entered into for the sale of a specific quantity of canned fruit to be packed in cases each containing 30 tins. When the seller delivered the exact quantity half the consignment was packed in cases containing 24 tins. The buyer refused to accept them. The Court held that as the delivered goods did not comply with their contractual description the seller had failed to fulfil a contractual obligation and the buyer was entitled to reject the consignment, relying on s. 30.

The above rules, however, requiring precise performance of contractual obligations can in practice, as has been seen, produce injustice. The law has therefore recognised certain exceptions.

a) *A divisible contract*   In some circumstances the courts are prepared to accept that a contract is a divisible one where part of the performance of the contract may be set off against part of the consideration to be given in return. Had the parties in *Sumpter* v. *Hedges* agreed a specific sum to be paid on completion of certain stages of the house building then the builder could have recovered compensation for part of the work done. In practice it is usual in a building contract to provide for payment of parts of the total cost at various stages of completion.

b) *Substantial performance*   If a party to a contract has substantially performed contractual obligations subject only to minor defects, the courts have recognised that it would be unjust to prevent the party recovering any of the contractual price. Therefore under this exception the contractual price would be recoverable, less of course a sum representing the value of the defects. It must be stressed that the exception will only operate where the defects are of a trifling nature. This is determined by considering not only the nature of the defects but also the cost of rectifying them in relation to the total contract price.

A claim of substantial performance of the contract was made in *Bolton* v. *Mahadeva* (1972). Here the plaintiff, a heating contractor, had agreed to instal a central heating system in the defendant's house for £560. On completion of the work the system proved to be so defective that it would cost £174 to repair. The defendant refused to pay the plaintiff any of the cost of the work and the plaintiff sued. The County Court accepted the plaintiff's claim of substantial performance and awarded him the cost of the work less the cost of repair. On appeal however the Court of

Appeal held that in the circumstances the plaintiff had not substantially performed the contract and he was not therefore entitled to recover any of the cost of the work. The exception would not operate where there were numerous defects requiring a relatively high cost of repair.

c) *The acceptance of partial performance* If a party to a contract partially performs their obligations and the other party accepts the benefit, then he or she is obliged to pay a reasonable price for it. Thus if a buyer in a sale of goods contract opts to accept rather than reject a delivery of less than the agreed quantity then the buyer is obliged to pay a reasonable price for it. In such circumstances the courts would allow an action on a *quantum meruit* basis (as much as he or she deserves). This exception however will only operate where the party receiving the benefit has the option of whether or not to accept or reject. In *Sumpter* v. *Hedges* the owner had no choice but to accept the work done on the half-completed houses and was therefore not obliged to pay for it.

d) *Where performance is prevented* Obviously if a party to a contract is prevented from fulfilling contractual obligations by the other party then the former will not be in default, eg if in a building contract the owner prevents the builder from completing. It these circumstances the builder can recover a reasonable price for the work done on a quantum meruit basis.

As well as the above exceptions to the general rule that the performance of contractual obligations must be precise, it is important to note that if a party to a contract makes a valid tender (offer) of performance this may be regarded as equivalent to performance. Thus if one party (a seller) cannot complete performance without the co-operation of the other party (a buyer), a valid tender of performance by the seller will be sufficient to discharge the seller from the contract, eg if a seller of goods attempts to deliver at the agreed time and place and the goods are of the correct quantity and quality and such delivery is wrongly refused by the buyer. Under the Sale of Goods Act 1979, s. 50, the seller in such circumstances could sue the buyer for damages for non acceptance of the goods.

2 *Discharge by agreement* This method of discharge occurs where the parties to a contract agree to waive their rights and obligations under it. It is called *bilateral discharge*. To be an effective *waiver* the second agreement must be a contract, the consideration for which being the exchange of promises not to enforce the original contract. The situation however is more complex where one party to a contract has already executed or partly executed consideration under it. Here for a waiver to be effective it must be embodied within a specialty contract or be supported by fresh consideration. This is called *unilateral discharge* and can only be achieved by *accord and satisfaction*. The accord is simply the agreement to discharge and the satisfaction is the

consideration required to support it, eg A contracts to sell goods to B for £50. A delivers the goods to B and then hearing of B's financial difficulties agrees to waive payment. Here the agreement of A to waive payment (the accord) is not enforceable unless supported by fresh consideration furnished by B (the satisfaction). The fresh consideration of course must be of value but need not be adequate. The position would be the same if A promised to accept £25 as full discharge of the debt of £50. There is a well known common law rule (referred to earlier under 'consideration') that payment of a lesser sum is not satisfaction of a liability to pay a larger sum even though the creditor agrees to take it in full discharge – *Pinnels Case*, 1602. The effect of this somewhat harsh common law rule would be to permit a creditor to renege on a promise. There are in fact a number of exceptions to the rule under which the courts will be prepared to accept that satisfaction, ie fresh consideration, has been supplied under the new agreement. Thus, if the creditor agrees:

a) A payment of a lesser sum before the due date would constitute consideration to discharge the £50 debt.
b) Payment in an altered mode, eg a £5 book would constitute consideration to discharge the £50 debt. Payment of a cheque however for less than £50 would not be a sufficient alteration in mode unless done at the request of the creditor (see *D & C Builders* v. *Rees* (1965).)
c) Payment of a lesser sum with something of value in addition, eg £10 and a bottle of brandy, would constitute consideration to discharge the £50 debt.
d) Payment of a lesser sum by a third party will discharge the £50 debt.
e) Payment of a lesser sum where the debtor is disputing the value of work that has been carried out by the creditor will discharge the debt, eg where a plumber has installed a central heating system for an agreed price, and when payment becomes due the creditor refuses to pay the full sum because of the alleged poor quality of the work performed.

A creditor's promise to accept a reduced amount may also be binding through the operation of the principle of *equitable estoppel* as enunciated by Denning.J in *Central London Property Trust Ltd* v. *High Trees House Ltd* (1947).

The *Central London Property Trust Ltd* v. *High Trees House Ltd* (1947) case involved the lease of a block of flats in 1939 from A to B at a rent of £2500 pa. In 1940 because of the lack of tenants in London caused by the war conditions the parties agreed in writing to a reduction of the rent to £1250 pa. As no time limit was set for the new agreement B continued to pay the reduced rent after the war had ended despite the fact that the flats were fully sublet. A, the landlord, now claimed rent at the rate of £2500 pa for the last

47

two quarters of 1945. The Court held that as the agreement for a reduced rent was intended to operate during the war conditions the full rent was payable on expiration of the war and therefore for the last two quarters of 1945. Denning.J also considered whether the common law rule that the 'payment of a lesser sum will not discharge the full debt' would render A's promise to accept a lesser rent unenforceable and enable him to claim back the full rent for the whole period. Relying on the earlier case of *Hughes* v. *Metropolitan Railway Co* (1877) Denning.J thought in such circumstances it would be inequitable to allow A to go back on his promise.

The principle of law relied on was termed equitable estoppel and still today is subject to much academic debate as to its limits. It may be stated as follows: if X, a party to a legal relationship, indicates by a promise to Y that he is not going to insist on his strict legal rights and as a result Y alters her position to her detriment, then although Y may not sue to enforce the promise she may use the promise as a defence if X purports to go back on it. For the principle to operate therefore it is necessary that the fresh promise was intended by the promisor to be acted upon and has in fact been acted upon to the promisee's detriment to the promisor's knowledge. It should be noted that the fresh promise cannot be enforced by court action brought by the promisee, but is available as a defence if the promisor attempts to go back on it. It is 'a shield not a sword': *Coombe* v. *Coombe* (1951).

It must be stressed that the equitable doctrine is not an attempt to remove consideration as a requirement of the simple contract, but rather a principle under which equity seeks to hold a promisor to a promise intended to be binding, and which has been acted upon by the promisee. The equitable doctrine only arises within the context of a pre-existing contractual relationship. It is worth pointing out that the High Trees decision is an authority which also supports the view that a deed can be varied by a simple contract. Prior to 1947 it had always been considered that because a simple contract is inferior to the more formal deed, that only a deed could vary a deed.

3 *Discharge by breach*   If a party to a contract fails to perform those obligations under it or performs them in a defective manner then the party may be regarded as being in breach of contract. Generally, the remedy of an innocent party who has suffered as a result of a breach of contract is to sue for damages. For some breaches of contract however the innocent party is given the additional remedy of *repudiation* (ie termination of the contract) and thus discharging himself or herself from obligations under it. It shall be seen in the later chapter on consumer protection that terms in a contract are classified into different categories and it is only when an important term in the contract has been broken that the remedy of repudiation is attached.

If a breach of contract occurs before the time set for performance of the contract it is called an *anticipatory breach*. This would occur where a party to a contract expressly declares that he or she will not perform their part of the bargain. Once an anticipatory breach has occurred the innocent party does not have to wait for the date set for performance but has the option of immediately suing for breach of contract.

> In *Hochster* v. *De la Tour* (1853) the defendant agreed in April to engage the plaintiff for work to commence in June. The defendant told the plaintiff in May that he would not require his services. The Court held that a cause of action for breach of contract arose on the anticipatory breach in May.

4 *Discharge by frustration* A contract may be discharged by frustration where as a result of an event subsequent to the making of the contract performance of the contract can no longer be carried out. The event must be subsequent to the contract for if the contract is impossible to perform at the time it is made then there *is* no contract. Originally the common law did not take such a lenient view of changes in circumstances and required that the parties to a contract should provide for all eventualities. If because of a subsequent event performance of an obligation became impossible the party required to perform the impossible obligation would be liable to pay damages for non performance.

> In *Paradine* v. *Jane* (1647) the King's Bench Court held a tenant liable to pay three years' arrears of rent to a landlord despite the fact that the tenant had been dispossessed of his house by soldiers during the Civil War.

Today however the courts recognise that certain supervening events may frustrate a contract and thus release the parties from their obligations under it, eg

a) *Changes in the law* If because of new legislation performance of the contract would become illegal this would be a supervening event to frustrate the contract. In *Denny, Mott and Dickson Ltd* v. *James B Fraser Ltd* (1944) the House of Lords held that a contract for the sale of timber was frustrated because of the subsequent passage of various Control of Timber Orders rendering performance of the contract illegal.

b) *Destruction of subject matter* If the subject matter or means of performance of the contract is destroyed this is an event which frustrates a contract.

> In *Taylor* v. *Caldwell* (1863) the plaintiff agreed to hire the defendant's music hall to give some concerts. Prior to performance the hall was destroyed by fire and this event, the

Court held, released the parties from their obligations under the contract.

c) *Inability to achieve main object* If as a result of a change in circumstances performance of the contract would be radically different than the performance envisaged by the parties then the contract is frustrated. It must be shown that the parties are no longer able to achieve their main object under the contract.

In *Krell* v. *Henry* (1903) the defendant hired a flat for two days to enable him to watch Edward VII's Coronation Procession. Due to the King's illness the Coronation was cancelled and the defendant naturally refused to pay. The Court of Appeal held that as the main object of the contract was to view the procession and this could no longer be achieved as the foundation of the contract had collapsed. The contract was thus frustrated and the parties released from their obligations under it. The cancellation of Edward VII's Coronation resulted in a similar case to contrast with *Krell* v. *Henry*. In *Herne Bay Steam Boat Co* v. *Hutton* (1903) a steam boat had been chartered to see the naval review as part of the Coronation celebrations and also for a day's cruise round the Fleet. The Court of Appeal had to determine whether the cancellation of the naval review released the defendant from his obligation to pay the hire charges. The Court held that there had not been a sufficient change in circumstances to constitute a frustration of the contract. Here the defendant could have derived some benefit from the contract and was therefore liable to pay the hire charges.

d) *Death or illness* In a contract for personal services the death or illness of the person required to perform will frustrate the contract. Temporary illness or incapacity will generally not release a party from obligations. The illness must be such that it goes to the root of the contract – *Condor* v. *The Barron Knights* (1966). The common law doctrine of frustration will not apply in the following situations:

(i) If performance of the contract has become more onerous on one party or financially less rewarding.

In *Davis Contractors Ltd* v. *Fareham U D C* (1956) the plaintiff building company claimed that a building contract should be regarded as discharged by frustration due to the shortage of available labour and resultant increased costs. The House of Lords rejected the argument that frustration had discharged the contract. Performance of the contract had simply been made more onerous than originally envisaged by the plaintiffs.

(ii) If the parties to a contract have made express provision for the event which has occurred then the common law doctrine of frustration is inapplicable. The courts will simply give effect to the intention of the parties as expressed in the contract.

(iii) Finally a distinction must be drawn between a frustrating event over which the parties have no control and a self-induced frustration. If it can be shown that a party to the contract caused the supposed frustrating event by his own conduct then there will be no frustration but there may be a contractual breach.

To determine the rights and duties of the parties following frustration it is necessary to consider the position at common law and under statute. Frustration of course will terminate a contract. However under the common law it does not discharge the contract *ab initio* (ie from the outset) but only from the time of the frustrating event. Therefore, if before that date work had been done or money transferred, the common law rule is simply that losses lie where they fall. It is thus not possible to recover money due or paid prior to frustrating events except if there is a total failure of consideration, ie there has been performance of consideration by one party and non performance of consideration by the other.

The common law position has been altered to some extent by the Law Reform (Frustrated Contracts) Act 1943. The Act however does not apply to certain contracts such as insurance, charter-parties (shipping contracts) and contracts for the sale of specific goods so the common law position is still relevant. Under the Act the following conditions apply:

a) Money transferred prior to the frustrating event may be recovered.
b) Money due prior to the frustrating event is no longer due.
c) Expenses incurred prior to the frustrating event may be deducted from money due to be returned.
d) Compensation may be recovered on a quantum meruit basis where one of the parties has carried out an act of part performance prior to the frustrating event and thus conferred a benefit on the other party.

The contractual bargain in the perfectly competitive market

The concept of a perfectly competitive market presupposes that neither side to the bargain, supplier or consumer, carries sufficient weight to significantly influence the other. Thus any supplier is bound by the market in determining the maximum price at which goods can be sold rather than being free personally to fix a price. Similarly no one consumer takes a sufficiently large share of the market to dictate contractual terms to the supplier. Therefore a contractual offer made by a consumer which contains terms which vary significantly from those with which the supplier is in accord will simply be rejected or met with a counter offer, since the supplier is always confident of finding an alternative buyer. Therefore in perfect competition the offer has the following characteristics:

1 it is usually similar in most transactions;
2 it will be rejected if conditions differ unfavourably to a significant extent.

But it has already been seen that perfect competition is a theoretical concept which rarely, if ever, manifests itself in practice. In most contractual bargains the reality is that one of the parties will usually have sufficient power to influence the terms of the contract. In the next chapter it is explained that most UK markets are oligopolistic. This type of market structure is reflected in the form of contracts which emerge from it.

Conclusion

The UK economy and the business environment which exists within it are obviously dynamic and complex entities. There are individual markets for specific goods and services which combine to form aggregate demand in the economy as a whole. The economy is essentially a free market one based on the interaction of demand and supply and theoretically should achieve an overall equilibrium which matches the demands of consumers with producers' willingness to supply. Each transaction in this process takes the form of a contract between buyer and seller and both the Government and the Judiciary, through the legal system, have established a set of rules and regulations which govern these transactions. In essence, the only need for government intervention in the market should be to establish the rules and then allow the courts to act as referees. However as already noted the market is incapable of providing some social goods, and supplies an insufficient amount of merit goods if allowed to operate in an uncontrolled manner. This chapter has concentrated on the theoretical workings of the free market and the basic law of contract which is necessary for it to operate efficiently. However in the following chapter it is necessary to relate theory to reality, assess how the market has developed and why the Government has felt it necessary to interfere with its working, using both economic and legal means.

2 Market reality

'The commerce of the world is conducted by the strong and usually it operates against the weak.'

Henry Ward Beecher
(Proverbs from the Plymouth Pulpit 1887)

The UK competitive structure

Perfect competition in perspective

The concepts of perfect competition and the implied conditions of a price-takers market were examined in the previous chapter. Economists have tended to the view that these conditions result in the market price and contractual terms being identical for all buyers and sellers. In fact each contractual bargain must be viewed in totality rather than concentrating on a single aspect, such as price. It is more realistic to examine the total substance of the bargain for the respective consideration exchanged by the parties will include all benefits and detriments arising under the contract. Thus, in a contract for the sale of goods consideration would include not only the price but also terms as to description, quality, rights of ownership and delivery time. For instance a purchaser may be prepared to pay a higher price in a perfectly competitive market if this is offset by some other benefit such as early delivery. However in perfect competition each contractual bargain made, when taken as a whole, will be economically equal. For this reason no buyer or seller, acting individually, carries sufficient economic power to significantly influence the other. Each has the freedom to buy or sell, and if the one decides to transact, there are many parties with whom to do so. The purchaser has a wide choice of potential suppliers and vice versa. The purchaser will in fact purchase on the supplier's terms but a contractual offer which contains provisions which differ considerably from those which prevail throughout the rest of the market will simply be rejected or met with a counter offer.

Perfect competition is however a theoretical concept which does not exist in practice except in certain limited cases which approach the perfectly competitive position, eg the Stock Exchange and the commodity markets. In almost all markets the reality is one of imperfect competition in which dominant suppliers inevitably use superior bargaining strength to negotiate terms which are most favourable to them and so produce a one-sided bargain. There are various examples of imperfect markets such as monopoly, monopolistic competition and oligopoly. Of these, oligopoly is the most common market form found in the UK. The last major industrial census found that in 20 of the 22 main industrial and service sectors an average of four organisations in each sector accounted for half the assets. Although some degree of competition may exist in oligopoly, business practice would tend to reflect a price-makers market, ie where the supplier is able to influence price and terms of the contract.

The growth of the oligopoly market

During the last sixty years the most noticeable characteristic of the changing industrial structure was the increasing predominance in most markets of a few very large organisations. This development has resulted in increasing concentration of output and resources into the hands of these organisations. Fig 2.1 illustrates this trend.

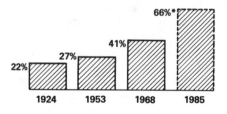

Fig 2.1   Share of the 100 largest companies in the UK net output: selected years
*1985 estimated figure

The market structure which has evolved has tended, in most cases, to be *oligopolistic*, ie a few large companies share the market between them. Table 2.1 shows oligopolistic characteristics in selected industries using the most common measure of concentration, the five firm concentration ratio.

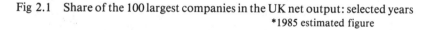

Industry	five firm seller concentration ratio %	illustrating % of market held by top five firms
Tobacco	99	
Manufactured fibres	98	
Sugar	97	
Cement	94	

Table 2.1   Concentration characteristics of selected industries in UK 1971
Source: Dept of Industry − Report on Census of Production 1971

A high degree of concentration in industry is often used as a measure of the level of competition. However in several instances there may be noticeable competition between organisations seeking to increase their market share. Oligopolies could result in excessive prices, a lack of efficiency and innovation and so be detrimental both to the consumer and the public interest. These consequences will be considered in more detail later.

Most consumers are unaware of the oligopolistic market structure as this is most pronounced at the production stage rather than at the retail stage. In buying most products, consumers have a wide choice of retailers but a much more restricted choice between the products of a few producers. If a person wishes to purchase a packet of soap powder there are a multitude of retailers available. The consumer may also believe that there exists a wide variety of choices available because of the many different brands on the shelf. In fact almost all soap powders are produced by either Procter and Gamble or Unilever. It is the retailer in the choice of which lines to carry who is faced with an oligopolistic supply structure.

International comparisons

International comparison of market concentrations is difficult because of the variations in statistical information. However it is clear that the trend towards a concentrated structure is more evident in the United Kingdom than in the United States or Europe. Between 1958 and 1970 UK concentration ratio increased from 32% to 39% while in the US this increase was only from 30% to 32%. The UK economy is also increasing its level of imports as a share of domestic demand and this unfortunately tends to disguise the facts on concentration and its relationship to the level of competition. If a large share of the domestic market is taken by imports then the concentration ratio (which is based solely on home producers) will underestimate the degree of competition which exists in the market. This is illustrated in Fig 2.2.

Industrial structure

A number of economic factors have probably contributed to this increasing degree of concentration. Organisational growth has traditionally been explained in terms of the *economies of scale* which result from such a development.

Economies of scale imply a reduction in average costs of production due to an increase in the size of companies at both plant and organisational level. They may be divided into *internal* economies of scale which are the result of large scale plants or organisations and *external* economies of scale which arise from industrial concentration in one geographical area.

Internal economies of scale are usually classified as follows: technical, managerial, commercial, financial and risk-bearing economies. A more detailed analysis of these economies is developed in

55

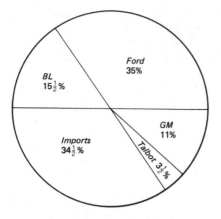

Fig 2.2   UK car sales November 1980 (Source: SMMT)

a later chapter, but generally, technical economies arise at plant level
while the other economies accrue at organisational level.

Plant level economies of scale

There is no doubt that technical economies of scale at plant level have
contributed to increasing company size in the UK. Much research has
been undertaken to establish estimates of *minimum efficient plant size*
(MEPS) over a wide range of UK industries. These estimates of MEPS
have varied from over 50% of UK production for goods such as electric
motors, TV tubes and tractors, to less than 1% for shoes or bricks.
Selected examples are given in Table 2.2.

Product	MEPS as % of UK produced sales
Aircraft	over 100%
TV tubes	c 100%
Tractors	76%
Electric refrigerators	69%
Diesel engines	56%
Cars	29 – 57%
Aluminium	36%
Detergent powder	20%
Car batteries	14%
Commercial vehicles	5 – 7%
Rubber tyres	6%
Bread	1%

Source: HMSO – A Review of Monopolies and Mergers Policy
* MEPS is defined as the minimum scale above which any possible subsequent
doubling of scale would reduce average total costs by less than 5%.

Table 2.2   Selected estimates of minimum efficient plant size*

For those products for which MEPS estimates are available, some assessment can be made of the extent to which high concentration is likely to be necessary if plant level economies of scale are to be realised. Where the MEPS % is above 20% this implies that efficient production is likely to require a high degree of concentration. Products in this category include cigarettes, sulphuric acid, electronic calculators, TV tubes, electric cookers, cars, and aircraft.

Insofar as it is possible to generalise, plant economies of scale are especially likely to be found in bulk chemicals and in operations where mass production assembly methods can be applied.

A number of qualifications must be considered when evaluating MEPS statistics. Understating the significance of technical economies of scale may have arisen for three reasons. Firstly, MEPS estimates are only available for a relatively small proportion of manufactured products and further research would reveal many more products for which MEPS is above 20%. Secondly, statistics relate to practice in the 1960s so in several cases MEPS may have increased since then. Thirdly, UK production includes export sales, so MEPS in relation to domestic sales may be even higher than suggested. Conversely, the MEPS figures may overstate the significance of scale economies for several reasons. For example, in many markets there is a demand for specialist products as well as the mass product, such as special sports cars and real ales and hence a role for smaller scale production. A number of practical considerations may limit the inducement to achieve maximum economies of scale, including

(i) the need to maintain flexibility in product range;
(ii) the problems of large plant management.

Despite these qualifications, however, it is a fact that production of many of the products identified above is very highly concentrated in the UK. For example, the five firm concentration ratio is over 90% for many products, such as cigarettes, detergents, TV tubes, and car batteries. This is an observation consistent with the existence of scale economies.

Organisation level economies of scale
The other economies of scale described earlier − managerial, commercial, financial and risk bearing − are chiefly the result of the size of the organisation and independent of plant size.

The fact that most of the growth in post war concentration has occurred through an increase in the number of plants owned by companies rather than increasing plant size (although average plant size *has* increased) suggests that these possible economies may have been an important stimulant. Unfortunately, there is very little real evidence about the importance of these economies and their role in explaining the increase in concentration. There is also some suggestion that positive diseconomies of scale occur in the growth of an organisation caused by factors such as industrial unrest and management problems.

The above analysis suggests that the complete reason for increased concentration cannot be found by reference to the internal economies of scale alone. Other possible explanations which have been suggested are the ambitions of managers for greater security, the desire for more market power and reduced competition. Analysis of these latter possible reasons is even more vague, and definite evidence is not available and so this remains an unresolved issue.

Merger activity

So far, possible reasons for the degree of concentration in the UK economy have been examined without considering how concentration may arise. This can result either from internal growth or from mergers. Evidence now suggests that much of the increased level of concentration has resulted from mergers between companies. Merger activity has varied in importance over the years, with peaks in 1965, 1968 and 1972 (see Table 2.3).

Year	No of mergers	Year	No of mergers
1963	888	1970	793
1964	940	1971	884
1965	1000	1972	1210
1966	807	1973	1205
1967	763	1974	504
1968	946	1975	315
1969	907	1976	353
		1977	482

Source: A Review of Monopolies and Mergers Policy

Table 2.3   Merger activity industrial and commercial companies 1963 – 72

The nature of mergers has also varied. *Horizontal* integration, that is, the acquisition of companies with similar products, has predominated. *Vertical* integration, that is, the acquisition of suppliers/distributors, and other mergers in which a company diversifies into various markets, has become increasingly common especially during the 1970s. The reasons for these other mergers which have produced increased concentration are both varied and complex. Many mergers certainly resulted in increased market share and have potentially or actually strengthened a monopoly or oligopoly position. This in itself may have been a prime motive for the merger. Other considerations may have played a role however. Apart from human motivations, financial factors such as the level of company liquidity and the difficulty in obtaining medium term finance, influence the ease with which mergers can arise. Other factors such as the advantages of growth by mergers rather than internal development, may also have contributed. Whatever the reasons for the mergers there is conclusive evidence of their important role in increasing the degree of concentration. Table 2.4 illustrates sources of changes in concentration between 1957 — 1969.

SIC industry group		Measure CR10 (% market share of top ten firms)		Change due to merger	Change due to internal growth
		1957	**1969**		
III	Food	62.1	80.5	12.9	5.5
IV	Drink	40.8	87.2	45.4	1.0
V	Tobacco	100	–	–	100
VI	Chemicals	80.6	86.4	2.0	3.8
VII	Metal manuf	58.7	74.3	16.7	– 1.1
VIII	Non electrical Eng	39.0	32.1	6.0	– 12.9
IX	Electrican Eng	60.4	81.2	22.0	– 1.2
X	Shipbuilding	80.3	93.3	10.5	2.5
XI	Vehicles & aircraft	67.2	85.8	20.0	– 1.4
XII	Metal goods	67.2	77.1	12.8	– 2.9
XIII	Textiles	55.9	74.2	23.4	– 5.1
XVI	Building materials	71.2	65.0	3.2	– 9.4
XVII	Paper & publishing	63.6	78.1	16.1	– 1.6

Source: L Hannah & J King — *Concentration in Modern Industry* (1977)

Table 2.4   Sources of change in concentration ratio

Theoretical behaviour of the oligopolistic market

The economic theory lying behind an analysis of the behaviour of the oligopolistic market is based upon an assumption that in a price-makers market which is created in oligopoly, producers are able to set a price which the market will bear and are able to raise it only by tacit agreement with competitors. It is known as an *administered price*.

The reasons why a few producers dominate a market is due to the optimal size of production unit for the type of industry. For example if a producer can continue to obtain economies of scale to a sufficient extent so that enough goods can be produced to meet total market demand, then a monopolistic situation will evolve. See Fig 2.3.

If the *optimal production* size is relatively small and each producer is only capable of providing a minor part of the total market demand, before diseconomies of scale set in and costs rise, then it is likely that the market will be made up of a large number of small scale suppliers. See Fig 2.4.

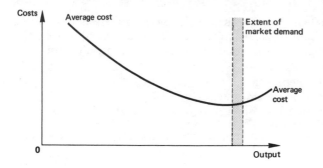

Fig 2.3　A monopolistic market

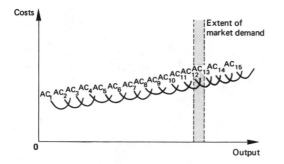

Fig 2.4　A highly competitive market

The oligopolistic market is likely to be one in which economies of scale continue to be possible for a substantial amount of the total market demand. This will mean that only a few suppliers can reach the optimal production size within the existing market. No one producer is able to totally dominate the market as it would be necessary to produce goods at an increasing cost if it were to meet total market demand. Therefore a few large suppliers will share the market. See Fig 2.5.

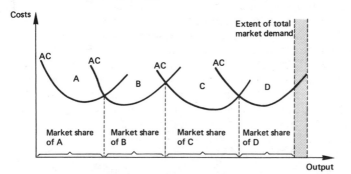

Fig 2.5　An oligopolistic market

Thus it is those industries where considerable economies of scale can be gained and where market demand is sufficient to accommodate several large scale producers which become oligopolistic.

If all producers in an oligopolistic market provide goods which are relatively similar, then even a small fall in price by one will tend to attract an expansion in sales of the other at the expense of competitors. However as all producers need to maintain high production levels in order to gain increasing economies of scale, the reaction of competing oligopolists is likely to be a reduction in their price to a competitive level with the producer who first cut the price. This would return market shares to their original level, but at a lower price, and so none of the competitors is likely to benefit. In fact all could be losers if sales have not increased by any great extent and prices have fallen. Thus all the oligopolists realise that it is in their *mutual* best interest to maintain price levels. Market shares therefore will tend to remain relatively static if prices stay constant. A brief illustration may help to explain.

A market is divided between three suppliers with the following market shares: A, 30%; B, 30%; C, 40%. A tries to increase its market share by lowering price, resulting in an initial re-alignment of sales: A, 38%; B, 26%; C, 36%; B and C are now producing below their most efficient level and so are forced to lower price to a comparable level with that of A. The market shares then return to their initial distribution with no producer gaining any marked benefit. In fact all are now worse off because the price has now fallen.

A theoretical example of this price rigidity is demonstrated by the *kinked* oligopolistic demand curve as shown in Fig 2.6.

If a producer cuts price market rivals will follow suit. That producer's market share will not increase although total sales will increase as market price falls. If the producer increases price and competitors do not, then the result will be a substantial fall in market share.

P_1Q_1 shows the original price and quantity sold. If the producer increases price to P_2 and competitors do not, sales will fall to Q_{2_1}. If competitors do follow suit then sales will only fall to Q_{2_m}.

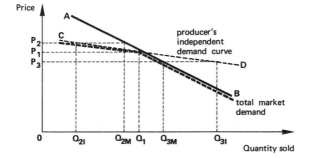

Fig 2.6   A 'kinked' demand curve

If the producer lowers price to P_3 independently, then sales increase to Q_{3_I} but competitors are forced to similarly comply and sales only increase to Q_{3_M}. Typical market trends would indicate a rigidity of price and the producers demand curve will be likely to be shown by the curve CB and thus the characteristic kinked demand curve.

Oligopolists realise the restrictions which this situation imposes upon them. They are therefore reluctant to compete with each other using price. However this does not mean competition is altogether absent in the oligopolistic market – far from it. If a producer is able to increase the extent of economies of scale and so raise the level of profitable output he or she may wish to attempt to increase market share. Because of the inherent dangers of trying to do this using price, the oligopolist seeks to use *non-price competitive measures* to increase sales. This usually means an increase in advertising budget in an effort to persuade consumers that this product is more desirable than the competitors, even though there is little price difference. Other means of sales promotion may include 'free' gifts, competitions and sales gimmicks. In the 1960s and 1970s the petrol industry was oligopolistic to a large degree. Competition tended to be based on advertising and sales promotions while prices remained relatively similar. Esso's 'Tiger in Your Tank', and other companies' use of free glasses and table mats were obvious examples of non-price competition.

The producer is in fact working on two demand curves – his or her own, if competitors do not alter their price as he or she does, and the total market demand curve.

The behaviour of dominant organisations

It has already been asserted that when suppliers enjoy a dominant market position it is usual to find that they will use their dominant bargaining strength for their exclusive benefit. By doing so they may prejudice not only the position of the buyers but also society as a whole. In most cases suppliers tends to be the dominant party. However, certain consumers in both the private and public sectors of the economy are so influential and take up such an important share of the total market supply that they are able to effectively determine the terms of the contract. For instance, Marks and Spencer, as consumers of manufacturers' products, have such a large market share that they are able to set very stringent conditions of purchase. Manufacturers desperate for the M & S contract, are forced to comply with conditions for M & S which they might not be willing to meet for other less important customers. Perhaps the most obvious characteristic of the behaviour of the dominant party is in relation to price. As a price maker, the supplier can successfully increase selling price to a level above that which would exist in conditions of perfect competition. Of course, the price at which goods or services are sold represents only one of the terms of the agreement the supplier concludes with customers. By using the ability to exploit people and situations, the supplier can provide for himself or herself a comprehensive set of favourable terms. The supplier will, for example, attempt to limit personal legal liability as far as it is permissable to do so under the law.

The terms which are negotiated and agreed upon by the parties make up the contents of the contract. They are its substance. Many contracts are concluded under which the terms agreed are of the most elementary kind. A mere identification of the subject matter of the bargain together with a statement as to price may be all that the parties expressly agree upon.

However as the economic value of a transaction increases it becomes more common to find that the parties incorporate into the contract a wide variety of express terms, each designed to specify precise contractual obligations and pre-empt any problems which arise before, during or after the contract has been performed. Clearly in the interests of cost, time and convenience, commercial organisations prefer to resolve contractual differences by reference to the provisions of the agreement itself, rather than seeking the help of the Courts. It is not only financially valuable transactions, such as building, engineering and manufacturing contracts that attract extensive and detailed terms. Contractual obligations may be of a detailed or technical nature even though the economic worth of individual transactions is small. For example a transport operator, such as British Rail, may carry a passenger a short distance for a relatively small charge, but the legal implications of the contract for the operator are considerable. What are the operator's obligations if the journey cannot be completed because of the weather, or industrial action? What if the passenger is injured during the journey? What if the train arrives late and the passenger suffers loss as a result? How long should the ticket be valid for, and what are the consequences if it expires during a journey? In a dominant market situation, such as that enjoyed by British Rail, terms can be imposed within the transactions it makes with its customers, which are both designed to benefit the stronger party and deal with any dispute which may arise. The dominant supplier can dictate terms for the customer is faced with a very limited range of alternatives.

Standard form contracts

Because it makes commercial sense to clearly and exhaustively set out the terms which will apply to the contract, the majority of organisations rely upon standard form agreements. These are printed forms consisting of a uniform set of terms for use by the organisation as the basis upon which it trades. A standard form agreement is an advantage to an organisation in two ways. Firstly it will help to save time by removing the need to regularly negotiate terms. Secondly it can, and usually will, provide the organisation with a set of terms which are entirely favourable to it, for instance, enabling it to increase prices, cancel the agreement in specified circumstances, impose obligations upon the other party as to minimum resale prices and other restrictive trade practices.

In the context of dominant firm behaviour the standard form agreement is a means of dictating terms to the weaker party. The weaker the party is, the more likely a 'take it or leave it' situation will emerge. The rail traveller who does not like the conditions of travel that are imposed will either have to accept them, or travel by some other means. The weaker party will have to accept the terms presented by the stronger party in total, or find that the other will refuse to transact at all. The only negotiation that takes place concerns whether or not the contract is actually made. It is not in a real sense negotiation at all, for the parties do not meet as bargaining equals. The agreement is totally unequal. Even so, the weaker party may be obliged to accept such domination because he or she cannot be deprived of the goods or services the supplier is offering, as they are essential to his or her livelihood (eg owning a garage and selling petrol to make a profit) or ordinary human needs (water, electricity and gas supplies). Such contracts are sometimes referred to as *contracts of adhesion*, for the weaker party is simply adhering to the other's terms.

Loss of bargaining freedom

Under the laissez-faire economic philosophy which flourished in the nineteenth century it was considered right and proper to allow contracting parties the freedom (with only a few legal limitations) to make whatever bargain best suited their individual interests. The parties themselves should and could look after their own needs and requirements. However this concept of *freedom of contract* presupposed the common ability of the parties to negotiate their bargain on an equal footing. The inequality that invariably exists in the modern bargaining situations especially in consumer transactions, underlines the illusory quality of freedom of contract if it is applied to many contemporary contractual situations. Parliament has recognised the imbalance of bargaining power as a common feature of modern transactions, and the result has been an ever-growing body of legislation designed to limit the powers of the dominant party, regulate particular transactions, and grant rights to certain classes of contract maker. Notable examples of legislative intervention in contract making are to be found in contracts of sale, contracts of employment and credit transactions of various kinds. A common device is to imply terms into the contract which the stronger party is unable to exclude, eg s. 12 of the Sale of Goods Act 1979 under which it is an implied condition of a contract of sale that the seller has the right to sell the goods. Thus if the seller does not own the goods then the seller is in breach of the contract and the buyer can terminate the agreement.

Before considering particular examples of standard contract terms it is important to note that the use of a standard form contract does not automatically exclude the possibility of negotiation upon the terms between the parties. As between bargaining equals, the standard form agreement that is put forward by one of them may be rejected in whole or in part by the other, who perhaps will wish to incorporate some of his or her own standard terms. This can sometimes lead to what has been called *the battle of conditions*. An example of this situation is seen in *Butler Machine Tools* v. *Ex-Cell-O Corporation (England) Ltd* (1978). It will be recalled that here the seller of a machine sent a quotation to the buyers. The quotation contained the seller's standard trading terms including a price escalation clause. The buyers ordered the machine on their own standard terms. These did not include a price escalation clause. The buyer's order included a tear-off slip which included a statement that they accepted the buyer's order 'on the terms and conditions stated therein'. The Court of Appeal held that the contract was made on the buyer's terms following the principle laid down in *Hyde* v. *Wrench* (1840) and applying the traditional rules relating to formation of contracts. The seller could not therefore increase the price under the escalation clause.

Particular industries produce standard conditions of contract for use within the industry. A good example is afforded in the case of the construction industry. By standardising terms in this way practical benefits are obtained. It becomes unnecessary to continually re-write the contract, and it becomes possible for members of the industry to familiarise themselves with terms, and gain an understanding of the nature and scope of the highly technical contracts they are involved in. In the case of the construction industry standard conditions of contract, of which there are various sets in use, have been produced through the involvement of various interested parties (eg builders, architects, civil engineers, etc). The aim is to provide a framework of terms which the parties can alter, amend, or remove if they care to do so. In other industries members combine to produce standard trading conditions which are not designed to be altered, for example, in the motor trade. Here it is unlikely that the supplier will negotiate on anything other than the predetermined terms.

Types of standard form contractual clauses
The dominant supplier may seek to include a variety of types of clauses in a contract of sale. The clauses could try to do three different things for the supplier:

1 *reserve the supplier's powers as the seller;*
2 *restrict the freedom of the purchaser.*
3 *force the purchaser to take a certain form of action;*

An examination of a wide selection of standard form contracts has produced the following examples of each of these categories.

Reserved powers of the seller

A general clause included in many suppliers' contracts of sale may simply state;

'Every contract of sale is subject to the seller's conditions of sale.'

This forces the buyer to accept a variety of clauses. The major type of clause usually specifies conditions of price or payment:

'Unless otherwise agreed, payment for the goods shall become due on completion of delivery in accordance with the contract.'

or

'Unless firm prices and charges are agreed upon, the seller shall be entitled to increase the agreed prices and charges by the same amount by which the prices or charges of the goods or their components including the costs of labour to be paid or borne by the seller have been increased between the date of quotation and the date of delivery.'

Clauses such as this mean that the supplier is able to escalate the price if production costs increase, eg wage rises or inflationary price rises for raw materials. The buyer will have no option but to bear the increased price.

The seller may also wish to retain ownership of the material sold until full recompense is received.

'Ownership of the material to be delivered by the seller will only be transferred to the purchaser when he has met all that is owing to the seller, no matter on what grounds. The seller and purchaser agree that if the purchaser should make (a) new object(s) from the material mix this material with (an)other object(s) or if this material in any way whatsoever becomes a constituent of (an)other object(s), the seller will be given ownership of this (these) new object(s) as surety of the full payment of what the purchaser owes the seller. To this end the seller and the purchaser now agree that the ownership of the article(s) in question, whether finished or not, are to be transferred to the seller and that this transfer of ownership will be considered to have taken place through and at the moment of the single operation or event by which the material is converted into (a) new object(s). Nevertheless the purchaser will be entitled to sell these objects to a third party within the framework of the normal carrying on of his business and to deliver them on condition that, if the seller so requires, the purchaser so long as he has not fully discharged his debt to the seller shall hand over to the seller claims he has against his buyer emanating from this transaction.'

In this case the seller is protecting his or her rights of ownership until the full selling price is received. The purchaser is not able to resell the goods in any form until this ownership is transferred.

Restrict the freedom of the purchaser

The seller may also require some protection against liability.

'The seller hereby excludes his liability for liability of or any consequential loss, damage, claims or liabilities of any kind arising from any cause whatsoever.'

or

'Under no circumstances shall the company be held responsible for any loss suffered by the customer through fire or any other cause, except in so far as such loss is solely attributable to the negligence of the company's employees within the course of their employment.'

Thus the clause attempts to place all liability on the customer.

Force the purchaser to take a certain form of action

Dominant suppliers have also attempted to force their distributors to resell their products only at specific prices and to certain customers. A clause such as this is known as a resale price maintenance clause. An example is given from *Dunlop Pneumatic Tyre Co* v. *Selfridge and Co* (1915).

"PRICE MAINTENANCE AGREEMENT

To be entered into by Trade Purchasers of Dunlop Motor Tyres. Messrs. Selfridge & Co. to Messrs. A.J. Dew & Co.

Dear Sir,

In consideration of your allowing us a trade discount of 10 per cent for prompt monthly payments off the list prices for motor tyres, covers, tubes and repairs contained in Dunlop Pneumatic Tyre Co's. list current from time to time . . .

(2) We will not sell or offer any Dunlop motor tyres, covers or tubes to any private customers or to any co-operative society at prices below those mentioned in the said price list current at the time of sale, nor give to any such customer or society any cash or other discounts or advantages reducing the same. We will not sell or offer any Dunlop Motor tyres, covers or tubes to any other person at prices less than those mentioned in the said price list . . .

(5) We agree to pay to the Dunlop Pneumatic Tyre Co. Ltd. the sum of £5 for each and every tyre, cover or tube sold or offered in breach of this agreement, as and by way of liquidated damages and not as a penalty, but without prejudice to any other rights or remedies you or the Dunlop Pneumatic Tyre Co. may have hereunder."

Each of the above clauses show how the dominant party in a contract of sale may attempt the promotion and protection of self-interests. The benefit to the weaker party will be the acquisition of property or the provision of some service, but the cost is the loss of rights which might otherwise have been enjoyed. The stronger party will, for instance, try to exclude any personal liability that would otherwise arise under or out of the contract, with the result that the weaker party who has a genuine grievance about the condition of the goods bought, finds he or she is prevented from obtaining any redress. This is the type of consequence which follows the conclusion of a one-sided agreement. The bargain which is struck is, often, totally unequal. Indeed it is arguable whether a contract which is based entirely upon the terms of one party alone, and where there is no possibility of negotiation, can be regarded as a bargain in the true sense at all.

Both Parliament and the courts have recognised that when a party is in a position to dominate trading in this way injustice will invariably occur. The response of Parliament to this imbalance has been the introduction over a number of years of a large and steadily growing body of legislation primarily, although not exclusively, designed to bolster the position of consumers in consumer transactions. A number of examples will be considered in the chapter on Consumer Protection, including the Sale of Goods Act 1979 which regulates contracts of sale, the Consumer Credit Act 1974 which regulates credit transactions of various types, and the Unfair Contract Terms Act 1977 which seeks to outlaw certain types of exclusion clauses and restrict the operation of others. The judicial response to bargaining inequality is less readily apparent. This is hardly surprising since Parliament possesses a far greater ability to implement radical and comprehensive legal changes than do the Courts, which are bound by the system of precedent. Nevertheless, there are areas in which the impact of the courts has been marked. The concept of undue influence developed as an acknowledgement by the Courts that circumstances can arise under which a contract should be set aside as being an unconscionable bargain:

> In *O'Rorke* v. *Bolingbroke* (1877) it was judicially stated that while 'In ordinary cases each party to a bargain must take care of his own interest . . . in the case of . . . persons under pressure without adequate protection, and in the case of dealings with uneducated ignorant persons, the burden of shewing the fairness of the transaction is thrown on the person who seeks to obtain the benefit of the contract'.

The courts have also traditionally shown a reluctance towards accepting the use of exclusion of liability clauses by stronger parties in their dealings with weaker parties. Manifestations of the disapproval of such clauses by the judiciary can be seen in the rules of construction (ie interpretation) that have been laid down to deal with them. The words of the clause will be strictly, not liberally, interpreted. Ambiguities are construed against the person relying on the written document (this is known as the *contra proferentem* rule).

Despite these examples the courts recognise that there is a limit to how far they should protect people from their own folly. It should be remembered that contracts spring from agreement, and it is the duty of the courts to uphold the sanctity of the agreement. Thus it is a fallacy to suppose that courts can or indeed will always wish to rectify every bad bargain. So, to take just one example, although the old common law principle *caveat emptor*, let the buyer beware, has been eroded both by the actions of Parliament and the courts, there still remain those circumstances under which a purchaser will find that there *is* no escape from the contract.

Earlier in the chapter some examples were given of clauses which are commonly found in standard form sale agreements. In the light of the comments that are made above regarding the statutory and judicial interference that can take place within a contract, it is helpful to identify in outline an example of how this will occur in practice. One clause, it will be recalled, attempted to exclude the seller's liability for 'loss damage claims or liabilities of any kind arising from any cause whatsoever'. It is, of course, a self-evident proposition that such a clause, like others, will largely be disregarded by the parties unless and until a disagreement arises between them, when it will come under close scrutiny. It is then that the standard of draftsmanship is tested. The party who claims that the clause does not apply to the dispute will commonly base this claim upon an assertion that it is contrary to statute or offends against the common law. Such an assertion will ultimately be tested before the court. Thus in the above clause it would be suggested that under the Unfair Contract Terms Act 1977, to the extent that the clause excludes liability for death or bodily injury arising through negligence, it would be void. It would also be pointed out that under the same Act the clause would have to satisfy a test of reasonableness. The question might then arise as to whether the clause *could* be reasonable if it is interpreted as applying to the breach of a major term of the contract. The answer to such a question would be found by looking beyond the Act itself to the Common Law, and perhaps referring to a decision of the Courts such as that of the House of Lords in *Photo Productions Ltd* v. *Securicor* (1980) which reaffirmed that it is possible to construct a clause which can effectively exclude liability for breach of a major term of the contract. The concept of fundamental breach of contract is dealt with in Chapter 5.

There may of course be clauses in a standard form agreement which legally are perfectly valid, in which event the nature of the dispute between the parties could be as to the meaning of the language used. Referring again to the clauses mentioned earlier in the chapter, one particular clause provided for ownership in the goods to remain with the seller until certain conditions as to payment were satisfied (known as a *Romalpa* clause). Under the Sale of Goods Act 1979 it is expressly provided that the parties to a contract for the sale of goods can determine for themselves when ownership shall pass. The clause therefore is simply the exercising of a right which Parliament clearly allows.

SECURICOR FREIGHT & PARCELS OPERATION
(PARCELS SECTION)

To: SECURICOR MOBILE LTD
Registered in England with No. 816887
Registered Office — 24 Gillingham Street, London SW1 1HZ

VAT Registration No. 238 5602 56
VAT Registered Address:
583, Fulham Road, SW6 5UE

T 430956

Receive and forward the consignment **SUBJECT TO THE STANDARD TERMS OF CONTRACT** of Securicor Mobile Limited ("the Company") **a** copy of which terms is available on request. An extract from such terms namely those relating to **limitation of the Company's liability to £50 per consignment** and to an indemnity by the customer, is printed overleaf.

CUSTOMER'S SIGNATURE

NAME OF SIGNATORY IN CAPITALS

FROM CONSIGNOR	TO CONSIGNEE	LABEL NUMBERS
		From _____
		To _____
POST CODE	POST CODE	inclusive

TICK
TYPE OF
SERVICE
REQUIRED

A ☐ *next working day by 1200
B ☐ *next working day
C ☐ *two working days
SAT A.M. ☐ by 1200 Saturday (if agreed)

*for total distances of 250 miles or more, and for transits in either direction between England and Scotland involving locations north of a straight line passing through Glenrothes and Greenock, add one working day.

WORKING DAYS DO NOT INCLUDE SATURDAYS, SUNDAYS OR PUBLIC HOLIDAYS

NUMBER OF ITEMS	TOTAL WEIGHT	DATE	TIME	COLLECTING BRANCH
	kgs.			

COURIER'S SIGNATURE... Order Number

Invoicing instructions if not charged to consignor _____

FOR SECURICOR OFFICE USE ONLY

Contract Number		Basic Charge	£	:
Excess Weight	kg	VAT at %	£	:
Temporary	Miles	Total	£	:
Account Number		Invoice Number	Invoice Date	

70

STANDARD TERMS OF CONTRACT

1. (i) "Consignment" means any article or articles of any sort which may be, or be intended to be, received by the Company from any one consignor at any one address for carriage and delivery at any one time to any one consignee at any one other address.

    (ii) "The Customer" means the person requesting the Company to transport the consignment.

    (iii) "The excepted risks" mean:—
    - (a) War, invasion, act of foreign enemy, hostilities (whether war be declared or not), civil war, rebellion, revolution, insurrection or military or usurped power, or loot, sack, or pillage in connection therewith, and/or
    - (b) Ionising radiations or contamination by radioactivity from any nuclear fuel or from any nuclear waste from the combustion of nuclear fuel, and/or
    - (c) Radioactive, toxic, explosive or other hazardous properties of any explosive nuclear assembly or nuclear component thereof, and/or
    - (d) Pressure waves caused by aircraft and other aerial devices travelling at sonic or supersonic speeds, and/or
    - (e) The absence, failure or inadequacy of packing or packaging.

LIABILITY OF THE COMPANY

Note: Where the Customer deals with the Company as a consumer the provisions set out hereunder do not and will not affect his statutory rights.

2. **WHEREAS:**
    (a) The value of the property intended to be carried and/or delivered under this Agreement and also the amount of any consequential loss which might arise from damage or loss to or of the said property are matters which are better known to and/or more readily ascertainable by the Customer than the Company; indeed to some extent they cannot be known to the Company, but are under the control of the Customer;

    (b) The potential extent of the damage (as defined in (f) below) that might be caused or be alleged to be caused to the Customer is disproportionate to the sum that can reasonably be charged by the Company under this Agreement;

    (c) The Company is not able to obtain insurance giving unlimited cover for its full potential liability to its customers under Agreements such as this and in any case even insurance giving limited cover for such liability is more difficult and more expensive to obtain than insurance in respect of any loss of or damage to his own property or of loss arising therefrom which insurance the Customer should be able to, and should, obtain;

    (d) The Company is concerned to keep down the costs of the services it provides to its customers under Agreements such as this;

    (e) In the circumstances the Company intends to limit its liability for any damage caused to the Customer (as defined in (f) below) to amounts which are not out of proportion to its charges hereunder, namely the amounts defined in (II) below;

    (f) In this Agreement "damage caused to the Customer" means any damage suffered by the Customer (including for the avoidance of doubt any loss of or damage to any Consignment and loss of any other kind whether direct or consequential), howsoever arising caused by any negligence, breach of duty or other wrongful act or omission (which phrase, wherever it appears in this Agreement, includes any deliberately wrongful act or omission and any breach, howsoever fundamental, of any express or implied term of this Agreement) on the part of the Company its servants or agents;

    (g) It is difficult to investigate claims received weeks after the loss or damage is alleged to have occurred.

THE COMPANY AND THE CUSTOMER AGREE TO THE FOLLOWING LIMITATION OF LIABILITY

   (I) Provision as to liability of the Company, its servants or agents
   So far as concerns damage caused to the Customer the Company shall be liable to the Customer (and then only to the limited extent set out below) only if and in so far as such damage is caused by the negligence, breach of duty or other wrongful act or omission of the Company itself or its directors or servants acting within the course of their employment.

   (II) Provision as to limitation of the amount of liability of the Company
   If, whether pursuant to the provisions set out herein or otherwise, any liability to the Customer shall arise on the part of the Company, its servants or agents (whether under the express or implied terms of this Agreement, howsoever fundamental, or in negligence or in any other way, however fundamental may be the breach of any duty) for any damage caused to the Customer, such liability shall in all cases whatsoever be limited to the payment by the Company on its own behalf and on behalf of its servants and agents by way of damages of a sum not exceeding £50 in respect of damage caused to the Customer in the case of any one Consignment and to a maximum sum of £10,000 in respect of all or any damage caused to the Customer during any one calendar year.

   (III) Provision as to notification of claims
   The Company its servants or agents shall not be liable to the Customer in any circumstances or to any extent whatever in respect of damage caused to the Customer unless written notice is received by the Company at its Head Office (stated hereon) within 7 days immediately following discovery of any damage caused to the Customer but in any event within 14 days of the date upon which the Consignment was collected or received by the Company.

   (IV) Special provision as to the excepted risks and as to strikes etc.
   - (a) The Company and its servants or agents shall not in any circumstances whatever be liable for any damage caused to the Customer arising directly or indirectly from or in consequence of any of the excepted risks, or for any expenses whatsoever resulting or arising therefrom.
   - (b) If the Company shall at any time be prevented from or delayed in starting, carrying out or completing any service referred to overleaf by reason of strikes, lockouts, labour disputes, weather conditions, traffic congestion, mechanical breakdown or obstruction of any public or private road or highway or any cause whatever beyond the Company's control, the Customer shall have no claim for damages or otherwise against the Company its servants or agents for any consequential loss as a result thereof PROVIDED that in the case of mechanical breakdown of one of the Company's vehicles the Company shall use its best endeavours to provide a replacement vehicle with the minimum practicable delay.

   (V) Special provision as to labelling
   The Company its servants or agents shall not in any circumstances whatever be liable for any late delivery or misdelivery or non-delivery caused or contributed to by any deficient or ambiguous labelling of the Consignment.

3. **PROVISION FOR INDEMNITY BY THE CUSTOMER**
    The Customer shall for all purposes be treated by the Company and its servants or agents as sole beneficial owner of any and every Consignment and it is agreed that if any other person shall in respect of any Consignment, or part thereof, make any claim against the Company its servants or agents arising out of the subject-matter of this Agreement whether arising out of any negligence, breach of duty or other wrongful act or omission by the Company its servants or agents or otherwise in respect of any loss or damage (including loss of any kind whether direct or consequential) outside or beyond the liability of the Company to the Customer, as limited herein, then the Customer shall indemnify the Company its servants or agents against any such claim (and all costs incurred therein) in respect whereof the Company is by this Agreement declared to be under no liability to the Customer, or in so far as any such claim shall cause the total liability of the Company to the Customer and all such claimants to exceed the limited sums set out above PROVIDED NEVERTHELESS that if any servant or agent of the Company shall have been guilty of any deliberately wrongful act or omission (relevant to such loss or damage in respect of which any such claim is made) such servant or agent shall not be, as between himself and the Customer, entitled to the benefit of this indemnity.

71

It is worth adding that in practice it is common to find provision made in standard form agreements for disputes to be referred to arbitration. This has the merit of enabling a dispute to be heard quickly and for less cost than if it were referred to the court. The arbitrator will also generally possess the technical expertise that is essential to the understanding or interpretation of detailed and specialised contracts. An example of an arbitration clause is given below. It is worth noting that it is not valid to attempt to remove the powers of the ordinary courts to hear contractual claims.

'The validity, construction and performance of this contract shall be governed by the law of England and any dispute that may arise out of or in connection with this contract, including its validity, construction and performance shall be determined by arbitration under the rules of the London Court of Arbitration.'

Some of these clauses are illustrative of the dominant bargaining position which can evolve if a customer has a limited choice of suppliers. Post-war governments have recognised this inequality and its potential dangers and have taken certain steps to attempt to redress this balance by their competition policy. This is now considered in detail.

Governmental policy on competition

The behaviour of the oligopolistic market in both practice and theory is likely to be detrimental to the consumer, in that it reduces choices available and could lead to increased price. It is also regarded as being against the best interest of the economy as a whole if it leads to inefficient production and an inflationary price level. Successive governments in the post-war period have recognised the inherent dangers of increasing market concentration. They have held that competition is, in essence, an objective that should be sought either by independent market forces or by government intervention.

Greater competition in the industrial service sectors of the UK economy has become either a stated or implied policy objective. The government however has had to be relatively pragmatic in its approach to competition policy. To enforce a more competitive approach in the UK economy may be at the cost of losing some of the advantages of the large scale economies which it brings. Its policy has therefore been based on three criteria:

(i)   *the structure of the market;*
(ii) *the conduct of individual producers;*
(iii) *the economic efficiency of these individual producers and the industry as a whole.*

The government has monitored the increasing concentration of industry and has by legislative means assumed power to intervene if one or more producers takes a significant share of an individual market. It has been realistic enough to allow this growing domination if it can be proved that the oligopolist is acting and is likely to continue to act in a manner which is not generally disadvantageous to a) the consumer, b) competing organisations, or c) the economy as a whole. A benevolent monopolist or oligopolist who acts in a manner which is not prejudicial to individuals as consumers or competitors or to the public interest, is tolerated as long as their market conduct does not change.

An efficient industry is also seen as being of vital need to the UK economy and if a producer can prove to the government that the level of production which most increases efficiency also happens to be so large that it creates an oligopolistic situation then this may be regarded as being acceptable. However if the evidence indicates that there are little or no substantial benefits to be gained from the existence of an oligopoly market then the government is clear in its intention to intervene in the market and influence it.

The Government's legislative power to intervene

The Government's legal power to intervene in the operation of the market is exercised by creating appropriate legislation. In this chapter there are many examples of government-sponsored legislation designed to manipulate the operation of market forces. The power of the government to legislate in this way is legally limitless. This is because Parliament enjoys *sovereign power*. The government of the day, having a voting majority in Parliament, can in general be assured that the legislation it presents to Parliament will be enacted. Nevertheless, despite the powers of government being legally unfettered there are in practice political pressures upon the government, of which it will take account when it is considering legal change. There are, for example, sectional interest groups such as employers' organisations and trade unions, whose views may be influential in determining the nature of the government's economic policy. The policy thus determined will be implemented through the passage of legislation. It is common to find that where the details of legislative proposals are complex, or technical, or where the legislation is intended to apply to future need or requirements which at present cannot be fully identified, then the framework of the proposals will be contained in the statute. Powers are then granted under the statute (*Parent Act*) to enable an individual, such as a Minister, or an organisation, such as a local authority, to make further subordinate legislation as and when the need arises. Such legislation, which is often termed *delegated* legislation, is a major source of legislative rules. These rules may be produced in the form of statutory instruments and orders. An example of legislation being created at these two levels can be seen in the government's attempts to protect the consumer in the field of credit transactions.

Under the Consumer Credit Act 1974 a variety of controls over the provision of credit facilities were introduced, and a number of consumer rights were granted. Among these were rights of consumers to protection from the seizure of hire purchase goods after a proportion of their price has been paid, and rights of cancellation. In addition powers were granted to the Secretary of State under the Act to make regulations as to the form and contents of regulated credit agreements.

Many regulations have now been produced by the Secretary of State, acting in accordance with the powers granted to him. Among examples of this subordinate legislation are the Consumer Credit (Advertisements) Regulations 1980 which makes provision for the form of credit advertisements and the Consumer Credit (Quotations) Regulations 1980 which indicates the details that the consumer is entitled to, when the creditor is providing information about the proposed transaction.

The return to the competitive market

The government in stating its policy aim to influence the level of competition within UK industry is basing its belief on the initial criteria for perfect competition. The government takes steps to move the economy towards the conditions prevailing in this type of market by recognising the need to redress the non-competitive aspects of current markets. To recap on the main conditions of a perfect market (outlined in Chapter 1) the government will attempt to counteract the increasing concentration of markets by encouraging many buyers and many sellers. It will attempt to allow in most cases, the freedom of movement of the factors of production so that they are used in their most efficient and profitable manner. Not only must land, labour and capital be free to move to the organisation or industry in which it will earn the highest rewards, but companies must also be able to enter a market in which they could be most profitable. And so the government will, in certain instances, reduce the *barriers of entry* into an industry or market.

The condition of *homogeneity* of products is not really enforceable by the government. However if producers state they are providing a product of a certain standard the government may legislate to ensure that minimum standards are adhered to and that goods correspond to the description given to them by the producers.

The government does not feel it is necessary to make every seller and buyer aware of prevailing market terms. This it believes should be the individual's own responsibility, but in some cases where non-disclosure of information may be prejudicial to one or both parties, the law requires disclosure of material facts, eg the government is currently considering legislation which would require second-hand car dealers to make customers aware of relevant information relating to the car's history.

Rational behaviour is also an assumption which must be open to question. Neither sellers nor buyers necessarily always act in their own best interests and while the law does not attempt to protect the foolish, it does seek to prevent practices which prey upon the irrationality of individuals.

The following section will look at each of these conditions separately and show how the law is used to increase the level of competition or reduce non-competitiveness in different markets.

Many buyers and many sellers — reduction of the growth of concentration

The prime condition for a competitive market is that there are many sellers who compete for the available custom. An absence of this criteria could tend to indicate to the government a lack of competition. As already stated the UK displays a high degree of market concentration in most sectors. The government has taken measures to monitor and control both the degree of concentration and the conduct of organisations in highly concentrated markets. It has done this through competition policy measures contained in legislation during the post-war period.

The Monopolies and Restrictive Trade Practices Act 1948 set up a body to be concerned with inquiring into industries where a monopoly or merger situation is thought to exist.* References of suspected monopoly or merger situations may be made to the Commission by the Government or the Director General of Fair Trading, who is also charged with the duty of assisting the Commission with investigating any reference. A reference may be made under two criteria.

(i) A monopoly situation exists if 25% of the goods or services in question in the UK is supplied by or to the same person (or group of interconnected corporate bodies).

(ii) There is a merger situation, if as the result of a merger either a monopoly situation exists, or the value of assets taken over will exceed £5 m.

The Commission may be required to report on the facts as to whether conditions of monopoly or merger exist and further as to whether these conditions operate or may be expected to operate in the public interest.

The public interest
The Fair Trading Act 1973 lays down factors to be taken into account by the Commission in determining what is in the *public interest*.

(i) the need to promote effective competition in the UK;
(ii) the need to protect the interest of consumers in relation to price and variety of goods;
(iii) the need to minimise the costs of production;
(iv) the need to develop new techniques and products;

---

* This body is now known as the Monopolies and Mergers Commission, and its powers are contained in the Fair Trading Act, 1973.

(v) the need to provide unrestricted entry into existing markets for new competitors;

(vi) the need to maintain the balanced distribution of industry and employment in the UK;

(vii) the need for promoting competition in markets outside the UK.

These factors may be somewhat contradictory in that some, for instance (i) and (iii) seek to improve economic efficiency either in the organisation or in the economy, while others such as (vi) aim to restrict the free movement of industry and so may impose constraints upon it making it less efficient. For example, an organisation may be most cost effective in the South East of England, yet the Commission encourages a more balanced distribution of industry and employment.

After investigation the Commission submits its report, stating whether there is a monopoly or merger situation and whether it is having adverse effects by operating against the public interest. If the Commission's report indicates areas of concern, the government has the following options open to it. It may by order:

(i) require the transfer of property from one organisation to another;

(ii) require the adjustment of contracts;

(iii) require the reallocation of shares in an organisation;

(iv) prohibit a merger taking place.

The above orders are enforceable by court action through *an injunction* (ie a court order prohibiting or requiring specified action).

Examples of mergers which were rejected by the government have been those between Ross Foods and Associated Fisheries and between Boots and Glaxo. In the first instance, the Commission regarded the two organisations as serious rivals, and felt that the proposed merger would reduce effective competition. In the second case, the two companies tried to argue that Research and Development would be enhanced as the joint company would have greater assets. However, the Commission did not believe there was sufficient evidence to justify this, and having considered the other possible consequences rejected the merger.

The Fair Trading Act 1973 includes provisions which relate solely to *newspaper mergers*. The transfer of a newspaper or its assets to another newspaper proprietor who would then own papers having a circulation of over 500 000, is presumed void unless the consent of the Secretary of State is obtained. The Secretary of State must refer the merger to the Commission *unless* he or she is satisfied that:

(i) the newspaper to be taken over has an average circulation of less than 25 000 copies;

(ii) the newspaper in question is not a going concern and urgent action is required.

This may be illustrated by the take-over of Times Newspapers by Rupert Murdoch's News International in 1981. This was not referred to the Commission because the Secretary of State was satisfied that without the merger The Times would not be a going-concern and the matter was of urgency because of the possible loss of jobs.

Freedom of entry into the market

One of the main criteria of a perfectly competitive market is that there must be no barriers to prevent the entry of new organisations. It is in the consumers' best interests that if high profits are being made in a particular market by existing suppliers there should be no restrictions on the entry of new organisations to that market and so preventing the achievement of healthy competition. The Government realises that competition may be reduced not simply by the number or size of organisations in a market per se (*the market structure*) but also by the way a dominant organisation or group of trading organisations enter into agreements which restrict trade and competition (*the market conduct*). This has led to legislation relating to restrictive trade agreements, the present law being consolidated in the Restrictive Trade Practices Act 1976, the Resale Prices Act 1976, and the Competition Act 1980.

Restrictive trade practices – adverse market conduct

Under the Restrictive Trade Practices Act 1976 the Director General of Fair Trading is charged with the duty of compiling and maintaining a register of restrictive trade agreements and also of bringing such agreements before the Restrictive Practices Court to declare whether they are contrary to the public interest. Agreements are *registerable* if made by two or more persons carrying on business in the UK in the production or supply of goods if they lead to a restriction in respect of:

a) the prices charged or recommended;
b) the terms and conditions of a supply of goods;
c) the quantities or description of goods to be produced;
d) the process of manufacture to be applied to any goods;
or
e) the classes of buyers and sellers.

The Restrictive Practices Court starts from the presumption that such agreements are contrary to the public interest and will only be justifiable and declared valid if it is satisfied as to the existence of one or more of the circumstances outlined in the Act. Briefly, the restrictive agreement could be justifiable if it is *reasonably necessary* to either:

a) protect the public against injury;
b) counteract restrictive measures taken by anyone not a party to the agreement;
c) enable the parties to negotiate fair terms with a monopolistic supplier or customer; *or*

the removal of the restriction would:

d) deny the public as purchasers other substantial benefits;

e) have an adverse effect on unemployment or exports.

Many parties to restrictive agreements have sought to justify them on the grounds that they are necessary for the protection of the customer.

In the *Chemists Federation Agreement* 1958 an agreement by the Federation to the effect that patent medicines should only be sold to the public by qualified chemists, was challenged as contrary to the public interest. The Federation claimed that under a) the restriction was necessary to protect the public against injury in view of the potentially dangerous nature of the goods being sold. The Court rejected this claim on the grounds that the risk was slight and declared the agreement void. The Chemists Federation was obviously seeking to reinforce a dominant position and the law recognised this as being undesirable.

Protection of the consumer under d) has been relied on successfully.

In *Re Net Book Agreement* (1957) the publisher had agreed not to permit the retailing of books below their published prices. The Court upheld the agreement considering that if it were declared void, many small specialist book sellers would be forced to close because of unfair competition from other outlets carrying fewer titles. Prices would be eventually higher and there would be fewer new titles published.

Protection of the economy has often proved to be a strong argument.

In *Re Water-Tube Boilermakers Agreement* 1959 an association of the majority of companies within the industry, by agreement, sought to maintain the prices of their boilers. The Court upheld the contention of the association under e) that if the restriction was set aside the members would lose export business which formed a substantial part of their whole market.

Protection of individual consumers or the economy as a whole is therefore a justifiable cause for a restrictive practice.

The justification of restrictive practices on the ground that they are necessary to protect competition has also received judicial consideration.

In the case of the *National Sulphuric Acid Associations Agreement (No. 1)* (1963) 50% of the imports of sulphur came from a US cartel, Sulexco. The UK acid manufacturers created a joint purchasing pool to negotiate with Sulexco under which the pool members bound themselves to a common price and to purchase solely through the pool. Sulexco had attempted to push prices up but the pool had been successful in reducing the increase in price. The restrictions were held to be reasonable under c), ie necessary to enable the parties to negotiate for terms with a monopolistic supplier.

Resale price maintenance — adverse market pricing

One of the most fundamental aspects of competition between retailers is that they should have the ability to charge whatever price they wish. However oligopolistic suppliers may seek to impose a *standard price* on all their retail outlets so as to stabilise their markets, maintain retail outlets and reduce the possibility of their products being used as competitive pawns by retailers. The government has recognised that this practice of *resale price maintenance* is not in consumers' best interests as they are denied the benefit of cut-priced purchases. Prior to the Resale Price Maintenance Act 1964 it was a lawful practice for a manufacturer to insist that a retailer sold the manufacturer's products at a stipulated retail price. To ensure compliance the producer could withhold or threaten to withhold supplies. The current law relating to resale price maintenance is contained in the Resale Prices Act 1976. The Act makes it unlawful for suppliers to make an agreement or arrangement to withhold supplies from dealers who do not observe resale price conditions; to offer them supplies only on less favourable terms than those applicable to other dealers; or only to deal with wholesalers who undertake to operate such restrictions. Subject to a claim for exemption and the power of the Restrictive Practices Court, any term of a contract for the sale of goods by a supplier to a dealer is void so far as it provides for the establishment of minimum prices to be charged on the resale of goods in the UK. It is also unlawful for the supplier actually to enforce a certain resale price by withholding supplies. However the producer may refuse to supply to a dealer who has within the preceeding twelve months been selling the same or similar goods as *loss leaders*, (ie where a retailer sells a product below cost price in order to attract custom for that and other products). The Act provides for enforcement of these provisions by way of court action for an injunction. If the producer, however, has other reasons for withholding supplies which are acceptable, then he will not be treated as withholding supplies for the purpose of the Act.

In *Oxford Printing Ltd* v. *Letraset Ltd* (1970) the plaintiffs applied for an injunction to prevent the defendants from withholding supplies. The court refused to grant the injunction on the grounds that the defendants had justification for this when they showed that their reason for withholding supplies was that the plaintiffs, as well as cutting the price, also used the defendants' products to promote the sales of the goods of a rival organisation.

Exemption criteria

The Restrictive Practices Court may exempt certain classes of goods where in default of a system of maintained minimum resale prices applicable to the goods, any of the following applies and so is detrimental to the public:

a) the quality of goods available for sale, or the varieties of the goods so available would be substantially reduced;
b) the number of establishments in which the goods are sold by retail would be substantially reduced;
c) the prices at which the goods are sold by retail would in general and in the long run be increased;
d) the goods would be sold by retailers under conditions likely to cause danger to health in consequence of their misuse;
e) any necessary services actually provided in connection with or after the sale of the goods by retailers would cease to be so provided or would be substantially reduced.

It must be shown that the detriment to the public would outweigh any detriment to them from a continuation of resale price maintenance. So far only three exemptions have been allowed. Those relating to books, maps and drugs.

In *Re Medicaments Reference (No. 2)* (1970) the Court held on application by the Association of the British Pharmaceutical Industry that drugs were exempt under the 1964 Act. Although when medicaments were prescribed under the Health Service they were not 'sold' within the meaning of the Act, they were available for sale. In addition, without resale price maintenance, distributors would emerge who would only stock popular drugs. Also the majority of chemists made small profits and would be likely to make even less if supermarkets undercut them forcing them out of business. Thus a declaration that drugs be exempted was made.

In *Re Chocolate and Sugar Confectionary Reference* 1967 the manufacturers' application for exemption from the general ban on resale price maintenance was argued under b). The argument was dismissed by the court on the ground that the evidence did not show that there was likely to be a substantial shift of trade to supermarkets and self-service grocers with a consequent closure of a large number of small confectionary shops.

EEC competition policy

As a member of the European Economic Community, Britain is subject to competition rules contained in Articles 85 and 86 of the Treaty of Rome. These Articles apply to *undertakings* which would include a company partnership or sole trader.

Article 85 states that the following shall be prohibited and automatically void 'all agreements between undertakings and decision by associations of undertakings which may affect trade between Member States and which have as their object or effect the prevention, restriction or distortion of competition within the common market, and in particular those which:

a) fix prices or trading conditions;
b) limit production, markets, technical development or investment;
c) share markets or source of supply;
d) apply dissimilar conditions to equivalent transactions with other trading parties;
e) make the conclusion of contract subject to acceptance of unconnected supplementary obligations.'

These provisions may be declared inapplicable however to agreements or practices which contribute to improving the production or distribution of goods, or to promoting technical or economic progress while allowing consumers a fair share of the benefit and which do not afford such an undertaking the possibility of eliminating competition. The European Commission is empowered to enforce these rules on competition and also grant exemptions. One important group exemption granted relates to two-party *exclusive distributorship* agreements. For instance if a German manufacturer agreed that an English importer should be the sole distributor in England of the German manufacturer's machine tools and the English importer agreed to limit himself to the German manufacturer as sole supplier, provided certain conditions are satisfied this agreement will be exempt from the 'competition rules'.

An example of the application of Article 85 is the case of *Miller Schallplatten* v. *E.C. Commission* (1978) heard before the European Court. Miller produced and distributed musical records on the German domestic market and in its conditions of sale imposed a ban on exports by the buyers (ie dealers). Despite Miller's argument that the records were intended only for the German speaking public and could be of little interest to the public of other member states the Commission decided that the export ban infringed Article 85. The European Court upheld this decision holding that a ban prohibiting export from Germany constituted a restriction on competition under Article 85. There was no requirement that the agreement had appreciably affected trade, only that it was capable of doing so.

Article 86 provides:

'Any abuse by an undertaking in a dominant position within the common market shall be prohibited. Such abuse may occur by
a) imposing unfair prices or trading conditions;
b) limiting production, markets or technical development to the prejudice of consumers;

c) applying dissimilar conditions to equivalent transactions with other trading parties;
d) making the conclusion of a contract subject to the acceptance of unconnected supplementary obligations.'

In 1978 British Petroleum appealed to the European Court against a decision of the European Commission that BP had abused its dominant position. As one of the seven undertakings that supplied motor fuel in Holland, BP had decided to cut its supply to its main customer, ABG, during a period of shortage caused by the restriction on production by OPEC countries in 1973 – 1974. The Dutch purchaser, ABG, claimed that the cut in supplies was significantly greater than that applied to other customers and therefore infringed Article 86(c) and the European Commission agreed. The European Court reversed the decision holding that there was no abuse, mainly on the ground that ABG had not been a regular customer of BP prior to the shortages, and to cut supplies to an occasional customer to a greater extent than a regular customer was reasonable, and not an abuse of a dominant position.

The increasing emphasis on competition in government legislation
The changing economic and political climate has led to the passing of new legislation which reflects the government's belief in a more openly competitive economy. The language of Article 85 of the Treaty of Rome which is intended to prevent *anti-competitive practices* between undertakings of member countries has been used by the British Parliament in the Competition Act 1980. The Act provides for selective investigation of anti-competitive practices which restrict competition. This is defined as comprising *a course of conduct which has or is intended to have or is likely to have the effect of restricting, distorting or preventing competition in the UK*. Previously, of course, under the Fair Trading Act 1973, power had been conferred on the Director General of Fair Trading to investigate the supply of goods and services in a monopoly situation. Now under the 1980 Act an individual practice by an individual organisation operating in either the public or private sector can be investigated and prevented without involving every organisation in the industry and without the need to prove a monopoly situation exists.

The procedure for investigation is shown in Fig 2.7, overleaf.

The Act does not give examples of anti-competitive practices to identify situations justifying a preliminary investigation by the Director General of Fair Trading, rather reliance must be placed on the broad definition of an anti-competitive practice, contained in section 2. The type of practices likely to be investigated are conditions restricting supply, eg

(i) *full-line forcing* – this involves a supplier requiring a distributor, who wishes to stock the supplier's major product, to carry the full range of products. (For example, a shopkeeper wishing to sell a major brand of baked beans may be required to carry the full range of the supplier's tinned products.)

(ii) *tie-in sales* – this is a less extreme form of the same arrangement, whereby the sale of one product is tied to the sale of others. (Thus, a distributor of a certain type of photocopier may also have to enter into a service agreement with the supplier to purchase all paper too.)

(iii) *reciprocal trading* – this involves organisations agreeing to purchase each other's products *exclusively*. Thus other competitors' products cannot be purchased where such an agreement is in force.

(iv) *long-term contracts* – here a distributor agrees to carry the supplier's products exclusively for a long period and therefore effectively restrict competitors from entering the market.

An anti-competitive practice does not include a course of conduct within the terms of an agreement which is registrable under the Restrictive Trade Practices Act 1976. This provision of the 1980 Act is included to prevent overlap of proceedings and control. Furthermore, companies with a turnover of less than £5 million, unless they have

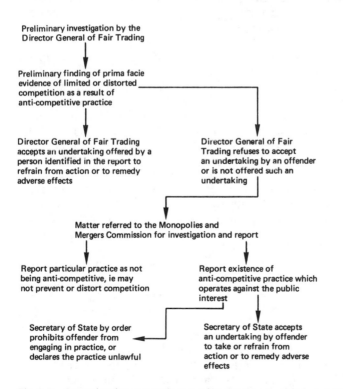

Fig 2.7   Investigation procedure under the Competition Act 1980

more than a 25% share of their particular market, are excluded from investigation.

It must be stressed, however, that such individual practices will only be regarded as anti-competitive and declared unlawful after a consideration of all the circumstances relating to their economic effect in the particular market situation. Of course, if this were taken to the extreme, *competition itself* could be regarded as anti-competitive, because if it is successful it could have the eventual effect of reducing the number of competitors by eliminating those which are least successful.

Public sector bodies are also brought under scrutiny. The Act empowers the Secretary of State to refer to the Commission for investigation any question concerning the efficiency and costs of the service provided or the possible abuse of a monopoly situation by a wide range of public sector bodies, eg Nationalised Industries, Passenger Transport Operators, Water Authorities and Agricultural Marketing Boards.

The reference may require the Commission to make a factual investigation and in addition to advise whether the body is pursuing a course of conduct which operates against the public interest. This recognition that public sector monopolies may not always act in the best interests of consumers is a radical step in government control of its own undertakings.

A good example of the contemporary attitude of Government towards free entry into the market is demonstrated by the Transport Act 1980. Previously the Road Traffic Act 1930 provided for exclusive provision of bus services by the public sector and acted as a bar to private operators. It was thought that uncontrolled development could lead to congestion and safety risks, and an Act to restrict competition was necessary to maintain control over standards. Under the Transport Act 1980 these earlier restrictions have been effectively removed. There is now a presumption in favour of granting a road service licence unless the traffic commissioners are satisfied that to do so would be contrary to the public interest. The Act therefore represents an encouragement towards the introduction of private operators into the public service vehicle system with a view to increasing the level of competition in the provision of bus services to the public.

Even protective legislation such as successive statutes providing for the protection of *patents*, which superficially appears to prevent competitive entry into a market, can be viewed as an encouragement to the development of new products and ideas. It is in the public interest that consumers should benefit from innovation and as such have the long term benefit of a wider choice of product. A legal patent provides the machinery by which this may be achieved. A patent grants a legal monopoly in respect of an invention to the inventor and is issued by the Crown through the agency of its Patents Office. The monopoly is granted to the person(s) named in the patent in respect of the invention described within it. The patent gives its holder (the patentee) a right to prevent others doing certain acts against the invention, namely, manufacturing according to his invention, using it, and/or marketing the patented product. To qualify for a patent the applicant must disclose a trade secret that amounts to an invention as defined in the Patents Act 1977. An invention amounts to an idea which may be for a new product, for applications of a new product, or for a new method of manufacturing or using a product.

Once granted, a patent will have a maximum life of twenty years. If the patent holder is in no position to exploit this personally by manufacturing or marketing, he or she can always try to get others to take up the idea, grant a licence and receive a royalty on the sales of the patented product.

Judicial intervention in the free market

Having considered how the government has intervened through legislative means in the post-war period, it is also appropriate to examine the attitude of the courts towards restrictive market practices. The courts, through the operation of the common law, have since the nineteenth century, been prepared to judge the validity of specific restrictive trade practices on the grounds of public interest. Two areas of concern have been the use by dominant suppliers of exclusive supply agreements with distributors and restrictions imposed on the sellers of business goodwill.

In the case of *exclusive dealership agreements* between two persons their validity is tested by the courts applying the criteria used to determine whether the contract is one in *restraint of trade*. Such practices are expressly excluded from Restrictive Trade Practice legislation.

Exclusive or sole supply agreements

Exclusive supply agreements may tie a retail outlet to a supplier for a fixed period. Usually, in return for benefits such as loans or discounts, the distributor agrees to stock the supplier's products to the exclusion of all others. This is a common practice in the petrol industry where large oil companies see the benefit of having a guaranteed chain of distribution to the public.

The validity of the exclusive supply agreements, known as *solus agreements*, has been questioned in the courts. It has been held that such agreements are to be classified as *contracts in restraint of trade*. This type of contract is discussed later in the chapter but generally the common law regards them as only valid if they do not offend the public interest.

In *Esso Petroleum Co Ltd* v. *Harper's Garage (Stourport) Ltd* (1968) the defendants owned two garages and entered into solus supply agreements in respect of each garage with the plaintiff oil company. The agreements tied the defendants to the plaintiffs' products and contained a continuity clause requiring the defendants, if they were to sell the garage, to persuade the buyer to enter into similar solus agreements with Esso. In relation to the Mustow Green Garage the agreement was to last for four years five months. As for the Corner Garage, Esso loaned the defendants £7,000 who then mortgaged the premises to Esso. Repayment of the mortgage was to be over 21 years with no right of redemption for that period. The mortgage also included the *tie covenant*. In an action by Esso to enforce the two agreements the House of Lords held that the rule of public policy against unreasonable restraints of trade applied to the solus agreements and the mortgage. The shorter period was reasonable and enforceable but the tie of 21 years went beyond any period for which developments were reasonably foreseeable and was therefore void. A solus agreement embodied within a 25-year sub-lease between a petrol company and a garage lessee *was* held enforceable by the Court of Appeal in *Cleveland Petrol* v. *Dartstone Ltd* (1969). The significant factor in this case was that unlike *Esso Petroleum* v. *Harper's Garage*, the lessee came to the land and to the tying covenant. He was not an existing owner giving up an existing freedom.

Restrictions on the seller of a business
It is usual practice in the sale of a business for the seller to undertake not to compete with the purchaser and thus restrict the freedom of entry back into the market. Such a restriction is designed to enable the seller to obtain an economic value for the *business goodwill*, that is, the value of trade custom attached to the business. These restraints are legally enforceable provided they are no wider than reasonably necessary.

> In *British Reinforced Concrete Engineering Co Ltd* v. *Schelff* (1921) the defendant who operated a business selling road reinforcements in the UK, sold his business to the plaintiff. In the contract of sale the seller agreed not to compete for a specified period in the 'sale or manufacture of road reinforcements' in the UK. The defendant took employment in the same type of business working for a competitor, and the plaintiff sued to enforce the restraint clause. The court held that had the clause been confined to 'sales' it would have been valid, but to include 'the manufacture of reinforcements' made the restraint wider than was reasonably necessary, and therefore void.

Therefore the courts recognise that a purchaser of a business has a right to protect the commercial interest in his new enterprise while at the same time acknowledging that excessive protection against competition is unreasonable and as such contrary to the public interest.

The freedom of movement of the factors of production

Freedom of movement by the factors of production between producers is theoretically essential for competition. Individuals must be allowed to have free choice of the nature of their employment and to whom they wish to offer their services. This allows the most efficient producers to attract the highest quality labour by offering the most substantial rewards. In practice an individual may, by contract, have restricted his or her future liberty to carry on his or her trade, business or profession. It has been seen that such contracts of employment are regarded by the common law as being in restraint of trade.

The common law relating to contracts in restraint of trade was expressed by the House of Lords in *Nordenfelt* v. *Maxim Nordenfelt Guns and Ammunition Co* (1894). The Court held that all contracts in restraint of trade are void as contrary to public policy unless reasonable in the interests of the parties and the public. To be reasonable between the parties a restraint must relate to a valid interest that the employer is attempting to protect and the clause used must be no wider than is necessary to protect that interest.

Restraint between employer and employee

It is usual in a contract of employment for an employer to expressly provide that on termination of the contract the employee will agree to limit his or her right to work for a rival business, or start a competing business. This is particularly so when the employee in question has a large degree of personal contact with the ex-employers' customers over whom there may be influence and also where the employee's work is of a confidential or secret nature. The courts recognise that for obvious economic reasons, such as the shortage of available employment, the parties to a contract of employment are not on an equal footing and therefore it may be one-sided in favour of the employer. It is also in the public interest that an employee should be free to use his or her professional skills as he or she wishes in order to make full use of the productive talents of available labour.

A restraint clause therefore, that is oppressive in nature either because the employer has no valid interest that requires protection, or is wider than is reasonably necessary, will be declared void by the courts as contrary to the public interest.

In determining the reasonableness of the restraint clause the courts will consider factors such as:

a) the interest that requires protection;
b) the consideration provided in return for the restriction;
c) the duration and area of the restraint.

In *Mason* v. *Provident Clothing & Supply Co* (1913) where a canvasser in the company's Islington Branch agreed not to work in any similar business for three years within twenty-five miles of London, the restraint clause was held to be unreasonable as it extended further than was legitimately necessary.

More recently in *Instone* v. *Schroeder* (1974) the House of Lords considered the validity of an exclusive service agreement that a young songwriter had entered into with a music publisher. The contract was to subsist for five years and provided for:

a) the assignment by the songwriter to the publisher of full copyright in songs both existing and those composed in the five-year period;
b) the right of the publisher to terminate the agreement with one month's notice;
c) the publisher was under no obligation to publish any of the songs.

The Court held that the contract, being one-sided and not in accord with standard trade practice, was void on the ground of being contrary to the public interest.

Lord Reid stated that:

'contractual restrictions which appear to be unnecessary or to be reasonably capable of enforcement in an oppressive manner . . . must be justified before they can be enforced'.

A similar copyright agreement was considered by the Court of Appeal in *Clifford Davis Ltd* v. *WEA Records Ltd* (1975). The agreement was entered into by two songwriters (members of Fleetwood Mac rock group) and their manager who was also a music publisher. It provided:

a) the assignment of full copyright in all their compositions for five years;
b) the right to extend the agreement for a further five years at the manager's option;
c) the publisher was under no obligation to publish any of the songs.

The Court held the contract to be void as one-sided, and not in the public interest, the inequality of the business skill and unequal bargaining power being a deciding factor.

The contemporary attitude of the courts in interpreting restraint clauses may be illustrated by two recent cases decided by the Court of Appeal.

In the first case, *Littlewood's Organisation* v. *Harris* (1977) the defendant was employed as a Director by Littlewoods who compete with Great Universal Stores Ltd for the major share of the mail order business in the UK. The defendant agreed in his contract of employment that on its termination he would not for twelve months enter into a contract of employment with GUS Ltd or any subsidiary company. Littlewoods by such a restriction were seeking to protect confidential information of which the defendant was aware relating to the preparation of their catalogue, upon which the success of their business depended. As GUS Ltd operated all over the world it was argued that the restraint clause was wider than reasonably necessary to protect Littlewoods' interests in the UK. A majority of the Court held however that the courts should interpret such clauses with regard to their object and intention and on a proper interpretation the clause was intended to relate only to the UK mail order business and was therefore enforceable.

In the second case, *Greer* v. *Sketchley Ltd* (1979) the Court of Appeal was faced with a similar agreement. The plaintiff was a Director of the defendant's dry cleaning business with responsibility for the Midlands area. In his contract of employment he agreed that following its termination he would not for twelve months engage in employment anywhere in the UK in any business which could make use of secret processes carried on by his employer. In fact the defendants' business only operated in the Midlands and London.

The Court held that as the restraint clause purported to extend to areas where the defendants did not operate it was wider than reasonably necessary and therefore void. The Court was not prepared to interpret the clause so that it applied only to the Midlands and London in a similar way that the clause in Littlewoods' case was limited to the UK. In attempting to restrain the employee throughout the UK the employer was unfairly preventing competition and the free movement of labour.

While these two cases appear difficult to reconcile they represent the present state of the law.

Thus the law assumes as a first premise that all contracts in restraint of trade are anti-competitive. However, restrictive clauses in contracts of employment may be enforced by the courts if it can be proved that the clause was entered into by parties who were fully aware of the economic consequences, and that it is not obviously against the public interest. The supposed economic freedom of individuals still predominates.

Homogeneous goods

A further condition is that all goods or services supplied by rival producers must be identical otherwise differences in product quality or standards can justifiably result in price differences and contract terms. For instance, if one petrol company offered three-star petrol for sale at below market price because it was of inferior quality and yet buyers believed that all three-star petrol was identical, then the petrol company would gain an unfair competitive advantage.

Of course, in reality, goods and services are by nature *heterogeneous*. The government would obviously not wish to reduce the variety of products available to the consumer. All that it has sought to achieve through legislation is the *maintenance of minimum standards* for certain goods and services. Recent examples of such legislation are the Consumer Safety Act 1978 and the Weights and Measures Act 1979.

Under the Consumer Safety Act 1978 the Secretary of State has power to make safety regulations designed to see that goods are safe and appropriate information is supplied with them and inappropriate information is not supplied. The regulations may relate to matters such as the design and composition of goods and may require the goods to comply with a standard, such as a British Institutes Standard, and may require a warning to be supplied with the goods. It is an offence for a person to infringe a requirement or prohibition in the regulations. The regulations relate to such things as electric blankets, oil room heaters, children's nightdresses, stands for carrycots, prams and pushchairs, cosmetics, toys and toxic paint, electrical equipment and colour coding of electrical appliances.

As far as contents of packages are concerned weights and measures legislation has traditionally adopted the rule of minimum contents, any shortfall giving rise to an offence. The severity of this rule has been motivated by the Weights and Measures Act, 1979, which adopts the average weights system to comply with EEC standards. The adoption of that system will move altogether away from attaching criminal penalties to the retailer who blamelessly provides a customer with short weight. Thus a short weight packet of itself gives rise to no offence and it is only when a batch of packages falls below the stated weight on averaging out their actual contents that an offence will occur. Nevertheless, an offence will still arise if a specified number of packages in the batch fall below a specified tolerance level.

Perfect knowledge of the market

Another criterion necessary to achieve the state of perfect competition is that the sellers and purchasers must have *perfect knowledge of the market*. This involves the purchaser being aware of the price and terms being offered by rival suppliers. Similarly, suppliers themselves should be fully aware of both their competitors' prices and terms, and the extent of demand. It is only when the supplier and purchaser are both aware of such information that they can be said to contract on an equal footing.

Disclosure of marketing information
Certainly there is no legal requirement that the parties to a contract

must have perfect knowledge of the market. In a contract for the sale of goods or a service there is no legal remedy for a purchaser who is unaware of the market price and pays a sum of money in excess of it. Generally the parties to a contract are free to make their own bargains whether good or bad and provided that there is no fraud, misrepresentation, duress or undue influence, the courts will not interfere.

As previously stated, the consideration transferred under a contract need not be adequate and so provided the consumer has not been misled, there is generally no requirement on a seller to disclose information relating to the contract, eg

a consumer purchases a package holiday to Greece for £400 from Tour Company X and is unaware that the same holiday could be purchased from Tour Company Y for £300.

Disclosure of contract information
Under the English law of contract there is no general duty of disclosure of information and it is only in certain exceptional contractual situations that the law requires the parties to disclose all material facts relevant to the contract. Lord Justice Kenney made the point in *London General Omnibus Co Ltd* v. *Holloway* (1912) when he said:

'No class of case occurs to my mind in which our law regards mere non-disclosure as a ground for invalidating the contract, except in the case of insurance.'

In contracts of insurance and also partnership contracts the law imposes a duty of total disclosure on both parties. They are known as contracts of utmost good faith – *uberrimae fidei*. In insurance contracts in particular, the insured may be in possession of certain facts relating to personal circumstances which are material to the contract and failure to disclose such facts could give the insurance company the right to treat the contract as voidable.

This duty of disclosure on the insured involves disclosure of all facts that are regarded as material of which he or she knows or which he or she ought to know. The insured is therefore presumed to be aware of material facts and by implication will be presumed to have made reasonable enquiries to become aware of such facts. Which facts are material may depend on the particular type of insurance but in the past the courts have regarded facts such as risk or vulnerability to the subject-matter and the insured's character as being of a material nature.

In *Locker and Woolf* v. *West Australian Insurance Co* (1936) the insured when negotiating a fire policy failed to mention a previous rejection of a motor policy because of fraud. The Court of Appeal held that the previous rejection was a material fact and the insurers were entitled to repudiate liability.

The insured, who has signed a proposal form, is taken to have constructive knowledge of its contents and is responsible for its omissions and inaccuracies.

> In *O'Connor* v. *BDB Kirby & Co* (1971) a broker completed a proposal form for the insured's motor policy in which the broker mistakenly stated that the insured garaged his car when in fact the insured had told him that the car was left in the street. Following a claim on the policy the insurers repudiated the contract on the ground of the inaccuracy. In an action in the tort of negligence by the insured against the broker the Court of Appeal held that there was no liability as the loss was caused by the insured himself signing and sending off an inaccurate proposal form.

As stated previously the relationship of the parties to a partnership contract is one of utmost good faith. It is uncertain whether the duty of full disclosure applies to intended partnerships but certainly during the course of the partnership partners are bound to render true accounts and full information of all things affecting the partnership to any partner or the partner's legal representative.

It must be stressed that the above are exceptional contractual situations. Thus there is *no duty* on the seller of poor quality goods to give a full description of the goods to the purchaser. Similarly, on the sale of land there would be no duty on the purchaser to inform the innocent seller that the purchaser is aware of rich mineral deposits which would make the land more valuable. In land contracts the law does require that some information must be transferred.

> In *Faruqi* v. *English Real Estate Ltd* (1979) the Court of Appeal recently held that if a vendor of land was aware of any defect in his ownership he is bound to make a full and frank disclosure.

If the parties to a contract do disclose information relating to the subject matter the law requires such information to be accurate. Under the Trade Descriptions Act 1968 a trader commits an offence if he or she supplies goods with a false trade description or to which a false trade description is applied.

The contractual remedies of an innocent party who suffers as a result of false information relating to a contract may be:

1 *an action for breach of contract;*
2 *an action for misrepresentation.*

Substantial rights are conferred on the customer in a consumer credit transaction under the Consumer Credit Act 1974 especially relating to the disclosure of information. The Act requires the credit agreement to be in a particular form and contain certain information. Because of the dangers of abuse of power Parliament has deemed it necessary to give the customer the right to *cancel* such an agreement without reason and even apply to the court to re-open the agreement. If the Court decides that the agreement is extortionate for the customer it has the power to alter or cancel the agreement altogether.

The Consumer Safety Act 1978 provides that a supplier of certain goods should supply the purchaser with certain information relating to the safe use of products and warn as to any dangers. To sum up therefore it is possible to state that the law does not require the parties to a contract to have perfect knowledge of the market but there are exceptional contractual situations where the common law or statute has intervened to require that certain information relating to the contract must be disclosed and that disclosed information must be accurate.

Thus, although the law does not and in most cases cannot, make all sellers and buyers aware of prevailing market conditions or even aspects of individual contracts, it seeks to protect those who are disadvantaged by falacious information or may be pressurised into buying or selling.

Rational behaviour

Rational behaviour by both producer and consumer is also assumed in a perfectly competitive market. Consumers should always attempt to maximise the satisfaction they gain from their purchase by seeking the *best overall bargain*. Similarly the producer is seeking to maximise profits by selling the optimum quantity for the maximum consideration that the market allows. It is a fundamental principle of the law of contract that both parties have the freedom to negotiate their own bargains. The law will not attempt to objectively value the respective considerations transferred under a contract. The law does not therefore intervene to ensure that the parties act in a rational manner. But to some extent Parliament has tried to protect the consumer from irrational conduct leading to a bad bargain. This is one of the main purposes of consumer protection legislation. Therefore, in particular, the Consumer Credit Act 1974 confers the right to cancel on the customer in a consumer credit agreement and determine the agreement without reason.

The effectiveness of government policy

The evidence appears to clearly indicate the growing concentration of industry in the UK economy. As a result the consumer is very likely to be faced with a dominant supplier situation when entering into a contractual bargain, unlike the assumed condition of equal bargaining in perfect competition. The degree to which the consumer can influence the terms of the contract is strictly limited and therefore government policy is generally one of attempting to limit the bargaining power of the supplier. Government policy is aimed at achieving this in its competition policy which imposes limitations on the behaviour of dominant suppliers.

Such suppliers are constantly endeavouring to safeguard their commercial interests. They do this by trading on terms which are most economically beneficial and which are legally permissable in the light of current legislation. By doing so trading practices will be revealed which, while not illegal, may be considered by the government to be socially or economically undesirable. The government will then introduce fresh legislation to outlaw the practice. Thus the relationship between the interests of suppliers and the policy of the government can be seen as one in which each side battles to pursue its own interests: the suppliers protecting themselves, the government protecting the public interest generally.

The success of this policy in the post-war period can only be judged in perspective by comparing the possible situation without government intervention. Concentration has continued despite monopolies and mergers legislation although notable modifications have been made to merger activity, for instance, the prevention of several major mergers, eg ICI-Courtaulds, Boots-Glaxo, Barclays-Lloyds, Ross-Associated Fisheries. However, in the main, the reduction of the trend towards concentration has been marginal. More noticeable success has been achieved in counteracting specific adverse behaviour of dominant suppliers. They have been required to set more competitive prices, consumer choice has been increased by the wider availability of products as producers have relaxed exclusive dealership contracts, and discriminatory pricing has been reduced in several instances.

It is evident that the government will continue to attempt to move towards a more competitive market economy by its own actions and through the actions of the courts. It will be necessary to monitor concentration trends and the behaviour of dominant organisations in the future in order to evaluate the success of this competition policy.

Case study on the oil industry

The oil industry is the biggest business in the world. This is because oil and oil-based products are vital in most industrial processes. All countries need oil and only a very few produce it. In fact, only the United States and the Soviet Union both produce and consume oil in large quantities. This means that very substantial quantities have to be moved from continent to continent and oil has become the major commodity in both bulk and value in international trade. Oil tankers account for over 40% of total shipping deadweight tonnage. Also the need to refine oil to manufacture petrol and other oil-based products has meant that a massive investment has had to be made in oil refineries and a distribution network. The post-war period, at least up until the late 1970's, has seen a continuous growth in the world's demand for oil and has led to the development of the multi-national oil companies whose objectives have been to meet these growing needs. Companies, having been established in one part of the business, have felt the need to spread into others. Refining companies have, for example, chosen to develop marketing and distribution networks to secure outlets for their products. Producers have found it necessary to meet part of their shipping requirements by building or buying their own oil tankers to reduce their vulnerability to fluctuating ship charter costs.

All of these influences have favoured the growth of very large organisations and the industry's development has been characterised by continuous technological advances and growing economies of scale. There has been a movement to reduce costs and maximise profits by concentrating the production of crude oil, its transportation, refinement and sale under the control of single companies or groups of companies. This can be termed the 'vertical integration' of the industry.

Structure of the industry

Seven private enterprise companies continue to dominate the transportation, refinement and sale of oil. This may seem remarkable in an industry which is so large, so international and so important to the economic well-being of the industrialised world. Furthermore, the ownership and corporate control of these companies is concentrated in just three countries, the United States, Great Britain and the Netherlands. This fact may not be clear at first glance for each of these seven major companies has established a variety of subsiduary companies registered throughout the world and through whose activities the business is undertaken. Nevertheless overall control tends to lie firmly with the head office of the mother company. This group of companies known jointly as the *Majors* or *International Majors*, collectively give the industry its characteristically *oligopolistic* nature at the level of production, refinement and sale.

The majors have developed massive organisations for the production, transportation, refining and distribution of petroleum and petroleum products. Because they have subsiduary companies in most countries in the world and transact business on a global scale they are known as *Multinationals*. These seven majors are among the biggest companies in the world as the table below shows.

Company	Country of Origin
Exxon (previously known as Esso) largest company in the world	USA
Shell Third largest company in the world	UK/Netherlands
Texaco Fourth largest company	USA
Mobil Sixth largest company	USA
Chevron (Standard Oil of California) Seventh largest company	USA
BP Eighth largest company	UK
Gulf Oil Eleventh largest company	USA

The majors account for over half of the activity of the oil business. However, their power has been undermined in the last fifteen years or so by the rise of two other forces, OPEC (which will be examined a little later), and other independent oil companies.

Other international oil companies
In recent years, some of America's domestic oil companies have sought expansion in the world market and now compete with the majors in many countries. This is particularly true in Western Europe and more latterly the developing nations. Brand names such as AMOCO, ARCO (Atlantic Richfield), Phillips and CONOCO (Continental Oil) are becoming increasingly familiar to British consumers.

Some of the European countries have established their own national oil companies which at first concentrated on domestic markets but have recently sought markets for their products not only in Europe but world-wide. The British National Oil Corporation does not fall into this category as its main concern is not with refining and sale but with extraction of North Sea oil. However, the major European oil company is 'Compagnie Française des Petroles' (CFP) which sells its oil under the Total brand. The Italian company 'Ente Nationale Idrocarburi' (ENI) has the brand name AGIP and finally there is the Belgium company 'Petrofina' which concentrates on purchasing crude oil produced by others and then refining and selling it under the brand names, Fina, Purfina and Perrofin.

A further major change in the structure of the industry has been the growth of the relatively small independent oil companies which have concentrated on refining and distribution rather than the extraction of crude oil. They are common in the USA and are increasingly playing a part in the European market. Here, they often buy oil from the Rotterdam Spot Market and are able to do so relatively cheaply if world prices are low and are then able to compete very favourably with the products of the majors. Conversely, if there is a shortage of oil on the world market, this will tend to push up the price in Rotterdam and so force these independents to raise their prices and lose their competitive advantage to the majors. Other companies, such as ICI may produce and sell oil as a by-product of their other industrial activities.

The Organisation of Petroleum Exporting Countries (OPEC)
The most significant development in the oil industry in the last twenty years has been the development of OPEC. This organisation acts as a cartel for the national oil companies of many of the major producer countries. Its actions as almost a monopoly producer have had far reaching repercussions on the world's economic development. Prior to the late 1960s the majors had worked a concession system with those countries having reserves of oil. This allowed the majors to explore for and extract crude oil and then sell it at the price they wished. The oil belonged to the majors for the period of the concession and they paid the producer government royalties and taxes on the level of production. At first, the Arab oil producers asked for 'participation' in the oil production process, taking part of the production costs and sharing the profits. This developed into a takeover by the host governments of the oil reserves which were then sold to the oil companies. This power to set the price of the crude oil has been dramatically used by OPEC. The most substantial increase came in 1973 following the Arab-Israeli war. The monopoly power of OPEC has allowed it to vary prices as it wishes and influence world prices by increasing or decreasing daily supply.

One of OPEC's major problems has been that of maintaining a common pricing policy among its members. Some, particularly those with relatively low reserves, would prefer to push up prices to whatever the market could bear in order to make short-term profits. Others, and in particular the major producer Saudi Arabia, have tended towards restraint in price rises for fear of causing further economic recession in the consumer countries of Europe and North America. The monopoly strength of OPEC is only possible because of the concentration of oil reserves in a relatively few hands and the widespread demand for oil with many consumers so producing an imperfect market. Oil itself has proved to have a relatively inelastic demand curve with few substitutes although conservation measures, particularly in the USA, have proved somewhat effective in the late 1970s.

Most of the OPEC countries, which include the Arab oil producers and others such as Nigeria and Venezuela, hope to develop their interests further. This 'downstream' involvement would take the form of establishing their own refineries, buying their own tankers and even becoming involved in marketing. Although this is still a relatively new idea it shows the increasing importance of the national oil companies of the producer nations.

Supply and demand for oil

Oil, as a commodity, provides an excellent example of the workings of supply and demand of the market. Despite the fact that the supply side of the industry is dominated by the OPEC producers providing about 50% of the free market capacity, there are still severe fluctuations in the supply of oil. The industry has developed on the premise of continuously expanding demand and so has built up its refining capacity. The major oil companies therefore have huge fixed investments while the small independents have relatively tiny overheads.

As prices have risen substantially due to the OPEC price rises, demand has tended to slacken leaving a substantial surplus of oil. Most of the majors have long-term contracts with the major producer countries and so have a fixed level of supply. Surplus oil is fed into the world market both by producer countries and the majors through the Rotterdam Spot Market. A surplus will clearly lower the price and this cheap oil is purchased by the independents for sale on the British market. The low spot market price allows the independents to offer the UK consumer relatively low prices. As the majors have a fixed contract price to pay for their oil, the independent companies are able to cut their price and so attract the majors' consumers. This is because petrol is a relatively homogenous product and there is little brand loyalty. The result may be a price war as the majors are forced to follow suit and drop prices. This competitive situation clearly benefits the consumer who is faced with a choice of lower prices.

However, in situations when oil is on short supply on the world market, the independents are unable to obtain cheap supplies from the spot market. The majors are able to increase their price without fear of competition and because of the oligopolistic nature of the market, there is a tendency for price leadership to occur. As one of the majors increases its price the others are able to follow suit and raise their prices. This accounts for the often fluctuating petrol prices seen on the roads of the UK.

One of the mechanisms used by the oil companies to vary prices is the discount system which they operate with their retail outlets. To increase prices they simply reduce the level of discounts they offer to their distributors who must increase their prices or lower their profit margins. There exists in the UK a complex system of distributor discounts which vary according to the situation of the petrol station. In city centres, outlets are faced with severe competition from rival brands and so the large petrol companies offer their retailers substantial discounts so allowing them to compete on favourable terms. This creates at times an almost perfectly competitive market for the consumer is faced with a relatively homogenous product and the market is characterised by a lack of consumer brand loyalty. Even a relatively small fall in pump prices at one station is sufficient to attract a substantial increase in trade. Falling sales will force the nearby competing petrol stations to follow suit and lower their posted prices. Both consumers and sellers are normally well aware of the alternative prices on offer for they are prominently displayed on the forecourt. The relatively small distance involved for consumers in travelling between rival petrol stations is usually insufficient to discourage a switch to a rival cheaper petrol.

An alternative situation often exits in rural areas with few petrol stations. One retailer may have a relative monopoly of the local market and so is able to increase the cost of petrol above that which prevails at the city centre market price. This is related in the discounts offered to such outlets by the oil companies. They are more likely to offer much smaller discounts to such outlets confident that higher pump prices will not significantly deter sales.

The petrol industry, therefore, illustrates the feasibility of regionalised markets growing up with completely different competitive conditions prevailing. On the one hand, a competitive price-conscious price-takers' market in urban areas with many buyers and many sellers, and on the other a much more pronounced monopolistic situation evolving in rural districts with relatively few petrol stations acting as price searchers and seeking to set a price which the market will bear.

Exclusive supply agreements and the oil industry

A contract in restraint of trade is one by which a party restricts future liberty to carry on his or her trade business or profession in such a manner and with freedom of choice. The law treats such contracts as prima facie void but binding if they prove to be reasonable in all the circumstances.

The doctrine of restraint of trade is based upon public policy which of course will inevitably change as economic conditions alter. As far as the oil industry is concerned the importance of the doctrine became evident in the mid 1960s when the courts were called on to determine whether the widespread practice of oil companies tying their distributors (garage owners) to long-term exclusive supply contracts (solus agreements) was in restraint of trade and so prima facie void. Such solus agreements normally contain the following covenants:

a) a *tying covenant* by which the garage owner agrees, in return for a rebate on the price and possibly a loan on favourable terms, to sell only the supplier's brand of petrol;
b) a *compulsory trading covenant* which obliges the garage owner to keep the garage open at reasonable hours and provide the public with an efficient service;
c) a *continuity covenant* which requires the garage owner, if he or she sells the business, to procure the acceptance of the agreement by the purchaser.

The House of Lords in *Esso Petroleum Co Ltd* v. *Harpers Garage (Stourport) Ltd* (1968), decided that solus agreements are in restraint of trade and so prima facie void but binding if justified as reasonable from the point of view of the parties and the community. Determining this question of reasonableness involves a complex process of balancing conflicting interests and a fine appreciation of both legal and economic considerations. To illustrate how this question is determined in practice, set out below is the background and decision in the Esso Petroleum case 1967 and also extracts from one of the House of Lords' judgements delivered, that of Lord Pearce.

Esso Petroleum Co Ltd v. *Harpers Garage (Stourport) Ltd* (1967) *HOUSE OF LORDS.*

This is an appeal by the appellants, Esso Petroleum Co Ltd from the judgement of the Court of Appeal allowing the appeal of the respondents, Harpers Garage (Stourport) Ltd from the judgment of Mocatta.J given in favour of the appellants.

The background
The first action, described as the 'Mustow Green action', concerned a solus agreement between the appellants and respondents, dated 27 June, 1963. The respondents agreed to buy from the appellants at the appellants' wholesale schedule price to dealers the respondents' total requirements of motor fuels for resale at a service station known as Mustow Green garage. The agreement was to remain in force for a period of four years and five months from 1 July, 1963. The appellants also agreed to allow the respondents a rebate of $1\frac{1}{4}$d per gallon on all motor fuels purchased by the respondents under the agreement and to extend to the respondents the advantages of the appellants' Dealer Co-operation Plan. The respondents agreed, inter alia,

a) to operate the service station in accordance with the plan, which included agreements on the part of the respondents to keep the service station open at all reasonable hours for the sale of the appellants' motor fuel and motor oils;

b) not to sell motor fuels for use in vehicles holding private licences except in accordance with the appellants' retail schedule prices; and

c) before completing any sale or transfer of the service station premises or business to procure the prospective purchaser or transferee to enter into an agreement with the appellants and the respondents whereby such person would be substituted for the respondents for all future purposes of the agreement.

The second action, which was referred to as the 'Corner garage action', concerned another solus agreement between the appellants and the respondents in the same terms as the Mustow Green agreement save that it related to a service station known as Corner garage, was made on 5 July, 1962, and was expressed to remain in force for a period of twenty-one years from 1 July, 1962. Under a legal mortgage made between the respondents and the appellants on 6 October, 1962, the respondents covenanted to repay the appellants £7000 with interest by quarterly instalments over a period of twenty-one years from 6 November, 1962; it was further provided in the mortgage deed that the respondents should not be entitled to redeem the security otherwise than in accordance with the covenant as to repayment. The respondents charged Corner garage by way of legal mortgage with payment to the appellants of all moneys thereby covenanted to be paid. The respondents further covenanted during the continuance of the mortgage to purchase exclusively from the appellants all motor fuels which the respondents might require for consumption or sale at Corner garage, so long as the appellants should be ready to supply the same at their usual list price, and not to buy, receive or sell or knowingly permit to be bought, received or sold at Corner garage any motor fuels other than such as should be purchased from the appellants.

From about the end of the year 1963 and from about August, 1964, the respondents sold at Mustow Green garage and at Corner garage respectively motor fuel that was not supplied by the appellants. On appeal to the Court of Appeal it was held, briefly stated, that the doctrine of restraint of trade applied to covenants in mortgages as well as to solus agreements; that the restrictions in the solus agreements and in the mortgage were unreasonable and void, and that the proviso in the mortgage prohibiting redemption for twenty-one years, taken with the tie of Corner garage for a like period, rendered the mortgage oppressive, and accordingly the tie was unenforceable.

The House of Lords revised the decision of the Court of Appeal as to the Mustow Green Garage and affirmed it as to the Corner Garage. (Set out below is an extract of the judgement of Lord Pearce in the House of Lords decision.)

LORD PEARCE. My Lords, on the assumption that the solus agreement relating to the Mustow Green Garage comes within the ambit of the doctrine of restraint of trade and that its reasonableness is a matter which the courts must decide, I am of opinion that it is reasonable.

The period of five years has been approved as a reasonable period for agreements of this nature in Canada (*British American Oil Co* v. *Hey*). In the courts of this country there is nothing which suggests that five years is an unreasonable length of time for a tie of this kind in a trade of this kind.

Since the war there has been a world-wide reorganisation of the petrol industry. The old haphazard distribution has, in the interests of economy, efficiency and finance, been converted into a distribution by the respective petrol producers through their own individual (and as a rule improved and more efficient) outlets. Vast sums have been spent on refineries, the improvement of garages and the like. Hand-to-mouth arrangements are no longer commercially suitable to the industry and considerable planning (involving inter alia the geographical spacing of the outlets) is obviously necessary. The garage proprietors were not at any disadvantage in dealing with the various competing producers of petrol. To hold that five-year periods are too long for the ties between the producers and their outlets would, in my opinion, be out of accord with modern commercial needs, would cause an embarrassment to the trade and would not safeguard any public or private interest that needs protection. I would, however, regard 21 years as being longer than was reasonable in the circumstances.

It is important that the court, in weighing the question of reasonableness, should give full weight to commercial practices and to the generality of contracts made freely by parties bargaining on equal terms. Undue interference, though imposed on the ground of promoting freedom of trade, may in the result hamper and restrict the honest trader and, on a wider view, injure trade more than it helps it. If a man wishes to tie himself for his own good commercial reasons to a particular supplier or customer it may be no kindness to him to subject his contract to the arbitrary rule that the courts will always reserve to him a right to go back on his bargain if the court thinks fit. For such a reservation prevents the honest man from getting full value for the tie which he intends, in spite of any reservation imposed by the courts, to honour. And it may enable a less honest man to keep the fruits of a bargain from which he afterwards resiles.

Where there are no circumstances or oppression, the court should tread warily in substituting its own views for those of current commerce generally and the contracting parties in particular. For that reason, I consider that the courts require on such a matter full guidance from evidence of all the surrounding circumstances and of relevant commercial practice. They must also have regard to the consideration. And although the court may not be able to weigh the details of the advantages and disadvantages with great nicety it must appreciate the consideration at least in its more general aspects. Without such guidance they cannot hope to arrive at a sensible and up-to-date conclusion on what is reasonable. That is not to say that, when it is clear that current contracts (containing restraints), however widespread, are in fact a danger and disservice to the public and to traders, the court should hesitate to interfere.

The onus is on the party asserting the contract to show the reasonableness of the restraint. When the court sees its way clearly, no question of onus arises. In a doubtful case where the court does not see its way clearly and the question of onus does arise, there may be a danger in preferring the guidance of a general rule, founded on grounds of public policy many generations ago, to the guidance given by free and competent parties contracting at arm's length in the management of their own affairs. Therefore, when free and competent parties agree and the background provides some commercial justification on both sides for their bargain, and there is no injury to the community, I think that the onus should be easily discharged. Public policy, like other unruly horses, is apt to change its stance; and public policy is the ultimate basis of the courts' reluctance to enforce restraints. Although the decided cases are almost invariably based on unreasonableness between the parties, it is ultimately on the ground of public policy that the court will decline to enforce a restraint as being unreasonable between the parties. And a doctrine based on the general commercial good must always bear in mind the changing face of commerce. There is not, as some cases seem to suggest, a separation between what is reasonable on grounds of public policy and what is reasonable as between the parties. There is one broad question: is it in the interests of the community that this restraint should, as between the parties, be held to be reasonable and enforceable?

In addition does the mere fact that a restraint is embodied as an obligation under a mortgage exclude it from critical scrutiny and prevent its being unenforceable if it would have been so apart from the mortgage? I think not.

The difficult question in this case is whether a contract regulating commercial dealings between the parties has by its restraints exceeded the normal negative ties incidental to a positive commercial transaction and has thus brought itself within the sphere to which the doctrine of restraint applies. If Esso had assured to the garage proprietor a supply of petrol at a reasonable price, come what may, in return for the garage proprietor selling only Esso petrol, it might be that the contract would have come within the normal incidents of a commercial transaction and not within the ambit of restraint of trade. But Esso did not do this. They hedged their liability around so that they had an absolute discretion in the event inter alia of a failure to their own sources of supply, whether or not Esso should have foreseen it, to withhold supplies from the garage proprietor (leaving him the cheerless right in such a situation to seek supplies elsewhere); and then at a later stage it would seem, if and when they were prepared to supply him once more, they could hold him to his tie with them. And the price was to be fixed by Esso. And for the duration of the contract he owed them a contractual obligation to continue to keep his garage open (or find a successor who would do so on like terms). When these contracts are viewed as a whole the balance tilts in favour of regarding them as contracts which are in restraint of trade and which, therefore, can only be enforced if the restraint is reasonable.

I do not here find help in the well-known phrases that a man is not entitled to protect himself against competition per se or that he is only entitled to protect himself if he has an interest to protect. It is clear that a restraint which merely damages a covenantor and confers no benefit on a convenantee is as a rule unreasonable. But here Esso had a definite interest to protect and secured a definite benefit. They wished to preserve intact their spaced network of outlets in order that they could continue to sell their products as planned over a period of years in competition with the other producers. To prevent them from doing so would be an embarrassment of trade, not a protection of its freedom. If all the other companies owned garages and Esso were trying for the first time to enter the market it would stifle trading competition rather than encourage it if Esso were prevented from being able to enter into a binding solus agreement for a sole outlet in order to compete with the others. And in a doctrine based on the wide ground of public policy the wider aspects of commerce must always be considered as well as the narrower aspect of the contract as between the parties.

Since the tie for a period of four years and five months was in the circumstances reasonable, I would allow the appeal in respect of the Mustow Green Garage. Since the tie for a period of 21 years was not in the circumstances reasonable, I would dismiss the appeal in respect of the Corner Garage.

3 Business organisations

'Persons are natural, created by God, and incorporate created by the policy of man, and these latter are either sole or aggregate of many.'

Lord Chief Justice Coke
1552 – 1634

Introduction

In the UK there are over two million business enterprises varying in size from the tiny one-man business to the massive multi-national organisation employing perhaps hundreds of thousands of people. They encompass every aspect of the business environment producing raw materials, manufacturing them into semi- and fully-completed products and then ensuring that they are distributed to millions of consumers. Business enterprises also provide all the vital, and sometimes not so vital, services which a modern society requires to meet its sophisticated needs.

This extensive variety of types of organisation obviously necessitates differing structures, aims and objectives which must be considered in this chapter.

Forms of business enterprise

The evolution of business, industry and commerce has meant that several distinct forms of business enterprise have developed to meet different types of need. The law recognises the following types of business enterprise:

a) *the sole trader;*
b) *the partnership;*
c) *the limited company.*

Each of these has distinct features which may suit them to particular trading activities. The law treats these forms of business in a different manner and there are various statutory and common law rules relating to each form.

One of the main criterion which will determine the form of the business is the type and scope of the activity which it intends to operate. A small business enterprise requiring limited capital such as a corner shop or small garage, could be efficiently operated on a *sole trader* basis. A business enterprise owned by more than one person may be

105

recognised in law as a *partnership* in which the respective partners will usually have made a capital contribution and may share profits and losses equally. As an alternative, joint owners of business may favour the *registered company*, limited by shares, as their form of enterprise. Registered companies confer on their members the benefits of corporate status and facilitate the raising of larger sums of capital by 'going public', ie offering ownership to members of the public by inviting them to subscribe for shares. A good example of this evolutionary process is the Courtaulds Group. Established by Samuel Courtauld in 1816, it grew through the partnership stage to become a private limited company in 1891 and a public limited company in 1904. It was reorganised under its present title of 'Courtaulds Ltd' in 1913 and has since diversified into a multi-national company operating throughout the world.

The objectives of the business enterprise

Before attempting to analyse the behaviour of the varying types of business organisation, it is necessary to try and assess the objectives which they may have, and to understand how these differing objectives have led to the establishment of such diverse legal forms of business organisation.

To use the term 'enterprises' to describe business organisations may give some indication as to the major objective that has in the past been attributed to them. The word enterprise suggests some adventurous and risky undertaking and it is true that many business organisations do have this characteristic. In return for the risk involved in investing capital and labour into a business, the entrepreneur or initiator, would seek to receive some monetary gain.

In theory, the entrepreneur would attempt to achieve as much return as possible. The entrepreneur would be a *profit maximiser*. It is from this basic assumption that all businesses are trying to gain most profit, that much economic analysis of organisational behaviour is developed. In the following chapter, the theoretical procedure by which an organisation will try to achieve this, will be examined.

However this is perhaps too general an assumption to make. Many enterprises do not in fact seek to maximise profits. They are content to accept sufficient profits to enable the organisation to survive, pay the bills, provide enough to allow employees to be paid and leave the owner or owners an adequate income to allow them to enjoy the life-style they are happy with. The enterprise does not seek maximum profit, merely *satisfactory profit*. This is obviously true for many small sole traders. A local shopkeeper may choose to close the store at 5.30 pm rather than practice late opening hours; staying open for another two or three hours each evening would increase profit but allow less leisure time at home.

This non-maximisation of profit is not restricted to the smaller one-man business. Many companies do not fully exploit the potential for expansion and profit growth. This may be for a number of reasons: fear of growing too large and encountering extra problems such as greater capital requirements (and perhaps greater risk) or increased industrial relations unrest. They are content to exist with a relatively small market share so as not to attract the attentions of competitors, fearful of their own market share, or the government which may be prompted into measures which would discourage the growth of a company leading to market dominance. Thus the company does not expand as much as it possibly could but as much as it feels it should.

It will be seen later in this chapter that the behaviour of business organisations is not always consistent with their overall objectives. Company policy may be decided by shareholders and directors, but often the actual performance of the enterprise depends on the attitudes, aspirations and abilities of its executives. If a manager prefers not to pursue maximum profit either because it may simply increase the workload or burden of worry, or because there is no personal incentive in increasing the company's profitability, then he or she may decide not to push the organisation to its maximum potential. In any business it is important to realise that there may be many conflicting interests and objectives. Yet the enterprise could and should be run in the most efficient manner and should aim to achieve one objective common to all business enterprises – *survival*. It is a rare instance indeed where a business or its managers would seek to see its demise. Most organisations realise that in order to survive, it is essential to attempt to reach optimal size, be as efficient as possible and make sufficient profit. In order to achieve this it is necessary for the business to be operated in the most appropriate form and the possible alternatives open to any enterprise will now be considered.

Unincorporated bodies

The sole trader

Small businesses are the most prolific form of enterprise in the UK. There are almost $2\frac{1}{4}$ million people trading as one-man businesses or as partnerships. Thus numerically, they would appear quite significant and yet their trade makes up only about $\frac{1}{3}$ of that in the private sector of the business environment. Most tend to be relatively small with a turnover of less than £25 000 pa and with only a small proportion of the employed workforce involved in their operation. And yet without the small business much of normal life would be unable to continue. Much of the food consumed in the UK is produced by independent farmers and sold by small shopkeepers. Many trades, such as plumbing and building, are undertaken by self-employed tradespeople and many professional services such as accountancy are carried on by individuals. The advantages to the small businessperson of remaining a sole trader are many: control over and in charge of the enterprise and profits.

There is, therefore, the personal incentive to work harder. In remaining small the risk involved with large-scale capital investment is minimised and by keeping the personal legal identity of an individual, acting as a sole trader, the myriad regulations and controls imposed on corporate bodies by the law do not have to be faced. Trading returns need not be published.

The attractions exist also for consumers, who feel they are receiving 'personal service' when dealing with the owner of the business who is not some employee of a faceless corporation. The sole trader, however, does have some distinct disadvantages as a form of business enterprise. Expansion is restricted by the individual limit on personal capital and the usual reluctance of banks and other financial institutions to provide funds on a large scale to one individual. The owner of an unincorporated business, although receiving all profits, is also personally liable for all debts incurred in trading. This can be an increasing concern if the entrepreneur allows the business to expand to any great extent.

Thus most sole traders tend to remain relatively small. The owner is content to earn sufficient profit to afford a decent living without the undue potential hazards inherent in an expanding concern. If the business does continue to grow, or as happens in many cases, the owner wishes to leave the business to a son or daughter, then he or she may decide to introduce others into the business. This action may be taken to share responsibility and provide extra capital and additional expertise in the running of the business, and so may transform the enterprise into a partnership.

The partnership

The advantages to a business enterprise of forming a partnership are somewhat similar to those enjoyed by the sole trader. The partners are capable of managing their own firm as they see fit, of sharing the profits and being able to deal directly with their customers or clients. The partnership is the most common form of organisation within the professions. Accountants, solicitors and other professional people are required by their professional associations to be *personally* liable for all their actions and so in most cases the formation of a limited liability company is prohibited.

The partnership provides the compromise of allowing an extension of skill and expertise and the possible influx of additional capital by the introduction of extra partners. This extra potential for capital allows many partnerships to grow to become substantial business enterprises.

Although it has always tended to be overshadowed by the limited company, the partnership remains a significant form of business organisation in the United Kingdom, and is the choice of many people either setting up a new business or modifying an existing one. Partnerships are *non-corporate bodies*. As such they do not enjoy a separate legal identity independent from their members. In fact the term partnership describes a legally-recognised relationship existing between the members of a defined type of business enterprise. The definition is contained in the Partnership Act 1890 which provides under s. 1(1) that a partnership is

'the relation which subsists between persons carrying on business in common with a view of profit'.

The Act goes on to state in s. 1(2) that the relationship between the members of a company or association registered under the Companies Acts or otherwise incorporated does not give rise to a partnership.

The heart of the partnership relationship lies in the law of agency: each partner is an agent of the co-partners and has the agent's power to bind them and himself or herself by acts within the ordinary course of the business. This fact, together with the non-corporate status of the partnership, has been judicially stated in the following terms:

'In English law a firm as such has no existence; partners carry on business both as principals and as agents for each other within the scope of the partnership business; the firm-name is a mere expression, not a legal entity' stated Lord Justice Farwell in *Sadler* v. *Whiteman* (1910).

It is worth adding that the expression 'the firm' is recognised under the Partnership Act, 1890. Under s. 4(1)

'Persons who have entered into partnership with one another are for the purposes of this Act called collectively "a firm", and the name under which their business is carried on is called the firm-name.'

The power of a partner to bind the other members of the firm by actions illustrates how important it is that each partner should trust and have confidence in their co-partners, not only in regard to their business ability but also as to their business ethics. It has been said that 'mutual confidence is the life blood' of the firm (Bacon, V-C in *Helmore* v. *Smith* (1886).) Indeed the partnership relationship is one of the *utmost good faith* (uberrimae fidei). As such the partners are under a duty to make full and frank disclosure to the firm of matters affecting it. (This concept of uberrimae fidei has already been considered on pp 91 – 4.)

The law governing partnerships is largely contained in the Partnership Act 1890, a codifying Act, whose provisions are intended to regulate the partnership. The Act is by no means a complete code, and many aspects of partnership law, such as the implied powers of partners, are found by reference to decided cases. In addition the Limited Partnerships Act 1907 provides for the creation of limited partnerships, a more specialised type of business organisation in which at least one partner must have limited liability for the firm's debts. This is in sharp contrast to the ordinary partnership in which each partner is fully accountable for the firm's debts and liabilities. All businesses, whether operated by individuals, partnerships or companies were, prior to the introduction of the Companies Act 1981, required to register under the Registration of Business Names Act 1916 if the name under which the business was operated was other than the true names of the owners of the business. Under the Companies Act 1981 the Central Business Names Registry is being abolished, and businesses are no longer obliged to register. However the Act does require a business carried out under a name other than that of its owners to provide its customers with the name of each owner together with a business or other address. This information must be provided on all business stationery and supplied to a customer or supplier on request. Additionally the information must be prominently displayed in any premises where the business is carried on. An example of such a notice is given below. In a partnership of more than twenty partners the names of the partners do not need to be included on business documents.

PARTICULARS OF OWNERSHIP
OF

_____

as required by section 29 of the Companies Act 1981

Full name(s) of Proprietor(s)	Address within Great Britain at which documents may be effectively served on the business

* Insert Name of Business

Failure to comply with these requirements is an offence, and may result in the business being unable to enforce its contracts.

Partnerships are based upon the existence of an agreement between the participators in the business, who become contractually bound, each to the other. Like most other contracts, a partnership can be created by an express agreement made orally or in writing, or can be implied simply by looking at the conduct of the parties; thus a partnership can arise even though the partners are unaware that the law regards them as such. The 1890 Act lays down no formalities. It is of course commercially desirable, and is common practice for partners to execute a deed of partnership, in which they provide for matters such as the capital contribution required from each member of the firm, and how profits and losses are to be divided. If the partners do not agree such details then the rights and duties laid down under the Act will apply to the partnership.

It will be recalled that the definition of a partnership under s. 1 requires there to be

(i) *a business,*
(ii) *carried on in common by its members,*
(iii) *with a view to making a profit.*

Under the Act 'business' includes every trade, occupation or profession. Although business is a broad term it does seem that it involves the carrying on of some form of commercial activity. This may be for a single purpose. In *Spicer (Keith) Ltd* v. *Mansell* (1970), the Court of Appeal held that two persons who were working together for the purpose of forming a limited company, and had opened a bank account and ordered goods in this connection were not in partnership prior to the incorporation of the company (which in fact was never formed). The reason was that at that time, they were preparing for business, rather than operating an existing one.

The business must be a joint venture which implies mutual rights and obligations existing between the members of it. There may still be a joint venture even though one (or more) of its members is a 'sleeping partner' who does not take an active part in the management of the business but simply contributes capital.

There must be a profit motive underlying the business. It will be a question of fact whether the partners aim to make a profit. Profit is considered in this instance as being simply a gain made over a determined accounting period based on the value of assets at the commencement of the period.

If any of the requirements of s. 1 are not satisfied the association will not be a partnership. It may nevertheless enjoy some form of alternative legal status, such as a trust. Whatever its form, the Act will not apply to it.

S. 2 lays down rules for determining whether a partnership does or does not exist. It provides that a person who receives a share of the profits of a business is, *prima facie*, a partner in the business, but adds that the test is not conclusive. Furthermore, the following situations set out under the section do not in themselves make a person a partner, namely where a person:

a) receives a debt or other liquidated amount out of the profits of a business, whether or not by instalments;
b) being a servant or agent is paid out of a share of the profits of the business;
c) being the widow or child of a deceased partner receives an annuity (an annual set payment) out of a portion of the profits of the business in which the deceased was a partner;
d) lends money to a person engaged or about to engage in business, on a written contract signed by, or on behalf of the parties to it that the lender shall be repaid either at a rate of interest, varying with the profits, or as a share of the profits;
e) receives by way of annuity or otherwise a portion of the profits of a business in consideration of the sale by the person of the goodwill of the business.

Such a situation occurred in *Pratt* v. *Strick* (1932), where a doctor sold his medical practice together with its goodwill, on terms that for the following three months he would remain living at the practice, introducing patients, and sharing profits and losses equally with the purchaser. It was held that the practice was the purchaser's as soon as he bought it.

Under s. 2(1) where persons own property either as joint tenants or tenants in common (the two forms of co-ownership of land), that co-ownership does not of itself make them partners, even if they share profits. Co-ownership can be created by operation of law, and thus such a relationship may occur without any express intention of the parties.

Under s. 2(2) the sharing of gross returns does not of itself create a partnership, even if the persons sharing the returns have a joint or common right or interest in any property from which, or from the use of which, the returns are derived. This draws a distinction between returns and profits. A return is the revenue obtained by a business, eg in a theatrical enterprise the amount of money received by a theatre from the sale of tickets, whereas a profit is the sum left after deducting costs from revenue, ie in the above example the profit would be the difference between ticket revenue and the costs incurred in putting on the play. Persons sharing returns are not sharing costs, but persons sharing profits are.

Once having determined that particular persons together constitute a partnership, certain statutory provisions need to be complied with by the firm. Under the Companies Act 1948 a partnership consisting of more than twenty persons is void, however the Companies Act 1967 provides that partnerships of more than twenty persons may be created in the case of solicitors, accountants and members of the Stock Exchange. This was to facilitate the growth of major professional firms, who by the nature of their professional bodies must remain as sole traders or partnerships. The Department of Trade has extended this privilege to other professional groups including surveyors, auctioneers and estate agents. The Companies Act 1967 raised to twenty the maximum permitted number of partners in a banking partnership, provided each member is authorised by the Department of Trade.

If the partnership chooses a name which is sufficiently like that of an existing business carrying on work of a similar kind that the public will confuse the two businesses, the established business may apply to the court for an injunction to prevent the use of the rival's name, and obtain damages if the rival used the name intending to cause confusion. (This is known as the tort of 'passing off'.) It should be noted that there is nothing to prevent a company becoming a member of a firm, subject to appropriate powers being included in the objects clause of its memorandum of association.

The partnership is thus recognised by the law as being an important form of business enterprise. However the majority of business undertaken in the UK is carried on by corporate bodies − either private or public limited companies.

Partnership contract

ARTICLES OF PARTNERSHIP BETWEEN TWO PERSONS SETTING UP IN BUSINESS AS A NEW FIRM

THIS DEED OF PARTNERSHIP made the _____ day of _____
BETWEEN A. B. of etc. of the one part and C. D. of the other part
WITNESSETH that it is hereby mutually agreed that the said A. B. and C. D. shall become partners in the trade or business of _____ upon the following terms:—

1. The partnership shall commence [or shall be deemed to have commenced] on the _____ day of _____ and shall continue [for the term of _____ years from that date and thereafter] until determined as hereinafter provided.

2. The name of the firm shall be 'B. and D.'

3. The business of the partnership shall be carried on at _____ in the County of _____ or at such other place or places as the partners shall from time to time agree upon.

4. The bankers of the firm shall be _____ Bank Limited _____ Branch and all cheques shall be signed by both partners [or. and each partner shall be at liberty to draw cheques upon the firm's account for payments on account of the business of the partnership].

5. The capital of the partnership shall be the sum of £_____ and shall be provided by and belong to the partners in equal shares. If at any

time hereafter any further capital shall be required for the purposes of the partnership the same shall, unless otherwise agreed, be contributed by the partners in equal shares.

6. The profits and losses of the business (including loss of capital) shall be divided between and borne by the partners in proportion to the capital for the time being credited to them in the books of the partnership.

7. The lease [tenancy agreement] under which A. B. now holds the premises situate at _____ at which the said business is now carried on shall on demand by C. D. be assigned to the partners as tenants in common to be held by them as part of the partnership property and it is hereby agreed that all liability under the said lease shall during the continuance of the partnership or until the said lease [tenancy agreement] shall determine whichever shall first happen be discharged as debts of the partnership.

8. Each partner may draw out of the banking account of the partnership sums not exceeding £_____ a month on account of his share of profits but if on taking the annual general account the drawings of either partner during any year shall be found to exceed his share of profits for the year he shall forthwith refund the excess.

9. All necessary and proper books of account shall be kept by the firm and on the _____ day of _____ 19____ and on the _____ day of _____ in each succeeding year a general account shall be taken of all the assets and liabilities and of the profits and losses of the partnership (including therein profits and losses earned or incurred but not actually received or paid) [or (but so that actual receipts and payments alone shall be taken into account)] for the preceding year and shall be signed by each partner. Such account when signed shall be conclusive and final between the partners as to all matters stated therein unless some manifest error shall be discovered within three months after the signing thereof in which case such error shall be rectified. So soon as the annual general account shall have been signed by the partners the net profits (if any) of the business shall be divisible between them in accordance with the provisions of this Deed.

10. Each partner shall—

a) Devote his whole time and attention to the partnership business (except during holidays)

b) Punctually pay and discharge his separate debts and engagements and indemnify the other partner and the partnership assets against the same and all proceedings costs claims or demands in respect thereof

c) Be just and faithful to the other partner in all transactions relating to the partnership business and at all times give to the other a true account of all such dealings.

11. Neither partner shall without the consent of the other—

a) Engage or be concerned or interested either directly or indirectly in any other business or occupation
b) Engage make any contract with or dismiss any employee
c) Enter into any engagement whereby the partners may risk the loss of or be made liable for one sum or any number of sums in respect of the same transaction amounting of £_____ or upwards
d) Forgive the whole or any part of any debt or sum due to the partners
e) Except in the ordinary course of trade dispose by loan pledge sale or otherwise of any part of the partnership property.
f) Become bail guarantor or surety for any person or do or knowingly suffer anything whereby the partnership property may be endangered
g) Assign or charge his interest in the firm or
h) Draw or accept or endorse any bill of exchange or promissory note on account of the partnership.

12. [After the expiration of the said term of _____ years] the partnership may be determined by either party giving to the other not less than [three] months' notice in writing [expiring on any anniversary of the commencement of the partnership] and on the expiration of such notice the partnership shall determine accordingly.

13. —(a) If during the continuance of the partnership either partner shall die or become bankrupt or become a patient under the Mental Health Act 1959 the surviving or solvent or other partner shall have the option [to be exercised by notice in writing to the personal representative of a deceased partner or to the trustee in bankruptcy of a bankrupt within [one month] after the death or bankruptcy or to the receiver of the patient duly appointed] to purchase the share of the other partner as at the date of his death or bankruptcy or becoming a patient as aforesaid in the capital and assets of the partnership.

(b) The purchase price shall be—

(i) A sum equal to the amount standing to the credit of the deceased or bankrupt partner as his share in the capital of the partnership and as undrawn profits belonging to him in the last annual general account prior to the death or bankruptcy or becoming a patient as aforesaid or if such event shall occur before the taking of the first annual general account the amount credited to him as his share in the capital at the commencement of the partnership;

(ii) A sum equal to the amount of any further capital brought by him into and credited to him in the books of the partnership after the taking of the last annual general account or commencement of the partnership as the case may be;

(iii) A sum equal to one [half] of the excess (if any) in the value of any freehold or leasehold property vested in the partnership over that shown in the said last annual general account and for this purpose the said property shall be valued by a professional valuer of such property to be agreed on by the personal representatives of the deceased partner or the trustee in bankruptcy or the receiver as the case may be and the surviving or other partner (*i*).

(iv) A sum in place of current profits equal to interest on the said share of capital and further capital (if any) of the deceased or other partner at the rate of _____ per cent per annum from the date of the last annual general account or from the commencement of the partnership as the case may be or in the case of further capital from the date when such capital was credited to such partner in the books of the partnership up to the date of the death or bankruptcy or becoming a patient as aforesaid.

after deducting from the total of the said sums any drawings by the deceased or other partner during the current year of the partnership such drawings being taken in satisfaction so far as possible the sum payable in respect of current profits.

(c) The purchase price shall be paid as to the sum payable in place of current profits on the exercise of the option and as to the balance of [twelve] equal instalments at intervals of [three] months from the date of the exercise of the option.

(d) The said purchase price or the balance thereof for the time being remaining unpaid shall carry interest at the rate of _____ per cent per annum from the date of the exercise of the option until payment and all interest due to date shall be paid on each date on which an instalment becomes payable.

(e) PROVIDED ALWAYS that if default shall be made in the payment of the sum payable in place of current profits or any of the said [twelve] instalments or of any part thereof [one month] after the same shall have become due and payable then the whole of the said purchase price or the balance thereof for the time being remaining unpaid shall forthwith become payable and be paid by the purchasing partner with interest thereon as aforesaid.

(f) Further upon the exercise of the said option the surviving or solvent or sane partner shall enter into a proper covenant to indemnify the representatives of the deceased partner or the insolvent partner and his trustee in bankruptcy and the estate of the deceased or insolvent partner or the receiver and the estate of the partner so becoming a patient as aforesaid against all proceedings costs claims and expenses in respect of the partnership.

14. Subject and without prejudice to the express provisions contained in this Deed on the dissolution of the partnership hereby constituted the same shall be wound up and the assets thereof sold as provided by the Partnership Act 1890 or any statutory modification or re-enactment thereof for the time being in force but so that each partner shall be at liberty to bid at any sale of any partnership assets.

15. Any notice required to be given hereunder shall be duly given if the same shall be delivered personally to the person to whom the same is intended to be given or left for him at or sent by post by registered letter to his usual or last known place of address in the United Kingdom or in the case of a notice to a partner left for him at the office of the partnership.

16. Any dispute or question in connection with the partnership or this Deed shall be referred to a single arbitrator (to be appointed by the _____ Chamber of Commerce) under the provisions of the Arbitration Act 1950 or any statutory modification or re-enactment thereof for the time being in force.

IN WITNESS, etc.

Corporate bodies

The limited liability company

There are more than 50 000 registered limited companies in this country and between them they employ the majority of the workforce and comprise about two thirds of the income made by the private sector. They vary greatly in size. A company can be formed having only two members but can also extend to the massive multi-national enterprises registered in the UK such as British Petroleum and Imperial Chemical Industries. They are strictly regulated by law and are much more likely to be the subject of scrutiny from bodies such as the Monopolies Commission and the Department of Trade and Industry. They have grown to become the most important entities in the business environment. Obviously with such a wide diversity of organisations it is difficult to generalise on their structure and behaviour but most have been formed to allow the company to expand by facilitating the raising of capital by the issuing of shares. As separate legal entities they also give the owners the protection of *limited liability* and so restrict the amount for which each of the shareholders can be responsible for the debts of the company. It was for this reason that they have become such a popular form of enterprise. Ownership can be divorced from management. An investor can stake capital in a company and without having to be involved in its running, can be assured of being responsible for, at worst, debts equal to the nominal share value held.

Companies can thus expand and diversify, raising additional capital if and when needed. The growth of this form of business enterprise and the recognition of the company as a separate legal entity has of course posed many problems and led to many abuses. The law has recognised these difficulties and has by various Companies Acts, the most important being the Companies Act, 1948, sought to clarify the legal status of companies and regulate their behaviour.

By creation of the limited liability company, the law has provided the means by which a large-scale commercial enterprise can operate in the business environment. The limited company is an *artificial legal person* having, in law, most of the powers and responsibilies of a natural person. It is capable therefore of owning property, entering into contracts such as trading contracts or contracts of employment and suing or being sued in its own name. It is a fundamental principle of company law that the rights and liabilities of a company belong to the company alone, and cannot be enforced by or against its members. Generally the members of a limited company are its shareholders and they incur no personal liability for any debts or obligations owed by the company to other persons. Even if a company fails, and is wound up, the liability of its members will be limited. The extent of such liability will depend on the nature of the company.

Companies can be divided into the following categories:

a) *Company limited by shares* Here the liability of the shareholder is limited to contribution of the nominal value of those shares, eg if X owns 100 £1 shares issued at nominal value known as the par value, and has paid £60 to the Company, liability is limited to the unpaid balance of £40. This is the most common type of company.

b) *Company limited by guarantee* Here the constitution of the company will state that its members are to contribute a stated sum in the event of it being wound up and each member's contribution will be limited to that sum. Such companies may have a share capital but this is rare in practice. This is the business form used by many clubs, charities and trade associations. The Business Education Council is an example of a company limited by guarantee.

c) *Unlimited company* Here the members have no limit to their liability and must contribute to the full extent of their personal wealth to satisfy the company's debts in the event of it being wound up. Again such companies are rare in practice.

The company limited by shares therefore is the usual form adopted by commercial and industrial undertakings. It provides the means by which large sums of capital may be raised from many investors who are also protected from personal liability.

Classification of registered companies
The Companies Act 1980 has made radical changes to the structure and regulation of companies. The Act makes provision for all existing companies to be re-classified over a transitional period (fifteen months) into two main categories:

118

1 *the public limited company,*
2 *the private company.*

To fully appreciate the new classification, it is necessary briefly to mention the categories of company provided for in the previous legislation (Companies Acts, 1948 and 1967). Under the 1948 Act, companies were similarly classified as public or private, and the general rule was that a company would be classified as a public company unless it satisfied the conditions necessary for it to be a private company. These conditions were laid down in s. 28 of the 1948 Act which provided that a private company is one whose Articles of Association contained the following:

a) a restriction on the right to transfer shares,
b) a limit on membership of fifty (with exceptions),
c) a prohibition on inviting public subscription.

The above restrictions necessarily meant that the private company was limited in size but existing members could retain control. It should also be appreciated that by far the majority of registered companies are small private companies.

Under the Companies Act 1980 it is the private company which forms the residual category, ie a company which is not registered as a public company. For a company to acquire the status of 'public' it must satisfy certain conditions laid down in the Act. The main condition relates to the size of share capital, the requirement being that existing companies limited by shares or guarantee must have an authorised share capital of £50 000 which must be issued in full though it need only be a quarter paid up (ie a minimum of £12 500 must have been paid to the company out of the £50 000 which may be called upon).

To comply with the new classification existing companies must re-register their new status, the Act requiring this to be done within a fifteen-month period. Existing public companies having the necessary share capital will re-register as public limited companies. In the unlikely event that the authorised share capital is less than £50 000 a further issue of shares will be needed prior to applying for re-registration. The names of re-registered public companies must also be changed to accommodate their new status, eg Courtaulds Company Limited (Co Ltd) would become Courtaulds Public Limited Company (PLC). Thus an outsider dealing with a new public company can determine its status from its name. Alternatively existing public companies who do not satisfy the condition can re-register as private companies.

Existing private companies are faced with a similar alternative. By satisfying the conditions they may re-register as public companies but if they intend to remain private, re-registration is not necessary. Under the Act an existing private company which takes no action is automatically re-classified as a new private company. It should be noted that the restriction preventing a new private company inviting public subscription remains. Also, while a private company need not restrict membership or the right to transfer shares it may still do so. The reclassification under the Companies Act 1980 is illustrated in Figs 3.1 and 3.2.

Public companies
Large trading concerns whose shareholders are members of the public and whose shares are freely transferable.

(End of 1976 numbered 16 716)

- *limited by shares*
- *limited by guarantee* either *with a share capital* or *without a share capital*
- *unlimited*

Private companies
A company which by its Articles:

a) restricts the right to transfer shares,
b) limits its membership to fifty (with exceptions),
c) excludes the right to invite the public to invest.

- *limited by shares*
- *limited by guarantee* either *with a share capital* or *without a share capital*
- *unlimited*

Fig 3.1   Classification of companies under 1948 and 1967 Acts

Classification of companies under the Companies Act 1980

Public Limited companies

A company whose
a) memorandum states that the company is a public company
b) authorised share capital is £50 000 with at least one-quarter paid up.

Private companies

A company that is not registered as a public company may not invite the public to invest.

Re-registration under the Companies Act 1980

Old public companies limited by shares

Such companies may either:
1 Re-register as public companies provided certain conditions are satisfied, ie share capital exceeds £50 000
   or
2 Re-register as private companies.

Old private companies limited by shares

Such companies may either:
1 Re-register as public companies provided certain conditions are satisfied, ie share capital exceeds £50 000
   or
2 Automatically be classified as private companies.

Fig 3.2   The effect of the Companies Act 1980

Corporate identity

The principle that a company has an independent legal personality distinct from its members was clearly established in *Salomon* v. *Salomon & Co Ltd* (1897).

> *Salomon* v. *Salomon & Co Ltd* (1897) Salomon, an established boot manufacturer and leather merchant, had formed a limited company. He transferred his business to the company for £30 000 and in return received 20 000 £1 shares and £10 000 in secured debentures (loan capital). The company failed and went into liquidation owing £8000 to unsecured creditors and having only £6000 in assets. Such assets were naturally claimed by the creditors, who argued that the company was a mere agent of Salomon, and that his claim as a debenture holder, and therefore secured creditor, should be set aside. The Court held that the company was a separate legal entity from Salomon, it had been properly formed and registered, and therefore Salomon as debenture holder was entitled to the available assets in priority to the unsecured creditors.

A company is also the beneficial owner of its own property in which its members have no legal interest.

> In *Macaura* v. *Northern Assurance Co Ltd* (1925), it was held that a majority shareholder had no insurable interest in the company's property. A fire insurance policy over the company's timber estate was therefore invalid as it had been issued in the plaintiff shareholder's name and not the company's.

The rule of separate legal identity also extends to the contractual and tortious liability of a company. A shareholder cannot therefore sue or be sued on a contract made by the company. Similarly a member of a company cannot sue in respect of torts committed against it, nor can that member be sued for torts committed by it.

Exceptions to the principle of corporate identity

The law has recognised, both in statutory provisions and the common law, that it is in the public interest that there should be certain exceptions to the general rule of separate corporate existence. The main motivation behind such exceptions has been to give effect to the economic reality of a particular case. These are as follows:

1 *Members liability for Companies debts* Under the Companies Act, 1948, if the number of members of a company falls below the statutory minimum and remains less than that number for six months, every person who becomes or remains a member of the company, while the situation continues after the six months has expired, is personally liable for the debts of the company incurred

while remaining a member and is aware of the position. The importance of this section has been substantially diminished by the Companies Act 1980, which reduces the minimum membership for all registered companies to two (previously it was seven for public companies and two for private companies).

2 *Liability for fraudulent trading* If, when a company is wound up, the court is satisfied that its business has been carried on with intent to defraud its creditors or the creditors of another person, or for any fraudulent purpose, the court may declare that any persons who were knowingly parties to carrying on its business in that way shall be personally liable for all the company's debts and liabilities. Under this provision therefore, personal liability may be imposed on any persons responsible for managing the company's business who have been guilty of dishonesty. Certainly, if a company carries on business and incurs debts when the directors are aware that there is no reasonable prospect of the creditors ever receiving payment, then it is a proper inference that the company is carrying on business with intent to defraud.

3 *Liability for the lack of formality* If an officer of a company or any person on its behalf:

a) uses the company seal and the company name is not engraved on it;

b) issues or authorises the issue of a business letter or signs a negotiable instrument and the company name is not mentioned;

c) issues or authorises the issue of any invoice, receipt or letter of credit of the company and again the company name is not mentioned;

that person shall be *personally* liable for debts incurred unless they are paid by the company.

In *Penrose* v. *Martyr* (1858) a bill of exchange was drawn up with the word 'limited' omitted after the company's name and the company secretary who had signed the bill on the company's behalf was held to be personally liable for it.

4 *Liability imposed in the public interest* In some cases the courts have disregarded the separate legal personality of a company and have in the public interest investigated the personal qualities of the shareholders. It is in the public interest that an enemy alien is unable to sue in British courts.

In *Daimler Co Ltd* v. *Continental Tyre and Rubber Co (Gt Britain) Ltd* (1916) the tyre company, which was registered in England, and had its registered office there, sued Daimler for debts incurred before the war with Germany had been declared. Daimler claimed that as all of the membership of the tyre company except one were German nationals and the directors were German nationals resident in Germany the claim should be struck out because to pay the debt would be to trade with the enemy.

The House of Lords held that although the nationality of a company is normally decided by where it is incorporated, in some cases the Court has power to consider who was in control of the company's business and assets in order that it might determine its status. Here, those in control of the company were enemy aliens and the action was struck out.

5 *Liability imposed for the evasion of legal obligations* In rare cases, the courts will disregard the separate legal personality of a company because it was formed or used to facilitate the evasion of legal obligations.

In *Gilford Motor Co Ltd* v. *Horne* (1933) the defendants had been employed by the plaintiff motor company and had entered into a valid agreement not to solicit the plaintiff's customers or to compete with it for a certain time after leaving employment. (A restraint of trade clause as explained on p. 87.) Shortly after leaving employment, the defendant formed a company to carry on a similar business to his previous employers and sent out circulars to his previous customers of the motor company. In an action to enforce the restraint clause against the new company the Court held that since the defendant in fact controlled the company its formation was a mere 'cloak or sham' to enable him to break the restraint clause. Accordingly an injunction was granted against the defendant and against the company he had formed, to enforce the restraint clause.

Similarly in *Jones* v. *Lipman* (1962) the defendant agreed to sell land to the plaintiff and then decided not to complete the sale. To avoid the possibility of an order of specific performance to enforce the sale the defendant bought a company (ie purchased a majority shareholding) to which he sold the land. The plaintiff applied to the Court for an order of specific performance to enforce the sale to the plaintiff against the defendant and the company. It was held that the formation of the company was a mere sham to avoid a contract of sale and specific performance was ordered against the vendor and company.

6 *Liability imposed because of an implied agency or trustee-ship* Occasionally the courts have avoided the principle that a company is a separate person and implied that the company was acting as an agent for its shareholders or that the company held its property as a trustee for its shareholders. Unfortunately it is not possible to determine at present when the courts will imply such an agency or trusteeship but the cases have shown that they are more likely to do so in revenue cases which could result in an injustice.

In *Firestone Tyre & Rubber Co Ltd* v. *Llewellin (Inspector of Taxes)* (1957) the appellant company was a subsidiary of an American company which made and sold branded tyres and had a world-wide organisation. The British subsidiary manufactured and sold tyres in Europe. The House of Lords held that the appellant company was in fact not trading on its own behalf but as agent of the parent company and the parent company was consequently liable to pay United Kingdom income tax.

Having considered the concept of corporate personality, it is now possible to consider how a corporate body (eg the registered company) may be created under the law.

Formation of a registered company

A company is incorporated and thus comes into being when the Registrar of Companies issues a document called the *certificate of incorporation*. This certificate is issued in response to an application by the persons who wish to form the company. Two of the main documents which must be included in such an application are:

1 The *memorandum of association* – which will include the constitution of the company, and
2 The *articles of association* – which will include the internal regulations of the company.

The Memorandum of Association
The Companies Act, 1948, provides that this document must contain the following matters:

a) the company name,
b) the situation of the company's registered office,
c) the company's objects,
d) the liability of the members,
e) the amount and division of share capital.

1 *Company name*
The form of the company name will depend, to some extent, on the company's status. Under s. 2 of the Companies Act 1980 the name of a public company must end with the words 'public limited company' and these words must not be preceded by the word 'limited'. For a private company the last word of the name must be 'limited'. In practice, although there is no requirement that the name chosen requires approval, there are in fact certain restrictions on choice. Statute has provided that, to prevent the public being misled, the use of a name which is associated with a registered charity is prohibited, eg the name could not include the words 'Red Cross' or 'Oxfam'. In addition, the Registrar of Companies is compelled to refuse to register a name which,

124

in the opinion of the Department of Trade and Industry, is undesirable. Such would be the case if a name was misleading as to the size of the company's resources or implied connection with Royalty or government or resembled too closely an existing company name. Of course, it is a tort for one person to represent his or her business as that of another and thereby obtain profit from that other's business goodwill. In such circumstances the innocent business could maintain the tort action of 'passing off' against the business guilty of the deception and recover damages and/or an injunction to prevent future trading as a remedy. It has previously been mentioned that failure by an officer of the company to conduct company business in the company name could make the officer personally liable for any debts incurred (see *Penrose* v. *Martyr* (1858)).

2 *Objects clause*

A fundamental feature of statutory corporations is that their activities must be restricted in their constitution. This is achieved by requiring that a registered company in its objects clause sets out the purpose for which it is formed and the kind of business or activities that it intends to carry on. The purpose of having restrictions on a company's activities is to protect investors and creditors. It is reasonable that an investor should know the purposes for which the investment is to be used and similarly a creditor is entitled to expect that the company's funds are not used for unauthorised activities. If a company purports to do anything beyond the limit of its permissable activities as expressed in the objects clause it is acting *ultra vires* (beyond the powers) and may be restrained by one of its members securing a court injunction. Prior to the European Communities Act 1972 the courts would also treat a transaction between a company and another, which was ultra vires the company, as being automatically void. This was the case even if a contracting party was unaware that the company was exceeding its powers as expressed in the Memorandum of Association, for such a contracting party was taken to have constructive notice of its content.

> These principles were clearly established by the House of Lords in the case of *Ashbury Railway Carriage and Iron Co* v. *Riche* (1875). Here the plaintiff company's objects included the power to manufacture or sell rail rolling stock and carry on business as mechanical engineers and general contractors. The company purchased a concession to finance the building of a railway in Belgium, but later the directors repudiated the contract. In an action for breach of contract against the company, the Court held that the contract was 'ultra vires' and void from the outset. Lord Cairns expressed the law when he said, 'This contract was entirely beyond the objects in the memorandum. . . . If it was a contract void at its beginning, it was void because the company could not make the contract'.

It is important to draw a distinction between the objects of the company and the powers given to achieve those objects. It has always been the intention of the courts that they should assist a company to achieve its expressed objects by implying all the powers necessary for it to do so.

The House of Lords held, in *Deuchar* v. *Gas Light and Coke Co* (1925), that a company is impliedly granted such necessary and incidental powers when it is incorporated. Here the defendant company had as its main object to make and sell gas and to convert residual products into a marketable state. One such residual product was napthalene and this was converted by the company into beta-naphtol, a substance used in the making of dyes. To achieve this conversion, caustic soda was necessary, the defendant purchasing its supplies from another company. However, having decided that it would be more economic to produce its own caustic soda, the defendant company began to do so. Naturally, the company who had been the supplier of caustic soda was aggrieved at the loss of business but could take no action in its capacity as a creditor. Deuchar, the Secretary of the supplier company, therefore acquired shares in the defendant company and in his capacity as a member sued for an injunction to restrain the defendant from undertaking the manufacture of caustic soda which it was claimed was an ultra vires act. The House of Lords held that the company's act was not ultra vires as there were express powers to convert residual products into a marketable state and there was thus a reasonable implication for the company to have the power to manufacture products which were reasonably incidental to these express powers.

To avoid the restriction placed upon a company by the ultra vires rule it became the practice to frame the object clause of a company in very wide terms, so as to state all the possible things that the company might wish to do at any time in the future. At one time the courts would interpret such object clauses containing wide powers in a very narrow manner by restricting all such powers only to the achievement of the company's main objects. This became known as the '*main objects rule*' and was eventually circumvented by a declaration in the Memorandum that each part of the objects clause was to be regarded as an '*independent main object*'. Where this is the clear intention of the memorandum the courts will interpret it in this manner.

In *Cotman* v. *Brougham* (1918) the memorandum clearly stated that each of a rubber company's many objects were to be regarded as independent. The main clause was to develop rubber estates abroad but another subclause authorised the company to deal with the shares of any company. When the company underwrote shares in an oil company the action was challenged as ultra vires. The Court held that the power to underwrite was clearly provided for in the memorandum and the action was therefore *intra vires* and valid.

Another method of conferring wide powers in the memorandum is to include a clause similar to the one included in *Bell Houses Ltd* v. *City Wall Properties Ltd* (1966). Here the main object of the company was to develop housing estates, but another clause allowed the company to carry on 'any other trade or business whatsoever which can, in the opinion of the board of directors, be advantageously carried on by the company with, or as ancillary to, any of the above businesses or the general business of the company'. The Court of Appeal held that such a clause was valid provided that the directors in forming their opinion acted in good faith.

In addition the Companies Acts provide power for a company by *special resolution* (a three-quarter majority of voting shareholders) to alter or extend its objects clause to enable the company to achieve any of the following stated ends:

a) to carry on business more economically or more efficiently,
b) to attain its main purpose by new or improved means,
c) to enlarge or change the local area of its operations,
d) to carry on some business which may be conveniently combined with its own,
e) to restrict or abandon any of its objects,
f) to sell its undertaking, or
g) to amalgamate with another company.

Enforcement of ultra vires transactions
As part of the aim of harmonising the company law of member states of the European Economic Community, the European Communities Act 1972 provides that in favour of a person dealing in good faith with a company, any transaction decided on by its directors shall be deemed to be within the capacity of the company to enter into validly and the other party to the transaction shall not be bound to enquire about the capacity of the company to engage in it and shall be presumed to have acted in good faith unless the contrary is proved.

This provision of course does not abolish the ultra vires rule but merely enables the other party to an ultra vires transaction to enforce it if certain requirements are met. Certainly a member may still secure an injunction to prevent a company entering into an intended ultra vires transaction, and the European Communities Act 1972 confers no right on a company itself to enforce an ultra vires transaction. As a result of the Act however, the rule that an outsider dealing with a company is presumed to have constructive knowledge of the contents of the memorandum has been abolished. Also to enforce an otherwise ultra vires transaction against a company an outsider, presumed by the Act to have acted in good faith, would have to show:

a) that the transaction has been decided upon by the directors (the board of directors) or
b) that the transaction has been authorised, effected or ratified by the resolution of the board.

The effect of this limitation is that relatively few transactions would be affected as only few, although usually important, contracts are formally resolved at board meetings.

It seems therefore that the common law doctrine of ultra vires is still important and all that the European Communities Act 1972 has done is to add to the complexity of this important area of law.

3 The registered office clause

All companies are required to have a registered office to which all communications may be addressed. The memorandum is required to state whether the office is in England, Scotland or Wales, and so indicate its country of registration. In this way the company's nationality is fixed and cannot normally be changed except by re-registration.

4 The liability clause

This clause merely contains a statement that the liability of the members is limited either by shares or guarantee. In the case of a company limited by guarantee a further clause must state the terms of the guarantee, which consists of a promise by the members to contribute a specified sum towards payments of the company's debts if it is wound up while they are a member or within a year after they cease to be members. For a company limited by shares the members' liability is, of course, limited to the nominal value of the shares.

5 The capital clause

Here the *nominal capital* of the company and the number and amount of shares is stated. The nominal capital is the total value of the shares that the company is authorised to issue. There is no legal limit to the amount. It is fixed by the founders of the company assessing the capital required for the acquisition of the business, its operation and possible emergencies. Usually, on formation, a company will not issue the whole of its nominal capital but will retain shares available for issue in case money is required later. The nominal value of each share must also be stated, this having been decided by the founders. It is rare for the nominal value to exceed £1 and it is quite common for it to be 50p or even 25p. The fact that there are different classes of shares, having different rights, will be discussed in Chapter 8.

The articles of association

While the Memorandum confers powers and defines a company's objects, the *Articles of Association* generally determine how such powers are exercised and how the objects are to be achieved. The

Articles will therefore contain rules relating to the internal management of a company and its organisation. These are matters left to the discretion of the founders of a company rather than being regulated by statute. Nevertheless, the Companies Act 1948 provides (in Table A in the First Schedule) a specimen set of Articles of a company limited by shares, and if no Articles are submitted, then the provisions of Table A become the Articles of the Company. Alternatively, Table A can be excluded in total or adopted in part. As a result of this wide discretion, the Articles of Companies may vary substantially in form but certain matters are normally included. They usually:

1 provide for the appointment of a board of directors and define their powers,
2 divide the shares into various classes and define the class rights,
3 provide for members' meetings and voting rights,
4 provide the company with power to deal with the share capital.

The Articles form an enforceable contract between the company and its members in respect of their ordinary rights as members. They are also regarded as forming a contract between each individual member and so one member, by court action, may require another to comply with the Articles' provisions. The Articles may be altered by a special resolution at a general meeting provided the alteration is passed *bona fide* for the benefit of the company as a whole. The courts will therefore restrain an alteration if it discloses oppression on a minority interest and cannot be justified as being in the company's best interests.

In *Brown* v. *British Abrasive Wheel Co* (1919) a majority of the shareholders (98%) were willing to provide the company with much needed extra capital if they could buy the 2% minority. As the minority were unwilling to sell, the majority proposed to alter the Articles so as to enable nine-tenths of the shareholders to buy out any other shareholders. The plaintiff, representing the minority, brought an action to restrain the majority. It was held by the Court that the alteration would be restrained as it was not for the benefit of the company as a whole but rather for the benefit of the majority shareholding.

The Companies Acts require, in addition to the Memorandum and Articles, (certain other documents, such as a *statutory declaration*) that the requirements of the Companies Acts have been complied with, to be filed with the Registrar as well as the registration fees, to obtain the incorporation of the company. Having examined all the documents filed and ensured that they are in order, the Registrar then issues a certificate under official seal which certifies that the company is incorporated. The certificate is conclusive evidence that all the requirements of the Companies Acts have been complied with and that the company is a company authorised to be registered and duly registered under the

Acts. A private company can enter into contracts, borrow money, and carry on business immediately on incorporation. Previously however, a public company could not commence business until it had satisfied certain conditions and obtained a *Trading Certificate* from the Registrar of Companies. This requirement has been repealed by the Companies Act 1980. However a public limited company registered under the 1980 Act cannot commence business until a certificate is issued by the Registrar that the share capital of the company is not less than the authorised minimum (ie £50 000 with at least one-quarter paid up). If more than a year after the incorporation of a public company it has not been issued with such a certificate the Secretary of State may petition the court for the company to be wound up.

CERTIFICATE OF INCORPORATION

ON RE-REGISTRATION AS A PUBLIC COMPANY

No.   27657

I hereby certify that

THE BOOTS COMPANY PLC

has this day been re-registered under the Companies Acts 1948 to 1980 as a public company, and that the company is limited.

Dated at Cardiff the   15TH MARCH 1982

**Assistant Registrar of Companies
C 455**

No. 27657

THE COMPANIES ACTS, 1948 to 1980

———————

COMPANY LIMITED BY SHARES

———————

Memorandum of Association

OF

THE BOOTS COMPANY PLC

(as altered and adopted by a Resolution of the Directors of the Company
passed on 25th February, 1982 pursuant to the Companies Act 1980).

———————

1st. The name of the Company is "THE BOOTS COMPANY PLC".

2nd. The Company is to be a public company.

3rd. The Registered Office of the Company will be situated in England and Wales.

4th. The objects for which the Company is established are all or any of the following, the Company having power to do any part of the matters mentioned in one section apart from any other of the said matters, and none of the general or other descriptions given in this Clause being subject to be limited or restrained to matters of the same or some similar kind to those elsewhere in this Clause mentioned or referred to, or to be otherwise limited or restrained by any other part of this Clause not containing an express limitation or restriction, nor by any inference to be drawn from such other part.

(A) To purchase or acquire the business of patent medicine vendors, dispensers, drug merchants, herbalists, manufacturers of proprietary articles, and general store-keepers, carried on by "THE MIDLAND DRUG COMPANY, LIMITED," at Goose Gate, Island Street, and Arkwright Street, in the Town of Nottingham; at High Street, in the City of Lincoln; at Snig Hill, and at High Street, Attercliffe, both in the Borough of Sheffield; and elsewhere; and the lands, shops, warehouses, buildings, machinery, plant, material, stock-in-trade, book debts, goodwill and assets of the said business; and to issue fully paid-up shares in the Company to all or any of the shareholders of the before-mentioned selling Company as the whole or part consideration for the purchase.

S207

(B)   To carry on and extend the said business, and generally to carry on the business of wholesale, retail, manufacturing and dispensing chemists and druggists, herbalists and patent medicine vendors.

(C)   To carry on the business of artists' colourmen, and of manufacturers of and merchants in oils, paints, colours and brushes, and artists' and painters' requisites of all descriptions.

(D)   To manufacture and deal in mineral and aerated waters, syrups, and other beverages of all descriptions.

(E)   To manufacture and deal in surgical, electrical, photographic, and other scientific apparatus, instruments, and requisites of all descriptions.

(F)   To establish and carry on stores in any place or places, and to buy, sell, manufacture and deal in goods, stores, consumable articles, chattels and effects of all kinds, both wholesale and retail, to transact every kind of agency business, and to carry on the business in all its branches of a store-keeper.

(G)   To carry on any trade, business or mercantile operation which in the opinion of the Directors of the Company may be incident, auxiliary or conducive to the objects aforesaid, or any of them, and whether on account of the Company alone, or with or for any other company or person.

(H)   To acquire by purchase or grant, or otherwise, or take out and to work and sell any inventions, patent rights or privileges in connection with the said business, or any other business for the time being carried on by the Company, and to procure foreign patents in respect of any such inventions, and to grant or sell all or any estate or interest of and in the inventions, patent rights, or privileges of or to which the Company may from time to time be possessed or entitled, and to grant licences to use, work, or vend the same.

(I)   To purchase or rent, or otherwise acquire and hold any freehold, copyhold or leasehold land, houses, factories, wharves, buildings, and hereditaments in the United Kingdom or elsewhere, and to sell, lease, let and dispose of the same, and to make, construct, and build any buildings or works for the purposes of the Company.

(J)   To sell the undertaking, assets, and property of the Company, or any rights or interests therein, or any portion of the same, to any other company, association, or person, for such price in money or shares, and on such terms, as the Company shall sanction, and to take over and acquire by purchase or otherwise the whole or any part of the undertaking, assets, and property of any other company or person, or to amalgamate with any other company established for objects similar in general character to the objects of this Company, and to take and hold any shares, stock, or debentures respectively in any company whatsoever in which the liability of the Members shall be limited to the amount of their shares or stock, and whether such company shall be established in the United Kingdom or elsewhere.

(K)   To establish agencies in connection with the business for the time being of the said Company in this country, or in such foreign places as the Directors of the Company may from time to time determine.

(L)   To draw, accept, endorse, and make bills of exchange, promissory notes, and other negotiable instruments.

(M)   .To borrow or receive deposits or loans of money at interest or otherwise, and to make and issue as security for the same, or for any moneys owing by the Company, debenture bonds or stock, or mortgage debentures, or mortgages, or charges, with or without powers of sale, of the whole or any part or parts of the undertaking and property of the Company (including its unpaid Capital, whether called or not), and to lend money upon such security as shall be thought fit, or without security, and to guarantee the payment of any money or the performance of any contract or work by any other company or person.

(N)   To maintain, establish, and aid institutions for the benefit of persons whether employed by or having dealings with the Company or not, including schools, libraries, dispensaries, infirmaries, provident societies, clubs, mechanics' and other institutions, and friendly societies.

(O)   To pay all or any servants and workmen employed by the Company such bonus, percentage, or share of the profits of the Company as the Directors of the Company may from time to time think desirable.

(P) to do all such things as are incidental or conducive to the attainment of the above objects.

5th. The liability of the Members is Limited.

See Notes below.

6th. The Capital of the Company is £80,000 divided into 800 shares of £100 each; which shares, and all other shares of which the present or any future Capital shall consist may be issued at a premium, and may be divided into different classes, and may have such preference, guarantee, or privilege, as between themselves, as shall be in conformity with the regulations of the Company from time to time, and may, when fully paid up, be converted into Stock.

NOTES:—

The Capital of the Company at 25th February, 1982 is £100,000,000 divided into 400,000,000 Ordinary Shares of 25p each, the original Capital having been increased from time to time and reduced, as follows:—

1. (A) On 21st December, 1900, increased to £180,000 by the creation of 100,000 new shares of £1 each.

(B) On 6th June, 1902, increased to £355,000 by the creation of 120,000 new shares of £1 each and 550 new shares of £100 each.

(C) On 11th September, 1905, increased to £600,000 by the creation of 245,000 new shares of £1 each.

(D) On 6th February, 1911, increased to £1,000,000 by the creation of 400,000 new shares of £1 each.

(E) On 23rd July, 1914, increased to £1,250,000 by the creation of 250,000 new shares of £1 each.

(F) On 3rd December, 1917, increased to £1,500,000 by the creation of 250,000 new shares of £1 each.

(G) On 5th January, 1920, increased to £1,750,000 by the creation of 2,500 new shares of £100 each.

(H) On 28th March, 1923, increased to £2,400,000 by the creation of 650,000 new shares of £1 each (on this date each of 3,600 shares of £100 each were divided into 100 shares of £1 each).

(I) On 12th January, 1926, increased to £2,900,000 by the creation of 500,000 new shares of £1 each.

(J) On 10th October, 1933, each of the 1,500,000 issued and fully paid Ordinary Shares of £1 each was divided into 4 Ordinary Shares of 5s. each.

(K) On 7th June, 1934, increased to £3,000,000 by the creation of 400,000 new Ordinary Shares of 5s. each.

(L) On 10th July, 1947, increased to £4,000,000 by the creation of 4,000,000 new Ordinary Shares of 5s. each.

(M) On 12th July, 1951, increased to £8,000,000 by the creation of 16,000,000 new Ordinary Shares of 5s. each.

(N) On 14th July, 1955, increased to £15,000,000 by the creation of 28,000,000 new Ordinary Shares of 5s. each.

(O) On 22nd November, 1960, increased to £40,000,000 by the creation of 100,000,000 new Ordinary Shares of 5s each.

(P) On 16th July, 1964, increased to £50,000,000 by the creation of 40,000,000 new Ordinary Shares of 5s. each.

(Q) On 31st March, 1965, reduced to £48,600,000 and immediately increased to £50,000,000 by the creation of £5,600,000 new Ordinary Shares of 5s. each (see Note 2 below).

2. On 31st March, 1965, pursuant to an Order of the High Court of Justice dated 22nd March, 1965, the Capital of the Company was reduced and subsequently increased. A copy of the Minute approved by the Court and set out in the Schedule to such Order and which, by virtue of Section 69 of the Companies Act 1948, is deemed to be substituted for the corresponding part of the Company's Memorandum of Association, is annexed.

3. Authorised Share Capital increased from £50,000,000 to £100,000,000 by Ordinary Resolution dated 17th July, 1975.

WE, the several persons whose names, addresses and descriptions, are subscribed, are desirous of being formed into a Company in pursuance of this Memorandum of Association, and we respectively agree to take the number of shares in the capital of the Company set opposite our respective names.

NAMES, ADDRESSES AND DESCRIPTIONS OF SUBSCRIBERS	Number of Shares taken by each Subscriber
JESSE BOOT, Mapperley, Nottingham, Drug Merchant ..	One
THOMAS CUTLER, 15 College Street, Nottingham, Drug Merchant	One
HY. G. JALLAND, Heathcote Buildings, Nottingham, Wine Merchant	One
WILLIAM NEVILLE, SENIOR, Sherwood Rise, Lace Agent, Nottingham	One
WILLIAM NEVILLE, JUNIOR, Chilwell, Notts., Lace Manufacturer	One
FRANCIS WILLIAM VICTOR MITCHELL, 204 Hagley Road, Edgbaston, Penmaker	One
GEORGE COLLISON TUTING PARSONS, 120 Colmore Row, Birmingham, Chartered Accountant	One

DATED the 5th day of November, 1888.

WITNESS to the signatures of JESSE BOOT, THOMAS CUTLER, HENRY GIBSON JALLAND, WILLIAM NEVILLE, Senior, and WILLIAM NEVILLE, Junior—

ALFRED ROBINSON, Solicitor,
Clerk to Messrs. WELLS & HIND, Solicitors,
Nottingham.

WITNESS to the signatures of FRANCIS WILLIAM VICTOR MITCHELL and GEORGE COLLISON TUTING PARSONS—

JOSEPH NICHOLLS,
54 St. Mary Street, Birmingham,
Clerk.

The objectives of companies

It has already been noted that business enterprise will have a wide diversity of organisational objectives because of the varying nature of their activity and size. However it should be understood that the objectives themselves will often determine the form of the enterprise and the nature of its behaviour.

The Companies Acts state that the objectives of the enterprise must be set down in the Memorandum and this would seem to indicate that all companies have clearly defined and stated objectives. In fact this is far from the truth. Most companies' Memoranda can be regarded more in a restrictive manner than as an indication of their likely actions. Unless the company exceeds its powers and performs an ultra vires act, it is relatively free to follow any objective and in whatever manner it sees fit.

Profit maximisation is not, as has already been mentioned, the sole objective of every company. In fact it may be that it is not a stated objective at all. The stated corporate objectives would outline the likely behaviour of the company if it were run and managed by individuals acting completely in the interests of the owners of the business. However as enterprises develop, and the ownership becomes divorced from the actual control and management (for instance where the founders of a company retain ownership through their shareholding and appoint executives to manage the business) it is possible that other 'corporate' objectives may either come to be explicitly part of company policy or implicitly demonstrated by the actions of the organisation.

One school of managerial thought suggests that executives tend to evolve organisational goals which serve their own best interests rather than simply seeking to profit maximise.

Alternative organisational objectives

Executives may often seek to promote those aspects of the organisation which give them the greatest personal rewards. For example, a sales manager, whose salary may be related to the organisation's sales revenue, may be more concerned with maximising sales than with considerations such as whether or not the company is producing at its optimum efficient size. Such a manager's salary may be determined either by the quantity he or she sells or by the revenue that those sales create. The problems that a policy such as this can cause may endanger the profitability of the organisation. An excess of sales may be as prejudicial as a lack of them.

Another possible objective of an organisation may be the achievement of *maximum rather than optimum growth*. This could mean not only overstretching the resources of the business but also may mean that the organisation expands into areas which are not the most profitable. Executives may choose to extend their own power and control, rather than seeking to achieve the maximum profit level for their organisation. A combination of these two managerial models has been suggested in which a number of variables are combined to give the executive the greatest *managerial utility*. This may involve an increase of the manager's power, the number of people under his or her direction and the size of his or her remuneration. Of course the management of the company is restricted to some extent by the requirement of the shareholders to make satisfactory profits, ie a sufficient return on capital, at least greater than that which they could receive by investing their money in some alternative form of capital.

Each of these managerial models tends to imply that organisational goals are clearly defined and delineated. In reality most business organisations tend to work to a set of ill-defined objectives which vary according to the development of the company, the executives who are in control and the state of the business environment in which the organisation is situated. Much of the behaviour of many organisations is not internally planned and co-ordinated but is the result of a series of both internal and external pressures. It may be based on expediency or in some cases can be the result of crisis management. If a company finds that it is reaching a situation in which the dissatisfaction of the workforce is so great that it cannot continue to function efficiently, then it may be forced into accepting managerial decisions which are basically contradictory to its organisational objectives. Also in a period of recession, an organisation may be forced to accept changes in its goals in an effort to remain in business. This leads us to, perhaps, the fundamental aim of any organisation, of whatever size or form – *survival*. Each enterprise realises that it must survive in order to achieve any of its objectives. In order to survive it must be financially viable. No organisation in the private sector can expect shareholders or other providers of capital to continue to finance a loss-making operation for a considerable period of time. Many enterprises manage to continue through a slump, which is either national or within its own industry, but usually only on the presumption that future profits will be forthcoming. Short-run losses must in the long run be compensated by an overall profit.

As stressed earlier the essential goal of any organisation is to survive. In order to do this it must be capable of making a profit, taking the long run with the short, and so profit, must be an essential pre-requisite. However there are many varying objectives which can be classified as secondary which contribute to the profit-making objective.

Secondary objectives

Economic
Each individual enterprise may be able to set a variety of individual internal objectives which will affect the whole organisation or merely one section or department. For instance, *efficiency or cost effectiveness* may be seen as a goal which will result in the lowering of cost and so will

provide a greater profit margin. This could occur in any or all of the organisation's departments. Other economic objectives such as *revenue maximisation* or *corporate growth* may also be sought in an effort to increase the profitability of the organisation.

Social objectives

The actions of a company may appear altruistic in that it aims to raise the satisfaction and welfare of its consumers or its employees. Companies having express or implied power, may sponsor activities seemingly unrelated to their business, such as sports or cultural events, and these acts may be regarded favourably by the general public. However, in doing so, most organisations are in reality simply attempting to contribute to their overall objective of financial gain. An improvement in a company's public image may serve to increase sales or bring the company's name to the public's attention. A paternalistic stance towards their employees' welfare may simply be an insurance policy against industrial unrest or an encouragement to retain staff and increase production. Few companies are charitable out of the goodness of their hearts.

Clearly stated objectives

There are substantial advantages to any organisation to be gained from having formally stated objectives. If there are no specific objectives outlined then it is possible that the organisation, or the decision makers within it, may pursue policies which conflict with the overall aims of the enterprise or which contribute to objectives which have been disregarded or modified. Thus, formally stated objectives allow a clear understanding within the organisation of its basic aims and facilitate the communication of these objectives to all levels of staff. If objectives are explicitly stated then it will become more obvious if some of these are contradictory and so will allow them to be more easily reconciled.

One of the most important reasons for having any objective is that it is then possible to measure the performance of the organisation against it. If, for instance, a clear objective of the business is to diversify into alternative markets, then a periodic examination of the extent of this aspect of the organisation's progress towards this goal is possible; a bench mark against which success or failure can be assessed is established. If objectives are realistically based on potential then it is feasible to consider the setbacks which may befall any organisation or to anticipate opportunities which may occur.

Objectives – their anticipated lifespan

An organisation should be able to classify its objectives into different time periods. These may be

a) immediate,
b) short term,
c) medium term,
d) long term.

It would be wrong to try and rigidly specify an actual period of time that each of these should cover. This would obviously vary according to the type of organisation in question and the industry in which it was situated. However as a rough guideline, immediate objectives could be those to be met in the coming six months, short term in the following two years, medium term in five years and long term within twenty years. Few organisations would seek to specify objectives which would extend beyond twenty years. It is essential that there is a strict coherence between objectives. It would be inadvisable for an organisation to set objectives which are expedient in the short term but which are in conflict with those outlined for the longer period. For instance the need to increase profitability in the immediate future could be achieved by a severe reduction in product quality. This could have adverse effects on long term sales if a clear aim is to extend output and sales in two or three years.

One consideration must always be borne in mind – realistic objectives are based on anticipation of future events. If such predictions are to be proved correct, then the information on which the forecasts are made must be as accurate as possible. If future sales figures are determined using unreliable data then the validity of objectives will clearly be questionable. The longer the time span is for objectives, then the less certain they will become. A prediction of consumer expenditure or inflation rates in ten years time must rely more on instinct and assumption than on hard facts.

4 The behaviour of organisations

'When producers want to know what the public wants, they graph it in curves. When they want to tell the public what to get they say it in curves.'

Marshall MacLuhan
'Eye Appeal', *The Mechanical Bridge*, 1951

Introduction

In the previous chapter the various objectives of the organisation were discussed and the primary objective in the private sector explained in terms of a satisfactory level of profit. Profit is the difference between the organisation's *Total Revenue* and *Total Costs* which results from its activities. In the next sections it is assumed that the organisation's primary objective will be to maximise its profit, ie operate at the point where the difference between total revenue and total costs is greatest. To determine when maximum profit occurs (or the organisation is in equilibrium) two sets of data are required. First, how *Total* or *Sales Revenue* varies at different levels of output or sales. (NB It is assumed that output or production is the same as sales with no stockpiling of unsold production.) Secondly, what total costs are incurred in order to produce the different levels of outputs. Only when the total costs and revenue at different levels of production are known is it possible to determine when maximum profit will be achieved. This means that the analysis must explain these two relationships before any answer can be given to the question: *what level of output will maximise the organisation's profit*? Since production must occur before sales are achieved it is with the cost and output relationship that the analysis begins.

Cost output relationship in the short run

Input-output relationship − the production function

Production of any goods or service requires combining the factors of production, land, labour and capital in varying proportions in the organisation. The proportions of each factor used depend upon the activity of the organisation and the methods of production currently used. For example, an oil refinery or chemical plant will be more capital intensive than a retail travel agency or a hairdresser. But even producing the same product such as wheat can be achieved by either *capital-intensive* methods (a high proportion of capital in relation to the two other factors) or *labour-intensive* methods (a high proportion of labour relative to land and capital). Which method is selected depends largely on the relative costs of the factors involved, eg if labour is plentiful and cheap then labour-intensive methods will prevail and vice-versa. Whatever proportions are selected, the organisation will combine those factors which it requires for its production.

In any productive activity at any one time there are some factors which cannot be increased and as such are classified as *Fixed Factors*. Fixed factors cannot be increased in the short run time period. No precise time period can be specified as the 'short run' since it depends to a large extent upon technical as well as economic factors. For example, most organisations, in the 'very short run', say one week, may be unable to change the quantity of any factors utilised. However in the short run, which may be months, a year or even more, only one of its factors may be fixed. Usually it is either land or capital which is fixed in the short run. A chemical plant may have a short run of several years before it can increase or renew complex plant whereas a light engineering company may be able to renew its capital machinery in a matter of weeks or months at most. But the organisation can perhaps alter its short run time span if it is prepared to incur higher costs. For example, by leasing factory space or machines at an excessive cost, it could reduce the time period considerably.

The factors whose quantity can be varied in this short run period are classified as *Variable* and usually could include labour and raw materials. The 'long run' period is when all factors can be varied by the organisation and so it is possible to reorganise its entire production process if necessary. This has significant results on costs which are dealt with later in the chapter. This division of factors is of course highly simplified, since in practice it is a good deal more complex. Each input used by the organisation will have its own time scale. For example, different types of labour such as production workers or senior management are variable over different time periods. Certain capital machinery such as a computer may be changed relatively quickly, whereas the plant in which it operates may take months or even longer to renew. To develop a *Cost-Output Theory* requires some simplification and it is assumed that the imaginery organisation uses only two factors of production, capital and labour. The time period involved is the short run when capital is the fixed factor and labour the variable factor. It is also assumed that all units of labour are equally efficient and can be combined with capital in any proportion. There are no changes in production technology which vary the production process. This relationship between the factors or inputs and the resulting output is called a *production function* and expresses a technical, not an economic relationship. The law or hypothesis explaining this relationship is called *Diminishing Returns*, *Diminishing Marginal Productivity*, or *Variable Proportions*.

Table 4.1 illustrates an imaginery relationship using capital as the fixed factor and labour the variable factor. The example could be a factory with a fixed quantity of capital, 100 units − (column 1). These 100 units could represent 100 machines which have been installed or simply the total amount of fixed capital used by the plant in the production process. It is possible to combine various quantities of labour with this capital − (column 2). The results in terms of output of finished products are shown in Columns 3, 4 and 5. Table 4.1 expresses a production function or input-output relationship.

1 Quantity of fixed factor capital	2 Quantity of variable factor labour	3 Total output or product in units	4 Average total output or product	5 Marginal output or product
100	0	0	0	0
100	1	20	20	20
100	2	50	25	30
100	3	90	30	40
100	4	120	30	30
100	5	140	28	20
100	6	150	25	10
100	7	150	21	0
100	8	140	17	− 10
100	9	120	13	− 20
			3 divided by 2	

Table 4.1   Input-output relationship

Total product is simply the total production figures achieved as different quantities of labour are used. *Average Total Product* is production per unit of labour, ie total product divided by the units of labour. It represents average productivity of labour. *Marginal product* is the extra production which results from employing one more (or less) unit of labour. It is that extra person's contribution to total production. It is now possible to see how production varies as the quantities of the variable factor, labour, are added to the fixed factor, capital. It will be noticed that as the two factors are combined total product increases to a maximum of 150 units when six units of labour are employed. But the rate of increase is not constant. At first, until the third unit of labour is employed, total product is rising at an increasing rate. Thereafter the rate of increase diminishes until maximum production is attained at 150 units. If further labour is added the effect is to cause production to decline after employing the seventh person.

The consequence of this behaviour can be clearly seen in average total product, and marginal product. Marginal productivity increases until the fourth person is employed and thereafter diminishing marginal returns occur as marginal product falls. Average productivity reflects this behaviour in a similar way, rising at first and then also diminishing. The law of diminishing returns is usually stated in terms of the behaviour of marginal productivity. If increasing quantities of the variable factor are added to the fixed factor, after a certain point marginal productivity will diminish. Note that the relationship between the average and marginal products is simply an arithmetic one. If the average is rising then the marginal product must be higher than the average whereas if the average falls the marginal product must be less than the average. It follows that in Fig 4.1b the marginal curve crosses the average at the latter's highest point.

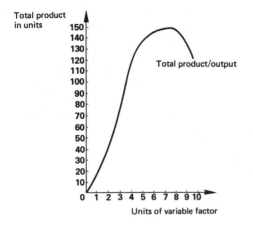

Fig 4.1a   Relationship between total product/output and variable factor

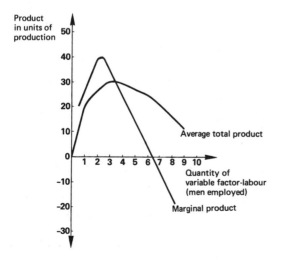

Fig 4.1b   Relationship between average total product and marginal product

The underlying behaviour of marginal product is explained by the varying proportions in which the two factors are mixed. Initially as the first three persons are employed in combination with the fixed capital, the 'factor mix' is increasingly more favourable in production terms. It is when the fourth person and beyond is employed that the capital-labour mix becomes less and less favourable. Clearly in any production situation different mixes of factors will result in less or more efficient combinations with consequent results on the production figures. In practical situations the mixture of capital and labour is certainly not varied over the wide range envisaged by the Tables, but this concept nevertheless remains true. In the example after employing the sixth person, production levels out and then actually declines if further labour is added to the capital, ie marginal productivity eventually becomes negative. This also is a valid assumption since with any production mix there must be some labour staffing which achieves maximum output. Further employees make no extra contribution to output. Beyond this point the over-staffing which will exist could well actually reduce output for several reasons. For example, the 'surplus' labour has to be employed in the production process and might be absorbed by 'job sharing', ie having three persons undertake a task when only two are necessary thus reducing the speed of the production line and reducing output. Alternatively restrictive working practices may be enforced to protect over-staffing levels.

Cost-output relationship – derivation of short-run cost curves

Having examined the input-output relationship it is possible to develop the cost-output links. It is essential for an organisation to know the relationship between its factor inputs and its output. But to determine profits, the management requires to calculate what are the costs of using the inputs to achieve a particular output level. The costs are incurred directly from using the factor inputs as shown in Table 4.1, p. 142.

At this point it is useful to reintroduce the concept of opportunity cost as explained in Chapter 1. To carry out production the organisation is using factor inputs, land, labour and capital. If the organisation uses inputs for one purpose it cannot utilise them for another. The true cost of using factors x and y is what the organisation must give up, ie the opportunity cost of x and y. The organisation places money values on the inputs used which reflect what has been given up in order to use it. In most cases the organisation is purchasing inputs and therefore paying *explicit* costs equal to whatever price it pays for the labour, raw materials, etc.

However, in addition to the obvious explicit costs there may be *implicit* or *imputed* costs to consider which arise from employing inputs owned by the organisation itself. These inputs, such as land owned by the organisation, may have alternative uses in most cases such as the possibility of leasing to another organisation. So although the organisation is paying no explicit rent it should include an imputed rent in its total cost calculations. Similar situations arise if the owner's own capital or management services are provided, ie an imputed interest or salary payment. To the economist (although not the accountant) the true cost of the inputs is their opportunity costs including both explicit and implicit. A further divergence between accounting and economic practice arises with the concept of *normal profit*. Even after adding both explicit and implicit costs, there remains one further economic cost − normal profit. Explicit and implicit costs apply to the factors land, labour and capital, but there is a fourth factor or input required − the services of the entrepreneur. If an entrepreneur combines inputs to carry out production a minimum rate of reward or profit is expected to justify those efforts. The level of this minimum reward will vary with the circumstances and indeed the objectives of the particular organisation, eg a high risk undertaking will require a higher normal profit than a low risk one. If this minimum reward or normal profit is not achieved then the entrepreneur will be better pursuing some alternative activity. Normal profit is defined as the minimum reward required to keep the entrepreneur or organisation in its particular line of business activity. It is the opportunity cost of the factor entrepreneurship or organisation and as such is equally valid as an economic cost. To summarise, the economic costs to the organisation are threefold:

1 Explicit costs ⎱ opportunity costs of the inputs land, labour and
  Implicit costs ⎰ capital
2 Normal profit − opportunity cost of the input from the entrepreneur

3 Total economic costs of all factors/inputs.

It is only when the organisation's sales revenue exceeds these total economic costs that the economist will regard a profit as having been made. This surplus of total revenue over total economic costs is defined as *super-normal profit*. It is these differences in approach which can result in an accountant showing a profit but an economist a loss when revenue just exceeds explicit costs.

For the purpose of this analysis costs are divided into fixed, variable and total costs. *Fixed costs* are those incurred from utilising the fixed factor of production and as such do not change irrespective of the level of production in the short run. These overheads, expenses or indirect costs as they are alternatively called, are usually incurred as a consequence of utilising the factors land or capital in some respect. They might include such accounting costs as rent, rates, insurances, interest charges or any fixed cost incurred in this way. *Variable costs* result from employing the variable factors and hence vary with the level of production. They could include production wages or indeed costs such as materials or power since in the input-output relationship the production mix utilises several factors, not just the two assumed in the example. Variable costs are often referred to as *production* or *direct costs*. In reality the simple division into fixed and variable costs is not precise as the definition depends upon the time period involved. In the very short run, when it is impossible to change any factor of production, all costs will be fixed. The short run implies a period when the variable factor can be altered, therefore some costs will be variable as production alters. In between are likely to be *semi-variable costs* which vary with output but not directly with it. An example might be the costs of administrative employees. Basically it depends upon whether that particular factor is classified as being fixed, variable or semi-variable in the short run period. In the long-run period, all factors are variable and so all costs will also become variable. As all factors are variable in the long run it is possible for the organisation to change its entire scale of production which will enable it to reduce average costs of production by benefiting from economies of scale. Cost behaviour in the long run is discussed later in the chapter.

Having explained how costs are divided it is now possible to derive the short-run cost-output relationship from the input-output figures. It is assumed that the organisation pays a fixed cost of £200 per week for the fixed factor and £100 per week in wages for each unit of the variable factor, labour. In addition, whatever quantity of labour the organisation employs, the cost remains at £100 per person, ie the price of labour is given and the organisation is faced with a perfectly elastic supply curve for labour. The cost-output relationships are given in Table 4.2. The first column is column 3 from Table 4.1 showing output or production figures. Column 6 shows the total fixed costs of £200 resulting from employing the fixed factor, naturally being constant at all levels of output. Column 7 gives the costs of employing the variable factor labour, hence total variable costs. Referring to Table 4.1, it requires one unit of labour (at £100/wk) to produce 20 units, therefore total variable costs are £100. Column 8 adds both total fixed and variable costs to obtain total costs of production. By dividing total fixed costs 6 and total variable costs 7 respectively by Output 3, average fixed costs 9 and average variable costs 10 are obtained. Column 11 average total costs, is obtained either by dividing total costs by output or alternatively by adding average fixed and average variable costs. *Marginal cost* is the cost of producing one extra unit of output. In the example used output increases not by single units but by 20, 30, 40 units, etc. The marginal cost is therefore the increase in total costs, £100, (or total variable costs) divided by the increase in output, eg to increase production from 50 to 90 units requires an extra £100 in variable cost, therefore marginal cost is $\frac{£100}{40}$ = £2.50. Since this marginal cost relates not to one unit but to the extra 40 units, graphically it must be plotted at an output level half way between 50 and 90 units.

3 Total output or product in units	6 Total fixed costs £	7 Total variable costs £	8 Total costs £	9 Average fixed costs £	10 Average variable costs £	11 Average total costs £	12 Marginal cost £
0	200	0	200	–	–	–	
10							5 – 00
20	200	100	300	10 – 00	5 – 00	15 – 00	
35							3 – 33
50	200	200	400	4 – 00	4 – 00	8 – 00	
70							2 – 50
90	200	300	500	2 – 22	3 – 33	5 – 56	
105							3 – 33
120	200	400	600	1 – 67	3 – 33	5 – 00	
130							5 – 00
140	200	500	700	1 – 43	3 – 57	5 – 00	
145							10 – 00
150	200	600	800	1 – 33	4 – 00	5 – 33	
							–
150	200	700	900	1 – 33	4 – 67	6 – 00	
							–
140	200	800	1 000	–	–	–	
							–
120	200	900	1 100	–	–	–	
			6 + 7	6 divided by 3	7 divided by 3	8 divided by 3 or 9 + 10	Increase in 7 or 8 divived by 5

Table 4.2   *Cost-output relationship (one week)*

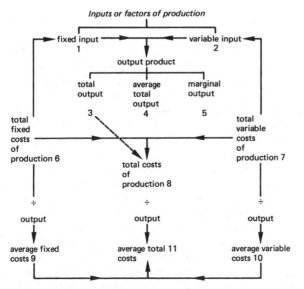

Fig 4.2   Cost-output relationship

Behaviour of short-run costs

Having explained the derivation of short-run costs it is now possible to examine how they behave as output varies. In doing so use is made of graphical analysis to present a clearer explanation. The cost schedules of Table 4.2 are plotted on two graphs, Figs 4.3 and 4.4. Fig 4.3 presents the total cost approach by plotting total fixed costs, total variable costs and total costs.

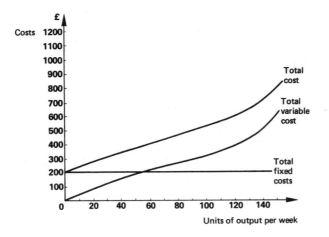

Fig 4.3   Behaviour of total costs in relation to output

The total fixed cost curve is parallel to the output axis at a constant £200 at all levels of production. Total variable costs are zero when output is zero and rise as production increases but not in a simple linear relationship. The shape of the curve reflects the input-output relationship described earlier by the law of diminishing marginal productivity. At first capital and labour are combined in an increasingly efficient mix and output is subject to increasing marginal productivity and hence decreasing marginal costs. Total variable costs are rising at a decreasing rate since each unit of the variable factor is costing the same to employ (£100) but is contributing more to production. When marginal productivity begins to decline and thus marginal costs rise, the total variable cost curve must rise at an increasing rate. The concave-convex shape of the curve is the direct result of the production function described earlier. Total costs are merely the sum of fixed and variable costs so the total cost curve reflects the same shape as variable costs but is merely £200 higher. Though the total cost curves are important, (in the context of break-even analysis especially) per unit cost curves are even more valuable in explaining the profit maximisation behaviour of the organisation in the short run. It is to the average-marginal cost curves that analysis must now be directed.

148

As shown in Fig 4.4 and Table 4.2 the average and marginal cost curves are derived from the behaviour of total costs. Average fixed costs decline as output expands since the fixed costs of £200 are being spread over more production units. The average variable cost curve is U-shaped reaching a minimum between 90 and 120 units of production. This is at precisely the point when average product reaches its maximum. If each unit of labour is paid a fixed £100 then while average productivity is rising, average variable costs must fall and vice-versa. It is because of 'diminishing returns' eventually occurring that average variable costs must rise. Average total costs is the sum of average fixed and variable costs, so it will reflect the U-shape of average variable costs. It will fall more quickly but rise more slowly because of the effect of average fixed costs. Marginal cost behaviour also produces a U-shaped curve since it reflects the marginal productivity of the variable factor, labour. The relationship between average costs and marginal costs is similar to that described earlier regarding marginal and average products. If average cost is falling, marginal cost must be below it since if the cost of a marginal unit lowers average cost, logically it must be less. Similarly when marginal costs are greater than average costs then average costs must rise. For this reason marginal cost must intersect both average cost curves at their lowest points.

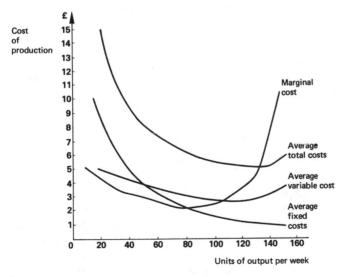

Fig 4.4   Cost-output relationship in the short run

To summarise, cost behaviour in the short run is based upon the law of diminishing marginal productivity which implies that average costs will eventually rise. Before leaving short-run cost behaviour it is important to comment upon the empirical evidence. Various empirical studies suggest that over the 'practical and relevant' ranges of output

149

produced by most plants, the diminishing returns principle does not operate. Marginal productivity is probably constant and therefore producing constant average variable costs equal to marginal costs. Since average fixed costs are falling, average total costs will exhibit a downward trend. This proposition is illustrated in Fig 4.5.

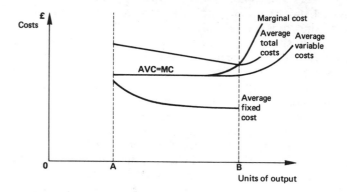

Fig 4.5   Short run cost behaviour as suggested by empirical evidence

Over the output range AB average variable costs are both constant and equal to marginal costs. This relationship also produces linear (straight line) total variable and total cost curves. It is at the extremes of production, beyond the normal output range that the 'diminishing returns' principle will probably operate and so cause both marginal and average cost curves to rise, ie beyond output OB. This basic difference of assumptions about the behaviour of marginal productivity explains the differences observed between the cost-output models of the economist and the accountant.

Cost-output relationship in the long run

As defined earlier, the long run time period is that when the organisation can change both its fixed and variable factors of production, capital and labour, thereby enabling it to change its entire scale of operations. It may decide to operate from a much larger plant or instal modern machines, eg the use of robotic machines in a car production plant. In the short run any increase in production by using more of the variable factor is subject to diminishing marginal productivity after some point, and therefore rising marginal and average costs of production. In the long run the organisation can choose whichever mix of capital and labour it desires, and therefore many different input-output relationships exist rather than just the one illustrated in Fig 4.4. This means that for each individual factor mix the different production function will give a separate cost-output relationship. In other words its average and marginal costs will be different in each situation. As the organisation expands the scale of its operation it is influenced not by the law of diminishing marginal productivity but by the effects of economies of scale.

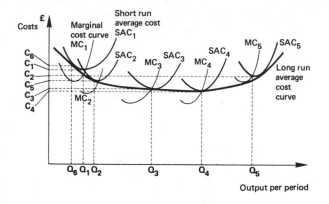

Fig 4.6   Long run cost output relationship

In Fig 4.6 is illustrated a situation where the organisation can produce using five alternative scales of plant. Each different capital-labour mix has its own production function and hence different short run cost curves associated with that particular time period and plant size. These are illustrated by curves SAC_1 to SAC_5. If the organisation builds a first plant of size 1 then with its fixed and variable factors it has costs as illustrated by SAC_1 and MC_1. Its lowest average costs using that plant size are shown by OC_1 producing OQ_1 output. Any increase in production beyond OQ_1 using only its variable factor results in increasing average costs as illustrated by SAC_1. In the long run however it can alter its entire scale of production and build a second plant of size 2 with resulting costs curves of SAC_2 and MC_2. At this larger scale of operations it is likely, as explained shortly, that its capital-labour mix will result in lower average and marginal short run costs associated with that plant size and time period. Output OQ_2 can be produced at a much lower cost of OC_2. An additional plant of size 3 reduces average costs still further and it is only when a fifth plant is operated that average costs of production rise again. In the long run the organisation can choose any scale of operations to suit a particular level of output. Therefore a long run average cost curve can be produced which shows the lowest average costs of production for each level of output. This is illustrated by the curve LRAC. If the organisation expected to produce at an output level of OQ_6 it would build a plant of size 1 and operate at point A where average costs are OC_6. If it wished to produce OQ_1 then it would build a plant of size 2 and operate at point B with average costs of OC_2. (The output OQ_1 can also be produced by plant size 1 but at higher average costs of OC_1) An output of OQ_3 is best produced by plant size 3

151

at point C and so on. The long run average cost curve represents these lowest average costs of producing any output when it is possible to produce that output level with the most appropriate scale of plant. The LRAC curve is the 'envelope' of all the short run curves. The short-run curves are tangential to the long run curve. This long run average cost curve illustrates the influence of the economies of scale in as shown in Fig 4.7.

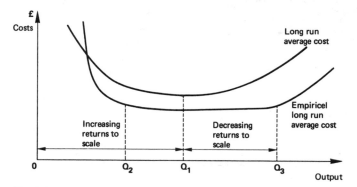

Fig 4.7   Long run average cost curves − theory and practice − illustrating returns to scale

As the scale of output increases, the organisation benefits from the economies of scale, thereby leading to a fall in long run average costs. At some point, OQ_1 in Fig 4.7, long run average costs reach their minimum. Beyond OQ_1 diseconomies of scale begin to operate thereby causing long run average costs to rise.

Empirically, the evidence tends to suggest a U-shaped long run curve, but with a flat bottom over a wide range of output as in Fig 4.7. This implies constant returns to scale over a wide range of output with economies and diseconomies operating only at the extreme ranges of output. Up to output OQ_2 economies of scale operate to produce a lowering of long run average costs. Point OQ_2 represents the 'Minimum Efficient Plant Size' described in Chapter 2, p. 56, and varies greatly between industries. Beyond output OQ_3 diseconomies begin to result in the long run average costs rising. The economies of scale may be classified as described earlier, as Internal and External economies of scale. The Internal economies may themselves be divided into plant level or organisational level economies. These are illustrated in Fig 4.8.

Internal economies of scale

Plant-level economies
Technical economies − if the scale of the organisation's level of production increases it may be possible to make economies as a result of the introduction of mass-production techniques. This could involve the

adoption of increased mechanisation, taking advantage of technological advances. The car industry, traditionally an innovator in the field of mass production, is currently undergoing the process of robotisation. This involves the use of highly-mechanised production lines using the minimum amount of labour. Not only is the use of machines likely to reduce staffing levels and overall cost but it is feasible for workers to become more specialised in their tasks and so becoming more experienced and therefore more productive.

Further economies can be gained in industries which can use process production methods such as the oil industry and chemical industry. In these instances the marginal cost of producing each extra unit can fall dramatically if large, expensive plant is used. It is only profitable if massive quantities are produced and the plant is utilised optimally.

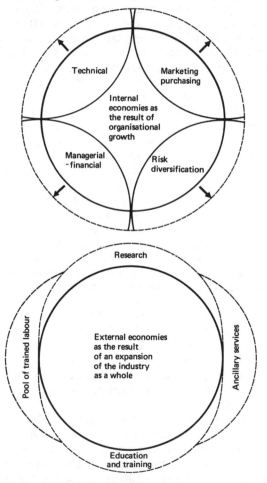

Fig 4.8   Economies of scale

Organisation level economies

(i) *Managerial/financial economies* – very large organisations have the distinct advantage of being able to afford to employ highly specialised managerial staff and apply sophisticated managerial techniques. A multi-national organisation will employ not just one type of accountant but a variety of specialists (eg cost accountants, financial accountants, tax accountants, etc).

The big company can also raise finance much easier. This is because banks and other financial institutions will be more willing to lend to large organisations with considerable assets and will normally offer cheaper 'corporate borrowing rates'. These companies are also usually more attractive to investors who regard them as a safe investment. Share issue becomes easier as speculators may be ready to accept a lower rate of return if their investment is safer. Shares of some very large companies such as BP, Marks and Spencer and Boots are called 'blue chip' shares and are recognised as being a very sound, if not exceptionally profitable, investment. It is also true that it is more economic to issue large numbers of shares at one time. The cost of issuing a relatively small number of shares, eg less than £500 000 worth, may be in excess of 10% of the capital raised. Larger issues, eg £5 m plus, may cost only 3% of return.

(ii) *Marketing/purchasing economies* – these two vital aspects of an organisation's operation may be reduced as a percentage of total cost as the enterprise expands. Advertising costs per unit may fall as more and more is sold during one advertising campaign. If a company can establish itself as a household name its advertising costs may decline substantially, eg Marks and Spencer spend relatively little advertising their St Michael brand. Average distribution costs can also be slimmed if more is sold. Obviously a full lorry delivering to one area is more cost effective than having to distribute small quantities over a number of regions.

Purchasing economies are also possible. The company can employ specialist purchasing staff and may enjoy the benefits of bulk buying and the discounts that can be gained. It is a wise company which realises the savings which can be made in purchasing. A pound saved in purchasing is a pound profit while an extra pound's worth of sales is not. Production and distribution costs must be deducted.

(iii) *Risk diversification* – small enterprises, because of their nature, almost always tend to be restricted to one type of product and to one industry. Large companies have often diversified into many different industries and produce a variety of products. This is in order to spread potential risk. A slump in one product market may be compensated by a boom in another (unless the whole economy is in recession). Losses in one subsidiary can be offset by profits in another.

Research and development projects can of course be initiated by enterprises of all sizes. However studies indicate that the most substantial advances have been the result of large amounts of risk capital invested by the large companies. Even though R & D may only take up a relatively small proportion of their overall budget, this could well be in excess of the amount of capital that smaller organisations could afford to divert to possibly profitless research.

External economies of scale

(i) *Research* – although it is the large organisations which produce the significant breakthroughs there is often a 'spin-off' for all enterprises within the industry and so the greater the size of the industry, the more likely it is that some company will achieve advances beneficial to all.

(ii) *Pool of trained labour* – if a relatively small organisation is producing some sophisticated product and the industry as a whole is undeveloped then there is unlikely to be a pool of trained and skilled labour available. As the industry grows a trained labour force will become available as more and more workers are attracted into the industry. An example of this is the microelectronics industry which has grown dramatically in the 1970s and has tended to concentrate in Southern California. There has now grown up in this area a pool of people able to work in this highly technical industry.

(iii) *Education and training* – as an industry expands its requirement for trained and educated staff will be met by the local and regional educational system. For instance as the offshore oil industry has expanded in the North East of Scotland, Aberdeen University has become a centre for the study of oil technology and the local further education system has geared itself up to providing trained technicians.

Revenue-output relationship

Having studied the relationship between costs and output in some detail, it is now possible to describe the relationship between the organisation's revenue and its output. The revenue of the organisation is simply the price of the product multiplied by its sales or output, ie *Total Revenue = Price × Output*.

Therefore in determining the relationship between output and revenue, it is the price charged for the product which will determine that relationship. The price charged depends upon the type of market structure in which the organisation operates. The result is that unlike the cost-output relationship, this relationship differs with each particular market structure. This relationship will be examined first in conditions of perfect competition and later in respect of specific forms of imperfect competition. When the revenue-output relationship is explained, it will then be possible to achieve the original objective of determining the organisation's equilibrium or profit maximising output.

Perfect competition

The assumptions of a perfectly competitive market were described in Chapter 1 and the results may be summarised as follows. The price which is charged by the organisation for its product is determined by the interaction of demand and supply in the overall market. This equilibrium price, OP, as shown in Fig 4.9 is the price taken by the individual organisation as a *price taker*.

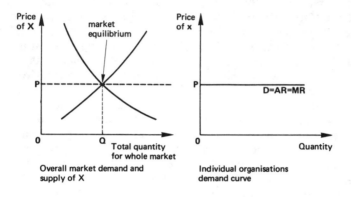

Fig 4.9   The determination of an individual organisation's demand curve in perfect competition

Because the market is composed of many small buyers and sellers, no single buyer or seller acting alone can influence market demand or supply and so influence market price. The individual organisation takes OP as the price to be charged for its product. But because the organisation's production represents such a small proportion of total market supply, it can effectively sell all it produces at this fixed price. The demand curve facing the supplier is perfectly elastic as in Fig 4.9. The organisation will not charge above OP as no consumer will buy at above market price (remember the assumptions of homogenity and perfect knowledge), neither will it sell at below OP, since its objective is to maximise profits. The organisation's demand or price curve is, in fact, its average revenue curve, ie

price × output/sales = Total Revenue
Marginal = price or *Average = Total Revenue ÷ Output*
Revenue   Revenue

156

Since the organisation can produce and sell each unit of output at a con
stant price of OP, its marginal revenue (the addition to total revenue
from selling an extra unit of output) is also OP. For the perfectly competitive organisation, its average and marginal revenue are both
identical.

As with the cost-output relationship, it is also possible to illustrate
the revenue-output relationship in terms of either total revenue or
average/marginal revenue. In Table 4.3 Column 1 shows output from
an imaginery plant with the market price per unit being assumed at £4
per unit shown in Column 2. The total revenue of the plant is shown in
Column 3.

1 Total output per week	2 Price or average/ marginal revenue £	3 Total revenue (price × output) £
0	4	0
1	4	4
2	4	8
3	4	12
4	4	16
5	4	20
6	4	24
7	4	28
$7\frac{1}{2}$		30
8	4	32
9	4	36

Table 4.3 The revenue/output relationship in perfect competition

	1 Total output per week	2 Price or average/ marginal revenue £	3 Total revenue (price × output) £	4 Total costs £	5 Total profits £
	0	4	0	4	-4
	1	4	4	10	-6
	2	4	8	13	-5
	3	4	12	15	-3
	4	4	16	16	0
	5	4	20	17	$+3$
	6	4	24	$18\frac{1}{2}$	$+5\frac{1}{2}$
	7	4	28	21	$+7$
Profit maximisation	$7\frac{1}{2}$	4	30	$22\frac{1}{2}$	$+7\frac{1}{2}$
	8	4	32	25	$+7$
	9	4	36	36	0

Table 4.4 The profit/output relationship in perfect competition

157

The equilibrium of the organisation in the short run

The short-run equilibrium of the organisation, ie the output which maximises its profit, is illustrated first in terms of total revenue and total costs. Table 4.4 shows Table 4.3 to which is added Column 4 showing the total costs of producing the various outputs of Column 1. Column 5 shows the total profit, ie total revenue − total costs. As can be seen, profit is maximised when output is at $7\frac{1}{2}$ units.

Equilibrium − marginal approach

Alternatively the equilibrium of the organisation can be illustrated by reference to the marginal cost and marginal revenue curves. The profit maximising output will be at that level of output where marginal revenue equals marginal cost. If the marginal revenue from a particular unit of output exceeds the marginal cost of production, then the organisation will earn a profit and so produce that unit. Clearly, if marginal cost exceeds marginal revenue, a loss is incurred and that unit will not be produced. However, *why will the organisation produce that unit of output where marginal cost equals marginal revenue*? The answer is that, as explained earlier, the costs of the organisation include an element of normal profit, therefore *at the point where MR = MC, normal profit is still earned on that single unit*. Consequently, whenever MR exceeds MC the organisation is earning super or abnormal profit on that unit of production. This equilibrium can be shown by reference to Table 4.5 and Fig 4.10.

Therefore to summarise, at the level of output where:

1 MR > MC super-normal profit is earned,
2 MR = MC normal profit is earned,
3 MR < MC a loss is incurred.

Column 1 shows output and Column 2 price or average/marginal revenue as in the previous table. In this case, the decision on output is made with reference to the average and marginal costs. These can be calculated as described in the earlier section on costs. Column 3 shows average fixed costs (total fixed costs divided by output) while Column 4 shows average variable costs (total variable costs divided by output). Average total costs as shown in Column 5 is obtained either by summing AFC and AVC or alternatively by dividing total costs by output. Finally as explained previously, marginal costs are calculated in Column 6 being plotted half way between the units of output. Equilibrium or maximum profit output will occur at 7.5 units when marginal cost equals marginal revenue. This situation is illustrated in Fig 4.10.

1 Output	2 Price/average/ marginal revenue	3 Average fixed costs	4 Average variable costs	5 Average total costs	6 Marginal cost
0	£4	–	–	–	
					£6 – 00
1	£4	£4	£6 – 00	£10 – 00	
					£3 – 00
2	£4	£2	£4 – 50	£6 – 50	
					£2 – 00
3	£4	£1 – 33	£3 – 67	£5 – 00	
					£1 – 00
4	£4	£1 – 00	£3 – 00	£4 – 00	
					£1 – 00
5	£4	£0 – 80	£2 – 60	£3 – 40	
					£1 – 50
6	£4	£0 – 66	£2 – 42	£3 – 08	
					£2 – 50
7	£4	£0 – 57	£2 – 43	£3 – 00	
					£4 – 00
8	£4	£0 – 50	£2 – 63	£3 – 13	
					£11 – 00
9	£4	£0 – 44 (TFC/ Output)	£3 – 56 (TVC/ Output)	£4 – 00 (AFC + AVC)	

Table 4.5 Producer equilibrium using marginal approach

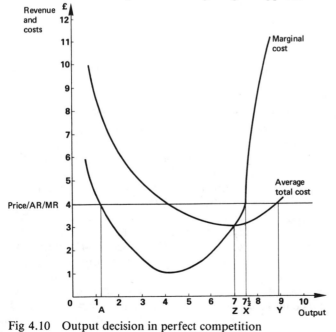

Fig 4.10 Output decision in perfect competition

In Fig 4.10 we have plotted the three relevant curves from Table 4.5. The maximum profit is earned when $MC = MR$, ie where the rising MC curve intersects the MR curve at $7\frac{1}{2}$ units. Clearly point OA cannot be equilibrium since although marginal cost and marginal revenue are equal, marginal costs are falling and so greater profits can be earned by expanding output. As long as marginal revenue is above marginal cost the organisation will continue to produce, until it reaches point OX ($7\frac{1}{2}$ units in our example) where profits are maximised. The organisation will not produce beyond OX since as the marginal cost exceeds the marginal revenue on every extra unit, the effect is simply to incur losses on these units and reduce overall profit. Total profits will still be earned however up to a production level represented by OY when average total costs equal average revenue. Neither will it produce at its optimum level of output where average costs are lowest (OZ) since this does not maximise its profits.

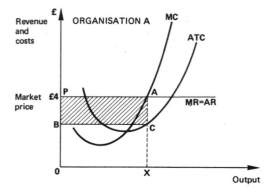

Fig 4.11   Efficient organisation in perfect competition earning supernormal profit

Consider three different organisations in a perfectly competitive market each with different levels of efficiency and so varying levels of costs. Each organisation will produce at the point where marginal cost equals marginal revenue but consider the differences in the profits which each will earn. Organisation A is the most efficient in that its costs are lowest. Its equilibrium output is at OX. At this level of output, total revenue is represented by the area OPAX (ie price or average revenue OP × output OX). Total costs are shown by the area OBCX (ie average cost CX × output OX). The remainder of total revenue BPAC, must be total profit to this organisation. More precisely it is abnormal or supernormal profit since normal profit is included within total costs. Organisation B is faced with the same average revenue/marginal revenue situation as Organisation A, but has higher costs since it is less efficient. Again its equilibrium output is OX where MR = MC. Total revenue and total costs are equal and represented by the area OPAX.

The organisation earns no supernormal profit but only normal profit. Since normal profit is the minimum required to persuade the organisation to remain in this industry, then this decision will depend upon its alternative profit levels in other industries.

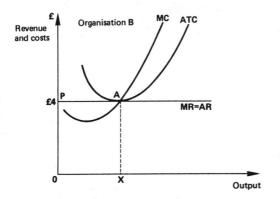

Fig 4.12   Marginal organisation in perfect competition earning normal profit

Organisation C is the least efficient of the three since its costs are higher than both A and B. As with both A and B, its equilibrium output is at OX where MR = MC but its total revenue equals area OPAX while total costs area is OBCX. The organisation incurs a loss equal to PBCA. Clearly in this situation the organisation must decide its future strategy. It cannot continue to incur such losses indefinitely so will be forced to close down or transfer production into some more profitable alternative product.

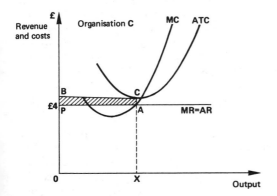

Fig 4.13   Inefficient organisation in perfect competition incurring losses

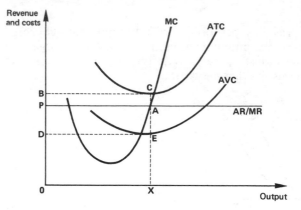

Fig 4.14 Inefficient organisation incurring losses but earning sufficient revenue to cover variable costs

However a situation can be illustrated in which the organisation may decide to continue to bear such losses for a limited period. Fig 4.14 shows Organisation C as before, but this time includes both the average variable costs and average total costs curves. As before the organisation is making losses as total costs exceed total revenue. Total costs are OBCX which include total variable costs of ODEX (AVC × output) and total fixed costs of DBCE. Since the organisation is earning total revenue of OPAX then the revenue is more than sufficient to pay for the cost of the variable costs of production and make a significant contribution, DPAE, towards covering the fixed costs of production.

The organisation may decide to continue for a limited period in this situation because it is the least disadvantageous option. If it ceases production, the variable costs would be eliminated as would any revenue. But assuming that the organisation is not totally wound up, then it still has its fixed costs or overheads to support. Providing total revenue covers the variable costs and makes some contribution to paying fixed costs then this is helping to reduce overall losses. This decision will be influenced by many external and internal factors. For example, the losses may be the result of a temporarily depressed market with its uneconomic price of OP. The management expects an upturn in the market in the near future and so decides to bear what they regard as short term losses. Moreover if they shut down production to eliminate variable costs there may be problems when the upturn comes. For example, valuable markets could be lost to competitors during the interim or there may be technical problems in restarting production, etc. Of course, if total revenue does not even cover variable costs then such a situation would not arise. In the commercial world however this scenario often arises when short term losses are temporarily incurred in the belief that times will improve or costs will be reduced by restructuring or rationalisation within the organisation. If there is an increase in market demand then this will result in raising market price and consequently the average revenue and total revenue of the organisation. To summarise the previous discussion, the determinants of the organisation's equilibrium − its level of output and its profits − are:

a) *The organisation's efficiency − its level of marginal costs, which are determined by the factor mix and resulting costs incurred.*
b) *The overall market demand and supply which determines the price at which the organisation sells its product and its marginal revenue.*

The organisation will produce that output where its marginal costs equal its marginal revenue and in so doing maximise its profits.

Equilibrium in the long run
In the previous analysis the organisation's equilibrium in the short-time period has been examined. Before leaving the perfectly competitive market it is necessary to consider the position in the long run. In the short run period it is possible for each organisation to be earning different profits or losses as with organisations A, B and C. Each equates marginal cost with marginal revenue but output is not necessarily at the point of lowest average costs. (A and B for example.) In the long run time period if some organisations are earning super-normal profits (as with A) then this will attract new entrants into the industry. The effect is to increase market supply, ie the supply curve shifts to the right, leading to a fall in market price.

Fig 4.15 shows the original situation with Organisation A earning its super-normal profits. The supply curve shifts to S_2 to produce a lower market price OP_2. The result on the Organisation is to reduce its price or marginal revenue as shown by AR/MR. As long as any organisation is earning abnormal profits new entrants will enter the industry and this process will continue until every organisation is only earning normal profits. All organisations will face the same cost situation as Organisation B in Fig 4.12. The organisation is in equilibrium with marginal cost equalling marginal revenue and average total cost. Free competition in the long run results in some organisations going out of business as with Organisation C, while all others earn normal profit with production or output always at the point of lowest average costs.

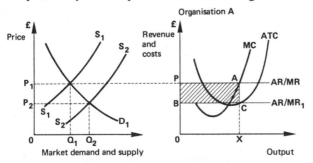

Fig 4.15   The effect of a shift in the market supply caused by new entrants on the profit level of an efficient organisation

In addition, as explained earlier, in the long run when all factors are variable it is possible for every organisation to operate at its most suitable scale of operations, ie where its costs are lowest.

It is this last point which underlies the attraction of the perfectly competitive model. Perfect competition represents the ideal market form in that it ensures that only the efficient producers can survive in the long run, and then only earning normal profits. No organisation can exploit the consumer by raising prices above the market level since to do so would eliminate sales entirely. It is a market form which is attractive perhaps not only in economic theory but to some extent to a government bent on moving industries towards a competitive stance. Of course no such market exists in reality but it is a yardstick by which the more real world markets of imperfect competition may be judged. These other market forms will now be considered.

Monopoly

Monopoly represents the opposite extreme of the competitive spectrum to the perfect market in that it comprises a single seller controlling the market in which there are no substitutes. The consumer is forced to purchase from this supplier or not at all. Strictly this situation is one of pure monopoly which is unlikely to exist in practice as all products will have some form of substitute. Given this assumption it follows that the market demand for the product is also the demand facing the single monopoly organisation, ie the market demand curve and the organisation's average revenue curve are identical. Unlike perfect competition therefore, the demand/price/average revenue curve of the monopolist is not perfectly elastic but downward sloping as illustrated in Fig 4.16. Furthermore, unlike perfect competition, the marginal revenue of the monopolist is always less than his average revenue.

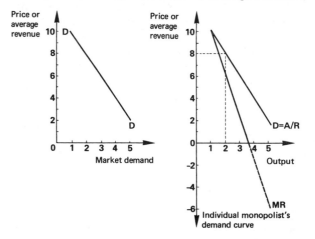

Fig 4.16 Derivation of the monopolist's revenue curves from market demand

This can be illustrated by using the numerical example below:

Market price/ average revenue £	Output	Total revenue £	Marginal revenue £
10	1	10	10
8	2	16	6
6	3	18	2
4	4	16	−2
2	5	10	−6

Table 4.6   Monopoly revenue/output relationship

If the market price is £8 then the monopolist produces and sells two units and average revenue is £8 with total revenue of £16. In order to sell an extra unit the monopolist must reduce the price to £6 thereby gaining an extra £6 by selling a third unit but losing £4 on the previous two units. Total revenue increases by £2, ie marginal revenue is £2 which is less than average revenue. The monopolist's marginal revenue will always be less than average revenue.

Having examined the relationship between revenue and output it is now possible to introduce the cost-output relationship into the analysis. Here the relationships and resulting cost curves are common to both perfect competition and monopoly. Therefore super-imposing the costs curves of the organisation upon the revenue curves as illustrated in Fig 4.16. As with the perfectly competitive situation it is possible to illustrate both revenue-output and cost-output relationships using total revenue and cost curves. In this case only the marginal analysis approach is discussed. The equilibrium of the monopolist is also where marginal revenue equals marginal cost (for the same reasons as before) and this equilibrium is shown in Fig 4.17. Equilibrium output is OX which will be sold on the market at a price of OP. Total costs are shown by area OBCX (average cost x output) and total revenue by area OPAX (average revenue x output). Area BPAC represents super-normal profits being earned by the monopolist. So far monopoly equilibrium has been similar to that of perfect competition. But a vital difference exists when comparing the long-run situation in monopoly with that of perfect competition. The monopolist is earning super-normal profits which in perfect competition would attract competitors into the market. The result in the long run was described earlier, so that only normal profits can be earned in perfect competition. Moreover when this occurs the organisation is producing at its minimum (most efficient) average cost level. The monopolist however can restrict the entry of new producers into the market and so super-normal profits earned in the short run can be earned also in the long run. There is no effective distinction in the behaviour of the monopoly in the short-or long-run periods. This possible existence of monopoly profits provides the main theoretical argument against the existence of monopolies.

This excessive price may be reinforced by selling the product on terms which are unfavourable to the consumer and restricting the consumer's effective choice.

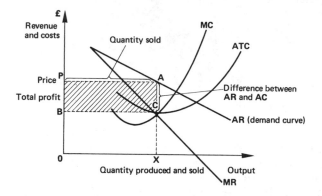

Fig 4.17   Monopolists pricing and output decision

For these reasons the state has pursued legislative policies which seek to regulate the behaviour of monopolies where the interests of the consumer are presumed to be at risk. Such legislation was examined in Chapter 2 p. 75. Of course the foregoing analysis assumes that the monopolist seeks to maximise profits and in practice this may be far from the truth. The monopolist may forego some profit by selling at a lower price than that which would maximise profit. Adverse publicity may moderate monopoly behaviour as might the threat of state action against the organisation. Nevertheless the danger of excessive profits still remains and can be accentuated by the practise of price discrimination between customers. Major conditions which facilitate price discrimination are that markets can be separated geographically (eg home and export markets), by differences in consumer demand or knowledge, by irrationality on the part of consumers or by restrictive resale agreements imposed by the supplier. In these cases the monopoly producer may well discriminate between its customers.

In fact, in the UK most of the monopolies are public corporations such as British Telecom, NCB, etc. In some cases large profits are earned but their objectives are not as straightforward as simple profit maximisation. A state monopoly could simply break even by operating at the point where average revenue equals average costs as shown in Fig 4.18 so that total revenue equals total cost (OPAX). Some output is produced at a profit (where MR > MC) while some is produced at a loss (where MC > MR). Examples of this are found in the loss-making operations of public corporations such as post being delivered to remote areas at the normal rate. In reality the public corporations charge a price which is somewhere between the point where MR = MC and AR = AC. The profits which result are used for reinvestment in the

166

industry to provide an improved service to the consumer. Despite this, however, many criticisms are levelled against state monopolies in terms of their overall behaviour being detrimental to the average consumer vis à vis price, conditions of sale, service, etc.

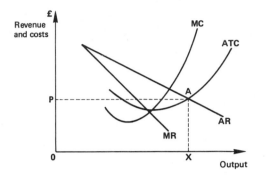

Fig 4.18   Average revenue pricing of a public corporation

Monopolistic competition

A second form of imperfect competition is that referred to as *monopolistic competition*. In some ways this is a hybrid mixture of perfect competition and monopoly. The market consists of many supplier organisations and buyers (similar to perfect competition) but each organisation produces a slightly differentiated product. This difference is created more by the organisation in the mind of the consumer than in the reality of physical differences. These differences may be the result of persuasive advertising linked to brand name policies or the consequence of differences in terms of sale such as servicing, etc. The organisation is therefore creating a mini-monopoly for its product in what is in fact a highly competitive market. The extent to which it succeeds depends upon how far consumers believe that competing brands are adequate substitutes.

The organisation is therefore faced with the downward sloping demand (average revenue) curve of the monopolist instead of the perfectly elastic curve of perfect competition. If the organisation raises its price it will certainly lose some customers to rival brands; but it will retain its loyal clients who have been convinced that there are no adequate substitutes. Similarly a price reduction cannot be expected to attract all customers from rival products.

The short run equilibrium is illustrated in Fig 4.19 where the organisation again equates marginal revenue with marginal cost. The organisation is like a monopoly in that it earns super-normal profits, BPAC, in the short run period, by producing an output of OX at a price of OP. But unlike monopoly, in the long run the existence of these super-normal profits attracts new organisations into the market with

167

slightly differentiated products (similar to perfect competition). The organisation will lose sales to these newcomers and this results in its demand (average revenue) curve shifting to the left. This process will continue as long as such profits exist until the position in Fig 4.20 is reached.

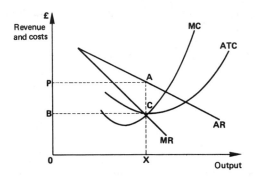

Fig 4.19   Price/output decision in the short run monopolistic competition

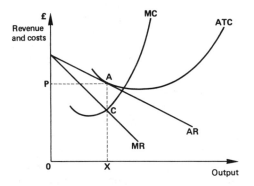

Fig 4.20   Price/output decision in the long run in monopolistic competition

Here the organisation is only earning normal profits since total revenue and total costs are equal (OPAC). It is also apparent however that in the long run the organisation is not producing at its most efficient level where average costs are at their lowest. They have excess capacity in the sense that any increase in production would lower unit costs. It can be argued that it is in this capacity that monopolistic competition with differentiated products is inefficient and wasteful.

Monopolistic competition is an attempt to move more towards the market reality than that expressed by the previous models of both perfect competition and monopoly. However its assumptions of many producers with complete freedom of entry into the market are not entirely consistent with the real world. As was examined in Chapter 2,

p. 58, the reality of the market place is more likely to be oligopolistic and so this must now be considered.

Oligopoly

The market forms so far discussed have been useful in explaining the behaviour of profit maximising organisations. But as shown in Chapter 2 the dominant market form in the UK economy is that of *oligopoly*. The typical oligopolistic market is one which is dominated by a few producers, selling either identical products (*perfect oligopoly*) or differentiated products (*imperfect oligopoly*). They are neither the price takers of perfect competition or the price makers of monopoly. The essential features of oligopoly are that first, the demand curve facing the organisation is less than perfectly elastic, and second, there is a high degree of interdependence between the decisions regarding price and output of the organisation. Each organisation must anticipate its rivals' reactions before it can predict the consequences of its own decision. This degree of uncertainty presents the economist with difficulties in constructing a general behavioural theory as with previous markets. In the industry itself this degree of uncertainty tends to lead to a noticeable feature of oligopolistic markets, that is, *price rigidity*.

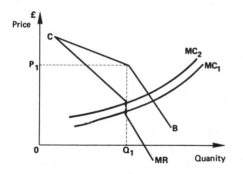

Fig 4.21   Oligopolist's 'kinked' demand curve

As explained in Chapter 2 a price cut by one organisation is likely to produce similar reactions by rival oligopolists. The result is likely to be to the detriment of all and so the rival organisations will avoid price competition between themselves. They are more likely to resort to non-price competition via extensive advertising campaigns or to a collusion policy on pricing. One theoretical analysis of oligopolistic behaviour which explains price rigidity was given by the 'kinked' demand curve of Chapter 2 illustrated in Fig 4.21. Because of this kinked demand curve the oligopoly's best pricing policy was to keep prices at the level shown by OP_1. Also as a consequence of the fact that the oligopoly demand curve CB is derived from two separate demand curves, AB and CD, there are also two marginal revenue curves derived from their respective demand curves. The combined marginal revenue curve reflecting CB is shown as MR with the distinctive 'discontinuity' shown by dotted lines. This discontinuity in the marginal revenue curve also provides theoretical reinforcement for the price rigidity observation when the marginal cost curve is added. As long as the MC curve cuts the discontinuity as shown, then even major variations in costs (shifting the marginal cost curve) will produce no change in price since MC = MR at the same price and output. (MC_1 or MC_2) The kinked demand curve theory is an attractive explanation of observed oligopolistic behaviour but it is only one theory based upon a specific set of assumptions about behaviour. Its major weaknesses lie in the fact that it is very difficult to test empirically and the possibility that price rigidity may be associated with factors quite unrelated to the kinked demand curve. So this cannot be presented as a general theoretical explanation of oligopoly by any means.

There are indeed several other explanations of oligopolistic behaviour each based upon its own set of assumptions. Lack of space precludes a detailed review but the more important versions are as follows. One other explanation is given by the *price leadership theory* in which the organisation plays the role of price leader and the others imitate its pricing policy. The question of uncertainty does not arise since rivals' behaviour is always predictable. The price leader may be the dominant organisation in the market but this may be a role adopted by a smaller member of the group. For example, in an oligopolistic market structure, all the organisations are likely to be affected by the same cost and demand conditions overall. A smaller member of the group may react quicker to changing conditions and so develop into the market 'barometer'. The other organisations through experience learn to follow its decisions. The general trend implied by this type of behaviour is an elimination of price competition with prices tending to drift upwards towards a monopolistic level.

A further possibility is that some form of collusion between organisations will occur either formally or through informal agreements if the former are outlawed by competition policy measures. In this case it is likely that price would be set well above the average costs of the organisations in the market. On the other hand, it is possible that the organisations may forego collusion and compete fiercely on price and terms. Price could be at or near average costs with minimal profit being earned.

This shows the difficulty in determining the price and output decision in oligopoly. Everything depends upon the degree of competitiveness and the behavioural variations assumed by the model which is constructed.

So far the chapter has attempted to analyse the behaviour of the organisation regarding price and output in different types of market structure. In all cases lack of space has made it necessary to strip away much of the detail and concentrate upon the basic framework. Omitted entirely from models has been any reference to situations in which the buyers are able to exert countervailing power against the producers. Further, only four basic market structures have been analysed. Nevertheless in all cases the attempt has been to construct models of organisational behaviour which can be of value in explaining the real world. It is by testing the models against the real market place and subsequently modifying the structures that the economist attempts to add to knowledge about the behaviour of organisations. Table 4.7 is a summary of the main behavioural predictions which result from our four models.

	Market structure		
Perfect competition (price taker)	*Monopolistic competition*	*Oligopoly*	*Monopoly* (price maker)
Many small sellers of homogeneous products with no entry barriers to new organisations.	Many sellers of differentiated products with no entry barriers to new organisations.	Few sellers of either identical products (perfect oligopoly) or differentiated products (imperfect oligopoly). Usually entry barriers.	One seller with entry barriers.
Organisation takes price as determined by market with equilibrium where MC = MR in short run. In long run equilibrium is where MC = AC = MR with normal profits only.	Organisation fixes price with equilibrium where MC = MR in short run. In long run equilibrium is where MC = MR with normal profit only with excess capacity.	Organisation's behaviour and therefore equilibrium depends upon assumptions of rivals' behaviour. No general oligopoly equilibrium.	Organisation fixes price where MC = MR. No difference between short and long run.

Table 4.7   Alternative market structures

Legal contraints on the behaviour of business organisations

Partnerships

As business organisations, partnerships regularly enter into transactions with other organisations and individuals, and inevitably these transactions are negotiated and executed on the partnership side by individual partners, rather than the firm as a whole.

The partner as an agent of the firm

It has already been stated that each partner is an agent of the co-partners, and it is now necessary to consider in more detail the consequences that flow from the partner's role as firm's agent. In short, the question that has to be answered is how can one decide whether or not the firm as a whole is bound by the particular contract made on its behalf by one of its partners. Under the law of agency, an agent will bind the principal (ie the person who has appointed the agent to act) by contracts made within the agent's *actual* and *apparent* authority. If the agent acts within either of these two branches the effect is that the contract concluded between the agent and the third party becomes the principal's contract, and hence it is the principal and the third party who become bound to each other. The actual authority of an agent is the express power given by the principal. A firm may for instance expressly resolve in a partnership meeting that each partner shall have the power to employ staff. Actual authority may also arise where the agent's power to make a particular contract or class of contracts can be implied from the conduct of the parties or the circumstances of the case. The apparent, or ostensible authority of an agent is the power which the agent appears to others to hold. Of a partner's apparent authority s. 5 Partnership Act, 1890, says:

> 'Every partner is an agent of the firm and his other partners for the purpose of the business of the partnership; and the acts of every partner who does any act for the carrying on in the usual way business of the kind carried on by the firm of which he is a member bind the firm and his partners, unless the partner so acting has in fact no authority to act for the firm in the particular matter, and the person with whom he is dealing either knows that he has no authority, or does not know or believe him to be a partner'.

Whether a particular contract is one 'carrying on in the usual way business of the kind carried on by the firm' is a question of fact.

An example of the operation of s. 5 is seen in *Mercantile Credit Co Ltd* v. *Garrod* (1962) where the court had to decide what could be considered as an act of a 'like kind' to the business of persons who ran a garage. It was held that the sale of a car to a third party by one of the partners, bound the other partner, despite an agreement between them that provided for the carrying out of repair work, and the letting of garages, but expressly excluded car sales. Not surprisingly the exact scope of an agent's apparent authority under s. 5 has been the subject of much litigation, and the following powers will usually fall within the agent's apparent authority:

a) in the case of all types of partnership the power:
   (i) to sell the goods or personal chattels of the firm,
   (ii) to purchase on the firm's account goods usually or necessarily employed in the firm's business,
   (iii) to receive payments due to the firm and give valid receipts for such payments,
   (iv) to employ staff to work for the firm. The agent has no authority to terminate the employment of staff against the co-partners' will,
   (v) to employ a solicitor to defend the firm.
b) in the case of a partnership whose business is the buying and selling of goods (a trading partnership) the following additional powers are within the agent's authority:
   (i) to borrow money for a purpose connected with the business of the firm. Here s. 7 should be noted. It provides that if a partner pledges the firm's credit for a purpose apparently not connected with the firm's business, the firm will not be bound, unless the partner was specially authorised to make the pledge;
   (ii) to draw, issue, accept, transfer and endorse bills of exchange (eg cheques).
   (iii) to secure a loan to the firm by pledging its personal property, or alternatively to create an equitable mortgage by a deposit of the title deeds of freehold or leasehold property which the firm owns.

However, a partner has no power to bind the firm by deed unless this power has expressly been granted by deed. This rule applies both to trading and non-trading partnerships. A deed must, for instance, be executed in order to transfer title to freehold land, and is necessary in order to create a lease for three years or more. The effect of this limitation upon a partner's apparent authority is that the firm will not be bound by a deed unless it has been signed by *all* the partners, or alternatively where it has been signed by one of them (or some other agent of the firm such as a solicitor) that the signatory has been given a power of attorney to do so and has acted within that power. Nor has a partner, whether in a trading firm or not, the power to:

   (i) bind the firm by giving a guarantee in the firm's name;
   (ii) compromise a debt owed to the firm, eg take something instead of money as satisfaction for the debt, such as fully paid shares. Acceptance of a cheque is not regarded as giving rise to a compromise;
   (iii) bind the firm by submitting a matter that is in dispute to arbitration. S. 6 lays down a general statement of a firm's liability for the acts of its authorised agents, by providing that: 'Any act or instrument relating to the business of the firm and done or executed in the firm-name, or in any other manner showing an intention to bind the firm, by any person thereto

authorised, whether a partner or not, is binding on the firm and all the partners'.

This does not however affect the law relating to the execution of deeds (mentioned above) or to the execution of negotiable instruments, such as cheques, which only bind the firm if the agent signs them for and on behalf of the firm (Bills of Exchange Act 1882). It will be noticed that s. 6 applies not only to the acts of the partners themselves but also extends to the acts of other authorised persons, such as employees of the firm, or its professional advisers such as solicitors and accountants. Similar rules of agency to those examined above apply to registered companies and are considered later in this chapter. The company itself is a principal, and its directors and other officers are its agents.

So far this examination of the partnership has been centred around the question of when the firm *as a whole*, will be held legally accountable for its agents' acts. It must however be remembered that a partnership is a group of closely linked associates, each acting in a dual capacity, that is, entering into transactions both as representatives of and for the general benefit of the firm, and also for their own, personal, benefit. But the firm that they represent is *not* a distinct legal entity, it is in fact no more than the aggregate of themselves. The problem this raises for a creditor who wishes to bring proceedings against the firm is who to sue. Similarly if an individual partner is being sued as a representative of the firm can he or she obtain a contribution from the other members? The Act lays down the liabilities of the partners in the following ways:

Under the Act every partner is jointly liable with the other partners for all the debts and obligations of the firm, incurred while being a partner. The effect of imposing joint liability is that while each partner is liable for the whole of the firm's debts, a creditor can only bring one action, where there is a single cause, to obtain satisfaction. The creditor's action may be brought against any one or more of the firm's members, however if the judgement obtained is not satisfactory, the creditor cannot sue the remaining partners for the creditor's right of action has been exhausted. This harsh rule is mitigated by the Rules of the Supreme Court which permit a plaintiff to sue a firm in its firm name, which has the effect of automatically joining all the partners in the action, and means that the judgement will be met out of the assets of the firm and, if necessary, the property of individual partners. Furthermore, any partner who is sued on a partnership debt may join co-partners in the action as co-defendants, and if a plaintiff has obtained a full judgement against one partner, that partner is entitled to claim contributions from the other partners.

The Act goes on to provide that the firm is liable for the 'wrongful act or omission of any partner' committed within the ordinary course of the firm's business. The term 'wrong' certainly embraces tortious acts although it appears that it does not extend to criminal acts.

174

The operation of this rule is seen in *Hamlyn* v. *Houston & Co* (1903). The defendant company was run by two partners as a grain merchants. One of the partners bribed the clerk of a rival grain merchant, and obtained information from him which enabled the company to compete at greater advantage. The Court of Appeal held that both partners were liable for this tórtious act. Obtaining information about rivals was within the general scope of the partner's authority, and therefore it did not matter that the method used to obtain it was unlawful. In the words of Collins, M.R.

'It is too well established by the authorities to be now disputed that a principal may be liable for the fraud or other illegal act committed by his agent within the general scope of the authority given to him, and even the fact that the act of the agent is criminal does not necessarily take it out of the scope of his authority.'

Nor will it operate as a defence for a firm to show that it did not benefit from the unlawful act of its agent.

The House of Lords in *Lloyd* v. *Grace, Smith & Co* (1912) held a solicitor's firm liable for the fraud of its managing clerk who induced one of the firm's clients into transferring certain properties into his name. In advising the client the clerk was acting within the scope of his authority, and that alone made the firm liable for his acts.

Although the Act does not apply to criminal matters two points are worth bearing in mind. Firstly, there may be occasions when one partner may be held *vicariously liable* for an offence committed by another. Secondly, a partner may be a party to an offence committed by another simply because it is in the nature of that partnership that they work together.

In *Parsons* v. *Barnes* (1973) where two partners worked together in a roof-repairing business, one of them was convicted of an offence under the Trade Descriptions Act 1968, by being present when his co-partner made a false statement to a customer.

If a partner acting within the scope of his or her apparent authority receives and misapplies the property of a third person while it is in the firm's custody the firm is liable to meet the third person's loss. Similarly when the *firm* has received property of a third person in the course of its business, and the property has been misapplied by a partner while in the firm's custody, it must make good the loss. The liability of partners for misapplications of property or wrongs of the firm, is stated by the Act to be joint and several. This means that if a judgement is obtained by a plaintiff against one partner, this does not operate as bar to bringing a further action against all or any of the others if the judgement remains unsatisfied. It will be remembered that where liability is merely joint this is not possible.

> In *Plumer* v. *Gregory* (1874) two of the partners in a firm consisting of three solicitors accepted on the firm's behalf and subsequently misappropriated money entrusted to them by the plaintiff, a client of the firm. The third member of the firm was unaware of these events, which only came to light after the other partners had died. The plaintiff's action against the remaining partner succeeded, for the firm was liable to make good the loss, and liability of the members was joint and several.

Changes in partnership constitution

It is common to find that the membership of a firm will alter from time to time. It may wish to expand its business by bringing in new partners to provide the benefit of additional capital or fresh expertise. Similarly existing partners may leave the partnership to join a new business, or on retirement. A changing membership poses the question of the extent to which incoming and outgoing partners are responsible for the debts and liabilities of the firm. While it will be clear from the foregoing that partners are responsible for matters arising during their membership of the firm, incoming partners are not liable for debts incurred before they joined, nor outgoing partners for those incurred after they leave, provided the retiring partner advertises the fact that he or she is no longer a member of the firm. This involves sending a notice to all who were customers of the firm while that person was a partner, and advertising the retirement in a publication known as the 'London Gazette'. If this is not done a person dealing with the firm after a change in its constitution can treat all apparent members of the old firm as still being members of the firm. As regards existing liabilities when the partner retires he or she may be discharged from them through the agreement of the new firm and the creditors, and himself/herself. This is known as *novation*.

So far all that has been dealt with is the liability of the firm, and its individual members, to those it deals with.

Rights and duties of the partners

Now attention must be given to the relationships that exist within the organisation between the members themselves. As to the terms which regulate this relationship, the Act states 'The mutual rights and duties of the partners, whether ascertained by agreement or defined by this Act may be varied by the consent of all of the partners, and such consent may be either express or inferred from a course of dealing'. Thus the provisions of the Act will apply in those cases where the parties are in dispute as to the nature or extent of their duties, and are unable to reach agreement amongst themselves. In a business enterprise like a partnership where a member's entire wealth lies at stake it is clearly of great value to execute a comprehensive agreement setting out in precise form the powers and responsibilities of the members. Thus, to take one example, it would be prudent for the agreement to provide grounds for the removal of partners for the Act makes no such provision. Because the members of a firm have the freedom to make their own agreement, without the statutory controls imposed upon other forms of business organisations, principally the registered company, the partnership stands out as a most flexible form of organisation, in which 'all the parties being competent to act as they please, they may put an end to or vary it at any moment' stated Lord Langdale in *England* v. *Curling* (1844).

The duties that the Act sets out, are based upon a single foundation of fundamental importance to all partnerships, namely that the relationship between the parties is of the utmost good faith − it is a contract uberrimae fidei. In Chapter 3 p. 111 it was explained that such a contract requires each partner to observe the utmost fairness and good faith in dealings with co-partners.

> This principle can be seen in *Law* v. *Law* (1905). A partner sold his share in the business to another partner for £21 000, but the purchaser failed to disclose to his co-partner certain facts about the partnership assets, of which he alone was aware. When the vendor realised that he had sold his share at an undervalue he sought to have sale set aside. The Court of Appeal held that in such circumstances the sale was voidable, and could be set aside.

A partner is under a duty to co-partners to render true accounts and full information of all things affecting the partnership. The Act imposes a duty upon a partner to account to the firm for any benefit derived without the consent of the other partners from any transaction concerning the partnership, or from any use of the partnership property, name or business connection. If the partner fails to do so the partnership will be entitled to recover the 'secret profit' made.

> In *Bentley* v. *Craven* (1853) one of the partners in a firm of sugar refiners, who acted as the firm's buyer, was able to purchase a large quantity of sugar at below market price. He resold it to the firm at market price, his co-partners being unaware that he was selling on his own account. When they discovered this they sued for the profit he had made, and were held entitled to it.

Finally, a partner is under a duty not to carry on any business of the same nature as and competing with that of the firm without the consent of the other partners. If the partner is in breach of this duty he or she must account to the firm for all the profits made and pay them over. If the partnership agreement prohibits the carrying on of a competing business an injunction may be granted to prevent a partner from competing.

Further rights and duties are set out in the Act, which states that subject to any agreement express or implied between the partners, the following rules are to apply:

(i) all partners are entitled to take part in the management of the partnership business;

(ii) any differences arising as to ordinary matters connected with the partnership business are to be decided by a majority of the partners, but no change can be made in the nature of the partnership business without the consent of all the partners;

(iii) no person may be introduced as a partner without the consent of all existing partners;

(iv) all partners are entitled to share equally in the profits of the business irrespective of the amount of time they have given to it, and must contribute equally towards any losses. The Act does not require the firm to keep books of account, although this will normally be provided for in the partnership agreement, together with specific reference to the proportions of the profits each partner is entitled to. If however there are partnership books they have to be kept at the principal place of business, where every partner is entitled to have access to them for the purpose of inspection and copying;

(v) if a partner makes a payment or advance beyond the agreed capital contribution he or she is entitled to interest at 5% p.a.;

(vi) a partner is not entitled to payment of interest on his or her capital until profits have been ascertained;

(vii) the firm must indemnify a partner in respect of payments made and personal liabilities incurred in the ordinary and proper conduct of the business of the firm, or in or about anything necessarily done for the preservation of the business or property of the firm (eg paying an insurance premium);

(viii) a partner is not entitled to remuneration for acting in the partnership business. In cases where the firm consists of *active* and *sleeping* partners the partnership agreement will often provide that as well as taking a share of the profits the active partners shall be entitled to the payment of a salary.

In the event of a breach of any of the terms of the partnership agreement damages will be available as a remedy, and an injunction can be granted to enforce a negative stipulation (eg not to compete).

Partnership property

Among the assets of a partnership will be the property which belongs to it, but it is important to point out that the mere use of property for partnership purposes does not automatically vest ownership of that property in the partnership.

In *Miles* v. *Clarke* (1953) the defendant started up a photography business which involved him in acquiring a lease and photographic equipment. After trading unsuccessfully he was joined by the plaintiff, a free-lance photographer, who brought into the firm his business connection which was of considerable value. The partners traded profitably for some time, on the basis of equal profit sharing. Later, as a result of personal difficulties, it became necessary to wind up the firm. The plaintiff claimed a share in all the assets of the business. The Court held that the assets of the business, other than the stock-in-trade which had become partnership property, belonged to the particular partner who had brought it in.

The Act provides that all property and rights and interests in property originally brought into the partnership or subsequently acquired by purchase or otherwise on account of the firm, must be held and applied by the partners exclusively for the purposes of the partnership and in accordance with the partnership agreement. Property coming within this provision is called partnership property and will normally be jointly owned by the partners. In the case of partnership land the persons in whom the property is vested hold it on trust for those beneficially interested under the partnership agreement. Because a partner is a co-owner of partnership property, rather than a sole owner of any particular part of the partnership's assets, he or she may be guilty of theft of partnership property if it can be established that his or her intention was to permanently deprive the other partners of their share as in *R* v. *Bonner* (1970).

Under the Act property bought with money belonging to the firm is deemed to have been bought on account of the firm, unless a contrary intention appears. There is nothing to prevent an individual partner taking out of the partnership a particular asset, provided the co-partners' consent is obtained. The asset may be purchased by the partner either by making payment, or by accepting a reduction in his or her capital. However if at the time of the transaction the firm is insolvent then the removal of the asset will not affect the interests of the firm's creditors, for they can require the asset to be returned.

Limited partnerships

Before considering the dissolution of a partnership, brief reference must be made to the limited partnership, which is a significantly different type of business enterprise, both legally and economically, from the general partnerships which have been dealt with in the foregoing pages.

179

Limited partnerships may be formed under the Limited Partnerships Act 1907 and must consist of:

a) one or more persons called general partners, who are liable for all the debts and obligations of the firm; and
b) one or more persons, called limited partners, who have contributed at the time of entering into the partnership a sum or sums as capital or property valued at a stated amount, and who are not liable for the debts or obligations of the firm beyond the amount contributed.

The Act allows a limited partner to be a *body corporate*. Once the limited partner has made the capital contribution he or she is disallowed from withdrawing any part of it, either directly or indirectly. By withdrawing it he or she becomes liable for the firm's debts and liabilities up to the amount withdrawn. Limited partnerships must be registered with the Registrar of Companies. This is achieved by sending to the Registrar a statement signed by the partners containing details of the firm's name, the general nature of its business, the principal place of business, the full name of each partner, the date of commencement and length of term of the partnership (if any), a statement that the partnership is limited, and particulars of each limited partner and the amount contributed by each whether in cash or otherwise. The registered statement is available for public inspection. If the partnership fails to register the limited partner becomes fully liable as a general partner. It will be appreciated that the principal difference between a limited partnership and a general partnership lies in the accountability of the partners of these respective organisations for the debts and liabilities of the firm. In a general partnership each partner has an unlimited liability for the debts and other liabilities of the firm, whereas in a limited partnership there must by definition be at least one member who, like a shareholder in a registered company, has a fixed or limited liability. Unlike a shareholder, however, the limited partner has no *right* to take part in the management of the organisation; a partner who does so becomes fully responsible for all liabilities incurred by the firm while acting as its manager. Nor does the limited partner have power to bind the firm. The limited partner is however granted the right to inspect the firm's books.

The limited partnership has been an unsuccessful rival to the private limited company largely, it would seem, because of the non-corporate status. The total number of partnerships registered in this way numbers hundreds, whereas there are many thousands of private limited companies.

Registered companies limited by shares

A business enterprise operating as a partnership is subject to few statutory regulations. The partners are left free to decide themselves such matters as meetings, the keeping of records and accounting methods.

180

As far as registered companies limited by shares are concerned, however, the fundamental principle of accountability of the directors to the members necessarily involves stricter regulation of the company's operation. The Companies Acts provide therefore that every company must in each year hold an *annual general meeting* of which every member is entitled to notice. In addition, the holders of not less than one-tenth of the paid-up capital with voting rights may at any time compel the directors to call an *extra-ordinary general meeting*. The proceedings at such meetings are usually laid down in the Articles. However the minutes of all meetings must be strictly recorded. Decisions at general meetings are usually taken by *ordinary resolution*, ie a majority of voting members present. For some types of business usually related to the company's constitution, such as the alteration of the Articles or objects of the company, a *special resolution* is necessary, ie three-quarter majority of voting members.

Another formality is the requirement that all companies must every year submit an annual return to the Registrar of Companies. The return must include details of the company's share capital, share division, debts secured by mortgages, the members and directors.

Also the Companies Act 1976 contains detailed provisions relating to the preparation of accounts, information to be included, and the need for submission of annual accounts to the general meeting and the Registrar of Companies. In general the accounting records must be kept at the registered office of the company and must be available for inspection. Company accounts must also be audited, and the auditor's report must be read before the company in general meeting, and must be open to inspection by any member. Other documents which a company is obliged to keep include a register of the interests of directors and their service contracts, a register of the company members, and debenture holders, and a register of members who have substantial interests in the company, ie one-tenth or more of the share capital of the company.

This strict regulation of the affairs of a registered company has proved necessary to prevent abuse, and ensure accountability to the members. The requirements as to publication of accounts provide a useful tool by which an outsider can assess the financial position of a company before transacting with it or investing in it. Generally a prospective investor in a company has two choices:

a) The prospective investor may lend money to the company in return for an issue of debentures. A debenture holder is a secured creditor of the company who is entitled to a fixed rate of interest on their investment;

b) The prospective investor may purchase a shareholding and become a company member. The rights of a shareholder will depend upon the nature of the shareholding but generally a shareholder has the right to receive a proportion of the profits of a company, vote in general meeting and share in the capital of a company if it is wound up.

Position of the members

Unlike a partner, a shareholder who has invested in a company and in so doing has become a *member* will play no part in its daily management. The company's Articles will usually confer power on the directors to operate the business. Nevertheless, ultimate control of the business is in the hands of the shareholders by the exercise of voting power in the general meeting. By the use of this power the Articles may be altered and if necessary the directors removed. Of course, it is the will of the majority of shareholders as expressed in general meetings that exercises the power, the view of the minority shareholders being of little significance. Certainly the law has been slow to assist the minority shareholder who claims oppression or prejudice by the majority.

> The case of *Foss* v. *Harbottle* (1843) laid down as a general principle that the courts will not interfere in the internal management of a company at the instance of the minority shareholders. Here an action had been brought by the minority alleging that the directors were responsible for losses that had occurred (these were caused by the sale, by the directors, of a piece of land to the company at an inflated price). The Court held that the action must fail as the proper plaintiff in such circumstances was the company itself. As the action to which the minority shareholders objected could have been ratified by the majority then it was the majority shareholders who should decide whether an action should be brought in the company name. The Court saw no merit in interfering in the internal management of a company by passing judgement on its commercial decisions. In *Pavlides* v. *Jenson and others* (1956) a company sold an asbestos mine for £182 000 when its real value was close to £1 000 000. The plaintiff minority shareholder brought an action for damages against the three directors responsible for the sale and against the company, alleging gross negligence. The Court held that the action could not be maintained by a minority shareholder because where negligence rather than fraud was alleged, it was the company itself which should decide whether to redress the wrong done.

It should be remembered that the process of incorporation, having invested a company with a separate legal personality, dictates that the company and individual members are separate. If a wrong is committed against the company it is the company, by virtue of a decision made by the Board of Directors at the general meeting, that should redress it.

Rights of the minority shareholder

Some of the individual shareholder's personal rights, arising under the common law, were considered in the previous chapter. Thus, a shareholder in an individual capacity may seek an injunction to restrain the company from performing an ultra vires act or altering the Articles so as not to benefit the members as a whole. In addition a member may act to prevent personal rights being infringed (ie voting rights or right to a *dividend*) and also to prevent the majority of shareholders inflicting fraud or oppression on the minority. Recently, the courts have held that a shareholder could take action based on the allegation that the directors were benefitting themselves at the expense of the company, without necessarily showing fraud.

In *Daniels* v. *Daniels* (1978) two company directors in 1970 instructed the company to sell land to one of them for £4250. In 1974 the land was resold for £120 000 and a minority shareholder brought an action claiming that damages should be payable to the company. The Court held that despite no allegation of fraud the action by the individual shareholder should be allowed to proceed.

In addition to the common law the Companies Acts confer certain statutory rights on minority shareholders. Such rights relate to the following matters:

1 *Re-registration under the Companies Act 1980*
The Companies Act 1980 provides that a special resolution by an old public company not to be re-registered as a public limited company, or a special resolution by a public company to be re-registered as a private company, may be challenged by the holders of 5% or more in nominal value of the issued share capital by application to the court.
2 *Variation of class rights of different shares*
If a company has issued different classes of shares then each class of share will have various rights attached to it (ie voting powers, rights to dividend). It is usual therefore for a company to provide in its Memorandum or Articles that the rights of each class of share may be altered with the consent of a certain majority of the holders of that class. The Companies Act 1948 provides that the holders of at least 15% of the issued shares of the class have a right to apply to the court to have the variation cancelled.
3 *Alteration of the objects clause*
As previously stated in Chapter 3, p. 127, under s. 5 of the Companies Act 1948 the objects clause of the Memorandum of Association may be altered to achieve certain defined objectives. The section also confers the right on the holders of at least 15% in nominal value of the company's issued share capital to apply to the court to cancel a special resolution altering the objects of the company.
4 *Members unfairly prejudiced*
The Companies Act 1980 s. 75 has replaced s. 210 of the Companies Act 1948 which provided the remedy of court action if a member could show that the affairs of the company were being conducted in a

manner oppressive to some members, including that member, and such oppression could justify the company being wound up. The new section gives a member the right to apply to the court for an order on the ground that the affairs of the company are being or have been conducted in a manner which is unfairly prejudicial to some members (including at least himself), or that any actual or proposed act or omission of the company is or would be so prejudicial. The position of the minority shareholder has been greatly strengthened by this new power. He or she need no longer show that the facts would justify winding up, nor show oppression but rather unfair prejudice, and finally the section applies to proposed action as well as past acts. If a case is made out under the section the power of the court to grant relief has also been extended. Generally the court may make such order as it thinks fit and this could include:

a) regulating the company's affairs in the future,
b) require the company to act or refrain from action,
c) authorise civil proceedings in the name and on behalf of the company by any person,
d) require the purchase of any member's shares by the company or other members.

It remains to be seen how the courts will interpret the expression 'unfairly prejudicial' but it is suggested that it must have been the legislature's intention for the expression to encompass conduct of a less serious nature than amounted to oppression sufficient to justify a winding up under s. 210. The conduct complained of must however affect the applicant personally.

In *Re: Five Minute Car Wash Service* (1966) the applicant alleged that the managing director of the company was 'unwise, inefficient and careless' in carrying out his duties. Such conduct, the Court held, was not sufficient alone to amount to oppression under s. 210. It is suggested that as there was no evidence that the managing director had behaved unfairly or unreasonably to any member, such conduct would not amount to 'unfair prejudice' under the Companies Act, 1980.

Also it is still necessary for an applicant for relief to show that it is his or her position as a shareholder that is being affected by the conduct.

Thus in *Re: Lundie Brothers Ltd* (1965) an application for relief was made by a shareholder who claimed that he had been unfairly ousted from his position as a working director. The Court held that no order for relief should be made as the applicant had suffered no oppression in his position as shareholder.

Having decided that relief should be granted, an example of how the court may regulate the affairs of the company is demonstrated by the case of *Re: H R Harmer Ltd* (1959). Here a company was run by an elderly father as chairman and his two sons as directors, the father having voting control. In practise the father largely ignored the wishes of the board of directors and ran the business as his own. On an application by the sons as minority shareholders under s. 210, alleging oppression, the Court held that relief should be granted. The father was appointed life president of the company without rights, duties or powers and ordered not to interfere in the company's affairs.

5 *Schemes of reconstruction and amalgamation*
There are situations where a company can propose to wind up voluntarily and transfer the whole or part of its business or property to another company. In such circumstances the Companies Act 1948 gives protection to minorities.
6 *Investigations by the Department of Trade*
The shareholders holding at least one-tenth of the issued shares of a company, or 200 shareholders whatever their shareholding, may apply to the Department of Trade for the appointment of inspectors if they feel that the affairs of the company require investigation. There is also power to apply to the Department of Trade by a similar minority if they feel that the membership of the company requires investigation.

Although the ultimate power of control of a registered company is in the hands of its owners (ie the shareholders at a general meeting) the responsibility for the general policy and management of a company is invested in the board of directors.

Position of the directors

The procedure for the appointment of directors is usually specified in the Articles which may provide that a director must hold a certain number of shares in the company. Notwithstanding anything in the Articles, however, the company may under s. 184 of the Companies Act 1948 remove a director by ordinary resolution. However, there is nothing to prevent the Articles conferring special voting rights on various classes of shares and following the decision in *Bushell* v. *Faith* (1970) it seems that such special voting rights may be given to a director on a resolution to remove him from office.

Bushell v. *Faith* (1970) Here the company's Articles provided that on a resolution to remove a director, the shares of that director should carry three votes per share. The company had an issued share capital of £300 with each £1 share carrying one vote. The defendant director and another shareholder each held one hundred shares and recorded two hundred votes in favour of a resolution to remove the plaintiff director who also held one hundred shares and had voted against it. The Court held that the resolution was defeated as the plaintiff's shares carried three hundred votes and there was nothing to prevent the Articles conferring such special voting rights.

The Companies Act 1980 s. 47 contains a new provision to prevent the abuse which could occur whereby directors, who possibly fear a s. 184 resolution for removal, enter into long term service contracts with the object of securing heavy compensation on removal. Such an action will now require the approval of the company in general meeting.

Directors' powers and duties

The powers of directors are conferred on them by the Articles and generally cannot be usurped by a general meeting without an alteration of the Articles. It is also possible for the shareholders in a general meeting to increase the directors' powers or ratify the ultra vires acts of the directors provided the acts are intra vires the company.

The Companies Acts do not define the term 'director' and merely state that it will include any person occupying the position of director no matter by what name he or she is called. In order to indicate their legal position the courts have described them as trustees, agents, or managing partners. However Lord Jessel stated in *Re: Forest of Dean Coal Mining Co* (1878), 'It does not matter much what you call them, so long as you understand what their true position is, which is that they are merely commercial men, managing a trading concern for the benefit of themselves and all other shareholders in it'. It is the directors who have control over the policy and management of a company and in this capacity as a *fiduciary*, that the law has imposed a number of duties that are owed by the directors to the company. The term fiduciary relates to the special position that a director occupies as an individual who, like an agent for a principal, must act in good faith and not make personal use of his or her position.

Fiduciary duties

1 *A director must act bona fide in what he or she considers is the interest of the company*

The powers that are invested in directors are to be used for the benefit of the company as a whole, ie the shareholders as a whole, rather than some sectional interest, ie a class of shareholders, the company employees, the directors, a holding or subsidiary company. Thus there has been abuse of power and a breach of duty where

a) The directors issue new shares to themselves, not because the company needs more capital but merely to increase their voting power.

In *Piercy* v. *S. Mills & Co Ltd* (1920) the directors used their power to issue shares to themselves solely in order to acquire the majority of voting power and defeat the wishes of the existing shareholders. The Court held that the issue was void as the directors had abused their powers.

b) The directors approve a transfer of their own partly-paid shares to escape liability for a call (a request to pay up an amount due on a share) they intend to make.

In *Alexander* v. *Automatic Telephone Co* (1900) the directors used their position to require all shareholders to pay 3s 6d on each share excluding themselves. The Court held that this was a clear abuse of power and the directors were required to pay to the company the same amount.

c) The directors negotiate a new service agreement between the company and its managing director simply in order to confer additional benefits on him/her or his/her dependants.

In *Re: W and M Roith* (1967) it was held that a new service contract negotiated between a managing director and his company was unlawful as it was solely to make a pension provision for his widow and that no regard had been taken as to whether this was for the benefit of the company.

d) The directors abdicate responsibility for the running of the company and appoint a manager with full powers (ie no board control), or they obey the majority shareholder without exercising any discretion.

e) The directors of a subsidiary company use their powers exclusively in the interests of the holding company and to the detriment of the minority shareholders of the subsidiary.

2 *A director must not place himself in a position where there is likely to be conflict between personal interests and duty to the company*
Directors act as agents on behalf of the company they represent and in such a capacity they must not enter into engagements where there is, or is likely to be, a conflict between the interests of the company and their own personal interests. The Companies Acts therefore require a director to give notice at the board meeting of personal interest – direct or indirect – in any contracts or proposed contracts in which the company is involved. Failure to disclose such an interest could result in fines being imposed and in addition any director who uses position to make personal profit may be made to account for such a profit to the company.

In *Cook* v. *Deeks* (1916) the directors of a railway company having negotiated a contract on behalf of the company decided to make the contract in their own names. The Court held that the benefit of the contract belonged to the company and the directors should account to the company for any profit made. The extent of this duty is also illustrated by the case of *Regal Hastings* v. *Gulliver* (1942). Here the company owned a cinema and decided to purchase two others with the intention of selling the whole undertaking as a going concern. A subsidiary company was formed which acquired the other cinemas, however the shares of the subsidiary were allocated between the company and its directors. Following a sale of the whole undertaking, involving a transfer of the shares of the company and its subsidiary, the purchasers brought an action to recover the profit on the sale by the directors of their shares in the subsidiary. Despite the fact that the purchasers had freely agreed to pay the share price, the House of Lords held that former directors must deliver up to the company the profit they had made. It was by the use of their special knowledge and opportunities as directors that they had made the profit. Of course the duty owed by a director is to the company as a whole and not to individual members and so in *Percival* v. *Wright* (1902) the sale of shares by the plaintiff to directors at a price which could have proved to be advantageous to the latter was held not to be a breach of duty. The directors did not disclose to the seller that they were negotiating a sale of the company's shares at a higher price to a third party. It is a general principle of law that there is no requirement on a contracting party to disclose all matters pertinent to the contract.

The power of directors to make use of their position for personal gain has been further regulated by the Companies Act 1980. Briefly, the Act now makes it a criminal offence for an *insider*, ie a director or officer, who is or has been during the last six months connected with a company, to deal in shares of that company, if that person has confidential information relating to such shares. This information could relate to any transaction or proposed transaction including of course a possible takeover. The offence also extends to communicating such information to others and is punishable by a maximum penalty of two years imprisonment and an unlimited fine.

The duty of skill and care: A director is obliged to exercise, in the performance of duties, the skill and care of a reasonable person. In exercising the powers connected with the position therefore, the director of a company must also exercise the skill and care that might reasonably be expected from a person with knowledge and experience. This is by no means an onerous duty and it is not surprising that there have been few cases where a director has been found negligent in the performance of duties and accountable to the company in damages. It has been held that a director is entitled to trust fellow directors and officers to perform their duties and may not be made responsible for wrongful acts decided on at board meetings he or she does not attend.

In *Re: Denham & Co* (1883) a situation had arisen where, for four years, a company's dividend was negligently paid out of capital. As the powers of management of the company had been vested in one individual, another director who rarely attended board meetings and had no reason to suspect misconduct, was held not liable for the negligence.

It does seem that, provided the directors act honestly, they usually fulfil the standards required of them.

In *Re: New Marshonaland Exploration Co* (1892) the directors approved a loan of £1250 and failed·to ensure that security was given. The Court held that in the absence of fraud the directors were not liable for this 'error of judgement'.

To sum up, therefore, it should be emphasised that the law imposes high standards on those who control and manage large business enterprises. They must have as their sole object the benefit of the enterprise, and act with total honesty. As far as the operation of the business is concerned, however, the law requires the director to demonstrate in the particular circumstances the business acumen of which he or she is capable, and no more. Justice Romer referred to this in *Re: City Equitable Fire Insurance Co Ltd* (1925).

'The position of a director of a company carrying on a small retail business is very different from that of a director of a railway company. The duties of a bank director may differ widely from those of an insurance director, and the duties of a director of one insurance company may differ from those of another . . . The larger the business carried on by the Company the more numerous, and the more important, the matters that must of necessity be left to the managers, the accountants and the rest of the staff.'

Transactions which bind the company

All business enterprises, whether corporate or non corporate bodies, will necessarily be involved in entering into business transactions with outsiders. In practise, it will be an individual acting on behalf of the business enterprise who would conclude such a transaction with an outsider. The problem that then springs to mind is what is the legal position if an individual concludes such a transaction and yet exceeds the authority delegated by the enterprise or fails to comply with procedures or conditions that the business enterprise has formulated. As far as registered companies are concerned the legal position where a contract is ultra vires the company has already been dealt with in Chapter 3 p. 127. It will be remembered that the enforceability of such a contract will depend on the operation of the European Communities

Act, 1972. Here the concern is with the situation where the contract is intra vires (within the powers of) the company but the individual who executes the contract has exceeded those powers, or the internal rules of the company relating to transacting have not been complied with. Of course any *outsider* dealing with a company is deemed to have notice of the contents of the Memorandum and Articles in which the company's contracting powers and procedures will be stated. An outsider who has notice of these requirements however may have no way of knowing whether they have been complied with. Following the decision in *Royal British Bank* v. *Turquand* (1856) an outsider dealing with a company is not bound to ensure that all the necessary internal rules have been satisfied, and may assume that there has been compliance.

> *Royal British Bank* v. *Turquand*, (1856) Here the company's directors borrowed £2000 from the plaintiff bank and issued a bond to the bank guaranteeing repayment. The company had powers to borrow money in this manner provided that the loan was authorised by a general resolution. The bank sued on the bond for repayment of the loan and the company claimed that it was not bound by the loan as no general resolution was passed. The Court held that the bank could sue on the bond, for it was entitled to assume that the resolution had been passed and thus the company's internal requirements had been complied with.

The rule in Turquand's case therefore provides considerable protection for outsiders contracting with companies. It will not apply, however, if the person dealing with the company is aware of the irregularity.

> Thus in *Howard* v. *Patent Ivory Manufacturing Co* (1888) the company's Articles empowered the company to lend up to a £1000 to a director. For loans in excess of that amount the sanction of the general meeting was required. A loan of £3500 secured by debenture was made to a director and not authorised by general meeting. It was held that the loan was only valid to the extent of £1000 as the director was aware that no resolution had been passed in general meeting.

Also, the rule cannot be relied on by a person who in the circumstances ought to have been put on inquiry as to the irregularity and therefore have investigated it.

> In *Underwood Ltd* v. *Bank of Liverpool* (1924) the sole director and principal shareholder of a company paid cheques made payable to the company into his own bank account and the bank did not enquire into the transactions. An action was brought by the company's debenture holders against the bank for the value of

the cheques. The Court held that the rule in Turquand could not apply, as the fact that the director had paid company cheques into his own account was suspicious and ought to have led the bank to investigate and discover whether the company had a separate account.

It has previously been stated that it will be rare for a registered company to enter into all transactions authorised collectively by the board of directors and thereby bring into operation s. 9(1) of the European Communities Act 1972. Despite the general company law principle that directors act collectively at board meetings, in practice many companies contain wide powers of delegation in their Articles. Accordingly, certain powers are often delegated to the managing director, individual directors or officers who will act as agents of the company. Under the general law of agency the acts of such agents within the scope of their actual authority will bind the company. In addition, an outsider dealing with such an agent is entitled to rely on the apparent authority of such a person (ie the powers which an agent of that kind normally has). For example, the managing director of a company will be invested with the apparent authority attaching to that office. This will include commercial matters such as the signing of cheques, borrowing money, giving security and guaranteeing loans. The fact that a company holds out an individual as managing director, despite the fact that this person has never been appointed, may be sufficient to bind the company for those actions made on its behalf.

In *Freeman and Lockyer* v. *Buckhurst Park Properties Ltd* (1964) the company's Articles contained power to appoint a managing director but none was in fact appointed. Nevertheless, to the knowledge of the board, one individual director acted as if he were the managing director and contracted with the plaintiffs for work to be done for the company. In an action by the plaintiffs for fees due under the contract the Court held that the company was liable under it. As the individual director was held out by the company as managing director, and had acted within the scope of the apparent authority of such a person in entering into the contract, the company was bound by it.

Dissolution of business organisations

The dissolution or winding up of a business organisation is important for a number of reasons. It is important to the members of the organisation since they will be concerned as to what share of the assets they are entitled to, and for much the same reason it will be of concern to the creditors: they will want to know what the assets of the business are, and how they are to be divided up amongst the creditors.

Dissolution of a partnership

This can occur either with or without the intervention of the court. Under the Partnership Act 1890 a partnership is dissolved without the intervention of the court, in any of the following circumstances:

a) if it was entered into for a fixed term, when that term expires;
b) if it was entered into for a single adventure or undertaking, by the termination of that adventure or undertaking, eg where the aim of the business is to acquire a single piece of property and resell;
c) if entered into for an undefined time, by any partner giving notice to the other or others of the intention to dissolve the partnership. If such a notice is served then the partnership is dissolved as from the date mentioned in the notice as the date of dissolution. If there is no such date dissolution operates from the time the notice was received, subject to the Articles providing for some other date;
d) by the death or bankruptcy of any partner. The Articles will often provide that in such an event the partnership will continue to be run by the remaining partners. In the case of the death of a partner the Articles may provide that the surviving partners will continue to run the business in partnership with the personal representatives of the deceased;
e) if a partner's share of the business is charged to secure a separate judgment debt, the other partners may dissolve the business;
f) by the happening of an event which makes it unlawful for the business of the firm to be carried on, or for the members of the firm to carry it on in partnership. This may occur, for example, where there is a partnership between a British partner and a foreign partner, the business is carried on in the United Kingdom, and war breaks out between the countries of the respective partners.

Dissolution can be granted by the court on an application to dissolve made by a partner in any of the following cases;

a) where a partner is suffering from a mental disorder;
b) where a partner other than the partner sueing
  (i) becomes in any way permanently incapable of performing their part of the partnership contract, eg through physical illness, or
  (ii) has been guilty of misconduct in business or private life, as in the opinion of the court, bearing in mind the nature of the partnership business, is calculated to be prejudicial to the carrying on of that business, or
  (iii) wilfully or persistently commits a breach of the partnership agreement, or otherwise behaves in a way in matters relating to the partnership business that it is impractical for the other partners to carry on in business with that partner. Cases on dissolution on these grounds have included a refusal to meet for discussions on business matters, the keeping of erroneous accounts, persistent disagreement between the parties, and in

Anderson v. *Anderson* (1857) where a father and son were in partnership together, the opening by the father of all his son's correspondence;
c) where the business of the partnership can only be carried on at a loss;
d) if circumstances have arisen which, in the opinion of the court, render it just and equitable that the partnership be dissolved.

Thus in *Re: Yenidje Tobacco Co Ltd* (1916) although the company was trading profitably the court held that it was just and equitable to wind it up on the basis that its two directors had become so hostile towards each other that they would only communicate by means of messages passed to each other via the Secretary, and that this amounted to a position of deadlock. It was pointed out that a private limited company is similar to a partnership, and that had the directors been partners in a partnership, there would have been sufficient grounds for dissolution. Lord Justice Warrington stated:

'. . . I am prepared to say that in a case like the present, where there are only two persons interested, and there are no shareholders other than those two, where there are no means of overruling by the action of a general meeting of shareholders the trouble which is occasioned by the quarrels of the two directors and shareholders, the company ought to be wound up if there exists such a ground as would be sufficient for the dissolution of a private partnership at the suit of one of the partners against the other. Such ground exists in the present case.'

Winding up of registered companies

Like a partnership, a limited company can be wound up either voluntarily, or compulsorily by order of the court. The grounds for winding up, whether on a voluntary or compulsory basis, are set out under the Companies Act 1948 and they recognise that winding up is a step which may become necessary not only in cases of financial instability, but also because the company, which is of course a creature of statute, has failed to comply with the statutory provisions which bind it, or simply because the members no longer wish to trade together. When examining the operation of the limited company it is common to draw an analogy with natural persons. Thus the company is said to be born when its certificate of incorporation is granted, and henceforth its brain, the board of directors, guides its actions and formulates its decisions, which are executed through those it employs. Following this analogy through to its conclusion the process of winding up is akin to the process of administering the estate of a deceased person. Assets are collected and used to satisfy debts owing, after which any property remaining can be distributed to those lawfully entitled, in the case of a company to its members. However the process of administering the estate of a deceased person commences with death, whereas winding up is a process which culminates in the dissolution of the company.

A company may be compulsorily wound up by order of the court under s. 222 Companies Act 1948 if:

a) the company itself has passed a special resolution that it be wound up by the court;

b) the company has defaulted in delivering the statutory report to the Registrar or in holding the statutory meeting;

c) the company has failed to commence business within a year of incorporation, or has suspended business activity for a whole year, although the court will only make an order if the company has no intention of carrying on business.

> In *Re: Middlesbrough Assembly Rooms Co* (1880) a shareholder petitioned for winding up where the company had suspended trading for over three years, because of a trade depression. The majority shareholders opposed the petition on the basis that the company intended to recommence trading when the economic situation improved. It was held that in the circumstances the petition should be dismissed;

d) the company is unable to pay its debts. This is the most common ground, and there are circumstances under which a company will be *deemed* to be unable to pay its debts, eg if the company has neglected to pay for a period of three weeks or more a debt in excess of £200 after a creditor of the company, to whom the sum is due, has served on the company a demand for payment. Of course in these circumstances the creditor will not be able to petition for a winding up if the company is bona fide disputing the debt;

e) the court is of the opinion that it is just and equitable that the company should be wound up. This ground covers a number of situations. For instance it will be available in cases where the substratum of the company has been destroyed.

> In *Re: German Date Coffee Co* (1882) the company was wound up on the basis that it had become impossible to carry out the main object in the Memorandum of Association, namely the acquisition and working of a German patent to make coffee from dates, because the patent could not be obtained.

The just and equitable ground will also apply in cases where there is oppression of the minority by the majority, (s. 75 Companies Act 1980 provides an alternative remedy in such cases), or where there is incompatibility between the members of the company, as in *Re: Yenidje Tobacco Co Ltd* (1916).

In *Re: Westbourne Galleries Ltd* (1971) Lord Wilberforce, in considering the scope of the words 'just and equitable' under s. 222 said:

'The words are a recognition of the fact that a limited company is more than a mere legal entity, with a personality in law of its own; that there is room in company law for the recognition of the fact that behind it, or amongst it, there are individuals, with rights, expectations and obligations inter se which are not necessarily submerged in the company structure'.

A petition for winding up may be presented to the court by the company itself (which is rare), by a member (in the context of a winding up referred to as a *'contributory'*), or by a creditor, which is the most common case. A contributory means every person liable to contribute to the assets of the company in the event of it being wound up (s. 213). In *Re: Othery Construction Ltd* (1966) Lord Buckley stated that if a fully paid up shareholder is to successfully petition to wind up

'. . . he must show either that there will be a surplus available for distribution amongst the shareholders or that the affairs of the company require investigation in respects which are likely to produce such a surplus'.

The Department of Trade and Industry also has certain statutory powers to petition for a winding up order.

In a compulsory winding up, the liquidator is appointed by the court and acts under its supervision, and under the supervision of the Department of Trade, and a committee of inspection appointed by the creditors and members. On appointment the liquidator takes over the functions of the directors, until such time as the company is wound up. The liquidator is a fiduciary agent of the company, and is also party to a fiduciary relationship with the creditors.

A company may be voluntarily wound up under s. 278 if it passes a special resolution to that effect or if it passes an extraordinary resolution that, by reason of its liabilities, it cannot continue its business and it is advisable to wind up. If a resolution under s. 278 is passed the directors may make a statutory declaration that they have formed the opinion, after examination of the company's affairs, that it will be able to pay its debts in full within a specified period not exceeding twelve months. The effect of making such a declaration is that the winding up becomes a *Members Voluntary Winding Up*, the members themselves then appoint the liquidator, and the liquidator will not be subject to supervision by the creditors. However if the statutory declaration is not made, the winding up becomes a *Creditors Voluntary Winding Up*, the directors must provide the creditors with a financial report, and the creditors enjoy the advantage of appointing, and supervising, their own liquidator. (Winding up is considered further in chapter 8.)

Case study on airline industry behaviour – the Laker Airways Skytrain

The structure and regulation of the industry

The present structure of the UK airline industry may be principally divided into three groups of operators. Firstly, the state-owned 'flag carrier' of British Airways, operating both international and domestic routes, and by far the largest UK airline. Included within this first group is British Caledonian Airlines which under the terms of the 1971 Civil Aviation Act was envisaged as a private enterprise second force carrier to complement British Airways. Secondly, there are the other airlines operating scheduled domestic and international services as well as charter flights. Such airlines include Laker Airways, Dan Air, British Midland Airways, Air UK and several other smaller operators. The third principal component of the industry consists of those airlines operating exclusively on a charter basis such as Britannia and Monarch Airlines and the recently formed Air Europe.

These airlines form part of an industry which has developed rapidly in the last thirty years and currently is one which is highly regulated in its operations and policies. The origin of regulation can be traced back to the Chicago Convention of 1944. The general philosophy to emerge from the Chicago convention was that scheduled traffic between countries was to be served by their respective national airlines. Within the rules suggested by the Convention it was for individual countries to conclude bi-lateral treaty arrangements covering airline operations. The bi-lateral agreements concluded were of two types. The first allowed the airlines of each country to operate unrestricted capacity on the route subject to periodic review. An example of such an agreement was the Anglo-American 'Bermuda Agreement' of 1946. Under this agreement each government was entitled to designate one or more airlines for specific routes between the UK and USA. The respective governments were then required to accept the designated airlines, providing they met national operating standards, and grant a licence to such an operator. Each country can still however impose conditions regarding prices to be charged, type of aircraft, etc before granting a permit. The second type of agreement concluded was more restrictive in that it allocated a fixed proportion of total route capacity to each country. Bi-lateral agreements normally only cover scheduled traffic and not charter flights. In 1977 the original 1946 Bermuda agreement was renegotiated by the UK and USA governments.

When agreements such as Bermuda are made between countries it is each country's responsibility to provide a suitable mechanism for deciding the designated airlines. In the USA and UK there were established official agencies to regulate the licensing procedure, called the Civil Aeronautics Board (CAB) and Civil Aviation Authority (CAA) respectively. Both agencies highly regulated their respective industries but in the late 1970s de-regulation of the US industry occurred. In the UK it was the Civil Aviation Act 1971 which established the CAA and set out its statutory duties. This Act sets up the CAAs functions as licensing airlines operating both internally and externally to the UK. Any aircraft beginning or ending its flight in the UK must have a licence to do so. An airline must make an application to the CAA as did Laker Airways, and more recently BMA (October 1981) to obtain the appropriate route licence. The CAA receives any objections to the applications and conducts a hearing before finally making its decision. In the Laker case the decision was positive whereas with BMA the licence to operate a Heathrow to Glasgow shuttle was refused. The refused applicant can appeal to the Secretary of State who has the power to direct the Authority to reverse or vary its decision. Additionally, the CAA also regulates fares and where inclusive tours are involved the price of the tour.

In carrying out its functions as described above, the 1971 Act sets out four general objectives. Section 3(1) of the Act states:
'It shall be the duty of the Authority to perform the functions conferred on it otherwise than by this section in a manner which it considers is best calculated

'a) to secure that British airlines provide air transport services which satisfy all substantial categories of public demand (so far as British airlines may reasonably be expected to provide such services) at the lowest charges consistent with a high standard of safety in operating the services and an economic return to efficient operators on the sums invested in providing the services and with securing the sound development of the civil air transport industry of the UK;

'b) to secure that at least one major British airline which is not controlled by the British Airways Board has opportunities to participate in providing, on charter and other terms, the air transport services mentioned in the previous paragraph;

'c) subject to the preceding paragraphs, to encourage the civil air transport industry of the UK to increase the contribution which it makes towards a favourable balance of payments for the UK and towards the prosperity of the UK; and

'd) subject to the preceding paragraphs, to further the reasonable interests of users of air transport services.'

These objectives were expressed in general terms, thus in accordance with the Act, the Secretary of State for Trade also gives the CAA policy guidance on how it should carry out its duties. Section 3(2) of the Act states:

'. . . the Secretary of State may from time to time, after consultation with the Authority, give guidance to the Authority in writing with respect to the performance of the functions conferred upon it . . . and it shall be the duty of the Authority to perform those functions in such a manner as it considers is in accordance with the guidance for the time being given to it . . .'. Section 3(2) stated that no guidance shall be given to the Authority . . . unless a draft . . . has been approved by a resolution of each House of Parliament.

Finally, Section (4) of the Act confers powers on the Secretary of State to override statutory licensing requirements and general objectives in exceptional circumstances such as national emergency or war. The directives which are issued cannot be challenged in the courts but only questioned by MPs in the House of Commons.

This distinction between the 'guidance' of section (3) and the directive of section (4) is important, and is referred to later.

Before leaving the description of regulation on the industry, the role of the other body involved must be described. The fixing of fares on international services has since World War II been determined by the traffic conferences of 'The International Air Transport Association' (IATA) subject to individual government approval. IATA was established in 1946 after the Bermuda conference since previously the airlines involved had fixed their own fares. IATA is principally a trade association of most of the world's scheduled airlines which derived its power over fare regulation principally because of the implicit approval given by governments. To its supporters it was a necessary body to facilitate a co-ordinated system of air transport. To its critics it was simply a producers' cartel aimed at eliminating price competition between airlines in the interest of mutually excessive profits. According to one critic IATA resulted in 'an over-priced product, an over-governed industry, and in turn inefficient airline operations'.

On the important and profitable North Atlantic route IATA regulation was particularly strong with the airlines of British Airways, Pan-American and TWA sharing the route. IATA in its post-war form came to an end in 1978 after the Montreal conference decisions. IATA changed its constitution to allow member airlines to voluntarily adhere to the fare decisions made or alternatively opt out and merely content themselves with the other benefits of the trade association. Under the various pressures to which they were subject, the US international carriers withdrew so leading to the de-regulation of the US industry. Of course, some airlines such as Laker Airways were not members of IATA and so were free to disregard its fare rules even before the 1978 change.

It was this tri-partite system of regulation – Bermuda agreement, CAA and IATA – which was in existence when the Laker skytrain operation first began. It is this aspect of the study which is now examined in more detail.

The Skytrain enterprise

Shortly after the formation of the CAA in April 1972 Laker Airways applied for a route licence to operate a non-reservation service between London and New York. The idea of such a service took the established airlines by surprise. Laker's submission to the CAA rested on his case that there existed a potential market demand for such a service which at present was uncatered for by existing airlines. They claimed that the creation of this service would not lead to a significant diversion of existing traffic from established carriers. During August 1972 the CAA conducted hearings into Laker's application. Until Laker's application the existing British carrier of British Airways was protected in its near monopoly position by an effective entry barrier in the form of the licensing procedure described. BA feared a loss of traffic to Skytrain and doubted the existence of such a market which they had never developed. Formal objections were lodged with the CAA supported by BCAL. In the event the CAA overruled the objections having taken into account its objectives under the Act, in particular s. 3(1)(a). They recognised that there was a demand for such a service and that the applicants had enough experience and finance to support the operation. The only reservation was the question of traffic diversion especially from Gatwick. Consequently the service was to operate from Stanstead not Gatwick as Laker had proposed and was to be limited to a daily capacity equivalent to a Boeing 707 during the winter period 1 October to 31 March. These modifications were to protect existing carriers from losing traffic especially in the winter months when load factors were low. The licence was granted for ten years starting in 1973.

A second step was to apply to the Civil Aeronautics Board for a permit in the US. The CAB response was favourable subject to approval by the President. In anticipation of a successful outcome Laker invested between £6-£7 million in three DC-10's and crew training. 1973 brought further delays in the US and it was not until December that the CAB positive decision was sent to the US President for confirmation. Despite pressure from the UK government on the US for an early decision, no confirmation was forthcoming. In December of 1974 events began to move in the UK but not in Laker's favour. Firstly, British Airways, supported by Dan Air, tried again to protect its monopoly position by applying to the CAA to revoke the licence. BA argued that since 1972 economic conditions had changed drastically for the worse. Market demand had fallen together with significant increases in costs caused by the rise in the price of fuel. This combination of increasing costs of production and decreasing market demand was a classic recipe for incurring substantial losses. Specifically BA made five points against Skytrain:

1 market demand for this service had disappeared;
2 there would be serious diversion of traffic because of the decrease in traffic volume;
3 the US carriers would retaliate; and
4 as a result the UK balance of payments would be adversely affected;
5 advance Booking Charters now catered for the market targeted by Skytrain. Any increase in market supply resulting from the introduction of Skytrain would exacerbate the difficult position of existing carriers especially British Airways.

Laker defended the licence by emphasising the investment already made in Skytrain as well as on other matters. The CAA hearings were in January 1975 and in February confirmed its original decision. They believed that the enterprise was likely to be commercially successful and but for US delay would already be in operation. At the same time permission was granted to increase capacity and transfer the operation to Gatwick. Despite protests from BCAL and the British Airports Authority the CAA granted these requests.

However, a second and more serious threat to Skytrain emerged in the announcement of December 1974 by the Secretary of State of a civil aviation policy review which resulted in a statement by the Secretary to the Commons in July 1975. It was a complete reversal of previous policy when the Secretary of State declared . . .
'in future it should be our general policy not to permit competition between United Kingdom airlines on long-haul scheduled services, and, therefore not to licence more than one United Kingdom airline on any given long-haul route . . . I have looked carefully at the Skytrain service . . . it would divert traffic away from existing services and, in particular, damage British Airways . . . in these circumstances the Skytrain service cannot be allowed to start'.

So in mid-1975 the Secretary of State had intervened and totally overruled the two previous decisions of the legally constituted CAA and protected the monopoly position of British Airways. The reaction by Washington was equally decisive in that upon learning of the UK decision, they withdrew the permit which was still unsigned by the White House.

In the UK the Secretary of State determined how the policy decision might be implemented and decided that a new policy guidance was required. In February 1976 the White Paper entitled 'Future Civil Aviation Policy' was issued which contained in paragraph 7 . . . 'In the case of long-haul scheduled services . . . the Authority should not . . . license more than one British Airline to serve the same route . . . The Authority should review existing licences and exemptions in the light of this paragraph and take appropriate action'.

In paragraph 8 it said that this should not prevent the licensing of another British airline to provide a scheduled service within the British Airways sphere of interest provided British Airways has given its consent.

In accordance with s. 3(2) of the 1971 Act the Secretary needed the approval of both Houses of Parliament to call on the CAA to follow the policy guidelines. Both Houses gave their approval despite reservations by the Lords. The impact on Laker Airways was immediate and potentially disastrous. At this point British Airways appeared to have successfully shut the door to any new entrant to the industry for the foreseeable future. The existence of a monopoly posed the threat of inefficient operations coupled with a lack of attention to market demand and customer choice.

Laker responded on the next day following parliamentary approval of the guidelines by issuing a writ claiming that the Secretary of State had acted unlawfully. Justice Mocatta heard the case with expedition and delivered judgement on 30 July 1976. He found that the Secretary of State had exceeded the powers granted to him by the Act and was not entitled to withdraw the designation of Laker Airways.

The defendants, the Department of Trade, appealed against this decision, which was heard before Lords Denning, Roskill and Lawton sitting in the Court of appeal. In his judgement Lord Denning stated that there were three issues of law. Lord Denning's judgment stated:

Ultra vires

'The first is whether the Secretary of State was acting beyond his lawful powers when he gave the new policy guidance to the Civil Aviation Authority.

In determining this point, I have found much help from the well-reasoned decisions of the Civil Aviation Authority, not only in 1972, when they granted the licence to Laker Airways, but also in 1975 when they refused to revoke it. It is plain that they applied most conscientiously and sensibly the four general objectives set out in s. 3(1)(a), (b), (c) and (d) of the 1971 Act, as amplified and supplemented by the 1972 policy guidance. The new policy guidance of 1976 cuts right across those statutory objectives. It lays down a new policy altogether. Whereas the statutory objectives made it clear that the British Airways Board was not to have a monopoly − but that at least one other British airline should have an opportunity to participate − the new policy guidance says that the British Airways Board is to have a monopoly. No competition is to be allowed. And no other British airline is to be licensed unless the British Airways had given its consent. This guidance was not a mere temporary measure. It was to last for a considerable period of years.

Those provisions disclose so complete a reversal of policy that to my mind the White Paper cannot be regarded as giving 'guidance' at all. In marching terms it does not say 'right incline' or 'left incline'. It says 'right about turn'. That is not guidance, but the reverse of it.

There is no doubt that the Secretary of State acted with the best of motives in formulating this new policy − and it may well have been the right policy − but I am afraid that he went about it in the wrong way.

Seeing that the old policy had been laid down in an Act of Parliament, then, in order to reverse it, he could have introduced an amending bill and got Parliament to sanction it. He was advised, apparently, that it was not necessary, and that it could be done by 'guidance'. That, I think, was a mistake. And Laker Airways are entitled to complain of it, at any rate in its impact on them. It was in this respect ultra vires and the judge was right so to declare.

Prerogative

The Attorney-General contended that the power of the Secretary of State 'to withdraw' the designation was a prerogative power which could not be examined in the courts. It was a power arising under a treaty which, he said, was outside the cognisance of the courts. The Attorney-General recognised that, by withdrawing the designation, the Secretary of State would put a stop to Skytrain, but he said that he could do it all the same. No matter that Laker Airways had expended £6 million to £7 million on the faith of the designation, the Secretary of State could withdraw it without paying a penny compensation.

Seeing that the prerogative is a discretionary power to be exercised for the public good it follows that its exercise can be examined by the courts. I turn, therefore, to examine the power in question in this case — the power to withdraw a designation.

In examining the power of the Secretary of State to withdraw the designation, it is necessary to see just how far Skytrain had got. Laker Airways, after full inquiry, had been granted a licence by the authorities in England. They had been designated as a carrier for the North Atlantic route. They had been granted a permit by the authorities in the USA. Skytrain was ready to take off. It only awaited clearance from control. The one thing that remained was for the President to sign the USA permit; but this was little more than a formality, seeing that the President was under a treaty obligation to sign it 'without undue delay'. He could be expected to do so in the near future. Unless someone intervened, he would do so. The question is: was it proper for the Secretary of State at that stage to stop it himself? Could he do it by withdrawing the designation, as he said in February 1976 that he intended to do?

In answering this question, it is important to notice that, if there was a proper case for stopping Skytrain, there were available some perfectly good means of doing it. They were already provided by the 1971 Act. One particular means was provided by s. 4. Under that section the Secretary of State could himself get the licence revoked. He could direct the Civil Aviation Authority to revoke it and they would have to obey. But this was only in carefully defined circumstances, such as in the interests of national security, or good international relations. For instance, if the Secretary of State thought that it was in the interests of good relations with the USA that Skytrain should be stopped, he could direct the Civil Aviation authority to revoke the licence; and they would have to obey without holding any inquiry or hearing Laker Airways at all. But in this case the Secretary of State did not give any direction under s. 4. So, presumably, the circumstances did not exist so as to permit him to do so. Another means of stopping Skytrain would be for the British Airways Board to apply again to the Civil Aviation Authority asking for the licence to be revoked — for instance, on the ground that traffic would be diverted from them. But, in that case, there would have to be a fresh inquiry. There would have to be a hearing at which Laker Airways could state their case. An independent and expert body would make the decision.

Seeing then that those statutory means were available for stopping Skytrain if there was a proper case for it, the question is whether the Secretary of State can stop it by other means? Can he do it by withdrawing the designation? Can he do indirectly that which he cannot do directly? Can he displace the statute by invoking a prerogative? If he could do this it would mean that, by a sidewind, Laker Airways Ltd would be deprived of the protection which the Act affords them. There would be no inquiry, no hearing, no safeguard against injustice. The Secretary of State could do it off his own head by withdrawing the designation without a word to anyone. To my mind such a procedure was never contemplated by the Act. The Secretary of State was mistaken in thinking that he could do it. No doubt he did it with the best of motives. Nevertheless, he went about it, I think, in the wrong way. He misdirected himself as to his powers. And it is well-established law that, if a discretionary power is exercised under the influence of a misdirection, it is not properly exercised, and the court can say so.

Conclusion
We have considered this case at some length because of its constitutional importance. It is a serious matter for the courts to declare that a Minister of the Crown has exceeded his powers. So serious that we think hard before doing it. But there comes a point when it has to be done. These courts have the authority, had I would add the duty, in a proper case, when called on to inquire into the exercise of a discretionary power by a Minister or his department. If it found that the power has been exercised improperly or mistakenly so as to impinge unjustly on the legitimate rights or interests of the subject, then these court must so declare. They stand, as ever, between the executive and the subject, alert, as Lord Atkin said in a famous passage, 'alert to see that any coercive action is justified in law': see *Liversidge* v. *Anderson*. To which I would add, 'alert to see that a discretionary power is not exceeded or misused'. In this case the judge has upheld this principle. He has declared that the Minister did exceed his powers. I agree with him. I would dismiss the appeal.

After the decision by the Court of Appeal the way was clear for the successful introduction of the Skytrain services which finally began on 26 September 1977 from Gatwick using a DC-10.

The economic implications of Skytrain

Having examined the long struggle which was necessary to secure the launch of Skytrain it is now possible to comment briefly on some of the economic factors involved. Laker was a UK government-designated airline operating services to New York and Los Angeles having a licence running until 31 December 1982. Prior to the Skytrain victory the North Atlantic route was reserved for the state-owned British Airways enjoying a monopoly position as far as British carriers were concerned. Laker Airways was formed only in March 1966 to operate charter flights and is wholly owned by Sir Freddie Laker. As a private enterprise organisation Laker Airways' success or failure was totally dependent upon market success. Under private enterprise freedom is laid upon the individual both as a consumer and factor of production. Laker as the entrepreneur had to co-ordinate the factors of production to produce a product which would satisfy market demand so that revenue would exceed costs. The reward is profit but since market demand can never be certain there was the considerable danger of failure. As a private company Laker did not have state financial support to cushion Skytrain against such risks.

On entering such a monopoly (or oligopoly if foreign carriers are included) market, Laker found itself confronted by obstacles from the existing carriers supported by the government. Both the Secretary of State Mr. Peter Shore, and his Under Secretary, made adverse statements about Skytrain. The disputes over Skytrain covered several areas. Firstly, the government and others denied the existence of a 'Skytrain market'. The Under-Secretary said, 'I do not accept that the market at which Skytrain is aimed will be neglected as a result of the service being scrapped'. The CAA clearly disagreed when they said, '. . . there is a substantial demand for cheap, no frills, short notice, mass travel which at present is not adequately catered for . . .'. Research undertaken in 1975 by Market and Opinion Research International (MORI) conclusively confirmed the existence of such a market. When Skytrain began operating there was no doubt about the existence of the market. In the summer of 1978 queues of up to 3000 people developed wanting Skytrain tickets. It was significant that the CAA recognised the existence of such a market and was prepared to accept its responsibilities under s. 3(1)(a) of the 1971 Act.

A second area of dispute was over the question to what extent Skytrain would divert existing traffic and seriously harm BA. Clearly, the attitude of the government was that serious diversion would occur. BAs attitude to Skytrain seemed to vary from objections in the early days to one which did not appear to regard Skytrain as serious opposition.

Another area of controversy concerned s. 3(1)(c) of the 1971 Act which takes into account the effects on the UK Balance of Payments. In 1975 the Under Secretary of State stated that his department estimated the loss to the UKs balance of payments to be of the order of £1 million per annum. Once again Laker disputed this statement and submitted detailed forecast figures to the government.

There was little doubt that the Skytrain enterprise was successful, since during the first nine months of operation nearly 144 000 passengers were carried. A second skytrain to Los Angeles commenced in September 1978. The response of other rival airlines was to follow suit and introduce various reduced fares on the North Atlantic service. This led to the current position where regulated pricing has virtually disappeared and been replaced by fierce competition for passengers. There is little doubt that Laker's Skytrain acted as the catalyst for this change.

Postscript 1977 – 82

In the first year of its introduction the Skytrain service proved enormously successful, so much so that the enterprise attracted adverse publicity caused by media coverage of large numbers of prospective passengers crowding Gatwick Airport for hours, even days, waiting for empty seats on Skytrain. Inevitably the success of the Gatwick to New York service lead to the extension of the Skytrain principle, and services to Miami and Los Angeles were introduced.

Applications to operate a Skytrain service to European cities and Hong Kong were not however successful. Throughout this period Laker Airways continued a policy of expansion by ordering no fewer than eight DC-10's and ten Airbuses, all of which were to be financed from bank loans. In April 1981 Freddie Laker said 'Today it would appear that our big competitors have accepted that we are here to stay; . . . I see 1982 and 1983 as very good years'. Four months later in August Laker's financial problems were such as to require a rescheduling of the vast debts of the Airline. Throughout the autumn of 1981 the banks involved attempted to solve this problem. In December, on Christmas Eve, Samuel Montagu, Laker's banking advisors, announced a survival package. However, by January 1982 severe problems faced the Airline. Passenger traffic and resulting cash flow to the Airline was well below expectations. In addition the Civil Aviation Authority refused to revise their requirement for a £5 million injection into the Airline's accounts. McDonnell Douglas and General Electric had agreed to loan this £5 million to Laker in December, but now General Electric withdrew its £1 million share of the loan. On February 3 the CAA stated that after further examination of traffic forecast and cash flow figures they were no longer certain that the £5 million was itself adequate. The following day Laker was summoned to the Midlands offices to hear the news that his company was in danger of trading while insolvent and losing the CAA licence. Despite eleventh hour optimism from Freddie Laker the inevitable end occurred on Friday 5 February when Laker requested the Clydesdale Bank to call in the receiver.

Summary of Skytrain history

1972
April 6	Application to CAA for licence.
August 1	Hearing by CAA Application granted.
Sept 26	10 year licence issued by CAA.
Oct 6	DC-10 aircraft contract signed.
Nov 16	Two DC-10 aircraft delivered.
Dec 28	Skytrain appeal by BCAL dismissed. No appeal by BA.

1973
Feb 6	Laker designated as carrier by UK government.
Dec 10	Hearing by CAB in Washington.

1974
March 13	CAB judge recommends in favour of Skytrain.
May 25	Third DC-10 aircraft delivered.
June 1	CAB recommendation sent to US President.
Oct 4	Secretary of State affirms in a letter to Laker of 'strong representations made to US . . . for early and favourable decision on Skytrain permit.
Dec 3	Department of Trade announces Civil Aviation Policy Review.
Dec 4	BA applies to revoke Skytrain licence. Dan-Air applies for licence suspension.

1975
Feb 5	CAA reject BA and Dan Air applications. No appeal by either party.
July 29	Secretary of State makes statement to the House of Commons reversing Skytrain decision.

1976
Feb	White paper 'Future Civil Aviation Policy' published.
Feb 20	House of Commons approval for Policy Guidance.
March 15	House of Lords approval for Policy Guidance.
March 16	Laker issues writ against Department of Trade.
July 30	Judge Mocatta delivers judgment in the High Court.
Nov 18 – 26	Hearing before the Court of Appeal.
Dec 15	Court of Appeal delivers judgement.

1977
Sept 26	Skytrain service begins from Gatwick to New York.

1982
Feb	Laker Airways goes into liquidation.

5 The consumer

" 'Scorn not the common man' says the age of abundance. 'He may have no soul; his personality may be exactly the same as his neighbour's; and he may not produce anything worth having. But thank God, he consumes.' "

Joseph Wood Krutch 'The Condition called Prosperity', Human Nature and the Human Condition, 1959

Consumers are the most important individuals in the business environment for it is their demand for goods and services which creates the need for the entire business environment. Consumers demand a variety of products and services ranging from the simple to the complex. These demands obviously vary with time and are affected by a number of both individual and interrelated factors. This chapter examines these influences on individual consumer demand, evaluates how suppliers, society and the government influence consumer expenditure and assesses how the law has evolved to regulate consumer transactions.

Theories of individual demand

There are three main theories suggested to interpret individual demand. They are:

  (i) *Marginal utility theory*,
 (ii) *Indifference curve analysis*,
(iii) *Revealed preference theory*.

Of these, perhaps the most easily understood and most widely used explanation of individual demand is marginal utility theory.

Marginal utility theory

In Chapter 1 p. 2 it was explained that products and services are only in demand if they provide consumers with some degree of satisfaction (or as it is termed *'utility'*). An individual product does not inherently possess utility. It only has utility when it provides satisfaction to an individual or a group of consumers. For instance one person may gain considerable enjoyment from a beef steak. The meat, if well prepared, may satisfy the hunger and also delight the taste buds. Another person may gain little or no enjoyment from eating an identical meal. The steak is exactly the same but the individual's perception of the amount of satisfaction that is gained from it differs. Some consumables such as water and air, are necessities for us all, but even these give differing degrees of satisfaction to individual consumers.

Perceived utility

Why then does a consumer enter into a contract to purchase an individual product? Because that consumer believes that it will provide a certain amount of satisfaction. This concept of *perceived utility* is crucial. It is not the *actual utility* that a person gains from a product which makes that person consume it, but the amount of satisfaction he or she *thinks* can be received from it. Obviously the consumer is more aware of the extent of satisfaction received from some goods than from others. If a person has eaten many steaks and has enjoyed them, then more steaks will certainly be enjoyed. But many of the things that consumers buy are first-time purchases. If a person has never eaten an Indian curry then the amount of satisfaction anticipated from that meal is based on the opinion of friends — they suggest enjoyment or otherwise. If a new toothpaste is introduced onto the market a consumer may buy it if he or she is persuaded that the amount of satisfaction (ie cleaner teeth, fresher breath, etc) will be greater than that gained from an existing brand. This will be influenced both by recommendation and by advertising. Thus, the important factor in determining whether or not a product is purchased by a consumer is if that person thinks it will meet individual *taste or preference*. What factors influence taste or preference will be discussed later in this chapter.

It may however be noted here that a total or partial failure of the utility a consumer anticipates in purchasing goods or services may give rise to a liability on the part of the seller who has created or enhanced the anticipation. Controls exist over advertising, some of which are statutory such as those contained in the Trade Descriptions Act 1968. Under this Act an advertisement containing a false trade description may give rise to an offence of applying a false trade description to goods, or supplying or offering to supply goods to which such a description has been applied.

Both the manufacturer in the false trade description, and the retailer who sells the goods may be guilty of an offence. Other less effective controls include the Code of Practice issued by the advertising industry watchdog the Advertising Standards Authority. The Independent Broadcasting Authority also has a detailed code of practice applicable to advertisements broadcast on television and radio.

It should be stressed that legal rights enabling dissatisfied consumers to obtain compensation where they have not obtained satisfaction from the product do not extend to situations where their perceived utility is based upon pure imagination, rather than what they have been told or encouraged to believe by others. An individual who buys a colour television anticipating viewing pleasure has no remedy when the majority of programmes do not appeal.

Quantifying utility
Utility, enjoyment, usefulness, satisfaction are all words which express
the benefit a consumer will gain from a product or service. However,
they do not measure the extent of the benefit. *Great satisfaction, very
enjoyable, nice, poor quality* are expressions which may be used to
indicate the consumer's satisfaction. It is necessary to quantify these
expressions in some way in order to be able to analyse an individual's
demand pattern. One way of doing this is to give a monetary value to
utility. This is not an entirely satisfactory approach as the measure of
utility is crude and inaccurate. For instance if you are extremely
hungry, how much would you be willing to pay for a hot dog − 50p? In
that case you are valuing the hot dog at 50p worth of utility. Even
though the price is only 25p, you would have been willing to pay 50p if
you had been forced to.

Diminishing marginal utility
One must be clear that as a person consumes more of a product the
marginal utility (ie the extra utility gained from each additional unit
consumed) he or she receives from each extra unit of that product will
tend to decline. This is despite the fact that total utility will be increasing
as long as the consumer gains positive satisfaction from each successive
unit consumed. For example if a person is hungry and is given one
cheeseburger, substantial satisfaction may be gained from eating it. It
will alleviate the pangs of hunger and perhaps give the taste buds a treat.
But what if a second cheeseburger is given? If he or she is still hungry it
will also satisfy the appetite and could still taste delicious. But will it be
enjoyed as much as the first? It is doubtful. He or she is likely to gain
less utility from it. And what about a third or a fourth cheeseburger?
The consumer may be very hungry or may be a glutton but it is probable
that satisfaction from each additional burger will decrease as they are
given more and more. This is a characteristic of most products −
greater consumption means a fall in marginal utility. This is termed
diminishing marginal utility and will certainly affect the level of consumption and the choice made between cheeseburgers and other
products which could be consumed. If the consumer is to choose
between three products each will have diminishing marginal utility but
of course each will have utility which diminishes at different rates. (You
may be able to eat ten meals out in a week but you may be reluctant to
spend the time watching ten movies − despite the fact that you may
prefer one movie in a month to one meal out.)

Utility expressed in money terms
In order to interpret a consumer's possible purchases it is necessary to
express utility in money terms. A normal consumer will not consciously
value the utility anticipated from everything that is bought. However if
utility is valued then it is much easier to explain why consumers act as
they do. Using steaks as an example, a meat lover may gain £2 worth of

209

satisfaction/utility from the first steak. He or she would enjoy a second, third and fourth steak but each would give less and less utility in money terms. Total utility would increase but at a decreasing rate. See Fig 5.1.

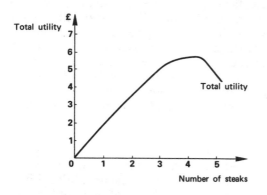

Fig 5.1 Total utility a consumer gains from eating steaks

It will be noted that the total utility actually declines if the individual consumes a fifth steak. This may be because the consumer has eaten sufficient and the last steak makes him or her feel ill. In fact it gives *disutility* and so total utility will fall. If the same situation is expressed in terms of marginal utility it could be shown either as a schedule or as a graph. These are shown in Table 5.1 and Fig 5.2.

Steaks	Marginal utility (in £)
1	£2
2	£1.75
3	£1.50
4	£0.75
5	− £1.75

Table 5.1 An individual consumer's marginal utility schedule for steaks

Some economists attempt to equate the consumer's marginal utility curve with the individual demand curve. This is something of an over-simplification. In fact the marginal utility curve simply shows the level of utility a consumer will gain from a succession of purchases and not what he or she will necessarily buy at different price levels.

Price of the product
There is clearly much more to a purchasing decision than the satisfaction that a particular product gives to an individual. A drinker may get considerable enjoyment from a bottle of whisky and yet buys beer which gives less satisfaction. Why? Because of the *price of the product*.

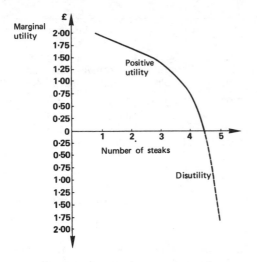

Fig 5.2   An individual's marginal utility gained from eating steaks

Either consciously or subconsciously each purchase made is, in fact, an evaluation of the relative value of perceived utility against the price. If a consumer believes he or she will gain £5.50 worth of utility from a bottle of whisky and yet a shop asks for £6 then the whisky will remain unsold.

Consumer surplus
A purchaser, if acting rationally, will only buy a product if it gives a *consumer surplus*, ie the perceived utility is greater than price. Using the same example if the person really wanted the whisky − to celebrate the New Year perhaps − then he or she may believe it will give £7 worth of utility. If the price is £6.50 then he or she would gain a 50p consumer surplus.

Purchases with an unlimited budget
Consider a consumer who has an unlimited budget and has only three things to spend money on − records, meals out and concert visits. Each of these costs £5 and each gives the consumer a different amount of utility. As already mentioned, the utility of additional purchases will decline, but not necessarily at the same rate. Table 5.2 illustrates a theoretical utility schedule for one consumer faced with these three choices.

Quantity	Records cost £5		Meals cost £5		Concerts cost £5	
	Marginal utility	Marginal consumer surplus	Marginal utility	Marginal consumer surplus	Marginal utility	Marginal consumer surplus
1	£7.50	2.50	8.00	3.00	9.00	4.00
2	7.00	2.00	7.15	2.15	8.00	3.00
3	6.50	1.50	7.00	2.00	7.05	2.05
4	6.00	1.00	6.95	1.95	6.50	1.50
5	4.70	−0.39	6.00	1.00	5.25	1.25
6	4.25	−0.75	5.00	0.00	4.75	−0.25

Table 5.2 An individual's utility schedule for records/meals/concerts in one month

In these circumstances what would a consumer with unlimited expenditure do? He or she would certainly buy four records for this would provide £7 worth of consumer surplus. He or she would also eat out on five occasions for again this would provide a consumer surplus, in this case of £10.10. It is clear from the Table that he or she would also see five concerts − £11.80 consumer surplus. But is that all that he or she would consume? This really depends on the individual. If a fifth record was bought or a sixth concert seen the consumer would certainly be acting irrationally for each would give a negative marginal consumer surplus (or more correctly, a *marginal consumer deficit*) − in this case 30p deficit on the fifth record and 25p deficit on the sixth concert. The difficult question is whether or not he or she would eat the sixth meal in a restaurant. Table 5b shows that the same value of satisfaction would be gained from the sixth meal as the consumer would be required to pay for it − marginal consumer surplus is zero. In that situation the consumer is indifferent as to whether or not he or she eats out. It makes no difference if he or she enjoys the meal (and gains £5 worth of satisfaction) or keeps the cash (£5 in his or her pocket). This is without doubt the last meal out the consumer will consider buying this month for any additional meal will be likely to give a marginal consumer deficit. So it is at this point the decision to consume or not to consume is most crucial.

However in most consumer purchases the idea can be simplified by saying that at the point of consumption where marginal consumer surplus is zero then there is usually an alternative product/service which gives a marginal consumer surplus and so the consumer will consume the alternative. Only in the situation where no product gives a distinct surplus will the consumer turn to the other main alternative − *saving*. But it must be noted that saving is in fact a form of *deferred consumption*, ie the consumer foregoes present utility for that which will be gained in the future from expenditure then. Only a miser gains satisfaction from saving for savings sake. Most people have saving so as to allow them to gain satisfaction from goods/services purchased at a later date. These will, or at least the consumer believes will, give a certain level of satisfaction/utility which is worth waiting for. If you save for retirement this is because you think that a 'nest egg' at sixty-five will give you more satisfaction than a life of extravagance at twenty, thirty or forty. As has been already noted, this is based purely on the individual's perception of the utility which may be gained. If the consumer dies at the age of 55 then a retirement pension is of no value, and of no utility whatsoever.

Utility in relation to price
The idea of consumer surplus is based on two factors:

   (i) *the amount of utility that the consumer believes he or she will gain from the product*;
   (ii) *the price of that product*.

A surplus is only anticipated if perceived utility is greater than the price which the supplier asks for the product. This is important if the price of a product changes for it will vary the extent of the surplus. In the example given in the table, if the price of records is raised to £6, either because of the manufacturer's decision or a government taxation increase, and this price change is not reflected in the price of alternative purchases, then the extent of a consumer's purchases will change. In this case the consumer may not buy more than three records. (Check this against Table 5.2.) The consumer will therefore be at the crucial decision point on the purchase of the fourth record. It is at this level of consumption that he or she becomes indifferent. Obviously if the price of all products changes then the consumer's surplus will be reduced. But it is clear that in the society in which the business environment is situated then the price level is almost certainly going to rise because of *inflationary circumstances*. To take this example to the extreme, all marginal consumer surpluses on any products will continue to fall with inflation and so eventually no product is worth buying. In reality the consumer's valuation of the marginal utility received from each product is adjusted in response to inflationary pressures. You might have thought that a record gave you £4 worth of satisfaction a year ago but because of your revaluation of prices it is now worth £5 − even though the record itself has not changed. Income, of course, will also usually rise with inflation.

Purchases within a limited budget
In the previous example it was assumed that the consumer had an unlimited budget and so could continue to purchase records/meals/concert visits until the marginal consumer surplus from each product was zero. Actually most people have a limited budget. Consider the purchasing decisions of the consumer if expenditure is restricted to £25 a month on these three things (refer back to Table 5.2).

In a situation where money is limited, a rational consumer will try to maximise consumer surplus. Thus in this instance he or she will buy the products in the order of decreasing marginal utility. If all prices were £5 then the first £5 would be spent on a visit to a concert (marginal utility surplus of £4.00) then either have a meal out or see a second concert (the consumer is indifferent since both give £3.00 marginal utility surplus). With £25 to spend the purchases will be:

	Cost	Total utility	Utility surplus
2 concert visits	£10	£17	£ 7
2 meals out	£10	£15.15	£ 5.15
1 record	£ 5	£ 7.50	£ 2.50
	£25	£39.65	£14.65

This will give maximum utility consumer surplus within the limited budget – ie £14.65. (Thus the consumer spends £25 and gains £39.65 of utility.)

Income as a determinant of consumer demand
If the consumer's income increases he or she will be able to extend the limit of total consumer surplus by buying extra products, as long as they provide a marginal consumer surplus. In the example an extra £5 in income would allow the consumer to have another meal out (£2.05 in marginal consumer surplus) an extra £10 would mean that not only could he or she have an extra meal but also another record or another meal out. Thus an increase will mean that a consumer will be likely to consume more of those products which will give the greatest marginal consumer surplus. There is however an exception to this trend. Some products can be described as *inferior*, ie they are purchased only because a consumer has insufficient income to purchase another product of better quality – a *superior product*. For instance an individual may be forced to buy 'cheap jeans' rather than 'Levis' because they cost less. If the consumer has more money to spend he or she may not necessarily buy more of the poorer quality jeans. In fact they may not be bought at all. The greater spending power allows the consumer the choice to buy 'cheap' or 'Levi' jeans and as greater satisfaction is gained from wearing 'Levis' he or she may not buy any of the cheaper jeans and transfer consumption spending to those of the higher quality (which necessarily cost more).

Because the pricing of goods raises varying expectations of utility for the consumer, if he or she is acting rationally the law provides a degree of protection if the price level suggests a standard or quality of product which is not in fact realised. In the case of goods the price at which they are sold is a major factor in deciding whether they meet the required legal standard of quality – known as *merchantable quality*. The legal rights of a consumer to return a pair of jeans costing £5.00 which have split with a minimum of use, are probably extremely limited. A consumer gets what he or she pays for.

Changing tastes or fashions
It would be wrong to assume that the marginal utility that a person gains from a product remains constant. The influence of taste or fashion will affect the amount of utility which is gained from purchases.

The price of other products
As the previous section noted the price of a particular product is obviously a major determinant of its demand. However the price of other products is also likely to influence it. This can be categorised as follows. The price of:

a) *substitute products*,
b) *complementary products*,
c) *other goods purchased by the consumer*, will all influence the demand for a particular good.

a) *substitute products*
These are products which a consumer is willing to substitute for the goods in question. For instance Levi jeans may be an acceptable substitute for Wranglers. A consumer will obtain about the same level of utility from either brand of jeans. Thus if the price of Levis falls and that of Wranglers does not then the consumer surplus will be greater if the consumer buys Levis. This results in a relationship between the price of Levis and the demand for Wranglers − a fall in the price of a substitute will result in the decrease in the demand for a product. The reciprocal situation is of course also true − a rise in the price of a substitute will mean an increase in the demand for a product. The closeness of the substitutability is important. The nearer that the level of utility a consumer gets from one product to the level of utility from another product, then the closer a substitute they are − and the more likely that a change of price will influence the demand for the other.

b) *complementary products*
If goods are complementary this means that the level of price of it will correspondingly affect the level of demand for its complement − but in the opposite direction. For instance if the price of large cars falls then the demand for a complementary product, eg petrol, oil, will tend to rise. Thus it is an inverse relationship between complements.

An increase in price of a complement results in a decrease in demand of the other product. A fall in price of a complement results in an increase in demand of the other product.

c) *other goods purchased by the consumer*
If the price of any good purchased by a consumer increases then it

would be likely that this would change the level of demand for other goods which he or she usually purchases. This is especially true if the good which suffers the price increase is a necessity, ie it has no close substitute. This would mean that the consumer has little alternative but to transfer expenditure from luxuries or less necessary products to be able to pay the higher price required to buy the necessity.

Perhaps the clearest example of this is in clothing. A woman may buy a blouse because of the perceived level of utility it gives her. The blouse is 'in vogue' and she gains satisfaction from the admiring looks of friends. However as fashions change the blouse may become 'passé'. Her friends no longer regard it as smart and despite the fact that the blouse itself has not changed it has decreased in value. That is value determined by the amount of utility or satisfaction that it gives to the wearer. A consumer may now think again about buying a similar blouse even though the price has stayed the same because the utility it will give − and of course the consumer surplus − will have fallen and so it is no longer a desirable purchase.

The influence of taste and fashion is crucial to many consumer purchases. Unfortunately it allows manufacturers, who are able to influence taste and fashion, to achieve a prime objective − *built-in obsolescence*. If a manufacturer was to produce a product advertised as 'long lasting' which disintegrated within six months of purchase, this could result in an action for breach of contract by a dissatisfied purchaser or even a prosecution for an offence under the Trade Descriptions Act. This would, in effect, be because the product failed to meet the suggested standard indicated by the producer's advertising statement. However this is exactly what a change in fashion does. The product itself is *essentially* still satisfactory but the consumer no longer gains the satisfaction he or she seeks from it and so is forced to purchase another product (which is, of course, often from the same producer). An item of clothing, which is no longer fashionable, does not lose its inherent characteristics: warmth, coverage, durability, but does lose its implied features − fashionableness, trendiness, and so will no longer provide the perceived utility which the consumer expected from it when first bought. This is the sales director's dream, a system of legitimate obsolescence.

Indifference curve analysis

The second method of interpreting the behaviour of the individual consumer is by using the *concept of indifference*. This overcomes the problem encountered in the previous method of having to quantify utility in monetary terms. This attempts to explain how an individual can achieve a balanced level of satisfaction through various combinations of two or more products consumed. A simplified example will explain it more clearly.

A consumer restricts purchases to two products – food and drink. A certain level of each must be consumed in order to survive but once the subsistence level is exceeded, the consumer is free to decide whether to consume more drink or more food. Like all consumers, he or she seeks to maximise levels of satisfaction and so attempts to achieve that mix of products which will give the most utility. However there are several alternative combinations of products which give the same level of satisfaction. With any of these purchase combinations the consumer is equally satisfied – indifferent to which combination of best alternatives to be chosen for no one specific combination gives a uniquely higher level of utility.

This is illustrated in diagramatic form in Fig 5.3.

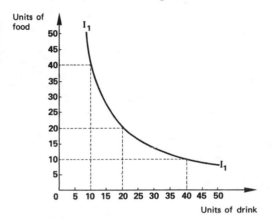

Fig 5.3 Possible combinations of food and drink giving equal satisfaction to a consumer

The figure shown is the consumer's indifference curve. The consumer gains an equal level of satisfaction from any combination shown by the curve, eg he or she is equally happy with 40 units of food and 10 units of drink, as with 20 units of each or 10 units of food and 40 units of drink. Neither gives any more or any less utility. The consumer is indifferent to these choices. Why then does the curve shape the way it does? This is because of the *diminishing marginal rate of substitution*. This means the more of a product that a consumer has then less of an alternative product he or she must be offered in order to persuade him or her to give up any of the initial product.

In the example if the consumer has 40 units of food and only 10 of drink he or she is willing to give up 10 food units in exchange for only $2\frac{1}{2}$ units of drink. Yet if he or she only has 15 units of food and 25 of drink then to be an acceptable exchange 15 units of drink must be offered if he or she is to lose 5 of food. The reverse case involving the diminishing marginal rate of substitution for drink is obviously also true.

If the consumer has only 9 units of food, this is the bare subsistence level and no matter how much drink is offered he or she will not give up any more food.

It is of course possible for the consumer to change the level of utility – either positively or negatively. Adapting the diagram previously used it is shown in Fig 5.4 that an increase in one commodity without a decrease in the other will improve the consumer's satisfaction.

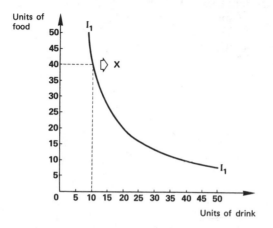

Fig 5.4   Increasing a consumer's level of satisfaction

If the consumer is currently at indifference level I, with 40 food and 10 drink units then in order to increase the level of satisfaction he or she must be given more of one or the other or both. The most dramatic increase in satisfaction would be noticed if the consumer were given more drink (with only 10 units of drink, each extra unit still gives considerable marginal utility). Thus if he or she were given 5 more units of drink without any reduction in food supply then the consumer would move to a higher level of satisfaction. At this new level the indifference curve obviously changes – and in fact would move to the right. (If he or she had 40 food and 10 drink units and lost some drink without gaining food the indifference curve would shift to the left.)

Fig 5.5 illustrates that consumers do not simply have one indifference curve but an infinite number – too many obviously to illustrate. But each indifference curve which is further from the origin means that the consumer is at a higher level of satisfaction (in Fig 5.5 any point on I_2 gives greater satisfaction than I_1 which similarly is a better situation than I_3).

Which indifference curve will the consumer be found on? This will depend on the extent of his or her budget and the prices of the respective products and is called the *budget line*. This is illustrated using the same example (see Fig 5.6).

218

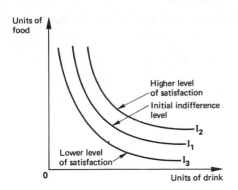

Fig 5.5 Varying levels of indifference

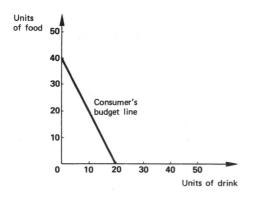

Fig 5.6 Relative prices of food and drink in relation to the consumer's budget

If one unit of food costs £1 and one unit of drink costs £2 and the consumer has £40 to spend he or she can have either 40 units of food or 20 units of drink — or a combination of the two, eg 10 units of food and 15 units of drink.

A rational consumer spending all his or her income on food and drink will never be at a point within the budget line as this will not maximise his or her satisfaction.

If the consumer's indifference curves are now superimposed on Fig 5.6 showing the budget line it is possible to identify the consumer's best combination of purchases (see Fig 5.7).

The consumer's budget constraint allows a number of alternatives. For instance he or she could buy 5 units of drink and 30 units of food (and be on curve I_3) or 5 units of food and $12\frac{1}{2}$ units of drink (and still be on I_3) or purchase 20 units of food and 10 drink and so be on I_1. This third alternative clearly gives the greater level of satisfaction. (Why can't a higher level be reached? — insufficient income.) So it is at the point where the budget line is just touching (tangential) to an indifference

219

curve that the consumer will gain the greatest level of satisfaction (point X in Fig 5.7).

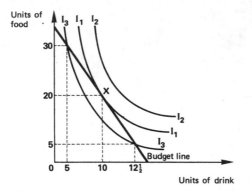

Fig 5.7 A consumer's best possible combination of purchases within an existing budget

Changes in income

The consumer's highest level of satisfaction was shown in Fig 5.7 to be at the point where the budget line just touches indifference curve I_1. However his or her level of satisfaction/utility could change if his or her income rises or falls. For instance if the consumer's income rises then the budget line will move to the right and will be tangential to an indifference curve giving greater satisfaction, shown in Fig 5.8.

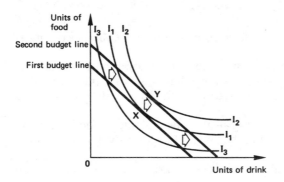

Fig 5.8 An increase in income leading to a higher indifference level

The consumer is now able to consume more of either food or drink or both or it allows choice for a better combination of the two products. Obviously a fall in income will have the reverse effect and move his or her optimum point of consumption to an indifference curve nearer the origin, ie at a lower level of satisfaction. In this example the consumer no longer purchases combination X but now consumes combination Y.

220

Changes in prices

If the price of the products change in relation to one another then the optimum consumption mix will change. For instance if the price of drink doubles while that of food remains constant, then the consumer will revise the combination of purchases. This is shown in Fig 5.9.

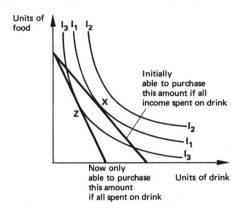

Units of food

I_3 I_1 I_2

Initially able to purchase this amount if all income spent on drink

X

Z

I_2
I_1
I_3

Now only able to purchase this amount if all spent on drink

Units of drink

Fig 5.9 An increase in price of one product with the consumer's income remaining constant

The consumer can now purchase only half as much drink as was possible at the previous prices (ie if total income was spent on drink). Thus although the consumer has the same amount of money to spend he or she will, in effect, be at a lower level of indifference (I_3) and so move from X to Z. Obviously if the price of both commodities rose (and the income he or she had to spend did not increase) the consumer would also move to a lower indifference curve.

This would be the result if, in times of inflation, prices increased and the consumer's purchasing power remained static. However in most inflationary situations income will rise as prices do and so the consumer will stay on the same level of indifference. If however prices rose faster than income most consumers would move to lower indifference levels (ie be worse off) – or as has happened, wages rise faster than prices then they would move to a more preferable level of indifference. This is known as the *income effect* and can be the result of an actual fall in prices – during times of *deflation* – or a fall in relative prices vis a vis income such as occurs when incomes rise faster than prices.

Revealed preference theory

The third method of explaining individual consumer demand is somewhat similar to indifference curve analysis but instead of illustrating a consumer's indifference between two products it shows the relationship between the price of a product and the quantity of it that he or she demands. The assumption is that a person will demonstrate preference for a particular product through willingness to exchange money for it. The curves illustrate the relationship between money and the product, in this case, records (see Fig 5.10).

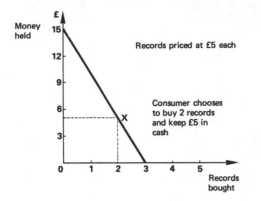

Fig 5.10   Consumer's possible levels of purchase with £15 to spend and records costing £5

If the consumer has £15 to spend he or she can buy three records — ie the line from £15 to three records is the budget line. In fact the consumer buys two records. This gives two records and £5 left. If three records were bought the consumer would have nothing left and if one record was purchased then this would have meant he or she still had £10. If this person is acting rationally (ie it is not an impulse buy) then it is possible to assume that two records and £5 in cash places this person in the situation he or she most prefers, eg better than one record and £10 cash. If records fall in price (assume a price war caused by new cut price record stores) to £3 then the new budget line is as shown in Fig 5.11.

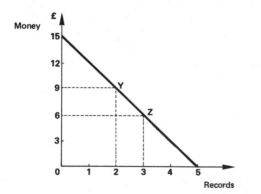

Fig 5.11   A fall in price of records to £3 each while the consumer still has £15 to spend

222

This results not only in a rise in *real income* (in terms of records, ie up to five if the consumer wishes to buy all records) but also allows choice as to whether or not to substitute more records for money or vice-versa. (The consumer can buy two records and have £9 left (Y) or still spend £10 and get three records and a £1 change (Z)). The two situations can be combined into one diagram (Fig 5.12).

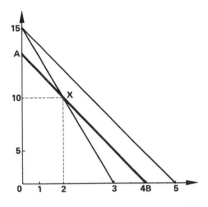

Fig 5.12   Fall in the price of records showing new budget line

If the effective increase in income is disregarded and the consumer is allowed, if he or she wishes, to purchase two records then a new budget line (AB) could be drawn parallel to that drawn in Fig 5.11 but passing through X. As the consumer previously chose two records and £5 cash as being the most preferred position within budget constraint, then if he or she chooses to move to any point on AB to the left of X, then he or she is acting inconsistently by buying less records even though they are cheaper. In fact, the consumer will buy more records, ie move further down and to the right along AB. This indicates that as price falls the consumer buys more of the product. This is the observation that would suggest a result similar to any demand curve. And, the more that the consumer moves to the right along AB, then the more of the product he or she will buy as price falls.

The shape of the demand curve

All three theories indicate that as its price falls consumers will normally purchase more of a product and this individual demand curve is shown in Fig 5.13. However none of them really shows what shape this demand curve will be. Will it be flat (indicating a large increase in demand caused by a small fall in price) or will it be steep (showing that little more is demanded if price falls)? This problem and the changing relationship between price and quantity demand is known as the *elasticity of demand.*

223

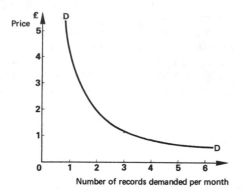

Fig 5.13   An individual demand curve for records

Elasticity of demand
The demand theories so far discussed have tended to concentrate on the influences causing changes in an individual's demand without assessing how great these changes will be. It is important for the consumer, the producer and for the government to know how much of a change in demand is likely to occur if price, income, taste, price of other goods, etc vary. For instance producers will need to be aware that increases in their prices are likely to substantially reduce the demand levels for their products – or the government would need to be certain that a tax increase on a particular commodity is not going to deter consumption to the extent that the revenue they would raise from taxation would actually decrease. Thus elasticity of demand is a means of measuring the responsiveness in the quantity of a product demanded to a change in price (or income/price of substitutes, etc).

Price elasticity of demand
To consider perhaps the most crucial form of elasticity, it is necessary to assess the *effect of a price change on quantity sold*. Considering extreme cases first, if an increase in price does not reduce sales at all this is known as *totally inelastic demand* (ie demand does not 'stretch' as price varies).

This can be shown in diagramatic form with a vertical demand curve. The price of the product is raised from P_1 to P_2 and yet the quantity purchased remains constant at Q. The reverse would obviously also occur – a fall in price would not encourage any more sales. This is rare in reality. For most products an increase in price would normally result in a falling off of demand. The only examples of inelastic demand would be either:

1 *absolute necessities*;
2 *products whose cost makes up a small part of consumers' spending.*

224

1 *absolute necessities*

Such products as bread may be used as examples. A price rise will not result in a fall in sales. Consumers must stop buying other products and divert expenditure into paying the higher price for the necessity. This presupposes that there is no suitable alternative – a substitute – to which consumers can transfer purchasing. If the price of bread went up people may prefer to buy crackers or biscuits instead. Thus there are few products which have no real substitute.

2 *products whose costs make up a relatively small part of the consumer's budget*

Some products, for instance salt or matches, may cost the consumer such a small part of overall expenditure that even a proportionately large increase in their price is unlikely to deter consumption. If a consumer buys one box of matches per week costing 5p even a doubling in price to 10p is not sufficient to encourage the individual to buy an alternative, eg a lighter.

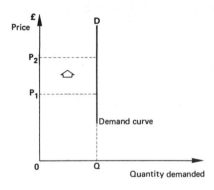

Fig 5.14   Totally inelastic demand curve

The other extreme situation is where even a relatively small increase in price will result in a substantial drop in the demand for a product. This is known as *elastic demand*. This is the result of consumers either totally discontinuing to purchase that product because they regard it as not being of suitable value in relation to its price or transferring their purchasing to another product (*a substitute*) which has remained at the same price. This is shown in the figure 5.15 using an *almost horizontal demand curve*.

This shows that even a relatively small increase in price from P_1 to P_2 results in a substantial fall in demand from Q_1 to Q_2. A producer who risked a price increase would find that the sales figures collapsed. Conversely, a drop in price would mean a massive increase in sales and so an elastic demand curve may prove advantageous to suppliers seeking to increase output.

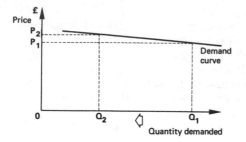

Fig 5.15   An almost totally elastic demand curve

Most products do not have an elasticity which is either totally elastic or totally inelastic. Most price changes will affect demand to some extent but usually less than demonstrated by these extremes. If the increase in price results in a less than proportionate decrease in sales then the product has an *inelastic demand*. If a price increase means a fall in sales which is proportionately greater, then the product has an *elastic demand*.

Simple mathematical illustration

It is important to realise that elasticity should be calculated in terms of proportionate (or percentage) changes in price and quantity.

For instance, consider these two alternatives:

a) Price | Quantity demanded
£10 | 100 units
price increase | quantity reduction
£15 | 80 units

b) £1000 | 100 units
price increase | quantity reduction
£1020 | 85 units

In the first instance price rose by five units (ie £5) while quantity fell by 20 units. This should be interpreted as a 50% increase in price (£10 increased by £5) and only a 20% decrease in sales (100 reduced by 20). This demonstrates *inelastic demand* as quantity falls at a less than proportionate rate than price increases.

In the second case, price rises by 20 units (ie £20) and quantity falls by 15 units. But this is in fact only a 2% increase in price and a 15% fall in demand and so is an *elastic response*.

The price elasticity of demand of product can be shown in the following equation:

226

Price elasticity of demand (E_P) = $\dfrac{\% \text{ change in quantity demanded}}{\% \text{ change in price}}$

For this it is possible to calculate that a product with totally inelastic demand will have a value of $E_P = 0$ $\dfrac{\text{zero change in quantity demanded}}{\text{any change in price}}$ must equal 0) and a product with a totally elastic demand must in the extreme have a value of $E_P = \infty$ (infinity)

$(\dfrac{\text{a large change in quantity demanded}}{\text{infinitely small change in price}} = \dfrac{\text{almost}}{\text{infinity}})$

If a change in price results in a proportionate change in quantity this is called *unit elasticity* and from the equation can be calculated as $E_P = 1$

$\dfrac{\text{equal \% change in quantity demanded}}{\text{equal \% change in price}} = 1$

If price elasticity of demand for a product (E_P) is greater than 1 then it is said to have an elastic demand. If E_P is less than 1 then demand is said to be inelastic.

Income elasticity

Income is the second factor which may determine a change in demand. If a consumer's income increases then more purchases of a product may be made. But how many more? If income increases by 10% and the consumer's demand for the product rises by less than 10%, then the income elasticity of demand (E_I) is less than 1 using the equation:

Income elasticity of demand (E_I) = $\dfrac{\% \text{ change in quantity demanded}}{\% \text{ change in income}}$

E_I is inelastic. Alternatively, if income rises by 10% and there is a more than 10% increase in demand then income elasticity is elastic, ie $E_I > 1$. Obviously for most products an increase in income will result in an increase in demand for that product and E_I will be positive. However in some cases as already mentioned, an increase in income will result in a fall in demand. These are *inferior goods* and for these E_I will be negative.

Cross elasticity of demand

The consumer's purchase of one particular product is also affected by the price of other goods and this relationship is measured using cross elasticity of demand (E_X). If the price of a substitute rises then demand for the product in question will increase.

Using the following equation this can be illustrated.

$\dfrac{\% \text{ change in quantity demanded of A}}{\% \text{ change in price of B}}$

If price of B rises by 20% and the quantity bought of A increases by more than 20% then E_X is elastic. If less than 20% then E_X is inelastic. Cross elasticity will be positive for goods which are substitutes. However for goods which are complementary, then a rise in the price of B may result in a decrease in demand for A, ie E_X will be negative. For example a rise in the price of large cars may result in decrease in a consumer's demand for petrol.

Summary of the relationships of elasticity
To summarise the relationships involved in elasticity refer to Table 5.3.

Price elasticity (E_P) = $\dfrac{\% \text{ change in quantity demanded of A}}{\% \text{ change in price of A}}$

    if E_P is > 1 then E_P is elastic
    if E_P is < 1 then E_P is inelastic

Income elasticity (E_I) = $\dfrac{\% \text{ change in quantity demanded of A}}{\% \text{ change in income}}$

    if E_I is > 1 then E_I is elastic
    if E_I is < 1 then E_I is inelastic
    Normally E_I will be positive
    if E_I is negative then A is an inferior good.

Cross elasticity (E_C) = $\dfrac{\% \text{ change in quantity demanded of A}}{\% \text{ change in price of B}}$

    if E_C is > 1 then E_C is elastic
    if E_C is < 1 then E_C is inelastic
    if E_C is positive then A and B are substitutes
    if E_C is negative then A and B are complements

Table 5.3   Elasticity of demand

Those seeking to influence the consumer's demand

The influences on a consumer's demand have been considered without examining the people who may influence the consumer's demand. These may be classified into three categories:

    (i)   *producers*,
    (ii) *the government*,
    (iii) *other individuals and groups in society*.

Each of these three have different motives in influencing the consumer and each will now be considered.

Producers
Suppliers usually have one motive in influencing the consumer – that is to sell more of their product. This can be achieved in a variety of ways. Advertising is the most common form of influence. It is used to inform consumers of the introduction of a new product, to bring to their attention a change in price. However in most cases its objective is to persuade the consumer that he or she will gain a certain level of satisfaction from the product. The advertisers hope that they may raise anticipated utility sufficiently to persuade the consumer that an adequate consumer surplus will be gained from the purchase of their product.

Later in this chapter it will be noted that the law protects consumers from untrue or misleading statements in the sale of goods or services. Nevertheless, advertisers use superlatives and innuendos, which although not contrary to the law, tend to mislead the unsuspecting. If a consumer is persuaded into believing that some product will give some unlikely amount of satisfaction, the law must decide whether these advertisements are likely to so influence a rational consumer. Clearly any statement of facts in advertisements must be capable of justification and the government has established the Advertising Standards Authority to act as a watchdog on advertising.

The producer when advertising is attempting to move the consumer's demand curve for that product to the right so that more of that product will be purchased at the same price. Advertisements also seek to influence the elasticity of demand by emphasising the uniqueness and unsubstitutability of their products. This allows the seller to increase price without experiencing a proportionate decline in sales.

Governmental influences on demand

The government also attempts to influence consumer demand for those products which it regards as producing either a social cost or benefit. The government through the Health Education Council promotes advertising which actively *discourages* the consumption of cigarettes or excess drinking. In so doing they are trying to lower the level of perceived utility which the consumer will gain from such consumption. Conversely the government will sponsor *positive* advertising which encourages people to insulate their houses, purchase new tyres for their cars, etc. This is because it regards these products as providing a social benefit.

The influence of other individuals or groups in society

As well as by the actions of producers and the government, consumers are influenced by the actions and attitudes of other consumers and individuals in society. Trends and fashions, although to some extent manipulated by producers for their own benefit, are also the result of changing attitudes in society. This holds particularly true of *conspicuous* items of consumption such as clothes or tastes in music. As the pendulum of fashion swings back and forth, clothes lose one of their characteristics of utility, their 'fashionableness'. While retaining their inherent qualities of warmth, durability, material quality and so on they provide the wearer with a much lower level of satisfaction as they are no longer smart or worn by others. The individual's desire not to be regarded as different plays an important role in determining the demand for products. The classic example is of blue denim which emerged from being the hard-wearing clothing of the worker to become the uniform of the majority of young people throughout many parts of the world.

Consumer protection

Consumer protection and the free market

One of the crucial aspects of consumer transactions is that both parties should be free to negotiate a bargain which is mutually satisfactory. The consumer, if acting rationally, should only purchase those goods or services which will provide a suitable level of utility in relation to the price he or she is asked to pay. The law, as epitomised by the principle of *caveat emptor*, regarded it as the consumer's responsibility to satisfy himself or herself that the product met the individual's requirements. Advocates of a free market approach argue that it is the consumer who should be responsible for self protection through the operation of the market and that government intervention in the form of imposed consumer protection is both unnecessary and unhelpful. The consumer is the best judge of self interest and, through the combined operation of the market as a whole, will act as a sufficient influence on producers' behaviour. A consumer or group of consumers who are dissatisfied with a supplier's product will simply not repurchase it in future. The resulting decline in sales will force the producer to review the standard of product or business practices. Competition also acts as a form of consumer protection, for if consumers are misled by one supplier, other more consumer-conscious suppliers of substitutes will gain the benefit from future sales.

The advocates of the free market argue that it induces more efficient results than government regulation. The State, by imposing strict standards on the producer and supplier, adds an extra cost which the cautious consumer must bear in an effort to protect the proportion of consumers who are not willing to use the law to protect themselves, or who act unwisely in their purchase.

The civil law remedy for the failure of the market

This support for the free market is perhaps *theoretically* sound but it is inadequate in the light of prevailing market practices. Markets, as explained earlier, are not normally competitive and oligopoly is the prevalent form of market organisation. Generally, products' defects will be revealed after purchase, and if the product is only bought occasionally, then the threat of turning for future buys to alternative competitors is illusory. A further competitive assumption is that rivals will try to inform consumers of defects or lower quality in rival products. However, in most cases, although not all, product advertising tends to concentrate only on the advantages of its own clients product and disregards competitors.

A further argument suggests that the middlemen in the distributive chain, the shopkeeper, travel agent, etc will attempt to inform their customers of the 'best buy' so forcing the poorer quality manufacturers to improve their products or suffer reduced sales. However this ignores the reality that retailers themselves are often unaware of the comparative qualities of the goods they sell. They may even push poorer products if they obtain a higher profit margin on them.

Civil law is also limited in its effectiveness in the protection of consumers. The civil law requires the wronged party, in this case the consumer, to take the initiative in seeking redress. Consumers are expected to be aware of their rights and to be sufficiently forceful to press them. In fact consumers frequently fail to utilise their legal rights in this way. They may not know their rights or do not take advantage of them. Other examples are where a relatively large number of people are affected by a defect in a product but only to some slight degree. None may be sufficiently harmed to complain and yet the supplier is able to escape liability from supplying a defective product. A slight overcharging of one consumer may not lead to complaint yet multiplied manyfold it provides a business with substantial profit gained from sharp practice.

Finally the advocates of the free market argue that self regulation of the market does not incur any costs while legal measures clearly do. In fact costs are involved if a consumer seeks redress through the civil law, and in the competitive readjustment of quality, etc. Thus although state intervention may be provided only at cost, this must be weighed against the cost of self regulation and the process of the law.

So far this Chapter has considered consumer demands for products and theories which are postulated to explain and measure these demands. Demands are created by real (and sometimes imaginary) needs, and they are met by the acquisition, use and enjoyment of the goods or services which satisfy them. Two points are apparent here. The first is that to be able to acquire goods or services a consumer must transact with a supplier. The second is that defects in the transacting activity may cause the consumer's perceived utility to be partially or wholly unfulfilled. In the remaining part of this Chapter these points are considered in more detail.

Consumer transactions

In the examples that have been given to explain consumer demand the consumer has been someone using or acquiring a product for his or her own private use or consumption. Clearly not all consumers can be categorised in this way. In many transactions the consumer will be a commercial body whose aim will be to pass on goods it has acquired, whether with or without alteration, for profit. Retail organisations fall within this group, as do manufacturers of sophisticated products requiring specialised component parts that the manufacturer cannot produce and must therefore purchase. A good example is provided by the motor manufacturers, who are the major or sole consumers of a large range of components – vehicle instruments, tyres, sparking plugs, lights and so on – supplied to them by other commercial organisations. Other commercial consumers are those who retain the purchased product with the aim of employing it for profit, for instance the transport operator acquiring new lorries to expand business, or the manufacturer of engineering products who replaces existing labour-intensive machinery with numerical-control machines requiring a substantially reduced staff of operators.

Consumers, then, can be commercial or non-commercial. The reason for distinguishing the separate categories here is that the non-commercial group, the private or *ultimate* consumers as they are sometimes called, possess a status as contract-makers which grants them a much greater protection from exploitation than that available to the other, commercial, consumers. This protection, which is almost exclusively legislative in origin, has expanded rapidly in recent years, most noticeably within the last decade. There are a number of reasons that account for the increasing involvement of governments in the regulation and supervision of consumer transactions through the creation of administrative machinery, among them an acceptance that market forces themselves do not generally appear to eliminate the trading malpractices of suppliers, and that the civil law does not provide an adequate deterrent against suppliers committing malpractices in their business dealings.

One advantage of regulating consumer transactions by creating regulatory criminal offences lies in its application as a means of prevention rather than cure. This can be achieved by means of penal sanctions such as those contained in legislation designed to maintain standards (for instance as regards the way in which goods may be described) and those prohibiting defined activities (such as doorstep selling of credit facilities). Apart from the undesirable publicity that may attach to an organisation which is convicted for breach of such matters, enforcement of criminal provisions is placed in the hands of independent agencies, in particular the local authorities, who employ trading standards officers for this purpose. Evidence suggests that if it is left to the dissatisfied consumer to take action over infringements of legal rights and duties, that lack of knowledge about these rights and duties, fear of possible legal proceedings and their costs, inertia, or a combination of any of these factors, will lure the consumer away from enforcing those rights against the commercial transgressor, especially when the economic value of the transaction is small. And certainly, commercial consumers in pursuing their business interests, are more likely to know their legal rights and of course have the resources to pursue them where trading strength alone is not enough.

In conclusion it is appropriate to make one further point. The raising of trading standards by legal means inevitably raises costs. Better materials and greater care are required in the manufacture of products, improvements are necessary in the field of testing and quality control, more attention must be paid to the marketing of products in the light of comprehensive legal controls in this area, while more comprehensive insurance cover becomes necessary as clauses excluding and restricting liability for all sorts of contractual and tortious matters are rendered void by legislation. It is the consumer who pays the price of consumer protection but it is probably a price worth bearing.

The nature of the transaction

The expression 'transaction' combines the idea of the pursuit of general business activity with the more precise legal notion of that activity affecting the legal rights of the parties to it. In other words it can be used to describe not only the contract itself, but also the events leading up to the making of the contract. These events have a legal significance of their own often giving rise to liabilities that are independent of the contract itself. It is therefore appropriate to examine them separately, and logical to do so before looking at the contract itself. For the sake of convenience these events may be classified as pre-contractual liabilities.

Pre-contractual liabilities

Contracts do not arise spontaneously. They result from agreement, and agreement is usually reached after a period of negotiation between the parties. How detailed these negotiations are will depend upon such factors as the nature and purpose of the proposed transaction, and the financial consideration involved. One would expect that the preliminaries attached to the granting of a lease of an office block would involve greater discussion than the negotiations attached to the purchase of a colour television by a private individual from a shop. Nevertheless in both instances statements are likely to be made during negotiations, which act as inducements, and encourage the making of the transaction. If these statements are found to be untrue, what is the effect upon the transaction? This is now considered.

Misrepresentation

It has already been noted that in the negotiations which lead to the making of the contract, statements will be made. Some of these statements will expressly or impliedly be incorporated into the contract itself — thus becoming *terms* whose breach will entitle the innocent party to *damages* or even *repudiation* of contract. Others will never become a part of the contract and will be regarded as *mere representations*, which if untrue, will not give rise to an action for breach of contract, but rather for *misrepresentation*.

These two forms of action differ in an important respect. If a term of the contract is broken it is irrelevant to consider the state of mind of the contract breaker. If however a mere representation has proved to be untrue, ie it has become a misrepresentation, the effect this has upon the liability of the misrepresentor depends upon the state of mind accompanying it. Thus it is recognised that the misrepresentor may act *innocently*, *negligently* or *fraudulently* in making the statement. Which it is, will determine the particular remedies available to the other

233

party – the misrepresentee. Before examining the remedies it is important to determine exactly what constitutes a misrepresentation. Many types of statement made prior to contract are not regarded as of sufficient significance to give rise to legal liability if they should subsequently prove false. A balance must be struck between protecting consumers' interests on the one hand, while recognising on the other that it is not the task of the courts or Parliament to regard consumers as totally naive contract-makers, who believe all the sales patter they hear.

A misrepresentation is a false statement of fact made by one party to the other which has the effect of inducing the other to enter into the contract.

A false statement of fact
In relation to the statement there are three points which are worth bearing in mind. Firstly the representation must be as to a fact, not law. This may raise difficulties, because often a single statement may implicitly refer to a proposition of law, for instance where in *Solle* v. *Butcher* (1950) statements were made that a flat which had been substantially altered did not come under rent control legislation.

Secondly a statement of fact must be distinguished from a statement of opinion, for the latter does not give rise to liability.

> In *Bissett* v. *Wilkinson* (1927) the appellant sold the respondent some land in New Zealand for sheep farming. It had never been used for this purpose and the purchaser knew this, however he relied on a statement by the vendor that the land could support 2000 sheep. The Court decided that in the circumstances it was not justifiable for the purchaser to rely on the statement, which was simply an expression of the vendor's opinion. By way of contrast in *Smith* v. *Land and House Property Corporation* (1884) the vendor of a hotel told the purchaser that it was let to 'a most desirable tenant'. The tenant was in fact in rent arrears, and the purchaser succeeded in an action to rescind the contract. In the words of Lord Justice Bowen 'if the facts are not equally known to both sides then a statement of opinion by the one who knows the facts best involves very often a statement of a material fact, for he impliedly states that he knows facts which justify his opinion'. Clearly sellers will invariably be in the best position to know the facts.

Finally a statement of future intention is not regarded as a statement of fact. However if it can be shown that when the intention was expressed it did not represent the real intention of its maker then an action in misrepresentation will lie, for again in words of Lord Justice Bowen 'A misrepresentation as to the state of a man's mind is . . . a misstatement of fact'.

Applying this principle, which provided part of the judgement in *Edgington* v. *Fitzmaurice* (1885) it was considered that the directors of a company had made a misrepresentation by inviting a loan from the public on the pretext of expanding the company's business, but which they intended to use to pay company debts.

Silence

It might seem to be self evident that if no statement is made, that misrepresentation cannot occur. In fact there are circumstances when silence, either total or partial, will give rise to liability. This will occur in the following circumstances:

a) *in contracts of the utmost good faith* (uberrimae fidei) where there is a positive duty to disclose all material facts. Perhaps the best example of such contracts are those involving the provision of insurance cover, where the insurer can avoid those obligations if the insured has failed in his or her duty to disclose. Other examples of such contracts include those when a fiduciary relationship exists between the parties (for example between solicitor and client), such as contracts for the sale of land, to the extent that a vendor is obliged to disclose defects in his or her title, *Faruqi* v. *English Real Estates* (1979) and finally contracts for the allotment of shares in companies, for 'Those who issue a prospectus . . . are bound to state everything with strict and scrupulous accuracy, and . . . to omit no one fact within their knowledge, the existence of which might in any degree affect the nature, or extent, or quality of the privileges and advantages which the prospectus holds out as inducements to take shares', stated Kindersley V-C in *New Brunswick and Canada Railway Co* v. *Muggeridge* (1860).

b) *if circumstances change*, rendering a previously made statement no longer true, and the representor remains silent.

> This happened in *With* v. *O'Flanagan* (1936) where a doctor sold his practice on the understanding that it had an income of £2000 pa. Although this was true at the time the statement was made, when the practice was sold the income was negligible as the doctor had fallen ill, and could not deal with patients. The doctor's silence about this material change amounted to misrepresentation.

c) *if a statement represents a half truth*, for instance a solicitor telling a purchaser of land that he or she is not aware of any restrictive covenants, when the reason for this lack of knowledge is the fact that he or she has not bothered to consult the deeds − *Nottingham Patent Brick and Tile Co* v. *Butler* (1886).

An inducement

A person will not have been induced into making the contract by a representation he or she is unaware of, or which he or she did not

235

believe, or on which he or she did not rely (for instance where the buyer of a vehicle takes it for a test drive to determine if it actually meets the claims made of it by the seller). The representation need not be the sole or major inducement. It will be enough that it had a material affect upon a person's intention to reach an agreement.

It is appropriate here to add that a statement may be made in a variety of ways. It may be oral, written, or arise by conduct. Thus the apparent condition of the item is a statement, eg in the case of a motor vehicle such features as the mileage shown constitute a statement.

The different categories of misrepresentation
There are recognised to be three categories:

1 *Fraudulent misrepresentation*
  In *Derry* v. *Peek* (1889) Lord Herschell stated that a false representation will be fraudulent where it has been made knowingly, or without belief in its truth, or recklessly, without caring whether it is true or false.

2 *Negligent misrepresentation*
  This will be established where it can be shown that the representor had no reasonable grounds to believe that the statement was true.

3 *Innocent misrepresentation*
  If a misrepresentation has been made without fraud or negligence then it will be regarded as a wholly innocent misrepresentation, but it may nevertheless give rise to legal liability. An example of a misrepresentation of this sort is seen in *Leaf* v. *International Galleries* (1950).

Remedies for misrepresentation
A variety of remedies are available to the misrepresentee. They include common law and equitable remedies, as well as those available under the Misrepresentation Act 1967. The following diagram indicates which remedies are available for each of the three categories of negligence (see Fig 5.16).

Rescission
This is an equitable remedy and therefore discretionary. It involves putting the parties back to the position they were in before the contract was made. The right to rescind may be lost in the following circumstances:

(i) *if the contract has been affirmed by the innocent party.*
    Affirmation occurs where the innocent party who knows of the misrepresentation elects to continue the contract. This election may be express or implied; in the latter case delay in bringing action to rescind may be enough.

In *Leaf* v. *International Galleries* (1950) the purchaser of a drawing described incorrectly but innocently by the seller as a Constable, was unable to rescind the contract when, five years later, he discovered the drawing was not a Constable after all.

	At Common Law	In Equity	Under Misrepresentation Act 1967
Fraudulent mis-representation	Damages in the tort of deceit (if contract is affirmed)	Rescission (and damages). If the contract is executory the fraud is a defence if the misrepresenta-tor brings action for specific performance	
Negligent mis-representation	Damages in the tort of negligence under the rule in *Hedley Byrne* v. *Heller* (1964), if a 'special rela-tionship' exists	Rescission	In addition to rescission, or, at the court's discre-tion instead of rescission, damages under s. 2(1) if as a result of the misrepresentation the innocent party has suffered loss. If the defendant can prove that up to the time of the contract he believed, with reasonable cause, that his state-ments were true, this will be a defence.
Innocent mis-representation		Rescission	If the grounds for rescission exist the court, in its discretion, may award damages instead, under s. 2(2).

Fig 5.16 *Remedies for misrepresentation*

(ii) *if restitution is impossible*, for example where the buyer has seriously damaged or significantly altered the goods. However precise restoration is not essential and the court can order financial adjustments to be made.

(iii) *if a third party, acting in good faith and providing value, acquires rights in the goods.*

It has previously been mentioned that representations may be incorporated into the body of the contract itself, becoming terms. If this occurs action will normally be brought for breach of contract, rather than for misrepresentation.

Trade descriptions legislation

Liability for a misrepresentation arises under civil law, but criminal liability for the use of false or misleading trade descriptions is imposed under the Trade Descriptions Acts 1968, 1972. These Acts do not provide civil remedies, but it is worth noting that the Criminal Law Act 1977 grants a magistrate's court the power to award compensation of up to £1000 to a person who has been affected by an offence under the 1968 and 1972 Acts.

Under the Act of 1968, s. 1, any person who, in the course of a trade or business a) applies a false trade description to goods, or b) supplies or offers to supply any goods to which a false trade description is applied, commits an offence. It is also an offence to make a false statement knowingly or recklessly regarding the provision of services, accommodation or facilities. 'Trade description' is broadly defined. Under s. 2 it includes, inter alia, quantity, size, composition, strength, performance, place and date of manufacture. Price is also part of the description, and if a supplier makes a misleading statement regarding price an offence is committed. Examples would include false statements that the goods are being sold at less than the manufacturers recommended price, or that they have been reduced, or that the sellers price is below that being charged by other sellers.

Obviously there will be occasions when the degree of falsehood will be trifling, and the Act provides that a trade description is only to be regarded as false if it is false to a *material degree*.

Compare the sale of a car described as having done 10 000 miles when the true mileage is 10 050, with a car described as having done 17 000 miles when it has done 36 000 miles. In the latter example a firm of car dealers were, hardly surprisingly, successfully prosecuted under the 1968 Act, even though the dealers had bought the car with the higher mileage shown. *Richmond-upon-Thames Borough Council* v. *Motor Sales* (1971).

S. 1 is broadly drafted, and an offence is committed simply by *applying* a false description to goods (ie by advertising). These need be

238

neither on sale, nor an offer to sell. The Act does however only apply to sellers contracting in the course of business, thus private transactions are excluded.

Certain defences are provided under the Act. In particular s. 24 states that it shall be a defence for a person to prove:

a) that the commission of the offence was due to a mistake or to reliance on information supplied to the defendant or some act or default of another person, an accident or some other cause beyond his/her control; and

b) that he or she took all reasonable precautions and exercised all due diligence to avoid the commission of such an offence by himself/herself or any person under his/her control.

In *Tesco Supermarkets Ltd* v. *Nattrass* (1972) the House of Lords had to decide whether, under s. 24, the manager of a supermarket employed by Tesco's could be regarded as 'another person'. It was decided that he was not sufficiently senior to be regarded as representing the 'mind' of the company for the purposes of criminal law, and the conviction against the company, which related to goods being sold with a false indication as to price, was quashed. The company was able to prove that it had exercised due diligence in the appointment of its managerial staff.

In the case of offences relating to the supply of services, eg by tour operators and dry cleaners, it will be a defence to show that the false statement was made without the knowledge of the maker and without recklessness.

Thus in *Sunair Holidays* v. *Dodd* (1970) the company advertised a hotel in their brochure, which had 'all twin bedded rooms with bath, shower and terrace'. At the time of making the statement the description was accurate, but it subsequently became inaccurate. It was held that no offence had been committed. Events occurring after the statement was made could not have the affect of rendering it reckless.

Other examples of pre-contractual liability

The broad range of legislation intervention in the sphere of pre-contractual activity is illustrated by the following statutory examples:

The Food and Drugs Act, 1955

This Act creates a number of offences in respect of the quality and labelling of food. In particular it is an offence to add any substance to food, use any substance as an ingredient in the preparation of food, abstract any constituent from food, or subject food to any other process or treatment rendering it injurious to health, with intention that the food shall be sold for human consumption (s. 1). If food coming within s. 1 is advertised for sale an offence is also committed. Furthermore under s. 6 it is an offence to publish an advertisement which falsely describes any food or which is calculated to mislead as to the nature, substance or quality of the food.

The Consumer Credit Act 1974

This Act applies to consumer credit agreements, that is, personal credit agreements under which the creditor provides the debtor with credit not exceeding £5000. In particular this includes hire-purchase agreements. The Act is a detailed piece of legislation, and all that is being noted here is the extent to which the Act creates rights and obligations prior to the completion of a credit transaction.

Firstly the Act requires that any person or body intending to carry on a business of providing consumer credit must obtain a licence to do so from the Director-General of Fair Trading (whose powers are contained in the Fair Trading Act 1973). The Director is bound to grant a licence when satisfied that the applicant is a fit person to engage in such a business, and the name(s) under which the applicant applies to be licenced are not misleading or undesirable. Under s. 40 an unlicenced trader is unable to enforce an agreement made with a creditor, unless the Director makes an order enabling the trader to do so.

Secondly the Act makes it an offence for a trader in an advertisement to include false or misleading information, or indicate a willingness to supply goods or services on credit terms when the trader is not also prepared to supply the goods or services for cash, or to infringe advertising regulations (eg the requirement that the true annual rate of interest be shown).

Finally it is an offence to canvass credit facilities off trade premises, that is to orally attempt to persuade consumers, usually in their own homes, and who have not requested a visit, to enter into a credit agreement.

The Unsolicited Goods and Services Act 1971

This Act was considered in Chapter I. It makes it an offence to send out certain types of unsolicited material, and demand payment, and it enables a person who has received unsolicited goods, eg books sent through the post without a request being made for them, to treat them as an unconditional gift if the sender fails to collect them within six months.

Exclusion clauses

Exclusion clauses are used as a means of reducing or removing legal liabilities. They are most commonly found as terms in contracts, and have been subject to both judicial and legislative control. These controls have become steadily more comprehensive and restrictive in response to greater demands for consumer protection, demands which have themselves often been a response to the commercial practice of seeking to avoid liability wherever it is legally possible to do so. Thus it is now sometimes an offence even to attempt to exclude or restrict liability. In particular the Consumer Transactions (Restrictions on

240

Statements) (Amendment) Order 1978 provides that liability for breach of implied terms in contracts of sale and hire purchase cannot by law be excluded — an example would be the implied condition that goods shall be of merchantable quality — s. 14(2) Sale of Goods Act 1979; it is an offence to *attempt* to do so (ie even though the exclusion would not be valid anyway).

Contractual liabilities

Such liabilities are determined by reference to the obligations of each of the parties to the contract. These obligations are the terms of the contract, and they arise in different ways, namely:

Important
The hirer must sign this agreement in the shop and not in the home.

This hire purchase agreement is made upon the date shown above between _____ _____ (hereinafter called 'the Owner') which expression shall include its successors and assigns and the Hirer named below (hereinafter called 'the Hirer') WHEREBY the Owner agrees to let and the Hirer agrees to hire the Goods described in the agreement (hereinafter called 'the Goods' which expression shall include any accessories before and any replacements or renewals thereof) upon the payment terms set out, and subject to the Conditions of Hire.

Description of goods and payment terms

Goods _____

Model _____
Hire purchase price _____
Balance payable by _____
Monthly rentals _____

NOTICE
Right of hirer to terminate agreement

a The Hirer may put an end to this agreement by giving notice of termination in writing to any person who is entitled to collect or receive the hire rent.

b He/She must then pay any instalments which are in arrear at the time when he/she gives notice. If, when he/she has paid those instalments, the total amount which he/she has paid under the agreement is less than £ ⟵ he/she must also pay enough to make up that sum unless the Court determines that a smaller sum would be equal to the Owner's loss.

c If the Goods have been damaged owing to the Hirer having failed to take reasonable care of them, the Owner may sue for the amount of the damage unless that amount can be agreed between the Hirer and the Owner.

d The Hirer should see whether the agreement contains provisions allowing him/her to put an end to the agreement on terms more favourable to him/her than those just mentioned. If he/she does, he/she may put an end to the agreement on those terms.

Restriction of owner's right to recover goods

a After £ has been paid, then unless the Hirer has himself/herself put an end to the agreement, the Owner of the Goods cannot take them back from the Hirer without the Hirer's consent unless the Owner obtains an Order of the Court.

b If the Owner applies to the Court for such an Order, the Court may, if the Court thinks it just to do so, allow the Hirer to keep either:—

i) the whole of the Goods, on condition that the Hirer pays the balance of the price in the manner ordered by the Court; or

ii) a fair proportion of the Goods having regard to what the Hirer has already paid.

Insert $\frac{1}{3}$ ⟵ and ⟶ Insert $\frac{1}{2}$ of the Hire Purchase Price

Particulars of hirer

Title   Forenames

Surname

First line of address

Second line of address

Third line of address

Telephone number _____
Married/single   Age _____
Present employer _____
Reference _____
Banker _____

The owner agrees:

If the hirer shall make payment of the monthly rentals then the hirer shall thereupon have the option of purchasing the Goods for the sum of five pence.

This document contains the terms of a hire purchase agreement. Sign it only if you want to be legally bound by them.

Signature of hirer _____

The goods will not become your property until you have made all the payments.
You must not sell them before then.

(i) *through express agreement* – as when the parties have discussed and settled the question of price, delivery dates and so on;
(ii) *by implication*.

Terms are implied into contracts by statute and the courts will sometimes imply terms to give a contract *business efficacy*, and there are sometimes occasions where terms will be implied into a contract on the basis of the commercial custom of a particular trade or area.

Whatever the sources of the particular terms of a contract may be, once they can be established then the parties are obliged to comply with them. If they fail to do so an action for breach of contract will be available to the injured party who may claim damages against the contract breaker. In some cases the injured party may even be entitled to repudiate the contract, treating himself or herself as discharged from any further liability. Clearly it is important to be able to identify which terms carry such weight that, if they are not fulfilled by one of the parties, the other is legally entitled to bring the contract to an end. A person who repudiates a contract under the misapprehension that he or she is justified in doing so will put themselves in breach. Ideally, then, the parties should expressly state that certain terms are to be regarded as so vital that if they are not complied with the innocent party shall have the right to repudiate. In practice however it is often the case that no such intention will have been expressed and it will fall to the court to adduce intention by examining the particular term in relation to the contract as a whole, in order to decide whether its breach has given rise to this right. In *Hong Kong Fir Shipping Co Ltd* v. *Kawasaki Kisen Kaisha Ltd* (1962) Lord Justice Diplock stated the test for the court to be whether the occurrence of the breach deprived 'the party who has further undertakings still to perform of substantially the whole benefit which it was the intention of the parties as expressed in the contract that he should obtain as the consideration for performing those undertakings'.

Terms which give rise to a right to repudiate are known as *conditions*. Terms which are not construed as being vital to the contract are known as *warranties*. They are said to be collateral or subsidiary to the main purpose or purposes of the contract. The Sale of Goods Act 1979, which implies into contracts of sale various conditions and warranties, defines the meaning of these two expressions for the purposes of the Act, (see later in this chapter). It is unfortunate that the twin expressions, conditions and warranties are used in a variety of ways, to mean different things in different circumstances. For instance contractual documents will often contain all the terms, under the title 'conditions' which will merely mean the provisions of the contract (eg booking conditions in a package holiday agreement). Again it may be that the contract as a whole is to take effect only if a certain contingency is met, ie the contract is dependent upon a condition being fulfilled.

An example of this use is seen in *Pym* v. *Campbell* (1856) where the sale of an invention was conditional on an express oral understanding that it should not be binding until a third party had approved the invention.

It may be stating the obvious to observe that the question of whether a term is a condition or warranty will usually arise only after the event of a breach, and reach the court if the contract itself fails to supply an answer. It can certainly be artificial, and may well be impossible to identify in advance whether a term is a condition or warranty if the parties themselves have not made this classification. If it is impossible for the court to do so the terms will be regarded as *intermediate*, or *innominate*, and the contractual remedies for its breach will be determined by how serious the consequences have been.

In the Hong Kong Fir Shipping case in 1962 a contract under which a ship was chartered stated that the ship would be 'in every way fitted for ordinary cargo service'. A combination of inefficient engine-room staff and old engines contributed to a number of breakdowns. During the first seven months of the charter the ship was only able to be at sea for eight and a half weeks. The charterers repudiated the contract. The Court of Appeal held that the repudiation was wrongful. The importance of the term as to seaworthiness should be determined by regarding the consequences of its breach when it occurred, not by looking at the term in isolation and classifying it as either a condition or warranty. Despite the non-availability of the vessel for the greater part of the charter this did not in the opinion of the Court deprive the charterers of 'substantially the whole benefit of which it was the intention of the parties they should obtain . . . under the charter party'.

Restricting and excluding contractual liability
There may appear to be something rather paradoxical in a situation where a party has voluntarily undertaken to fulfil certain contractual obligations but has provided within this same contract that should they fail in some way to carry out these obligations they will incur no legal liability, or possibly only a restricted liability, for their failure. In its most extreme form, exclusion of liability for breach of a major term of the contract, it does appear that sometimes English law will permit a person to escape their primary contractual obligations, for example an organisation undertaking to provide a service while broadly excluding liability for any consequences of a failure to provide it. It has been made clear in examining the law of contract that the principle of contractual freedom has played an important part in the formulation of contractual rules. Similarly it has been noted that this freedom requires some checks upon its operation. The way in which the common law and Parliament have regarded the use of clauses restricting and excluding liability

reflects these conflicting forces. Firstly the approach of the common law is examined, and secondly the approach of Parliament.

The common law approach

The initial question that has to be asked is whether the clause has become a part of the contract, for, in accordance with the basic rules of contract, if it has not been agreed upon either before or at the time of making the contract the person seeking to rely on it will be unable to do so. If the agreement containing the clause has been signed, the signatory will be bound by all the terms of it. It will be of no help to plead, as the plaintiff did in *L'Estrange* v. *Graucob Ltd* (1934), that the contract had not been read. But if misrepresentations have been made as to the meaning of the terms, it may be impossible for the excluder to rely on those terms.

> In *Curtis* v. *Chemical Cleaning and Dyeing Co* (1951) an assistant in a dry cleaners told a customer that a clause in a document the customer had to sign merely excluded liability for any damage caused to sequins on the customer's satin dress. The clause actually excluded liability for *any* type of damage. The Court held that the cleaners could not rely on the clause when the customer complained about bad staining of the dress itself, for the scope of the clause had been misrepresented.

In circumstances where the clause is contained in an unsigned document, or on a notice, the excluder must show that reasonable steps have been taken to bring the clause to the attention of the other party, and the document or notice containing it might be reasonably regarded as a contractual one, and likely to contain terms.

> It has been held for instance that a deck-chair ticket, which contained an exclusion clause, was reasonably regarded by the hirer of the deck-chair as being nothing more than a receipt. The exclusion clause it contained did not therefore bind the hirer. (*Chapelton* v. *Barry UDC* (1940)). In contrast the court in *Thompson* v. *LMS Railway Co* (1930) held that the plaintiff was bound by an exclusion clause contained in the company's conditions and regulations which were available for inspection in the booking office, although these conditions and regulations were merely referred to on the back of the railway ticket she bought. By providing this reference on the ticket the company had done all that could reasonably be expected of them, to make normal passengers aware of the conditions and regulations. It was consequently of no assistance to the plaintiff that she was illiterate.

If the clause is post-contractual, for example where it is contained in a notice on the back of a bedroom door in an hotel (*Olley* v. *Marlborough Court* (1948)) or on the back of a car-park ticket issued by a machine after the customer has inserted money into the machine (*Thornton* v. *Shoe Lane Parking* (1971)), it will not be a part of the contract and therefore ineffective. It does seem that sometimes knowledge of express terms gained by previous repeated dealings with the other party may be enough to incorporate those terms into a subsequent contract by *implication*, even though they have not been expressly incorporated on that particular occasion – *Spurling (J) Ltd* v. *Bradshaw* (1956).

If the clause has been incorporated into the contract the mere fact of the incorporation does not mean that the clause will be effective, for this will only occur if the court construes the clause as covering the liability in question. Among the rules of construction used by the courts the following are of particular importance:

(i) *the clause will be strictly interpreted*: this means that the court will only permit reliance on an exclusion clause where it clearly and unequivocally covers the liability in question.

An example of this approach is seen in *Baldry* v. *Marshall* (1925). The plaintiff purchased a Bugatti car from the defendants on the understanding that it would be 'suitable for touring purposes'. It was not, and in an action to recover the price paid the plaintiff found himself faced by a written term in the agreement which excluded any 'guarantee or warranty, statutory or otherwise'. The court held that the term as to purpose was a condition, and therefore did not come within the exclusion. As Lord Justice Scrutton pointed out in *Alison (J Gordon) Ltd* v. *Wallsend Shipway and Engineering Co Ltd*, (1927), 'if a person is under a legal liability and wishes to get rid of it, he can only do so by using clear words'.

(ii) *the contra proferentem rule*: by applying this rule, which can only be used where there is ambiguity or doubt about the meaning of an exclusion clause the words of the clause will be construed to resolve the ambiguity or doubt *against* the person relying on the clause (ie contra proferentum), in favour of the other party. In other words the excluder will not be allowed to exploit his or her own weakness of expression to his or her own advantage, and argue that the words used *can* be construed as covering the breach. The principle is that a person will be held responsible for his or her own lack of clear expression.

(iii) *the main purpose rule*: in construing an exclusion clause the court, in applying this rule, will presume that the excluder did not intend to defeat the main purpose or object of the contract.

In *Glynn* v. *Margetson* (1893) a contract was made for the shipment of oranges from Malaga to Liverpool. Clauses in the contract entitled the shipowners to call into any ports in the Mediterranean area. After leaving Malaga, the ship did not proceed direct to Liverpool, but first travelled to Valencia, only then doubling back and proceeding to Liverpool. On arrival the delay had caused the oranges to deteriorate. The House of Lords held the shipowners liable. The main purpose of the voyage was the shipment of a perishable cargo from Malaga to Liverpool. The broad terms entitled the ship merely to call into ports along the route but not to deviate. Lord Halsbury stated 'looking at the whole of the instrument, and seeing what one must regard . . . as its main purpose, one must reject words, indeed whole provisions, if they are inconsistent with what one assumes to be the main purpose of the contract'.

Fundamental breach

While a court may feel itself entitled to interpret broadly-framed clauses by reference to what the excluder may be presumed to have intended, a very different situation is faced when a clause is clearly and accurately framed to cover potential breaches of 'the main purpose of the contract', ie breaches of those fundamental terms which make up the very core of the contract. Whether to permit a party who has agreed to perform such fundamental obligations, then simply exempt himself or herself in the same contract from any liability should he or she fail for any reason to comply with these obligations, has perplexed the courts for a number of years. The issue is really whether there exists a rule of law preventing such an exclusion of liability, or whether the matter is one of construction, it being for the court to decide on the facts of any case whether the clause in question covers the fundamental breach in question.

The case of *Karsales (Harrow) Ltd* v. *Wallis* (1956) graphically illustrates the concept of breach of fundamental contractual obligations. The defendant took a second-hand car on hire-purchase terms from a finance company. A clause of the agreement stated 'No condition or warranty that the vehicle is roadworthy or as to its age, condition or fitness for any purpose is given by the owner or implied therein'. After the agreement was concluded the car was delivered to the defendant one night. It was totally incapable of self propulsion, and many parts were either missing or replaced by older parts. Thus the defendant found it the following morning. He refused to accept it. The Court of Appeal held that the exemption clause was not intended to cover such a fundamental breach as this. 'A car that will not go' said Lord Justice Birkett 'is not a car at all'. Dealing with such situations as this Lord Wilberforce, in the *Suisse Atlantique Case* in 1967 said,

'Since the contracting parties could hardly have been supposed to contemplate such a mis-performance, or to have provided against it without destroying the whole contractual sub-stratum, there is no difficulty here in holding exemption clauses to be inapplicable'. In *Photo Production v. Securicor Transport* (1980) the House of Lords have now made it clear that a party can, by clear and unambiguous language, construct an exemption clause to cover fundamental breach. In this case Securicor agreed to provide limited security services at a factory owned by Photo Productions. One night the duty patrol lit a fire inside the factory. The fire became out of control completely destroying the factory and its contents, a loss of £615 000. In an action brought against them Securicor relied on an exclusion clause which stated 'Under no circumstances shall [Securicor] be responsible for any injurious act or default by any employee of [Securicor] unless such act or default could have been foreseen and avoided by the exercise of due diligence on the part of [Securicor] . . .'. The House of Lords held that the clause clearly exempted Securicor from liability and therefore the question of whether the breach was such that Securicor lost the right to rely on the exclusion clause did not arise.

It must be appreciated that this examination of exclusion clauses is based upon the general position at common law. The passing of the Unfair Contract Terms Act 1977 has significantly extended the limitations upon the freedom of organisations and individuals to exclude or restrict various forms of legal liability, and this important Act merits special consideration.

The legislative approach

The long title of the Unfair Contract Terms Act 1977 provides an outline of its purposes. This explains that it is 'An Act to impose further limits on the extent to which . . . civil liability for breach of contract, or for negligence or other breach of duty, can be avoided by means of contract terms and otherwise . . .'. The reference to the imposition of 'further' limits indicates that it is not the first attempt by Parliament to legislate in this field, but to date it is unquestionably the most comprehensive measure introduced.

Fig 5.17 identifies the main provisions of the Act. Two points are worth noting before considering it. Firstly most of the provisions apply only to cases where there has been a breach of what the Act calls a *business liability*. Essentially this is liability occurring from things done by a person in the course of a business (whether it is his business or someone elses), or from the occupation of business premises. The legal duties imposed upon occupiers of premises are explained in the Chapter on Land. Secondly private consumers are afforded special protection, going beyond that granted to business consumers, who should be better placed to look after their own interests. A person deals as a *consumer* (ie

247

a private consumer) if he or she is not making the contract in the course of a business, while the other party *is* making the contract in the course of a business.

It will be noticed from Fig 5.17 that in many cases the survival of the term or notice excluding or restricting liability will depend upon it satisfying a test of reasonableness. The Act indicates the factors to be applied in such circumstances. Thus in the case of a contract term whether it will be a fair and reasonable one is found by having regard inter alia, to the circumstances known to or in the contemplation of the parties when the contract was made. It is clear that the economic foundations upon which a contract is based may also provide guidance as to the reasonableness of a term. In the case of a contract term or notice which seeks to limit a person's liability to a specific sum notice must be taken of resources likely to be available should any liability arise, and how far it was open to the person to insure against the risk. The burden of proving that a contract term or notice is reasonable always rests with the person who claims that it is reasonable. Although the Photo Productions case was decided on the basis of the law as it stood before the passing of the Act, it is clear that the Act deals with such an exclusion clause in the same way, namely that its validity is a matter of construing it, to determine whether it satisfies the requirement of reasonableness.

Manufacturer's liability to the consumer

a) *Civil liability*

In certain circumstances it is possible for a consumer who has suffered harm as a result of using or consuming defective goods to bring an action against the manufacturer under the tort of negligence. Such rights arise where a duty of care is imposed upon the manufacturer who fails to take reasonable precautions in producing the goods, and as a result a consumer suffers injury to property or person. This duty was laid down by a majority decision of the House of Lords in the case of *Donoghue* v. *Stevenson* (1932).

In *Donoghue* v. *Stevenson* (1932) the House of Lords had to decide whether a manufacturer could be made liable, under the tort of negligence, to a consumer in the following circumstances. Here, the consumer's friend had purchased a bottle of ginger-beer for her from a retailer. When she consumed some of the ginger-beer, the remainder, from the opaque bottle, was poured into her glass with what was later discovered to be the remains of a decomposed snail. The presence of the snail in the bottle caused shock and distress to the consumer which later developed into illness. She therefore sued the manufacturer of the ginger-beer in negligence, claiming that he was responsible for the presence of the snail and consequently had failed in his duty towards her. (Note the

Nature of exclusion/restriction	Effect of exclusion	Applicability	Section
Tortious liability			
Liability for negligence arising in any way which: (i) causes death or personal injury	void	these provisions apply whether the	s.2(1)
(ii) causes any other loss or damage	only valid if reasonable	exclusion/ restriction is contained in a contract or a notice	s.2(2)
In cases (i) and (ii) awareness of or agreement to the term or notice does not in itself constitute acceptance of it			
Contractual liability			
Misrepresentation			
A term excluding or restricting liability for a misrepresentation or regarding a remedy available to a misrepresentation by reason of the misrepresentation	only valid if reasonable	*all* contracts	s.8(1)
Sale or supply of goods			
(i) *Implied terms*: a) implied condition as to title (s.12 SGA 1979 for sales, s.8 SG(IT)A 1973 for hire purchase)	void	*all* contracts	s.6(1)
b) implied conditions as to description, quality, fitness for purpose (ss. 13 – 15 SGA 1979 for sales, ss. 9 – 11 SG(IT)A 1973 for hire purchase)	void in consumer sales valid in other sales if reasonable		s.6(2)(3)
(ii) *Guarantees*: A term or notice contained in, or operating by reference to a guarantee of the goods, excluding or restricting liability for loss or damage arising from the goods proving defective whilst in consumer use, where the defect is due to negligence either in manufacture or distribution	void	if goods are of a type ordinarily supplied for private use or consumption	s.5(1)(2)
Other contractual liability			
(i) *Breach of contract*: A contract term under which a person seeks to exclude or restrict liability for breaches of contract that he has committed. (ii) *Substituted or non-performance*: A contract term entitling a person to either a) render performance of the contract substantially different from that expected of him, or b) render no performance at all regarding either the whole or part of his contractual obligation(s).	only valid if reasonable	To contracts where either one of the parties deals as a consumer *or*, contracts on the other's written standard terms of business	s.3(1)(2)

Key SGA 1979 = Sale of Goods Act 1979
SG(IT)A 1973 = Supply of Goods (Implied Terms) Act 1973

Fig 5.17   Exclusion of Liability under the Unfair Contract Terms Act 1977

consumer had no right of action against the retailer in contract as she had not entered into a sale of goods contract with him as the ginger-beer had been purchased by her friend.) By a majority decision, the House of Lords held that as the manufacturer of a product can reasonably foresee harm as a result of his acts or omissions to the ultimate consumer of his products, then he owes them a duty of care in the tort of negligence. This is particularly so where there is no opportunity of an examination of the products in question before consumption (ie the opaque bottle prevented examination of the ginger-beer). By allowing the presence of the snail in the bottle, the duty of care was broken and, as damage resulted, he was liable in negligence to her and damages were awarded. This case, more than any other, established the principle that manufacturers should bear in mind the interests of consumers when producing goods for their consumption. A manufacturer must therefore ensure that he acts as a reasonable manufacturer would have acted in the circumstances, to fulfil the duty of care which he owes to the ultimate consumer of his products.

In *Vacwell Engineering Ltd* v. *BDH Chemicals Ltd* (1971) the defendants, who were chemical manufacturers, were held liable under the tort of negligence when one of their products caused an explosion. The defendants were liable for failing to warn prospective users their if the product came in contact with water it could lead to an explosion.

In suing under the tort of negligence, the consumer can take advantage of a well-known rule of evidence *res ipsa loquitur*. (This means 'let the facts speak for themselves'.) Under this rule the courts will infer negligence of the defendant, where there is no reasonable explanation for the damage caused, eg a stone in a cake, a new car with faulty brakes, poison in a bottle of lemonade. In addition, the activity causing the damage must be something totally within the control of the defendant, and would not be expected to occur if reasonable care had been exercised. The rule has the effect of shifting the burden of proof to the manufacturer to prove that he or she was not negligent. If the individual who suffers damage as a result of defective equipment (eg plant, machinery, vehicles or clothing), is an employee in the course of employment, then, following the Employer's Liability (Defective Equipment) Act 1969 he or she may recover damages from the employer who is deemed to be negligent. This then, leaves the employer to sue the manufacturer of the defective equipment to recover any damages paid to the employee.

Criminal liability

The Consumer Safety Act 1978 is a broad piece of legislation passed with the purpose of consolidating all the previous legislation on consumer safety in relation to dangerous goods. Under the Act, the Secretary of State is given wide powers to make regulations to ensure that goods are safe, and appropriate information is provided. Existing regulations relating to oil heaters, electrical goods, toys, pencils, night-dresses and children's clothing will eventually be replaced. Many of the regulations will simply specify existing safety standards (eg approved British Safety Standards) in respect of particular categories of goods. If the Secretary of State believes there is a risk of danger connected with the supply of goods, he has power to make a *prohibition order*, prohibiting the supply of specified goods. A supplier in breach of the regulations commits a criminal offence which will carry with it sub-stantial penalties. The Act provides a defence, if the supplier can show he or she took all reasonable steps and exercised all due diligence to avoid committing the offence. The duty of enforcing the Act is placed upon local authorities who are given wide powers of entry, search, seizure and testing. (This is the responsibility of the *Consumer Protection Department* and the *Weights and Measures Department*.) Trading Standards Officers employed by the Department fulfil the dual role of advising traders and enforcing the legislation.

Consumers and the law of sale

As a consumer a business organisation has a number of options available to it when it wishes to acquire non-human resources. Which option it chooses depends upon the relative costs attached to the particular form of acquisition, its own particular needs, and the market availability of the chosen form.

An organisation may obtain full ownership of property to take effect when the transaction is completed eg purchasing the freehold of a site for factory development. It may obtain ownership fixed by time — a 10-year lease; or have the mere expectation of acquiring property eg the right to buy certain land if and when the present owner decides to sell (*an option*). It may have possession and use without ownership by hiring machinery, or possession and use with the option of purchase, at some future time, by means of hire-purchase. It may pay for its resources by means of a lump sum or by means of instalments, using its own funds to do so, or by borrowing.

In the final part of this chapter one particular form of property is examined in conjunction with the legal rules by which it can be acquired and which regulate the rights and obligations of the parties dealing with it. The property in question is goods, and it is considered here because all organisations, their suppliers and their customers are parties to the daily process of buying and selling goods. This process represents the life blood of the economy, and it is hardly surprising that for nearly a hundred years the major source of law applicable to it has been legislative, namely the Sale of Goods Act, which is now examined. It should be pointed out that this examination is in no way intended to be exhaustive. It simply seeks to cover the following aspects of the law:

(i) *which contracts the Act applies to*;
(ii) *what the main obligations of the parties are*;
(iii) *when ownership will pass from the seller to the buyer*;
(iv) *some of the remedies available.*

The Sale of Goods Act 1979

This Act regulates all contracts for the sale of goods. It is a consolidating statute which combines the provisions of the original Sale of Goods Act 1893, with the various amendments made to it. The importance of the Sale of Goods Act 1979, to the commercial activity of the United Kingdom cannot be underestimated, for it provides the framework of rights and obligations applicable to all buyers and sellers of goods, and is thus a principal reference for the resolution of disputes involving buyer and seller, ie consumers and those who supply to them. When the 1893 Act was introduced it was drafted to codify (ie put into statutory form) the common law rules then existing that related to sales. These rules were primarily developed for the benefit of the business community, as an aid to contracting, rather than a judicial attempt to lay down a set of mandatory principles of law. Not surprisingly therefore the 1893 Act reproduced this underlying feature of the law of sale by granting parties the freedom to exclude its provisions if they so chose. The Act was there to regulate the contract of sale only to the extent that the parties themselves had failed to do so and as a result subsequently found themselves in disagreement. It was not for Parliament to dictate to a businessperson what the contract should be. This freedom to exclude is still contained in the 1979 Act, but it is now a very limited freedom. This is because it is subject to the provisions of the Unfair Contract Terms Act 1977, which restricts, and in certain cases, prohibits a seller from excluding his liabilities which arise under the 1979 Act. The effect of such restrictions is that the 1979 Act is not simply an aid to the business world, it is also a creator and defender of the rights of the economically weaker sections of the community, and thus qualifies for inclusion in the growing body of legislation which grants protection to the consumer. The main features of the Act are considered below.

Definition of a sale of goods transaction

The Act defines a contract for the sale of goods as one by which the seller transfers or agrees to transfer the *property* in goods to the buyer for a money consideration called the price. To understand this definition and therefore identify those transactions which fall outside the Act, an explanation of the terms *property*, *goods* and *money consideration* is necessary.

Property is ownership. It follows that the Act does not apply to transactions in which ownership does not pass from one party to the other, for example where goods are hired or borrowed, for the hirer or borrower is simply obtaining possession, not ownership. Such a transaction is known as a *bailment*. One of its consequences is that the person taking possession (the bailor) owes a duty of care towards the goods in custody. Hire-purchase agreements are similarly excluded from the Act. This is because a hire-purchase agreement consists of a simple hiring of goods, to which there is attached an option to purchase. Since the hirer is not compelled to purchase the goods he or she is not a 'buyer' for the Act defines a buyer as a person who *buys* or *agrees to buy* goods.

> In *Helby* v. *Matthews* (1895) the House of Lords made it clear that an option does not give rise to a firm commitment. In that case a piano dealer agreed to hire a piano to a customer for a period of 36 months on payment of 10/6d per month. The agreement provided that on completion of all the monthly payments the customer would become the owner of the piano, being liable to pay any arrears of the monthly payments outstanding at the date of termination. During the hire period the customer disposed of the piano to an innocent third party. The Court held that the dealer was entitled to recover the piano from the third party for the customer was not an owner and therefore could not pass a *good title* (ie ownership) to the third party.

The expression *goods* includes all personal property (called *chattels personal*) − such things as cars, furniture, tools, and books − but not land which forms a separate category of property, termed *real property*. Things which are attached to or form part of the land and which are agreed to be severed from the land either before the sale or under the contract of sale are treated as goods. However such goods must be identifiable from the land itself.

> In *Morgan* v. *Russell and Sons* (1909) a sale of slag and cinders was considered not to be a sale of goods because these materials had merged into the land upon which they had been deposited.

Annual growing crops such as barley, and industrial growing crops, like pine trees, are also goods within the meaning of the Act. However the following do not constitute goods:

(i) choses in action, such as shares and patents;
(ii) money, unless sold as something other than currency, such as a collector's item;
(iii) contracts whose substance is the supply of labour and materials where the value of the materials supplied under the contract is of lesser value than that of the labour involved. In *Robinson* v. *Graves* (1935) a commission to paint a portrait was held to be a contract for labour and materials. In contrast the following have been held to be contracts of sale: a contract to supply and lay a carpet (*Philip Head & Sons Ltd* v. *Showfronts Ltd* (1970),

a contract to make a fur coat (*J Marcel Furriers Ltd* v. *Tapper* (1953), and a contract to prepare and supply food in a restaurant (*Lockett* v. *A & M Charles Ltd* (1938).

The expression *money consideration* excludes from the definition of contract of sale gifts, and any transaction where goods are exchanged for other goods – a barter – although where the consideration is partly in goods and partly in money the contract will be one of sale.

Price

It might be expected that in a commercial transaction the parties will at very least determine the price for the goods. The Act says that the price may be fixed under the contract or left to be fixed in a manner agreed by the contract, or, where the parties have dealt with each other before, by reference to their previous course of dealing. In the event of no price being fixed the buyer must pay a *reasonable* price. Although this is likely to be the *market* price it is necessary to consider the circumstances of each particular case.

The transfer of property

The object of a sale is the transfer of property (ie ownership) in the goods from the seller to the buyer. The Act lays down a set of rules for determining when this vitally important event takes place, but these rules apply only if the parties have not expressed their own intention as to when property shall pass. The rules are examined later but it is helpful at this stage to identify why the time at which property passes is so important.

(i) The Act states that *risk* passes with property, unless the parties agree otherwise. This means that it is the owner of the goods who bears the risk of them being stolen or accidentally damaged. A person may be an owner although not in actual physical possession or control of the goods, as for example where a buyer of a painting leaves it at the auction rooms for collection at a later date, or where a seller allows the buyer to take possession of the goods, but provides in the contract that ownership shall only pass to the buyer when all outstanding sums owed by the buyer to the seller have been paid – a *Romalpa clause*. A prudent owner will usually insure the goods, and this will be especially important where the goods are not under his or her own control. The Act also provides that if delivery of the goods has been delayed through the fault of one of the parties the goods are then at the risk of the party at fault.

(ii) It is a general rule of law that a non-owner of goods cannot transfer ownership in them to another. This is expressed by the Latin maxim *nemo dat quod non habet* (no one can give what he has not got). The rule is subject to a number of exceptions, but as a general principle a seller who is not an owner is unable to effect a valid transfer of title.

(iii)   The seller can sue for the price of the goods only after property
        in them has passed, unless the parties have agreed that payment
        should be made at some other time.

It will be recalled that the definition of a contract for the sale of goods
makes reference to the transfer of property. It goes on to add that where
property in the goods is transferred at the time the contract is made,
there has been a *sale*, whereas if the transfer is to take place at some
future time or subject to some condition to be fulfilled later the contract
is called an *agreement to sell*. In this connection two points relating to
the passing of property are worth noting. Firstly the Act provides that if
a seller sells goods to a buyer and is unaware that the goods had *perished*
at the time the contract was made the contract will be void on the
grounds of *impossibility*. They may for instance have been stolen or
destroyed by fire while in a warehouse without the seller's knowledge.
Secondly the Act provides that where goods perish *after* the contract
has been made, but before the risk has passed to the buyer, then the
contract becomes *frustrated* and void, (frustration was examined in
Chapter I). Exactly when goods reach a stage at which they can be said
to have perished is not clear, however in *Asfar* v. *Blundell* (1896) a
consignment of dates that became unsaleable through contamination
with sewage were held to have perished.

Conditions and warranties
Even the most simple type of contract contains promises given by one
party to the other. Most will include a variety of mutual undertakings.
These undertakings are the contractual obligations which each party
owes to the other and they represent the terms of the agreement — its
contents. They generally arise through express agreement, however
certain terms may be implied into specific types of contract by statute.
The courts may sometimes be prepared to imply terms which the parties
have not expressly agreed. If a term is broken the consequences for the
contract will depend upon the importance of the term in relation to the
contract. Obviously the more important it is the more serious will be the
effect if it is broken. Terms are classified into conditions, warranties
and innominate terms, and have already been considered earlier in the
chapter.

In relation to sales the Act describes conditions and warranties by
referring to the effect on the contract if they are broken. A condition is
a stipulation, the breach of which gives rise to a right on the part of the
innocent party to treat the contract as *repudiated* (ie rejected) and/or
recover damages. A warranty on the other hand is a stipulation whose
breach entitles the innocent party to claim only damages, but the
contract still stands. A warranty is thus of less importance to the
purpose of the contract. Where there has been a breach of condition
there may still be sound reasons for continuing the contract. For
instance the buyer may have no other source of supply than the seller

255

and is unlikely therefore to repudiate when the seller notifies him or her that he or she cannot deliver the goods on time. It should be added that the courts will usually regard the delivery date in a commercial transaction as being a condition, or 'of the essence of the contract' as it is sometimes expressed.

> In *Richards.(Charles) Ltd* v. *Oppenheim* (1950) the seller agreed to build the buyer a car. When it had not been completed by the agreed delivery date the buyer requested the seller to complete it as soon as possible. Over three months later the car was still not ready, and the buyer told the seller that if it was not ready at the end of a further four weeks the contract would terminate. It was held that since the car was still incomplete at the end of that period the buyer was under no obligation to buy. He had waived the original delivery date, but had replaced it by serving a reasonable notice on the seller to complete the work.

Whether a particular term is to be treated as a condition or a warranty is a matter of interpretation for the courts. The label placed upon a term by the parties, for instance goods sold 'warranted free of all defects', does not mean that the court is bound by that label. In the example above defects in the goods would more likely be regarded as breaches of condition, enabling the buyer to repudiate, than warranties limiting him or her to damages alone.

Under sections 12 – 15 of the Act a wide range of conditions (and two warranties) are implied into all sales of goods. Before considering them in detail it is appropriate to point out that taken together they impose upon sellers who attempt to comply with them stringent trading standards. These occur notably in relation to the descriptions applied in the marketing of goods, in the emphasis placed upon customer reliance on a seller's skill and judgement, and in respect of product standards.

Statutory conditions implied into sales

S. 12 implies into a contract of sale a condition that the seller has a *right to sell the goods*. If there is an agreement to sell it is an implied condition that the seller will have this right to sell by the time ownership is to pass. The words 'right to sell' mean that the seller must have the legal *power* to sell. The seller will not have this power if the goods are not owned (unless the true owner has authorised the seller to sell them) or if he or she is the owner but can be prevented by legal means from selling them.

> In *Niblett* v. *Confectioners Materials Co* (1921) a buyer purchased 3000 tons of preserved milk in tins, some of which bore labels marked 'Nissly Brand'. This constituted an infringement of the trade mark used by the Nestlés Company, who could have obtained an injunction restraining the sale of the tins by the

purchaser. The purchaser was obliged to suffer a loss of profits by selling the tins without the offending labels, and it was held that the original sellers were in breach of the condition under s. 12. 'If a vendor can be stopped by process of law from selling he has no right to sell,' said Lord Justice Scrutton.

S. 12 also implies a warranty that (i) the goods are free, and will remain free until the time property is to pass, from any undisclosed charge or encumbrance (an example would be where a third party has the right to retain the goods until the seller pays the money owed – a *lien*), and (ii) that the buyer will enjoy *quiet possession* of the goods.

The meaning of this expression can be seen in *Microbeads* v. *Vinhurst Road Markings* (1975) where the buyers of road-marking machines found that shortly after purchasing them another company, not the seller, had obtained a patent relating to such machines, which enabled the company to bring action against the buyers to enforce the patent. The sellers were held liable in damages to the buyers, the buyers being unable to enjoy the machines undisturbed in the future.

It should be stressed that any clause excluding these s. 12 terms is treated as absolutely void by virtue of the Unfair Contract Terms Act, 1977.

In transactions between buyers and sellers of goods it is usual to find that some description will be applied to the goods. For instance the nature of the goods themselves is likely to be described, perhaps by the seller verbally, 'a fully-automatic washing-machine', or by reason of labelling on the goods 'Low Fat Natural Yoghurt'. Weight, size, quantity, contents and packing may also constitute part of the description. If goods are sold by description there is an implied condition, under s. 13, that the goods shall correspond with the description. Some examples may illustrate the commercial importance of this condition and demonstrate how liability under it is strict.

In *Arcos* v. *Ronaasen* (1933) a contract for the purchase of staves stated that they should be $\frac{1}{2}$ " thick. When they were supplied only 5% of the total corresponded to the size specified, the rest being slightly under 9/16" thick. The buyer's action to reject the goods succeeded. Lord Atkin observed that '. . . a ton does not mean about a ton, or a yard about a yard. Still less when you descend to minute measurements does $\frac{1}{2}$ " mean about $\frac{1}{2}$ ". If the seller wants a margin he must and in my experience does stipulate for it . . .'.

In *Re: Moore & Co Ltd and Landauer & Co* (1921) the buyers of a quantity of canned fruit, which the contract required to be packed in cases each containing thirty tins, sought to reject the whole consignment when on delivery it was found that half the consignment was packed in cases containing twenty-four tins. The buyer's action was successful despite the fact that no commercial loss would be suffered by the buyer through the incorrect packing.

As a counter balance it seems that a buyer who purchases on the basis of a *trade* description applied to goods cannot rely on s. 13 if the goods correspond to that description while failing to comply with its literal interpretation. Thus when buyers of 'safety glass' to be fitted into goggles discovered that the glass splintered they were unable to reject the glass since it in fact conformed to the technical trade meaning of 'safety glass' – *Grenfell* v. *E B Meyrovitz* (1931). In addition microscopic deviations as to size, weight, etc will in general be disregarded. It would be wrong to assume that a defect in goods will automatically give rise to liability under the section.

Goods may of course correspond with description but still suffer from some major defect of substance. A leaking hot water bottle is still a hot water bottle, even though it is not of sound quality. S. 14(2) assists the buyer in such a situation by implying a condition on the part of the seller that the goods shall be of *merchantable quality*. This means that the goods must be 'as fit for the purpose or purposes for which goods of that kind are commonly bought as it is reasonable to expect having regard to any description applied to them, the price (if relevant) and all other relevant circumstances'. For s. 14(2) to apply the seller must have sold the goods in the course of a business, thus a single private transaction would not attract the implied condition. 'Business' is broadly defined to include a profession, the activities of any government department or local or public authority. Thus the sale of steel by the British Steel Corporation or coal by the National Coal Board will be with the benefit to the buyer of the implied condition. The following points in relation to the merchantable quality provisions are worth noting:

(i)   The seller need not be a manufacturer. The seller may be simply the distributor of goods, but he will still be responsible under the section as a seller.

(ii) If sellers, in particular manufacturers, are to comply with the section they will be obliged to exercise some system of quality control over the products they sell, which will increase their costs of production.

(iii) Some flexibility in product quality is granted to sellers – they may adjust their prices to act as an indicator of quality.

(iv) The seller is not bound by the conditions where he or she has pointed out the defect to the buyer prior to the contract, or where the buyer has examined the goods before purchasing them, and ought to have discovered the defect.

The case law regarding merchantability tends to reveal the more extreme examples than the commonplace complaints about products failing to work properly or at all. Thus the following have been held to constitute breaches of s. 14(2) as non-merchantable items: beer contaminated by arsenic (*Wren* v. *Holt* (1903)), woollen underpants containing a chemical that caused dermatitis (*Grant* v. *Australian Knitting Mills* (1936)), 'Coalite' containing a detonator which exploded when thrown into a fire (*Wilson* v. *Rickett Cockerell & Co* (1954)), and a plastic catapult which splintered on use causing the child who bought it to lose an eye (*Godley* v. *Perry* (1960)).

That liability under the section is strict is illustrated by *Frost* v. *Aylesbury Dairies Ltd* (1905), where the dairy supplied milk containing typhoid germs and was held to be in breach of the section despite establishing that it had taken all reasonable precautions to prevent such contamination.

It would be wrong to assume that a defect in goods, will automatically give rise to liability under the section. For instance it is clear that because all relevant factors, in particular the price, should be considered to determine merchantability, that second-hand goods with defects *may* still be of merchantable quality eg: the sale of a used vehicle with defects of the bodywork or mechanical parts.

An additional benefit to a buyer is granted by s. 14(3) which states that where a seller sells goods in the course of a business and the buyer, either expressly or impliedly makes known to the seller any particular purpose for which the goods are being bought, then there is an implied condition that the goods supplied under the contract are reasonably fit for that purpose. The condition is not implied in circumstances which show that the buyer did not rely, or that it was unreasonable to rely, on the seller's skill and judgement. For instance if goods are purchased by their trade name and in such a way as to indicate that the buyer is satisfied that they will fulfil the purpose, the condition will not apply. Nor will it apply where the buyer has knowledge about particular market conditions which the seller does not possess.

In *Teheran-Europe Co Ltd* v. *S T Belton (Tractors) Ltd* (1968) the buyer purchased air compressors from the seller for export and resale in Iran. In fact the goods infringed that country's regulations, the buyer was fined, and sued the seller. The action failed, for the buyer, as an Iranian incorporated company, must have been relying on its own knowledge and judgement of the suitability of the goods for the Iranian market.

However it may happen that the buyer places only partial reliance on the seller. If this occurs the buyer will only have a claim against the seller where the unfitness relates to a matter on which the buyer did rely on the seller.

259

In *Cammell Laird & Co Ltd* v. *Manganese Bronze & Brass Co Ltd* (1934) the buyers supplied the sellers with a specification for ships' propellers which the sellers were to manufacture for the buyers. Reliance was placed upon the sellers regarding matters outside the specification, such as the appropriate thickness of metal to be used. On delivery the propellers were unsuitable, being too thin. The sellers were held liable, because the unfitness concerned a matter on which the buyers relied on the sellers' skill.

It will be noticed that even if there has been reliance, the standard required of the goods is only that they should be *reasonably fit*, and that like s. 14(2) the provisions of s. 14(3) apply only where the seller sells in the course of a business. Although a buyer may expressly state to the seller the particular purpose for which the goods are required, it is clear that if the goods have only one usual purpose, for example a radio, then merely by purchasing the goods the buyer will be implicitly making known that purpose.

Goods may be merchantable under s. 14(2) while failing to be fit for their purpose under s. 14(3), although in practice there is considerable overlap between them. The contaminated milk in *Frost* v. *Aylesbury Dairies* (1905) was both unmerchantable and unfit for its purpose, namely to drink.

The implied conditions imposed upon sellers under the Act, in particular ss. 13 and 14, place a considerable burden upon them, and their combined effect may be seen as a reversal of the old common law principle 'caveat emptor' – that it is for the buyer to beware. The justification for s. 14(3) was perhaps partially alluded to by Lord Wright in *Grant* v. *Australian Knitting Mills* (1935) when he observed that in retail sales '. . . a buyer goes to the shop in confidence that the tradesman has selected his stock with skill and judgement'. Sellers are expected to know something of their own business.

A sale is often made on the basis of sample goods being examined by the buyer who, satisfied as to such matters as quality, will then purchase the bulk item or items. Commercial buyers, who require large quantities of goods, purchase by sample, so do private consumers when buying items such as carpets. S. 15 provides that if the parties agree to contract on the basis of the sample, either expressly or impliedly, then there is an implied condition that a) the bulk shall correspond with the sample in quality, b) the buyer shall have a reasonable opportunity of comparing the bulk with the sample, and c) the goods shall be free from any defect, rendering them unmerchantable, which would not be apparent on reasonable examination of the sample.

Exclusion of seller's liability

A breach of the implied conditions will in most cases mean lost profit for the seller, since it will be recalled that the remedy for breach of a condition is repudiation. It is hardly surprising that with this in mind the natural reaction of a seller will be, in most cases, to attempt to exclude or restrict liability under ss. 12 – 15. The seller may do so by trying to exclude the provisions in their entirety, or limit liability to a fixed sum. The seller may impose a time limit upon the buyer's right to reject, or reduce the buyer's remedies (eg obliging the buyer to have the defective goods repaired). The Unfair Contract Terms Act 1977 (already considered earlier in this Chapter) limits the seller's freedom to exclude and restrict liability. The Act distinguishes business trans-actions (non-consumer deals) from consumer deals; under the 1977 Act a person deals as a consumer if he or she does not make the contract in the course of a business, the other party *does* make the contract in the course of a business, and the contract goods are of a type ordinarily supplied for private use or consumption. If the contract satisfies these criteria any attempt by the seller to exclude or restrict ss. 12 – 15 of the Sale of Goods Act 1979 is void (see Fig 5.17 p. 249). If the contract does not satisfy these criteria, for example where both parties are acting in the course of business, then the effect is that the seller is unable to exclude or restrict liability under s. 12 of the Sale of Goods Act 1979. The seller may however do so in relation to ss. 13 – 15, provided the term by which it is done satisfies a further test, that of reasonableness. In determining whether this test has been satisfied the 1977 Act lists a number of matters or *guidelines* to which reference must be made in reaching a decision. These are:

a) The respective *bargaining strengths* of the parties relative to each other. This involves considering possible alternative sources of supply, hence a monopolist seller may have difficulty in establishing the reasonableness of a widely drafted exclusion clause.

b) Whether the customer received an *inducement* to agree the term, or in accepting it had an opportunity of entering into a similar contract with other persons, but without having to accept a similar term. The reference to *other persons* involves account being taken of other suppliers within the market and their terms of trading. Sometimes suppliers combine to produce standardised terms of trading, giving buyers no opportunity of finding improved terms.

A customer may receive *an inducement* by an adjustment of the contract price.

c) Whether the customer knew or ought reasonably to have known of the *existence of the term*. This involves the customer's knowledge of the trade in general, its terms and customs, and knowledge of the seller, with whom the customer may have previously traded on the same terms.

d) Where the term excludes or restricts any relevant liability if some condition is not complied with, whether it was reasonable at the time of the contract to expect that it would be *practicable to comply with the condition*. It might not be practicable, for example, to oblige the buyer to notify the seller of defects occurring in a large consignment of goods within a limited time period and to couple that requirement

261

with a term excluding liability if it is not complied with.

e) Whether the goods were manufactured, processed or adapted to the *special order* of the customer.

If a contract term excluding, or restricting liability under ss. 13 – 15 fails to satisfy the test of reasonableness then it will be void.

A seller may also seek to exclude or restrict liability for failure to comply with other terms of the contract, such as time and place of delivery, delivery of the wrong quantity, or even the rendering of no performance at all.

S. 3 Unfair Contract Terms Act 1977 applies in such cases where the seller's liability is a *business liability*. It provides that where goods are purchased by a buyer who either 'deals as a consumer', or who purchases on the seller's written standard terms of business the seller cannot exclude or restrict liability for personal breaches of contract. Nor can the seller claim to be entitled to either (i) render contractual performance substantially different from that which was reasonably expected of him, or (ii) in respect of the whole or any part of the contractual obligations, to render no performance at all, unless the exemption clause satisfies the test of reasonableness. The 'guidelines' used to determine the question of reasonableness (mentioned above) are not required to be applied under s. 3, although they are likely to be taken into account by the court. The following points arising from the section are worth bearing in mind:

a) a buyer who purchases on the seller's written *standard terms* will include business organisations;

b) standard terms is not defined, but it seems likely that even if the only standard part is the exclusion clause or clauses that the section will still apply;

c) the section will apply to the seller's *fundamental breaches* of contract. A fundamental breach of contract is a breach which deprives the innocent party of substantially the whole benefit that it was intended should be obtained under the contract, and such breaches have been the object of considerable judicial discussion over the years. Fundamental breach was dealt with earlier in the chapter.

The passing of property

At some stage after the contract between the buyer and the seller has been concluded ownership will transfer from the seller to the buyer. This transfer of ownership is the principal obligation of the seller under the contract. Earlier in the chapter reference was made to the rule that risk is borne by the owner of the goods. It is obviously important to know who owns the goods for other reasons. For instance if either party becomes bankrupt that person's *trustee in bankruptcy* is obliged to gather all the property belonging to the estate of the bankrupt (in the same way that a liquidator collects the property of a company that is being wound up) in order to sell it and pay off debts. The trustee or company liquidator must know which property he can lawfully realise. Also the buyer can be sued for the price of the goods once he or she has become the owner of them.

Section 17 says that if the goods are *specific* or *ascertained*, ownership in them passes when the parties intend it to pass. Specific and ascertained goods are those *identified and agreed upon at the time the contract is made*, such as a motor vehicle identified by its registration number. The question of intention is determined by looking at the contract itself and all the surrounding circumstances. Because ownership is such a vital concept it will often be expressly referred to under the terms of the agreement.

A good illustration is provided by *Aluminium Industries Vaasen DV* v. *Romalpa Aluminium Ltd* (1976) where a reservation of title clause was inserted into a contract under which the plaintiffs sold aluminium foil to the defendants. The defendants would use the foil in their manufacturing process for the purposes of resale, and the plaintiffs clause provided firstly that ownership would only pass to the defendants when all payments owing by the defendants had been met, and secondly that if the foil was processed into other articles, that ownership in these articles would pass to the plaintiffs. The Court upheld the validity of the clause.

If the clear intention of the parties regarding the passing of property cannot be found, five rules to ascertain this question come into operation. The rules are contained in s. 18.

Rule 1

When there is an *unconditional contract* for the sale of *specific goods* in a *deliverable state* the property in goods passes to the buyer when the contract is *made*, and it is immaterial whether the time of payment or the time of delivery, or both, be postponed. Goods are in a deliverable state when the buyer would be bound to take delivery of them. In *Philip Head & Sons* v. *Showfronts* (1969) the plaintiffs had sold the defendants a quantity of carpet which the plaintiffs had agreed to lay. After the carpet had been delivered to the defendants' premises in bales, prior to being laid, it was stolen. Since it was not in a deliverable state at the time of the theft it was held that property was still with the plaintiffs under Rule 1 and the defendants were not liable to pay the price. It should be noted that although Rule 1 enables property to pass even though payment and/or delivery occur at a later date, in the case of sales in supermarkets and cash and carry stores the implied intention is that ownership shall only pass when the price is paid.

Rule 2

In a contract for the sale of specific goods where the seller is bound to do something to the goods to put them into a deliverable state, the property does not pass until that thing is done, and the buyer has notice of it.

In *Underwood* v. *Burgh Castle Brick & Cement Syndicate* (1922) a 30 ton condensing machine was to be sold under terms that the seller would be responsible for removing it from its site and loading it on to a train for delivery to the buyer. During the removal it was damaged and the Court held that the seller's action to recover the price must fail since, applying Rule 2, ownership had not passed. This was because something remained to be done to the engine.

Rule 3

In a contract for the sale of specific goods in a deliverable state, but where the seller is bound to weigh, measure or do something to the goods in order to ascertain the price, ownership will not pass until that thing has been done and the buyer has been given notice of it.

Rule 4

When goods are delivered to the buyer on approval or on sale or return property passes to the buyer when he or she either signifies his or her approval or acceptance or does some act adopting the transaction, or alternatively if the buyer retains the goods without giving notice that he or she is rejecting them within the time specified (eg goods delivered on 14-day approval) or if there is none, within a reasonable time. In cases where the buyer resells the goods he or she will be treated as having *adopted* the transaction. By the resale the buyer is asserting rights of ownership over the goods.

In *Kirkham* v. *Attenborough* (1897) the pledging of goods with a pawnbroker was held to constitute an adopting of the transaction.

Rule 5

This rule applies only to *unascertained goods*, unlike the four previous rules which apply to specific goods. Specific goods, it will be remembered, are those that are identified and agreed upon at the time the contract of sale is made. If the contract of sale is not for specific goods, then it must be for unascertained goods. Examples of such transactions include the purchase of 100 tons of coal, or 500 tons of wheat out of a cargo of 1000 tons of wheat on board a named ship (*Re: Wait* (1927)), or animal feedstuff to be produced by the seller according to a formula supplied by the buyer (*Ashington Piggeries* v. *Hill* (1971)). In each of these examples it is impossible to identify at the time of the contract the particular goods which are to become the buyer's property, even though they have necessarily been described.

Under Rule 5 ownership in such goods passes to the buyer when goods as described, and in a deliverable state, are unconditionally appropriated to the contract either by the seller with the buyer's assent or vice-versa. The expression *unconditionally appropriated* is vital.

In *Carlos Federspiel* v. *Charles Twigg & Co* (1957) the plaintiffs bought from the defendants a quantity of eighty-five bicycles. The contract required the seller to deliver them to the ship they were to be carried in and load them. Before they had left the seller's premises a Receiver was appointed who claimed the bicycles which were packed and marked with the plaintiff's name. The Court held that property had not passed to the plaintiffs, firstly because in a contract of this type (known as an f.o.b − free on board contract) the intention is that property shall pass when the goods are loaded, and secondly because in any event there had not been an unconditional appropriation. Pearson.J stated that 'To constitute an appropriation of goods to the contract the parties must have had, or be reasonably supposed to have had, an intention to attach the contract irrevocably to those goods'.

Rule 5 requires that the appropriation must be made by one party with the assent of the other. This may be *implied*. A clear illustration is provided in the case of purchasing petrol. It has been held that if petrol is put into a car by a petrol pump attendant the petrol is being unconditionally appropriated with the implied assent of the buyer (*Edwards* v. *Ddin* (1976)) and if it is the buyer who personally fills the car at a self-service petrol station there is an unconditional appropriation with the implied assent of the garage as seller when the petrol is being poured. (*R.* v. *McHugh* (1977)).

Under Rule 5, delivery of the goods by the seller to the buyer, or to a carrier for delivery to the buyer amounts to an unconditional appropriation.

Remedies available to buyers and sellers
In the event of a breach of the obligations owed by one party to the other under a sale of goods contract the injured party may seek redress against the other. The principal obligations that arise may be summarised as follows:

a) *the seller must transfer ownership in the goods to the buyer*; physically deliver them to the buyer unless the contract provides otherwise; fulfil the implied conditions and warranties contained in ss. 12 − 15 of the 1979 Act.
b) *the buyer must accept the goods and pay for them*. Note that payment and delivery are concurrent obligations, unless the parties agree otherwise. This means they occur at the same time, for instance cash sales in shops.

The remedies of a seller

If the seller is owed money by the buyer the Act gives the seller the following rights, even if the buyer has become the *owner* of the goods:

(i) *a lien over the goods*, ie a right to retain possession until he or she is paid;

(ii) *if the goods are in transit and in possession of a carrier, a right to regain possession of them during the transit if the buyer has become insolvent*;

(iii) *a right of resale* in certain circumstances, for instance when the goods are of a perishable nature, or where the seller gives the buyer notice of the intention to resell and the buyer does not within a reasonable time pay for the goods. In the event of a resale the seller can claim damages representing any loss suffered. Such a loss could be the reduced profit on a resale because of a drop in the market price of the goods, including the cost of advertising them, etc;

(iv) *an action for the price of the goods*;

(v) *an action for damages* where the goods are still owned by the seller and the buyer refuses or simply fails to accept them. Damages awarded will represent the loss directly and naturally resulting from the non acceptance. Prima facie, this will be the difference between the *contract* price, and the *market* or *current* price at the time when the goods should have been accepted, assuming of course there is an *available market*. So if supply exceeds demand and there is a fixed retail price for the goods damages will then represent the loss of profit that would have been made on the sale, but if demand exceeds supply then damages will only be *nominal* as the goods can be readily resold.

The remedies of a buyer

(i) *an action to recover damages when the seller wrongfully fails or refuses to deliver the goods*. Again damages are measured in the same way as outlined above in a seller's action for non-acceptance. It should be stressed that in the case of a non-delivery by the seller, or a non-acceptance by a buyer it is the market price *when the breach occurs* that is used to determine the measure of damages.

In *Pagnan* v. *Corbisa* (1970) Lord Justice Salmon made it quite clear that other market fluctuations are not relevant, '. . . the innocent party is not bound to go on the market and buy or sell at the date of the breach. Nor is he bound to gamble on the market changing in his favour. He may wait if he chooses; and if the market turns against him this cannot increase the liability of the party in default. Similarly, if the market turns in his favour, the liability of the party in default is not diminished'.

(ii) *recovery of the price paid if the goods are not delivered.*

(iii) *rejection of the goods* where there has been a breach of condition, and damages for breach of warranty — the amount being the difference between the value of the goods as delivered, and their value if the warranty had been complied with. A buyer may elect to treat a breach of condition as a breach of warranty.

The administrative machinery of consumer protection

The Fair Trading Act 1973 provides valuable protection to the consumer by adding to consumer protection law and the law relating to competition. Local enforcement of the Act is delegated to local authorities (the Department of Weights and Measures or Consumer Protection). The Act creates the post of *Director General of Fair Trading*, a new watchdog for consumer affairs. Wide powers have been granted to the Director General in relation to:

a) *Protecting the economic interests of consumers* — This involves collecting information relating to commercial activities in the UK with a view to discovering practices which adversely affect consumers.

b) *Protecting the general interests of consumers* — This involves receiving evidence of commercial activities which may adversely affect consumers' general interests (eg economic, health, safety interests).

c) *Assisting the Secretary of State for Consumer Affairs* — The Act imposes a duty on the Director to give information and assistance to the Secretary of State in respect of matters connected with those duties and also to recommend action.

d) *Seeking court orders in respect of detrimental courses of conduct* — Power is conferred on the Director to seek orders from the Restrictive Practices Court against persons who persistently maintain conduct which is unfair to consumers (ie contravenes the criminal law, Trade Descriptions Act 1968; or civil law, Sale of Goods Act 1979). The Director must first attempt to obtain an assurance from the person that he or she will refrain from the conduct, but if none is given or observed, the Director should seek a court order to direct the person to refrain, or accept an undertaking that he or she will refrain from the course of conduct. To break the court order will place the individual in contempt of court and make them liable to imprisonment.

The role of local government in consumer protection

All county councils including metropolitan county councils have a multitude of duties placed upon them by consumer legislation. These wide ranging duties are beyond the scope of the weights and measures departments so that many authorities have renamed them (Consumer Protection Departments or Trading Standards Departments). It is the duty of trading standards officers employed by the above departments to enforce much of the consumer legislation including:

a) Any legislation recommended by the Director General of Fair Trading under the Fair Trading Act 1973 to deal with unfair trade practices. Information on such practices is, of course, often communicated to the Office of Fair Trading by trading standards officers.

b) Regulations made under the Consumer Safety Act 1978 in relation to the supply of dangerous goods (mentioned previously).

c) The investigation of complaints made under the Trade Descriptions Acts 1968 and 1972 (mentioned previously).

d) The duties imposed under the Food and Drugs Act 1955 (mentioned previously) involving the sampling of food for analysis and the investigation of direct complaints.

e) Provisions of the Consumer Credit Act 1974 parts of which are still being brought into force by regulation. The Act provides for criminal, civil and administrative sanctions which may be imposed on persons who infringe its provisions.

f) Finally, duties are also placed on local authorities in relation to the enforcement of the Unsolicited Goods and Services Act 1971.

Summary

This section on consumer protection has attempted to set out the numerous common law and statutory rules that affect the consumer during transactions. It should be stressed, however, that the basic principle of 'caveat emptor' (let the buyer beware) is a paramount one; and a consumer of goods/services is presumed to have acted in a rational economic manner and will have no redress if a transaction he has entered into fails to meet his perceived utility, when this has been raised by lawful means.

Case study on the retailing industry

An examination of the industrial structure of the UK would reveal that this country has moved away from its traditional base of manufacturing and, in common with most of the developed countries of the world, has established an important tertiary sector providing the service requirements of a sophisticated society. It is suggested that this sector is unproductive in that it does not manufacture tangible products. However this view may be disregarded if production is considered in its widest sense. The aim of production in the economy is to satisfy the wants of the consumer and as such, the service sector plays an equally important part. It is for this reason that this case study will undertake a consideration of the retailing industry.

The distribution of food and manufactured products requires a chain of wholesalers, distributors, transport organisations and retail outlets but it is not the object of this study to examine the entire distribution process, but merely to concentrate on the final link in the chain between manufacturer and consumer − the retailer.

In the UK there are approximately 500 000 retail outlets which roughly equates to 1 shop to every 500 of the population. The retail trade is a major employer and because of its vulnerable position as the market place for consumer transactions is extremely susceptible to fluctuations in consumer demand. It has evolved over the last hundred years from a collection of small individual outlets to its present state which, although still containing the numerous small one-man businesses, has at its heart a relatively few major companies controlling chains of department stores and supermarkets.

Structure of the industry

There are several distinct categories which can be identified in the retail business. The most prolific business unit is the small shop often run on a sole trader basis which may specialise in one area of merchandise such as fruit and vegetables, or tobacco and newspapers. Alternatively, it may handle a variety of goods from food and drink to clothes and fancy goods. Traditionally such shops were located close to the market they served and customers made frequent, relatively low value purchases. An analysis of the consumer group using this type of store indicates that the majority live within walking distance and tend to shop daily or every two days. Often they may have children and/or no motor car and so travelling is restricted. There is also a tendency for the customers of small shops to come from lower income bracket families. Such outlets have much to recommend them as regular customers are often known to the shopkeeper who in most cases also provides personal service from behind the counter. However this proximity and friendly service may be offset to some extent by the higher prices charged by the small shops and the smaller range of products on offer. Increasingly the small shopkeeper has been unable to compete on a price basis with the supermarkets who gain economies of scale associated with bulk buying and centralised control. About one-third of all retail outlets are now part of voluntary groups such as Spar, VG or Wavyline which allows a continuance of the personal control while providing the advantages of mass purchasing. Often such shops have relatively small rates of return on capital. However the proprietors may be willing to accept this in return for the benefit of being their own boss.

The second category of retail outlets is the supermarket chain such as Tesco or Fine Fare. This type of store began to develop in the middle 1950s. The growth has been a notable feature of the retail trade. They have the advantage of relatively low staff costs in relation to turnover as they are self-service. Because of their rapid turnover of stock and a relatively large number of outlets they are able to buy direct from the manufacturer, often at a considerable discount. Centralised buying also enables them to impose quality standards on their suppliers in a way that the small one-man business is unable to do. The lower supplier prices and small overheads give the supermarkets the advantages of being able to compete vigorously with cut-price offers and bargain buys. The supermarkets have been criticised from some quarters in that their actions have led to a decline in the number of small retail outlets. However this argument is something of a two-edged sword for although the aggressive marketing and pricing policies of the supermarket chains have clearly reduced the number of competitors in the market place, they have been influential in reducing consumers' shopping costs and in so doing having created more market-related prices.

A further prominent element in the retailing industry has been the increasing share of the nonfood market taken by the department store chains. Companies like C & A, Littlewoods, Currys, Marks and Spencer and Woolworths all have turnovers in excess of £100 m per annum and the larger chains have even greater turnovers. Most of these stores have established a high reputation with the public in one or more areas of the market and have also developed a store character. For instance, C & A concentrate on clothing and Currys on electrical goods. They both have a reputation for good quality at a reasonable price. Others like Marks and Spencer have an almost idealist approach to retailing believing in high quality products, customer service and their ability to meet customer needs in a socially conscious way. Marks and

Spencer products are worn by the majority of people in the UK at some time and there has almost developed a 'St. Michael' look which usually reflects quiet conservatism mixed with a gradual acceptance of changing fashions. These large retailers are usually in a dominant position with regard to their suppliers and so enforce rigidly their own ideas on style, quality and price.

There remains a variety of other retail outlets in all sectors of the industry which are not connected to large chains. They market manufacturers' brand products and rely on their own reputation and the advertising of the manufacturers to survive.

The following table gives an indication of some of the major chains in the retail industry and their areas of activity.

Some Market Leaders in the Retailing Industry

Marks and Spencer	– the market leader in clothing and also has a substantial food market.
Co-ops	– over 10 000 retail outlets divided between about 250 societies with varying membership among consumers. Activities vary from food, clothing, furnishing to travel, etc. Declining share of market. Purchasing centrally undertaken by the Co-operative Wholesale Society Ltd.
Woolworth	– American owned, biggest retailer of a variety of cheaper products. In last twenty years has sought to move upmarket and has experienced difficulty in doing so.
Tesco	– Largest supermarket chain in UK with almost 1000 supermarkets and stores.
Boots	– Largest chain of retail chemist shops specialising in chemist's goods and related products but successfully diversifying into electrical goods, records, stationery.
Sainsbury's	– chain of supermarkets and shops. Well established in the South of England but gradually extending operations throughout the UK.
Spar	– voluntary chain of independent retailers providing central purchasing and advertising to its members.
Debenhams	– department store chain trading under its own name but also as Harvey Nichols, Marshal and Snelgrove Swan and Edgar and others. Mainly established in London and South East but seeking to extend geographically. Also owns chain of Cater supermarkets and Cresta fashion shops.

W H Smith & Son Ltd	– newsagents and newspaper distributors diversifying into books, records, fancy goods.
House of Fraser	– department store chain throughout the UK including the most prestigious name in UK retailing, Harrods, but also trades as Dickens and Jones, DH Evans, Derry and Toms, Binns and others.
John Lewis Partnership	– established as department store now with branches throughout the country. Also owns Waitrose chain of supermarkets.
Menzies (John) Holdings Ltd	– newsagents, originally based in Scotland but now geographically diversified. Also retailing, records, books, fancy goods, etc.
British Home Stores	– chain of department stores throughout UK often having to live in the shadow of Marks and Spencer.
Great Universal Stores	– holding company control stores, shops and warehouses. Particularly strong in men's clothing shops such as John Temple, Willerby and in furniture stores including Times Furnishing, Astons. Largest catalogue mail-order business in Europe.
Currys Ltd	– chain of stores specialising in electrical consumer durables such as TVs, hi-fi.
Peter Dominic Ltd	– wine and spirit retailers. Subsidiary of Distillers. Trades under names Peter Dominic, concentrating on up-market city centre sites, and Westminster Wines, usually situated in 'corner shop' sites.
Safeway Food Stores Ltd	– supermarket chain, UK subsidiary of Canadian and US holding company.
Mothercare	– established in 1963, chain of retail outlets specialising in babies', children's and mothers' clothing and accessories. Rapid growth in UK and Europe.

Retailers own brand products

An important feature of many of the chains of both department stores and supermarkets has been the emergence of retailers' own brand range of products. This adds the retailer's reputation to the goods and increases customers' confidence in them. In some circumstances such as in food retailing, a retailer's own brand offers national brand quality, but at a lower price.

Perhaps the most well-known example of a retailer's 'own brand' is the St Michael range sold by Marks and Spencer. Everything that the store sells carries this brand and because of the very large orders which the company places with its suppliers it is able to enforce rigorous contractual conditions with regard to such matters as specification or quality control. Other stores pursue the same type of policy, eg Boots, who produce 'Boots No. 7' cosmetics established as a product leader. Other examples include Woolworths 'Winfield' brand, and British Home Stores 'Prova' brand. The primary advantage of a store having its own brand is that if customers are satisfied and wish to repeat purchases they must come back to the same retailer or another member of the same chain. With national suppliers brands they are free to buy from any store stocking the product. Therefore the own brand policy can encourage repeat business not only for the same product but also for other goods sold in the store. This of course is only true if the retailer ensures that quality is maintained and has a sufficient reputation among consumers so that they will trust the 'own brand' in the first place. Finally for a retailer's own brand to succeed there must be a relatively large market for the product to permit mass production so that they may compete with the products of national manufacturers sold through many outlets.

Credit facilities offered by retailers

If a retailer is to offer credit to customers as many now do, this retailer is acting both as a shopkeeper and a credit financer. Clearly without credit facilities many consumers could not afford to purchase large value consumer durables. Traditionally bank lending for such purchases was restricted to the middle classes while the poorer sections of society made use of hire-purchase to buy larger items. In recent years it has become more usual to find retailers offering their own credit facilities either directly or acting as agents for finance houses. In times of economic recession when sales are slack, retailers tend to improve the credit facilities on offer either through longer periods of repayment, cheaper interest rates or substantial periods of interest-free credit, subject to prevailing statutory restrictions. In times of inflation credit favours the consumer who is able to purchase at the current price with repayments over a period in which currency is depreciating. Of course the main determinant is the relationship between the rate of inflation and the interest rates being asked. There have been certain periods in the 1970s when interest rates were below inflation and so a credit sale offered by a retailer could cost money in real terms. A further problem with credit is that the retailer offering it is forced to write off a percentage of sales as bad debts. Thus, some retailers, notably Marks and Spencer, and many food retailers only trade for cash or cheques. They believe that the extra costs incurred by the retailer in offering credit would eventually have to be passed on to the customer in the form

273

of higher prices and so they would lose some of their competitive edge. However for many retailers dealing in large consumer durables such as TVs, domestic appliances, furnishing, and so on, providing credit facilities is a fact of life which they must live with if they hope to compete. The use of retailers' credit varies with the socio-economic group to which the consumer belongs. Above average income families more often use bank lending as a source of credit. Middle-income groups tend to rely on hire-purchase facilities and the extensive credit offered by the mail order companies. At the bottom end of the income bracket consumers find credit much more difficult to obtain either because they are unable to afford it or are regarded as a poor credit risk.

The growth of retailers' budget accounts, where consumers have a set credit limit and pay a regular monthly repayment, has been of increasing importance in recent years. They tend to be more widely used by the middle and upper middle income groups but they impose extra costs on the retailer who is in effect offering up to a month's free credit on purchases. This is as a result of the time lag between the date of purchase and the requested payment date. Accounts which are not settled at the end of each month are now normally charged a rate of interest on the outstanding balance equivalent to that asked by the major credit card companies.

Retailer advertising

The retail industry uses advertising to bring its outlets, merchandise and prices to the public's attention. In character this type of advertising differs from that of product manufacturers as its attitude tends to be more objectively based. Factors such as value for money, friendly and convenient service are emphasised greatly. The fantasy engaged in by product manufacturers is inappropriate to retailers who are more concerned with supplying the consumer with information, eg that the store has a special offer for that week. When compared with manufacturers, retailers spend a relatively small proportion of their turnover on an advertising budget, often less than 1%. Of course, the opening of a new outlet may be accompanied by an impressive publicity fanfare but once customers are established, retailers often rely on return sales and word of mouth recommendation. Some of the large food retail chains such as the Co-op, Tesco and Safeway do use television and press advertising to promote their value for money character and this is necessary because of the highly competitive nature of food retailing. Of the large non-food chain stores Boots and Woolworths spend the greatest amounts on advertising. This is perhaps for different reasons. Boots are attempting to promote their own brand products in direct competition with manufacturers' brands and so to some extent have a similar outlook to manufacturers as regards advertising. Woolworths on the other hand are currently having difficulty in re-establishing a store character with the consumer population. Having been regarded up to the 1950's as a sixpenny bazaar it has sought to push its image upmarket by the introduction of more expensive consumer durables such as hi-fi, garden equipment and electrical goods.

It has also established Woolco as a hypermarket outlet. Because they now have no recognised specialism for which the consumer always turns to them, they have been forced to invest heavily in promotional advertising. Disastrous trading figures with less than £1m profit in the UK in 1980 – 81 has illustrated their dilemma.

Perhaps the most interesting growth without recourse to extensive advertising is the case of Marks and Spencer. They have an almost negligible promotional budget and rely on the prominence of their locational sites and long-established reputation for good quality and customer service. Other chains to follow such a policy include Sainsburys, the John Lewis Partnership and British Home Stores. Retailers without a clearly defined market or in a more competitive situation may rely more heavily on advertising. However dangers may exist if advertising includes references to national brands for this may prove beneficial to competitors retailing the same product. Therefore advertising needs to concentrate on the store's own specific advantages and in so doing create a corporate image. It is wiser to concentrate on the store's differences from its rivals rather than its similarities.

To summarise this examination of retail advertising it may be suggested that it has a number of clear objectives. First and foremost it is to bring the store and its name to the public's attention. Secondly to attempt to establish a character for the chain, whether it be high quality, friendly service, or good value, etc. Thirdly to encourage consumers to concentrate a substantial proportion of their shopping budget with the store. This is particularly true of food retailing where supermarkets attempt to persuade shoppers that they should acquire their entire week's requirements from one shop. Fourthly to promote special offers, sales, remnant days, etc when the store seeks to attract a substantial inflow of customers and achieve a rapid turnover.

The legal liability of retailers

The retailer is a middleman – goods are bought from a distributor or direct from the manufacturer, for the purpose of reselling to the consumer at a profit. The consumer may make the purchase for his or her own private use or consumption, but in practice many consumer transactions involve purchasing a product that the consumer shares with others such as the rest of the family, or gives to someone else as a gift. A number of persons are involved in the chain of buyer/seller relationships. All of them possess rights and some of them owe responsibilities. These rights and responsibilities are of particular concern to the retailer who is central to the chain of transactions, acting as both a buyer and a seller. If a consumer buys goods that fall short of the standards he or she expects of them then it is to the retailer that the customer will generally make complaint, rather than the manufacturer. Contractual liabilities are only owed by the parties to the contract and in consequence a consumer who buys goods from a retailer *strictly speaking* has no contractual relationship with the manufacturer at all. They are not privy to, or parties to the same contract, for neither has supplied the other with consideration, and so the consumer has no choice but to return the goods to the retailer if something 'goes wrong'.

Many manufacturers however provide the consumer with a product guarantee. Indeed thousands of transactions are entered into on the basis that if things do go wrong the consumer can look to the manufacturer for repair or replacement under 'the guarantee'. Manufacturers' guarantees play an important part in the marketing of products that are highly competitive, such as electrical goods and motor vehicles. A product guarantee is a selling point which the retailer will be quick to exploit, and because of the undertakings given in them by the manufacturer, guarantees have helped to persuade the buying public that the principal responsibility of the defective product *does* lie with the manufacturer. Retailers often compound this misapprehension by instructing their customers who return defective goods that because the goods are under guarantee they should be returned to the manufacturer, the shop bearing no responsibility in such a situation. The manufacturer may indeed be responsible under the guarantee, but the primary liability rests with the retailer. At best the guarantee will operate as a collateral contract between the manufacturer and the consumer, the consideration provided by the consumer for the benefits gained under the guarantee being his or her purchase of the product from the retailer. But the guarantee does not operate as a device to enable the retailer to avoid personal liabilities as a seller. What it may do is to deflect the consumer away from seeking a remedy against the retailer. A comprehensive guarantee will certainly be regarded by the retailer as giving an opportunity to redirect contractual liabilities towards the manufacturer if the product proves defective. This will save what might otherwise be the loss of profit on a sale if the product was returned as unmerchantable, the consumer demanding a return of the price paid.

It is not only manufacturers who provide guarantees, for retailers themselves will often do so, usually as a promotional device. If the guarantee provides for repair or replacement of parts the retailer will require expertise and access to suitable parts to meet the requirements of the guarantee.

Guarantees will not always be as beneficial to the consumer as they appear. Although they cannot be used to cut down statutory rights, nor exclude in the case of manufacturers' guarantees liability for negligent manufacture, they may certainly be designed to raise expectations in the consumer's mind of a valuable benefit which may last anything up to five years. In the event of claims the guarantee may prove to be worth little or nothing, for instance because the retailer can actually charge for the work he carries out, or the replacement parts he fits. As Lord Denning said in *Adams* v. *Richardson & Starling Ltd* 1969:

'We all know what happens. Be it a motor car, a refrigerator, or a washing machine, the supplier will "guarantee" it for two, three or five years, as the case may be. It sounds splendid. It looks fine. It is often headed in ornamental lettering "GUARANTEE", sometimes with a seal attached, as if to show it is of great value. The salesman asks the customer to sign an acknowledgement and return it to the supplier. It is in the customer's interest, he says, to do so. The customer does so, believing it is worth a great deal to him. He does not read it, of course. No one ever does. He takes it on trust that it is what the salesman says it is — a guarantee for those years. But when it comes to the pinch — when something goes wrong with the thing and he reads it — then he will discover that he would have done better without it. The guarantee gives him no more than the law would have done anyway.'

A further circumstance in which a consumer may bring legal proceedings directly against a manufacturer, other than under a manufacturer's guarantee, is if the goods are not only unmerchantable but cause actual harm to persons or property. Here the retailer may step out of the legal arena, although if defectively produced goods are stocked and sold, the retailer may become liable to a consumer who suffers harm in the tort of negligence. Of a manufacturer's liability Lord Atkin in *Donoghue* v. *Stevenson* (1932) said:

'A manufacturer of products, which he sells in such a form as to show that he intends them to reach the ultimate consumer in the form in which they left him with no reasonable possibility of intermediate examination, and with the knowledge that the absence of reasonable care in the preparation of putting up of the products will result in an injury to the consumer's life or property, owes a duty to the consumer to take reasonable care.'

The legal liabilities of the retailer arise out of both the civil and the criminal law, and they are detailed and extensive. The Sale of Goods Act 1979 obliges the retailer to sell a product which he or she has the legal power to sell, which meets the description that it has been sold under and that it is of merchantable quality. If the customer requires the product for a particular purpose and the retailer is aware that the customer is placing reliance on the retailer to supply a suitable product, it will be in breach of contract if the retailer fails to supply a suitable product, even if it is quite fit for other purposes. If the retailer fails in any of these respects the statute regards the retailer as having broken fundamental obligations. The consumer can return the goods and lawfully demand a return of the price paid. The contract is over. In addition to these private responsibilities statute places public obligations on the retailer, for instance under the Trade Descriptions Act 1968. This prohibits the retailer from misdescribing goods and services and giving false and misleading indications as to the price at which goods are sold. The retailer will be criminally liable if such acts are committed and can be fined up to £1000 by a Magistrate's Court, and if the matter is tried by a Crown Court the fine may be unlimited and in addition up to two years' imprisonment may be imposed. While the power to imprison is rarely used, the power to fine has been utilised. In 1977 for example, some ten years after the passing of the Act, fines imposed under the Act upon the sellers of motor vehicles and accessories exceeded £128 000. It must be pointed out however that if annual fines provide a guide to the standards operated by the various sectors of the retail trade then the motor trade is at the top of the league of offenders. During the same year of 1977 fines imposed upon clothing suppliers totalled just over £5500.

These two statutes, one concerned with civil liability, the other criminal liability are central to the business of retailing within the law. There are however many other rules of law which the retailer is bound by. The legislation above represents only a part of the statutory controls that exist. Criminal legislation concerning the retail trade is particularly extensive. It extends to weights and measures, food and drugs, advertising, prices, trading stamps, credit facilities, and hallmarking, to take just some examples. This daunting body of rules could lead one to consider that the burden placed upon the retail trade might be regarded by the trade itself as intolerable. This is patently not the case. Retailing activity still flourishes. It has obviously been able to withstand the deluge of rules which now govern it. Invariably the cost of legislation designed to benefit the consumer is passed on by the retailer to the consumer in the form of higher prices. In any case the gradual disappearance of the smaller retail outlets in favour of bigger retailers, such as the supermarket chains, has ensured that the turnover levels achieved by such organisations enable them to readily absorb the cost of greater controls over pricing, packaging, and the costs of fines and loss of profit on returned goods.

It may be asked, not unreasonably, why it is the retailer rather than the manufacturer who possesses primary liability in selling the product. This apparent anomaly is perhaps most strikingly demonstrated by the retailers' liability towards the standard of quality of the goods they sell, under the Sale of Goods Act, 1979. Since these goods will commonly have been manufactured by someone else, upon what basis is it just or reasonable to make the retailer responsible for their defects, especially if the goods are complex by nature? As the *Molony Committee Report on Consumer Protection* (1961) pointed out:

'[The last half century] has seen a growing tendency for manufacturers . . . to appeal directly to the public by forceful national advertising and other promotional methods . . . a further influence during the same period has been the development of a mass market for extremely compled mechanical and electrical goods . . . Their performance cannot in some cases be accurately established by a short trial; shortcomings of design are not apparent to the inexpert eye; inherent faults may only come to light when the article breaks down after a period of use.'

The reason seems to be that the philosophy which guided the establishment of liability on retailers in the nineteenth century has not been replaced by a more appropriate philosophy applicable to the conditions of the twentieth century. A hundred years ago the retailers exerted a real control over product quality, and could also be regarded as possessing an expertise in the nature of their business: they should know their trade. As late as 1935 Lord Wright, in the case of *Grant* v. *Australian Knitting Mills*, discussing the statutory rule that goods must be fit for their purpose where the seller's skill and judgement has been relied on by the customer, said

'. . . thus to take a case like that in question of a purchase from a retailer the reliance will be in general inferred from the fact that a buyer goes to the shop in confidence that the tradesman has selected his stock with skill and judgement'.

Although the modern retail trade is doubtless in many ways far more efficient than its nineteenth century counterpart, it is unrealistic to suggest that in selling products of modern technology, such as televisions, micro-wave ovens and the like, the retailer can directly control quality. Quality is a matter for the manufacturer. At best the retailer can refuse to stock products which consumer complaints show to be of a consistently poor quality. Only the dominant retail chains like Marks and Spencer exercise real control over the quality of the products they sell. This they achieve by requiring manufacturers to supply products made to the retailer's own specification, to be sold under the retailers own brand-name (St Michael for Marks & Spencer, Canda for C&A's, Winfield for Woolworth, etc). Nevertheless there are matters over which the modern retailer does have considerable control. It is for instance presumably quite reasonable to expect sellers to satisfy themselves that the goods they are selling have not been incorrectly priced or otherwise inaccurately described, or that foodstuffs have been properly stored or cooked, and at the time of selling are fit for human consumption.

Finally it should be pointed out that legal controls over sales by retailers do often provide them with a measure of sales flexibility. A good example is provided by the statutory requirement that goods must be of merchantable quality, for in deciding the question of what determines this important standard account must be taken of the price and description applied to goods. The retailer is permitted therefore to adjust prices as an indicator of the quality the consumer may expect to find, and indications that the goods are 'substandard', 'seconds', or 'manufacturer's rejects' will be a means of reducing the standard that might otherwise be required. Relief from liability under criminal legislation may also be available, for example the Trade Descriptions Act 1968, provides the retailer with a number of defences. Of these the defence most frequently put forward is that the offence was due to the act or default of another person, but the retailer may also plead that the offence was caused by reliance on information supplied, or a mistake, or an accident, or some other cause beyond the retailer's control.

Thus, even in circumstances when liability is strict (ie when the state of mind accompanying the prohibited act is irrelevant) the retailer may nevertheless escape liability.

In recent years both retailers and manufacturers have sought to show that profit is not always the sole motivator of business organisations. They have produced detailed codes of practice, as a method of business self-regulation, in their concern to demonstrate social responsibility. The Director General of Fair Trading is under a duty to encourage such codes, which impose only voluntary obligations upon the members of the trade associations which adopt them. The Office of Fair Trading has approved a number of major codes. Because they now play such an important role in regulating the relationship between consumers and suppliers, an example of a code of practice is given below. Many codes are considerably more detailed than the example given.

Code of Practice Statement
As a member of the Association of British Launderers and Cleaners Limited we undertake not to restrict our liability under the general law and shall so far as is reasonably practicable:

1 Handle all clothes, linens, furnishings and other items accepted by us for processing with proper and due care and attention.
2 Investigate any complaint promptly and, if requested, re-process, free of charge, any article which is unsatisfactory due to fault on our part.
3 Pay fair compensation for loss or damage due to negligence on our part.
4 Train our staff to be competent, courteous and helpful at all times.
5 Keep our shops, vans, containers and premises clean and tidy.
6 Maintain the highest possible standard of quality and service consistent with the price charged.
7 Display in shop premises a list of prices for standard articles.
8 Have all orders ready or delivered at the time stated, unless prevented by exceptional circumstances.

The ABLC's customer advisory service is available to help resolve any disputes which arise between members of the association and customers. The association's address is: Lancaster Gate House, 319 Pinner Road, Harrow, Middlesex HA1 4HX.
Telephone no 01-863 7755

6 Labour

'Industrial relations are like sexual relations.
It's better between two consenting parties.'

Vic Feather
Guardian Weekly,
8 August 1976

Labour as a factor of production

For most organisations, it is the workforce which is their most important factor of production, for without the appropriate number of workers, holding the requisite skills and experience the operation of a business cannot be undertaken efficiently. In this chapter the central focus will be the organisation's labour force. It will be necessary to consider the number of workers an organisation should employ, the different types of contract of employment under which the workforce can be hired, and the wage rate which will be acceptable both to the employer and employees. This will involve an examination of the legal implications to both employer and employee of entering into a contract of employment. Finally the effect of trade union activity and its impact on the labour market will be considered.

The demand for labour

The demand for labour, in common with the demand for the other factors of production, is *derived demand*. This simply means that it is the demand for the products or services which the labour force helps to produce which is the determining factor. A bricklayer is only in demand if the construction industry is flourishing. This may be regarded as an oversimplification, for many workers have talents which could be used to produce a variety of products. The demand for typists is not related solely to the demand for one particular product. The typist is capable of moving from organisation to organisation or industry to industry as fluctuations in product demand influence the demand for typists and their wage levels in different jobs. However, it has already been noted in earlier chapters that the overall level of demand in the economy as a whole – *aggregate demand* – may also fluctuate according to the changes in combined demands of all consumers for all products. Therefore a decline in aggregate demand will be reflected in a fall in derived demand for labour and greater unemployment within the economy as a whole. Conversely a rise in aggregate demand will mean a general rise in the demand for labour. This relationship is important for the government when it is seeking to control the level of unemployment within the economy. It is in the government's power to influence the level of aggregate demand for goods and services in order to increase or decrease the number of people employed. This is known as *demand management*. However, this control of the overall demand for goods and services will be considered in some detail in the chapter on Government Economic Policy. This chapter concentrates on the demand for labour generated by individual industries and organisations.

Individual organisation's demand for labour

Clearly any organisation will attempt to employ the most appropriate number of workers to efficiently meet the demand for its products. The two main factors which it should take into account when deciding how many people to employ are:

a) *the level of output from each employee*;

b) *the cost of employing each extra worker*. This takes into account the wages or salary they must be paid, plus any additional cost of hiring workers such as national insurance contributions, administrative overheads, etc.

The output of employees

It is often difficult to measure precisely the output of each worker. If the worker is performing a relatively straightforward repetitive manual task such as a machine operator then it may be simple enough to count the number of units produced in a day or a week. However, it is much more difficult to calculate the output of a person performing a variety of tasks or one task which may differ in length or complexity each time it is undertaken. So, for instance, in attempting to assess the output of an administrator making decisions, it is not feasible to simply summate the number of decisions such a person has made in a day. It is necessary to consider the complexity of the decisions and the time taken over them and the efficiency with which they are made. Often this is a matter of comparing one worker's performance against another's. In this way the organisation must make a more subjective assessment of an employee's output.

In an attempt to quantify such output, assessment of each worker's performance is made in terms of their *physical product*. This may be stated in actual tangible units produced, eg a worker produced 100 light fittings in one hour. When this is not possible, it may be expressed in terms of work units, eg an administrator performed the equivalent of 100 work units in a day.

All workers will not produce the same physical product doing the same job. Some may work harder, be more skilful, experienced, or have a greater understanding of the job to be done. In theory it would be in the organisation's best interests to value each worker's contribution in terms of physical product and so be able to compare differing levels of productivity.

Another factor which will influence the productivity of individual workers is the number of fellow workers employed by the organisation contributing to the same overall task. This concept is known as the *division of labour* and basically it illustrates the fact that if one person is required to carry out an entire process alone then that person must develop a level of expertise in each stage of the process. If the task is divided among several workers, each of whom concentrates on one aspect of the operation, then it is probable that they would acquire a higher degree of expertise in that one particular aspect and thus a greater level of productivity than if they were required to undertake the whole operation. Organisations find that as they employ more people their total output increases in a greater proportion than the increase in the workforce. The organisation benefits from *labour economies of scale* by developing expertise, and employing specialists to undertake particular tasks.

A simple numerical example may help to illustrate the point.

Number of employees	Total output (physical product) units per week
1	25
2	56
3	88

Table 6.1 Output in relation to Number of employees

From the above figures each extra worker contributes to the total output. But this total output is increasing at a greater rate than the addition of each extra worker. The extra output from each additional worker is expressed as *marginal physical product* (MPP). (The concept of the margin has already been introduced in earlier chapters.) Using the same figures the MPP may be expressed as follows:

Number of employees	Total output total physical product	Marginal physical product
1	25 (0 – 25)	= 25
2	56 (25 – 56)	= 31
3	88 (56 – 88)	= 32

Table 6.2 Marginal Physical Product in relation to number ôf employees

This does not necessarily mean that the second worker is more efficient than the first, *simply* that working together they can produce more than two individuals working separately. Unfortunately, this increasing marginal physical product will not continue indefinitely as more and more workers are employed. Eventually the organisation will reach that *optimum level of production* at which additional workers, although adding to the overall output, do so at a diminishing rate. This is called the point where the organisation gains *less than proportionate returns to scale* or *diminishing returns*. Using the same figures but employing more workers the example becomes:

Number of employees	Total output total physical product	Marginal physical product
1	25 (0 – 25)	= 25
2	56 (25 – 56)	= 31
3	88 (56 – 88)	= 32
4	119 (88 – 119)	= 31
5	147 (119 – 147)	= 28
6	174 (147 – 174)	= 27
7	198 (174 – 198)	= 24
8	209 (198 – 209)	= 11

Table 6.3 Marginal Physical Product relationship with workforce

These figures are obviously simplified to illustrate the point, but it is clear that in employing the fourth, fifth, sixth, seventh and eighth workers the organisation, while still benefiting from additions to total output, is gaining a smaller MPP from each extra worker. The marginal physical product for this situation can also be shown graphically:

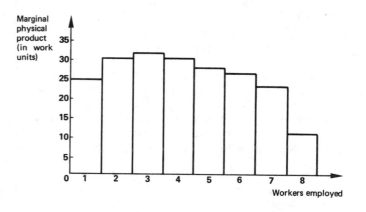

Fig 6.1   Marginal physical product

It is clear that the third worker adds the greatest additional output to the organisation's production. However this does not necessarily indicate to the organisation that it should only employ three workers.

So far, workers' output has been valued in terms of *tangible products made* or in *work units*. In order to assess a worker's worth to an organisation these quantities need to be expressed in a monetary value. This will then indicate not only how much the employee has produced, but also the revenue that this output will generate for the organisation when it is sold. This is called the *revenue product*.

From the example previously used if it is assumed that each unit produced can be sold for £3 then the total revenue product from the first worker would be £75, from the first and second workers £168, and so on. The *marginal revenue product* would be the extra value of the output of each additional unit of labour.

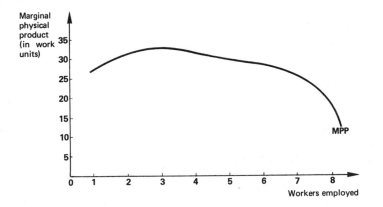

Fig 6.2   Marginal physical product curve

Number of workers	Marginal physical product (work units)	Marginal revenue product £
1	25	75
2	31	93
3	32	96
4	31	93
5	28	84
6	27	81
7	24	72
8	11	33

Table 6.4   Marginal Revenue Product in relation to workforce

The factor determining how many workers to employ will be the relationship between the marginal revenue product and the cost of employing each extra worker. To simplify this, the cost of employing each worker could be regarded as the prevailing wage rate, and the assumption is made that the wage rate remains constant for all workers employed. In the example given, if the wage rate was £60 per week and the workers' marginal revenue product was as shown in the previous table the following relationship could be shown graphically:

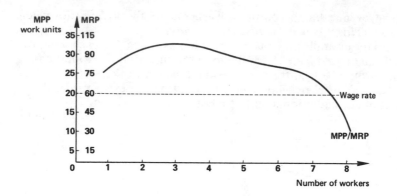

Fig 6.3   Marginal physical/marginal revenue product in relation to wage rate in determining number of employees

Clearly only those workers whose marginal revenue product exceeds the wage rate should be employed. Therefore the seventh worker who produces £72 worth of MRP is employed while the eighth worker who only produces £33 worth of MRP and is paid £60 should not be employed.

Changes in the level of employment
The level of employment in an organisation will not remain static. Changes in certain factors will influence the number of workers who should be employed. If wage rates rose (due to pressure from within the organisation or to an increase in nationally negotiated pay levels) and productivity did not, then it may mean that less workers could be employed.

Fig 6.4 illustrates an increase in wage rates with static productivity levels.

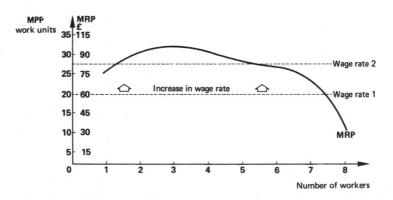
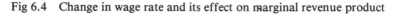

Fig 6.4   Change in wage rate and its effect on marginal revenue product

If the wage rate rose from £60 to £80 per week it is now no longer profitable to employ either the seventh or eighth worker as their MRP is less than £80. Only the second, third, fourth, fifth and sixth workers' MRP exceeds £80 and because it is a prerequisite that to employ these workers the organisation must also employ the first person, and as he or she is employed at a loss, it would be necessary to total the MRPs of all six workers and compare it with the total wage bill to ascertain if production is profitable at all. In this case the total revenue product for the first six workers is £532 (£75 + £93 + £96 + £93 + £84 + £81). So as a result of the wage rise, the organisation may be faced with a *redundancy situation* with regard to the seventh worker. The process of redundancy is considered in some detail later in this chapter.

However, the shedding of labour is not the only option open to the organisation in these circumstances. One alternative is to increase the price at which the product is sold. This has the effect of raising the value of the marginal revenue product of all workers. Obviously this is only possible if the demand for the organisation's product is relatively inelastic and the price increase will not deter consumers. For instance, if the price of the product was increased by 20% thus also increasing each worker's MRP by 20% then the seventh worker would have an MRP in excess of £80. A further alternative which often accompanies an increase in wage rates is an agreed rise in worker productivity (a *'productivity deal'*). Here the workers agree to produce more in return for higher wages. This has the effect of raising their marginal revenue product without the organisation having to increase its price to consumers. In the situation used as an example, a 20% increase in productivity would have the same effect as a 20% rise in price for it would mean that the organisation would not face the cost of possible redundancies. These two alternatives can be illustrated in the same diagram showing the rise both in wage rates and in marginal physical product.

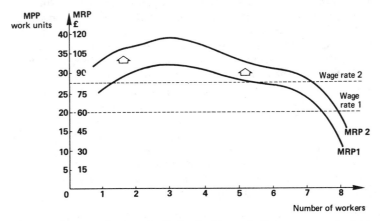

Fig 6.5   Increase in marginal physical/marginal revenue product caused by increase in productivity

In many circumstances a *rise in wages is accompanied by both an increase in productivity and an increase in price.*

A fall in the value of the MRP of workers may be due either to a drop in productivity or a decline in demand for the organisation's product. If the latter occurs the workers would still be producing an identical quantity but its value (MRP) is less as a fall in demand reduces the price for which it can be sold.

Changes in the price or availability of other factors of production

Labour is just one of the factors of production which must be combined with others to produce a finished product. The proportionate amounts of each input will depend on the cost and availability of the various factors. For example in those parts of the world where population growth has led to a plentiful supply of cheap labour, such as India, most productive activity will be *labour intensive* and thus use little machinery. In the industrialised West, the reverse is true. Relatively few workers produce much more using sophisticated productive techniques. This type of production is *capital intensive.* Clearly there are other contributing factors such as the size of productive unit but this example illustrates the point. If wage rates in India rose sufficiently, machines would be substituted for the workforce. This is only possible if machines are capable of performing the tasks currently undertaken by people. However history has demonstrated that as people's ingenuity has grown and greater technological advances are made, increasingly jobs currently performed by men and women will be taken over by machines. A contemporary example has been the rapid development of micro electronics. The demand for many clerical jobs and occupations such as shop assistants may be reduced dramatically as cheaper and more sophisticated machines are introduced to replace human labour.

In this first section we have considered how an organisation determines the number of workers it should employ and how factors such as: the level of demand for the organisation's final product; the productivity of its workers; the prevailing wage rate; and how the cost and availability of other factors of production which can be substituted for labour, affect the demand in the labour market. Later in this chapter there is an analysis of how the interaction of the supply of labour with the demand for labour establishes the total number of people employed in the economy and the wage rate they are paid. First it is necessary to examine the process by which an organisation employs its workers once it has decided how many it should employ. The relationship between employer/employee is one of contract. Organisations offer to pay workers' wages and salaries in return for the work they perform and the law recognises the uniqueness of this *contract of employment* by the formulation of specific rules to govern it.

The nature of the contract of employment

A major resource of any business organisation is the labour that it employs. The relationship which exists between a business organisation as an employer and its workforce is based upon contract.

Essentially, two types of contract of employment are recognised under the law:

a) *The contract of service*: This contract applies to employed persons and governs the relationship between the employer and the employee;

b) *The contract for services*: This contract applies to *self employed persons* and governs the relationship between the employer and the *independent contractor*.

The classification of the above contracts is crucial since both of them will confer rights and impose duties which vary considerably under the law. A comparison of some of the main rights and responsibilities under the two types of contract can be seen in Table 6.5 overleaf.

How the contracts are distinguished

If it were left to the parties alone to determine the type of contract of employment entered into, this could lead to abuse and injustice. A dominant employer, aware of the many advantages that the contract for services relationship could provide, could choose to employ the whole workforce on a self-employed basis. This is why it is generally left to the courts to determine as a question of law a worker's status by examining the reality of the relationship. In the past the courts have adopted a number of tests to decide this question.

The control test: Originally this test was applied in isolation and basically involves posing the question whether or not an employer could tell individual workers not only what to do but also how and when to do it. If the answer to this question is yes, then the worker will be employed under a contract of service.

In *Performing Right Society Ltd* v. *Mitchel and Booker* (1924) McCardle.J said that 'the test to be generally applied, lies in the nature and degree of detailed control over the person alleged to be an employee'. Unfortunately, the application of this test was found to be unreal when applied to highly skilled and qualified workers (eg consultant surgeons) and so a more up-dated test was suggested by Lord Denning in *Stevenson, Jordan and Harrison Ltd* v. *MacDonald and Evans* (1952) called the Organisation test.

The organisation test: Here a worker was said to be employed under a contract of service if employed as part of the business with the work as an integral part of it. By the application of this test a consultant surgeon could be said to be an integral part of the activities of a hospital and therefore employed under a contract of service. Again this test was unable to provide a suitable solution in all cases.

Contracts of service (employed persons)	Contracts for services (self-employed persons)

Employer's liability

1 An employer may be made liable under the law for torts committed by employees during the course of their employment.

1 As a general rule an employer is not liable for torts committed by independent contractors during the course of their employment.

2 The law imposes a high standard of care on an employer with regard to the health and safety of employees both under Statute and common law.

2 Generally a lesser standard of care is owed by an employer towards contractors with regard to health and safety both under the common law and Statute.

Economic implications

3 An employee's income tax is deducted by the employer from wages under the pay as you earn scheme, ie PAYE (Schedule E).

3 A self-employed person is responsible for his own tax liability and pays tax under Schedule D on a preceeding year basis. This can prove to be a more advantageous method for the taxpayer.

4 Under the *Social Security Act, 1975*, both employer and employee must contribute to the payment of Class 1 National Insurance contributions.

4 Under the *Social Security Act, 1975*, a self employed person is individually responsible for the payment of lower Class 2 National Insurance contributions.

5 As a result of making Class 1 contributions, an employee is entitled to claim all the available welfare benefits, eg unemployment, sickness, industrial injuries benefit.

5 A self employed person who makes Class 2 contributions has no entitlement to certain welfare benefits, eg unemployment, industrial injuries, but may claim others – sickness benefit.

Other statutory rights

6 Employment legislation, (*Employment Protection (Consolidation) Act, 1978*), has conferred a number of rights and benefits on employed persons, eg
  a) the right to a written notice of the details of employment within the first 13 weeks of employment;
  b) the right to receive certain minimum periods of notice on dismissal;
  c) the right to a redundancy payment in appropriate circumstances;

6 The majority of statutory rights under the *Employment Protection (Consolidation) Act, 1978*, are not available for self employed persons.

d) the right to protection against
   unfair dismissal;
e) the right to be a member of a
   Trade Union and engage in
   Trade Union activities;
f) the right to protection against
   the employer's insolvency.

Table 6.5 Comparison between employed and self-employed status

The multiple test: Today reliance is placed upon the 'mixed' or 'multiple' test under which all the features of a contract of employment are subject to scrutiny to determine the relationship.

> In *Ready Mixed Concrete (South East)* v. *Minister of Pensions* (1968) the Court was asked to determine the contractual status of drivers employed by the plaintiff company. The question for the court was to determine which National Insurance category the drivers fell into. The lengthy contract of employment under which they were engaged provided: that the drivers purchased the RMC lorries they drove; placed the lorries exclusively at their employer's disposal; used them solely for the employer's purposes; wore the company's uniforms; maintained the lorries; paid their own National Insurance and Tax; could in some circumstances delegate the driving. After examining all the features of the contract (particularly the right to employ substitutes) the Court held that the drivers were self employed under a contract for services. In his judgment MacKenna.J stated that a contract of service exists if:
> (i) The worker agrees for a wage that he will provide his own work in performance of a service; and
> (ii) The worker will submit to his employers control; and
> (iii) The majority of the contractual provisions are consistent with it being a contract of service.

Certainly, self-employed status cannot be achieved simply by including an express provision in a contract. The courts will look to the *substance of any employment relationship* to decide a worker's status.

> In *Ferguson* v. *John Dawson Ltd* (1976) a builder's labourer agreed to work on what was known as 'the lump' and described as a 'self-employed labour only subcontractor'. Having suffered injuries as a result of the employer's breach of a statutory duty, the labourer could only succeed in an action for damages if he could show that he was an 'employee' and therefore protected under the Statute. The Court held that 'the lump' was no more than a device to attempt to gain tax advantages and in reality, taking all the circumstances of the employment into account, the relationship was one of employer and employee and a contract of service.

Formation of the contract of employment

The general contractual rules governing offer and acceptance considered in Chapter 1 p. 26 are relevant to determine when a contract of employment has been entered into, eg

a) An advertisement of a job is a mere invitation to treat.
b) An employer will make an express offer of a job to the successful applicant on specific terms which may differ with the advertisement.
c) A counter offer by the applicant will extinguish the original offer.
d) The contract is concluded on the communication of the applicant's acceptance and, if the postal rules of acceptance apply, the acceptance is complete on posting.

Of course, this whole process may take place over a period of time involving conversations, exchange of letters and interviews.

A contract of employment is not a contract of uberrimae fidei (utmost good faith) so there is no duty of disclosure of material facts on the parties.

> In *Hands* v. *Simpson Fawcett and Co Ltd* (1928) the plaintiff obtained a job as a travelling salesman with the defendant company and failed to inform his employer that he had been convicted for a drunken driving offence. When the employer became aware of the conviction, he dismissed the plaintiff without notice. The plaintiff claimed damages for *wrongful dismissal*. The Court held that the plaintiff should succeed as failure to disclose the conviction did not invalidate his contract of employment.

Following the *Rehabilitation of Offenders Act 1974* there is no duty on a job applicant to disclose certain less serious convictions which have become '*spent*' under the Act. A sentence of 30 months or less may become 'spent' (ie disregarded for all purposes) after a fixed period has run.

During the negotiations leading to employment, it is imperative therefore that the employer should discover, by skilful questioning, all important matters. Certainly any false statements made by a job applicant could lead to an action for damages in tort or misrepresentation, together with the right of the employer to rescind the contract.

> In *Torr* v. *the British Railways Board* (1977) the plaintiff job applicant untruthfully stated on his application form for a job as a guard that he had never been convicted of a criminal offence. His employer dismissed him on discovering that he had been imprisoned for 3 years in 1958 for an offence. The plaintiff claimed *unfair dismissal* but failed in his action since the *Tribunal* considered that the information required by his employer in the application was fundamental to the relationship of trust required by the

job. Accordingly the employer was entitled to terminate the contract. NB the provisions of the Rehabilitation of Offenders Act 1974 did not apply in this case.

There are no special formalities that need to be adhered to in entering into a contract of employment. The contract may be written or oral, however the Employment Protection (Consolidation) Act 1978 provides that within 13 weeks of starting employment an employer must provide his or her employees with written details regarding certain minimum information surrounding their employment or draw the employees' attention to such details, eg remuneration, hours, holidays, incapacity, pensions, continuity of employment.

This requirement is one example of the many statutory provisions relating to employees' rights. Other statutory rights are examined later in the chapter following a consideration of the interaction of supply and demand for labour and how this will determine the number of contracts of employment entered into. Employers are now much more aware of the importance of the contract of employment and in order to clarify the precise rights and duties it is becoming more usual for them to draw up a formal written agreement.

The supply of labour

In the previous section it was considered how an organisation decides how many people to employ and the mechanisms by which the organisation can employ labour. Now it is proposed to examine the broader perspective of the supply of labour to the economy as a whole, to specific industries and specific areas.

Supply of labour to the economy

The number of people available and looking for work in the UK varies over time. Demographic factors such as the age and sex structure of the population influence the number of employable people. However it is also necessary to consider how much work these people are willing to do which is referred to as their *activity rate*.

The working population

Out of the total population of about 56 million the UK has a potential workforce of about 25 million. The size of the workforce is restricted by legislation as young people are not allowed to undertake full-time employment until they are over 16 years of age. Also the government has set the retirement age at 65 for men and 60 for women and although this does not mean that they cannot then work by law, it may affect their pension rights if they do.

Other people such as married women or students may be physically capable of working but *choose* not to have a full-time job. These people, with the addition of those who are of working age but are per-

293

manently unfit for work, are classified as the *economically inactive*. Present trends are increasing this inactive element of the population. These trends are a combined result of delaying the entry of young people into the employment market by encouraging them to remain in further and higher education, and of increasing early retirement opportunities. They are to some extent a *secondary source of workers*, for if the wage rate rose sufficiently they may be attracted into giving up their studies, housework or retirement and taking on a job.

The primary workforce of the UK is made up of the *economically active* and this includes not only those in employment but also those who are currently unemployed but are seeking a job and registered as unemployed with the Department of Employment. At the end of 1981 there were 3 000 000 unemployed out of the workforce of 25 million.

The activity rate
The amount of work a person chooses to do will vary according to individual preference. Some may opt for substantial periods of leisure. Others work for as many hours as possible. This choice is related to individual levels of income and expenditure and their chosen life styles.

It is normally assumed that as wage rates rise people will be willing to substitute work in place of leisure hours and so work longer. The extra incentive of higher rates for overtime working is used to induce people to give up leisure. This is once again the concept of opportunity cost as people subconsciously value the leisure time that they must forego in order to do more work. It is only if the wage rate paid is higher than the value put on the leisure time that people will substitute work for leisure. This is an example of the *substitution effect*. So, for many people, an increase in the wage rate will mean that the supply of their labour increases. This can be shown diagrammatically in Fig 6.6.

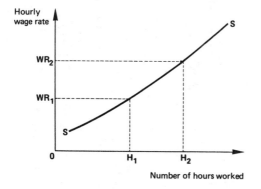

Fig 6.6 Supply of labour in relation to hourly wage rate

As the wage rate rises from WR_1 to WR_2, the number of hours worked also increases from H_1 to H_2. However this example disregards the fact that as a worker continues to work longer hours and have less leisure time, then the value of the remaining leisure time becomes greater. Therefore the worker may reach a stage when he or she will not give up any more leisure whatever the wage rate. In fact in certain circumstances as the wage rate rises, some people actually work less because they have reached a certain level of income sufficient to meet their needs and so they prefer to have increased leisure time. This is another example of the *income effect*. This results in a backward sloping supply curve for labour and can be shown graphically in Fig 6.7.

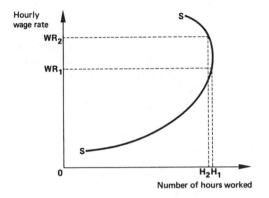

Fig 6.7   Backward sloping supply of labour curve

Once the wage rate exceeds WR then the worker earns sufficient from fewer hours to allow him or her to work less and enjoy more leisure.

These examples of increases in wage rate refer to individual workers but could be summated to find the *aggregate supply of labour in relation to the wage rate*. From this it is clear that it would be unwise to assume that a general increase in wage rate is likely to produce a proportionate rise in hours worked, and even if more hours are worked this does not always mean that there is greater effort being exerted. The supply of labour is not solely determined by the wage rate but also by workers' attitudes to their jobs, commitment and the job satisfaction that they receive.

An extension of this misconceived assumption is the belief that a reduction in income tax rates (and so an increase in workers' take-home pay) will necessarily be an incentive to the workforce to work harder. Evidence suggests that certain sectors of the working population will show a positive response to a fall in the marginal tax rate. This is particularly true of those workers whose committed expenditure tends to exceed their regular income, who are therefore willing to work extra hours if the rewards are sufficiently high. However it has already been noted that some workers will actually work less if tax rates fall as their previous income level, now achieveable by working shorter hours, is sufficient to meet their needs. Changes in the tax rates will not affect the working hours of the majority of people because they work a set number of hours fixed by their employer and cannot work longer even if the attraction of lower taxes was sufficiently strong. The extensive research which has been undertaken into the relationship between income tax changes and work effort has failed to produce conclusive evidence of a simple connection, except in marginal cases.

Labour supply to specific industries

The supply of labour to a specific industry or occupation is determined by several factors. These include the *wage level* offered by that industry, trade or profession and its comparability with other similar occupations, the *amount of skill*, or expertise required to do the job and the *number of people in the workforce* who have such skills, and finally the *length of training or academic qualifications* required. Obviously if an occupation required little particular skill and no formal training and happened to be very well paid, this would attract considerable numbers of people eager to be employed in that way. But in such circumstances the forces of supply and demand would dictate that with excess supply of labour over demand (more people wanting jobs than there are vacancies) the result should be a fall in the wage rate. Therefore in society those occupations which receive the highest remuneration should be those where demand is high but few people are willing or able to do the job either because of its nature, the skills required, or the qualifications needed. This is true in professions such as surgeons, barristers, architects, etc. However, later in this chapter, it will be noted that in some industries or occupations the strength of the trade union or professional association is such that wages and salaries are kept high even though many people not employed in that industry, who are capable of doing the job and wish to do so, cannot find employment because of the lack of available vacancies.

Normally the wage or salary a person receives reflects the value which society or consumers place on his or her talents. For instance, the salary paid to computer experts has risen as more organisations instal computers. A bi-lingual secretary can demand higher wages as more organisations become involved in international business. However many anomalies exist where people carrying out valuable tasks are relatively lowly paid. This is often the result of the satisfaction inherent within the job which persuades people to accept such jobs despite receiving a comparatively small remuneration.

However, for most people, the choice to enter a profession or occupation is determined by a combination of *monetary reward and job satisfaction*. In order to attract workers into less satisfying jobs, wage rates must be higher. An example would be the mining industry where hard and dirty working conditions must be compensated by high wages. Conversely, jobs such as nursing, which provide considerable job satisfaction, may be handicapped with regard to monetary rewards as some people are more willing to work for lower wages (often below the value of the job to society). Recent evidence of this has been seen in the Police Service. The Edmund Davies Report introduced in 1979 substantially increased police's wages and so attracted more recruits to a job which is difficult and possibly dangerous. Some jobs require a considerable period of training or apprenticeship during which earnings may be relatively low. A person must decide to accept relatively low earnings initially on the basis of expected high future wages. For instance, many professions (eg medicine, accountancy) require long periods of training at extremely low rates of pay before a person is qualified and can earn a higher salary.

Locational factors affecting the supply of labour

The supply of labour is often restricted by regional factors. Some industries require a particular skill or expertise and this may have developed in one particular area. This effectively dictates the location of that industry. Workers are also often restricted to their local labour market, ie they do not seek jobs in other regions because of the *immobility of labour*. The reasons for the immobility of labour may be the result of family ties, age (both the school leaver and older workers tend to be less mobile), the inability to finance a movement to another area (for example house prices tend to be highest in areas with low unemployment – or a person who is a council tenant and cannot arrange an exchange), or simply a lack of knowledge of job vacancies in other areas.

These factors affect a worker's geographical mobility and the government has attempted to help the regional unemployment problem by facilitating geographical mobility. This has been done by helping with the cost of moving from depressed areas and by increasing workers' knowledge of job vacancies in other areas through job centres and employment exchanges. Employers themselves may encourage job mobility by providing financial assistance towards resettlement expenses.

A second similar factor is *industrial immobility of labour* and this refers to a worker's ability to shift from one occupation or industry to another. The more highly specialised a person's talents or skills are, the more difficult it is to find another job if he or she has to.

Again the government's labour policy has been designed to encourage retraining in those skills or professions which are in demand and it has established the Manpower Services Commission and its subsidiary the Training Services Agency to plan and provide training and retraining for those workers who are industrially immobile. Government Skill Centres and training opportunity schemes within colleges (TOPS) are examples of how this has been achieved.

It is the interaction of the forces of supply and demand which, in a perfect employment market, will determine the details of the contractual bargain in any given employment relationship. There are in fact many imperfections in the labour market which combine to interfere with the free working of supply and demand, and hence the terms under which an individual may be employed. It is now proposed to examine the origins of these employment terms, and their scope.

Contents of the contract of employment

The contents of a contract of employment are its *terms* which include the mutual promises of the parties. These are called *express terms* and in addition to them there are *terms implied* into a contract of employment from various external sources. These include collective agreements entered into between employers' associations and trade unions, statutory terms and common law terms.

Express terms

When contractual negotiations are completed the parties will in writing, or orally, expressly state the terms which form the basis of the contract, eg remuneration, hours, duties, holidays, sick pay, pensions, etc. As a general rule these terms cannot be varied by either party without the other's consent, unless an express term confers this right on one of the parties. Breach by the employee of a contractual term may be a ground for dismissal. Similarly breach by an employer may be sufficient ground for the employee to treat the contract as at an end and bring a claim for *constructive* dismissal.

Implied terms:

a) *Collective agreements*
   Such agreements are made by a trade union and an employer or employers' association, which provide for terms and conditions of employment of those covered by the agreement, eg *'union rates of pay'* or *'union conditions'*. These agreements may be nationally or locally entered into. However they are not enforceable in law. They will however be legally binding on the employer and employee if incorporated into the individual's contract of employment by express reference.

b) *Work rules, custom and practice*
   If the employer issues instructions to workers in the form of rule books or notices the courts are unlikely to consider such rules as terms of an individual's contract of employment.

298

In *Secretary of State for Employment* v. *Associated Society of Locomotive Engineers and Firemen* (1972) railwaymen operated a work to rule campaign by working strictly according to the rule book which had been issued to them. Lord Denning held that the work rules were in no way terms of the railwaymen's contract of employment and by working to it the employees could still be in breach of their implied contractual duty of good faith. However if the contents of the rule book are mutually agreed and then varied, they could be part of the contractual terms, and a failure by an employee to obey obligations contained within them could amount to a breach of his duty to obey lawful and reasonable orders.

As far as customary practices are concerned the courts may regard them as part of an individual's contract of employment and legally enforceable if they are *certain, reasonable and notorious*.

This was the case in *Sagar* v. *H Ridehalgh Ltd* (1931) where a custom that deductions were to be made from the wages of a weaver was held to be legally enforceable as a contractual term.

c) *Statutory terms*
The Employment Protection (Consolidation) Act 1978 provides extensive rights for employees which are inserted by implication into their individual contracts of employment. An employee's remedy for infringement of these rights lies by way of complaint to an *industrial tribunal*. The rights, which will be examined in detail later, relate to dismissal, redundancy, wages, and health and safety. The majority of additional rights relate to trade union membership. The 1978 Act specifically provides that an employee has the right to be a member of a trade union and take part in trade union activities. In addition an employer must permit an employee who is an official of an *independent trade union* recognised by that employer to take time off during working hours to carry out official duties or undergo relevant training.

d) *Common law terms*
   (i) *Imposing duties on the employer* The major common law duties of an employer relate to the payment of wages and the provision of a safe work system and these are examined later under separate heads. As far as providing work is concerned the courts have consistently asserted that no such'duty exists as long as the employer provides the contractual remuneration. If however an employee's pay depends upon the performance of work (piece-work) then the employer is under an obligation to provide sufficient work to enable a reasonable wage to be earned. A further exception is where the employee's occupation

is such that the opportunity to work is an essential part of the contract because of the possibility of loss of reputation, eg an actor, entertainer or journalist.

Similarly, there is no legal duty on an employer to provide employees with a reference on the termination of their employment. If a reference is given, however, the tort of *defamation* will provide a remedy for an employee if the employer has maliciously included false statements which damage the employee's character. Also, an employer could be sued for the tort of *deceit* or *negligent misstatement* by another employer who suffers loss as a result of hiring someone following an unwarrantable good reference. It may be added that under the common law, an employee is entitled to be *indemnified* for loss or expense incurred in the course of employment. In most cases, of course, expenses are provided for expressly in the contract of employment.

(ii) *Imposing duties on the employee* The most important duty of an employee may be described as the duty of good faith which gives rise to a number of obligations.

Duty to respect trade secrets: Since all employers' trade secrets and confidential information (eg lists of customers) are regarded as part of the employers' property then all employees are under a continuing duty to respect them. This duty may be enforced by a court injunction.

In *Printers & Finishers Ltd* v. *Holloway* (1965) an ex-employee was restrained from showing secret documents to a competitor and disclosing confidential information he had obtained during his employment.

It follows that there would be a flagrant breach of contract if an employee were to disclose trade secrets or other confidential information *during* the course of his or her employment. Of course an employer who wishes to guard against the practice of an employee revealing trade secrets following the termination of his or her employment may insert an express *restraint clause* in the employee's contract of employment to achieve this. The law relating to such clauses was dealt with in Chapter 2, p. 87.

Duty to account for money received: There is an implied duty on an employee not to accept any bribes, commissions or fees in respect of work.

In *Boston Deep-Sea Fishing & Ice Co.* v. *Ansell* (1888) an employee, who received a secret commission from other companies for placing orders with them, was treated as being in breach of this duty and his dismissal was justified.

APPENDICES

a) <u>Date of commencement of employment</u> _____

b) <u>Agreement</u>

Your terms and conditions of employment will be as laid down
in the National Agreement.

c) <u>Reference</u>

The appointment is subject to satisfactory references as
discussed at your interview.

d) <u>Hours of duty</u>

Your normal hours of work are 38 per week, Monday to Friday.
The office is closed on Saturdays. Time worked in excess of
these hours will be treated in accordance with the provisions
set out in the Agreement. A flexible working hours scheme is
currently in operation.

e) <u>Holidays and sickness</u>

Your entitlement to paid annual and public holidays and the
terms and conditions relating to sickness absence, including
entitlement to sick pay, are set out in the Agreement.

f) <u>Superannuation</u>

On reaching the age of 20 years you will, if eligible, be
required to join the Superannuation Scheme, details of which
will be made available to you.

g) <u>Trade Union membership</u>

Your attention is specifically drawn to the provisions of the
Agreement under which you are required to become a member of
one of the trade unions signatory to the Agreement within
30 days of commencing employment.

h) <u>Grievance procedure</u>

The grievance procedure relating to your employment is set out
in the Agreement. If you have a grievance, you should raise
it in the first instance, either orally or in writing, with
your immediate supervisor. If the matter is not resolved by
this means you may ask for it ot be referred to your Depart-
mental Head. At both stages you may be accompanied and assisted by your Staff Committee/Trade Union Representative if you
so wish.

301

Failing a settlement by these means you may, if you are a
member of a recognised trade union, raise the matter with your
union for further discussion and if a settlement is not then
effected the matter may be referred to the Staff Committee.

i) Termination of employment

The appointment may be terminated by one calendar month's
notice in writing from yourself or by the following notice
in writing from the firm.

(i)   Less than 5 years
      continuous service
      in the firm   One calendar month

(ii) 5 years or more
      continuous service
      in the firm but less
      than 12 years   1 week for each completed
                                     year of service

(iii) 12 years or more
      continuous service
      in the firm   12 weeks

j) Disciplinary rules

A statement on disciplinary rules relating to serious
misconduct is the Agreement referred to above.

NB The agreement referred to is too lengthy to be included.

Employees working in their spare time for a competitor would be in
breach of this duty.

In *Hivac* v. *Park Royal Scientific Instruments Co* (1946) an
employee was restrained from working for a competitor engaged
in work of a similar nature.

Duty to obey reasonable orders: This duty could be included within
the general obligation to render faithful service. To be reasonable an
order must be lawful for there is no duty to obey an unlawful order, eg
to falsify some records.

In determining the reasonableness of an order, all the circumstances
must be considered including a close examination of the contract of
employment.

In *UK Atomic Energy Authority* v. *Claydon* (1974) the defendent's contract of employment required him to work anywhere in the UK. Accordingly it was held to be a reasonable order to require him to transfer to another base. Also, in *Pepper* v. *Webb* (1969) a head gardener, when asked to plant some flowers replied 'I couldn't care less about your bloody greenhouse or your sodding garden' and walked away. The court held that the refusal to obey the instructions, rather than the language which accompanied it, amounted to a breach of contract.

The determination of wage levels

In a perfectly competitive market, wage levels would be established simply by the interaction of supply and demand.

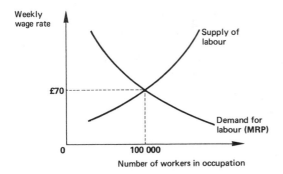

Fig 6.8   Determination of wage rate

Figure 6.8 illustrates the equilibrium of the supply and demand for labour establishing the wage rate. For £70 a week 100,000 people are willing to offer their services and employers seek 100,000 employees. A lower wage rate would create a shortage of workers and a higher wage rate a surplus.

As explained previously, the demand curve is, in fact, the *Marginal Revenue Product curve*. This is true because as the value of the additional work produced by each worker falls, then the worker will only be employed if the wage rate similarly falls. If productivity increases, then employers demand more labour and the demand curve for labour may shift to the right and so increase wage levels.

This simple supply and demand relationship would exist if the labour market was perfectly competitive. However, it will be pointed out later that there are imperfections in both supply and demand and this will affect the wage level.

In most instances, the wage rate set for a job tends to be the same for all employees doing that particular job. Variations obviously occur with seniority or length of service but if the assumption is made that all workers are on an equal grade doing the same job, it is clear that some workers would be willing to do the job for a lower wage rate than that which they are paid. A simple example will explain.

If, for a particular job, one woman is willing to work for £50 a week because she cannot get another job at a higher rate and her next best paid job gives her £49 a week, then she would work for any wage above £49 (eg £50). The £49 she could receive is called her *transfer earnings*, ie the wage she could get by transferring to the next best paid job she can find. Any income above £50 is a *profit* to her as she would have worked for £50. A second person is willing to work for £55 (his transfer earnings are £54), a third for £60 (he could get £59 doing another job), a fourth £65 (transfer earning £64). This 'profit' above the person's transfer earnings is called *economic rent*. (The term rent is a little misleading. This is due to the fact that the same concept is used when assessing the rent of a piece of land.)

So the supply of labour in this case would be:

Wage level £	No of men/women willing to work
50	1
55	2
60	3
65	4
70	5
75	6

Table 6.6 Supply of labour in relation to wage level.
This can be shown graphically as in Fig 6.9

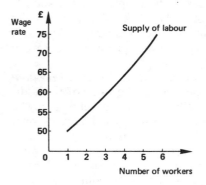

Fig 6.9   The supply of labour in relation to the wage level

If the demand curve were added the wage rate that would be offered could be found.

304

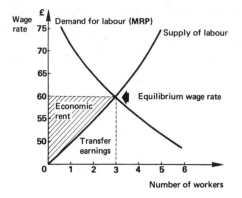

Fig 6.10   Equilibrium wage rate showing economic rent earned.

The wage rate offered would be £60 a week and three workers would be employed. The first worker would have worked for £50 and so gains £10 economic rent (£60 − 50) and the second person has £5 economic rent (£60 − 55) as he would have worked for £55. Thus the area above the supply curve and below the wage rate is economic rent and the area below the supply curve shows the employee's transfer earnings.

For the majority of employees the remuneration that they receive is the prime motive for working. The law has recognised the pre-eminence of this contractual term in an employment relationship and through the operation of common law and statute has regulated the form, method and, in some cases, the level of wages payable.

Payment of wages

One of the most fundamental terms of a contract of employment is the agreement by the employer to pay a wage in return for the service rendered. This is usually expressly agreed by the parties or is expressly incorporated into a contract of employment by referring to a collective agreement in which the wage rate has been negotiated. In the absence of any express term it is implied at common law that the employer should pay a *reasonable* remuneration which in the event of a dispute would be determined by the court. The law has intervened in various ways to regulate the payment of wages and more recently, as wages are recognised as a dominant factor in the regulation of the economy, there have been attempts to determine by statute the level of wage increase, eg counter-inflation legislation in the early 1970s.

The form of payment

The earliest legislation relating to the payment of wages was the Truck Act 1831 designed to prevent the exploitation of workers by employers, operating the practice of paying them in goods or tokens rather than

305

cash. It requires that wages must be paid in current coin of the realm and a contractual term specifying any other manner of payment is void. The Act also provides that deductions can be made from a worker's wages only for certain purposes acknowledged by the worker in a signed agreement.

> In *Daley* v. *Radnor* (1973) an oral agreement between an employer and employee provided that the employer would let premises to the employee at £10 per week rent, such a sum to be deducted from the employee's weekly wage. The employee claimed £1570 which had been deducted from his wages for this purpose. The Court held that the sum was recoverable on the ground that the deduction was unlawful.

In order to permit the payment of wages in forms other than cash, the Payment of Wages Act 1960 was passed. The Act provides that by written agreement employees may be paid by cheque, bank giro, direct bank account debit, etc. Under the Employment Protection (Consolidation) Act 1978 every employee is entitled to a written itemised pay statement on or before receipt of wages which includes the following:

a) the gross amount,
b) deductions and their purpose,
c) the net amount,
d) if the net amount is paid in different ways the amount and methods.

Determining the level of the wage rate

Generally, the parties to a contract of employment are free to negotiate the wage rate, individually or by their representatives, eg Employers' Association or Trade Unions. Of course, if no wage is expressly agreed, in the event of a dispute the courts will value the service provided and imply a reasonable wage. Because of the state of the economy, however, recent governments have found it necessary to *regulate the level of wages* payable by passing legislation (eg imposing a wage freeze). So far, this state intervention by statute in *free collective bargaining* has only been a temporary measure. A more permanent measure with the intention of securing equal pay and conditions for both men and women was the Equal Pay Act 1970 (as amended by the Sex Discrimination Act, 1975). The requirement of equal treatment under the legislation only applies where the sexes are engaged in similar work and higher rates for either sex can be justified where greater skill or responsibility is demanded. However, any differences based on physical strength and time when the work is to be done are to be disregarded.

In *Electrolux* v. *Hutchinson* (1977) female workers engaged in broadly similar work to their male counterparts were held to be entitled to equal pay despite the condition that the men could exclusively be required to work overtime, at weekends or at night. The fact that the men were rarely called on to do this was a major consideration.

The decision as to whether similar work is being carried on demands a comparison not between the contractual obligations of the parties but rather a consideration of the things that are *actually* done and the *frequency* with which they are done.

In *Coombes (Holdings) Ltd* v. *Shield* (1978) the female counter-clerks in bookmakers' shops were paid a lesser rate of pay than their male counterparts. The employer sought to justify the differences because of the male employees' extra duties of acting as a deterrent to unruly customers and transporting cash between branches. The Court of Appeal held that in deciding the question as to 'like work' it was necessary to:

(i) consider the differences between the things the men and women were required to do;
(ii) consider the frequency with which such differences occur in practice; and
(iii) consider whether the differences are of practical importance.

This approach should enable the court to place a value on each job in terms of demands placed upon the worker and if the value of the man's job is higher he should be paid an increased rate for the job. In this case the differences were not of sufficient importance to justify a different rate of pay.

One of the main effects of the Sex Discrimination Act 1975 in amending the Equal Pay Act 1970, was to provide that every contract of employment is deemed to include an *equality clause*. This clause automatically:

a) modifies a term of a woman's contract which is less favourable than a term of a similar kind in a man's contract where he is employed on similar work *and*
b) includes in a woman's contract any term benefiting a man employed on like work.

The equality clause however will not operate if the employer can show that the differences between the contracts is 'genuinely due to a material difference' other than one of sex. In cases where there are differences involving benefits and detriments the disadvantage of one term may be complemented by the advantage of another.

Fair wages clauses

Another example of government intervention in the determination of wage rates is the *fair wages resolution* passed by Parliament in 1946. In any contract concluded by a Government Department and a contractor for the completion of work, the fair wages clause is included so as to ensure that the contractor pays the currently accepted rate of wages to employees for the work undertaken. Such a clause then operates for all the contractor's employees whether or not they are engaged in government work, and all subcontractors employed are similarly bound in respect of their own employees.

Comparable employment conditions

The Employment Protection Act 1975 provides machinery whereby complaints may be made by either an employers' association or a Trade Union that an employer is offering terms and conditions of employment less favourable than those normally granted in comparable employment elsewhere in that particular trade or industry. Such complaints may be made to the *Advisory Conciliation and Arbitration Service* (ACAS) for settlement, with a possible further reference to the *Central Arbitration Committee* (CAC). The Committee has power to require an employer to observe recognised terms and conditions, and power to imply such terms into an individual employee's contract of employment.

Wages councils

Many employees who are not represented by large influential trade unions have their interests protected by wage councils, established under the Wages Councils Act 1959. There are at present about 50 wages councils protecting the interests of around three and a half million employees. Wage councils are set up by order of the Secretary of State for Employment following application by a joint industrial council or an organisation representing employer and employees, or on the Secretary of State's own initiative. ACAS first must consider the issue and make a recommendation to the Secretary of State. The Service will recommend the setting up of a wages council if it is felt that there is no effective negotiating machinery for a section of workers to ensure a reasonable standard of wages. Wages councils are composed of an equal number of representatives of employers and employees, together with three independent persons. They have power to make a *wages order* setting out the minimum wages payable to workers in a specified industry, and other stipulated terms. The order takes effect as an implied term in the contract of employment of every employee whose work falls within its scope, and it is enforced by inspectors employed by the Department of Employment.

Imperfections in the labour market

In earlier sections of this chapter, it has been assumed that the conditions of supply and demand are allowed to interact freely in the labour market. In fact, there are many factors affecting the perfect competitiveness of the market and this section will consider these imperfections.

Imperfect demand for labour

The demand for labour is the result of employers seeking to hire workers. Clearly employers will attempt to influence the wage rate they must offer and may also discriminate regarding whom they employ. This discrimination may be outright against certain races or against women, or more covert in a policy of not employing older people and married women. The government has attempted to legislate against blatant discrimination although the more subtle forms of discrimination are much more difficult to prevent. This can be seen in the repeated attempts by successive governments to successfully define and enforce race relations legislation.

Discrimination

Discrimination occurs in employment when a person, on the grounds of race or sex, is treated less favourably in either securing a job, working conditions or promotion prospects. Various studies have shown that discriminatory practices are still widespread in Britain and this has led to the passing of legislation with the aim of introducing protection against discrimination and hopefully re-educating those who are guilty of it. Many organisations now operate *codes of practice* to govern their actions in this area. Of course, the main difficulty with any form of discrimination is that of detecting it. The provisions relating to discrimination are now contained in the Race Relations Act 1976 and the Sex Discrimination Act, 1975. Both pieces of legislation have basically the same format. The principal features of these Acts are contained in Fig 6.11 overleaf.

Race discrimination

The 1976 Act is concerned with discrimination on *racial grounds* which is based on colour, race, nationality or ethnic or national origins. Any such discriminatory practice which comes within the three categories shown in Fig 6.11 is unlawful. In addition, the publication of an advertisement showing an intention to commit an act of discrimination is also unlawful, such as 'no coloureds need apply. In some cases discrimination is lawful and justifiable on racial grounds if membership of a particular racial group is a *Genuine Occupational Qualification*. Examples may include:

1 Drama and entertainment, eg employing only a black actor to play 'Uncle Tom'.
2 Artist's or photographic models to achieve authenticity, eg a photograph depicting a national scene.
3 Bar or restaurant work where the setting requires an employee from a particular race, eg Chinese restaurant.

Race Relations Act 1976	Sex Discrimination Act 1975

1 Direct discrimination

This occurs where one person: treats another less favourably on racial grounds such as by segregating workers.	This occurs where one person: treats another less favourably on the grounds of sex such as providing women with different working conditions.

2 Indirect discrimination

This occurs where one person: requires another to meet a condition which as a member of a racial group is less easily satisfied because	This occurs where one person: requires another to meet a condition which as a member of a particular sex is less easily satisfied because
a) the proportion of that group who can comply with it is smaller and	a) the proportion of that sex who can comply with it is smaller and
b) the condition is to the complainant's detriment and is not justified.	b) the condition is to the complainant's detriment and is not justified.
There would therefore be indirect discrimination if an employer required young job applicants to have been educated only in Britain.	There would therefore be indirect discrimination if an employer advertised for a clerk who is at least six feet tall.

3 Victimisation

This occurs where one person: treats another less favourably because the other has given evidence or information in connection with, brought proceedings under, or made allegations under the Act against the discriminator.	This occurs where one person: treats another less favourably because the other has given evidence or information in connection with, brought proceedings under, or made allegations under the Act or the Equal Pay Act, 1970, against the discriminator.

4 Enforcement

Complaints alleging any of the above may be made to the Commission for Racial Equality which, in an attempt to eliminate discrimination, has investigatory powers and will attempt a settlement or institute proceedings. Complaints are heard before an industrial tribunal and if a settlement cannot be reached the tribunal can, if the complaint is just	Complaints alleging any of the above may be made to the Equal Opportunities Commission which, in an attempt to eliminate discrimination, has investigatory powers and can issue a *non-discrimination notice* which will place a requirement on an employer. Complaints against such a notice or original complaints are heard before an industrial tribunal and if a settlement cannot be reached the tribunal can, if the complaint is just
(i) make an order declaring rights	(i) make an order declaring rights
(ii) award compensation of up to £5200 or 104 weeks pay whichever is smaller	(ii) award compensation of up to £5200
(iii) recommend action to reduce the adverse effect of the discrimination, eg promotion.	(iii) recommend action to reduce the adverse effect of the discrimination, eg promotion.

Fig 6.11   Principal features of race relations and sex discrimination legislation

Sex discrimination

The 1975 Act is concerned with discrimination on grounds of sex either by males against females, or vice versa, and on grounds of marital status by treating a married person less favourably than an unmarried person either directly or indirectly.

> In *Nemes* v. *Allen* (1977) an employer in an attempt to cope with a redundancy situation dismissed female workers when they married. This was held to be unlawful discrimination on the grounds of sex and marital status.

Any discriminatory practice which comes within the three categories shown in Fig 6.11, p. 310, is unlawful. In addition, the publication of an advertisement showing an intention to commit an act of discrimination is also unlawful, such as 'salesman required' or 'barmaids required'.

In some cases discrimination is lawful and justifiable on grounds of sex if a person's sex is a genuine occupational qualification. Examples may include:

1 Where the job requires a man or woman for physiological reasons other than physical strength, eg a female stripper or a male model.
2 Where there are considerations of decency or privacy, eg male toilet attendant.
3 Where there are statutory restrictions, eg women may not work underground in coal mines.
4 Where the work location makes it unreasonable to provide separate facilities for sleeping or sanitation, eg an oil rig.
5 Where the service is most effectively provided by a man or woman, eg a female social worker.

> In *Peake* v. *Automotive Products Ltd* (1978) Lord Denning in the Court of Appeal held that the ground of safety and good administration was a justifiable reason for discrimination. Previously, the Employment Appeals Tribunal had held that the practice of allowing women employees to leave work five minutes before the men was unlawful discrimination against the men. This decision was reversed on appeal, Lord Denning maintaining that it was not unlawful discrimination to treat women with the chivalry and courtesy they deserve.
>
> This decision was subject to a great deal of criticism and eventually in 1979, Lord Denning himself cast doubt on its validity by stating that it had been given without reference to certain relevant parts of the Act and in the modern age, chivalry is no longer a consideration. These statements were made in *Ministry of Defence* v. *Jeremiah* (1980). Here the employers created a working practice that if men examiners volunteered for overtime they could be required to work it in shops where colour bursting shells were

made. Women examiners, working overtime, were never required to work in these shops because the working conditions required protective clothing to be worn and showers to be taken and there were no facilities for women in that part of the factory. A male examiner complained to a tribunal that despite extra pay for working in these shops, the employer's practice unlawfully discriminated against him by subjecting him to a detriment. Both the Tribunal and Employment Appeals Tribunal agreed. In the Court of Appeal it was held that subjecting a person to detriment meant no more than putting a person under a disadvantage. This was the case here and the fact of extra payment could not remove the detriment because the employer could not purchase the right to discriminate. The practice amounted to discrimination by the employer against the male examiners and was therefore unlawful.

Monopoly employers in the labour market

In some areas or specific industries, a situation exists when there is only one employer of labour, in fact a *monopoly employer*. For instance in some parts of the country, workers have little choice but to seek a job with a single employer such as the National Coal Board or British Steel. In cases such as these, where the employer is a nationalised industry, the wage rates are normally negotiated collectively on a national basis by the employer and the trade union involved. However, if the monopoly employer in question is a private sector organisation, then like all organisations in a monopolistic or monopsonistic position, it will attempt to influence prices (and in this case wages) to its own best advantage. As workers have little chance of another job, they may be forced to accept relatively low wages. Fortunately for the workers faced with monopoly employer they are able to belong to a trade union capable of matching the power of the employer and maintaining wage levels.

Trade unions

Probably the most important development in the labour market in this century has been the growth of the trade union movement. The *collectivisation of labour* has given workers substantial strength to improve their relative bargaining position and this has led to significant advances in wages and conditions. Before considering how trade union pressure has encouraged the government to legislate to workers' advantage, it is worth briefly considering the major characteristics of trade unions, the structure of trade unions and the position of the *Trades Union Congress* (TUC) in co-ordinating the movement and acting as a pressure group in society.

312

Trade union characteristics

Although the nature and status of work carried out by the membership of the various trade unions, professional bodies and workers' organisations is diverse, they share a common aim, namely to *improve the position of their members* with regard to pay, conditions of working and job security. In order to promote these and other aims workers combine to gain collective strength and unity. Clearly, the fundamental characteristic of all trade unions is that they have a *corporate identity*; the National Union of Seamen, the Royal College of Nursing, the National and Local Government Officers' Association are all bodies who act as a trade union for their members. Some of these organisations may in fact be professional bodies in such areas as medicine, accountancy or the law but they fix their professional qualification standards to restrict entry into the occupation and so maintain wage levels by reducing the supply of suitable job applicants. Of course these professional bodies also have functions such as education, training and maintenance of high standards of work. It is less likely that these professional associations while demonstrating many of the characteristics of trade unionism, are affiliated either to the TUC or the Labour Party, while most of the more conventional unions are. However it is fair to say that if an organisation acts as representative of its members in the collective negotiation of pay and conditions it may be regarded as a trade union in the widest sense. So the traditional view of a trade unionist as a blue collar worker may be considered no longer appropriate in the sphere of organised labour.

Structure of the trade union movement

Trade unionism covers most areas of employed labour in the UK. From its emergence as a series of craft unions covering such trades as printers, carpenters and engineers in the nineteenth century, it has developed to encompass white collar workers such as the National Union of Bank Employees, industrial unions such as the National Union of Mineworkers and general unions containing members in many different jobs and industries such as the Transport and General Workers' Union. The degree of union membership varies from industry to industry and it is often the *percentage of an industry's total workforce* which is unionised which demonstrates the relative strength of that union *rather than the total membership*. For instance in the coal mining industry there is almost 100% membership and although it is a comparatively small union with about 300 000 members its bargaining strength is often much greater than that of larger unions such as the Union of Shop, Distributive and Allied Workers which has a relatively small percentage union membership in its industry.

The gradual decline in employment in basic industries such as coal, steel, etc and the substantial increase in the numbers employed in the tertiary sector of the economy in clerical, administrative and service jobs has meant that the most pronounced union growth in the last twenty years has been in the *white collar unions*. Particularly rapid growth in public sector employment combined with the government's encouragement of unionisation of its employees has meant dramatic gains in membership for unions such as NALGO and the National Union of Public Employees. Another change in union membership structure has been the increasing recruitment of female workers. For many reasons women have been reluctant to join unions and have often worked in industries without a strong trade union. However, as more jobs were established for women in the service and administrative sectors and as an increasing number of women began to work full-time, the percentage of female trade unionists has continued to grow.

Union membership is also more pronounced in industries which have large work units such as factories, mines, shipyards, etc. Small businesses employing a few workers are often non-unionised and consequently workers may face poorer pay and conditions. This lack of unionisation in such organisations is due to the difficulty of recruitment and organisation of the union when there are few workers. As the size of industrial units has continued to grow as employing organisations sought to achieve economies of scale, the result has been increased unionisation which has brought both positive advantages in collective bargaining and adverse outcomes in some instances with a greater potential for industrial unrest.

The number of trade unions

There are now only about 450 trade unions in the UK since numbers have dropped substantially as amalgamations have taken place to form certain unions with a membership in excess of one million members. This trend is illustrated by the development of the TGWU which has grown by taking over smaller, less significant unions. This has the obvious advantage of increasing the potential strength of the union in that a greater number of workers may be asked to support, perhaps militantly, an aim of the union. To some extent it has had the disadvantage of submerging some of the individual objectives of smaller groups who must submit to the overall view of the union. Similarly some unions who had maintained a rigid entry procedure such as a long apprenticeship have been submerged in a larger union operating an *open entry* membership at the cost of being less able to restrict the supply of labour to their particular industry.

Some industries have the added complication of being *multi unionised*, ie that in one industry the workers are represented by a variety of unions. This can lead to difficulties in collective bargaining as employers are faced with a variety of attitudes and claims rather than one single union view. It can also result in problems of inter-union conflict such as *demarcation* disputes where it is claimed that a member of one union is carrying out a task which is the responsibility of the

314

member of another union. Other circumstances may occur where the militant action of one union may endanger the employment prospects of the members of another. Attempts have been made to reduce this problem in some cases by forming a confederation of unions to act as a joint representative body, eg the Confederation of Shipbuilding and Engineering Unions. However many unions are jealous of their independence and prefer to exist in an industry with a splintered union structure.

Internal union structure

Most trade unions are intended to be democratic organisations whose actions reflect the views of their members. This necessitates a complex representative system allowing the voice of grass roots members to be heard by the national executive. Unions are normally organised in *local branches*, each with an elected committee to promote the branch's opinion on both specific and general matters. The branch reports to the *regional or district office* which may combine the opinions and views of its constituent branches and pass these on to the national head office. Each region will normally have a representative on the *national executive* which has overall control of the union's affairs and formulates union attitudes in general. Often the most powerful person in the union is the *general secretary* who is a paid employee of the union and is often seen as its public spokesperson. Union policy is given its direction through motions carried at the annual national conference and the general secretary and the national executive are required to adhere to such policy in making their decisions.

The role of the Trades Union Congress is to act as a focus and a forum for the trade union movement. At the annual conference, the constituent member trade unions making up the majority of union members agree to pursue national policies and act as a pressure group on the government of the day. In the past, governments who have blatantly opposed the TUC have found the combined strength of the labour movement a powerful force indeed. The Heath Government in 1974 fought a general election basically on the issue of 'who rules Britain', following which the Labour opposition became the new government.

The functions of trade unions

As stated earlier the major function of trade unions is to protect the interest of their members. They do this through the process of collective bargaining which involves the union acting as a negotiating body either at a local or national level with the employer or in some cases the employers' association. The union is able to use the combined strength of its membership to seek improvements in pay or conditions. Unions attempt to set a level of wages below which their members will not

315

work. Obviously the more members of a union there are in an industry the more able it is to maintain wage levels and secure better conditions for its workers. Currently about seventy-five per cent of all workers have their wages fixed through collective bargaining between trade unions and employers. Often, these collective agreements affect all other workers to some extent by establishing the 'going rate' for other wage agreements outside the collective bargaining framework. At certain times governments have attempted to *restrict free collective bargaining* by the imposition of an *incomes policy* and the motives and methods of incomes policy will be considered in some detail in the chapter on Government Economic Policy.

Trade union attempts to fix a wage rate

If the trade union and employer agree a wage rate through a process of collective bargaining, the result may be shown graphically in Fig 6.12 using a supply and demand diagram for that particular labour market.

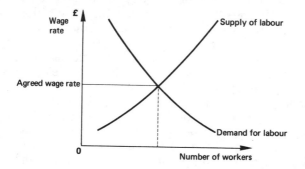

Fig 6.12   Effect on wage rate of union collective agreement.

The agreed wage rate is shown at the point where the demand for labour intersects the supply. If the employer attempts to cut wages, the unions may impose sanctions which lead to a strike or work stoppage, thus effectively reducing the supply of labour to zero, and so below the agreed wage level the supply curve for labour becomes horizontal.

In certain circumstances, such as during periods of high unemployment, demand for labour may well be below potential supply, ie those looking for jobs.

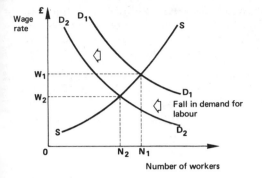

Fig 6.13   Fall in demand for labour

A fall in demand for labour from D_1 to D_2 should reduce the number of workers employed from N_1 to N_2 and so lower the wage rate from W_1 to W_2. However, if the union has fixed the wage rate at W_1, then it may not be allowed to fall and a situation results where supply of labour exceeds demand.

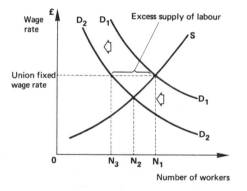

Fig 6.14   Fall in demand for labour with fixed wage rate

As you can see, if this situation prevailed and the wage rate was maintained, then the number of employees might fall from N_1 to N_3. Unions are obviously acutely aware of the need to protect the employment prospects of their members and may fight such redundancies. The legal implications of redundancy are considered later.

Trade unions and the law

Certainly the role of the trade union as a representative of labour is of paramount importance in the business environment and this importance has been reflected by the position given to the trade unions under the law. The majority of rights and duties of independent trade unions

317

and the members they represent are contained in the Trade Union and Labour Relations Acts 1974 and 1976, the Employment Protection Act 1975, and the Employment Act 1980. Among the rights of independent trade unions contained in this body of legislation include:

a) Disclosure of information to an independent recognised trade union during the course of collective bargaining and the right to be consulted concerning proposed redundancies.
b) Rights and duties in relation to the establishment of a *Closed Shop* or *Union Membership Agreement.*
c) Rights of individual employees against insolvent employers including claims against the Redundancy Fund.
d) Rights of officials of independent Trade Unions to time off work for trade union duties.

It would not be practicable to include in a work of this nature a detailed examination of Trade Union law. However it is proposed to examine at a later stage one of the most controversial areas of Trade Union law, that of the closed shop.

As well as rights and duties contained in statute, and regulations made under these statutes by delegate bodies many of the rules relating to industrial relations are contained in codes of practice. So far such codes have been produced by the Advisory, Conciliation and Arbitration Service but the 1980 Act confers similar power to make codes to the Employment Secretary. Codes do not have the same force as rules embodied in statute or regulations but may be used in evidence in any civil or criminal proceedings. So far under the Employment Act, 1980, two codes have been produced, one in relation to the closed shop and one in relation to picketing.

Legislation to protect the worker

One of the major strengths of the labour movement has been its ability to act as a pressure group in achieving improved protection for workers under the law. In this section of the chapter, the important areas of health and safety at work and industrial injuries will be considered.

The present law relating to an employer's duties in relation to the safety of the workforce is so comprehensive that it is necessary to consider it in a separate section.

Duties are imposed upon an employer by:

a) *The common law*: An employer owes a duty of care towards employees under the tort of negligence, which involves providing them with a safe system of work.
b) *Statute*: Statutory duties are imposed upon an employer under various Acts, eg The Factories Act 1961 and the Office Shops and Railway Premises Act 1963, the contents of which are being incorporated by regulation into the Health and Safety at Work Act 1974.

Common law duties

An employer must under the common law, exercise reasonable care with regard to the safety of employees by providing a safe system of work. This common law duty arises under the tort of negligence and is by far the most important duty imposed on an employer. The tort of negligence is composed of three basic elements:

(i) An employer will owe a *duty of care* towards employees if the employer can reasonably foresee harm.

(ii) An employer *breaks the duty of care* by failing to exercise the reasonable care expected of a reasonable employer.

(iii) If, as a result of the breach, *damage results* (ie physical injury, damage to goods), the employer may be made liable under the tort of negligence.

Such a duty of care is imposed on an employer who can reasonably foresee harm to the employees under his or her control. The standard of care which an employer must observe is the care which a prudent employer would take in all the circumstances. It should be emphasised therefore that the duty imposed on an employer is not a strict duty and may be fulfilled by the exercise of a reasonable degree of care.

In *Latimer* v. *AEC* (1953) after a factory was flooded the employer asked his workforce to return, warning them of the dangerous state of the factory floor. Sawdust had been used to cover most of the damp areas but not enough was available and the plaintiff slipped and was injured. To determine whether the employer had broken the common law duty of care he owed to his employees, the Court weighed the cost of avoiding the injury against the extra risk of injury, and held that the employer had acted reasonably in the circumstances.

Another relevant factor to determine the standard of care required of an employer is to consider not only the risk of injury but also the possible serious consequences of injury.

In *Paris* v. *Stepney BC* (1951) the plaintiff, a one-eyed motor mechanic, lost the sight of his good eye while working at chipping rust from under a bus. Despite there being no usual practice to provide mechanics with safety goggles, the Court decided that they should have been provided to the plaintiff. The defendants were liable as they could foresee serious consequences for the plaintiff if he suffered eye injury.

The above case illustrates the principle that the standard of care required of an employer will vary with each individual employee, ie more care in relation to a young apprentice than an experienced worker.

The common law duty of an employer has been described as to provide a *safe system of work*.

Safe system of work
This duty may be broken down under three main headings:
a) *Provide safe fellow employees*
An employer should employ workers who will fulfil their contractual duties without causing dangers to fellow employees. If an employer is aware of an employee who by incompetence or stupidity is creating dangers then the employee must be dismissed after due warning.

However, in *Coddington* v. *International Harvester Co of Gt Britain* (1969) an employee caused severe injuries to a fellow employee by kicking a burning tin of paint thinners in his direction. The employer was held not liable as there was nothing to suggest in his previous conduct that the employee in question would act in such a manner.

NB Under the doctrine of *vicarious (substituted) liability* an employer may be made liable for the negligence of his employees arising during the course of their employment both in relation to fellow employees and third parties.
b) *Provide safe plant and machinery*
The duty on an employer is to provide employees with equipment that is safe. However the employer is taken to have fulfilled this duty by purchasing equipment from a reputable supplier. Since 1969, the burden upon an employer has been made more onerous following the Employers' Liability (Defective Equipment) Act 1969 if an employee suffers injury as a result of defective equipment provided by the employer and the defect is caused by a third party (supplier). In such circumstances the injury is deemed to be attributable to the employer. The employer can then look to recover damages from the supplier at fault.

An extreme example of an employer being made liable under the common law for providing his employees with defective equipment is the case of *Bradford* v. *Robinson Rentals* (1967) where an employee driver suffered frost bite after being required to drive an unheated van on a journey of 400 miles in winter. The employer was held to be liable in negligence for the damage which was reasonably foreseeable.

c) *Provide safe working methods*
This involves ensuring that safety precautions are taken in relation to the work to be done. There should be adequate training and supervision, the provision of warnings, clear instructions and safety

equipment where necessary. Obviously the more dangerous the work the greater is the need for stringent safety precautions. An employer must ensure that workers are aware of safety precautions and similarly provide safety equipment and make it available for use. In some cases particularly where there is a serious risk of injury the employer's duty extends to ensuring that workers make use of the safety equipment provided.

In *Nolan* v. *Dental Manufacturing Co* (1958) it was held that an employer was liable in negligence when he failed to ensure that safety goggles were worn by a toolsetter who was injured while working on a grinding wheel.

Alternatively, if an employer gives proper instructions which the employee fails to observe then the employer will not be liable if the employee is subsequently injured.

In *Charlton* v. *Forrest Printing Ink Co Ltd* (1978) the employer gave proper instruction to an employee who was given the job of collecting the company's wages. The instructions required the employee to vary his collecting arrangements to prevent robbery. The employee failed to do this and suffered severe injuries when he was robbed. The Court of Appeal held that the employer was not liable as he had taken reasonable steps to cut down the risk.

Vicarious liability

Vicarious liability is a legal doctrine under which one person may be held responsible for the unlawful acts of another. Its modern significance lies primarily in the employment relationship. The courts have considered that because an employer chooses staff and has a degree of control over their activities it is reasonable that the employer should be made accountable for their actions. Moreover the fact that the employer gains the economic benefit of employees' activities and is in a position to compensate third parties who suffered loss (usually by insuring against the risk) reinforces the rationale underpinning the doctrine. The application of the doctrine is restricted to the extent that an employer will only be made liable for the acts of employees carried out during the course of their employment. It should be stressed that an employer is responsible for the actions of *employees* under direct control as opposed to *contractors* employed. The distinction between the two forms of employment was dealt with earlier. Exceptionally the act of a contractor will be treated as if it were the employer's act. For instance where the employer expressly authorises the unlawful act or the work carried on is particularly hazardous.

Course of employment

To determine whether an employee is acting within the course of his or her employment, the courts will pose the question – *at the time of the act can the employee be said to be doing their job?* It is recognised that an employee may still be doing the job despite performing it in an unlawful manner.

> In *Century Insurance Co Ltd* v. *Northern Ireland Transport Board* (1942) the driver of a petrol tanker, while delivering petrol struck a match which caused an explosion. His employer was held to be vicariously liable as the employee was doing his job at the time of the negligent act and therefore within the course of his employment.

It should be mentioned that an employee is personally liable for his or her negligent acts and even though not sued may be required to contribute to damages paid by the employer under the Law Reform (Married Women and Joint Tortfeasors) Act 1935. In addition, of course, a negligent employee is in breach of contract of employment and may be justifiably dismissed. If the employee commits an act outside the course of his or her duties the employer will not be made responsible.

> In *Warren* v. *Henley's Ltd* (1948) a petrol pump attendant argued with a customer who he thought was intending to drive off without paying for his petrol. The customer having threatened to report the attendant to his employer was assaulted by him. The Court held that the employer was not liable for the outrageous conduct as the attendant's action was provoked by personal malice which took it outside the scope of his employment.

Nevertheless, even if an employer gives an employee an express instruction intended to prohibit particular conduct, the employer could still be made liable if the conduct is regarded as being within the scope of the employee's job.

> In *Rose* v. *Plenty* (1976) the employer instructed his milkman not to engage help from young children. In breach of this instruction, a milkman hired a young boy to help him and, as a result of the milkman's negligent driving, the boy was injured. The Court held that the milkman was nevertheless still within the scope of employment and thus the employer was vicariously liable.

Statutory duties

Health and safety

The Health and Safety at Work Act 1974 is a comprehensive body of law which governs the health and safety of all persons who are affected by the activities of an employer. Under the Act, the *Health and Safety Commission* has been created with the major task of incorporating

322

safety regulations in relation to all industries (eventually replacing the provisions of the Factories Act, 1961, and the Offices Shops and Railway Premises Act, 1963). Also the *Health and Safety Executive* (replacing the Factory Inspectorate) has been set up to enforce the Act's provisions. The Act provides for criminal penalties for employers and employees who are in breach of its obligations by way of prosecution in the Magistrates Court and in some cases the Crown Court for serious offences. Also a person who suffers harm as a result of failure to comply with specific regulations made under the statute can maintain an action for damages for breach of statutory duty. The Act imposes a general duty on all employers to ensure *so far as it reasonably practicable*, the health, safety and welfare of all employees while they are at work. This general duty involves:

(i) *providing and maintaining safe plant and work system,*
(ii) *making arrangements for the use, handling, storage and transport of articles and substances,*
(iii) *providing any necessary information, instruction, training and supervision,*
(iv) *maintaining a safe place of work and a safe access to and exit from it,*
(v) *maintaining a safe working environment.*

One of the major innovations of the Act is the introduction of *constructive sanctions* which can be used by an inspector employed by the Executive. If an inspector believes that a person is contravening one of the statutory provisions, the inspector may serve on that person an *improvement notice* requiring that the contravention be remedied within a specified period. In cases where the contravention involves a risk of serious injury, the inspector may serve a *prohibition notice* which will direct that the particular activity be terminated until the contravention is remedied.

The comprehensive nature of the Act makes it impracticable to describe all its provisions in a text of this nature but it should be stressed that duties are not limited to the employer but also include manufacturers, designers, importers and suppliers of equipment or substances, and also employees and contractors in relation to health and safety.

Industrial injuries benefit

Many injuries are caused at work without the employers being at fault or in breach of a statutory duty. They are simply caused by *accidents*. In the mid-sixties a new state scheme was introduced under which compensation is payable to an employee injured at work by an accident. The present provisions are contained in the Social Security Act 1975. Employees (contractors are excluded) are entitled to benefit if they suffer *personal injury caused by an accident arising out of and in the course of employment, or contract a prescribed industrial disease* (prescribed under regulation by the Secretary of State for Social Services). Benefit is payable therefore only if the claimant suffers physical or mental injury rather than damage to clothes or tools.

If the claimant can show that the accident arose during the course of his or her employment (during contractual hours) there is a presumption that it arose 'out of' the employment. It is necessary however for the claimant to show that the nature of the employment upon which he was engaged gave rise to the accident rather than the risk of injury being shared by all persons.

In *R* v. *National Insurance Commissioner Ex parte Richardson* (1958) the question was whether a bus conductor who had been assaulted by a gang of youths while he was standing on the platform of his bus was attacked because of the nature of his employment. It was held that he was not attacked for any reason connected with employment but merely in his capacity as a member of the general public and therefore he was not entitled to benefit.

As far as injuries occurring during permitted breaks are concerned, an employee will still be within the course of his or her employment. Even if the employee is injured while engaged in a sporting activity at work he or she may still recover benefit if it can be shown that the activity relates to the job. Thus a fireman injured playing volleyball attempting to keep fit was held to be entitled to benefit. Benefits have also been payable to workers injured as a result of the misconduct of others provided that the claimant did not contribute to the misconduct. Finally, the Act also provides for benefit to be payable to an employee who suffers injury travelling to and from work on a vehicle operated by and on behalf of his employer.

The termination of employment

In order to complete this analysis of labour, it is necessary to examine the process of termination of employment and to consider the measures the law has imposed on employers wishing to reduce their labour force.

A contract of employment must inevitably terminate at some time either by the death of the employee or the dissolution or winding up of the business. If the contract is expressed to be for a fixed term or for the completion of a particular project then under the common law it will terminate either on the expiration of the fixed term or the completion of the project. In addition, either side may terminate the contract by serving the *required notice*. However, since 1971, employees are now given statutory protection against arbitrary dismissal without good reason. *Industrial tribunals* have been set up with jurisdiction to decide disputes relating to *unfair dismissal* with a possible right of appeal against their decision to the Employment Appeals Tribunal and from there to the Court of Appeal.

Wrongful dismissal

The expression *wrongful dismissal* refers to the situation where an employee has been dismissed without being given the minimum period of notice required under the Employment Protection (Consolidation) Act, 1978, or payment in lieu of notice. The periods are shown below and generally depend on seniority and length of service.

Periods

After Continuous Employment for:		*Period of Notice*
4 weeks up to 2 years	–	1 week
2 years up to 12 years	–	1 week for each year
12 years or more	–	12 weeks

Of course, if the contract of employment provides for a longer period, then that is the period of notice that applies. Even though the 1978 Act lays down minimum periods a longer period may be justifiable as reasonable under the common law.

> In *Hill* v. *Parsons* (1972) the Court of Appeal thought that a chartered engineer who had been employed continuously for thirty-five years was entitled to at least six months' notice.

If an employee is *summarily dismissed* (instant dismissal) without justification then he or she can bring an action for damages for wrongful dismissal in the ordinary courts (the County Court or High Court).

Gross misconduct

Under the common law, summary dismissal may be justified in cases of *gross misconduct*. The employee must have acted in a grossly improper way by reason of disobedience, dishonesty, incompetence, negligence or misbehaviour to amount to gross misconduct. In *Pepper* v. *Webb* (1969) the action of the head gardener in wilfully disobeying a reasonable order was sufficient to amount to gross misconduct and give grounds for summary dismissal despite the contract of employment providing for three months' notice.

It should be stressed however that the reaction of the gardener in the previous case was the culmination of a long period of insolence and the isolated use of choice obscenities by an employee to an employer may not amount to gross misconduct if there is provocation.

> In *Wilson* v. *Racher* (1974) a gardener who proved to have an even wider knowledge of bad language for which he was dismissed instantly was held to be wrongfully dismissed in the circumstances. His employer had provoked the outburst by his own conduct.

Certainly, instant dismissal may be justified on the grounds of:
a) *dishonesty*

Sinclair v. *Neighbour* (1967) Here the manager of a betting shop who 'borrowed' £15 from the till and left an IOU in its place, was held to be summarily dismissed justifiably,

or
b) *absenteeism*

Ross v. *Aquascutum Ltd* (1973) Here a night watchman who was absent from his post for two hours each night was held to be summarily dismissed justifiably.

Unfair dismissal

The concept of unfair dismissal was first introduced by the Industrial Relations Act 1971. Today law relating to unfair dismissal is contained in the Employment Protection Act 1978, the Employment Act 1980 and their interpretation in the many reported cases. A dispute relating to dismissal is first dealt with by an industrial tribunal, with the possibility of appeal to the Employment Appeals tribunal and from there in certain circumstances to the ordinary courts. *Every employee to whom the 1978 Act applies has the right not to be unfairly dismissed.* The basic qualifying period of continuous employment is 52 weeks for an employee to obtain protection except in cases where the dismissal was for attempting to join or refusing to join a Trade Union or on the grounds of sex or race discrimination. Under the 1980 Act the period is two years for employees of small firms (less than 20). However, the *compensation* has also been increased by the 1980 Act to a possible £17 060 comprising £6250 *compensation*, £4050 *basic award* and £6760 *additional award* which may be made if an employer unreasonably refuses to carry out an order of reinstatement or re-engagement. It should be pointed out that sometimes a successful applicant may be awarded reduced compensation because of his or her own contributory conduct.

Dismissal

Once an employee brings a complaint of unfair dismissal against the employer, within a short period of time a *conciliation officer* will visit both parties in an attempt to resolve the conflict and reach a settlement. It should be stressed that in many cases an amicable agreement is reached at this stage because of the conciliation officer's intervention. However, if the employee wishes to proceed with the claim before a tribunal, then to succeed he or she must firstly show that they have been dismissed. There is no dismissal if the employee:
   (i) *Resigns*. This may occur by the employee expressly terminating the contract by giving notice, or constructively where the employee by his or her conduct is taken to have brought the contract to an end, eg refused to work.

(ii) *Is a party to a contract which is frustrated.* Frustration of the contract of employment occurs when performance of the contract has become impossible because of some event, eg illness of the employee where the employee is unlikely to return to work for a long period.

(iii) *Completes a particular project.* If the employee is employed to complete a particular task, on completion the contract is terminated.

(iv) *Terminates the contract by agreement.* If it can be shown that the employer and employee have expressly agreed that the contract should terminate on the happening or non happening of a specified event then the contract will terminate on its occurrence.

In *British Leyland* v. *Ashraf* (1978) the employee was given five weeks unpaid leave to return to Pakistan and he expressly agreed that if he failed to return to work on a particular date his employment would terminate. The failure of the employee to return to work on the due date was held to amount to a mutual termination of the contract of employment.

(v) *Enters into a fixed term contract of twelve months or more and agrees in writing to exclude his or her statutory rights on unfair dismissal.*

A dismissal will be taken to have occurred if either:

a) An employee's contract of employment is terminated by the employer with or without notice.

b) An employee's fixed term contract terminates without being renewed (subject to the exception above).

c) An employee justifiably terminates the contract of employment with or without notice (constructive dismissal).

(i) *Express termination*

If an employer expressly informs an employee that the contract is at an end by saying 'collect your cards', or 'you're fired', the dismissal is clear and explicit but in practice tribunals are often faced with the problem of placing an interpretation on the language used.

In *Futty* v. *Brekkes* (1974) a fish filleter was told by his foreman 'If you do not like the job you can fuck off'. The Tribunal held that the language used had to be interpreted in the light of the work, where such expressions were not unusual, and so the words did not constitute a dismissal when the employee walked out.

Of course there is no doubt that telling an employee to 'fuck off' or 'piss off' can constitute a dismissal in the right circumstances but in

Davy v. *Collins (Builders) Ltd* (1974) the tribunal drew a distinction between the expression 'If you are not satisfied you can fuck off' and 'I am not satisfied so you can fuck off' where only the latter amounted to a dismissal.

(ii) *Fixed term contracts*

This has been defined as a contract which must run for a fixed period and one which cannot be terminated except by a gross breach of a contractual term by either party. The possibility of an employee giving up statutory rights relating to unfair dismissal for a fixed term contract over one year has already been mentioned. Quite simply therefore, a fixed term contract which does not come within this category will result in a dismissal if it is not renewed.

(iii) *Constructive dismissal*

This occurs where the employee terminates the contract of employment in circumstances where he or she is entitled to do so because of the employer's conduct. To determine this issue has always proved to be a difficult question but it now seems that the test to be applied is at least certain.

In *Western Excavating (EEC) Ltd* v. *Sharp* (1978) the Court of Appeal held that to decide what constitutes constructive dismissal the 'conduct test' should be applied, ie was the employer guilty of conduct which was a significant breach of the contract of employment showing that he or she no longer intended to be bound by one of its terms?

It now seems therefore that an employee has to show that his or her employer was in some way in breach of the contract of employment to demonstrate that the employee walking out amounted to a constructive dismissal. This would occur if the employer attempted to change employment terms unilaterally without the employee's consent (less pay, holidays, change of work place). The breach, of course, is not limited to the express terms of the contract but would also cover the breach of implied obligations.

In *British Aircraft Corp* v. *Austin* (1978) the employer was held to be in breach of his implied duty of safety when he failed to investigate a complaint relating to the suitability of protective glasses. This conduct would be a sufficient ground to entitle the employee to terminate the contract of employment and seek a remedy for unfair dismissal.

Quite often, of course, the employee who walks out is aggrieved not at the employer's conduct but at the conduct of a fellow employee for whom the employer is responsible, eg

In *Isle of Wight Tourist Board* v. *Coombes* (1976) the applicant walked out following a remark not by the employer but by a superior employee:

'She is an intolerable bitch on a Monday morning.' This was held to amount to a fundamental breach of the contract of employment and constructive dismissal.

Having established that a dismissal has taken place, the next question to be considered is whether the dismissal was fair or unfair. This is determined by considering the facts of each individual case and whether the employer acted reasonably in the circumstances.

Fair dismissal

The first stage in proving a fair dismissal is for the employer to show that he or she *had a reason* to dismiss the employee and secondly that it is *a reason falling* under one of the categories laid down in the Employment Protection (Consolidation) Act, 1978, eg.

a) *related to the capability or qualifications of the employee*;
b) *related to the employee's conduct*;
c) *that the employee is redundant*;
d) *that the employee, in continuing to work, is in contravention of a statutory provision*;
e) *that it was some other substantial reason of a kind to justify dismissal*.

The second stage was, having shown a reason within the 1978 Act, for the employer to prove that he or she acted reasonably in treating it as a sufficient reason for dismissing the employee. This burden of proof has now been shifted from the employer by the Employment Act 1980 however the tribunal must still be satisfied that the employer acted reasonably and this will be decided by examining all the circumstances of the case (including the size and resources of the employer).

A reason

If the employer fails to show a reason for dismissal falling within the categories laid down in the 1978 Act the dismissal can never be justified.

In *Price* v. *Gourley Bros Ltd* (1973) the applicant worked in a cake shop for seven years and received top wages for her grade. She was dismissed, and when she asked for the reason, was told by her employer 'it was just one of those things'. Later at the tribunal the employer relied on *capability* as his reason but had no evidence to support it. In any event, if capability was the reason the employer had waited too long before taking action. The tribunal held that there was no statutory reason for dismissal, the reason was reduction of overheads, and the dismissal was accordingly unfair.

Statutory reasons

1 *Capability or qualifications*

'Capability' is given a wide definition and includes skill, aptitude, health, physical or mental quality for the job for which the employee was dismissed.

329

In *Fitzpatrick* v. *Hobourn Eaton (Manufacturing) Co* (1973) an employee contracted dermatitis in the course of his work and was dismissed. He was unable to do his job as a machine operator which involved contact with oil. The tribunal held the dismissal to be fair as the employee was no longer capable of performing his contractual duties.

'Qualification' means any degree, diploma or other academic, technical or professional qualification relevant to the position held.

In *Blackman* v. *The Post Office* (1974) the applicant was recruited for a particular job on an unestablished basis. Under the terms of a collective agreement his job could only be continued if he proved to be successful in a written aptitude test. Despite showing aptitude for the job the applicant failed the test three times and was dismissed. The tribunal held the dismissal to be fair on the grounds of lack of qualification and also on capability, ie his failure to pass the test.

2 Misconduct

This category, of course, is the widest and covers action such as the outburst of the gardener in *Pepper* v. *Webb*. It also includes a refusal to obey a reasonable order, and conduct such as that in *Ramroop* v. *Goldman* (1974) where the applicant was dismissed for taking home the warehouse cat and negligently losing it.

Misconduct at work

It is a question of fact in each case whether an act of misconduct at work is sufficient to justify dismissal. For serious cases of gross misconduct (eg theft, gross negligence) one act may be sufficient whereas for less serious matters (eg bad timekeeping) a course of conduct with a number of warnings may be necessary. Certainly there is a duty on the employer to mount a thorough investigation of the misconduct and in dealing with it he is entitled to consider all the circumstances of the case including the individual employee's record.

In *Sherrier* v. *Ford Motor Co* (1976) two employees were caught fighting and after a full investigation by the employer it was impossible to discover who was responsible. The employee who had a long exemplary record was suspended while the other, who in two years' employment had been disciplined on a number of occasions, was dismissed. The tribunal held that the applicant's dismissal was justified in the circumstances.

In *Trust House Forte Hotels Ltd* v. *Murphy* (1977) a night porter admitted stealing liquor from his employer and was dismissed. The Appeals Tribunal held the dismissal to be a fair one.

However, in *Pringle* v. *Lucas Industrial Equipment Ltd* (1975) an employee, who absented himself from work for one hour without permission in breach of a works rule, was summarily dismissed. The tribunal held that, without prior warning, the misconduct was insufficient to justify the dismissal which was therefore unfair.

Misconduct outside of work
Generally misconduct outside of work to justify dismissal must in some way affect the employee when doing his or her work.

In *Cassidy* v. *Goodman Ltd* (1975) the applicant was dismissed because he refused to terminate his relationship with a former female employee. As the private conduct was in no way damaging to his work or the employer's business the tribunal held that the dismissal was unfair.

Alternatively, in *Singh* v. *London County Bus Services* (1976) the applicant driver of a one-man operated bus was convicted of an offence involving dishonesty committed outside his employment. Here the tribunal held the misconduct was sufficient to affect the way the employee did his work and was dismissed justifiably.

The ground of misconduct was relied on in *Bradshaw* v. *Rugby Portland Cement Co Ltd* (1972) the applicant being dismissed following a conviction for incest with his own daughter for which he was on probation. The tribunal held that the dismissal was unfair as the offence had no bearing on his work as a quarryman, and the relationship that he had with fellow employees had not deteriorated to any grave extent.

3 *The redundancy of the employee*
A *redundancy situation* will exist if the employer closes down the business or part of the business and no longer requires the services of the particular employee. It does not follow that a redundancy situation will automatically produce a fair dismissal. The employer must have had consultation with the workforce, observed proper selection procedures and considered possible alternatives. A redundancy situation could be dealt with otherwise than by dismissing employees, eg reducing overtime, short-time working, restricting recruitment.

This point was argued in *Attwood* v. *William Hill Ltd* (1974) where the employer closed down betting shops and declared the managers redundant without warning or offering alternative employment. The tribunal held that a redundancy situation existed but the employees did not have to be made redundant and more effort should have been taken to find them alternative work.

4 *Statutory contravention*

A dismissal will be fair if the employer can show that to continue employing the worker in that particular job would infringe a statutory provision. The usual example of course, is where a driver has been disqualified from driving under the Road Traffic Acts.

In *Appleyard* v. *Smith (Hull) Ltd* (1972) a motor mechanic who required a valid driving license to test vehicles was disqualified from driving. The tribunal held that, as he worked for such a small firm, who could not find him alternative employment, his dismissal was in the circumstances fair.

5 *Some other substantial reason*

This is the residual category upon which an employer can rely to justify dismissal. It was relied on as a ground in *Foot* v. *Eastern Counties Timber Co Ltd* (1972) where the employer was held to have acted reasonably in dismissing an employee who had access to confidential information when her husband started a rival business.

These then are the five categories upon which an employer could rely to justify a dismissal. In addition of course a tribunal must also be satisfied that the employer acted *reasonably* in treating the reason as being sufficient to dismiss the employee. This is a question of fact for each tribunal to determine after examining all the circumstances of the particular case. Now that the Employment Act 1980 has removed the burden of proof of this second stage from the employer the question is how will it affect claims. It is suggested that this change will produce little difference, for an employer will still find it necessary to bring to the tribunal's attention evidence to demonstrate the reasonableness of the action. The ratio of successful applicants has remained around the same (one-third) since the unfair dismissal provisions were first introduced in 1971.

Statutory fair or unfair

Finally some mention may be made of the statutory provisions which *designate* certain reasons for dismissal as either fair or unfair – Employment Protection (Consolidation) Act 1978 as amended by Employment Act 1980. The Act states that if the principal reason for dismissal is that the employee:

a) was or proposed to become a member of a Trade Union, or
b) had or proposed to take part in Union activities, or
c) had refused or proposed to refuse to become or remain a member of a *non independent* Trade Union,

then the dismissal is *necessarily* unfair. On the other hand, a dismissal is to be regarded as fair if:

a) It is the practice for employees of the same class to belong to an *independent* Trade Union in accordance with a *Union membership agreement.*

b) The reason for dismissal was that the employee was not a member of the specified Union or had refused or proposed to refuse to remain a member.

This section provides therefore, that if a valid *closed shop agreement* is in force, then an employee who refuses to join the independent Trade Union may be dismissed fairly by the employer. The 1978 Act provided, however, that an employee dismissed in this situation would be dismissed unfairly if he or she objected to being a member of a Trade Union on religious grounds. Now the 1980 Act replaces this exception with some new ones.

(i) That the dismissal in these circumstances shall be regarded as unfair if the employee *genuinely objects on grounds of conscience or other deeply-held personal conviction* to being a member of any Trade Union whatsoever, or a particular Trade Union, or

(ii) the employee in question has been among

a) the class of employees to whom the union membership agreement relates since before the agreement required membership, *and*

b) has not at any time while the agreement had effect been a member of a trade union in accordance with it.

In addition, the 1980 Act provides that a new union membership agreement (ie closed shop) must be approved by a ballot and *not less than 80% of those entitled to vote* in the ballot voted in favour of the agreement.

Redundancy payments
In 1965, a scheme was introduced whereby an employee who is dismissed because there is no longer a demand for his or her work can claim a redundancy payment in respect of the loss suffered. The present provisions relating to such payments are contained in the Employment Protection (Consolidation) Act 1978. Of course the making of such awards, as well as compensating for the loss of employment, has the additional economic advantage of helping to provide a more mobile labour force to ensure that labour skills may be redistributed.
Entitlement
Individuals qualifying for an award are *employed persons* (as opposed to self employed) who have served a minimum of *two years continuous employment*, over the age of *eighteen*, and have been *dismissed* for reason of *redundancy*. There is a dismissal if either:

a) the employer terminates the contract of employment;
b) a fixed term contract expires;
c) there is a constructive dismissal;
d) the employer has died, the business dissolved or wound up.

333

If the employee does not establish a dismissal then he or she loses entitlement to a redundancy payment.

> In *Morton Sundour Fabrics* v. *Shaw* (1966) the employee in question, having been warned of the possibility of redundancy left to take other employment. The Court held that as he had not been dismissed, he was therefore not entitled to a redundancy payment.

Dismissal due to redundancy
There is a presumption under the 1978 Act that, if an employee is dismissed, it is for reason of redundancy unless the contrary is proved. If the employer does show another reason for dismissal, eg illness or misconduct, it will then be necessary to determine whether the dismissal is fair or unfair. The Act specifies that certain reasons for dismissal will 'constitute redundancy including:

   (i) If the employer stops or intends to stop carrying on the business altogether;
  (ii) If the employer stops or intends to stop the type of business in which the employee is engaged;
 (iii) If the employer reduces or intends to reduce the workers due to a fall in demand;
 (iv) If the employer stops or intends to stop carrying on business at a particular location;
  (v) If the employer reduces or intends to reduce the workers at a particular location.

An employee could also be classified as redundant if the employer attempts to change the contract of employment by requiring him or her to work at a different location not within travelling distance of the present work, or transfer to a different type of work which in the circumstances involves less beneficial conditions of employment. However, there is nothing to prevent an employer including an express term in the employee's contract of employment which gives the employer the right to vary the employee's contract without his or her consent.

Surplus workforce
Nowadays, one of the main reasons for redundancy is the fact that the employer finds that a number of the workforce have become superfluous, perhaps because of new working methods, machinery, the need for new skills, or a fall in demand for the product. If the employer decides to dismiss for this reason, the question is whether it is a redundancy situation, or a dismissal on grounds of incapability.

> In *Cannon* v. *William King Ltd* (1966) a french polisher who refused to do painting was held to be redundant, and in *Smith* v. *AK Purdy Trawlers Ltd* (1966) a seaman who could not operate a new diesel driven trawler was held to be redundant.

However, in *Hindle* v. *Percival Boats* (1969) the applicant was highly skilled and built and repaired wooden boats. His employers began to concentrate on producing fibreglass boats and the demands for the applicant's work were greatly reduced. Eventually his work became so uneconomic that he was dismissed as unsatisfactory. As the type of work on which he was engaged was still in existence, the Court held that this was not a redundancy situation.

Had there been a genuine rundown in the above case and the applicant's job had been totally swallowed up, then the Court might have been convinced of a redundancy situation. Nevertheless, the decision above has been subject to criticism.

Suitable alternative employment
There can be no redundancy if the employer makes an offer of suitable alternative employment which the employee rejects. The offer will be suitable if:

(i) the provisions of the new contract are similar to the previous contract;

or

(ii) the provisions of the new contract *do* differ but the offer constitutes an offer of suitable employment.

Whether the alternative offer is suitable or not will depend on examining all the circumstances of the particular case, eg work, pay, hours, conditions, travelling, fringe benefits, accommodation, social and family links, children's education and so on.

In *Devonald* v. *JD Insulating Co Ltd* (1972) the applicant was required to move from a factory in Bootle to another at Blackburn. He refused, and on his claim for redundancy, the tribunal held that suitable alternative employment had been offered as he was already required under his present employment to do outside contract work.

Similarly, in *Fuller* v. *Stephanie Bowman Ltd* (1977), the applicant typist refused to move from Mayfair to a new office in Soho. She found the move distasteful particularly as the new office was above a sex shop. The tribunal found that the refusal to move was unreasonable in the circumstances based upon undue sensitivity and the claim for redundancy must fail.

Redundancy payment procedure
The 1978 Act lays down a particular procedure which must be followed by an employer who intends to make redundant an employee belonging to a group of workers represented by an independent trade union. The procedure involves consultation with trade union representatives, notification to the Secretary of State for Employment, and advance

warning of redundancies to enable alternative jobs to be found. Certain details must be disclosed by the employer to the trade union representative including reasons for redundancies, numbers, how selected, etc. The Secretary of State administers the *redundancy fund* which is made up of contributions from employers and employees. A claim is met by an employer in full but he or she is entitled to a 41% rebate from the fund.

To calculate the amount of a redundancy payment it is necessary to establish the following facts;

  (i) *the relevant date*, ie the date that the contract of employment terminated;

 (ii) *week's pay*, ie the minimum remuneration to which the employee is entitled in the week preceeding the relevant date (maximum of £135);

(iii) *years of continuous employment*, ie the number of years employment calculated in weeks in which the employee works 16 hours minimum. Certain matters will break the continuity such as long absence through illness, and certain periods although not breaking continuity will not count, eg strikes or lock outs after July 1964.

Having established the above matters the calculation of redundancy payment is as follows:

For each year employed between the ages of:	Amount of redundancy payment:
18 – 21	half week's pay × no. of years worked
22 – 40	one week's pay × no. of years worked
41 – 65 (Men) 41 – 60 (Women)	one and a half weeks' pay × no. of years worked

The maximum length of reckonable service is 20 years and maximum weeks' pay is £135, eg maximum payment under the scheme is for a man over 60, with 20 years continuous service, on a wage of £135 per week.

$$20 \times 1\tfrac{1}{2} \times £135 = £4050$$

When making the payment, the employer should give the employee a written statement of how it has been calculated and any lump sum given to a redundant employee. Failure to provide such a statement could lead to the payment being regarded as simply voluntary rather than a redundancy payment.

It should be noted however that much larger sums are payable under private schemes for redundancy payments entered into by employers and Trade Unions.

The provision of redundancy payments in addition to providing compensation for loss of employment has encouraged free movement of labour as the redundant worker has sufficient capital either to seek employment elsewhere or to establish a new small business.

Case study of the national newspaper industry

The National Newspaper Industry or 'Fleet Street' as it is more colloquially known proves an excellent if complex example of the labour
market in one particular industry. It shows the interrelation of
employers and organised labour. For example, it demonstrates how
new technology can dramatically influence the demand for labour and
how the unions can oppose its introduction; it demonstrates the factor
of derived demand for labour and the manner in which a declining
demand for national morning papers has reduced the number of
publications and with it the demand for labour; and finally how industrial law has had an important effect on the industry.

The structure of the market

In 1981 there were ten national daily papers which can be arbitrarily
divided into the *quality* papers: the Times, Guardian, the Daily
Telegraph and the Financial Times; and the *popular* press: the Daily
Mirror, the Daily Express, the Daily Mail, the Sun, the Star and the
Morning Star. Of these the Financial Times and the Morning Star while
published in London and distributed nationally, both have relatively
small circulations and the Star after a rather unsuccessful launch is now
concentrating its publication in Manchester. The Sunday papers published and distributed nationally are – *quality*:- the Sunday Times, the
Sunday Telegraph and the Observer; and *popular*:- the Sunday Mirror,
the Sunday Express, the News of the World, the People and the Mail.
Also published in London on the national presses is the sole remaining
London evening paper, the New Standard. The ownership of these
papers is concentrated in a relatively few hands and can be regarded as
an oligopolistic market. The following table shows how control is
centred with certain companies.

Ownership	National Daily Newspapers	National Sunday Newspapers
News International	Times Sun	Sunday Times News of the World
IPC Ltd	Mirror	Sunday Mirror People
Daily Telegraph Ltd	Telegraph	Sunday Telegraph
Express Newspapers	Express Star	Sunday Express
Manchester Guardian and Evening News Ltd	Guardian	–
Observer Ltd	–	Observer
Associated Newspapers	Mail	Mail

Other holdings by these groups include substantial shares in the provincial newspaper market as well as interests in magazines, independent television and book publishing. As such this relatively small group has a considerable influence on the media as a whole.

Competition in the market

Newspapers compete in two ways – for readers and for advertisers. Competition is, of course, not only with other newspapers but also with the other branches of the media, television, local radio, magazines, etc. While the growth of commercial TV and radio has not seemed to reduce the amount of money spent on newspaper advertising, it has certainly caused a reduction in national newspaper circulation. Thus, the last ten years have seen both a reduction in the number of national newspapers and a substantial reduction in the circulation of those that have remained in existence. However as advertising expenditure has not fallen in proportion, this has led to an increase in the size of newspapers and the growth of free supplements containing extensive advertising. This decline in the number of titles and an increasing concentration of ownership as mergers and takeovers reduced the spread of control has had a considerable impact on the demand for labour in the industry.

A further factor which has contributed to the decline in demand for newspapers has been the rapid increase in the cost of newsprint prices in recent years which has led to substantial rises in the cost of newspapers particularly the Sunday papers. The result of all these factors has led most of the newspapers to attempt to reduce production costs in two ways: firstly by a cut in staffing levels and secondly by introducing new technology. This clearly illustrates the effect of derived demand in the product market on the demand for labour.

The organisation of production in the industry
The process of producing a national newspaper has been established over a considerable period of time. It is divided into a series of almost separate operations linked in the production chain. Each separate operation tends to be staffed by members of a different union. To briefly outline the process it can be subdivided into five sections:

(i) *Editorial process* – news gathering either by the paper's own journalists or from news agencies. Also advertisement copy submitted direct from advertisers or through ad agencies. Copy selected and edited. These tasks almost exclusively carried on by members of the National Union of Journalists (NUJ).

(ii) *Composing process* – typesetting of the copy and special display setting of headlines, photos, etc. This is then made up into pages on the 'stone', a flat metal table. These tasks are undertaken by members of the National Graphical Association (NGA) and to a lesser degree by the Society of Lithographic Artists, Design Engineers and Process Workers (SLADE). At this point in the composing process, the pages are re-assessed and proofed by page readers. This is done by members of NGA with assistance from members of the National Society of Operative Printers, Graphical and Media Personnel (NATSOPA).

(iii) *The foundary* – once the pages are complete and checked they are made into metal plates which are hot pressed and trimmed by members of the NGA.

(iv) *Machine room* – the actual printing of the paper. The operation is segregated between time-served machine operators who are members of the NGA and machine assistants who are semi-skilled and belong to NATSOPA.

(v) *Publishing room* – once printed, the newsprint is cut and folded into newspapers and transferred by conveyor to the publishing room where they are bundled, labelled, packaged and dispatched to the distributors or railway stations. The publishing room work is carried on by members of the Society of Graphical and Allied Trades (SOGAT).

As this examination of the production process illustrates, the industry has a labour structure which is splintered between several different trade unions. Each negotiates on behalf of its own members. All journalists are represented by the NUJ while the NGA and SLADE represent craft unions and SOGAT and NATSOPA represent unskilled or semi-skilled workers. To further complicate matters, plant maintenance is carried out by members of the Amalgamated Union of Engineering Workers (AUEW) and the Electrical, Electronic Telecommunications and Plumbing Union (EETPU). Each union has its own branch (known in the industry as *chapels*) for each paper and the chairperson of the branch is known as the Father or Mother of the Chapel.

Management of the industry

The national newspaper industry is somewhat unique in the extent of the control by the respective trade unions over the actual productive process. The most significant level of bargaining is between the employers and the union chapels. There are some industry wide conditions negotiated between the employers' association, the Newspapers Publishers Association, and the national trade unions which give overall guidelines relating to different wage rates, holidays, responsibilities, bonuses, etc. However it is a chapel level where the most crucial agreements are reached.

Each newspaper may have to negotiate with a dozen or so independent chapels who each jealously guard their own independent rights. This results in a highly complex structure of pay rates often well above (and in many cases twice) nationally agreed levels. This can also mean a 'leap-frog' effect is established as once one chapel gains substantial pay or conditions improvements, the chapels of the other unions attempt to emulate them.

Another significant element in the management of the production process is the level of actual control which management has allowed to be assumed by the individual Fathers or Mothers of the chapels.

The amount of overtime which is allocated to individual workers, the division of particular jobs and the disciplinary matters are all largely undertaken by the chapel. A further area of control by the unions is in the recruitment of new employees. The unions enforce a strict closed-shop policy restricting employment to union members who have served a long period of apprenticeship. In some instances the unions nominate particular individuals who the employer must hire to a specific vacancy. The national newspaper industry does not train many printers but recruits them from the general printing industry. However long waiting lists exist of people trained in the general printing industry seeking employment on the national papers with their much higher wage levels. These are carefully vetted by the unions and instances frequently exist of preference given to those with family or friendship ties. Once appointed, promotion tends to be based on seniority with the union chapel reserving the right to veto any up-grading or promotion which does not meet with its approval.

Management is also restricted in its ability to vary its level of staffing by the employment of casual workers. All such extra workers must be union members, be on the union's register of casual workers and be paid union rates.

Control by the trade unions of labour activity

In effect the relationship between employers and trade unions is one of almost subcontracting of the process of producing national newspapers. Management leave the majority of workplace control in the hands of the Fathers or Mothers of the chapels. This has resulted in a number of restrictive labour practices. These were defined in the Donovan Commission report on Trade Unions and Employers' Associations as 'rules or customs which unduly hinder the efficient use of labour'. Examples of such practices include excessive overstaffing levels negotiated between the employers and the unions. Estimates have suggested that for some of the productive processes involved, reduction in staffing levels, and subsequent savings in wage bill, of up to 50% could be achieved without a loss in production. Instances of 'ghost crews' being employed have been reported where ficticious workers are added to the payroll for particular shifts and their wages shared out between other less phantom colleagues. These and other practices while opposed by employers in public are often overlooked in the workplace.

Wage levels in the industry
The effect of the collective agreements with the unions as a whole and the specific negotiations with chapels within the industry has been a significantly high level of earnings for workers. No clear data is available but indications are that many workers earn 75% above the average wage in manufacturing industries and some more than twice as much. There is no set rate of pay per job throughout the industry and the pay position of different workers on the same paper changes over time as agreements are re-negotiated with each industrial group. The continually changing pay structure leads to rivalry between chapels as pay differentials open and are then sought to be closed. This aggravates the already shaky industrial relations position and has led to numerous disputes.

Attempts to introduce new technology
A further notable feature of the national newspaper has been the proprietor's difficulty in introducing the new technology which has become available. The overstaffing which is already prevalent in the industry could be reduced by the impact of computer-based typesetting and printing techniques.

The collection, editing, composing and printing processes can now be carried out much more efficiently using a much lower level of labour. These techniques have been used in other parts of the world and also in British regional newspapers. However the unions have strongly resisted the change over in most newspapers. Some advances have been made since the middle of the 1970s but with the introduction of each new process the employers have been faced with the problem of negotiating new demarcation agreements. The new technology removes the need for many of the skilled jobs currently undertaken by members of the NGA and would allow NATSOPA members to undertake the control of new mechanised printing machines. This movement has been severely resisted by the NGA. Many other such instances exist of the unions attempting to prevent the reduction in the demand for their members' labour by the introduction of new technology. Employers argue that without substantial changes in the production process they will be unable to maintain costs at a level which will allow them to compete with the other media forms.

Industrial unrest in the industry
The industrial environment in which national newspapers are published and the relationship existing between employers and organised labour has proved to be a setting for many industrial disputes. The industry has been described as 'strike prone'. The industrial action ranges from all-out union-backed officials strikes on a particular paper as with Times Newspapers in 1980 and 1981, to short hold-ups in production caused by inopportunely called chapel meetings which delay production for only a short time but sufficient to ensure that papers do not reach the necessary trains. (There is nothing as unsaleable as a newspaper which out of date.) Newspaper disputes are not restricted to a particular group of newspapers. All the nationals have had problems of a varying degree and some such as the Times and the Sunday Times have lost millions of issues and pounds through periods of industrial action. Those newspapers who have managed to survive with fewer disputes have often been those who have management willing to make concessions on pay and conditions to the unions. This has been possible usually only for those newspapers who have remained profitable because of their ability to hold on to readers and advertisers. However there has been an increasing tendency for proprietors to become tougher in their dealings with the unions and threats of closure or sale unless the industrial relations situation improves have been made against such papers as the Times and the Observer.

It would be a fruitless task in a case study of this size to attempt a comprehensive examination of industrial law as it relates to the national newspaper industry. Rather it is proposed to consider in some depth one aspect of industrial law, the extent that trade unions enjoy immunity from tort action. This aspect has been chosen because of its controversial nature and also because it was the subject of a major case decision involving the newspaper industry – *Express Newspapers Ltd* v. *McShane* (1980) which itself promoted legislative change in the form of the Employment Act 1980 s. 17. In order to appreciate a detailed consideration of the McShane decision it is necessary to set the scene by outlining the area of law involved.

Immunity from tort action
The position of the Trade Unions in relation to the committal of certain wrongful acts is both unique and controversial. Since the early part of this century Parliament has conferred on Trade Unions certain 'immunities' from legal action the most important of which is now contained in s. 13 of the Trade Union and Labour Relations Act 1974 as amended by the Trade Union and Labour Relations (Amendment) Act 1976. Under s. 13(1) an act done by a person in contemplation or

furtherance of a trade dispute shall not be actionable in tort on the ground only —

a) that it induces another person to break a contract or induces any other person to interfere with its performance, or
b) that it consists in his threatening that a contract (whether one to which he is a party or not) will be broken or that he will induce another person to break a contract of employment to which that other person is a party.

The effect of the section is to extend protection to an individual who induces another to break a contract of employment or commercial contract (an otherwise wrongful act), in relation to a trade dispute. It prevents liability therefore in a situation such as when a union official induces employees to take industrial action (eg strike) without the required notice, or when that employer persuades drivers not to cross a picket line to deliver goods.

The Act goes on to define the term 'trade dispute' in some depth to include disputes between 'employers and workers', or 'workers and workers' in connection with matters such as terms and conditions, discipline, allocation of work, etc. The fact that the dispute in question is unreasonable or impracticable has no bearing on whether it amounts to a trade dispute.

In addition to there being a trade dispute, the act in respect of which the statutory immunity is claimed, must be *'in contemplation or furtherance'* of it. These words were the subject of a number of Court of Appeal decisions in which it was held that they must be viewed *objectively* in determining whether the acts in question were *reasonably capable of achieving their objective*. Thus, if the court felt that the action taken was too remote in relation to the dispute, it would not be protected by the statutory immunity. This approach effectively placed a curb on secondary action in relation to a trade dispute. This was the position until the decision of the House of Lords in *MacShane and Ashton* (appellants/defendants) v. *Express Newspapers Ltd* (respondents/plaintiffs).

The MacShane decision
The case arose out of a strike called by the National Union of Journalists on 4 December 1978 against provincial newspapers. As the local papers also obtained new copy from the Press Association, the Union called upon its members employed by the Press Association to also come out on strike. About half the Press Association journalists however remained at work, thus enabling the local newspapers to carry on. The union also ordered its members employed by national newspapers to *black* Press Association copy. On 6 December, the managing director of the Daily Express wrote to the Father of the Chapel warning him that if NUJ members refused a proper instruction to handle PA copy they would be in breach of their contracts of employment. The

chapel replied that they could not ignore an instruction from the union's national executive.

The Express sought an injunction restraining the President and General Secretary of the NUJ from inducing their employees to breach their contracts of employment. The High Court, Queen's Bench Division (Mr. Justice Lawson) granted the injunction, holding that the actions were not immune from liability by virtue of s. 13 of the Trade Union and Labour Relations Act as amended, since they were not '*in furtherance of*' the trade dispute between the union and the provincial newspapers. The judge rejected the argument put forward by the union officials that action which merely has the effect of keeping up morale or which is for the sake of solidarity is 'in furtherance' of a trade dispute. The Court of Appeal dismissed an appeal against this decision reaffirming that there is an objective element in whether an act is taken 'in furtherance' of a trade dispute within the meaning of s. 13. For an act to be held to be in furtherance of a trade dispute, the party taking the act must establish both a genuine intention to achieve the objective of a trade dispute and that the acts pursuant to that intention were reasonably capable of achieving the objective.

The House of Lords (Lord Wilberforce, Lord Diplock, Lord Salmon, Lord Keith of Kinkel, Lord Scarman) *allowed a further appeal holding* that the Court of Appeal had erred in granting an injunction restraining the defendants from instructing NUJ members employed on national newspapers to 'black' copy from the Press Association. In addition the Court of Appeal had incorrectly concluded that the defendants were not likely to be held to have acted 'in furtherance' of the union's trade dispute with the provincial newspaper employers within the meaning of s. 13(1) of the Trade Union and Labour Relations Act.

The test of whether an act is done 'in furtherance' of a trade dispute so as to fall within the protection of s. 13(1) is a purely subjective one. The ordinary and natural meaning of the words 'in furtherance' refer to the purpose and state of mind of the person who does the act. If the party who does the act honestly thinks at the time it may help one of the parties to the trade dispute to achieve their objective and does it for that reason, the party is protected by s. 13(1).

An act is entitled to immunity even if the doer knows full well that it cannot have more than a minor effect in bringing the trade dispute to the successful outcome that he favours, but nevertheless is bound to cause disastrous loss to the victim. Although the belief must be honest, it need not be wise nor need it take account of the damage it will cause to innocent and disinterested third parties. If the doer is acting honestly, Parliament leaves the person the choice of what to do.

The MacShane judgment

To illustrate the approach of the judiciary in arriving at their decision in McShane the judgments of two of the judges involved, Lord Salmon and Lord Diplock are included below.

Lord Salmon: My Lords, towards the end of 1978 a trade dispute arose between a trade union, the National Union of Journalists (NUJ) and most of the provincial newspapers which are represented by the Newspaper Society (NS). The NUJ asserted that the journalists employed by the provincial newspapers were being underpaid and demanded an increase in the journalists' wages. The NS refused to agree to any such increase in wages. As a result the provincial journalists came out on strike on 4.12.78. The provincial newspapers normally obtain most of their news from the journalists in their employment. They also obtain much of their news from the Press Association (PA) as do the national newspapers and some radio and television networks. PA employ about 250 journalists, some of whom are members of the NUJ. As long as the PA were able to supply the provincial newspapers with its usual service, they could carry on business, may be with some difficulty, in spite of the fact that the journalists whom they normally employed were out on strike. Accordingly, on 4 December, the NUJ who had no dispute with the PA, called out on strike all their members who were employed by the PA, the NUJ's object in calling this strike was to reduce the provincial newspapers' supply of news from the PA to such an extent that the provincial newspapers would be obliged to cease publishing their newspapers unless they agreed to increase the wages of their journalist employees, and so brought them back into the fold.

At the meeting on 4 December, 86 of the members of the NUJ who were employed by the PA voted against the strike and 76 for it. The chairman told the meeting that any copy produced for the PA by those who had been instructed to strike but had disobeyed the instruction, would be 'blacked'. The 76 members who had voted for the strike went out on strike and were shortly joined by 32 others. This meant that the PA were able to render a little less than half its normal services to its usual customers.

On 3 December, no doubt because they foresaw the difficulties which did arise in persuading their members in the PA to come out on strike, the NUJ wrote to their members employed by the national Press, including the Daily Express, instructing them to 'black', ie not to make use of, any copy coming from the PA after noon on 4 December. The NUJ had at that time no dispute with any of the owners of the national Press. Their instructions to 'black' amounted to the commission by the NUJ of the tort of procuring its members to commit a breach of their contracts of employment with the national Press. The NUJ would be liable in damages for this tort unless s. 13(1) of the Trade Union and Labour Relations Act 1974 (as amended) entitles the NUJ to immunity for committing this tort. This would depend upon whether the giving of instructions by the NUJ to its members employed by the national Press to 'black' all news obtained from the PA amounted to 'an act done . . . in furtherance of a trade dispute'.

The evidence seems to me to prove clearly that the NUJ gave its instructions in relation to 'blacking' for the purpose of furthering on behalf of its provincial members the trade dispute between them and their employers the provincial newspapers. If the NUJ members employed by the national Press consented to handle the newscopy compiled by the PA's NUJ strike-breakers this might well undermine the morale of the PA's NUJ strikers and induce them to abandon the strike: it certainly would not encourage any of the PA's NUJ non-strikers to join in the strike. Accordingly, there would then be a real danger that the strike of the PA's NUJ members would collapse and thus enable the PA to resume its normal services to the provincial Press, which would help to break the strike of its NUJ employees. Morale, and the lack of it, are, in certain circumstances, just as likely to win or lose a trade dispute as a battle.

I recognise and regret how much the national Press must have been incommoded and put to serious expense by the strike at the PA and the 'blacking' of PA's newscopy. In my opinion, however, the strike at the PA and the 'blacking' may well have helped the NUJ members to succeed in their trade dispute with the provincial newspapers. It appears the strike ended quite quickly by the provincial newspapers' journalists having their pay substantially increased. In any event, I do not think that the evidence before the court could justify a finding that no sensible officers of the NUJ could reasonably have believed that the strike at PA and the 'blacking' would further the trade dispute to which I have referred.

The words 'an act done by a person in . . . furtherance of a trade dispute' must be given their ordinary and natural meaning in their context. That meaning, in my view, is that the person doing the act must honestly and reasonably believe that it may further the trade dispute. If he does not honestly and reasonably believe that, but does the act out of spite or in order to show his 'muscle' or is an embittered fanatic who believes, wholly unreasonably, that the act he does is in furtherance of a trade dispute, I do not think that s. 13(1) was intended by Parliament to afford protection to such persons as these.

I entirely agree that the courts are not the appropriate places in which trade disputes should be decided. S. 13(1) however deals with the commission of a tort, ie a breach of the law, and the circumstances in which the tortfeasor may be entitled to immunity when those against whom the tort is committed may suffer seriously. This, in my opinion, is a matter to be decided in the courts; and I have no doubt that the courts will be very slow to hold that an act is wholly unreasonable if those of great experience in the trade give evidence that the act had a reasonable prospect of furthering the trade dispute in question.

On the other hand, there have been cases in which tortious acts have been done which constituted inhuman conduct causing the most grievous harm. For example, quite recently patients in the Charing Cross Hospital being treated for cancer were brought near to death because industrial action had been taken to prevent fuel oil from being brought into the hospital. This made the hospital intolerably cold when

346

warmth was necessary in order to provide any chance of keeping the patients alive. No doubt some of those who were responsible for preventing the fuel from entering the hospital firmly, but certainly not reasonably, believed that they were doing an act 'in furtherance of a trade dispute' within the meaning of those words in s. 13(1) ibid, and were therefore immune. They may have been: but if this is the law, surely the time has come for it to be altered.

My Lords, I am satisfied that in the present case the evidence established that the officers of the NUJ honestly and reasonably believed that the action which they took was fairly 'in furtherance of a trade dispute', and for these reasons I would allow the appeal.

Lord Diplock: My Lords, during the past two years there has been a series of judgements in the Court of Appeal given upon applications for interlocutory injunctions against trade union officials. These have the effect of imposing on the expression 'an act done by a person in contemplation or furtherance of a trade dispute' for which immunity from civil actions for specified kinds of torts is conferred by s. 13(1) of the Trade Union and Labour Relations Act, 1974, (as now amended), an interpretation restrictive of what, in common with the majority of your Lordships, I believe to be its plain and unambiguous meaning. The terms in which the limitations upon the ambit of the expression have been stated are not identical in the various judgements, but at the root of all of them there appears to lie an assumption that Parliament cannot really have intended to give so wide an immunity from the common law of tort as the words of ss. 13 and 29 would, on the face of them, appear to grant to everyone who engages in any form of what is popularly known as industrial action.

My Lords, I do not think that this is a legitimate assumption on which to approach the construction of the Act, notwithstanding that the training and traditions of anyone whose life has been spent in the practice of the law and the administration of justice in the courts must make such an assumption instinctively attractive to him. But the manifest policy of the Act was to strengthen the role of recognised trade unions in collectively bargaining, so far as possible to confine the bargaining function to them, and, as my noble and learned friend Lord Scarman recently pointed out in The Nawala (*NWL Ltd* v. *Woods and another* (1979) IRLR 478), to exclude trade disputes from judicial review by the courts. Parliament, as it was constituted when the Act and the subsequent amendments to it were passed, may well have felt so confident that trade unions could be relied upon always to act 'responsibly' in trade disputes that any need for legal sanctions against their failure to do so could be obviated.

This being so, it does not seem to me that it is a legitimate approach to the construction of the sections that deal with trade disputes, to assume that Parliament did not intend to give to trade unions and their officers a wide discretion to exercise their own judgement as to the steps which should be taken in an endeavour to help the workers' side in any trade dispute to achieve its objectives. And if their plain and ordinary meaning is given to the words 'An act done by a person in contemplation or furtherance of a trade dispute', this, as it seems to me, is what s. 13 does. In the light of the express reference to the 'person' by whom the act is done and the association of 'furtherance' with 'contemplation (which cannot refer to anything but the state of mind of the doer of the act) it is, in my view, clear that 'in furtherance' too can only refer to the state of mind of the person who does the act, and means: with the purpose of helping one of the parties to a trade dispute to achieve their objectives in it.

Given the existence of a trade dispute (the test of which, though broad, is nevertheless objective, see The Nawala) this makes the test of whether an act was done 'in furtherance of' it a purely subjective one. If the party who does the act honestly thinks at the time he does it that it may help one of the parties to the trade dispute to achieve their objectives and does it for that reason, he is protected by the section. I say 'may' rather than 'will' help, for it is in the nature of industrial action that success in achieving its objectives cannot be confidently predicted. Also there is nothing in the section that requires that there should be any proportionality between on the one hand the extent to which the act is likely to, or be capable of, increasing the 'industrial muscle' of one side to the dispute, and on the other hand the damage caused to the victim of the act which, but for the section, would have been tortious. The doer of the act may know full well that it cannot have more than a minor effect in bringing the trade dispute to the successful outcome that he favours, but nevertheless is bound to cause disastrous loss to the victim, who may be a stranger to the dispute and with no interest in its outcome. The act is none the less entitled to immunity under the section.

It is, I think, these consequences of applying the subjective test that, not surprisingly, have tended to stick to judicial gorges: that so great damage may be caused to innocent and disinterested third parties in order to obtain for one of the parties to a trade dispute tactical advantages which in the court's own view are highly speculative and, if obtained, could be no more than minor. This has led the Court of Appeal to seek to add some objective element to the subjective test of the bona fide purpose of the person who did the act.

In the reported cases, which have already been cited by my noble and learned friend Lord Wilberforce, three somewhat different tests have been suggested. They are conveniently stated in summary form by Ackner J in *United Biscuits* (UK) *Ltd* v. *Fall* (1979) IRLR 110. First there is a test based upon remoteness. The help given to the party to the trade dispute must be direct. 'You cannot' said Lord Denning MR, in Beaverbrook Newspapers v. Keys (1978) IRLR 34 at p. 36, 'chase consequence after consequence after consequence in a long chain and say everything that follows a trade dispute is in "furtherance" of it'. The second test, suggested by Lord Denning in the instant case, is that the act done must have some 'practical' effect in bringing pressure to bear upon the opposite side to the dispute whose cause is favoured are not protected. Thirdly there is the test favoured by Lawton and Brandon LJJ in the instant case: the act done must, in the view of the court, be reasonably capable of achieving the objective of the trade dispute.

My Lords, these tests though differently expressed, have the effect of enabling the court to substitute its own opinion for the bona fide opinion held by the trade union or its officers, as to whether action proposed to be taken or continued for the purpose of helping one side or bringing pressure to bear upon the other side to a trade dispute is likely to have the desired effect. Granted bona fides on the part of the trade union or its officer this is to convert the test from a purely subjective to a purely objective test and for the reasons I have given I do not think the wording of the section permits of this. The belief of the doer of the act that it will help the side he favours in the dispute must be honest; it need not be wise, nor need it take account of the damage it will cause to innocent and disinterested third parties. Upon an application for an interlocutory injunction the evidence may show positively by admission or by inference from the facts before the court that the act was not done to further an existing trade dispute but for some ulterior purpose such as revenge for previous conduct. Again, the facts in evidence before the court may be such as will justify the conclusion that no reasonable person versed in industrial relations could possibly have thought that the act was capable of helping one side in a trade dispute to achieve its objectives. But too this goes to honesty of purpose alone not to the reasonableness of the act, or its expediency.

My Lords, upon what I have held to be the true construction of the Act, I agree with your Lordships that this appeal must be allowed. There was unquestionably a trade dispute between provincial journalists and their employers. There was, I think, what could properly be described as a continuing dispute between the PA and the NUJ as to the 'blacking' by PA of provincial newspapers whose journalists were on strike, which flared up whenever such a strike occurred but in the meantime remained quiescent. This dispute, however, did not qualify as a trade dispute under s. 29. The withdrawal of PA copy from the provincial newspapers would be a crucial factor in strengthening the bargaining position of the striking journalists, but in view of PA's attitude this could only be achieved by forcing it to close down or at any rate to reduce its services drastically, by withdrawing journalistic labour from it. PA was not an NUJ closed shop and for economic reasons even the NUJ members on its staff were not likely to be enthusiastic at the prospect of being called out on strike. For my part I see no reason for doubting the honesty of the belief held by Mr MacShane and Mr Dennis, that the response of their members to the strike-call at PA might well be less numerous and less enduring if they knew that fellow members of their union on the national newspapers were continuing to make use of copy produced by those whom they would regard as 'blacklegs' at PA.

I would allow this appeal.

The response to MacShane

The effect of the MacShane decision was that a person who engages in secondary industrial action (ie action against a person who is not a party to the dispute in question) is immune from tort action if they honestly believe that the secondary action is in furtherance of a trade dispute. The House of Lords had therefore rejected the objective approach of the Court of Appeal. Secondary action, even that which causes disastrous loss, was effectively made lawful.

The response of the Thatcher Government to this decision was almost immediate. A new section was added to the 1980 Employment Bill as it went through Parliament − now s. 17 of the Employment Act 1980. The effect of this section is to overrule the MacShane decision and remove the statutory immunity for secondary action beyond certain limits which is done in contemplation or furtherance of a trade dispute. The section provides that for secondary action to be lawful and protected, it must be restricted to where the principal purpose of the action is to interfere with the supply of goods or services, during the dispute between the employer in dispute and a first supplier or customer, whose employees are taking the action and, where from an objective viewpoint, it is likely to achieve that purpose. Certainly secondary action such as the blacking which occurred in MacShane would now be regarded as unlawful. To summarise therefore we have now reverted to the objective approach of the Court of Appeal in determining statutory immunity.

7 Land and business property

'It should be remembered that the foundation of the social contract is prosperity and its first condition that everyone should be maintained, in peaceful possession of what belongs to him.

J-J Rousseau
A Discourse on Political Economy 1798

The division of property

All business enterprises make use of economic resources to enable them to operate. Traditionally economists have classified economic resources into land, labour and capital. This chapter considers land as a resource and to gain a full appreciation of its significance it is necessary to examine land as part of the property of a business. Land is one of the most valuable forms of business property and as a resource may be used in a number of ways. An area of land could be used for agriculture, mining, recreation, housing or business premises. However, it is important to stress that under English Law, land is only one form of property and it is necessary before considering types of land ownership and use to show how property is classified.

The classification of property

The expression *property* simply means under English law anything that is capable of ownership, eg land, buildings, cars, debts. The most obvious way of classifying property would be to distinguish between *movable property* (eg goods, shares in companies, cheques, etc) and *immovable property* (eg land and buildings) as they do in many European countries. Unfortunately, the English classification of property is not as simple as that, due mainly to the long historical development of English land law. Under English law, the basic division is between *Real* and *Personal* property, see Fig 7.1 overleaf.

Real property

The only category of real property is *Freehold land* because originally it was the only type of property which was protected by a *real* action in court. This meant that, if a freehold owner was wrongfully dispossessed of land, he or she could bring a real action to recover the land itself rather than compensation for its loss. For all other types of property, *personal property*, originally if an owner was wrongfully dispossessed, he or she could only rely on a personal action which gave no right to

351

recover the property lost since the owner had to be content with compensation. As early as the fifteenth century however, the courts began to recognise exceptions to this rule so that today, an owner wrongfully dispossessed of personal property can normally recover the thing lost. The classification of real and personal property however remains the same! Real property then is freehold land, and any form of property which is not freehold is classified as personal property.

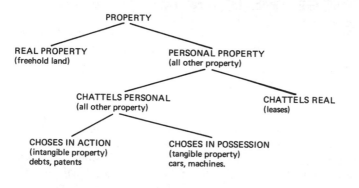

Personal property

Personal property (otherwise known as chattels) is further sub-divided into *chattels real* (leases) and *chattels personal* (all other personal property). Under a *lease*, the tenant has the right to possession of land for a term of years, (a fixed period), and despite being very similar to a freehold interest in land it was not protected by the real action and so is classified as a form of personal property. The expression chattels real is used to distinguish leasehold interests in land from all other personal property, chattels personal.

As far as chattels personal are concerned, there is one further sub-division into *Choses in Action* (intangible property, eg cheques, debts, patents, copyrights, goodwill) and *Choses in Possession* (tangible property, eg cars, typewriters, radios, etc). The word 'chose' comes from the French for 'thing' and a chose in action is simply a thing which may be owned but has no physical existence.

Choses in possession

These are tangible things that may be physically possessed by their owner. A business enterprise will own many types of property in this category including cars, furniture, machinery, stock in trade, etc. Of course, the owner of a chose in possession who is wrongfully dispossessed, has the right to recover it by direct *physical* action without the need for court action, eg having paid less than a third of the price repossess a car where the hirer, in a hire-purchase contract, defaults on payment.

Choses in action
These are intangible things that have no physical existence but nevertheless may form an important part of the assets of a business. The main feature of a chose in action is that the only effective way to assert a right to it is by *court* action. Because of their importance in the business world it is now proposed to consider the main characteristics of various choses in action in some detail.

a) *Debts* Debts are often one of the most important circulating assets of a business and one of real value to a creditor as they will represent money owed. If necessary, a creditor can by court action require payment of a debt by the debtor. Alternatively, a creditor can raise money on a debt by assigning it (transferring the debt) to some third party in return for valuable consideration.

b) *Patents* A registered patent will grant to the holder a legal monopoly over a particular invention and confer to that holder, for a specific period, all rights in relation to it − Patent Act 1977.

c) *Copyrights* A copyright grants to the holder a legal monopoly over the reproduction of subject matter such as books, songs and films to prevent copying − Copyright Act 1956.

d) *Negotiable instruments* The most important types of negotiable instruments are bills of exchange and the law relating to them is contained in the Bills of Exchange Act 1882. A bill of exchange is a written order addressed by one person to another requiring the person to whom it is addressed to pay a sum of money to a particular person or to the bearer. Nowadays, bills of exchange are used mainly in the export trade.

B. Sykes having sold goods valued at £2000 to Kurt Komment (a German importer) addresses a bill of exchange to Komment requiring him to pay B. Sykes (or indeed anyone to whom B. Sykes owes cash) £2000, three months from the date of the bill. When Kurt accepts the bill by signing it, B. Sykes may either:

(i) Hold the bill for three months and then require payment of it when it matures; or

(ii) Discount the bill at a bank or *discounting house* who will be willing to take the bill for less than its face value; or

(iii) Use the bill to satisfy a debt by *endorsing* it over to one of his creditors.

The most common form of bill of exchange is the *cheque* which is simply *a bill of exchange drawn on a banker and payable on demand*.

e) *Business goodwill* All business organisations by operating over a period of time will acquire trade connections and custom which will amount to a valuable asset. This is described as business goodwill and is usually only valued when the business is sold as the purchaser will be required to pay for its acquisition.

Freehold and leasehold estates in land

It may surprise the reader to know that since the Norman conquest the ownership of all land in this country has been in the hands of the Crown, so that *absolute* ownership of land by an individual or business organisation is impossible. Individuals or business organisations hold land as *tenants* since they do not own the land itself. To determine the extent of their interest over the land it is necessary to examine the *estate* that they hold. An estate is simply the measure of a person's interest in land from the viewpoint of time. The two most important estates are the *freehold* estate and the *leasehold* estate. Before the two types are examined, the following points should be noted in relation to estates in land:

(i)   The type of estate owned by an individual will depend upon the terms on which the land was granted to him.

(ii) Several individuals may simultaneously own distinct and separate estates in the same piece of land.

(iii) The type of estate granted will depend upon the length of time it is to endure.

Freehold estates

The main characteristic of estate of freehold is that they are of *uncertain duration*. The two categories of freehold estate are the *fee simple* estate and the *life* estate.

a) *The fee simple absolute in possession*
This is known as the fee simple estate and is the freehold estate which is normally associated with *absolute* ownership. The word 'fee' indicates that the estate is inheritable, 'simple' means that there is no restriction on who may inherit, 'absolute' refers to the fact that the estate is not subject to any condition and 'possession' means that it is to take effect immediately. The holder of a fee simple estate has therefore the right to sell or leave it to anyone he or she wishes.

b) *The life estate*
This estate of freehold is a much less common form and arises where an interest in land is granted to last for an individual's life. If granted for the life of the owner, it will terminate on the owner's death and if granted 'pur autre vie' (for the life of another) it will terminate when that other life ends.

Leasehold estates (term of years absolute)

The main characteristic of this estate is that it is of *certain duration* or *capable of being made certain*, eg a lease for ten years will expire after ten years and a monthly tenancy by giving a month's notice. A leasehold is held under the terms ie *covenants* of a lease, the effect of which is to give the tenant the right to occupy the land to the exclusion of all others, including the landlord. When the period of the lease expires or in the case of a periodic tenancy, when one party gives notice (eg a monthly tenant gives one month's notice), the landlord has the right to re-occupy the land subject to the rights of a tenant to *security of tenure* that is the right of the tenant to remain in possession. The rights of a private residential tenant to security of tenure after the contractual lease has expired are contained in the Rent Act 1977. Now, under the Housing Act 1980, the council tenant of a local authority has equivalent security of tenure. As far as a *business tenant* is concerned, those rights to security are contained in the Landlord and Tenant Act, 1954, Part II.

The covenants
Leases impose on the parties to them contractual obligations, some of which are expressly agreed in the lease and some implied under the common law and by statute. In the case of a business lease, the express terms usually relate to such matters as the payment of rent and rent review, the right to transfer the lease or sublet, the obligations to repair, and a restrictive covenant relating to the particular use to which the premises may be put.

In addition to express terms, except in so far as the lease provides otherwise, certain terms are implied under the common law. It is implied that the landlord will

(i) not interfere with the tenant's *enjoyment* of the land by harassing in any way;
(ii) not *derogate from his grant* ie detract from the value of the premises by committing an act which makes the premises less fit for the purpose for which they were let;
(iii) ensure that *furnished premises are fit for human habitation* on the commencement of the lease.

As far as the tenant is concerned, it is implied that he or she will

(i) pay such *rates and taxes* as the landlord is not obliged to pay;
(ii) treat the property in a *tenant-like manner* which involves doing the repairs to the premises you would expect a reasonable tenant with the same lease to carry out.

Failure to comply with the express or implied covenants in a lease may entitle the party who has suffered to bring an action for damages or in some cases to *exact a forfeiture* ie terminate the lease.

How estates in land are acquired
It has already been stated that the two usual types of land holding are the freehold (fee simple estate) and the leasehold (term of years absolute). Which of these types is best suited to a business organisation will depend upon a number of factors such as the type of business carried on, the respective costs, market availability and the period for which the land is required. The acquisition of the fee simple will involve high initial cost but as the holder is for all practical purposes the absolute owner, he or she has an important asset which will increase in

value and is freely disposable. Nevertheless it should be made clear that even the freehold owner is subject to restrictions both under the common law and statute on the right to use the land as he or she pleases.

TENANCY AGREEMENT

Date   19

Parties   1.   The Landlord

                 2.   The Tenant

Property

Together with the Fixtures Furniture and Effects therein and more particularly specified in the Inventory thereof signed by the parties

Term   from

Rent   (subject as provided in the Letting provisions) clear of all deductions for every   of the term

Payable   in advance by equal   instalments on

First Payment   to be made on

A.   The Landlord lets and the Tenant takes the Property for the Term at the Rent payable as above.

B.   The Agreement incorporates the Letting Provisions printed overleaf with the following variations or additions:

Signed by the

in the presence of

356

LETTING PROVISIONS

INTERPRET-
ATION
1. Where the context admits—

   (a) "The Landlord" includes the persons for the time being entitled in reversion expectant on the tenancy.

   (b) "The Tenant" includes the persons deriving title under the Tenant.

   (c) References to the Property include references to any part or parts of the Property and to the Fixtures Furniture and Effects or any of them.

INCREASE
OF RENT
2. Where and whenever there is in respect of the Property under the Rent Acts a registered rent which is greater than the rent hereby reserved then the rent hereunder may be increased (whether or not as increased it will for the time being be fully recoverable from the Tenant) up to the amount of the registered rent by a notice of increase served by the Landlord on the Tenant and specifying the date from which the increase is to operate but so that the date so specified shall not be earlier than the date on which the rent was registered or earlier than four weeks before the service of the notice.

TENANT'S
OBLIGATIONS
3. The Tenant will

   (a) Pay the Rent at the times and in the manner specified.

   (b) Pay for all gas and electric light and power which shall be consumed or supplied on or to the Property during the tenancy and the amount of the water rate charged in respect of the Property during the tenancy and the amount of all charges made for the use of the telephone (if any) on the Property during the tenancy or a proper proportion of the amount of such charges to be assessed according to the duration of the tenancy

   (c) Use the Property in a tenant-like manner.

   (d) Not damage or injure the Property or make any alteration in or addition to it.

   (e) Preserve the furniture and effects from being destroyed or damaged and not remove any of them from the Property.

   (f) Yield up the Property at the end of the tenancy in the same clean state and condition as it was in at the beginning of the tenancy and make good pay for the repair of or replace all such items of the Fixtures Furniture and Effects as shall be broken lost damaged or destroyed during the tenancy (reasonable wear and tear and damage by fire excepted).

   (g) Leave the Furniture and Effects at the end of the tenancy in the rooms or places in which they were at the beginning of the tenancy.

   (h) Pay for the washing (including ironing or pressing) of all linen and for the washing and cleaning (including ironing or pressing) of all counterpanes blankets and curtains which shall have been soiled during the tenancy (the reasonable use thereof nevertheless to be allowed for).

   (i) Permit the Landlord or the Landlord's agents at reasonable hours in the daytime to enter the Property to view the state and condition thereof and of the Fixtures Furniture and Effects.

   (j) Not assign underlet charge or part with possession of the Property without the previous consent in writing of the Landlord.

   (k) Not carry on on the Property any profession trade or business or let apartments or receive paying guests on the Property or place or exhibit any notice board or notice on the Property or use the Property for any other purpose than that of a strictly private residence.

   (l) Not do or suffer to be done on the Property anything which may be or become a nuisance or annoyance to the Landlord or the tenants or occupiers of any adjoining premises or which may vitiate any insurance of the Property against fire or otherwise or increase the ordinary premium for such insurance.

   (m) Permit the Landlord or the Landlord's agents at reasonable hours in the daytime within the last twenty-eight days of the tenancy to enter and view the Property with prospective tenants.

4.   PROVIDED that if the Rent or any instalment or part thereof shall be in arrear for at least fourteen days after the same shall have become due (whether legally demanded or not) or if there shall be a breach of any of the agreements by the Tenant or if the Property shall (save by arrangement with the Landlord) be left vacant or unoccupied for over a month the Landlord may re-enter on the Property and immediately thereupon the tenancy shall absolutely determine without prejudice to the other rights and remedies of the Landlord.

**LANDLORD'S
OBLIGATIONS**

5.   The Landlord agrees with the Tenant as follows:—

(1) To pay and indemnify the Tenant against all rates taxes assessments and outgoings in respect of the Property (except the water rate and except charges for the supply of gas or electric light and power or the use of any telephone).

(2) That the Tenant paying the Rent and performing the agreements on the part of the Tenant may quietly possess and enjoy the Property during the tenancy without any lawful interruption from the Landlord or any person claiming under or in trust for that party.

(3) To return to the Tenant any rent payable for any period while the Property is rendered uninhabitable by fire the amount in case of dispute to be settled by arbitration.

**HOUSING
ACT 1961**

6.   The Tenancy Agreement shall take effect subject to the provisions of Section 32 of the Housing Act 1961 if applicable to the tenancy.

The alternative to acquiring a fee simple estate is that adopted by many business organisations and it is to acquire possession of land under a leasehold. Clearly any organisation or individual wishing to acquire a freehold or leasehold estate will have to enter into a contract for its purchase. Contracts for the sale of land, to be legally binding, require written evidence under the Law of Property Act, 1925, section 40. In practice this is rarely fulfilled immediately and the usual procedure is that an oral agreement for the sale of land is entered into and the formal contract is drawn up at a later stage after certain matters have been investigated by the purchaser's solicitor. Prior to the formal contract, the land is *sold subject to contract*. This rule relating to the requirement of written evidence is subject to one major exception – it is called the *rule of part-performance*. All this means is that if one party to the contract has performed an act which clearly demonstrates intention to sell or purchase, this act may be sufficient to persuade a court to enforce the contract by ordering *specific performance* of it ie require the other party to fulfil obligations under the contract. Such an act could be spending money on the land or moving in.

In *Rawlinson* v. *Ames* (1925) the prospective tenant of property required the landlord to carry out conversion work which the tenant supervised. On completion of the work, the prospective tenant backed out. The court held that the act of the landlord, in paying for the conversion for the prospective tenant's benefit, was a sufficient act of part-performance to require the tenant to enter into the lease, and awarded specific performance.

Also, in *Wakeham* v. *McKenzie* (1968) the Court awarded specific performance in the following circumstances. A widower of 72, asked his neighbour, a widow of 67, to come and look after him with the promise that he would leave his property to her when he died. The widow left her council flat and moved in agreeing to pay 'her own board and her share of the coal'. The widower died but there was no provision in his will leaving the property to the unfortunate old lady. The Court ordered that the property should be transferred to her because of her act of part-performance in leaving her council flat and looking after the old man in return for his promise.

Of course, the contract is only the first stage in the purchase of a legal estate: it is simply the agreement to buy and sell. To transfer ownership, *a deed of conveyance* is necessary. This is a detailed description of the property transfer.

The law has, for a long time, recognised that a leasehold for a term of less than three years may be transferred without the need for a deed of conveyance.

Business leases, which are the predominant method of land holding for commercial organisations, are normally for a fixed term and will be contained in the form of a deed. Because of their widespread use in the business environment they are considered in detail below.

The business lease

To create a valid lease it is essential that the term of the lease is certain by being fixed or determinable by notice, the tenant being given exclusive possession of the land and the parties to the lease intending to create the relationship of landlord and tenant. Basically, there are two kinds of leases which would be of use to a business tenant:

a) *Fixed term lease* This is the most popular type of business lease which is granted for a specified period, eg one, three, five, ten years. In general, such leases come to an end automatically once the agreed term is over and no *notice to quit* is required.

b) *Yearly tenancies* A yearly tenancy will continue from year to year until one side or the other brings it to an end by serving the required notice to quit. The tenancy may be created by express agreement or be implied when the landlord accepts payment of annual rent. This would be the case if, on the termination of a fixed term lease, the landlord allowed the tenant to remain in possession and accepted payment of annual rent. A tenancy is merely the term used to describe a short lease, eg of a year or less.

Formalities in the creation of a business lease

Under the Law of Property Act, 1925 ownership in land can only be transferred by means of a formal deed. The only exception is in the case of a lease for a term of three years or less (eg an annual business tenancy) at a market rent. Such leases may be granted informally. Failure to execute a deed where it is necessary will not prevent ownership from being transferred because it is enforceable in *equity*. Historically through the intervention of the law of equity, the lack of formality (ie a deed) will not prove fatal provided there is sufficient evidence of the parties' intentions. The contract containing the agreement for a lease is therefore sufficient evidence of such an intention and will survive as an *equitable lease*. As between the landlord and tenant an equitable lease will have the same effect as a legal lease. The vulnerability of an equitable lease is that it requires registration under the Land Changes Act 1972 otherwise it will be void as against a subsequent purchaser of the landlord's interest.

Security of tenure for business leases

Leases of business premises were first given protection under the law by the Landlord and Tenant Act 1927 which provided for compensation from the landlord for a business tenant who improved the property or who had attached goodwill to it by establishing a trade custom. If the tenant could not be adequately compensated, the Act provided that he or she could obtain a new lease and was thus a secure tenant. The security provisions are now contained in the Landlord and Tenant Act 1954, Part II. The 1954 Act applies to leases where the property in the lease is or includes premises occupied by the tenant for the purposes of business. The term 'business' encompasses many activities including 'a trade, profession or employment and any activity carried on by a body of persons, corporate or unincorporate'. The definition is very wide and includes not only obvious business premises such as shops, offices, and workshops, but also residential hotels, restaurants and clubs.

The broad effect of the Act is that a lease fulfilling these conditions is automatically continued until terminated in a way provided by the Act, and the tenant can then apply for a new lease. The Act provides that a business lease will not come to an end on the expiration of the term but will continue until terminated by:

(i) The *landlord* serving a *notice under s. 25* of the Act specifying the date for termination, giving at least six months' notice, and requiring the tenant to notify the landlord whether he or she is willing to relinquish possession. The notice should also state the ground upon which the landlord intends to rely if wishing to oppose an application for a new tenancy.

Alternatively,

(ii) A request by the *tenant under s. 26* for a new tenancy, specifying the date for termination of the current tenancy, giving at least six months' notice, and stating the proposed terms of the new tenancy. Having received a s. 26 request, the landlord must give notice to the tenant that he or she intends to oppose an application for the grant of a new tenancy and state the ground that will be relied on.

If the parties fail to reach agreement on the grant or the terms of a new tenancy, then an application may be made to the court to resolve the dispute. If the rateable value of the property does not exceed £5000

T H I S   C O N V E Y A N C E   dated the

day of   1980 is made

BETWEEN

(1) The Vendor

of

and

(2) The Purchaser

of

1. The Vendor acknowledges the receipt from the Purchaser

£   the purchase price of the land known as

                                        (the Property).

2. The Vendor as beneficial owner conveys to the Purchaser

his freehold estate in the Property.

3. The Purchaser covenants with the Vendor by way of indemnity

only to perform and observe such of the covenants conditions

restrictions and stipulations contained in a Conveyance dated

the   day of   19   and made between

of the one part and   of the other

part so far as they are still effective and to indemnify the

Vendor from any liability resulting from their breach or

non-observance.

4. It is certified that this transaction does not form part

of a larger transaction or of a series of transactions in

respect of which the amount or value of the consideration

exceeds Fifteen Thousand Pounds.

IN WITNESS whereof the parties hereto have set their hands and

seals the day and year hereinbefore written.

Signed sealed and delivered
by the Vendor in the presence
of

Signed sealed and delivered
by the Purchaser in the presence
of

361

the court is the County Court, otherwise it is the High Court. The Act lays down a number of individual grounds that may be relied on by a landlord to oppose an application by the tenant for a new tenancy. If the landlord relies on grounds a), b), c) or e) which are set out below, the court has a discretion to decide whether a new tenancy 'ought to be granted'. The other grounds listed are absolute grounds and if proved the tenant's application for a new tenancy must be refused. The grounds are set out in s. 30 of the Act. They are as follows:

a) That the tenant has failed to fulfil obligations with regard to *repair and maintenance* of the premises.
b) That the tenant has been guilty of *persistent delay in paying rent.*
c) That the tenant has committed *other substantial breaches* of obligations under the tenancy.
d) That the landlord is willing to provide *suitable alternative accommodation.*
e) That the current tenancy was created by the letting of part of the property and the landlord *requires that part in order to let the whole* property which it is reasonable for the landlord to do so in the circumstances.
f) That the landlord intends to *demolish or reconstruct* the premises or a substantial part of it or carry out substantial work of construction on the premises.
g) That the landlord intends to *operate a business* from the premises.

If the landlord fails to establish one of the above grounds then the court must order the grant of a new tenancy.

Obviously it is a question of fact in each particular case whether the landlord has fully satisfied the ground relied on, the court being influenced by the evidence placed before it.

The new tenancy

In the absence of agreement between the parties the new tenancy will be 'such as may be determined by the court to be reasonable in all the circumstances'. Obviously, the court will consider closely the provisions of the current tenancy to decide the content of the new tenancy, eg the length of the current tenancy. The main restriction on the court, as far as the new term is concerned, is that it must not exceed a fourteen-year fixed period. The court will decide the rent payable by considering the open market value. If in fact the tenant fails in an application for a new tenancy because the landlord proves one of the s. 30 grounds e), f) or g), the tenant may make a claim for compensation for the *disturbance* moving out has caused. The amount of compensation that may be claimed is either:

(i) the rateable value of the premises; or
(ii) twice the rateable value, if the occupier had carried on a business for the fourteen years previous.

In addition to the disturbance payment, under the Landlord and

Tenant Act 1927, a tenant may recover compensation from the landlord for improvements which the tenant has made to business premises if these have added to their letting value.

The scarcity of land as an available economic resource

One of the most characteristic aspects of economic goods are their scarcity in relation to demand. Economic resources are also liable to become scarce in times of excess demand and this is even more true of land which in some circumstances becomes exhaustable or non-reusable. Of all the economic resources, land is the most pronounced example of a resource fixed in supply. Each nation has a finite amount of agricultural and industrial land and a limited amount of natural resources such as coal, oil or minerals. Of course, at any one time a country may not be aware of its total stock of resources or even capable of utilising those resources of which it knows. The UK is certainly not positive about the extent of its North Sea Oil reserves as new discoveries are made periodically. Even on the mainland, new coalfields are found and developed from time to time. In other countries large tracts of seemingly infertile land may be made arable once irrigation or fertilization projects are introduced. Areas of the UK may be transformed into prime industrial or commercial sites once an effective *infrastructure* of rail or road transport is extended to them. Despite these examples of apparent increases in the stock of land or resources, in fact there is no actual increase in the finite amount. A country cannot usually expand its supply of land or natural resources without some form of territorial gain at the expense of some other country. Therefore the problem remains that as a country's population grows and continues to place increasing calls on limited resources then land will become scarcer in relation to demand.

One further problem with land and natural resource utilisation is that some uses will indefinitely preclude any other possible reuse. Farming land may have wheat grown for one year and barley the next. An open-cast mine may be returned successfully to agricultural use once the coal has been extracted. However, the coal itself, once burned, cannot be reused by future generations. This leads to a distinction between different categories of land and natural resource use.

Categories of usage

One possible means of classifying the factor of land is into

a) *reusable,* and
b) *consumable.*

One of the most important aspects of this classification is the effect it will have on the price of the land or natural resources. A simplified example may be seen in the difference in price one must pay for a leasehold estate in land for a fixed term of twenty years and a freehold estate. The freehold owner who lets the land for a fixed period knows that after the expiration of the lease he or she can repossess the land (subject to security of tenure). Similarly the owner of a finite consumable resource such as coal or oil will seek full recompense for the sale of this resource as he or she will not gain any future income once it has been consumed.

The alternative uses to which land can be put

Land and natural resources clearly have a variety of uses. Agricultural land may be converted for industrial use. A city centre plot may be turned into an office block, a shopping centre or cinema. Similarly natural resources can be used in different ways. Oil can be used to make plastics, fuel power stations or lubricate engines. The factor which determines the use to which land and natural resources are put is the relative prices offered by the competing alternatives. Like all the factors of production, demand for land is *derived demand* and so it is the value of the final product which determines the price people are willing to pay for the land or natural resource. For instance, if there is a growing demand for office space in a city centre, property values rise. Of course this will mean that alternative users of the land would also be asked to pay more and so, for example, residential rents may also increase so forcing inner city residents to move to the suburbs. This once more illustrates the concept of opportunity cost. The government and local authorities have had to intervene and influence the use to which land is put by imposing planning and development restrictions or encouraging specific development elsewhere by giving grants and loans to industrial and commercial users who move out of city centres to certain development areas. The whole process of government intervention to influence location of industry is covered later in the chapter.

The immobility of land

One characteristic of land, as distinct from other natural resources, is its total immobility. Clearly it is impossible to move a prime agricultural site from one part of the country to another. Vacant residential land cannot be moved from the North to the South East of England. This immobility is not just restricted to geographical mobility. Once land is used for a specific purpose it becomes more difficult to put it to other alternative uses. If an office block is built it will take considerable time and capital investment to convert it into a block of flats. Therefore the cost of land to an organisation will be determined by the following factors:

a) the duration of ownership (leasehold or freehold);
b) its location position;
c) its existing use and the cost of converting it to alternative use;
d) any alternative uses to which it may be put, for this will influence its

cost as competition for alternatives may push up its value.

Location of industry

The choice of where to locate is one of the most important questions facing any organisation. For organisations which have been long established the choice may be whether or not the existing location is the most suitable for the business' needs. There will be considerations of cost and availability of suitable premises, an appropriate labour force, access to markets or accessibility of sources of raw materials or suppliers. Those organisations who are in the process of being established will have more freedom of choice in their locational decision. The next part of this Chapter will consider these factors which are influential in this locational decision.

Factors affecting organisational location

Regional location

A substantial proportion of all organisations in the UK may be described as 'foot-loose'. That is, they are capable of establishing in any region and are not tied to any specific area. Estimates suggest that about 70% of organisations in the UK's manufacturing industry fall into this category. This does not mean that they are necessarily dispersed or scattered all over the country. It simply means that they are *capable* of moving to those areas where economic conditions are most suitable. They are seeking a region which will provide a number of factors. These considerations would include:

a) labour costs, and
b) manufacturing costs.

The types of organisations which characterise foot-loose businesses could be those concerned with light engineering or assembly capable of locating or relocating in almost all the industrial regions in the country.

Labour costs
In the UK wage rates differ substantially from region to region. The South East of England has wage rates often 50% higher than those in Northern Ireland, 25% higher than in Scotland and the North East and 15% higher than in the West Midlands. These are the results of traditional wage patterns and the level of unemployment and demand for labour in the respective areas.

Although in many industries there are nationally negotiated wage rates agreed between the unions and the employers which can lead to a levelling of pay in all regions, there is still a tendency for a *wage drift*, where employers in areas of full employment pay above nationally agreed wage levels in order to attract and hold workers, while in those regions with higher unemployment, employers are capable of only offering nationally agreed minimums. There is much greater likelihood that there will be a nationally agreed wage level in those industries which are highly unionised. Also employers who have workers throughout the country such as the civil service or the nationalised industries are more likely to have standardised wage levels.

Differential wage levels will tend to be attractive to those organisations seeking cheaper labour. However it should be emphasised that this may only be attractive to businesses which do not require labour with a particular skill, for this may be only available in a certain region.

Manufacturing or operating costs
The costs of production or operation may vary from area to area and so may act as an influence on the location of industry. The cost of capital tends to be relatively homogeneous throughout the country because of the comprehensive banking system which is operated nationwide. However smaller organisations may be more restricted in their sources of capital and tend to have to raise it from established connections. This can well act as a limiting factor on the mobility of industry and prevent it from moving to different areas.

The government has used the availability of capital as a means of inducing industrial mobility by offering cheaper means of finance to those businesses willing to move to development areas. Other important operational costs will be those incurred in the acquisition of offices, factories or other premises. In practice this may be one of the major considerations in influencing locational decision. Property prices and rent are often much higher in those areas with a high level of economic activity. This may act as a sufficient incentive to move industry out of city centre sites, or away from the South East of England. Also the central government and local authorities have made conscious efforts to attract industry to depressed regions by offering subsidies and grants such as rent-free properties or low rents for a period of years. The availability of suitable sites may also be a considerable attraction to foot-loose industry and the government has used a policy of 'sticks and carrots' in restricting industrial development in the South East while facilitating sites for new organisations in other regions. One of the latest attempts to attract industry to development areas is to create *enterprise zones*. Notable features of these zones are the less rigid adherence to planning restrictions and rate relief. Town and Country Planning legislation restricts development in other areas, so making these enterprises zones more attractive. Property values will always reflect development potential.

These measures have been successful to some extent in attracting companies but unfortunately, there are instances of organisations who, having sited in the development areas, abandon them once the incentives have expired. Often there are examples of businesses taking advantage of free factories, capital allowances and so on and then moving on after these costs move back to their unsubsidised levels.

Organisations tied to a particular area

It was noted that some organisations may be described as foot-loose in that they are capable of locating in a variety of areas. However, many organisations are tied to particular regions because of the need to be close to markets, suppliers of raw materials or components, or the availability of a pool of labour with a specific skill.

Accessibility of markets
It is often the nature of the product or service produced which restricts an organisation's choice of location. Most service organisations requiring personal contact with the public will obviously be sited conveniently for their customers. Banks, retailers, restaurants must be near to centres of population. This is because the service which they sell cannot easily be transported. In manufacturing industry too, it is the *portability* or ease of transport of the final product which can determine whether or not a manufacturer must site close to customers. If the product has high value in relation to its bulk then transport costs may add little to the final selling price and so the producer may site a considerable distance from customers. Other products may be costly to transport and so make it necessary to locate near to markets. In the past transport costs were much more important both nationally and internationally in determining the location of industry but as transport systems have developed, this has become much less of a constraint. However as the European market has developed, there has been a drift of industrial location to areas with access to European markets.

Supply of skilled labour
Certain businesses require a specific skill or talent in their labour force. If workers of this type are available throughout the country then this does not pose a constraint. But if an organisation requires workers with a particular talent and such people are found only in certain regions this will act as a pull to an organisation requiring such workers. For example a business hoping to establish as glass manufacturers may require experienced glass blowers and so choose to locate in St Helens or Sunderland with their long-established tradition of glass making and pool of skilled labour. However it is not only the type of labour which may act as an attraction for an organisation to a particular region, it may also be the attitude of the workforce. For example, a tradition of shift working or female workers may prove attractive. The region's record on industrial relations may prove to be a deciding factor. An area which is regarded as 'strike prone' may be unattractive while those regions with a comparatively good industrial relations history may attract and hold industry.

In those regions which have faced the industrial decline of major employers such as Scotland, Wales and the North East, a large pool of redundant labour may develop. This may appear attractive to potential new employers but they may have to retrain their new labour force and the costs of retraining may offset the benefits achieved by relatively low wage levels. As part of the government's policy to attempt to alleviate unemployment in the depressed regions, it has instigated wide-ranging retraining schemes for redundant workers.

The availability of the supply of raw materials

If an organisation requires large supplies of raw materials for its productive process, and if the raw materials used are bulky and costly to transport then it may be most suitable for it to locate close to suppliers. As noted in the comments on the access to a market, transport costs were much more of a determining factor in the past and particularly during and after the industrial revolution when the manufacturers of products such as steel tended to move close to their suppliers of coal, iron ore, etc. This trend is clearly not so prominent now as transport costs have reduced and movement of raw materials is easier. However manufacturers do tend to congregate in areas where suppliers of parts and components are situated. This infrastructure of suppliers and services related to their particular industry tends to keep down costs. Examples include the concentration of much of the motor industry in the West Midlands and another example is in the United States where many of the micro-electronics manufacturers have located in California's so-called 'Silicon Valley'. The advantages of concentration of an industry in a particular area are referred to as *external economies of scale*. These would include such gains as the development of a skilled labour force, the provision of education and training facilities by local colleges and training centres and the growth of mutually dependent systems of suppliers and subcontractors.

The decision by management on location

While it has been noted that the economic factors of labour, materials and market accessibility may play an important part in determining the most appropriate location for an organisation's operation, it is often the managers of the business who will have the final say. This decision may be influenced by the management's decision where to live and work. One of the major factors quoted for many organisations' reluctance to move from the South East to the regions is the unattractive impression these areas have in the eyes of senior management. They prefer to live in the South East and work in London than move to the North East or Northern Ireland despite the obvious economic advantages to their organisation of moving. Despite the fact that this may be an irrational judgement it could nevertheless prove to be a crucial factor in locational decisions.

Of course in the public sector there has, in recent years, been a conscious effort on the part of the government to move civil service departments out of London to the regions. Examples include the siting of the Motor Vehicle Licencing Centre in Swansea and the Department of Health and Social Security in Newcastle. This has been done because many of the organisations attracted to the regions have been manufacturing industries and so to balance the employment pattern in these areas, the government provides 'white collar' jobs.

Government regional policy

In the UK different regions have always experienced widely varied levels of economic prosperity. This variation in prosperity has expressed itself in various ways but the most obvious signs are to be found in differing unemployment levels between the UKs regions. Table 7.1 illustrates such variations between UK standard regions.

Region	Percentage unemployment
North	15.6
Yorkshire & Humberside	12.7
East Midlands	10.9
West Midlands	14.2
North West	14.4
East Anglia	9.4
South East	8.3
South West	10.0
Wales	14.8
Scotland	14.1
Northern Ireland	18.8
UK	

Table 7.1 UK regional unemployment rate, July 1981

Source: Monthly Digest of Statistics, July 1981

The table illustrates the wide differences which exist in regional unemployment, ie from 8.3% in the South East to 18.8% in Northern Ireland. To some extent the rising unemployment of recent years has reduced the disparities between regions compared to more prosperous earlier years. Nevertheless the variation is sufficiently wide to point to a serious regional problem in the UK. Such a problem is not unique to the UK however since similar situations are to be found throughout Europe.

In addition to varying unemployment levels regional differences are also to be found in income per head, economic growth rates and associated social conditions. These variations have resulted in all governments recognising the existence of a *regional problem* in the UK economy. The recognition of the regional problem led naturally to the implementation of policies aimed to correct the economic imbalance between the regions. Historically such government policy can be traced

369

to the 1930s when very high regional unemployment rates prompted the government to legislate with the Special Areas Act 1934 which established the idea of designating selected areas and providing various financial incentives to encourage companies to establish in such areas. In practice the effects of the legislation on the problem were marginal and it was only after the Second World War that balanced regional development became part of the government's overall economic objectives.

The justification for implementing a regional policy which seeks to reduce the economic imbalance between regions can be expressed at various levels. At the most fundamental level, no democratic government could allow a policy which divided the UK into different nations of rich and poor without facing serious social and political consequences. But moreover such regional imbalance implies an overall waste of economic resources to the nation which results in everyone being poorer in the long run. Consequently the post-war era has seen a long succession of regional policy measures which although differing in detail, have reflected two parallel aims. Most of the measures implemented have sought to solve the problem by encouraging companies to develop in these problem regions using a wide range of financial incentives. Concurrently the government has sought to develop measures aimed at improving the mobility of labour both between regions and industries.

Current regional policy measures are based to a large extent upon the Heath government's 1972 Industry Act with modifications made in the intervening years. This Act continued a long tradition by dividing the UK into areas, known respectively as *special development areas* (SDAs), *development areas* (DAs), *intermediate areas* (IAs) and *non assisted areas*. Northern Ireland was given special category status because of the particular severity of its economic and social problems. In the assisted areas there is a variety of financial assistance available to companies; regional development grants for buildings, new plant and machinery; selective assistance in the form of either loans or interest relief grants; removal grants and certain tax allowances. In addition to these financial incentives the government also encourages development by advance factories on industrial estates on attractive terms. Apart from this UK government financial aid there exist funds from the EEC via such institutions as the European Investment Bank. A summary of these current policy measures is provided in Table 7.2.

Regional policy — success or failure?

Regional policy measures have existed in one form or another since 1934 and yet as Table 7.1 illustrates, there are still considerable inequalities between the regions whatever economic indicator is used as a measure. If one were to judge the success or failure of regional policy then it is vital to first identify the policy objective accurately. If the objective is expressed in terms of eliminating entirely such regional disparities in unemployment, then the conclusion must be that regional policy has failed to achieve this objective. If however the yardstick of success or failure is set in less extreme terms than this, then it is possible to claim some success for regional policies. Two questions can be suggested. Firstly have regional policy measures had any impact in providing additional employment that would not have occurred in their absence? Secondly, would the regional problem have been much worse if the measures had not existed?

Incentive	SDA	DA	IA
Regional development grant for new buildings, plant and machinery	22%	15%	–
	Minimum value of assets which qualify – £5000 for buildings + works £500 for plant + machinery		

Selective assistance

Selective assistance is available usually in the form of a grant for projects creating or safeguarding jobs.

Firms in office and service industries can get up to the following maxims for each extra job created

SDA	DA	IA
£6000	£4000	£2000

Employees can get a £1500 grant for removal expenses.

Factories Factories available rent free for limited periods.

Tourist projects Firms investing in tourist projects can get grants up to 50% of the capital cost of a project or interest relief grants.

Training 40% of the eligible costs of the basic wages of trainees/instructors/materials will be given to manufacturers with projects creating or safeguarding 25 jobs or more in SDA or DA to provide skilled labour in new technology areas. A matching 40% is available from the European Social Fund.

Table 7.2 Summary of incentives

The empirical evidence which has emerged over several years does seem to suggest that regional policy has been successful in terms of creating extra employment and investment. A comprehensive study was undertaken by Moore and Rhodes, involving the period from 1960 to 1976, into the impact of regional policy measures. The results of their investigation indicated that in the period to 1971 regional policy measures did create extra jobs and factories, about 250 000 and 800 respectively. The period after 1971 was one where the effectiveness of policy appears to have been less. It should be remembered however that as with many enquiries, there is criticism of both the method and conclusions in the Moore and Rhodes study.

Alternative evidence comes from other studies into investment grants during 1966 – 68 which indicates that development areas experienced greater investment in plant and machinery per employee than non-assisted areas. The empirical evidence therefore seems to suggest a positive answer to the first question, indicating that regional policy measures *have* had a significant impact. The second question is impossible to answer positively. Would the regional problem have been much worse in the absence of policy measures? The policy itself has been costly to promote and it has been estimated that the cost of each job created was in excess of £2000. However, most observers agree that without such positive government intervention the situation in these regions would be much worse.

The cost of land

As has already been noted the cost of land will vary from area to area and site to site. It is usual to refer to the payment for land as a factor of production as rent, although it is important to distinguish between *economic rent* which is the earnings of any of the factors of production over and above that which it would receive in its next best paid alternative use, and *commercial rent* which is the total cost the organisation must pay for the use of its premises. It is an important decision for any organisation to decide whether it should purchase the freehold estate of land or acquire a leasehold estate under which rent is payable.

Alternatives – freehold or leasehold?
The main disadvantage of purchasing the freehold of a site including the buildings upon it is that it must commit a large amount of capital. Such a substantial outlay may come from accumulated reserves or alternatively it may have to be borrowed. In either case the organisation is assuming one of two things. Either that the rent it would have had to pay under a leasehold would rise faster and so cost more than interest it must repay on the loan, or alternatively that the loss of revenue which it could have gained by using its reserve capital for other purposes such as other investments or new machinery is worth less than the benefit it gains from acquiring the freehold. The revenue it could have gained by using its capital in these alternative ways is the opportunity cost of choosing to allocate the capital for purchasing the freehold.

If the organisation decides instead to rent the property under a lease it will clearly cost less initially but could mean that in the future the rent could be subject to review and could fluctuate as market values change.

The lease of rents or property values although by no means stable throughout the country as a whole, is the result of the interaction of supply and demand. A high level of economic activity in the economy as a whole will tend to push up property prices. If organisations anticipate an upturn in demand for their goods and services in the future, then they may seek to expand their premises. This extra demand will shift the demand curve for land to the right and property values and rents will increase.

This process of supply and demand is also reflected in the private housing market. If mortgage rates are low and the building societies are willing and able to lend, then housebuyers will compete with each other and force prices up. Other actions can affect house prices. For instance a decision by a local authority to sell off part of its stock of council houses. This may reduce private house prices initially by increasing the supply of houses for sale. However in the long term there is a reduction in the supply of rented accommodation in the future and this could then push up house prices. The Rent Acts, passed in the 1960s, to strengthen the position of tenants in rented accommodation (now covered by the Rent Act 1977), by granting security of tenure and providing the means by which a fair rent could be registered (often below market rent), meant that some private landlords were reluctant to let property. Rents asked by landlords rose and so prospective tenants were discouraged and turned to the building societies in an attempt to buy their own homes and, as mortgages were relatively cheap and available, this resulted in an increase in demand for private houses and in a doubling of property prices in 1971 and 1972.

Property speculation
Throughout the 1970s successive governments became increasingly concerned about the practice of property speculation. The rapid inflation of most of the period led to rocketing rents and property values. Speculators bought and then resold property at very large profits. The increasing demand for property led to land prices rising more rapidly than inflation and so some speculators bought commercial property and kept it vacant. This was because they hoped that the real market value of the property would go up and so did not wish to enter into long leases which would quickly become unrepresentative of prevailing market prices. The growing concern on the part of the public pressurised local authorities into placing compulsory purchase orders on some properties which remained unlet. This resulted in the speculators having to let property and so market supply was increased. The property speculators were reluctant to let business premises even for short periods at a rent which could quickly fall below the prevailing market value because, since the Landlord and Tenant Act 1954 Part II, the occupier of premises let for business has security of tenure.

Restrictions and liability relating to landholding

Individuals or organisations in occupation of land for business

373

purposes will not enjoy an unrestricted freedom to exploit the land as they please. In practice the holder of a freehold or leasehold estate will be subject to restrictions which have been expressly agreed upon on the acquisition of land, and be subject to limitations as to use imposed under the general law.

Restrictions on the use of land

On the sale of a freehold or leasehold it is common practice for the *vendor* to impose express restrictions on the *purchaser* in relation to his use of the premises. Such restrictions are known as *restrictive covenants*.

Restrictive covenants

A lease of business premises may contain a covenant that the premises are not to be used other than for specified business purposes. Such a covenant will bind the tenant and also anyone who takes possession of the premises if he or she has notice of the restriction, such as a sub-tenant. To be valid restrictive covenants must be negative in nature and are enforceable by injunction. If such a covenant is broken it could result in the payment of damages or a forfeiture of the lease. An example of a covenant of this nature would be a requirement that the premises are to be used only for the purposes of operating a retail travel agency.

When a freehold estate in land is sold the parties may enter into covenants which bind the land, often for the benefit of land retained by the vendor, eg use the land only for the purpose of a private dwelling house. The *benefit* of such a covenant will pass automatically to the subsequent holders of the vendor's retained land and it will be enforceable by them. The *burden* of a restrictive covenant will similarly 'run with the land' and be binding on those who acquire the land from the original purchasers, but only if they have notice of it. If under the Land Charges Act 1972, such covenants are registered at the *Central Land Registry* as a *land charge*, a subsequent purchaser of the freehold is taken to be aware of them, and they are then binding on the purchaser.

Usually, when land is developed (eg a housing estate is built) the developer may require each purchaser to enter into restrictive covenants designed to maintain the general character of the estate and the value of the property on it (eg not to keep a chicken coop in the back garden). Every holder of a freehold property on the housing estate can enforce such covenants against every other holder. There are, however, statutory provisions which ensure that in some cases, restrictive covenants can be *modified* or *discharged* with or without the payment of compensation. The matter is dealt with by the *Lands Tribunal* which takes into account the changes in the character of the neighbourhood or the fact that the covenant impedes some reasonable user of the land.

Easements

These are rights which may exist over land a) expressly as part of a land transaction or special agreement and b) by implication if in existence for more than twenty years. An easement could confer the right to use the land of another in a particular way (*a positive easement*, such as a right of way) or the right to *prevent* another from using the land in a particular way (a *negative easement*, such as a right of light to prevent building on an adjacent property). Easements, like restrictive covenants, may bind sucessive owners of the land but in all cases, to be valid, there must be one piece of land which enjoys the benefit of the easement and one piece of land which bears the burden.

Planning

The rights of an individual or business organisation in occupation of land to carry out any *development* on the land are subject to the overriding control of *local planning authorities* (eg country councils and district councils) who have wide powers conferred on them under the Town and Country Planning Act 1971. The term 'development' is defined as including 'the carrying out of building, engineering, mining or other operations in, on, over or under land, or the making of any material change in the use of any buildings or other land'. Certain changes in operation or use are specifically declared not to be development under the Act, for example the use of a light industrial building for one purpose could be changed to light industry of another kind without constituting development. The Act also contains machinery whereby an occupier can discover whether a proposed change would constitute development under the Act. This is by means of obtaining *outline planning permission* for any proposed development to ascertain whether *full* planning permission is likely to be granted. A planning authority may then issue an *outline planning consent*. Having determined that proposed work amounts to a development under the 1971 Act it is illegal to carry it out until the required permission is obtained. Such consent may be obtained by either:

1 The Secretary of State making a *development order* which has the effect of granting consent to classes of development set out in the order, eg the Town and Country Planning General Development Order 1973; or
2 Permission for development being granted by the local planning authority. Here an application for planning consent must be made by the developer to the district planning authority which has power to grant consent unconditionally, subject to conditions, or refuse consent. A prospective developer who is aggrieved at the decision of a local planning authority may appeal against the decision to the Secretary of State who has power to confirm, reverse or vary it. Alternatively, an aggrieved developer, who can show that as a result

of the planning authority's decision the land is incapable of reasonably beneficial use in its present state, may serve a *purchase notice* on the district council requiring the authority to purchase the developer's interest in the land. If any development takes place without consent or in breach of a conditional consent then the planning authority may serve an enforcement notice on the developer requiring restoration of the land to its original state or compliance with the conditions. Such notices may be enforceable by the authority restoring the land in default and charging the cost to the owner, or by proceedings in the Magistrates Court which has power to impose fines.

Compulsory purchase

Wide powers have also been conferred on local authorities with regard to *compulsory purchase*. The holder of a freehold or leasehold estate can be required to sell his interest in the land to a local authority exercising compulsory purchase powers, usually in order to facilitate some development scheme. An individual or organisation can, of course, object to a compulsory purchase order and then a *Public Inquiry* will have to be held to consider the views of those affected. Such inquiries are conducted by an inspector who will recommend a course of action to the appropriate Minister (the Secretary of State for the Environment) − the *Minister's* decision being final.

Liability arising from the use of land

Statutory nuisance

An individual or organisation operating a trade or business should also be aware of the multitude of statutory offences which could constitute the crime of *statutory nuisance* and render that individual or organisation liability to prosecution. In particular the Public Health Act 1936 makes the following statutory nuisances:

a) deposits on land or animals kept in such a state as to be prejudicial to health or a nuisance;
b) dust or effluvia (ejected steam) caused by any trade, business, manufacture or process and being prejudicial to the health of, or a nuisance to the inhabitants of the neighbourhood;
c) a workplace, which is not provided with sufficient means of ventilation, or which is not kept clean or which is so overcrowded while work is carried on as to be prejudicial to the health of those employed there.

The meaning of the term 'nuisance' is explained later. Local authorities are under a *statutory duty* to inspect their areas for statutory nuisances, the task of which falls on the *Environmental Health*

Departments. In many cases, complaints of statutory nuisance (often by a tenant of property in disrepair) are made direct to the local authority which, if it feels a statutory nuisance exists, must serve a notice on the person responsible to require it to be *abated* (ended). If the person responsible, usually the owner, takes no action then the local authority can do the work itself and recover the cost from the person or obtain a court order to require the person to act. If the nuisance is such that the local authority feels immediate action should be taken to abate it, for instance where through lack of repair a dwelling-house has become unfit for human habitation, it may rely on a procedure laid down under the Public Health Act 1961 which involves the local authority serving a notice to abate, and giving it the power to undertake the work itself if the work is not carried out by the creator of the nuisance within nine days.

In cases where the local authority fails to take action, a victim of a statutory nuisance can bring a case before the Magistrates Court on his· or her own initiative. If the victim is successful, the court has power to find the person responsible and order the abatement of the nuisance. The inclusion, as a statutory nuisance, of noise and vibrations under the Noise Abatement Act, 1960, and the emission of dark smoke under the Clean Air Act 1968 has led to a large number of prosecutions against trading organisations. The ultimate aim of this legislation is, of course, to ensure minimum environmental standards for occupiers of property, workers at their place of work and people generally in the environment in which we live. One of the latest examples is the Control of Pollution Act 1974 which places responsibility on local authorities for the control of waste, noise, atmospheric pollution, and the pollution of waterways. Failure by an organisation to comply with the statutory requirements will constitute a criminal offence.

Private nuisance

An individual or business organisation in possession of land which suffers harm as a result of interference by an adjoining occupier can turn to the common law to provide a remedy, such as damages, or an injunction to prevent the interference from continuing. To succeed in such an action the plaintiff has to establish the tort of private nuisance. Private nuisance has been defined as *an unlawful interference with a person's use or enjoyment of land or of some right over or in connection with it.* For an action to succeed in this tort the plaintiff must prove the existence of three essential elements:

(i)   That there has been an *indirect* interference with the enjoyment of his land as opposed to a *direct* interference such as trespass to land. The types of interference could include excessive noise, smoke, smells, heat, vibrations and encroaching roots or branches of trees.

(ii) That the interference has caused some sort of damage in the

377

form of physical harm to the land or discomfort or inconvenience to the occupier.

The case of *Halsey* v. *Esso Petroleum* (1961) provides an example of actual physical harm. Here smuts from the defendant's chimneys caused damage to the plaintiff's clothes which had been hung out to dry. In contrast *Kennaway* v. *Thompson and Another* (1980) provides an example of damage in the form of discomfort and inconvenience. Here the plaintiff occupied a house adjacent to a lake where the defendants carried on motor boat racing during the summer months. As a result of the discomfort caused by the excessive noise the plaintiff sued under the tort nuisance for damages and an injunction to restrain the activity. The Court of Appeal awarded an injunction to restrain the defendants racing to such an extent that it could not be said to constitute an unreasonable interference with the plaintiff's use of her land.

(iii) That the interference is an unlawful one. The determination of this issue is of course crucial. It involves the court in examining all the circumstances of the particular case. The following may be relevant considerations.

a) *The sensitivity of the plaintiff*
An occupier of land is only entitled to reasonable comfort in the enjoyment of that land and can hardly complain if he or she is peculiarly sensitive to a neighbour's conduct. A balance must always be sought between the interests of an owner to enjoy the use of the property without restriction, and the freedom of an adjoining occupier to use his or her premises as desired. An occupier therefore who suffers harm because he or she is overly sensitive to the interference cannot complain of it.

In *Robinson* v. *Kilvert* (1889) the plaintiff stored brown paper above his landlord's cellar and claimed damages because it had dried out, and diminished in value, as a result of heat rising from the cellar. The Court held that as the level of heat would be harmless to most goods there could be no nuisance for damage caused to delicate brown paper.

b) *The reason for the interference*
The fact that the defendant shows that his or her activities which constitute the alleged nuisance are in the public interest is of no bearing in determining whether or not they are unlawful.

Thus in *Adams* v. *Ursell* (1913) the defendant claim that his fried fish shop in the East End of London performed a public service in providing cheap food for the working classes was held to be an irrelevant consideration in deciding whether it constituted a private nuisance. The fact that the defendant is acting from a malicious motive has been held to be relevant consideration. In *Hollywood Silver Fox Farm* v. *Emmett* (1936) there was a dispute between the defendant who had a farm adjacent to the plaintiff's silver fox farm. In an attempt to interfere with the foxes' breeding, the defendant asked his son to fire guns as near as possible to the plaintiff's land. The Court held that the malicious intent was sufficient to make the interference an unlawful one and damages and an injunction were awarded for private nuisance.

c) *The locality of the nuisance*
The location of the interference is an important factor in determining whether it is unlawful. In the words of Lord Justice Thesiger in *Sturges* v. *Bridgman* (1879), 'What would be a nuisance in Belgrave Square would not necessarily be so in Bermondsey'. It would be unreasonable therefore for an occupier of property in a heavy industrial area to complain of smoke from his neighbour's fire if the atmosphere is already to a large extent polluted.

d) *The duration of the nuisance*
Although the act complained of must usually be of a continuous nature, such as constant emissions of smoke from a factory, nevertheless one single serious act could constitute a nuisance if it is evidence of a dangerous situation. An explosion may be the consequence of a dangerous state of affairs.

In *Miller* v. *Jackson* (1977) the regular hitting of cricket balls from a cricket ground on to adjacent property was held to be a sufficient course of conduct for the purpose of nuisance.

Defences
The defences to an action in nuisance include:

1 *Volenti non fit injuria*, ie consent of the plaintiff.
2 That the nuisance was caused by the act of a stranger of whom the defendant was unaware.
3 *That the nuisance has been in existence for twenty years or more* – Prescription Act, 1832. Of course, it is the 'nuisance' rather than the interference which must have been in existence for the twenty-year period.

In *Sturges* v. *Bridgman* (1879) a confectioner caused noise and vibrations in the course of his trade which had been in existence for more than twenty years. No actual damage was caused however until the adjoining occupier, a physician, built a consulting room in his garden. The Court held that as the nuisance was not created until the damage was caused, the Prescription Act 1832 provided no defence.

4 Statutory authority

The established rule that where a statute specifically authorises an act there can be no liability in tort for harm caused by the act, has been subject to recent scrutiny by the House of Lords.

In *Allen* v. *Gulf Oil Refining Ltd* (1979) the Gulf Oil Refining Act 1965 authorised the defendants to acquire land for the construction of a refinery. The oil refinery was built and began operations, but following complaints by adjoining occupiers of noxious odours, vibrations and unreasonable noise an action in nuisance was finally brought. The defence of statutory authority was accepted in the High Court. The Court of Appeal however interpreted the Gulf Oil Act differently, stating that although the Act authorised the building of the refinery there was no specific statutory authority to operate it. The operation of the refinery was carried on by the company under its common law right to use its land as it pleases. Consequently, if the operation of the refinery constituted a nuisance, those affected by it could exercise their common law rights to bring an action to enforce them. Lord Denning MR made the point that where private enterprises seek statutory authority to conduct and operate an installation which might cause damage to people in the neighbourhood, it should not be assumed that Parliament intended that damage should be done to innocent people without redress. The diverse opinions of the judiciary in relation to the use of this defence of statutory authority is shown by the decision of the House of Lords on further appeal in January 1981. The Lords reversed the decision of the Court of Appeal and held that the defendants *could* rely on the Gulf Oil Act as a defence to an action in nuisance resulting from the operation of the refinery, but only to the extent that the nuisance was the *inevitable result* of such operation.

Remedies

The various remedies for the victim of a private nuisance include an action for damages, abatement of the nuisance (eg cutting off offending roots or branches of a tree that cross the boundary) or an injunction to prevent the defendant continuing the nuisance. It should be noted that an injunction is a discretionary remedy and need not be granted if the court feels that the circumstances of the case do not merit its grant.

In *Miller* v. *Jackson* (previously mentioned) it was held that the cricket club was liable in nuisance but the Court refused to grant an injunction to prevent the playing of cricket after weighing the loss of the club to the community, against the risk of injury to adjoining occupiers. This decision may be contrasted with the approach of the Court of Appeal in the later case of *Kennaway* v. *Thompson and Another* (1980) where an injunction *was* granted but only to the extent that the interference was unreasonable.

Relationship between statutory and common law nuisance
It has already been noted that the expression 'nuisance' is contained as part of the definition of statutory nuisance in the Public Health Act 1936. So, premises kept in such a state as to constitute a nuisance may amount to the crime of statutory nuisance, as well as giving rise to civil liability under the tort of private nuisance, ie a double liability. It is apparent therefore that these separate forms of nuisance are serving different purposes, statutory nuisance imposing criminal sanctions, and private nuisance providing a means of redress to the victim.

Quite independently of statutory nuisance the common law has indentified certain types of conduct harmful to others as giving rise to criminal liability in the form of public nuisance.

Public nuisance

Public nuisance has been defined under the common law as comprising *an act or omission which materially affects the reasonable comfort and convenience of a class of Her Majesty's subjects.* As the definition is very wide the crime of public nuisance may cover many types of conduct and although it is not restricted to the use of land it may include various ways land may be unlawfully used such as:

   (i) Selling or serving food in unhygienic conditions.
   (ii) Causing an obstruction of the highway for instance in *Fabbri* v. *Morris* (1947), by selling ice-cream from a shop window and causing queues.
   (iii) Keeping a disorderly house.
   (iv) Carrying on a dangerous activity near to the highway.

In *Castle* v. *St Augustine's Links* (1922) the Court held that the proximity of a hole on a golf course to the public highway constituted a public nuisance.

Certainly, it is a requirement of the offence that a number of persons must be affected by the act or omission. In *Castle* v. *St Augustine's Links* these were the persons using the highway. However, if an individual can show that a public nuisance exists and as a result of it he or she has suffered some *special damage* beyond the discomfort of the public at large he or she can succeed in an action in tort against the creator of it. Therefore in *Castle* v. *St. Augustine's Links*, the plaintiff taxi driver, who lost an eye as a result of a golf ball striking the windscreen of his cab, succeeded in a tort action against the defendants and recovered damages.

Also in *Campbell* v. *Paddington Corporation* (1911) the defendants were guilty of public nuisance in unlawfully erecting a stand and blocking the highway so that members of the council could watch Edward VII's funeral procession. As the stand blocked the view from the plaintiff's house and she was unable to make a profit by letting spectators view the procession, she was held to have suffered damage and could succeed in tort against the defendants.

Finally it should be mentioned that acts that constitute a public nuisance may also amount to offences under statute, eg the Highways Act, 1959 (obstructing the highway), the Sexual Offences Act, 1959 (keeping a disorderly house) and the Public Health Act, 1936 (emitting noxious substances into the atmosphere).

Occupiers liability

All occupiers of business premises owe a duty under the law with regard to the safety of those who come into their buildings and on to their land. As far as lawful entrants are concerned, classified as *visitors*, the law imposes a duty on the occupier in relation to their safety. This duty is imposed under the Occupiers Liability Act 1957 and is referred to as 'the common duty of care'. All other entrants are classified as *trespassers* and the rules relating to their safety are contained in the common law.

The common duty of care

Under the 1957 Act this duty is owed by an occupier to all visitors. Visitors are those having an express or implied right to enter, and include such persons as employees, consumers, guests and contractors. The common duty is a duty to 'take such care as in all the circumstances of the case is reasonable to see that the visitor will be reasonably safe in using the premises for the purposes for which he is invited or permitted by the occupier to be there'. Notice that the duty is owed by the *occupier* ie the person in control of the premises. Thus it will include an owner in possession, a business tenant, or a landlord as regards the parts of the premises he or she controls, or under an obligation to repair. Also, the duty relates to *premises*, which is defined to include not only land and buildings but also fixed or moveable structures such as caravans, vehicles, houseboats or even aircraft. The Act also gives further guidance as to the standard of care required of an occupier in relation to the duty owed, namely:

a) *Children* – In relation to child visitors, the Act states that an occupier must be prepared for children to be less careful than adults. This suggests that a higher standard of care is owed towards children and therefore, a warning sign which may be sufficient to protect an adult may be insufficient for a child.

b) *Contractors* − In relation to independent contractors who are carrying out their specialist job, the Act states that an occupier is entitled to expect such a person to be aware of the risks inherent in their trade, eg the electrician who fails to turn off the electricity and suffers a shock could not complain of that injury.

In *Roles* v. *Nathan* (1963) despite being warned of the danger, two chimney-sweeps carried on working on a boiler and were killed by carbon monoxide poisoning entering from the ventilation system. The employer was held not to be liable. Lord Denning MR stated 'when a householder calls in a specialist to deal with a defective installation on his premises, he can reasonably expect the specialist to appreciate and guard against the dangers arising from the defect'.

Satisfying the common duty of care
The duty of care imposed upon an occupier can be satisfied in one of two ways: either −

a) ensuring that the premises are reasonably safe and free from dangers; or
b) giving effective warning of any danger which is sufficient to enable the visitor to be reasonably safe. This can be achieved by a warning notice which is prominently displayed.

Prior to 1977 an occupier had a further option available. He could simply exclude or restrict the duty owed to his visitors. In *Ashdown* v. *Williams* (1957) the defendants had posted notices on their land to the effect that persons on the land were there at their own risk and should have no claim against the defendants for any injury whatsoever. The plaintiff visitor suffered injury by the negligent shunting of railway trucks but the Court held that her action must fail as liability had been excluded.

This right to exclude liability has been modified to a large extent by the Unfair Contract Terms Act 1977. The Act applies mainly to duties that arise in the course of a business. Under the Act, liability for negligence including breach of the common duty of care under the Occupiers Liability Act, causing death or physical injury, cannot be excluded or restricted. Occupiers of business premises, who hope to rely on the provision of an exclusion clause to prevent liability, must therefore think again. The Act also states that liability for other loss or damage can be excluded or restricted but only to the extent that such provision satisfies the test of reasonableness laid down in the Act.

Finally it should be noted that where injury is caused to a visitor because of the negligent workmanship of a contractor, then the liability of the occupier will depend upon whether he or she acted reasonably in entrusting the work to the contractor. The occupier will have acted reasonably therefore, if a reputable organisation was selected to do the work rather than the local handyman.

> In *O'Connor* v. *Swan and Edgar* (1963) the plaintiff was injured by a fall of plaster when she worked as a demonstrator on the first defendant's premises. The fall of plaster was due to the faulty workmanship of the second defendants who had been engaged as contractors to work on the premises. The Court held that as the first defendant had acted reasonably in entrusting the plastering work to a reputable contractor, as occupier he had satisfied the duty owed. However, the second defendants were held liable in damages under the tort of negligence for the faulty workmanship.

The duty owed to trespassers

A trespasser is not a lawful visitor therefore the Occupiers Liability Act 1957 does not impose a duty on an occupier in relation to such a person. The duty owed towards trespassers is found by referring to the common law, and the traditional attitude of the courts was that, so long as an occupier did not set out to injure trespassers intentionally, then the occupier would not be made liable for their injuries.

> This approach is illustrated in *Addie* v. *Dumbreck* (1929) where the defendant occupier of a colliery was held to owe no duty of care under the common law towards a child trespasser who was crushed in the wheel of the defendant's haulage system.

The harshness of this attitude was mitigated to the extent that if *children* habitually trespassed and an occupier took no steps to warn them off the land the child trespasser could be regarded as a lawful visitor and was thus owed a duty of care.

The contemporary approach is reflected in the following decision of the House of Lords which effectively overrules the precedent of *Addie* v. *Dumbreck*.

> *British Railways Board* v. *Herrington* (1972) Here, British Rail had negligently failed to maintain fencing which ran between their railway track and a park frequently used by children. A six-year old climbed through the fence, wandered on to the track, and suffered severe injury on the electrified rail. The House of Lords held the Board liable in negligence to the child trespasser. The Court stated that, '. . . if the presence of the trespasser is known or ought reasonably to be anticipated by the occupier then the occupier has . . . a duty to treat the trespasser with ordinary humanity'. Among the factors to be taken into account in such cases are the degree of potential harm faced by the trespassers, the financial resources of

the occupier, and in the case of children whether the premises act as an allurement. In this case the Board were aware of a known and potentially lethal danger, which would act as an allurement, and they possessed sufficient financial resources to have prevented the harm suffered by the child. The standard of care required of an occupier in such circumstances was to act as a conscientious humane man with the knowledge, skill and resources at his disposal could reasonably be expected to act in the hope of avoiding the harm.

It should be noted that the duty owed to a trespasser is a restricted duty and much less than the standard of care owed to a lawful visitor.

The rule in Herrington has been applied in later cases, for instance in *Pannett* v. *McGuinness Ltd* (1972). Here a demolition contractor was made liable for injuries caused to a five-year old trespasser by an unguarded fire. This was despite the fact that the contractor, aware of the danger, had posted workmen to guard the fire. The fact that the men were absent when the injury occurred meant, as far as the injured child was concerned, nothing was done to safeguard him.

Also, in *Harris* v. *Birkenhead Corporation* (1976) the defendant local authority, who failed to board up an empty house under their control, were held liable to a child trespasser who wandered inside and was injured. The presence of the child, the court decided, was foreseeable, as he was attracted to the derelict property and the failure to prevent his entry was not the conduct to be expected of a conscientious humane local authority.

The tort of Rylands v. Fletcher

In some circumstances the common law imposes strict duties upon occupiers of premises in relation to the use of land. An example of this is the tort of *Rylands* v. *Fletcher*, which receives its name from the famous case of 1868.

Rylands v. *Fletcher* (1868) The case concerned a mill owner who had employed a competent contractor to build a reservoir on his land. The owner was not aware that an old mill shaft was underneath the land and when the reservoir was filled in, it caused flooding to a neighbour's mine. Despite the absence of any negligence on the part of the mill owner the Court held that he was strictly liable for the escape of water. Blackburn.J stated the following rule which has now been given status as a separate tort:
'A person who, for his own purposes, brings on his land and collects and keeps there anything likely to do mischief if it escapes . . . is prima facie answerable for all the damage which is the natural consequences of its escape'.

It is possible to appreciate the scope of this tort by examining its various elements.

a) *Brings and collects the thing on the land* — The occupier must have brought something non-natural to the land which could include water in a reservoir, gas, electricity, oil in a refinery, etc.

In *Pontardawe RDC* v. *Moore-Gwyn* (1929) it was held that there could be no liability, under the tort, for an outcrop of overhanging rock which had not been brought on to the land.

b) *The thing collected must be likely to do mischief if it escapes* — It follows therefore that the range of things to which the tort applies is potentially enormous and has been held to include: fire, gas, electricity, animals, water, filth, oil and vibrations.

In *Attorney-General* v. *Corke* (1933) the defendant allowed caravan dwellers to occupy his land and they caused damage by breaking fences on neighbouring land where they were not permitted. The Court held that Rylands v. Fletcher applied and an injunction was granted against the defendant.

c) *The thing must have escaped* — Liability under the tort depends upon the mischievous thing escaping from the land.

In *Read* v. *Lyons* (1947) a munition inspector who was injured by an explosion while inspecting a factory could not succeed under the tort as there had been no escape of the thing from the premises.

Defences

A number of defences to the tort have been recognised including:

a) The consent of the plaintiff to the thing (volenti non fit injuria).
b) An escape due to the plaintiff's action.
c) Statutory authority to collect the dangerous thing.

In *Pearson* v. *North-Western Gas Board* (1968) the plaintiff's house was destroyed by a gas explosion caused by the fracture of a pipe. As the defendants were under a statutory duty to supply the gas, there was no liability under the tort.

d) An escape due to the act of a stranger.

In *Rickards* v. *Lothian* (1913) the defendant was held not liable for the escape of water from his premises when he showed that the escape was due to the act of a stranger, who had blocked up the waste pipe and turned on a tap.

These then are the various restrictions which exist in relation to land ownership. Even the holder of a freehold estate does not have absolute freedom to use the land as he or she wishes because of the various constraints under the law. In addition, various duties are owed by a landowner imposing obligations in relation to the state of the land for the purpose of protecting persons who come on to it, and in relation to the use made of the land for the purpose of protecting adjoining occupiers. There are of course economic consequences attached to restrictions and liabilities in relation to land. Thus, the government's decision to protect the environment by imposing high standards on organisations in relation to pollution − Control of Pollution Act 1974 − will obviously have the effect of raising an organisation's operating costs by forcing them to modify their production processes or installing pollution control equipment. This added cost will, in most cases, be passed on to the customer in higher final prices. The consumer must therefore pay the price of a clean environment.

8 Capital and financial resources

> 'I finally know what distinguishes man from the other beasts; financial worries.'

Jules Renard
Journals
1887–1910

Introduction

In this chapter it is proposed to examine how business organisations obtain the financial resources they require to function, and the responsibility they then owe to those who have provided such finance. Initially it is important to define what is meant by financial resources. An economist refers to any material resource as *Capital* and this would include money held and debts owed, plant and machinery and all stock held by the organisation. These are all capital assets of the business but in this chapter it is intended to use the term capital to refer primarily to the monetary assets of the organisation for it is money which provides the means of purchasing not only the other capital assets but also land and labour.

Demand for capital, as for the other factors of production, land and labour, is a *derived demand*. Money in itself provides no satisfaction to a business or an individual. It is the final product or service from which satisfaction is derived and money is simply the means by which these are obtained. Only a miser would enjoy holding money for its own sake and a machine is worthless unless it is used to produce something of value. If the demand for the machine's product decreases and the machine is only capable of making that product, then the value of the machine and the demand for similar machines will consequently fall. This is most obvious when one considers tangible capital assets such as plant or machinery, however it applies equally to the demand for money. If economic activity in the country is buoyant and aggregate demand for products and services is high then the demand for money will accordingly increase. From the earlier analysis of supply and demand it was shown that as demand rose for a product then its price should increase. This also applies to some extent to money. The price of money is the rate of interest which must be paid by an organisation or individual to acquire it by borrowing. However because of its importance in the economy, later in the chapter it will be shown that the government intervenes to influence the level of interest rates, so affecting the free working of supply and demand in the money market.

Functions of money

In the modern UK economy, money is in the form of *currency*, ie notes and coins, and bank deposits. Originally societies used a variety of forms of money including animals and precious metals. Each was more or less successful in achieving the functions of a monetary system. The inability of these commodities to perform the monetary requirements of a sophisticated economy has led to establishment of today's system. The functions of money may be classified as follows:

a) *The form of money used must be an acceptable means of exchange*
So that a developed economy may exist, there must be some means by which individuals and organisations may exchange their respective assets. Acting independently, an individual is only capable of producing a relatively limited range of products. Thus to satisfy other needs the individual will find it necessary to acquire goods and services provided by others. This necessitates a process of exchange in which he or she gives labour or the product(s) of that labour in return for that of others. This would require a *mutual coincidence of needs* where respective wants coincide. (A farmer wanting clothes would have to find a hungry tailor, a homeless school teacher would be looking for a builder with uneducated children.) The inherent difficulties involved in this form of barter stimulated the use of money as a means of exchange by which assets could be converted into a form of currency. (The farmer sells food to the tailor for money and then buys clothes from the tailor. The teacher buys a house from the builder who pays taxes to the local authority who employ the teacher to educate the builder's children.) Money acts as a medium by which these transactions can take place.

b) *The form of money must be able to be used as a unit of account*
In order to value assets, it is necessary to have a system of account. It would not be practicable to value one asset in terms of another, eg is one suit equal to 300 loaves of bread? As it is not easy to value alternative assets a common unit of account has been set and in the UK — it is the pound sterling. Thus, a suit may be valued at £50 and a loaf of bread at 40p.

c) *Money must act as a store of value*
The form of money must have the characteristic that it is easily storable. This allows an individual to defer consumption and enjoy the benefits of accumulated wealth at a later date. Pounds earned throughout the year may be saved in a bank account to pay for a summer holiday.

d) *Money must act as a standard for deferred payments*
Finally, a monetary system must allow individuals and organisations to defer payment for goods and services purchased, ie it

389

must facilitate the use of credit. The vast majority of business transactions are undertaken using credit. In credit transactions, the seller must be confident that the value of the money to be received for the product will reflect the 'consideration' the seller seeks at the time of the transaction.

A variable factor which will complicate all these functions of money is the *level of inflation*. This will not only influence the acceptability of a currency in certain places at a set value but will also reduce its use as a means of stored value and as a means of deferred payment. (The problem of inflation will be analysed in considerable detail in the Chapter 11.)

Characteristics of money

In order to be acceptable as a means of currency, the form of money used should have most, if not all, of the following characteristics:

a) *It must be universally acceptable*
   The prime characteristic of any form of money is that it must be acceptable as a means of exchange to the majority of the population. Most of the UK money supply is not in fact legal tender (ie a means of payment which a creditor is legally bound to accept – coins up to a limited value and bank notes up to an unlimited value). It is the form of bank deposits which can be transferred by means of cheques, credit cards, etc (a creditor is not legally bound to accept payment in these forms).

b) *It should be divisible*
   A divisible currency will allow transactions of different values to be carried out. A pound is sub-divided into one hundred pence to enable a consumer to make relatively small purchases although the trend in recent years has been to make the currency divisible into fewer units by the deletion of specific coins (farthings, threepenny bits) and decimalisation. This is sometimes claimed to have an inflationary effect.

c) *It should be portable*
   The form of currency must be capable of being easily carried. Large denomination notes enable substantial sums of money to be transported with ease, cheques and credit cards provide even greater convenience.

d) *It should be uniform*
   All pound notes and coins are essentially similar to ones of the same value and so those transacting can be reasonably confident of the value they represent.

e) *It should be durable*
   Ideally, a unit of currency should last and would be of little value if it lost shape, colour or form after one transaction. This is clearly a disadvantage of paper as it must be replaced quite regularly

although coins may last decades or even longer.

f) *It should be difficult to counterfeit*

If a means of exchange were adopted using notes or coins which were easy to counterfeit, then unscrupulous people would soon flood the country with counterfeit money and so devalue the worth of the currency. The government must therefore take great pains to ensure that the currency cannot easily be reproduced.

g) *It should have a stable value*

This characteristic is one of the most desirable attributes of a currency. In the UK and in many other countries, inflation has meant that the currency used has not required a stable value and so successive governments have sought to control the amount of money in the country and in so doing regulate its value.

All these characteristics are prerequisites for an efficient monetary system. This is particularly true for some of the characteristics, for instance, a currency with an unstable value will be less suitable as a unit of account and ultimately could collapse as a means of exchange. A clear example of this was the German hyper inflation of the early 1920s, when the value of the mark fell hourly and eventually became unacceptable as a means of exchange.

The need to achieve these characteristics has meant that in Britain as in all developed economies, a monetary system based on notes, coins and bank deposits has evolved. It is important to consider how much money there is available in the country and the form that it takes.

The money supply

The amount of money circulating in the UK varies from day-to-day and even the level of currency varies over the year (eg it is increased at Christmas). It is usually growing and since the mid 1970s it has become a primary government objective to attempt to *regulate the growth in the money supply*. The money supply is difficult to delineate as it comprises not only notes and coins in circulation but also bank deposits held by individuals and organisations both in sterling and non sterling in the commercial banks, other financial institutions and the Bank of England.

The commercial banks do not have a stock of notes and coins equivalent to the amount of the deposits they hold. Most banking transactions take the form of paper transfer, ie by cheque. The cheque itself is not money merely a means of transferring a deposit from one account to another. Consequently the major proportion of the money supply is simply in the form of list of figures in banks' accounts. Good commercial banking practice demands that a certain percentage of the banks' total deposits should be held in cash in their till. This enables the bank to meet the demand for withdrawals by depositors. However, the banks work on the basis that all depositors will not attempt to withdraw all their money in the form of cash at the same time, for if they did the bank would not have sufficient cash in hand to meet all withdrawals. This practice is known as holding part of the bank's assets in a *liquid form*. (This concept of liquidity essentially means how easily an asset can be transferred from one use to another. Cash is the most liquid asset. Other capital assets such as plant or machinery are less liquid in nature for they must first be sold to raise cash to spend on alternatives. Similarly bank loans are less liquid than cash for it may take time for the bank to recall loans and so be able to have money available.)

The government has attempted to define the money supply using banking terminology. A *sight deposit* in a bank is one which can be withdrawn immediately ('on sight') and this includes most current accounts. A *time deposit* is one which requires a period of notice to be given to the bank prior to withdrawal ('time required') and many deposit accounts or savings accounts may require a week, month or longer notice by the depositor before they can be withdrawn. The commercial banks must keep more money in cash form available in their tills to cover sight deposits because it could be required immediately, but they will have some future warning of a withdrawal of a time deposit and so are able to call in a loan to cover the withdrawal. Clearly as time deposits allow the banks to lend out money more easily (and so earn interest for the bank) they will carry a higher interest rate for their depositors than sight deposits. (Current accounts normally pay no interest rate.) All the monies held by the UK commercial banking system are not in the form of pounds sterling. Some is also held by UK residents in the form of foreign currencies and this too makes up part of the money supply. Table 8.1 below illustrates how the UK government has defined and valued the money supply.

	£ million(Unadjusted)
Notes and Coin in circulation with the public	10 256
UK Private Sector Sterling Sight Deposits:	
Non-Interest Bearing	17 524
Interest Bearing	5 007
M1	32 787
UK Private Sector Sterling Time Deposits	38 809
UK Public Sector Sterling Deposits	1 569
Sterling M3	73 165
UK Residents deposits in other currencies	9 859
M3	83 024

Table 8.1   The money supply (Second Quarter 1981)

Source: Bank of England Quarterly Bulletin, September 1981.

From Table 8.1 it is clear that the commercial banks play a crucial role in the monetary system for it is the banks that hold the vast majority of the money supply. The commercial banking system is dominated by four big banks, Barclays, Lloyds, National Westminster and Midland. These are known as commercial clearing banks and carry on most of the domestic 'high street' banking in the UK. Other smaller banks such as the Co-operative, the Trustees Savings Bank and the Yorkshire Bank have been expanding in recent years but are still relatively small in comparison to the 'Big Four'.

There is also a secondary banking system comprising of Merchant Banks, branches of Foreign Banks in the UK and UK Overseas Banks. These institutions provide a service to business, industry and commerce in the form of accepting deposits, arranging loans and other financial services.

Finally, there are other financial institutions such as the Discount Houses (which will be considered later in this chapter), Finance Houses, who provide money for hire-purchase and other credit transactions, the Building Societies and other smaller financial organisations which play a part in the monetary system. These organisations all interact in the money and capital markets providing the short, medium and long term loans which are required by a variety of borrowers including the Central Government, local authorities and foreign and domestic businesses.

The growth of the money supply

If the money supply consisted simply of notes and coins then the only way in which it could grow would be by the printing of new notes or minting of more coins. Although the number of notes and coins is increased by the Bank of England at times when many cash transactions are being made, for instance at Christmas, this is not the most important form of money growth. This results from the creation of credit through commercial bank lending. A simple example will help to illustrate how a commercial bank creates money through lending, (see overleaf).

This example could be extended as the money continues to be spent, deposited in bank accounts and lent to borrowers. At this stage the initial £100 has grown. A still has £100 in the bank, C has a £92 deposit and E has an £84.50 deposit. F has £78 in cash to spend. Therefore the money has grown although £100 in cash are the only notes in the system. It is the amount held by the banks and not lent to borrowers which will determine the growth of the money stock.

The cost of money

As previously mentioned, money like the other factors of production has its price which is the *rate of interest* that must be paid to borrow it. From the earlier analysis of the market mechanism, it was clearly shown that the price of most goods and services are reached through the free interaction of supply and demand. In a completely 'free' economy this would also be true of the rate of interest. However, because of the prime importance of money in the economy and because it is also the biggest borrower, the Government intervenes to affect interest rates. It does not do this by passing laws or regulations but simply by using the supply and demand mechanism to its own advantage. The process of control of the money supply (called monetary policy) will be considered in detail in Chapter 11 p. 510 so it is sufficient here to briefly explain how the government affects interest rates.

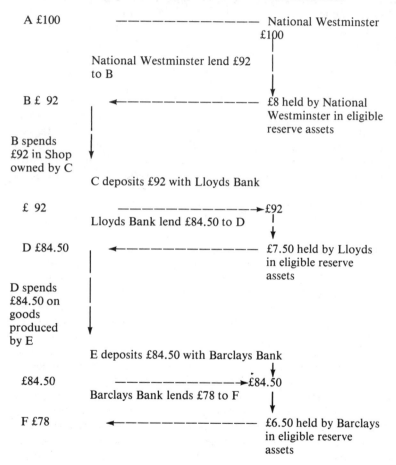

A deposits £100 with National Westminster Bank

Table 8.2

Banks, when they lend money to individuals or organisations, seek a combination of two factors – *profit* and *security*. Banks take many factors into account when considering loans such as the borrower's ability to repay, the purpose of the loan and the collateral provided by the borrower. The most attractive borrower is one who combines absolute security with a willingness to pay a high rate of interest. The security of a borrower varies with the amount of assets that they hold. Thus the government is a very safe risk and also the largest borrower in the country, whereas smaller organisations or individuals have fewer assets and are more likely to default on loans. Therefore, if the government is willing to pay a certain rate of interest for a loan, ie 12%, then other borrowers, who are less secure must pay a rate of interest which is not equal but higher than this (perhaps 14%). Unsecured borrowers who are therefore a relatively high risk will be required to pay an even higher rate.

Business finance

A trading organisation in the private sector which intends to carry on business will require capital to finance its activities. To function an organisation will need to acquire fixed assets such as land, plant, machinery, etc which may be termed *fixed capital*. It will also require finance to pay for raw materials, labour, etc which may be termed *circulating capital*. In this section it is proposed to consider how trading organisations meet their financial requirements. Generally the smaller the organisation, the less options it has with regard to the raising of finance.

The financing of unincorporated bodies

A new trading organisation which intends to operate as a sole trader or partnership (unincorporated bodies) will usually find great difficulty in raising finance from external sources and will often be forced to contribute its own initial capital. A sole trader therefore will be the major provider of his or her own capital and similarly a partnership firm will rely heavily on the capital contribution of the partnership members. The ease with which finance can be raised by borrowing from external sources will depend upon a number of economic factors. Thus any prudent lender of finance will seek a reasonable rate of return on investment, the loan guaranteed by security, and an assurance of the borrower's healthy economic prospects. Many new trading organisations operating as unincorporated bodies would have difficulty in satisfying these criteria. In addition, of course, as a general rule interest is payable on a loan whether or not the borrower is making a profit so in order to survive an organisation with many debts must trade profitably.

On the creation of a trading partnership, it is usual to include in the partnership agreement the rights of the individual partners in relation to their capital contributions. Such an agreement would provide, therefore, that each partner is entitled to be credited with the value of finance that partner brings into the firm. If the agreement makes no provision for capital, then under the Partnership Act 1890 the partners are entitled to capital in equal shares regardless of their capital contributions. Also, unless the partnership agreement provides for it and there are sufficient profits, no interest is payable on capital contributions. The initial capital contributions of the partners must be distinguished from a situation where a partner makes an additional loan to the firm. Here the partner lending the additional money is in the same position as any external lender and interest is payable on the loan whether or not the partnership makes a profit.

External borrowing by unincorporated bodies

Sole traders or partnerships can raise capital by borrowing either from individuals or, as is more likely, from financial institutions such as commercial banks. Short-term borrowing from banks is usually facilitated by means of an *overdraft* by which the borrower is given a specific level of credit on which he or she can draw. If part of the overdraft facility is not used, ie the borrower does not withdraw all the money the bank is willing to lend, then interest will only be paid on that part borrowed. Overdrafts are a means by which a trading organisation can raise short-term working capital, eg pay day-to-day bills which cannot be met because debtors have not paid up. If a long term loan is required, for instance, to increase productive capacity, then this is normally in the form of a secured or unsecured loan whereby a set amount is loaned by the bank and repayments are either in instalments over a period, or in total after a set time.

If the loan is secured, the bank will hold *security*, for instance, the deeds to property, which it can then realise (turn into cash) if the debtor defaults. One of the most common forms of raising finance under a secured loan is the mortgage which is usually on freehold or leasehold interests in land but may also be made on chattels personal. Under a *mortgage*, the mortgagor (borrower) in return for a loan from the mortgagee (lender) will transfer the ownership of the mortgaged property to the mortgagee with a stipulation that the property be retransferred to the mortgagor on repayment of the loan plus interest. A mortgage may be entered into by drafting a mortgage deed (a legal mortgage) or simply depositing the title deeds of freehold or leasehold land with the mortgagee (an equitable mortgage). This method of raising finance is used widely by both sole traders and partnerships. Incidentally, the creation of an equitable mortgage is within the implied individual powers of a partner in a trading firm, however a legal mortgage requires a deed and therefore the consent of all the partners.

Borrowing by means of an unsecured loan simply means that the lender has no rights over the borrower's property in the event of default in repayment. The lender is limited to bringing a court action on the debt if default occurs and this could of course lead to the borrower having to sell property to make repayment or alternatively to the borrower's insolvency. Certainly in the present economic climate, it is more usual for the lender to require the added protection of a secured loan.

396

County and district . . . .

Title number . . . .

THE HALIFAX BUILDING SOCIETY - MORTGAGE DEED

Dated the   day of   19

The Borrower :

The Society : **THE HALIFAX BUILDING SOCIETY** of Halifax, West Yorkshire HX1 2RG

The Advance : £	The Initial Repayment Period	years
Monthly Payment : £ (variable)	Interest Rate : (variable)	% per annum

The Property :

A. The Borrower acknowledges receipt of the Advance

B. The Borrower as Beneficial Owner **Charges** the Property **by way of Legal Mortgage** with the payment of all moneys payable by the Borrower to the Society

C. This Mortgage is governed by the Mortgage Conditions 1975 - 1978 which have been prescribed by the Board of Directors of the Society and of which a copy has been supplied to the Borrower

D. This Mortgage is made for securing further advances

SIGNED SEALED and DELIVERED
by the Borrower in the presence of :-

The financing of corporate bodies

The most important trading organisation in the private sector is the registered company limited by shares. The initial capital of such companies is raised by the *issuing of shares* which have the effect of conferring on the shareholder a long term interest in the company and various rights depending on the class of share acquired. Alternatively, registered companies may raise long term finance by the issuing of debentures. Borrowing by means of debentures is considered later in the chapter, the debenture being a document which is issued by a company to acknowledge a specified debt to the holder. Unfortunately, the uses of the term 'capital' when applied to companies can have numerous meanings, so in order to minimise confusion brief explanations of the more widely used expressions are given below:

a) *Nominal (or authorised) capital*
   This expression refers to the value of shares that a company is authorised to issue and is included in the Capital clause of its Memorandum of Association.

b) *Issued capital*
   This refers to the value of capital in the form of shares which have been actually issued to the shareholders.

c) *Paid-up capital*
   This is the amount of capital which has actually been paid up on the shares issued, ie the amount of capital that the company has actually raised and received. Under the European Communities Act 1972 if a company makes a reference to share capital on its business stationery or order forms, it must refer to its paid-up capital.

d) *Unpaid capital*
   If shares which have been issued are not fully paid for, the amount outstanding is referred to as unpaid capital, eg if 5000 shares issued have a nominal value of £1 each and only 50p has been paid up on them, then the paid up capital is £2500 and the unpaid capital is £2500. Shareholders may be required to pay up the unpaid amount on their shares by the company making a '*call*' on them to do so.

e) *Reserve capital*
   A company, by special resolution (75% majority vote) may declare that any portion of its unpaid capital shall not be called up except if the company is being brought to an end (liquidated) by a winding up. This is called reserve capital and cannot be converted into ordinary capital for use in the operation of the company without the court's permission.

Having dealt with the various types of capital in a company, it is now proposed to show how the capital may be divided into different classes of shares. This division is included in the Articles of Association which will also specify the rights attaching to each class of share and how the shareholders' rights can be varied.

Classes of shares

There is nothing to prevent a registered company limited by shares from having one class of shares with equal rights. Usually, however, different classes of shares are issued with varying rights attaching to them relating to such matters as voting, payment of dividend and return of capital on liquidation. The three main types of shares are:

a) *Preference shares*
b) *Ordinary shares*
c) *Founders shares*

a) *Preference shares*
The main characteristic of a preference share is that it will have the right to a preferred fixed dividend. This means that the holder of a preference share is entitled to a fixed amount of dividend, eg 6% on the value of their share, before other shareholders are paid any dividend. They are presumed to be cumulative which means that if in any year the company fails to declare a dividend, the shortfall must be made up out of profits of subsequent years. A preference share is therefore a safe investment with fixed interest, no matter how small or large is the company's profit. As far as return of capital on a winding up is concerned, the preference shareholder will rank equally with the ordinary shareholder for any payment due, unless the preference shares are made 'preferential as to capital'. Normally, preference shares do not carry voting rights and therefore the preference shareholder has little influence over the company's activities.

b) *Ordinary shares*
Ordinary shares are often referred to as the 'equity share capital' of a company. When a company declares a dividend and the preference shareholders have been paid, the holders of ordinary shares are entitled to the remainder. It follows therefore that an ordinary shareholder in a well-managed company, making high profits will receive a good return on his investment and consequently the nominal value of his share will rise, eg a £1 ordinary share could have a market value of £1.25. Unfortunately, the reverse is also true and they may fall in market value so that ordinary shares inevitably involve a certain risk. This risk is reflected in the amount of control that an ordinary shareholder has over the company's business. While voting rights are not normally attached to preference shares, they are to ordinary shares enabling the ordinary shareholder to voice an opinion in a general meeting and vote on major issues involving the running of the company.

c) *Founders shares (or deferred ordinary shares)*
Such shares are now quite rare but were orginally granted to the founders of a company (ie those people who established the company − promoters). Their main characteristic was to confer on the holder the right to the remainder of the distributed profit after a dividend had been paid on the ordinary shares.

ORDINARY SHARE CERTIFICATE

THE BRITISH PETROLEUM COMPANY p.l.c.

INCORPORATED UNDER THE COMPANIES (CONSOLIDATION) ACT 1908

THIS IS TO CERTIFY THAT

IS/ARE THE REGISTERED HOLDER(S) OF

CERTIFICATE NUMBER	NUMBER OF SHARES OF 25p EACH (IN WORDS)	(IN FIGURES)

ORDINARY SHARES OF TWENTY FIVE PENCE EACH, FULLY PAID, IN THE COMPANY, SUBJECT TO THE MEMORANDUM AND ARTICLES OF ASSOCIATION.

THE COMMON SEAL OF THE COMPANY WAS AFFIXED PURSUANT TO ARTICLE 113 OF THE COMPANY'S ARTICLES OF ASSOCIATION.

EXAMINED

PRINTED IN ENGLAND BY METCALFE CALDWELL

THE COMPANY WILL NOT REGISTER THE TRANSFER OF ANY SHARE WITHOUT THE PRODUCTION OF THE RELATIVE CERTIFICATE.
REGISTRAR'S OFFICE: BP HOUSE, THIRD AVENUE, HARLOW, ESSEX, CM19 5AG.

Raising share capital

The basic classification of registered companies limited by shares is between *public* and *private*. Under the Companies Act 1980 a public limited company is one which is classified by Memorandum of Association as a *public limited company*, having an authorised share capital of at least £50 000, of which at least one-quarter is paid up. All other companies are classified as private companies which are now the

400

residual class. It is still the position that private companies have no right to invite public subscription for shares and only public limited companies are permitted to do this by issuing a *prospectus*, ie an advertisement offering shares or debentures for sale. This restriction effectively limits the capacity of a private company to raise large amounts of capital. Private companies must necessarily, therefore, rely on those individuals who are aware of its existence and who may be willing to subscribe for shares. On the other hand, to acquire its initial capital or increase its issued capital, a public limited company will issue a prospectus to invite the public to subscribe for shares or debentures. By law, the prospectus must however contain certain information including:

a) particulars of all material contracts entered into by the company in the last two years which are likely to influence prospective investors;
b) an auditor's report showing the company's assets and liabilities, profits, losses and dividends paid over the last five years;
c) if the proceeds of the share issue are to be used to acquire property or a business, a statement giving particulars of the prospective vendors and the purchase price.

An investor who can show that he or she was induced to buy shares in a company by false statements of fact in the prospectus may sue to reclaim any money paid, terminate the share issue, and possibly obtain damages from the persons responsible. It is usual practice when a company makes an invitation to the public for share issue, to have the issue underwritten. In return for a commission, an underwriter, eg a merchant bank, will agree to subscribe for any shares which the public do not take up.

External borrowing by corporate bodies
All trading companies have an implied power to borrow finance for the purposes of their business activities. In the case of non-trading companies, there is no such power unless expressly provided for in the Memorandum of Association. Power to borrow money is usually conferred on the company directors in the Articles of Association. However there is nothing to prevent a company from restricting its own borrowing powers to a specific amount stated in the Memorandum, eg borrow an amount which is no more than two-thirds of the value of the company's paid-up capital. If a power to borrow has been conferred, then this will also carry with it an implied power to offer company property as security for a loan. As previously mentioned, if a company borrows beyond its powers then the loan and any security given for it, is void on the grounds of ultra vires and the lender cannot sue for the return of the loan. Under the rule in *Royal British Bank* v. *Turquand* (1868) if the company has power to borrow money, the lender is under no obligation to discover the purpose for which the money is to be used.

In the short term, registered companies make use of overdraft facilities offered by the commercial banks to finance a temporary cash flow difficulty. This type of borrowing is increasingly used during temporary financial and economic recession, when the cash receipts of the company are anticipated to rise in the future.

Longer term loans may be borrowed either through the commercial banks or on the capital market (which will be discussed later in the chapter). These loans are normally secured against some collateral offered by the company which may be realised by the lender in the event of a default on the loan.

In addition, trading companies may borrow money by means of issuing a debenture or series of debentures which may be secured or unsecured. The definition of *'debenture'* is very wide and includes all forms of securities (undertakings to repay money borrowed) which may or may not be secured by a charge on the company's assets. Indeed a mortgage of the company's property to a single individual may be regarded as a debenture within the definition. Debentures are usually made by means of a trust deed which will create a *fixed charge* over specific company property by mortgage and/or a *floating charge* over the rest of the company assets. The distinction between a fixed and floating charge is essentially that a company is not free to deal with assets subject to a fixed charge, ie selling or mortgage, but a company is free to deal with any of its assets covered by a floating charge. However, on the occurrence of a particular event, a floating charge is said to *crystallise* and is then converted into a fixed charge. Such an event would be when money becomes payable under a condition in the debenture, eg repayment of interest, and the debenture holder takes some steps to enforce his or her security because the interest due is unpaid. The principal rights of a debenture holder are contained in the debenture deed and will include:

a) the date of repayment of the loan and the rate of interest;
b) a statement of the assets of the company which are subject to fixed or floating charges;
c) the rights of the company to redeem the whole or part of the monies owing.
d) the circumstances in which the loan becomes immediately repayable, ie if the company defaults in repayment of interest;
e) the powers of the debenture holder to appoint a receiver and manager of the assets charged.

A further means of raising capital open to organisations facing a cash flow problem is *factoring*. Essentially this means that an organisation with outstanding monies owed to it, sells the right to this money to a *factor* (an organisation willing to provide immediate cash in return for the right to collect and keep the monies owed from the organisation's debtors). The factor will usually pay the organisation less than the face value of the debts − 3% − 10% − and so if the debt can be collected in full, this percentage is the factor's profit on the transaction.

ISSUE OF DEBENTURES FOR £

Carrying interest (payable half-yearly) at the rate of   per cent. per annum,
in   Debentures of £   each, all ranking pari passu without preference
or priority on account of date of issue or otherwise, and secured by Trust Deed
dated the   day of   19   and made between the Company
of the one part and   of the other part.

Such issue is made under the authority of clauses   and   of the Articles of Association
of the Company, and pursuant to a resolution passed by the Directors of the Company on the
day of   19 .

No.   **Debenture**   **£**   .

1.   *LIMITED*

(hereinafter called " the Company "), for valuable consideration received hereby covenants
with
of
that the Company will pay to him or other the registered holder for the time being of
this Debenture, the sum of £   on the   day of
*   19   , or on such earlier day as the said sum shall*
become payable pursuant to any of the Conditions endorsed hereon, and also in the meantime
on the   day of   and the   day
of   in every year interest on the said sum of £   by
equal half-yearly payments at the rate of   per cent. per annum, the first of
such half-yearly payments of interest or a proportionate part thereof calculated from the
date of the issue of this Debenture, to be made on the   day of
next.

2. *This Debenture is issued subject to and with the benefit of the Conditions*
endorsed hereon, which shall be deemed to be incorporated with and to form part of the
Debenture.

Given *under the Common Seal of the Company this   day of   19   .*

The Common Seal of
*   Limited*
was hereto affixed in the presence of

      Directors.

--**Secretary.**

THE CONDITIONS within referred to.

1.   This Debenture is one of a series of   Debentures, each for securing the sum of £

2.   The registered holders of all the Debentures of this issue will be entitled *pari passu* to the benefit and subject to the provisions of a Trust Deed dated the   day of   19   , and made between the Company of the one part and
and   (hereinafter called " the Trustees ")
of the other part, whereby the Company has charged its property in favour of the Trustees for securing the payment to the holders of the said Debentures of all principal moneys and interest secured thereby.

3.   The Company may at any time after the   day of   19   , give not less than months notice in writing to the registered holder for the time being of this Debenture, or his personal representatives, or, in the case of joint holders, to that one whose name stands first in the register as one of such joint holders, of the intention of the Company to pay off the principal moneys secured hereby with interest to the date of payment, and on the expiration of such notice the principal moneys hereby secured shall become payable with all interest accrued due and not previously paid.   For the purposes of this clause a notice shall be deemed to have been duly given if given in accordance with the provisions of the said Trust Deed, which shall be deemed to be incorporated herein. Interest shall cease to run on this Debenture on the due date for redemption thereof unless upon production of this Debenture payment of the amount due on such redemption shall be refused.

4.   A register of the Debentures of this issue will be kept by the Company.   Such register shall contain the names, addresses and descriptions of the registered holders for the time being of such of the said Debentures as shall for the time being be outstanding or have been re-issued, and particulars of any which have been redeemed or purchased, and shall be open for inspection by any such registered holder or his personal representatives or any person authorised in writing by him or them at all reasonable times during business hours, but the register may be closed during the fifteen days preceding each day on which interest is hereinbefore covenanted to be paid.   Nothing herein contained shall be deemed to preclude the Company from re-issuing any Debentures under any circumstances or in any manner under or in which Debentures may be re-issued in accordance with the provisions of the statutes for the time being in force.

5.   All persons may act for all purposes on the assumption that this Debenture is the exclusive property of the registered holder for the time being thereof or of his personal representatives, and the Company shall not be under any obligation to enter in the register notice of any trust or to recognise any person as having any claim to or equitable or other interest in the same except as herein expressly provided : Provided nevertheless that in the case of joint registered holders this Debenture shall on the death of any of them be deemed to be the exclusive property of the survivors or survivor.

6.   The following provisions shall have effect with respect to the transfer of this Debenture—

   (A) Every such transfer must be in writing under the hand of the registered holder thereof or of his personal representatives.

   (B) Every such transfer must be delivered at the registered office of the Company together with a fee of twelve and one half pence.

   (c) Such evidence must be furnished as to the identity and title of the transferor in each case as the Directors of the Company may reasonably require before any such transfer will be registered.

   (d) No transfer will be registered while the register is closed.

   (E) The Company will be entitled to retain the transfer.

7.   The principal moneys and interest secured by this Debenture will be paid by the Company without regard to any equities between the Company and any other person except the registered holder hereof or his personal representatives, whose receipt for the same shall be a good discharge to the Company.

8.   The principal moneys and interest hereby secured will be paid at the
Bank Limited, No.   Street,   , or at the registered office of the Company.

9.   The Company may at any time purchase any of the Debentures of this issue in the open market or by tender or by private treaty at any price not exceeding [par plus accrued interest].

10.   In respect of each half-year's interest on this Debenture a warrant on the Company's Bank payable to the order of the registered holder, or in the case of joint holders to the order of that one whose name stands first on the register as one of the joint holders hereof, will be sent by post to the registered address of such registered holder, and the Company shall not be responsible for any loss in transmission.   The payment of the warrant shall be a good discharge to the Company.

11.   The principal moneys hereby secured shall immediately become payable if the Company makes default in the payment of any interest hereby secured for a period of   weeks after the same shall become payable, or if an order shall be made or a resolution effectively passed for the winding up of the Company, or if the security constituted by the said Trust Deed shall become enforceable and the Trustees or Trustee for the time being of the said Trust Deed shall determine or become bound to enforce the same.

Central government provision of business finance

Central government may provide organisations in the private sector with capital in two ways:

a) by direct grants or subsidies;
b) through the purchase of part of the organisation's share capital.

a) *Direct grants and subsidies*

These are given specifically to organisations established in the development regions of the country. (The government's regional development policy was considered in Chapter 7, p. 369.) Direct grants and subsidies are part of the government's overall policy to attempt to influence the location of industry in the UK. They take the form of cash grants or tax allowances and are for specific periods, eg within three or five years of establishment. Industries which are capital intensive tend to benefit most. Tax allowances allow an organisation to write off part of the depreciation (fall in value) of capital equipment against tax. This, in effect, makes the purchase and operation of plant and machinery cheaper and so encourages organisations to invest.

b) *Purchase of part of an organisation's share capital*

The government established two bodies with the intention of providing equity (share) capital for the private sector.

(i) The first of these was the National Enterprise Board which was set up in 1975. Although in the period from 1975 – 80 it controlled the share capital of such important organisations as British Leyland and Rolls Royce. Under the Thatcher government, its role was changed slightly so that it acted as a catalyst for new organisations producing high technology products such as microelectronics, computers, biotechnology etc. It was later merged with the National Research and Development Corporation (the NRDC) to form one body.

(ii) Finance for Industry Ltd (FFI):

This has been established jointly by the Bank of England and the clearing banks as a holding company (to hold the controlling share capital) for *Industrial and Commercial Finance Corporation Ltd* and *Finance Corporation for Industry Ltd*. These two organisations provide certain medium sized and small companies with finance for the short and long term if they are unable to raise finance elsewhere.

Government action to encourage investment in small businesses

In 1981 the government introduced measures which it hoped would encourage private investors to place *risk capital* in small businesses. It has already been noted that small enterprises experience greater difficulty in raising capital than public companies and this is particularly true for businesses which are just establishing or wish to expand. The government has responded by introducing two schemes to help small private organisations raise equity and loan funds.

The *Business Start-Up scheme* is designed to promote an injection of capital from outsiders other than the initial entrepreneur and associates. This allows a tax incentive in the form of tax relief on up to £10 000 per individual in each year invested in a new independent limited company starting up a genuinely new business venture in certain kinds.of trade. The capital introduced must remain in the business for at least five years in order to qualify for the tax relief and the relief will be given at the investors' marginal rate of income tax.

Secondly, the government introduced a pilot *Loan Guarantee Scheme* which aims to help those businesses who are unable to raise loan finance because of the entrepreneur's previous lack of experience or unwillingness to provide private loan guarantees on borrowed capital. The scheme also introduced in 1981 will last for three years and comprises a maximum commitment of £50 m on behalf of the government. Loans of up to £75 000 are available to individuals for a period of between two and seven years. The government will act as guarantor on 80% of the loan and the borrower will pay normal commercial rates for the loan and a premium of 3% to the government which acts as a guarantee provision.

The government also took measures in 1980 and 1981 to reduce the tax burden on small businesses. This has meant a lower rate of *corporation tax* is applied to small companies than to other larger organisations and greater tax relief for those businesses investing in new small business premises. These and other measures reflect the government's belief that it is necessary to encourage small enterprises and create a fiscal climate which is more favourable to the small organisation. Although action such as this cannot completely redress the imbalance which results from the substantial economies of scale enjoyed by large organisations both in raising capital and in the costs of operation, it does go some way to promote the regeneration of small businesses in the private sector.

The markets for raising capital

Having considered the different methods which may be used by organisations to raise finance, it is now proposed to examine the markets in which this is done.

Individuals or organisations may invest their money either directly by buying shares or debentures or indirectly through banks or other financial institutions who pay interest on these deposits and re-invest the capital so earning a return.

The Stock Exchange
The Stock Exchange is the market for permanent or as it is known

equity capital and here most transactions in securities (the collective name for stocks and shares) are carried out. The process of sale or purchase is carried on through intermediaries, stock brokers and jobbers. Each has a specific function. Brokers act on behalf of buyers and sellers of securities (for private individuals are not permitted to transact in their own right in the Stock Exchange). The broker, on behalf of a client, buys or sells to the jobber acting as a middleman who in turn is seeking to make personal profit by buying at a price which is cheaper than his selling price. Jobbers tend to specialise in particular securities (eg mining or industrial shares) and will buy without having a specific seller in the hope that they can make a profit on the transaction. It is obviously a skilled and risky business to know at what price to buy shares and when prices will be sufficiently high to give a profit on resale.

All transactions on the Stock Exchange are in 'second-hand' shares as a company wishing to offer a new share issue to the public usually does this through direct advertisement by prospectus. This is called the 'New Issue' Market although no such market exists in one discrete place.

Functions of the stock market
The stock market performs a number of roles:

a) it allows investors, both small and large, to be confident that they will have a market for the resale of the securities they buy (of course, there is no guarantee as to the price they may obtain on resale);
b) it gives an indication of the confidence of investors in the state of the economy. If investors are competing to buy shares, this would indicate that they have confidence in the economy's future and expect high dividends from their investment (the reverse is clearly true if confidence is low). This is why the most widely used index (the Financial Times Index) is watched by individuals, organisations and the government in order to get some indication of investors' confidence.

The 'closed shop' system of the Stock Exchange restricting entry to a selected number of jobbers and brokers has recently come under scrutiny and has been criticised as likely to lead to unfair competition and may amount to a restrictive practice. The Stock Exchange Council which regulates the market is considering a possible review.

The money and capital markets
The Stock Exchange does not provide money or capital direct to organisations but merely encourages share purchase in the knowledge that they can easily be resold. Most direct capital is raised in two areas:
The Money Market (used for short term loans),
The Capital Market (used for longer term loans).

a) *The money market*

The London Money Market comprises various financial institutions whose sole function is to act as middlemen in the monetary system. They borrow money (or accept deposits) at certain interest rates and then relend it out at higher rates and so make a profit. At first sight this may appear a rather mercenary operation but in fact they perform a vital service. They are the focus for those who seek to deposit short-term funds (and so earn interest) and those who require to borrow money for a short time. These institutions are called *Discount Houses*. Their lending tends to be short term, sometimes overnight thereby allowing other institutions such as the commercial banks to have money 'at call' (easily recoverable into hard cash) and also permitting organisations who are temporarily short of funds to find immediate financing.

In addition, the discount houses play an important role in financing government short-term borrowing for they agree to purchase all the Treasury Bills which remain unsold each week following their offer by the government. Treasury Bills are simply loans to the government for 60 or 91 days. The government offers to repay a certain sum (eg £10 000) after 91 days and each week financial organisations bid to buy them. The government accepts the highest bids made. For instance, a building society may bid £9500 for a £10 000 bill to be repaid in 91 days. The £500 extra it earns on the maturity of the bill is the equivalent of earning interest on a loan to the government. These are then resold to banks and other institutions. Discount houses will also purchase Treasury Bills from other holders at less than their maturity value ('at a discount' – hence the name) and this gives the holders of Treasury Bills the opportunity to convert them into cash immediately.

b) *The capital market*

The capital market is the collective term which describes the actions of a variety of financial institutions such as merchant banks, insurance companies, pension funds, who are willing to provide longer term loan capital to organisations in both the private and public sectors. These loans are usually secured by assets or future revenue of the borrowing organisation and they provide an important source of long term large scale finance.

The Euro currency market

Finally a mention may be made of the international money market known as the Euro Currency Market, which deals in the buying and selling of currencies. It handles transactions in vast amounts of money which are used either in international trade or borrowed by governments or multinational companies to finance their operations. Initially most of the money changing hands was in the form of dollars ('Eurodollars') but now many currencies are bought and sold either for use in transactions or for speculative purposes. (International currency transactions will be considered in more detail in Chapter 9, on International Trade, p. 423.)

Termination of business enterprises

Having examined the means by which trading organisations raise business finance and the markets in which they do this, it is now possible to consider the legal consequences for an organisation experiencing serious financial difficulty. This can occur as a result of insufficient capital or because of excess debts (liabilities) over current assets which may result in *insolvency*. Insolvency can lead to the termination of a business enterprise and it is now proposed to consider in detail the consequences of this occurring for unincorporated and corporate trading bodies.

Termination of unincorporated bodies

Sole traders may terminate their business at any time subject to the limitation that all debts of that business must be repaid. However the death of an individual trader does not automatically terminate the business, for it can be passed by the trader's *will* or on *intestacy* (if there is no will) to the successors in title, eg wife or children. Similarly a partnership may be terminated by the express agreement of all the partners. However the death or bankruptcy of an individual partner will automatically terminate the partnership by operation of the law. If the remaining partners (of which there must at least be two) wish to carry on in business, a new partnership agreement is required. In addition, partnerships are sometimes entered into for a fixed term or to achieve a particular object and so when the fixed term expires or the object is achieved, the partnership will fold.

In relation to the termination of unincorporated bodies due to a lack of finance, it is necessary to distinguish between the terms, insolvency and bankruptcy.

a) *Insolvency*

This occurs when an individual or organisation is unable to meet current liabilities (ie pay money due to creditors). If the insolvency is merely a temporary situation, then the creditors may be willing to wait for payment. If, however, financial recovery is unlikely, the creditors may decide to sue for payment of their debts, enforce any security they hold and this may eventually lead to the termination of the business. For an unincorporated body, whether an individual or a firm, this is called *bankruptcy*.

b) *Bankruptcy*

The law relating to bankruptcy is contained in the Bankruptcy Act 1914 and the Insolvency Act 1976. If an individual or organisation commits an *act of bankruptcy*, either

(i) performs an act with the intention of defeating or delaying creditors such as transferring property to another;

or

(ii) fails to comply with a 'bankruptcy notice' (a notice served by a creditor to pay a debt ordered to be paid by the court, – a *judgment debt*)

then its assets are transferred to a *trustee in bankruptcy* for distribution among the individual or the organisation's creditors.

Following an act of bankruptcy, any creditor who is owed at least £200 may present a bankruptcy petition in the County Court or High Court. If the petition is accepted by the court, it will make a *receiving order* under which an official receiver is appointed to control the affairs of the individual or organisation in question. After the submission of a written statement of affairs, there is usually a court examination of the individual or organisation in which the creditors are given the opportunity to pose questions to the debtor. At this point the creditors will then decide whether to make the business bankrupt or to accept what is called *a composition*. This is an agreement to accept part payment of the debts owed, eg 50p for every £ owed. If the creditors opt for bankruptcy, a trustee is appointed to sell off the business property and distribute the money received among the creditors in proportion to their debts. Bankrupt individuals, however, are allowed to keep the tools of their trade, clothes and bedding for themselves and their family and sufficient money to maintain them. The distribution of money is subject to the priority claims of creditors some of which are *preferred debts*, eg rates and taxes, wages and redundancy payments. The bankruptcy of an individual partner in a partnership will operate to automatically dissolve the partnership from the date of the commencement of the bankruptcy. When a partnership firm is dissolved, the assets must be used to pay off debts and liabilities, then individual loans to partners, then repayment of the partners' capital contributions. Finally the residue is divided among the partners in the proportion that the profits were divided.

Termination of corporate bodies

If a registered company becomes insolvent or the members wish it to terminate or for any other reason it becomes desirable that the company be terminated, it may be *wound-up*. There are three methods of winding up:

a) a compulsory winding up by the court;
b) a voluntary winding up by the members or creditors;
c) a winding up under the supervision of the court.

All three methods involve a *liquidator* being appointed to administer the company's property with the intention of paying off creditors and distributing the residue among the shareholders.

Compulsory winding up

A petition to wind up a company may be presented in the County Court or if the paid up share capital exceeds £120 000, the High Court. A company may be wound up by the court if any of the following apply:

(i)   it is unable to pay its debts;
(ii) it has not commenced business within a year of formation;
(iii) if the number of members has fallen below the statutory minimum;
(iv) if the company fails to submit its statutory report or hold a statutory meeting;
(v)   if the company resolves to wind up by special resolution (75% majority vote);
(vi) the court is of the opinion that it is just and equitable that the company be wound up, eg there is deadlock between the members.

As far as (i) is concerned, a company is unable to pay its debts if:
the court is satisfied *as to this fact* on evidence; or
a judgment creditor of the company has not been able to satisfy his debt by execution on the company's property (ie confiscation); or
a creditor who is owed £200 or more has demanded payment and the debt has not been paid for at least three weeks.

A petition for winding up may be presented by a contributory (eg a shareholder), a creditor, the company itself or the Department of Trade. The court, of course, is not forced to make a winding-up order, but if it does it will appoint a liquidator to realise the assets, in other words sell them off, and pay the creditors. When the company's affairs are fully wound up, the court will make an order to dissolve the company.

Voluntary winding up

The events which entitle a company to voluntarily wind up are:

(i)   if the company was set up for a period fixed in the Articles, that period has expired and the company has passed an ordinary resolution (50% majority vote) to wind up;
(ii) if the company has to be dissolved on the occurrence of a specified event (included in the Articles) and that event has occurred;
(iii) if the company resolves by special resolution (75% majority vote) to wind up;
(iv) if the company resolves by extraordinary resolution (75% majority vote with notice of the resolution) that it cannot continue in business because of its liabilities.

There are two types of voluntary winding up:

a) *Members voluntary winding up*:
   If the company is solvent, a majority of the directors may make a *declaration of solvency* which is a statutory declaration that in the

411

directors' opinion the company will be able to pay its debts in full within twelve months. When this has been made, the members in a general meeting are in control of the winding up and may appoint a liquidator to carry it out. If having examined the affairs of the company the liquidator is of the opinion that the company will not be able to meet its debts within the period, the liquidator must summon a meeting of creditors and from then on meetings must be held as in a creditors' winding up.

b) *Creditors winding up*:

If there has been no declaration of solvency and the directors call a meeting at which the resolution for voluntary winding up is to be proposed, they must also call a meeting of the creditors to be held the same day or the day after. Both creditors and members may nominate a liquidator, and if there is a dispute as to who should be appointed, it will be settled by the court. If the winding up takes more than one year, then a meeting of the company and creditors must be called so a report on the liquidator's actions can be taken. When the affairs of the company are fully wound up, the liquidator must call further meetings of the company and creditors to show how it has been achieved.

Winding up under the court's supervision

In rare cases, when the company has voluntarily resolved to wind up, the court may make an order that the voluntary winding up shall continue under the court's supervision. The voluntary liquidation can then continue but is subject to the court's power to make orders in connection with it. The intervention of the court may result from a creditors' petition for a compulsory winding up of a company already in voluntary liquidation. The court then makes an order that the company be dissolved on an application by the liquidator that the affairs of the company have been fully wound up.

412

9 International trade

'Dirty British coaster with a salt-cake smoke stack,
Butting through the Channel in the mad Marchdays,
With a cargo of Tyne coal,
Road-rail, pig-lead
Firewood, iron-ware and cheap tin trays.'

John Masefield (1878 – 1967)
Cargoes

Introduction

The United Kingdom, in common with all other industrialised nations, is dependent on the process of international trade in order to achieve its present level of economic development and the standard of living enjoyed by its citizens. Without imports from other countries, the UK would be denied many of the raw materials on which its industries are dependent and much of the foodstuffs necessary to feed its population. Conversely, if foreign countries did not buy the products which the UK exports, the UK would not be in a position to pay for the foreign produced goods which it buys. International trade is of benefit to all participating nations in a similar way. It provides the means by which nations can obtain those goods and services which they cannot, or choose not, to produce. It also increases the size of the market available to producers, who are not then confined to their domestic market. Each country has particular resources such as labour, raw materials, industrial expertise. These can be combined to produce a variety of products and services. These resources are not uniformly distributed among the countries of the world. Third World countries have considerable resources of unskilled labour while Western economies have a highly industrialised base which relies upon skilled labour.

The UK is an economy with a workforce capable of producing a range of sophisticated manufactured products but it lacks certain raw materials such as iron ore and bauxite. If each country in the world attempted to be self-sufficient without recourse to international trade, then they would be considerably poorer. Many products would be unattainable, eg the UK could not produce aluminium as it has no bauxite. In addition many of the products the UK can produce efficiently would have to be foregone. The reason is that resources would have to be diverted from producing them to producing alternatives at which the UK is less efficient, eg the UK may be forced to reduce its industrial workforce to meet all its food requirements.

If this happened this country would be worse off as the value of the

413

food produced would be less than that of the manufactured goods. Thus international trade is based on the concept of *specialisation* in which each country is producing those things at which it is most efficient. This idea is explained by examining the theory of international trade.

The theory of international trade

Most countries produce some of their basic necessities themselves and so they are not totally dependent on foreign trade. The UK produces about one-half of its food requirements despite the fact that it could be produced cheaper elsewhere. Nevertheless, a country should in theory concentrate on the production of those products in which it has a comparative advantage over other nations. For instance, Argentina is capable of producing beef more cheaply than the UK and this country is capable of producing chemicals more efficiently than Argentina. Consequently Argentina has a comparative advantage over the UK in respect of beef and the reverse is true in respect of chemicals. Therefore Argentina concentrates on beef production and the UK on the manufacture of chemicals. In this way relatively more beef and chemicals are produced by both countries through specialisation. This is of course just one example and is repeated with many products and in many countries. In this way international trade not only encourages specialisation but also makes it feasible.

Some countries are in an even more favourable position in that they are capable of producing many products more cheaply and efficiently than the rest of the world. They could therefore become almost self-sufficient. The USA is perhaps such a country but nevertheless it still trades with less efficient countries so that it can concentrate resources on the production of those goods and services for which it has the *greatest comparative advantage*. A less efficient country would produce those goods and services for which it has the *least comparative disadvantage*.

A simple example will illustrate this point. Assume that there are two countries − Eurabia and Britland. Eurabia is an agricultural nation with vast amounts of arable land and Britland is a manufacturing country with a large industrial base. If both countries specialised in the production of that product for which they had the greatest comparative advantage then Eurabia could produce 10 million units of food and Britland could manufacture 20 million units of industrial products. They could then trade exchanging Eurabian food for Britland's manufactured goods. However if trade did not take place and both countries required both food and manufactured goods then Eurabia could only produce 5m units of food and 8m units of manufactured goods. Similarly Britland must divert resources previously used in manufacturing to food production and so could only make 10m units of manufactured products and 3m units of food. The combined food production of the two countries would now be 8m units (5 + 3) and the combined manufacturing output would be 18m units (8 + 10). Therefore the total combined productive capacity of both countries has fallen by 2m units of food and 2m units of manufactured goods. This makes both countries worse off and so to maximise their combined use of resources they should specialise in that product for which they have the comparative advantage and then trade. Fig 9.1 below will illustrate the position.

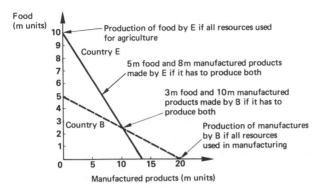

Fig 9.1 Comparative advantage of international trade

This example is relatively straightforward as each country has a comparative advantage in the production of one of the two products. However it has already been noted that some countries have a productive advantage over other nations in most products. Assuming this is the case and Eurabia has resources sufficient for it to outstrip Britland in both food and manufactured products then the less productive country should concentrate on that product for which it has the *least comparative disadvantage*. Fig 9.2 shows that Eurabia could produce 10m units of food or 15m units of manufactured products if it concentrated all its resources towards one or the other. In the same way, Britland could produce 4m units of food or 13m units of manufactured products.

Both countries could also produce a combination of products. Clearly Britland is at a least comparative disadvantage in the production of manufactured goods as it can produce 13m to Eurabia's 15m units while in food manufacture it can only manage 4m units in comparison to Eurabia's 10m. Therefore to achieve the greatest combined production, Britland concentrates all its resources in industrial manufacture and Eurabia either produces all food or a suitable combination of both depending on the relative needs of the two countries.

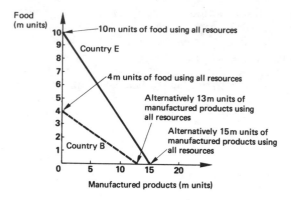

Fig 9.2 Least comparative disadvantage

The reality of world trade

The theory of international trade explained above shows, in a simplified way, that countries should attempt to concentrate their productive resources into making those goods and services for which they have the most efficient comparative advantage or least comparative disadvantage. However certain real world concentrations mean that in practice this does not always occur. Many countries such as the UK have developed an *industrial base* over a long period of time. This has resulted in considerable investment in plant and machinery, the development of a labour force with specific skills and the establishment of a sophisticated infrastructure. This situation may prove incompatible with the most efficient deployment of UK and world resources today. The employment of more than one million people in the UK motor industry is a considerable investment in plant and labour which cannot be easily disregarded. This is despite the fact that other countries such as Japan can and do produce motor cars more cheaply and efficiently than the UK. It could be argued that the UK car industry should be allowed to run down and resources diverted to other products for which the UK has a greater comparative advantage. However the cost of change both in the waste of economic resource and the social upheaval involved would be so drastic that it may be better for the country to support the industry in the short and medium term.

Other influences such as security or political factors may indicate that certain industries should be maintained domestically despite the availability of cheaper products abroad. Most nations prefer to supply a substantial part of their food and energy needs domestically to prevent loss of supplies in time of war or other such crisis. Also some countries clearly have political motives in discouraging trade with nations holding conflicting views. Trade embargoes between East and West have occurred in order to exert political pressure although trade may be mutually advantageous. For example, the Arab countries attempt to

416

force some of their trading partners to sign an agreement by which they will boycott trade with Israel in an attempt to pressurise and isolate that country.

UKs trading partners

The UK has traditionally been dependent on international trade to meet its needs and develop its economy. In recent years, Britain has tended to trade more with the other members of the Common Market and less with its old Commonwealth trading partners. This trend was apparent prior to joining the EEC and has continued. Today the EEC and the USA are our most important markets as well as suppliers.

During the world recession of the late 1970s and early 1980s many commentators have argued that the UK should impose restrictions on imports in order to protect domestic employment. Many industries, such as cars, paper and textiles, are suggested as examples of where the government should impose *import quotas and tariffs*. These would either reduce the quantity of foreign products imported or reduce their competitiveness by increasing their price. Later in this chapter the arguments for and against imposing such measures will be considered but certainly such moves would be against the general trend of reducing trade restrictions throughout the world. Britain is a member of the *General Agreement on Tariffs and Trade (GATT)* and through this body it has sought in conjunction with most of the other trading nations of the world to move towards an elimination of quotas and a reduction of tariffs. GATT has been a considerable success since it began in 1947. This is despite certain weaknesses which have become apparent. Examples include the failure to agree on the liberalisation of agricultural trade; loopholes which permit a country to impose quotas if it has a 'temporary' balance of payments problem or to protect vulnerable domestic industries; and the subsidisation of exports by some governments to increase their world competitiveness. Nevertheless it has achieved a reduction in the number of tariffs and quotas restricting world trade.

Britain's membership of the *European Economic Community* is somewhat restrictive since the common external tariff imposed by the Community on many imported products from outside the EEC raises prices substantially. Any further tariff restrictions introduced by the UK independently which only relate to non EEC countries because of the EEC structure, would increase import prices still further and fuel domestic inflation. This is considered in detail later in the chapter.

The currency of international trade

The importance of international trade to the world economy is self evident. However, it would be impossible to achieve international trading between numerous countries in diverse commodities without a *means of exchange.* Some of the world's trade is in the form of barter. This is a notable feature of East-West trade agreements, eg the USA builds power stations in China in return for textiles. This is because the West does not wish to accept 'weak' Communist currencies as they tend to be overvalued officially. They are of limited value to the West which does not need Eastern bloc imports as much as the Eastern bloc needs Western exports. However *barter* is only possible if there exists a *mutual coincidence of needs,* that is, one country has what another needs and vice versa. Therefore most trade in the world is paid for using some form of currency. In the past, gold and silver were used as acceptable currencies in world trade as their weight indicated their value. Although gold is still used to a limited extent, most trade is now transacted using paper currencies. The US dollar has become the most frequently used means of exchange, for example oil, which makes up a substantial amount of world trade, is valued in dollars. However it is necessary to set an *exchange value* for the currency used against the trading partners' own currency. A Swedish manufacturer's workers will not be paid in English pounds or US dollars and so if this manufacturer exports to the UK payment is required in Swedish krona. Alternatively, the pounds paid may be exchanged into krona. Thus, either the English importer must transfer the pounds into krona prior to purchase, or the Swedish seller must exchange the pounds after the sale. In either case an international currency exchange must take place and there must be a rate of exchange by which it is possible to give a comparative value, eg £1 sterling is equivalent to 9.75 Swedish krona. Each country's currency will then have a value not only domestically, but also in relation to the amount of other currencies which can be exchanged for it. This changing relationship and the importance of the value of the pound to the UK economy is considered in the last part of this chapter but first it is necessary to look at the measure of the UKs annual trade which is covered in the annual Balance of Payments Accounts.

The UKs balance of payments

The UK annually imports and exports goods and services to the value of more than £140 000 million (1980 figures). These imports and exports take the form not only of tangible products such as food, cars, machinery, etc but also of non tangible services such as tourism, transport, insurance. This distinction is important for it gives some indication as to the UKs world standing as a manufacturing nation or as a provider of services. The distinction is illustrated in the way that the government measures the amount of trade which is transacted between the UK and foreign countries. The importance of this is assessed through the *balance of payments*.

A country's balance of payments statement is simply a calculation of the value of the country's trade and other financial transactions with the rest of the world. It is a comprehensive summation of all the individual trading activities in which both the private and public sectors of the economy take part. The balance of payments statement covers a specific period and although it is published every three months, the most important time period is the full year. At this time the government uses the figures to assess whether or not the country has bought or sold more in the previous twelve months.

Current account

The balance of payments is made up of not one but several accounts which are combined to give the overall picture. The first account is the *Current Account*. This covers the import of all goods and services and can be subdivided into the *Visible trade account* and the *Invisible trade account*.

Visible trade

This part of trade is vital for the UKs survival. About half the country's food requirement is produced abroad and although the UK is a major manufacturing nation many of the raw materials it needs must be imported. The UK must buy rubber, zinc, copper, iron ore, etc from abroad. In fact the UK spends about 30% of its national income on imports. (This proportion has grown as the country has become richer and this is characteristic of most developed nations.) Of course the UK could not continue to import on such a large scale unless it was capable of also earning foreign currency by selling its products abroad and in fact the UK is able to sell a variety of items abroad enabling it to pay its way in the world.

Table 9.1 illustrate the components of visible trade of the UK.

Exports	%
Food, beverages and tobacco	7.2
Basic materials	2.8
Fuels	14.5
Manufactured products	72.5
Others	3.0
Total	100.0

Imports	%
Foods, beverages and tobacco	13.1
Basic materials	8.2
Fuels	14.4
Manufactured products	61.6
Others	2.7
Total	100.0

Table 9.1 *Visible trade of the UK*
Source: Monthly Digest of Statistics, March 1981 (HMSO)

Since the Second World War, the UK has tended, in most years, to import more goods than it has exported. This has resulted in a continuing *balance of visible trade deficit* (ie more money going out of the country for visible imports than coming in for visible exports). However, in recent years, particularly since the discovery of North Sea Oil, the UK has not needed to import so much fuel oil and has in fact become a net oil exporter. This has meant that exports have improved relative to imports and the UK has moved into a position of *visible trade surplus*.

This changing situation can be illustrated by comparing the visible trade balance for the twelve years between 1969 and 1980.

Year	Exports £m	Imports £m	Visible trade balance £m
1969	7269	7478	− 209
1970	8150	8184	− 34
1971	9043	8853	+ 190
1972	9437	10185	− 748
1973	11937	14523	− 2586
1974	16394	21745	− 5351
1975	19330	22663	− 3333
1976	25193	29120	− 3927
1977	31734	34012	− 2278
1978	35070	36643	− 1573
1979	40687	44184	− 3497
1980	47376	46199	+ 1177

Table 9.2   UKs balance of visible trade

Source: Economic Trends, March 1981

Invisible trade

From the figures it is clear that the UK had a *massive visible trade deficit* for many years. If this were the only type of trade in which this country were involved then it would have accrued a greater and greater debt. Fortunately, another important aspect of the UKs trade is the import and export of services. As these are not tangible products, this is known as *Invisible trade*. Examples of invisible exports from the UK are the provision of shipping, banking and insurance services to the rest of the world. For these services the UK receives payments and although it will at times have to pay out large sums, eg as insurance claims on shipping losses, its receipts outweigh its payments and it has a *net positive balance*. A further important invisible earner is tourism and foreign visitors bring in invisible earnings as they spend money in this country (this has the equivalent effect of selling a UK product abroad). Of course, UK tourists on holiday abroad have the reverse effect and act as invisible exports. Two other major items of invisible trade are the earnings from UK investment abroad and government spending overseas on such things as a military presence, diplomatic and consular services and the contribution to the EEC. Investment returns on the UKs previous investments abroad produces a net positive balance of almost £1 000 million. This includes both dividends and interest paid to British individuals and organisations and the profits made by British subsidiaries abroad.

Government expenditure abroad is substantial and despite the decline in the UKs role as a world military power, the accession of the UK to the EEC together with the substantial annual contributions which are made and which are not balanced by receipts has meant that the effect on the balance of payments has been detrimental. The following table shows the balance of invisible trade in the UK for recent years.

Year	Exports £m	Imports £m	Invisible trade balance £m
1969	4388	3708	+ 680
1970	5082	4269	+ 813
1971	5649	4763	+ 886
1972	6242	5305	+ 937
1973	8430	6900	+ 1530
1974	10400	8429	+ 1971
1975	11307	9468	+ 1659
1976	14799	11932	+ 2867
1977	16582	14510	+ 2072
1978	18582	16378	+ 2280
1979	22832	20965	+ 1867
1980	25023	23463	+ 1560

Table 9.3 UKs balance of invisible trade

Source: Economic Trends, March 1981

The sum of visible and invisible trade is called the *Current Account of the Balance of Payments* and may be seen as the country's ability to pay its way in the world without recourse to borrowing or using accumulated reserves of foreign currency.

Some help on interpreting the balance of payments may be useful. If the figures for the balance of visible or invisible trade have a minus sign (−) in front this meant that more money has left the country than has come into it, *a trade deficit*. If there is no sign or a positive sign (+) this indicates that more money has come into the country than has been taken out, *a trade surplus*. Thus on its current account, the UK had a trade deficit for the following years: 1973, 74, 75, 76, 77 and 79, and a trade surplus for 1969, 70, 71, 72, 78 and 80.

The current balance for visible and invisible trade since 1969 is shown in Table 9.4:

Year	Visible trade balance £m	Invisible trade balance £m	Current balance £m
1969	− 209	+ 680	+ 471
1970	− 34	+ 813	+ 779
1971	+ 190	+ 886	+ 1076
1972	− 741	+ 937	+ 189
1973	− 2586	+ 1530	− 1056
1974	− 5351	+ 1971	− 3380
1975	− 3333	+ 1659	− 1674
1976	− 3927	+ 2867	− 1060
1977	− 2278	+ 2072	− 206
1978	− 1573	+ 2280	+ 707
1979	− 3497	+ 1867	− 1630
1980	+ 1177	+ 1560	+ 2737

Table 9.4 Current balance of UK trade
(Visible and Invisible trade)

Source: Economic Trends, March, 1981

It is worth pointing out that the UK tends to act as a middleman for a considerable amount of the world's trade. Many of the imports recorded on the debit side of the current account are often re-exported following processing or manufacture into finished products and thus appear again as exports with value added on the credit side of the current account.

Despite these exports and re-exports it is clear that in the post war period the visible account has been in deficit more often than in surplus and this has been known as the *Trade Gap* (generally the visible trade account is called the *Balance of Trade*).

The invisible balance, normally in surplus, has offset the Trade deficit and this stresses the importance of invisible trade to the UK economy. It is hoped that with the increased exploitation of North Sea Oil the current account should move into a considerable surplus in the 1980s.

Investment and captial flows account

The second part of the balance of payments is often called the *Capital Account* although its correct title is the *Investment and Capital Flows Account*. This lists the transfer of capital into and out of the country. It is the result of investments, government lending or borrowing and the transfer of money through bank accounts.

The Account is subdivided into:

a) *official capital flows*,
b) *private capital flows*.

a) *Official capital flows*

The UK government lends money to other countries (usually less developed countries — ldc's). Most of this money is in the form of official development assistance (ODA) which is defined as government-financed aid given or lent on concessionary terms for non-military purposes. Part of this money will be repaid and usually with some interest, and so represents a future credit to the balance of payments, but its immediate effect on being given is to be a deficit. ODA from Britain has tended in recent years to fall as a percentage of the UK Gross National Product and despite the recommendations of the *Brandt Commission* in 1979 that all developed countries should contribute about 0.6% of gnp to help the ldc's, Britain currently gives less than 0.4% in economic aid. This has been as a result of lessening ties with the Commonwealth, the feeling that some ldc's, eg Brazil, Korea, Turkey, are no longer in need of so much aid, and the domestic budgetary constraints felt in the UK during the recession.

b) *Private capital flows*

UK individuals and organisations invest money abroad in the hope of earning profit. This may be invested in foreign owned operations or in the foreign subsidiaries of UK companies. Prior to 1979, the government sought to restrict the outflow of UK funds through strict *currency controls*. However, once these capital transfer restrictions were lifted, the attraction of higher potential investment earnings abroad resulted in a substantial increase in the annual outflow of capital funds. Of course, should these investments prove profitable they will result in a net influx of earnings in the future but the investment lost to the UK acts as a brake on domestic economic growth. To some extent this is compensated for by foreign investment in the UK. However, the UK domestic recession has had a somewhat negative effect on earning potential of investment in this country and so it has tended to decline in real terms.

Clearly it would be more beneficial to the UK economy if foreign investment in this country was always greater than UK investment abroad since this would improve employment and increase the demand for capital goods in the UK. This is obviously of concern to the government.

Currency speculation

A further complication in this part of the balance of payments is the influx and outflow of money not used for investment but simply placed in UK banks as *interest earning deposits*. This is done by foreign governments, companies and individuals who seek to place their available cash where it is able to earn the greatest rewards. Some of these flows are used to finance international trade transactions but much is in the form of *'hot money'* so called because it can be quickly and easily transferred between different countries in search of the highest level of return. This return depends on two major factors:

(i) *the rate of interest offered in the country*;
(ii) *the continuing stability of the value of the currency in which it is held*.

Interest rates offered to depositors of capital in commercial banks vary from country to country and are determined by the monetary policy of each particular country's government. If interest rates are high in the UK relative to the rest of the world, this will encourage foreign speculators to deposit capital in this country. This will be shown as a *credit* in the investment and capital flows account. If these speculators then withdraw their deposits and move them to another country, this has the effect of being a *debit* in the account. This country may be reluctant to lose substantial sums of money through such withdrawals and so an increase in interest rates abroad, particularly in the USA, may force the UK government to raise its own interest rates in order to retain deposits.

A further influencing factor on foreign currency speculation is the *strength of the pound*, for speculators are in effect buying pounds when they deposit cash in UK banks. The money is normally held in pounds sterling and so if the pound were to fall in value, they could lose out, despite having a high rate of interest paid. A simple example will illustrate this point. If an American deposits $4m in a London bank and the prevailing exchange rate is $2 = £1, then £2m is credited to that account. The American gains 10% interest per annum and so after one year has a value of £2.2m. Later on this American wishes to withdraw the capital and transfer it back into dollars. However in the meantime the value of the pound has fallen to £1 = $1.75. Thus for £2.2m only $3.85m (2.2 × 1.75) is received and in real terms the American's assets have fallen.

Because of these two factors of interest rates and the changing value of currencies, it is possible to understand why countries with different interest rates are capable of receiving deposits from different countries.

The importance of hot money speculation and its effect on the value of the pound will be considered later in the chapter when looking at floating exchange rates.

A final item must be included in the balance of payments to allow for any errors or omissions which can quite easily result as the statistics are collected and collated. These can be caused by mistakes on the part of traders who may incorrectly record prices or exchange rates for their transactions. Also there is a possibility of statistical error on the part of the government's Statistical Office in the collation of the figures. To counteract any discrepancy an extra entry into the accounts called the *balancing item* is included. When this adjustment is added the accounts should give a reasonable indication of the state of the country's position with regard to trade, capital movements and currency transactions.

Official financing

If the overall balance of payments taking both current and investment and capital flows accounts results in a deficit, this indicates that the country has spent more abroad in the year than it has earned. As with any case of overspending, this must be financed either through borrowing or from a depletion of reserves accumulated in earlier good years. If the country decides to borrow foreign currency, the government has usually turned to the *International Monetary Fund* (IMF) or occasionally to central or commercial banks in other parts of the world.

The IMF acts as a banker to a group of 138 member countries. Each member pays an annual deposit to the IMF known as a *quota* and its amount is determined by the size of the respective country's economy. Obviously the USA has the largest quota to pay although the United Kingdom pays more than France or Japan or West Germany. Quotas are made up of 25% in dollars and 75% in the member country's currency. This results in the Fund having substantial reserves of relatively useless weak currencies. Each member country is entitled to withdraw a percentage of the quota – up to 50% – in foreign currency with few conditions. Additional withdrawals – up to almost 500% of the quota – are available but with increasingly stringent conditions imposed. These loans facilities are usually there on standby and the full amount available is rarely withdrawn.

The IMF is controlled by a board of directors representing the USA, UK, France, West Germany, Japan and Saudia Arabia (who have a directorship as a major IMF creditor) plus 15 other director countries which are elected on a rota basis by the other member countries. The IMF intends its loans to be *short term* and act as means of *solving immediate balance of payments difficulties*. Stringent conditions usually include a declaration by the borrowing nation that it will heed 'advice' to meet certain economic criteria such as a reduction in Public Spending, money supply, imports, etc. This declaration is in the form of a *'letter of intent'* outlining agreement to the main conditions of the loan. Britain last had to turn to the IMF in 1976 and the restrictions imposed have been a strong influence on domestic economic policy in the late 1970s. Once the loan is repaid the conditions obviously need not be adhered to. The strict monetary restrictions imposed by the IMF often may be against a country's economic strategy and thus the IMF tends to be a *lender of last resort*. However, by negotiating standby credit from the IMF, countries often find that commercial banks are willing to make loans to help.

Of course, an alternative to borrowing is the use of a country's *foreign currency reserves*. The UK amasses these in profitable trading years but during periods of balance of payments deficits and during the two world wars these were depleted. The government is reluctant to leave itself without any reserves and as they are by no means limitless, the continual use of them is not feasible. In the next part of the Chapter it will be noted that the government also uses these reserves to maintain the value of the pound when it is under pressure. However before considering how the value of the pound is established it is worth analysing a full balance of payments account and means of financing.

Visible trade (balance)		+ 1 177
Invisible trade (balance)		
services	+ 3 753	
Interest, profits and dividends	− 86	
Transfers	− 2 107	
Total		+ 1 560
Current balance		+ 2 737
Current balance		+ 2 737
Investment and other capital transactions		− 1 490
Balancing item		− 55
Balance for official financing		+ 1 192
Financed as follows:		
Allocation of SDR's and gold subscription to IMF		+ 180
Official reserves (drawings on, + additions to, −)		− 291
Other official financing		− 1 081
		− 1 192

Table 9.5 Balance of Payments (1980)

Source: Economic Trends, March 1981

Establishing the value of the pound

Sterling as a reserve currency

Earlier in the chapter it was noted that much of the world's trade is carried out using dollars (and to a lesser extent using other major currencies such as pounds sterling and Deutschmarks). These are known as *reserve currencies*. In the past, countries also held considerable reserves of gold but this has become less popular as its production is concentrated in particularly sensitive hands, South Africa and the USSR. Now, about 80% of all reserves are held in dollars, 8% in Deutschmarks, 2% in pounds sterling and the remainder in a mixture of other currencies including *Special Drawing Rights* (a composite paper currency issued by the IMF based on a basket of 16 of the world's major trading currencies). This means that the value of these currencies can be influenced not only by the actions of their own countries' governments and trade but also by those of other countries, organisations and individuals. Despite the fact that the pound plays a relatively small part today as a reserve currency, the UK government has expressed the wish to see the pound no longer regarded as a reserve (as have the Germans).

This has been one of the reasons for the development of the SDR system although this has proved slow and unpopular.

Fixed v. floating exchange rates

Prior to 1971, the pound's value was *fixed* in relation to other currencies until the government decided to change it (from 1967 – 71 it was fixed at $2.40c to the pound). This system of *fixed exchange rates* caused difficulties in international trade for it meant that a country which had a higher rate of inflation than its trading partners would tend to lose exports (as they became more expensive to foreigners) and buy more imports (as they tended to become cheaper). A simple example will illustrate the point.

UK manufacturer produces a product for £1.
Exchange rate is $2.40 = £1
and so asks $2.40 for the product in the USA
UK inflation rises at 10% and so the manufacturer's costs rise and the price increases to £1.10p.
With a fixed exchange rate the manufacturer must now ask $2.40 + 10% = $2.64.
If US inflation is low (say 2%) then this is an effective price rise and so discourages purchase.

This is despite the fact that the British manufacturer receives the same real value, ie £1.10 is the same value as £1 a year ago because of inflation.

Because the UK tended to have greater inflation and less attractive products than the rest of the world, the balance of payments was continually in deficit. The problem was mirrored in countries such as Germany and Japan who had continuous large surpluses. There developed a series of international liquidity crises when certain countries continually could not pay their way. So in 1971, a system of *floating exchange rates* was introduced. In theory, this was based on the supply and demand for a currency determining its exchange rate. If the UK does not sell much abroad then foreigners do not have a demand for pounds in order to pay the British exporter. Demand for pounds falls and so does its price – the exchange rate. As the rate falls, the UK exports become cheaper on the world market and so more attractive. Foreigners now buy more British goods and in order to pay for them they must have more pounds. Demand for pounds goes up and the value of the currency stabilises at a point when the balance of payments is *in equilibrium*. Conversely if the UK is selling more abroad than it is importing the demand for pounds in relation to other currencies is high and so the exchange rate goes up, the result being that exports are less competitive and so less are bought and imports become cheaper and so increase.

Thus the price of the pound – the exchange rate – will rise or fall according to demand and supply of currency until demand equals supply, ie when imports match exports and the balance of payments actually balances.

Complications for floating the pound
There are two main problems with allowing the pound to float freely:
1 *Influence of specialisation*
The idea of floating the pound is that the demand for currency with which to trade will be the main determining factor in setting the exchange rate. However, as we have already noted, there is considerable speculation in world currencies using moneys not as a means of financing trade but as a commodity in itself from which profit can be made. There are vast sums of money involved in these capital movements (eg it is estimated that there is approximately $100 billion owned by the Arab oil countries in circulation through the foreign exchange markets of the world in 1981). These vast sums can influence the value of sterling irrespective of the UKs balance of payments situation. If speculators decide independently that they will transfer all their money from sterling to dollars, this will cause a massive growth in demand for dollars and a similar drop in demand (and an increase in supply) of pounds with the result that the pound falls in value against the dollar. This manipulation of the value of sterling, whether intentional or not, by foreign speculators is obviously not a satisfactory state of affairs. During 1980 and early 1981 the pound remained remarkably high in relation to other currencies (approximately $2.40 = £1) because of the high interest rates being offered in London. This made imports into the UK cheap but made British exports abroad more expensive and thus less competitive. The drop in interest rates introduced in the March 1981 budget went some way to discourage holding of sterling and brought the exchange rate down from its artificially high level.
2 *Effect of exchange rate on inflation*
The exchange rate also has a significant effect on the rate of domestic inflation in the UK. The UK is dependent on imports for food, raw materials and many other necessities. These products must be bought even if prices goes up − they have an inelastic demand. A price rise for imported products will be inflationary. Thus if the exchange rate falls 5% this is estimated to result in approximately a 1% increase in domestic inflation,

eg $2.40   = £1
   falls to
   $2.16   = £1 − ie 10% fall
   result   = 2% increase in inflation.

So if a government is seeking to minimise inflation it should attempt to keep the value of the pound as high as possible. However, if they do this it can result in less exports (as they are more expensive abroad) and more imports (because they are cheaper in the UK) and so can lead to a worsening of the balance of payments. This is clearly a dilemma in which the government must decide what it regards as its most urgent priority − inflation or balance of payments problems.

Dirty floating

If the government allows the free operation of the forces to supply and demand then this could result in the pound being too strong (result − possible Balance of Payments deficit) or too weak (result − inflationary consequences) and so the government intervenes and influences the floating of the pound − this is known colloquially as *'dirty floating'*. The government intervenes by manipulating supply or demand for the currency. For instance if the pound is too high then the Bank of England can sell pounds on the world currency markets and so increase supply and thus reduce the exchange rate. Or if the pound is falling too far or too fast, the Bank of England uses its foreign currency reserves and buys pounds on the foreign exchange markets. This causes an increase in demand and so forces the exchange rate up.

However, government intervention of this sort to *'support the pound'* can be expensive for the country as it places a drain on its foreign currency reserves which must be used. It is only really feasible if at other times the pound is strong enough to allow the Bank of England to sell pounds and so use the foreign currency purchased to restore the strength of the reserves.

Future prospects for the UK balance of payments

As we have already noted, the UK has been in balance of payments deficit for most of the last 30 years. However, recently the discovery of North Sea Oil has meant that the large debits created by oil imports have no longer been necessary. The UK has become a net exporter of oil, thus also adding to the credit side. We are also fortunate in some respects that oil prices have been rising because of the cartel pressure of OPEC in forcing massive increases. This has meant that the UK is gaining more in money terms from exporting the same quantity of oil. If oil continues to be in short supply, and there would be little to suggest that demand will drop drastically in the foreseeable future, and if North Sea Oil production continues to rise, as it will, the UK will move more and more into a balance of payments surplus. This situation is also influenced by the fact that UK domestic demand has been declining and so the level of imports has fallen, as a result of domestic recession. However, the favourable balance of payments surplus is somewhat misleading in that UK exports in products or commodities other than oil have not really risen. The high rate of exchange brought about by high interest rates and foreigners' confidence in the pound because it is an 'oil-backed' currency has made the exporters' job even more difficult. Thus, the balance of payments surplus is something of a false picture with regard to UK industrial competitiveness with the rest of the world.

429

If this situation continues what are the possible alternative solutions open to the UK government?

Governmental influence on international trade
There is considerable pressure in this country to try and protect some of our industries from imported competition. Growing unemployment in industries such as textiles, motor cars, steel and coal caused by cheaper imports has led to calls for a *'siege economy'*. This is a colloquial phrase meaning that imports should be restricted by the use of:

a) *Tariffs* – taxes which can be levied on all imports or on specific commodities.
or
b) *Quotas* – restricting the quantity of certain commodities which are allowed to be imported into the UK.

There are several problems involved in the introduction of tariffs and quotas. Firstly, the UK is party to a general agreement which discourages tariffs, GATT (General Agreement on Tariffs and Trade). Secondly, the UK is a member of the European Economic Community (EEC) and this restricts our freedom to influence trade not only to and from the member countries but also in relation to trade from outside the EEC.

Thirdly, there is the possibility of retaliation in that, if the UK imposes tariffs and quotas on imports from specific countries, foreign countries could retaliate and do the same to our exports to their country. (However it has been pointed out that Japan, whose imports are often suggested as a possible target for import control, does not import massively from the UK and so any retaliation would be relatively ineffective.)

Import controls have been suggested as a possible short-term solution which would allow a gradual readjustment of the UKs industries without the rapid upheaval of massive unemployment. Conversely it is argued that this is merely *'featherbedding'* industries which should be allowed to decline and whose resources should be transferred into other more competitive industries.

Tariffs and quotas also make import prices higher and reduce the free choice of the UK domestic consumer.

Another alternative suggested and tried is the encouragement of UK industry to invest and so become more competitive. This may mean giving loans at cheaper rates to exporters or giving them specific tax relief on investment. This can prove difficult in practice as was found in the early 1970s by the Heath Government who sought to encourage British industry to reinvest prior to entry into the EEC. Cheap loans were often not used for investment in exporting industry and, because of lack of control, cheap money was used for property speculation and domestic consumption so helping to fuel inflation.

Other alternatives to a longer term deficit could be to allow (or even

430

force) the value of the pound down so that exports will become cheaper and imports increasingly prohibitively priced. As we have mentioned earlier this may solve the immediate balance of payments problem but exacerbates inflationary pressures.

Finally, if the balance of payments deficit was sufficiently large, as in 1975 – 6, the government may be faced with the need to *deflate the economy* and so reduce the demand for imports. Unfortunately this will have the side effects of making it also more difficult for exporters to produce and can lead to higher domestic unemployment.

The UK is fortunate to have the cushion of North Sea Oil which will hopefully mean that the balance of payments is not a serious problem for the next twenty years or so – but when the oil runs out the country could be faced with a repetition of the difficulties it was presented with in the '50s, '60s and '70s and therefore it should, during the next few years, be attempting to revitalise our export industries and ensure that domestic products are capable of competing with imports.

10 The State

> 'The executive power of the State is simply a committee for managing the common affairs of the entire bourgeois class.'
>
> Karl Marx
> The Communist Manifesto

> 'The State is the servant of the citizen and not his master.'
>
> John F Kennedy
> State of the Union Message
> January 11th 1962

The United Kingdom of Great Britain and Northern Ireland is a geographical area with defined and internationally accepted boundaries, comprising some fifty-six million inhabitants who together constitute a vast but nevertheless highly organised and interdependent community. The administration of this organisation is in the hands of an elected government recognised by the community as being responsible for making and administering those rules considered necessary for the internal regulation of the United Kingdom. In an industrialised society these rules are diverse, complex, sophisticated and affect nearly every aspect of individual and organisational activity. The rules included in this book represent only a fractional part of the total. Annually some sixty to seventy Acts of Parliament are enacted, added to which there are estimated to be in the region of 400 000 precedents.

In addition to internal matters, the government is responsible for the external affairs of the United Kingdom, that is its relationship with other states in the economic and diplomatic spheres. The United Kingdom is therefore a state, an organised political community, and this chapter is concerned with an examination of administrative machinery of this State, its institutions and the relationship of its citizens to these institutions. It is also concerned with the aims of governments and the means they have available to implement them.

The functions of government

Traditionally three principal functions of government are recognised. These are the *legislative function*; the *executive* and the *judicial* function. In order that each of these functions can be carried out there must be governmental institutions to achieve this, namely a *legislature* (Parliament), an *executive* (the Government, the Civil Service) and a *judiciary* (the judges within the courts). In this analysis Parliament creates the rules of law considered appropriate for the government of the United Kingdom. It is then the task of the executive to ensure that they are implemented, as well as carrying out the administration of the

State at a central level. Finally it is for the judiciary to arbitrate in the event of disputes or alleged breaches arising out of any of these matters. The same traditional school of thought which recognises these three basic classes of government functions regards it as essential to a democratic state that each function should be placed in the hands of separate individuals or institutions. The lawmakers should not be authorised to adjudicate over court proceedings concerning laws they have laid down, the administrators should not be allowed to make laws, and so on. This concept of the separation of powers provides a useful starting point in an examination of the workings of the State, but it is important to appreciate two points about it. The first is that the concept of the separation of powers is a theoretical notion which does not accord with the practical reality of the government of modern Britain. Many examples can be put forward to demonstrate that functions are invariably shared. The Law Lords sit as legislators in Parliament and as members of the judiciary, Cabinet ministers perform major roles within the executive as heads of the government departments, while sitting as Members of Parliament, and in addition receive from Parliament delegated legislative powers. The second point is that there is no reason to regard such sharing of functions as necessarily harmful to the liberty of the individual citizen provided that adequate safeguards are available to prevent or overcome abuse.

A notable feature of the system of government in the United Kingdom is the special place of the judiciary. Judges of the superior courts hold office during their 'good behaviour', and since the Act of Settlement 1701, which introduced this requirement, no judge has been dismissed from office. This illustrates the high ethical standards of the judiciary. The provision of the Act of 1701 also asserts the independence of the judiciary from political influence. Judges are able to reach their decisions without fear of political interference or pressure, and are thus able to act impartially in disputes of a politically sensitive nature. The Tameside case 1977, examined later, provides a good example. An independent judiciary can be regarded as the most valuable safeguard in a State such as ours where there is overlap between legislature and executive.

The characteristics of the British Constitution

The constitution of a state is the body of fundamental principles and rules which a) define the compositions and powers of the organs of government, and b) describe the relationship of the organs of government both towards each other and to the individual citizen. The constitution is therefore fundamental to the legal system for it defines the legislature and identifies its powers. The British Constitution is a product of many centuries growth during which various influences have moulded it. Among the characteristics of the British Constitution the following features are worth noting:

(i) *Its unwritten character*   Although constitutional documents do exist, for instance Magna Carta 1215 and the European Communities Act 1972, no single document or group of connected documents contains the Constitution. This illustrates the long period over which the Constitution has evolved. It is in fact a combination of common law, statute and *convention*, ie legally unenforceable rules which are observed for practical reasons. The place of convention in the government of the United Kingdom is one of the most remarkable features of the Constitution. The Monarch has wide powers, both statutory and prerogative, and it is for instance necessary for the Monarch's approval to be given to bills passed by Parliament. By convention this approval is not withheld, although strictly speaking the Monarch does have the prerogative power to refuse assent. The Government of the day is led by a Prime Minister and assisted by a Cabinet, although there is no statutory or common law rule requiring this. By virtue of the existence, through convention, of a Cabinet comprising government ministers, there is a further convention that the Monarch acts in accordance with Ministerial advice, although possessing the prerogative power to dismiss Ministers according to the Monarch's pleasure. One final convention is worth noting, namely that of the courts following the doctrine of binding precedent. Under this doctrine a court is guided by past decisions of the courts, and is bound to follow those decisions where the facts established in the present case are materially the same as those occurring in previous decisions.

(ii) *A limited monarchy*   Despite possessing considerable legal powers, in practice the power of the Monarch in matters of state is very limited.

(iii) *Parliamentary sovereignty*   The Queen in Parliament has the power to make any law, or revoke any law. No other body has the power to override Parliament. This law-making supremacy enables Parliament to effect constitutional change by ordinary legislation. As a consequence of the accession of the UK to the European Economic Community there has been a loss of Parliamentary Sovereignty. The law-making institutions of the Community can make laws which become binding on all the member states as soon as they are created. Such laws are known as *regulations*, and in the UK these 'self-executing' regulations become a part of our law without reference to Parliament. To this extent there is a body with legislative powers exceeding the powers of Parliament, but it must be remembered that community law is not concerned with many domestic matters, for instance criminal law. In addition it is a fundamental feature that in the same way that entry into the community was achieved, that is by an Act of Parliament, so the same means can be used to *withdraw* from the community. What the political and economic consequences of such action might be are of course the subject of much debate.

(iv) *Flexibility* Since there are no special procedures laid down for altering constitutional rules the Constitution can be regarded as very flexible.

(v) *Executive influence over the legislature* Creating legislation is the ultimate means at the disposal of the Government of the day for implementing its policies. Since the Government will command majority support in Parliament there is little danger of it being unable to pass the legislation it sponsors, thus it is not Parliament which governs, but rather the Government which governs through Parliament. Nevertheless the Government *is* likely to take note of the opinion of Parliament as a whole, especially the back-benchers of its own party, and of the opinion of the electorate as a whole.

The judiciary

The independence of the judiciary has already received mention. It is regarded as essential that not only should justice be done in the courts, but also be seen to be done. Little confidence in the impartiality of the judiciary would exist if appointments were politically based, for judges would be regarded as servants of the Government in legal proceedings in which the Government had an interest. Independence is maintained in the following ways:

a) Members of the judiciary are prevented from becoming members of the House of Commons under the House of Commons Disqualification Act 1975 (although judges who are made peers can sit in the House of Lords).

b) By convention judges do not take sides in politically controversial matters, although they may criticise the content of legislation and the way it is expressed, and may criticise the conduct of members of the Executive, for instance when executive powers have been misused. The statements of the judiciary are not regarded as matters which members of the Executive, or Parliament, should make comment on.

c) It appears that all members of the judiciary enjoy immunity from liability in damages arising out of their judicial activities, for example trying a case. This was the view of the Court of Appeal in *Sirros* v. *Moore* (1975) where the plaintiffs action against a circuit judge for false imprisonment failed. The reason for this immunity, in the words of Lord Denning, 'is not because the judge has any privilege to make mistakes or to do wrong, it is so that he should be able to do his duty with complete independence and free from fear'.

It is appropriate to add here that barristers and it seems solicitors, representing their clients in court proceedings enjoy immunity from action founded in the tort of negligence brought by the client in respect of the proceedings: *Rondel* v. *Worsley* (1969).

d) Mention has already been made of the fact that judges hold office during their good behaviour. This is an important safeguard of their independence for it means that they cannot be removed from office for displeasing the Government of the day.

e) Appointments of Magistrates, circuit judges and High Court judges are made by or on the advice of the Lord Chancellor, who is a member of the Cabinet and head of the judiciary. In the case of appointments to the Court of Appeal (whose judges are known as Lords Justices of Appeal) and to the House of Lords (whose judges are known as Lords of Appeal in Ordinary) the Prime Minister makes the appointment acting on the advice of the Lord Chancellor.

These appointments, apart from the appointment of lay magistrates, are not in practice based upon political considerations.

The legislature

Legislation may be defined as the formulation of law by the Queen in Parliament, the law begins life as a bill and becomes an Act of Parliament after the Royal Assent has been given. The United Kingdom Parliament sits at Westminster, and is *bicameral*, ie consists of two Chambers, an upper House and a lower House. The upper House is the House of Lords. Its members are non-elected. They include the Lords Spiritual – the Bishops and Archbishops of the Church of England, and the Lords Temporal – hereditary peers, and life peers, a larger group, whose titles are created under the Life Peerages Act 1958.

The House of Commons, the lower House, is composed of Members of Parliament elected by universal franchise for each of the parliamentary constituencies of the United Kingdom, a total of 635 seats. A substantial body of legislation controls the franchise, including the Ballot Act 1872, which provides for the secret ballot, and the Representation of the People Act 1969, which fixes the age of eligibility to vote at 18.

'A parliament' sits between the Royal proclamation that summons it and dissolves it. The Monarch attends the opening of a new parliament. A meeting of Parliament is known as a *session*, of which there are usually two each year. The sessions are divided into sittings which are separated by adjournments, and may be on a day-to-day basis or for a longer period. A Parliament automatically dies at the end of a period of five years from the first summoning of it, if it has not already been dissolved.

Functions of Parliament

It is during parliamentary sessions that the legislative, or law-making function is carried out. If a bill has not passed all the stages necessary to become an Act before the end of a session it *lapses* and must be reintroduced again in the next session. Parliament is also concerned with the granting of consent to the spending of public revenue. It is furthermore regarded as a guardian of the interests of the nation with the duty of controlling the Government. This occurs in two ways – the accountability of Ministers during *question time*, and *debates* on proposed legislation. The publicity connected to these activities helps to act as a deterrent towards corrupt or unethical practices.

Types of legislation

(i) *Government bills* – most legislation passed by Parliament is introduced by the Government, and sponsored by it during its passage through the various stages. Such legislation is the most tangible form of the implementation of Government policy.

(ii) *private members bills* – all MPs and members of the Lords are entitled to present their own Bills before Parliament, but they can only do so during time allocated for the purpose by Parliament. Usually such legislation is only successful if adopted by the Government. A further classification of bills is into:

a) *public bills*   these relate mainly to government policy and they are of general application, unless otherwise stated. Examples include the Competition Act 1980, and the Employment Act 1980.

b) *private bills*   these are of limited operation, applying to a specific organisation, or even individual, and usually conferring powers, for instance the Glamorgan Act 1976 which conferred powers on Glamorgan County Council. Private bills do not affect the general law.

How legislation is made

The task of drafting bills is largely carried out by *Parliamentary Counsel to the Treasury*, a staff of barristers. Legislation passes through the following stages:

First reading   This is simply a formality. The short title of the bill is read out ie it is a notification of the Bill to the House. It is then printed.

Second reading   This takes the form of a general debate on the Bill. Since 1965 this reading may take a purely procedural form, on the giving of 10 days notice, unless more than 20 members rise to object. If it is debated there is a *division* and if the Bill survives it moves to the committee stage.

Committee stage   Here details to proposed *amendments* are discussed, the Bill being dealt with clause by clause. The committee will usually be a *standing* committee consisting of between 20 and 50 members, appointed at the beginning of the session, and reflecting in its constitution the relative strengths of the parties in Parliament. The House may refer the Bill to a *select* committee which is smaller than a standing committee. Money Bills, in particular the annual Finance Bill ('the Budget'), are dealt with at the committee stage by the *whole House*.

Report stage   After the committee stage the Bill is reported to the whole House, where further amendments may be made. Amendments made in committee stage may also be discussed although the Speaker has the power to select amendments and may decide not to call one that has been fully discussed in committee.

Third reading   After the Report stage the Bill is 'put down' for its third reading. This is the final debate. If the motion that 'the bill now be read a third time' is carried it is deemed to have passed the Commons and is sent to the Lords.

The Lords   The procedure followed in the Lords is similar to the Commons. The Lords may (i) agree the Bill, or (ii) amend the Bill and return it to the Commons 'endorsed'. If so, the Commons may give their assent to it or amend and return it to the Lords. Under the Parliament Act 1911, a Bill certified by the Speaker as a money Bill and having passed through the Commons must be passed by the Lords within one month, without amendment, or the Royal Assent may be given without the concurrence of the upper House.

Under the Parliament Act 1949, any public Bill passed by the Commons in two *successive* sessions and rejected by the Lords in both cases may receive the Royal assent without their agreement, provided a year has elapsed between the second reading of the first session, and the third reading during the second session.

The Royal Assent   After completion of these stages the Bill is sent for the Royal Assent, which is now merely a formality. By the Royal Assent Act 1967, the Bill becomes an Act of Parliament when the Royal Assent is notified by the Speaker to each House sitting separately.

Delegated or subordinate legislation

For a variety of reasons it is not possible for Parliament to provide sufficient legislation to meet the needs of such a complex industrialised society as the United Kingdom. As a response, Parliament grants restricted powers to other bodies and individuals, for example local authorities and Ministers, to create legislation themselves. Such legislation is known, not surprisingly, as delegated or subordinate legislation, and it represents a vital and extensive source of law making.

The main advantages, and reasons for the growth of this form of legislation are:

a) *Insufficient Parliamentary time* to satisfy all legislative needs. In particular, detailed rules are best dealt with at Ministerial level or by subordinate bodies set up for the purpose, for instance the Health and Safety Commission created under the Health and Safety at Work Act 1974.

b) *The lack of a rapid Parliamentary procedure* for the creation of legislation, and the fact that Parliament is not always in session prompts the need for a means of legislating rapidly and efficiently. It must be added however that Parliament itself can, in exceptional circumstances, enact legislation in a matter of hours.

c) *Future problems* arising out of Parliamentary legislation are often best dealt with by Executive action.

d) *Parliament may lack sufficient knowledge* to legislate in areas of technical complexity. Such matters can be more appropriately dealt with by experts within the appropriate government departments.

ELIZABETH II

Sale of Goods Act 1979

1979 CHAPTER 54

An Act to consolidate the law relating to the sale of goods.   [6th December 1979]

BE IT ENACTED by the Queen's most Excellent Majesty, by and with the advice and consent of the Lords Spiritual and Temporal, and Commons, in this present Parliament assembled, and by the authority of the same, as follows:—

PART I

CONTRACTS TO WHICH ACT APPLIES

1.—(1) This Act applies to contracts of sale of goods made on or after (but not to those made before) 1 January 1894. Contracts to which Act applies.

(2) In relation to contracts made on certain dates, this Act applies subject to the modification of certain of its sections as mentioned in Schedule 1 below.

(3) Any such modification is indicated in the section concerned by a reference to Schedule 1 below.

(4) Accordingly, where a section does not contain such a reference, this Act applies in relation to the contract concerned without such modification of the section.

Despite the inevitable need for delegated legislation, there are a number of criticisms levelled at it. It is suggested that Parliamentary control over legislation is reduced, that the diversity and quantity of this form of legislation makes it impossible to keep up with changes in the law, (ignorance of a statutory instrument is not a defence), that there is a lack of publicity attached to such legislation, and that on occasions powers are granted in the parent Act enabling others to legislate on the matters of principle. There are however two important safeguards which operate to control the operation of delegated legislation. Firstly the courts have the power to scrutinise the exercise of delegated law making functions, and may declare as *ultra vires* (beyond the power) any such legislation which falls outside the legal boundaries imposed by the parent Act. In such circumstances the legislation will be rendered void. Secondly Parliament itself has provided certain checks, for instance the 'Scrutinising Committee', a select committee which has the task of examining subordinate legislation laid before Parliament, and must report any matter requiring special attention. These matters include legislation which the committee consider requires elucidation.

Types of delegated legislation

a) *Orders in Council* These grant extensive powers to the Privy Council, and are used to deal with emergenices such as the government of Northern Ireland following the Suspension of the Northern Ireland Parliament of Stormont under the Northern Ireland (Temporary provisions) Act 1972.

b) *Statutory instruments* These are the legislative documents made by Ministers, and must be laid before Parliament.

c) *By-laws* District Councils and the London Boroughs have general powers conferred on them under the Local Government Act 1972, to make by-laws for the good rule and government of the areas for which they have responsibility, and for the suppression of nuisances within them. This general power is supplemented by numerous specific powers contained in other legislation relating to highways (Highways Act 1980), housing (Housing Act 1957), public health (Public Health Act 1936), and local recreational facilities (Local Government Planning and Land Act 1980).

Offences created under the general power deal with such matters as:

    (i) Music near churches or hospitals,
   (ii) Dangerous games in the streets,
  (iii) The fouling of footpaths by dogs,
  (iv) Cycling on the footpaths,
   (v) Indecent language,
  (vi) Nuisances contrary to public decency.

There are two main limitations on the by-law making powers of local authorities:

a) All by-laws require confirmation by the confirming authority (Secretary of State).

b) If challenged as invalid, a by-law must satisfy the court's scrutiny.

a) *Confirming authority* (Secretary of State) — there is a strict procedure that a local authority must adhere to in exercising its by-law making powers. Notice of intention to submit the by-law for confirmation must be published, after which it is submitted to the confirming authority who will both determine whether the by-law is necessary and also decide whether the by-law is likely to satisfy judicial scrutiny.

    The confirming authority has the power to confirm or reject the by-law, but even if confirmed, the by-law may still be subjected to scrutiny by the courts.

b) *Judicial scrutiny* — in the case of *public* statutes the courts have no power to question their validity. As far as by-laws are concerned, however, the courts have developed a number of rules so that their validity may be tested. They will be invalid if they are

1 *Ultra vires* — In exercising by-law making powers a local authority must ensure that the strict limits of the power given by the statute are not exceeded.

    In *R* v. *Wood* (1855) the Public Health Act 1848, conferred power on Boards of Health to make by-laws relating to the removal by an occupier of dust, ashes, rubbish, and soil. A by-law made by a board requiring the occupier to remove snow was held to be invalid as ultra vires the enabling power;

2 *Inconsistent with the general law* — If a by-law attempts to permit what a public statute forbids or forbid what a public statute permits, it may be declared invalid as contrary to the general law.

    In *Powell* v. *May* (1946) a local authority made a by-law to prohibit betting in a public place despite the Betting and Lotteries Act 1934 allowing such betting in certain circumstances. The by-law was held to be invalid as contrary to the general law;

3 *Uncertain* – To be valid, a by-law must be positive and unambiguous in its terms.

> In *Nash* v. *Finlay* (1901) a by-law provided that 'no persons shall wilfully annoy passengers in the street'. It was held to be void on the grounds of uncertainty:

4 *Unreasonable* – While the attitude of the courts is that a by-law should be supported if possible, they will nevertheless declare one invalid if it is obviously unjust in its operation, demonstrates bad faith, or was shown to involve an oppressive interference with individual rights.

> The ground of unreasonableness was relied on in the case of *Burnley Borough Council* v. *England and others* (1977). Here the local authority had infuriated dog owners by introducing a by-law to prohibit the entry of dogs (except guide dogs) into its public parks and pleasure grounds. The validity of the by-law was challenged on the ground of unreasonableness in its operation. This challenge was rejected by the Court who felt that the by-law was not discriminatory in nature.

The relationship between legislation and case law

Since Parliament is free to alter all law, a power not vested in the judiciary, it follows that the instruments of Parliament's law-making power, statutes, should take priority whenever they are in conflict with case law, ie the law contained in precedents, and that developments of common law shall not take priority over existing statute. Nor do the courts have the power to declare an Act of Parliament ultra vires, although it has been seen that this power is available in relation to delegated legislation. It is worth remembering that statute, unlike case law, never becomes obsolete, and that Parliament is for obvious reasons far better placed to institute legal change than the judges.

The executive

The executive composes the central government and the central administration, and there are four distinct bodies which together constitute the executive.

1 *The Privy Council*
   This is headed by the Lord President of the Council, and its members include the Monarch, members of the Cabinet, and Lords Justices of Appeal. Its main responsibility is the issue of Orders in Council, a powerful form of delegated legislation.

2 The Government of the day

This is lead by the Prime Minister, a post which became established during the nineteenth century as the party system emerged. Since the turn of the century the Prime Minister has additionally held the sinecure post of First Lord of the Treasury. The functions of the Prime Minister are:

a) to form a government and preside as Chairman of the Cabinet, choosing who shall serve on it;
b) to act as the principal channel of communication between the Cabinet and the Monarch;
c) to ensure that Cabinet decisions are implemented by the various government departments, and to generally supervise the administration.

The Cabinet

The Cabinet consists of approximately 20 Ministers. The majority of them are heads of government departments, such as the Home Office, the Department of Employment, etc. The Cabinet may meet up to twice a week. In addition to Cabinet appointments the Prime Minister will make a number of other government appointments – junior Ministers, Parliamentary secretaries and under-secretaries. The term 'the Ministry', 'the Government' or 'the Administration' is the collective term used to describe all holders of Ministerial office, most of whom will be Members of Parliament, although occasionally members of the House of Lords hold such office.

The Cabinet is the nucleus of the Government. The members are bound by the doctrine of *collective responsibility*, which requires them to accept and support every Cabinet decision, so that both inside and outside Parliament a common front is presented. The doctrine is simply a convention, but it may be seen as a means of preserving confidence in government policies. It is worth noting that if a government is out-voted on a major policy issue it is a convention that it should resign. Cabinet members are also bound to observe secrecy.

> In *Attorney-General* v. *Jonathan Cape* (1975) an injunction was sought to prevent publication of extracts from the Crossman Diaries, a record of Cabinet meetings held between 1964 and 1970. The court held that in the circumstances it was in the interests of the public that they be kept informed of these matters, and that after ten years had passed, matters referred to in Cabinet discussion had lost their confidentiality. It was also decided that publication did not affect the doctrine of collective responsibility.

Cabinet Ministers are also responsible for the wrongful acts carried out by their Ministries.

Nowadays the title *Secretary of State* is used in place of the title Minister, to describe members of the Cabinet.

443

3 Government departments

These form the heart of the central administration, and there are over 20 of them. (They are known collectively as 'Whitehall'.) Each department is under the political control of the appropriate Minister of State, and consists of a staff of permanent officials (civil servants) headed by a *Permanent Secretary*. In total there are approximately 700 000 civil servants. It is not possible here to exhaustively examine all those departments whose activities affect organisations, but Fig 10.1 identifies four major central government departments and their functions.

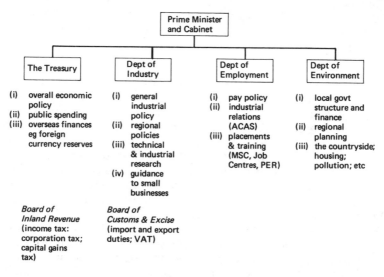

Fig 10.1   Major central government departments and their functions

Other important departments which affect the activities of organisations are the Department of Trade and Consumer Affairs, the Department of Transport and the Ministry of Agriculture, Fisheries and Food (MAFF).

The three departments which may be described as the centre of British Government are the Treasury, the Civil Service Department and the Cabinet Office. *The Treasury* is the most powerful of the three, having responsibility for the control of public spending and the economic performance of the country. As the *First Lord of the Treasury*, the Prime Minister is its nominal head, whereas its working head is the *Chancellor of the Exchequer*.

The *Civil Service department* is responsible for the recruitment, training, organisation and management of the civil service and is headed by the Lord President of the Council. Finally, there is the *Cabinet Office* which is run by the Secretary to the Cabinet and is

444

under the Prime Minister's instructions. It draws up the agenda for Cabinet meetings and includes the individuals who form the *Central Policy Review Staff* (the 'think tank') who have the important function of advising the government on its strategy after investigating specific areas of policy.

4 *Government agencies*
These institutions are responsible for the organisation and provision of what may be called government services, that is those areas of activity falling outside the responsibilities of the government departments, but which are nevertheless government provided. Such institutions are ultimately government controlled, through supervision exercised by the appropriate minister. These areas of activity fall into the following categories. Government agencies are responsible for the organisation of what can be called government services, that is areas of activity outside those of government departments, which are ultimately government controlled, through supervision by an appropriate Minister. These activities fall into three main categories:

(i) the supply of certain nationalised *commodities* – coal, steel, iron, etc.
(ii) the supply of certain *public services* – postal and telecommunications, gas, electricity.
(iii) the supply of *welfare services* – the NHS, pensions, supplementary benefits.

The Administration of local government
Local government administration is performed by the local authorities. In England and Wales these authorities are:

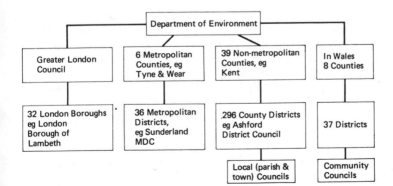

Fig 10.2   Local authorities

445

Local authorities have *elected members* who decide policy, and they employ *permanent staff* who carry out policy decisions and actually operate and run services, in particular education, housing, police and fire services, environmental health, etc.

The activities of local authorities are controlled by:

a) *Parliament – which grants them their powers.* The Local Government Act 1972, which puts into effect the new local government structure (see Fig 10.2) – except for London which was reorganised in 1965 – is one of a number of Acts which grants legal powers to local authorities. In particular S. 111 of the LGA 1972, confers general power on an authority to do anything which is calculated to facilitate, or is conducive or incidental to the discharge of any of its functions. Of course the powers of local government can be altered or removed at any time by an Act of Parliament.

b) *Central government departments*, notably the Department of the Environment. Most of the spending by local authorities is met out of the rate support grant from central government.

c) *The courts*, which are able to exercise control over all administrative action, central and local, and can award certain legal remedies to persons and organisations who having a sufficient interest in the matter are aggrieved by some act or omission of a member of central or local government. Remedies include:

  (i)   damages;
  (ii) injunctions and specific performances (except against the Crown);
  (iii) declaratory judgements.

In addition to these 'ordinary' remedies judicial control is exercised by means of the prerogative orders which are dealt with later.

The United Kingdom and the European Economic Community
It has previously been noted that the accession of the United Kingdom into the European Economic Community (EEC) by the European Communities Act, 1972, caused a partial loss of parliamentary sovereignty. This occurred voluntarily, and the powers lost by Parliament are now in the hands of the law making institutions of the Community. These are the *Council of Ministers* and the European Commission. Between them they can make three distinct types of law, *Regulations, Directives and Decisions*. These laws are concerned with general matters of trade and are designed to promote the primary objective of the Community, namely the establishment of a single economic unit made up by the individual member states in which there will be a free movement of labour, goods and capital.

Regulations: these apply in all the member states as soon as they come into force. No reference has to be made to Parliament.

446

Directives: these are also binding on the individual members states, but they are brought into operation by each state issuing statutory instruments to this effect, ie they are not *self executing*.

Decisions: these apply only to a particular state, organisation or individual.

In addition to the Council and the Commission there are two other major Community institutions, the European Parliament and the European Court of Justice. The Parliament is essentially a consultative body, and it consists of elected representatives representing constituencies throughout the countries of the Community. In the United Kingdom these constituencies represented by the 'Euro MPs' are considerably larger than those represented by MPs elected to Parliament at Westminster. The European Court has the task of interpreting the meaning of the three Treaties upon which the Community is based. It was the Third Treaty, the Treaty of Rome 1957, which set up the EEC. The Court also hears disputes involving the Commission, the Council, individual member states, and sometimes even individuals. Of particular importance is the jurisdiction of the European Court under Article 177 of the Treaty of Rome, 1957. This provides that where a case is before a national court from which there is no further right of appeal (in the United Kingdom this is the House of Lords) and the case involves the interpretation of one of the Treaties, the action must be suspended and a preliminary ruling of the European Court obtained. Once the preliminary ruling has been issued the national court will then proceed with the case, applying the ruling of the European Court as appropriate, which cannot be questioned. In relation to Community law, therefore, the jurisdiction of the House of Lords as the highest appellate court in the UK is cut down. It may be noted that in those cases which the European Court has heard and issued a judgement it has no means of enforcing the judgment. This is provided by means of the enforcement systems of the individual member states. Finally a gradual harmonisation of laws is taking place, as Parliament brings United Kingdom law into line with community law. An illustration of this is provided by the Competition Act, 1980. The Act uses the wording of Article 85 of the Treaty of Rome to define 'anti-competitive practices' within the United Kingdom, thus harmonising domestic law on this matter with Community law.

Methods of dispute resolution

The interaction between individuals, organisations and the state generates a large number of conflict situations. These conflicts are dealt with in a variety of ways, both informal and formal. The courts and tribunals provide the formal means of conflict resolution, and they are now considered.

The structure of the courts

The structure of the courts in England and Wales consists of two separate sets of courts. There are the civil courts dealing with private disputes between individuals and organisations, and the criminal courts which are concerned with prosecutions brought against individuals or organisations for alleged breaches of the criminal law. In distinguishing the rules of the civil law from those of the criminal the words of Lord Diplock in *Knuller* v. *Director of Public Prosecutions* (1972) are most helpful. 'Civil liability is concerned with the relationship of one citizen to another; criminal liability is concerned with the relationship of a citizen to society organised as a state.' There are many examples throughout this book of criminal rules and civil law rules to identify the purposes for which they exist. It has to be said that there is no universally accepted definition of what a crime is or ought to be, although it is clear that criminal law, as a branch of public law, concerns behaviour which can be regarded as affecting the interests of society as a whole. Criminal conduct includes in addition to the traditional offences of murder, theft etc, a wide range of regulatory offences. Such would include when an organisation causes environmental pollution or operates a factory in a manner which represents a threat to the health or safety of the workforce.

Civil disputes

Contrary to what is commonly believed most private disputes never reach the courts for trial. In many cases the matter will be resolved without the parties resorting to litigation at all, and this outcome will carry with it the advantage of savings in time and money for the parties concerned. Indeed the cost of proceedings may in itself act as a deterrent to a party with a legal grievance. It is common to find specific provision made in commercial agreements for disputes to be referred to *arbitration*. Referring a dispute to arbitration, for example in the case of an important civil engineering project, has a number of advantages over court proceedings. For as well as being cheaper and much quicker, the arbitrator will be someone with technical knowledge who will be more readily able to grasp the complexities of the problem. And, unlike court proceedings, arbitration proceedings will be heard in private, which will prevent undesirable publicity, and is particularly useful if the dispute involves commercial or trade secrets. The court has certain powers in relation to arbitration agreements under the Arbitration Act 1951. It can for instance *stay a court action* brought by a party in breach of an arbitration agreement, until such time as the arbitrator has made the award. Any attempt by the parties to an arbitration agreement to oust the jurisdiction of the courts is however void on the grounds of illegality, and the court will have the power to hear the matter. In *Ford* v. *Clarksons Holidays Ltd* (1971) it was held that a provision in an arbitration agreement that the award of the arbitrator 'shall be accepted as final' did not oust the court's jurisdiction. It is appropriate to add here that arbitration provisions are a common feature of contracts between tour operators and holiday makers.

Even in cases where the process of litigation is commenced, by the plaintiff issuing the defendant with a *writ*, a settlement will invariably be reached by the parties before trial (an out of court settlement).

The Civil Courts

The two *first instance* courts administering civil jurisdiction are the County Court and the High Court.

a) *County Courts*   County Courts were created by the County Courts Act 1846, with the original aim of dealing with civil disputes relating to small claims. There are over four-hundred such courts in England and Wales, presided over by *Circuit Judges* who are appointed from barristers of at least ten years standing. The administrative work of County Courts is carried on by a *Registrar* who is a civil servant and must be a solicitor of seven years standing. The majority of civil disputes which lead to court action are now heard in the county courts as their jurisdiction, which is contained in the County Courts Act 1959, has been extended to cover such matters as cases in contract and tort (up to a limit of £5000), housing and landlord and tenant disputes, hire purchase, undefended divorces, many employment disputes, bankruptcy and the winding up of small companies.

Only a small percentage of the numerous county court cases that are begun ever go to full trial. This is often because, when proceedings are commenced against individuals or organisations, they are more likely to back down and fulfil their obligations by repaying a debt, etc.

The county courts operate a *small claims arbitration procedure* which was introduced by the Administration of Justice Act 1973. If the sum involved in a claim does not exceed £500, the matter is referred to the Registrar for arbitration. The dispute can only be heard in open court on certain grounds eg if a complex point of law is involved, or if both the parties have agreed to a trial in open Court. Usually the arbitrator will be the registrar who will hear the case in private and decide the dispute on the basis of statements and documents submitted by the parties without the need for legal representation. This procedure, with the minimal cost attached to it, has proved of great value to the individual, particularly in consumer disputes.

b) *The High Court* − the High Court of Justice was created by the Judicature Acts 1873−5, and is based anywhere in England and Wales. It has a wide jurisdiction over civil disputes and, as a matter of convenience, is split into three divisions − *Queen's Bench*, *Chancery* and *Family*. Judges of the High Court are called *puisne (younger) judges*, and they are allocated to each division by the *Lord Chancellor*.

Two copies of the Plaintiff's particulars of Claim are required before a plaint can be entered, and if there are two or more Defendants to be served, an additional copy for each additional Defendant.

In the   County Court

Entered   19   Plaint No.

To   served by

Statement of Parties

1. **PLAINTIFF'S** names in full and residence or place of business.

2. If suing in a representative capacity, state in what capacity.

3. If a minor required to sue by a next friend, state that fact, and names in full, residence or place of business, and occupation of next friend.

4. If an assignee, state that fact, and name, address and occupation of assignor.

5. If co-partners suing in the name of their firm, add "(Suing as a Firm)".

6. If a company registered under the Companies Act 1948 state the address of the registered office and describe it as such.

7. **DEFENDANT'S** surname and (where known) his or her initials or names in full; Defendant's residence or place of business (if a proprietor of the business).

8. Whether male or female.

9. Whether a minor (where known).

10. Occupation (where known).

11. If sued in a representative capacity, state in what capacity.

12. If co-partners are sued in the name of their firm, or a person carrying on business in a name other than his own name is sued in such name, add "(Sued as a Firm)".

13. If a company registered under the Companies Act 1948 is sued, the address given must be the registered office of the company, and must be so described.

The Defendant is not a person under disability

(Signed)
       Plaintiff

                                                 [P.T.O.

What the Claim is for

Amount Claimed	£
Fee on Entering Plaint	£
Solicitor's Costs	£
TOTAL	£

*[I apply for this action, if defended, to be referred to arbitration.]

*Strike out if inappropriate

Notes

1. Any claim for £500 or less which is defended will be referred to arbitration automatically, but the reference may be rescinded on application.
2. Where a defended claim is arbitrated the right of appeal against the arbitrator's award is very limited.

Solicitor's Name and Address for Service:

oyez The Solicitors' Law Stationery Society, plc, Oyez House, 237 Long Lane, London SE1 4PU

F1060-3.81

County Court 10

★★★

451

Writ indorsed with
Statement of Claim
[Liquidated
Demand]
(O.6, r. 1)

IN THE HIGH COURT OF JUSTICE   19 .— .—No.

·   **Division**

[Group   ]

[District Registry]

Between

Plaintiff

AND

Defendant

(1) Insert name.   **To the Defendant(¹)**

(2) Insert
address.   **of(²)**

This Writ of Summons has been issued against you by the above-named Plaintiff in respect of the claim set out overleaf.

Within 14 days after the service of this Writ on you, counting the day of service, you must either satisfy the claim or return to the Court Office mentioned below the accompanying **Acknowledgment of Service** stating therein whether you intend to contest these proceedings.

If you fail to satisfy the claim or to return the Acknowledgment within the time stated, or if you return the Acknowledgment without stating therein an intention to contest the proceedings the Plaintiff may proceed with the action and judgment may be entered against you forthwith without further notice.

(3) Complete
and delete as
necessary.

Issued from the(³) [Central Office] [District Registry]
of the High Court this _____ day of _____ 19 .

NOTE:—This Writ may not be served later than 12 calendar months beginning with that date unless renewed by order of the Court.

IMPORTANT

Directions for Acknowledgment of Service are given with the accompanying form.

452

(Signed)

_____

If, within the time for returning the Acknowledgment of Service, the Defendant pay the amount claimed and £   for costs and, if the Plaintiff   obtain an order for substituted service, the additional sum of £   , further proceedings will be stayed. The money must be paid to the Plaintiff   ,   h   Solicitor or Agent

(1) If this Writ was issued out of a District Registry, this indorsement as to place where the cause of action arose should be completed.

(¹) [(²) [The cause] [One of the causes] of action in respect of which the Plaintiff claim relief in this action arose wholly or in part at(³) in the district of the District Registry named overleaf.]

_____

(2) Delete as necessary.
(3) Insert name of place.

(⁴) **This Writ** was issued by

of

[Agent for

of   ]

(4) For phrase-ology of this indorsement where the Plantiff sues in person, see *Supreme Court Practice,* Vol 2, para 3.

Solicitor for the said Plaintiff whose address   (²) [is] [are]

(i) *The Queen's Bench Division* – this is the largest and most important division of the High Court and has jurisdiction over any civil matter not specifically allocated to the other divisions. In particular, the Queen's Bench hears contract and tort cases and has a separate *Commercial court* and *Admiralty court* within the division. The head of the division is the *Lord Chief Justice* and Queen's Bench judges also sit in *Crown courts* where they hear criminal and civil cases. The court also hears appeals on matters of law from the *Magistrates court* and for this purpose the judges sit as *Divisional courts*. The Queen's Bench has *supervisory control* over all inferior courts and tribunals and acts as a check on the abuse of power, which is considered later.

(ii) *The Chancery Division* – this division is in practice headed by the *Vice Chancellor* and is the smallest of the three. Its jurisdiction is related to specialist matters including company and partnership law, bankruptcy, mortgages, taxation, land, and probate (disputes over wills).

(iii) *The Family Division* – the Family Division is headed by the *President*, and is concerned with civil disputes relating to family law including divorce, nullity (making a marriage void), legitimacy, wardship and marriage property disputes.

c) *Civil Appeals Courts* – The majority of cases that have been quoted in this book have been decisions which have involved important points of law and created precedents. Generally, these have been cases which have gone on appeal to the *Court of Appeal* or the *House of Lords* and hence have become regarded as the most authoritative decisions of the civil courts.

(i) *The Court of Appeal (Civil Division)* – this court is headed by the *Master of the Rolls* and has sixteen *Lords Justices of Appeal*. As an individual appeal court, three judges preside, hearing appeals involving questions of fact and/or law. In practice, the evidence is not reheard but rather reliance is placed on the record of the previous trial. The majority of appeals come from the High Court, County Courts and the Restrictive Practices Court. The court has power to *reverse, affirm or amend* the previous decision and in some cases order a *retrial*.

(ii) *The House of Lords (Judicial Committee)* – as an appeal court rather than a legislative body), the House of Lords is composed of the *Lord Chancellor* and *Lords of Appeal in Ordinary* (Law Lords). It is the highest court of appeal for England, Wales, Scotland and Northern Ireland in civil disputes, and similarly in criminal cases (except for Scotland). Usually, five judges will form a court and the relatively small number of cases which go to it come mainly from the Court of Appeal. In cases involving a point of law of general public importance, an appeal may go direct to the House of Lords from the High Court. This is known as the 'leap-frog' procedure and it was introduced by the Administration of Justice Act 1969.

The Criminal Courts

The two courts which try criminal cases are the Magistrates Court and the Crown Court.

a) *The Magistrates Court* – This is the lower of the two courts but nevertheless, deals with the majority of criminal cases. Judges in the majority of Magistrates courts are laymen who have no legal training (*Lay Magistrates* who are also known as *Justices of the Peace*). Their role in a criminal trial is to determine guilt or innocence and then pass sentence. As far as matters of law and procedure are concerned, they rely on the advice of the *Clerk to the Court* who is a barrister or a solicitor. The court's jurisdiction extends to dealing with *summary offences* (ie less serious offences), however Magistrates may also try more serious crimes known as *hybrid offences* (eg theft) if the prosecution and accused agree. Otherwise, they are triable in the Crown Court. As far as imposing sentences is concerned, the Magistrates are restricted to a fine of up to £1000 and/or six months imprisonment. Otherwise they may commit the accused for sentence to the Crown Court.

Finally, it is their role to act as *Examining Magistrates* determining whether there is sufficient evidence against the accused for there to be a *case to answer* in an *indictable offence* (eg an offence triable in the Crown court with a judge and jury, such as murder. This is called a *committal proceeding* and, if the Examining Magistrates decide that a 'prima facie' case has been established, then they must commit the accused for trial to the Crown court and also decide whether he should be remanded in custody awaiting trial or allowed *bail* (ie set free until the trial date subject to conditions). The provisions relating to the granting of bail are contained in the Bail Act 1977.

b) *The Crown Court* – Crown courts were introduced by the Courts Act, 1971. They are situated in all major towns and cities in England and Wales and are responsible for trying all serious criminal cases (ie *indictable offences*). For this purpose, the offences dealt with are classified into four groups ranging from the very serious (eg murder or treason) to the less serious (eg hybrid offences – theft). There are also three types of judge who will preside over a crown court ranking in order of importance and the offences they deal with will reflect this, eg

(i) High Court judges,
(ii) Circuit judges,
(iii) Recorders (barristers or solicitors of at least ten years standing who sit as part-time judges).

455

The role of the judge is to determine questions of law and evidence and generally ensure a fair trial. It is the jury, however, who will decide the accused's guilt or innocence and, if the accused is found guilty, the judge will fix the sentence. Juries are selected at random from the electors of the particular area. The *Central Criminal court* (ie the Old Bailey) is the Crown Court with jurisdiction over the London area.

c) *Criminal Appeal Courts* — It has been seen that the Queen's Bench Division of the High Court fulfils the role of a criminal appeal court when appeals are made on questions of law from the Magistrates court. The Crown court also sits as an appeal court when appeals are made on questions of fact from the Magistrates. Appeals in serious cases tried in the Crown court, however, are made to the Court of Appeal (criminal division) and in rare cases may go further to the House of Lords.

  (i) *Court of Appeal (Criminal Division)* for the purpose of hearing criminal appeals, the Court is presided over by Lord Justices of Appeal and puisne judges of the Queen's Bench Division, three of whom will constitute a court. Appeals may be made *as of right* if a *question of law* is involved, (eg the interpretation of the wording of an offence), but only *with leave*, (eg permission of the court or a High Court judge), if it is made on a *question of fact* (eg insufficient evidence to convict). The court may allow the appeal and quash the conviction, substitute a conviction for a lesser offence, alter the sentence, (but not increase it) or in some cases order a retrial.

  (ii) *The House of Lords* in rare cases. Appeal may be made to the House of Lords from the Court of Appeal or also from a Divisional court of the Queen's Bench Division. Appeals are only heard where:
      the court below certifies that a point of law of general public importance is involved; and
      either the court below or the House of Lords grants leave to appeal.

Administrative disputes
Since the Second World War, there has been a dramatic increase in the exercise of government functions, eg

a) An increase in social legislation (pensions, industrial injuries, sickness and unemployment benefits).
b) An increase in powers to acquire land by compulsory purchase.
c) In housing an increasing intervention in the private rented sector by conferring upon tenants rights of security of tenure, and by establishing a system whereby rents of dwellings may be controlled.

In addition, there is an ever-increasing amount of statute law in relation to employment, covering such matters as redundancy, unfair

456

dismissal, equal pay, sex and race discrimination.

To resolve disputes arising in these areas machinery has been set up in the form of administrative tribunals. Tribunals are thought to be better equipped to deal with administrative disputes rather than the overloaded ordinary courts because:

a) They will include a specialist expert in the area concerned to help resolve the dispute.
b) They are speedier and less costly than the ordinary courts.
c) They have wide discretionary powers which are necessary to enable them to resolve administrative disputes.

Administrative tribunals

Administrative tribunals are set up by statutes which will also define the extent of their power. Different tribunals have been created to deal with the various types of administrative disputes, including:

a) *Social Security tribunals* These tribunals hear disputes arising from individual claims for welfare benefits, eg supplementary benefit. For this purpose, the tribunal will consist of a chairperson appointed by the Secretary of State and one representative of employers and one of employees. Similar local tribunals have been set up to deal with disputes arising from claims for industrial injuries benefit.
b) *Lands tribunal* This is a highly professional body whose main function is to decide questions surrounding the value of land particularly when land has been compulsorily acquired.
c) *Rent tribunals* These are bodies which were created under the Rent Acts to determine the rents of certain types of private rented accommodation and grant limited security of tenure to a tenant. Under the Housing Act 1980, the functions of Rent Tribunals have been transferred to the Rent Assessment Committees. It should also be mentioned that when dealing with a Rent Tribunal function, the 1980 Act provides that the Rent Assessment Committee is known as 'the Rent Tribunal'.

Tribunals

a) *Industrial tribunals* These are bodies created under employment legislation and are not concerned with administrative matters but rather with disputes relating to employment, eg unfair dismissal and redundancy.
b) *Domestic tribunals* Domestic tribunals are simply *disciplinary committees* of particular professions, eg doctors, lawyers, dentists, etc with power to discipline members of the various professions for professional misconduct.

Administrative enquiries

Some areas of administrative action by government or local authorities, eg housing and planning, provide no appeal route to tribunals from decision making. Rather, provision is made under statute for an aggrieved individual to argue their case at a *public local enquiry*. The majority of such enquiries arise out of the compulsory acquisition of land by public authorities. They are conducted before a Minister's inspector who, after hearing the evidence, will report to the Minister concerned. The final decision is made by the Minister.

The Tribunals and Inquiries Act 1971

Following a great deal of criticism of the workings of Tribunals in the late 1950s, a committee (the Franks Committee) was given the task of inquiring into the criticism and, following its recommendations, the Tribunals and Inquiries Act 1958, was passed. Most of the law is now embodied in the Tribunals and Inquiries Act 1971. The statutes provided for the setting up of a review body, the *Council on Tribunals*, which is given the task of reviewing the working of tribunals and reporting annually to Parliament. In addition, it is now a requirement that in most cases, if the parties request it, *reasons for decisions* must be given. This provision, of course, enables an individual who is aggrieved at a decision to more easily challenge the decision in the ordinary courts. The ordinary courts have power to supervise the decision making of Tribunals and administrators (eg the Executive) generally.

Judicial control of the action of public bodies

The High Court has a supervisory jurisdiction over the acts of any executive agency (eg nationalised industries, local authorities, government departments, ministers, and inferior courts and tribunals). This jurisdiction covers matters such as granting various orders, eg (mandamus, prohibition and certiorari) issuing declarations and injunctions, and hearing statutory appeals.

a) *Mandamus*   The order of mandamus may be issued by the Queen's Bench Division of the High Court to compel the performance of a public duty imposed by the law on some person or body. It should be stressed however that this order is only available where;

  (i) there is no other remedy provided by statute or the common law to redress the grievance;

  (ii) the applicant for the remedy has a substantial personal interest in the matter;

  (iii) the complaint relates to the non-performance of a public duty rather than the exercise of a discretionary power. Thus mandamus would not be granted to require the making of a particular by-law by a local authority.

Wherever statutory duties are imposed on public bodies therefore, for instance duties in relation to Education, Housing, Public Health and Highways imposed on local authorities, and they are not fulfilled, then *mandamus* may be issued from the High Court to require performance.

b) *The use of mandamus in administrative supervision*   Mandamus will not lie as a remedy to compel the exercise of a discretionary power conferred on administrators. However, of a power is conferred by statute, mandamus may be issued to compel its exercise one way or the other and ensure at least that an individual case is dealt with fairly and according to the law.

In *R* v. *London County Council, Ex parte Corrie* (1918) a by-law was made by the defendants, prohibiting the sale of articles in the parks under their control without their consent. The defendants resolved to revoke existing permissions to sell already granted and not to grant new permissions. The Court held that as the defendants had a power to grant permission they had a corresponding duty to hear applications and decide them on their merits. Mandamus was granted to require the defendants to hear applications. (Of course, if the council did not want the power it could amend or repeal the by-law.)

It is not uncommon for particular statutes to include mandamus as a remedy to require compliance with its provisions, eg under the Education Act 1944, s 68, the Secretary of State for Education has power to issue directions to local education authorities which in his opinion are proposing to act *unreasonably* in the exercise of their powers and the performance of duties conferred to them by the Act. The extent of this wide ministerial discretion was examined in the recent Tameside case, 1977.

R v. *Tameside Metropolitan Borough Council, Ex-parte Secretary of State for Education and Science* (1977). The case concerned a decision by the newly-elected Conservative Council at Tameside to postpone a half completed scheme to convert five grammar schools into three comprehensives and two sixth-form colleges. This scheme had been introduced by the then Labour Council and approved by the Minister in 1975. The Secretary of State, believing that the scheme had progressed too far to be stopped by the Conservative Council, directed them to carry out the change-over (ie under s. 68 Education Act 1944). When the Council ignored this direction, the Secretary of State applied successfully to the High Court for an order of mandamus to require the council to fulfil their duty and carry out the change-over. On an appeal by the Tameside Council to the Court of Appeal, the court acknowledged that a postponement of the change-over to comprehensive schools would cause disruption. Nevertheless, the power of the Minister to intervene depended on whether the newly-elected Council at Tameside were acting *unreasonably* in taking the course they proposed to take. Lord Denning put forward the view that a 'body' could not be labelled as unreasonable unless they were not only wrong but unreasonably wrong, so wrong that no reasonable person could take that view. Thus, for the Council to be acting unreasonably it must have been following a course which it did not feel was in the best interests of the community and would not work. This was not the case here, so therefore the Council were not acting unreasonably and the Minister was not entitled to mandamus. On a further appeal to the House of Lords this decision was upheld.

The Tameside decision is an outstanding example of the principle that even where wide discretions are conferred on administrators in central and local government in this country, the courts are, nevertheless, willing to intervene and supervise the exercise of their powers if they feel that there has been an abuse.

c) *Prohibition and certiorari* These orders may be issued from the Queen's Bench Division of the High Court in cases where a judicial body (eg an inferior court or tribunal) has acted or is proposing to act unlawfully or has otherwise exceeded its powers. The order of *certiorari* has the effect of quashing such a decision already made and the order of *prohibition* will restrain a body from completing an act already begun. Today, the orders are most frequently used when a body in reaching a decision ignores what are called the *principles of natural justice*. These principles are not easily defined but generally require the body reaching the decision to:

(i) act fairly without bias and in good faith;
(ii) give both sides to a dispute an opportunity to put their case;
(iii) ensure that no party to the decision making has an interest in the matter before them.

To recap, therefore, the orders of certiorari and prohibition may be available where a body either:

(i) acts ultra vires;
(ii) acts unlawfully (ie adopts an incorrect procedure or its decision discloses an error of law);
(iii) infringes the principles of natural justice.

In deciding to which bodies these orders apply, it is possible to consider the words of Lord Justice Atkin in *R* v. *Electricity Commissioners* (1924) where he said that they will apply 'whenever any body of persons having legal authority to determine questions affecting the rights of subjects, and having a duty to act judicially, act in excess of their legal authority'.

The orders extend, therefore, not only to the actions of inferior courts but also to administrative tribunals.

In *R* v. *Northumberland Compensation Appeal Tribunal, Exparte Shaw* (1952) the tribunal's decision contained the reasons for it, and from these reasons it was clear that the tribunal had made an error of law. The Court of Appeal granted certiorari to quash the decision and stressed that the supervisory control of the courts extended not only to seeing that inferior tribunals keep within their jurisdiction but also to seeing that they observe the law.

The importance of these orders as far as government administration is concerned is that there are many occasions where administrators decide questions *affecting the rights of individuals* and act in a judicial manner. It is now recognised that if such decision making discloses any abuse of power then the courts will intervene.

In *Ex-parte Ladbroke Group* (1969) the proceedings of a licensing committee appointed under the Gaming and Lotteries Act 1963 were put under the scrutiny of the Queen's Bench Division of the High Court. The complaint related to the decision of the committee as to whether a license should be granted and the statutory requirement that objectors should be heard. The evidence showed that the committee's decision was not a corporate one but rather that of the dominant chairman, who sat so far from the rest of the committee that it was impossible to confer with them. The chairman also had made it plain that he was willing to make a decision before hearing all the evidence. These, the Court held, were sufficient grounds to issue certiorari to quash the eventual decision made.

It is also clear that the orders will now lie in relation to purely administrative decisions. In *R* v. *Barnsley Metropolitan Borough Council, Ex-parte Hook* (1976) a licensed street trader, in breach of local authority by-laws, urinated in a side street after the market had closed. When spotted by a security officer and rebuked by him for his conduct, the trader exchanged words of abuse. The matter then escalated, the market manager was informed, he reported the incident to the relevant local authority committee and they decided to ban the trader for life from the market. In a subsequent appeal to the local authority sub-committee against this decision, the trader's representatives were given the opportunity to put his case. The problem was that during the committee's deliberations, the other side to the dispute (the market manager) was present throughout, and the committee decided to confirm the ban. Failing to obtain a remedy from the High Court on the grounds that the committee's decision was a purely administrative one, the trader appealed to the Court of Appeal. The Court unanimously held that certiorari would lie to quash the committee's decision on the grounds that the rules of natural justice had not been complied with. The presence of the market manager throughout the decision making was a violation of the rule against bias. On the question as to whether certiorari would lie to quash an administrative

461

decision, the Court held that the order was relevant as the local authority *was determining questions affecting the rights of subjects*. Lord Denning emphasised the point when he said 'Certiorari will lie to quash not only judicial decisions but also administrative decisions'. The fact that the prerogative orders will now extend to purely administrative proceeding has far reaching affects for administrators particularly in relation to the rules of 'fair play' in decision making.

d) *Declarations and injunctions*   As an alternative to seeking a prerogative remedy, an aggrieved individual may question the legality of the action of a public body by requesting the High Court to *declare the law* and/or grant an *injunction* to refrain from action.

In *Prescott* v. *Birmingham Corporation* (1955) a ratepayer requested the High Court for a declaration that the granting of free bus travel to old age pensioners was ultra vires. The Court declared that the practice was illegal in the absence of clear authority under statute.

Such authority has now been granted and the practice would probably be justified anyway under the Local Government Act 1972.

It should be noted, however, that where it is a *public grievance* that is complained of, eg a public nuisance or non compliance with an Act of Parliament, then an action must be brought in the name of the *Attorney-General*, (the protector of public rights), unless an individual can show that he or she has suffered special damage. Normally, the Attorney-General will permit his name to be used, the Attorney-General suing *at the relation of* the aggrieved individual (a *relator action*).

e) *Statutory appeals*   Finally, it is worth pointing out that many statutes give a right of appeal to an individual who is aggrieved at non compliance or supposed compliance with their provisions, for example under the Public Health Acts.

The role of the Parliamentary Commissioner for Administration
Another body which has been created in order to resolve administrative disputes is the *Parliamentary Commissioner* (or *'Ombudsman'*) appointed in anticipation of the Parliamentary Commissioner Act 1967. The Parliamentary Commissioner's functions under the Act include the investigation of complaints in relation to actions by various government departments and authorities in the exercise of administrative functions. The power of the Commissioner to investigate is limited to complaints referred by a member of Parliament. An individual who claims to have sustained injustice in consequence of *maladministration* must therefore make a written complaint to a member of the House of Commons who will refer it to the Commissioner. There are still a large number of complaints referred to the

Commissioner which are outside his jurisdiction for he has no right to investigate cases where there is a possible right of appeal to a tribunal or a remedy exists through legal action in the courts. Having investigated a complaint, the Commissioner will send a report to the member of Parliament who referred the matter and the Department concerned. However the Commissioner has no power to require action to be taken but can only make recommendations. The Commisssioner also makes an annual report to Parliament which is subject to review by a Select Committee. In Britain, where there is no free access to information (as there is in the United States of America) the investigatory powers of the Commissioner, which include the right to obtain documentary and other evidence from departments, may provide a useful tool for the private individual who has suffered at the hands of a large government department.

Local Commissioners for Administration
Under the Local Government Act 1974, machinery was established for the investigation of complaints by individuals who have suffered as a result of maladministration by local and other authorities. The Act provides for the appointment of *local Commissioners for Administration* (*local Ombudsmen*), who are given responsibility for particular areas. Their jurisdiction is limited in the same way as the Parliamentary Commissioner in that they will only hear complaints referred to them by a councillor of the authority covered, unless there is evidence to show that a councillor has failed to pass a complaint on. Thus the local authority has an opportunity to put the matter right before a referral is made. Local ombudsmen have no power to investigate matters where there is a legal remedy. In addition, recent case law suggests that the investigatory power of the local ombudsman in relation to obtaining documentary evidence is much more restricted than that of the Parliamentary Commissioner. Finally, it should be mentioned that even where a conclusion of maladministration is reached, by either the Parliamentary or Local Ombudsman, they have no power to require remedial action but can only make recommendations. As far as local ombudsmen are concerned, however, where local authorities are found to be guilty of maladministration, remedial action is taken by over ninety per cent of the authorities concerned.

The reasons for state intervention in the market economy

In Chapter 1 the functioning of the market economy through the mechanism of demand and supply was examined. In this way an attempt is made to solve the basic economic problem of allocating scarce resources between the competing demands placed upon them. However, as noted, the market economy is subject to several defects which, if left uncorrected, would result in inefficiencies and misallocation of resources. In this section, it is proposed to examine these deficiencies in more detail and explain why and how the state has intervened in order to correct or modify the free working of the market economy.

The provision of public goods (social and merit)

Even in the laissez-faire economy of the eighteenth century, it was acknowledged by Adam Smith that the price mechanism was an inappropriate method for providing those wants which were collectively demanded by society rather than by individuals alone. In Book VIII of his 'Wealth of Nations' published in 1776, he wrote that the 'expenses of Sovereign or Commonwealth were of three categories:

  (i) defending society from the violence and injustice of other independent societies;

  (ii) securing internal justice between citizens; and

  (iii) erecting and maintaining those public institutions . . . and works which, though they may be in the highest degree advantageous to a great society, could never repay the expense to any citizen'.

Smith's words provide the traditional justification for the government's intervention in the market system in order to provide such *collective wants*. The market responds to individual demands very efficiently and supplies private goods or services. But where wants are collective, as with public goods or services, market provision will be absent or at best inadequate. To understand why this is so it is necessary to look more closely at the characteristics of private and public goods.

Private goods

Private goods have the two important characteristics: *exclusion* and *competitive consumption*. It is possible for an individual consumer to purchase and enjoy the benefits from a product or service alone to the exclusion of all others. If a private business organisation is to supply such a product, then exclusion is necessary for two reasons. Firstly, unless it is possible to exclude from its benefits those individuals who choose not to purchase the product, then supplying it becomes an economic nonsense. Secondly, why should any rational consumer elect to pay for the product when they can enjoy the benefits from a fellow consumer's purchase? Exclusion is a necessary requirement for market provision of goods or services. Furthermore, consumption of private goods is competitive in that an individual consuming *more* means another individual consuming *less*.

A further characteristic of private goods is that generally the payment by the consumer and the satisfaction (utility) received is either simultaneous, for instance the payment for a drink is made immediately prior to its consumption, or at least is seen to be reasonably immediate so in the case of buying a television set the satisfaction extends over time. In addition to this characteristic, in most cases with the purchase of a private product, the payee and the beneficiary are identical. Even a gift of jewellery or clothing purchased for a personal friend gives satisfaction not just to the respective wearer but also to the payee concerned.

With most private goods, it is possible for the consumer to clearly understand and so evaluate the prospective benefits from the purchase. It is therefore possible to make an informed and rational choice.

Finally, in the case of the majority of private goods, they only give rise to private costs and benefits. Only the minority present serious problems of externalities.

By combining all these six characteristics, it is possible to appreciate why private goods can be market provided successfully. As a result of exclusion and competitiveness a producer will be willing to supply and a consumer willing to pay. The consumer can make a rational choice to purchase as not only does he or she understand the benefits but is also the immediate beneficiary. The lack of externalities, for the most part, means that the purchase is a matter entirely between buyer and seller and of no concern to society as a whole.

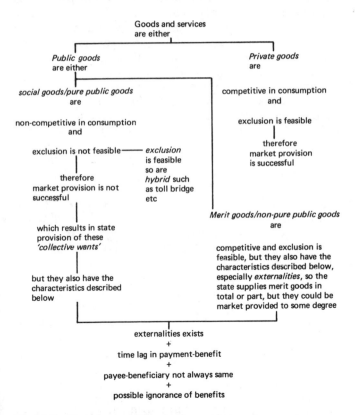

Fig 10.3   State intervention in the market economy

465

Public goods

It is because public goods have opposite characteristics to those described above that they are unsuited for market provision. Exclusion is difficult because of either technical or economic reasons. In many cases it is simply not possible to exclude individuals from consumption of the product or service. It is also 'non-rejectable' in that all consumers cannot opt out. Also they are usually non-competitive in consumption unlike private goods. The cost of one extra consumer, ie the marginal cost, is zero or negligible. This is the case of collective wants described in Chapter 1 and is the reason for state provision of services such as external defence and internal law and order. Provision also extends beyond this to such services as street lighting, highways and so on. These are the category of *social goods* or *pure public goods*, supplied mainly because of their collective consumption characteristics. It should be noted however that while pure public goods are both non-excludable and non-competitive, goods which are non-competitive can sometimes be excludable. For example, a hybrid product such as a bridge or highway is non-competitive (up to its capacity limit) but exclusion can be practised by means of toll charges.

With public goods, the payment (via taxation) and the benefits are not only *not* simultaneous but there may be a considerable time lag. Part of the policing function is the protection of private property, however it is only when an individual is the victim of a theft that he or she will appreciate the recovery of the property. Furthermore unlike private goods, the payee and the beneficiary may be quite distinct individuals. There may also be contradictory views as to the benefits to be gained from such public goods, eg the clear controversy over the provision of nuclear weapons.

Finally, with most public goods there are considerable externalities resulting. Public goods which are state provided mainly because they result in important externalities, and to a lesser extent because they have some of the other characteristics, are classified as *merit goods*. Examples are health and education provision in the UK. Unlike the social or pure public goods previously described above, a free market system can supply merit goods. In practice, the UK has elements of both private and public health and education services. However private provision of these is not likely to be comprehensive or socially adequate. For example, private health provision is efficient for certain forms of treatment and specific social groups but is unlikely to be adequate for the entire spectrum of medical provision. The same holds true for educational provision. Of course, arguments exist in favour of extending or curtailing the provision of merit goods.

Private and social costs and benefits

As described in Chapter 1, the market economy only takes into account the private costs of, and the private benefits from, any production or consumption activity. In many cases however, the activity will have economic and social effects upon other groups in society, either in the form of social costs or social benefits. These are called *externalities*. It is the existence of these externalities which chiefly result in the state providing merit goods and legislating to modify the market system. Some examples may be used to illustrate these points more clearly. For example, education and health are both consumed by individuals who obviously gain individual private benefits. A better education will enable someone to perhaps obtain a better job. But there will also be wider social benefits to society resulting from a more educated work-force which matches the needs of the economy. Similarly while an indi-vidual will derive benefits from good health, society also directly benefits from a healthy population. In both these cases, the social benefits are greater than the private benefits. It is quite possible to charge consumers for both these services by provision through the market system. But a possible consequence of this is that some indi-viduals may not buy much of the service for a variety of reasons. They may be too poor, or because of ignorance of benefits, decide to opt out of purchase. They will only take account of the value to themselves rather than to society as a whole, with the result that the community is losing some benefit. The service or product is underconsumed in a free market. Society intervenes by provision of health and education as merit goods to correct this underconsumption. The *hybrid* system of the UK is such that the state pays for some of the merit goods entirely and pays in part for the consumption of others. For instance, education is provided free up to 16 years but thereafter a contribution may be required from consumers. A similar situation applies to dental treat-ment in the Health Service.

Another example of the result of external effects can be seen when there is a divergence, not between private and social benefits as above, but between the private and social costs of an *activity*. For example, some goods or services consumed by individuals involve costs to society and not just the individual alone. Consumption of alcohol can have adverse effects much wider than the direct effect on the individual involved in excessive consumption. Excessive drinking may result in harmful anti-social behaviour such as violence in the street and home, and road accidents. Where private costs are less than social costs there is likely to be overconsumption in a free market with the result that the state intervenes to regulate the activity by either prohibition or influ-encing consumption through the mechanism of demand and supply. Legislation restricting the age and hours of drinking are an example of this prohibition, as is legislation dealing with drugs, etc. Consumption of cigarettes is influenced by health advertising although so far the government has been reluctant to use taxation to restrict consumption. Differences between costs can occur with production activities as where a chemical plant is producing a product whose manufacturing process has harmful results on society. The organisation will take full account of the private costs to itself in producing the chemical, but not necessarily the social costs to the environment of pollution damage or the danger of explosion. Similarly, petrol companies at present are producing petrol containing lead which has very harmful effects upon children who absorb lead into their brains. Again, there is the danger of over-production of these activities if left completely to the free market. The state intervenes to regulate these activities usually through legislation. To conclude, therefore, the existence of externalities is a powerful justification for state intervention, although it must be remembered that most activities will produce external effects felt beyond the immediate parties. It is a question of the state deciding which externalities justify intervention and which do not.

Imperfect markets

The market mechanism described in Chapter 1, assumed the existence of a perfect market. The reality as exposed in Chapter 2 will be an imperfect market in some form such as monopolistic competition, oligopoly or monopoly. This reduced level of competition can have several possible disadvantages to the consumer. The unequal bargaining position between consumers and producers may result in unwarranted high prices, a lack of consumer choice, indifferent service or the sale on terms unfavourable to the consumer. The state has recognised these dangers and so legislated to promote competition and control practices unfair to the consumer.

Of course monopoly dangers do not just exist on the business side of the market. The growth of powerful trade unions which resulted from a need to balance employer power in the employment bargaining situation may be quoted as an example. The state itself has of course created some of the most important monopolies in the economy in setting up the nationalised industries. There has been both an economic and political rationale behind the impetus towards nationalisation. Until 1980 however the behaviour of such state bodies was not brought within the scope of competition policy legislation.

Distribution of income and wealth

Since market demand consists of wants plus income to purchase the product, it is clear that for individuals to be able to express demands, their income must be sufficient to permit this. In this way the economic system will respond by producing what consumers require. But if society is unevenly divided in terms of the distribution of income and wealth, then the production response will not necessarily reflect the needs of the majority. Different political judgements will colour to what extent such redistribution should occur, but all governments have been committed to a redistribution policy implemented mainly through a progressive taxation system of income tax and a comprehensive range of welfare benefits.

Cyclical fluctuations in the market economy

Other inherent failings of the free market economy have resulted in growing state intervention over a number of years. A major criticism has been the tendency for the unregulated economy to be subject to cyclical variations in employment, output and the level of national income. The state has found this politically and economically unacceptable and has intervened to establish *economic policy targets* and has acted through the use of various policy instruments to achieve the targets. The aim has been to regulate aggregate demand to achieve a low level of unemployment coupled with price stability and growth. Over the post-war period, the instruments used have varied but have all involved active intervention in the economy either via policies on taxation, spending and money or the use of legislation to control prices and wages directly. In addition to such policy objectives, there has been constant intervention in the area of industrial location as described in p. 369 the chapter on Land. Such intervention policies are now one of the major roles of the modern state.

Technology and capital provision

One other reason for increasing state intervention in the modern economy has been the inability of the private market to provide sufficient capital funds for projects requiring very large capital contributions. Since many of these projects provide benefits to society, (social benefits) if they are not undertaken, then society overall will suffer a loss. Of course many projects undertaken using public funds, such as Concorde and possibly the Humber Bridge, have proved less successful than originally hoped for. But major capital programmes such as the Tyneside Metro passenger transport system could not be financed from private funds. This is because of the sums involved and the long period required before a return of the investment is received. Additionally there is the question of externalities. Assessed on private cost and benefit criteria alone, the Metro system would have been a non-starter.

Another example of increasing state intervention in the private sector was the establishment of the *National Enterprise Board* (NEB) by the 1975 Industry Act and also the Industry Act 1972. The 1972 Act made the provision that state grants might be given in return for a state shareholding in a company. This provision was used in the financial rescue of British Leyland in 1975. The policy was extended by the establishment of the NEB which was empowered to assist organisations in financial difficulty under the terms of the 1972 Act and manage other companies already in public ownership such as Rolls Royce, BL, etc. The present government has proposed modifications to the National Research and Development Corporation (the NRDC) to form one body.

The forms of state intervention in the market economy

The state has attempted to remedy the various failures in the market economy in three main ways; by finance, provision and regulation. It is necessary to examine each in turn.

Finance – public sector income and expenditure

The state uses its powers of *finance* in two ways. Firstly, through the use of taxation and secondly through the use of government spending. The state uses taxes to influence the allocation of resources between the private and public sectors and also to influence individual production and consumption patterns. Table 10.1 p. 474 illustrates the main components of the income and expenditure of the public sector planned for the financial year ending 1982. The income side of the account is examined first.

Of the total receipts of the public sector of £106.4b, over 92% comes from various forms of taxation. The objectives of taxation may be outlined as follows. Firstly, the primary objective of taxation is to raise income or revenue for the government which is necessary to finance the public expenditure also shown in Table 10.1. In effect the state is using taxation to reduce private demand for goods and services so releasing the resources which can be used in the public sector to satisfy collective wants, etc. Secondly, taxation in the modern economy is also used to achieve additional objectives such as shifting patterns of consumption or production between goods. For example, it would be possible to discourage smoking by imposing much higher taxes on tobacco and so reducing the social costs involved. Thirdly, the use of taxation in redistributing income and wealth within the economy is a major objective, although its importance varies between political parties. Fourthly, taxation is used as a means of changing the level of aggregate demand in order to achieve the economic policy objectives mentioned earlier.

Table 10.1 clearly illustrates the main components of the state's income. Broadly, taxes fall on income, expenditure or capital. *Income tax* is by far the most important single tax, accounting for nearly 29% of all taxation. The major expenditure tax is *Value Added Tax* which when combined with income tax and insurance contributions accounts for 58% of all tax receipts.

State expenditure

The second way in which the state uses its finance powers is through its expenditure activities. It can influence demand for selected commodities by giving subsidies. In the past this has meant the subsidisation of certain foodstuffs by central government. At local government level subsidies may be used to reduce the cost of such services as housing and public transport. The expenditure figures of Table 10.1 show transport subsidies to currently be around £0.7 billion. Public money is also used to influence the location of industry as explained in the Chapter on Land p. 351 and is forecast as £1 billion in the 1981–2 estimates. Financial support for industry is a further element of intervention. For example the budgeted support for BL in the estimates is seen to be £0.6 billion. By far the most important example of financial intervention and the biggest single expenditure element is spending in the form of *transfer payments*. The social security benefits paid out alone add up to over £27 billion. In all these various ways that state is intervening through finance to modify the free market system in a particular desired direction.

Provision

The state itself provides many goods and services to society. The taxation levied is used to transfer resources so that the state can supply the public goods, both social and merit, which it regards as economically and socially desirable. Such goods and services may be supplied at either central or local government level, although local provision is for the most part centrally finance aided. Obvious examples of social goods are the Defence and Law and Order services accounting for about £17 billion. In practice, state spending on merit services such as education and health is considerably higher at £27 billion.

Other goods and services which are perfectly marketable are the products of the nationalised industries, where the state has taken the entire industry into public ownership. The nationalised industries are Public Corporations established by specific Acts of Parliament. They have a board appointed by the Industry Minister and although they operate with considerable independence, they are ultimately responsible to the Minister and to Parliament. The government lays down general policy guidelines for the board which is then charged with the day-to-day management of the industry. The first areas of nationalisation were the basic staple industries such as coal and rail. More recently the motive has been primarily one of job preservation followed by a rationalisation of the industry, as with British shipbuilders.

Regulation

Regulation of various activities can be either in a positive or negative form. The law regulates in a positive manner in many areas where citizens are forced to follow a course which the state regards as desirable. For example, as education is regarded as having considerable social benefits, it is compulsory under the Education Acts, to provide children with 'approved' education, usually at a school. The compulsory fitting (and as proposed the wearing) of seat belts is yet another example. Negative regulation can take such form as licensing drinking hours, the hours of public transport drivers and restrictions on planning and development.

Finally, the major merit services of education and health include elements of all three methods of state intervention. Education, for example, includes elements of *finance*, such as grants for higher education, *provision*, in that it is predominantly state maintained, and *regulations* in that all children must receive education to a required standard until the age of 16.

Income, expenditure and borrowing

An examination of Table 10.1 shows that total state income or revenue was £106.4 billion whereas expenditure equalled £117 billion, an excess of spending of £10.6 billion. The state therefore must borrow the shortfall to finance its expenditure activities. This borrowing is called the *Public Sector Borrowing Requirement* (PSBR). The three areas of the public sector, the central government, the local authorities and the nationalised industries and other public corporations, borrowed £5.8 billion, £1.0 billion and £2.4 billion respectively in 1981 − 2. The balance is made up of the unallocated £1.4 billion. The size and financing of this public sector borrowing requirement is of major importance to government economic policy and therefore requires a closer study. Table 10.2 shows in a more structured way, how the figures for the PSBR of 1981 − 2 were arrived at using the government's own accounts system.

The *Consolidated Fund* is the account which receives all government revenues as classified in Table 10.2 giving a total revenue of £75 524 million. From this fund flows government expenditure which is either *Supply Services* or *Standing Services*. The former is voted annually by Parliament whereas the latter is a standing charge against revenue. Total expenditure was £83 697 million. Since expenditure exceeded revenue, the deficit was £8173 million. The *National Loans Fund* is the other main account which broadly covers the lending activities of central government. Receipts from interest payments on government loans are paid into this fund together with the contribution from the Consolidated Fund for paying national debt interest, as written into the Standing Services estimates. Against such total receipts of £11 100 million are the payments made from the National Loans Fund totalling £23 307 million. These comprise the payments involved with servicing the national debt and also the net lending activities of the government. Such lending is to nationalised industries and other public corporations as well as private sector organisations. The final payment is the deficit brought forward from the Consolidated Fund. Balancing receipts against payments gives a net borrowing requirement by the National Loans Fund of £12 207 million. After taking into account central government's net debt to certain official funds as shown, the figure of £11 497 million represents the Central Government Borrowing Requirement (CGBR). Since the public sector also includes local authorities and public corporations, their respective borrowing from outside the public sector must be added to the Central Government Borrowing Requirement. Local authorities borrowed £100 million but Public Corporations made a net repayment of £1031 million instead of borrowing. The three figures add up to the Public Sector Borrowing Requirement of £10 566 million for 1981 − 2. This Public Sector

Borrowing Requirement is financed by borrowing from the other sectors of the economy, namely the non-bank private sector, the banking sector and the overseas sector. Using figures for 1980 – 1 when the PSBR was £13 192 million, the financing was as follows:

Financed by the:	£million	
Non-bank private sector	9 282	(70%)
Banking sector	3 231	(25%)
Overseas sector	697	(5%)
Total	13 192	(100%)

The borrowing takes a number of forms such as notes and coin, government securities, Treasury Bills, National Savings and other types of debt. To the extent that the PSBR is financed by borrowing from the banking sector, it can have an expansionary effect upon the money supply although this relationship is not a simple one.

In conclusion, having examined the reasons for state intervention and the forms used in the market economy, the next chapter concentrates on one area of state intervention, namely how the government seeks to regulate the economy to achieve its economic policy objectives.

The consolidated fund

Central government revenue		*Central government expenditure*	
Inland Revenue	39 100	Supply services	73 741
Customs and excise	26 000	*Standing services*	
Vehicle excise duty	1 628	Payment to NLF for debt interest	6 200
National Insurance surcharge	3 809	Payments to Northern Ireland	1 279
Miscellaneous receipts	4 987	Payment to EEC	2 450
		Other payments	27
Total	75 524	Total	83 697

Consolidated Fund Deficit
− 8173

The National Loans Fund

Receipts		*Payments*	
Interest on loans, profits of		Payments on the National Debt	11 100
the Issue Dept of the Bank of		Consolidated Fund Deficit	8 173
England, etc	4 900	Loans (net)	4 034
Contribution from Con. Fund			
for payment of debt interest	6 200		
Total	11 100	Total	23 307

Net borrowing by NLF − 12 207

Government net indebtness to official funds	+ 710	
Central Government Borrowing Requirement	− 11 497	CGBR
Local Authorities Borrowing Requirement	− 100	LABR
Public Corporations Borrowing Requirement	+ 1 031	PCBR
equals Public Sector Borrowing Requirement	10 566	PSBR

Table 10.2   The public sector borrowing requirement (£ million) 1981 – 1982 (forecast)

Source: The Financial Statement and Budget Report 1981

	£ billion
Where the money comes from	
Income tax	28.2
National Insurance and health contributions	16.4
of which, Employees	9.1
Employers	7.2
Value Added Tax	12.6
Local authority rates	10.3
of which, Domestic	4.5
Commercial	5.8
North Sea taxes	5.9
of which,	
Petroleum revenue tax	2.2
Supplementary petroleum duty	1.9
Oil royalties	1.2
Corporation tax	0.6
Oil duties	4.8
Corporation tax (excl. North Sea)	4.0
National Insurance surcharge	3.8
Other taxes	12.5
of which, Tobacco	3.2
Spirits, wines etc	3.2
Vehicle excise duty	1.6
EC duties	1.0
Stamp duties	0.8

	£ billion
Where the money goes	
Social security and personal social services	30.3
of which benefits for the:	
Elderly	13.8
Disabled and sick	3.8
Unemployed	3.8
Family (child benefit etc)	4.7
Widows	1.0
Personal social services	2.1
Administration of social security	1.2
Education and science, arts and libraries	14.1
of which, Schools	7.8
Higher and further education etc	4.6
Research councils etc	0.5
Arts and libraries	0.6
School meals, milk and transport	0.6
National Health Service etc	13.4
Defence	12.3
Housing	5.5
of which, Subsidies (incl. rent rebates & allowances)	2.6
Capital expenditure (net)	2.8
Other	0.1
Other environmental services (excl. support for nationalised industries)	4.9
of which, Water	1.0
Other	3.9
Law, order and protective services	4.4
of which, Police	2.4
Fire services	0.6
Other	1.4
Transport (excl. support for nationalised industries)	3.7
of which, Roads	2.4
Subsidies	0.7
Other	0.6

£ billion		£ billion	
Car tax	0.6	**Industry** (excl. energy and support for nationalised industries)	2.5
Capital gains tax	0.6	of which, Regional support	1.0
Betting tax	0.5	Support for BL	0.6
Capital transfer tax	0.4	Other	0.9
Tax on bank deposits	0.4	**Employment**	2.4
Other	0.2	of which, Manpower Services Commission	0.9
TOTAL TAXES AND NATIONAL INSURANCE CONTRIBUTIONS	**98.5**	Special employment measures	0.5
		Other	1.0
Interest and dividends	4.0	**Nationalised industries' total net external finance**	2.4
		Overseas aid and other overseas services	2.0
Local authority housing, rent	3.2	of which, Overseas aid	1.0
		EC contributions (excl. overseas aid)	0.5
Other receipts	0.7	Other	0.6
		Agriculture, fisheries, food and forestry	1.5
		of which, Market support under CAP	0.4
		Other	1.1
TOTAL RECEIPTS	**106.4**	**Energy**	**0.4**
		Trade	**0.2**
		Other public services	**3.0**
		of which, Tax collection	0.9
		Civil service pensions	0.8
Borrowing requirement	10.6	Other	1.3
		Contingency reserve	2.5
		General allowance for underspending	− 0.9
		Special sales of assets	− 0.2
		PUBLIC EXPENDITURE PLANNING TOTAL	**104.2**
		Debt interest	12.8
TOTAL	**117.0**	**TOTAL**	**117.0**

Table 10.1 Public income and expenditure 1981 – 2

Source: Economic Progress Report, September 1981

Case study on the National Health Service

The National Health Service in the UK provides an excellent example of state intervention through legislation into a market system in order to finance and provide a service which it regards as a merit good giving substantial social benefits to the community.

The NHS was established in 1946 by the National Health Service Act. The aim of this act was 'to secure improvement in the physical and mental health of the people of England and Wales and the prevention, diagnosis and treatment of illness'.

The decision to establish the NHS came after a considerable period of debate and reflected the growing characteristic in the UK of state provision through the welfare state. Prior to 1946 the medical services in this country had been moving towards public control and ownership. There had been a long tradition in the local authorities of the provision of municipally financed hospitals and also in the establishment of facilities to cater for the mentally ill and the homeless. The 1912 National Health Insurance Scheme had begun the pattern of providing medical facilities for the poor and this was supplemented by a variety of private health insurance schemes. Charitable organisations had for many years provided a valuable service to the needy related to the patient's ability to pay. However this tended to be unevenly spread throughout the country and as such did not meet the needs of the rapidly urbanised population.

The pressure on medical facilities caused by the two world wars had meant that the government was posed with a national problem. During the Second World War the government decided to introduce an Emergency Hospital Service which was controlled through the central government's Ministry of Health. This Ministry was also instrumental in producing a number of reports on health provision. The most influential of these was the Beveridge Report published in 1942. This advocated a national health service which would be freely available to all. This was formulated into the 1944 White Paper on the National Health Service. The White Paper provided the basis for discussion and negotiation with the local authorities, and those bodies already responsible for providing health care. Considerable political debate between the two main political parties over the rationale for providing a socialised health system took place, but the election of the Labour government in 1945 under the premiership of Clement Atlee meant that the country had as its first post-war government a political party firmly committed to the introduction of the NHS. The government passed the National Health Service Act in 1946 and this was implemented at the beginning of 1948.

Original structure of the NHS

The initial system was based upon a voluntary decision whether or not to join. This choice was open to both patients and to medical practitioners. Individuals were required to contribute to National Insurance if they decided to join the system and doctors and other medical staff were paid a salary if they chose to join. The system was organised on a national and regional basis. Central control lay with the Ministry of Health and central funds provided about 85% of the costs of the service. The remainder was to come from NHS contributions and certain charges which were levied for some elements of the health service such as dental and optical treatment. The local authorities also maintained a substantial responsibility for social work and environmental health control which they had developed in the inter-war years.

One of the most striking features of the Act was that it did not prohibit private health care but allowed this to continue in parallel. Private hospitals and clinics continued and many practitioners were permitted to retain private practices while registering as part of the NHS. This also allowed a demand for 'pay beds' within the state hospitals where patients paid either for the bed or treatment or both at an economic rent. At the time this provision of retaining a private sector was felt necessary to gain agreement of the medical profession to the Health Service as a whole.

The 1946 Act established a structure which was controlled overall by the Ministry of Health (later renamed the Department of Health and Social Security) but under this body, control was vested in three areas:

   (i) the Regional Hospital Boards and Hospital Management Committees responsible for the running of the hospitals and employment of consultants, specialists and other hospital staff;
  (ii) the Local Authorities in charge of Health Centres, Health Visiting, Community Health Care and other home-based health services;
 (iii) Executive Councils controlling the General Practitioners, Dentists, Pharmaceutical services, etc.
       This structure was to remain relatively unaltered until the early 1970s when it was felt that the local authorities' responsibilities

in the main should be brought more directly under the control of the NHS.

Reorganisation of the Health Service

The 1973 NHS Reorganisation Act altered the entire structure of the service and was implemented in 1974 and followed the substantial changes in local government brought about by the Local Government Act 1972. It is interesting to note that the 1973 NHS Reorganisation Bill was in fact initially proposed in the House of Lords. The relatively lower level of debate in the House of Commons demonstrated that support for the reorganisation was evident on both sides of the House.

The NHS reorganisation attempted to impose a managerial structure which would not only be more unified but also more professional in character. The Act established Regional Health Authorities in place of the Regional Health Boards and also established Area and District boards to administer their decisions. The Health Authorities took under their control the Family Practitioner Services and also the Community and Home-based Health Services previously run by the local authorities. Only environmental and public health services remaind with the local authorities. This restructuring of the NHS is not inconsistent with the policy of central government in the 1970s to try and rationalise and to some extent centralise the provision of many public services.

Until the 1974 reorganisation, the NHS had been severely criticised for its duplicity of services, its inefficiency and its lack of professional management. Prior to this time much of management had been in the hands of lay committees and members of the medical profession. The new structure integrated the management teams and introduced a new more positive role for administrators, treasurers and others. In the period since the reorganisation there has been a mixed reaction to the new structure with criticism of the increased bureaucracy and extra costs which have resulted. Nevertheless the period in which the new system has been operating has been one of increasing economic stringency with the deteriorating economic condition and the consequent cut-backs imposed by central government through the Department of Health and Social Security. There has also been the continuing controversy over the abolition of pay beds from the system. It is interesting to note that despite having a Labour government in power from 1974 until 1979 there was no positive phasing out of pay beds from the system. The 1974 – 9 Labour government by enacting the Health Services Act 1976, had established the Health Services Board charged with the responsibility of reporting to the Secretary of State as to arrangements which could suitably be made to run down private facilities within the Health Service. The response of the 1979 Conservative government towards this proposal in relation to pay beds was to provide for the abolition of the Health Services Board by the Health Service Act 1980.

478

The arrangements, structures and institutions which have been discussed so far are now generally governed by the Health Service Act 1977. This is a consolidating measure aiming to gather together a number of diverse legislative provisions relating to health services under one Act. The effect of the mass of criticism (ie over-administration and over-delay in the provision of service) that the 1973 reorganisation has led to, promoted the consultative paper 'Patients First' issued by the Department of Health and Social Security in December 1979 as provided for in the 1977 Act. In consequence of this paper and following a great deal of Parliamentary debate the Health Services Act 1980 has been enacted. The Act envisages a further reorganisation of the Health Service, to be achieved however in a different manner than the 1973 provision. Power has been conferred by the 1980 Act on the Secretary of State for Health and Social Services to make changes in organisation; in particular to establish district health authorities to replace the area health authorities as constituted under the 1973 reorganisation. The objectives of the new legislation seem to be to simplify the structure of the Health Service and devolve more responsibility at local level to those in hospital and community services. The broad task of the Regional Health Authorities has been identified under the 1980 Act as being to initiate and supervise changes in health service structure in the direction of a district-based administration, and to stand back from the actual operational activities of the new districts.

Once again then the structure of the Health Service is undergoing a period of change in an attempt to ensure that as efficient a service as possible is provided. Now it is proposed to consider the arguments for and against the provision of socialised medicine.

The arguments for a free market system
The most extreme proponents of the free market approach argue that the existing National Health Service should be abolished and replaced by a system of privately provided health facilities and paid for by the patients taking out private insurance policies. The arguments centre around the contention that the tax financed medical system is less efficient than medicine which would be marketed. This assumption is based on several criteria.

The first is that as the health provision of the NHS is, for the most part, free then the consumer (the patient) takes no account of the cost and so this leads to excess demand. This can be illustrated by waiting lists for treatment, queues in doctors' surgeries, etc. In effect, the argument suggests that with zero cost the demand curve is almost horizontal indicating infinite demand.

The mirroring case is seen on the supply side. There exists a situation of severe under-supply which is seen by staff shortages, below standard buildings and medical facilities. The reason that the supply is not increased is that it is state-provided. Electors are not fully aware of the social benefits to be gained from the NHS and thus are not willing to vote for an increase in expenditure, and no government is sufficiently determined in its aim to improve the Health Service that it is willing to risk the consequences of raising tax levels sufficiently to meet the increased expenditure required to finance the expansion. It is somewhat illogical although not surprising that most people regard the level of health service provision as being too low and yet regard their tax bill as being too large.

Empirical evidence indicates that less is spent per capita in this country on health provision than is spent in many European countries and substantially less than in the United States which has a predominantly market-provided health service. Proponents of this type of system point to this as an indication that under the British system, people are restrained from showing the true extent of their demand for health provision. If it was market-determined then the average consumer would wish to spend more on their health. In fact consumers are provided with a lower level of provision and a poorer quality of service than that which they really want and would be willing to pay for if they could purchase it, and recognise the individual benefit gained from the price they are asked to pay.

Many of the other arguments which those advocating a free market in medical provision put forward, are direct challenges to the assumption that socialised medicine is a merit good which provides substantial benefit to society by being free and available for all.

It is suggested that the system should be free to all because it is a basic right and necessity of life to have good health, and the state should provide this right to all its citizens. However the argument contrary to this is that there are many other necessities of life such as food which the state does not provide and so why should health provision be made the exception?

Secondly socialised medicine is said to provide considerable externalities or social benefits. Without the Health Service the spread of contagious diseases and infection would affect not only the immediate sufferer but the rest of the community as well. However it is also true that these diseases are not widespread in countries such as the United States, without a centralised health service, and a study of the actual work of hospitals and GPs would show that the majority of their treatment was for non-contagious diseases, accidents, old age and rheumatism. There are in fact more days lost from work through cold, influenza and rheumatism which the NHS has only been partly able to affect. The argument that the NHS in fact keeps people healthy and therefore benefits the nation economically by preventing the loss of working days through illness, is countered by the view that even if the NHS increased its provision to the extent that it managed to eliminate the working days lost through illness rather than from causes such as accidents, this would only add about 0·5% to the present number of days worked. The argument is also added that the Health Service is in fact not wealth producing but wealth consuming in that a considerable part of its effort is directed to keeping old people alive and by increasing longevity it is raising that percentage of the population which is dependent on the rest of the working population.

Two further arguments which support the socialisation of medicine are also challenged. The first is that a free health service is necessary in order to try and redress the inequality of income and wealth which exists in society. However, the argument is put forward that this has basically nothing to do with health provision but with the basic problem of mal-distribution, and if it is thought necessary should be tackled by giving money to the poor sections of society and so allowing them to have the choice to spend on health provision if they so wished. By the process of state intervention and provision the individual's freedom of choice is removed.

The final argument that the free market advocates seek to oppose is that without a free health service, individuals might disregard the possible consequences of not insuring against illness or injury if there was a market-provided system. This may be countered by evidence in the United States of widespread insurance and also the contention that this is rather a case of ignorance on the part of individuals and the state should simply concentrate on a policy of health education and a programme promoting the need for health insurance rather than having to provide the health provision itself.

Despite the seemingly persuasive nature of some of the arguments, successive British governments have continued to support the NHS while at the same time allowing private medicine to continue relatively unhindered. However they have tended to move the NHS away from being a completely free service by increasing the cost of prescriptions, dental care, optical care, etc. Therefore in the UK we have accepted the arguments counter to those put forward by the free market advocates. The points for the system may be summarised as follows.

The NHS *is* providing an important merit good which as such creates considerable beneficial externalities. As society may not be willing to pay individually for benefits to the community as a whole, the state must ensure that the benefits continue to accrue and finance them through taxation. Consumers are also sometimes unaware of the actual private benefit to be gained from health care or if they realise it are irrational enough to ignore it. So for instance the benefit of a regular dental check up might only be apparent if the patient had not had the treatment and developed toothache. Given the freedom of choice whether to pay and receive treatment, or not pay and receive no benefits might mean that the more irrational consumer, or those who are perpetually optimistic about their dental health, would choose not to pay and so risk the toothache. This example is clearly a relatively trivial one as toothache is purely a private cost. However what of the irrational parent who decides not to spend more on post-natal medical care for a child? The long-term consequences are not felt by the decision maker with freedom of choice, the parent, but by the person who benefits (or in this case does not benefit) from the decision, the child, who has no voice in the decision whatsoever. The argument that all will insure against illness or injury is also open to question. In the United States, it has been found that there is considerable under insurance particularly by the poorer sections of society. The government has found it necessary to provide state-aided health schemes for the poor and the aged. Even the more affluent find themselves in financial difficulty if faced with very substantial hospital fees. It is argued that the American system of market provision is fine as long as you act as a rational individual, are relatively affluent and do not become seriously ill!

The cost of operating a system of marketed medicine may somewhat counter the claim that it would improve the efficiency of the system. The cost may be judged in two ways. Firstly the actual cost of each individual hospital or doctor having to chase patients for payments, buy their own equipment, etc and secondly the opportunity cost of providing duplicated facilities and services within a particular area, each competing with the others for patients.

The argument that the problem of wealth redistribution should be undertaken by transfers of money rather than services in order to allow the individual freedom of choice, may be opposed in two ways. The state does provide money to the poor, eg social security and unemployment benefits, and in so doing allows freedom to spend as they wish. However wealth transfer in the form of services is often much more acceptable to the taxpayer who sees taxes clearly being used for a beneficial purpose, whereas if money itself were provided it may be felt that the poor would spend it on goods which might be less beneficial.

To conclude therefore, the state continues to provide a health service in this country because it regards it as a merit good providing the externalities of social benefits and helping to redistribute income and wealth by providing free services to all, even those who could not otherwise afford them. In this case, as with public goods, it is difficult to precisely quantify the full extent of the benefits to society involved, and to assess whether such benefits outweigh the considerable costs of the NHS. However the government is willing to make a value judgement based on its principles and beliefs and in so doing this country continues to have a state-provided National Health Service.

11 Government economic policy

'In general, the art of government consists in taking as much
money as possible from one part of the citizens to give to the
other.'

Voltaire
'Money' Philosophical Dictionary
(1764)

The objectives of government economic policy

Since 1945 all governments have attempted to achieve various economic
policy objectives which they have regarded as desirable. These objectives may be identified as follows. Firstly, a commitment to maintain
full employment in the economy and never again to return to the levels
of unemployment experienced between the two World Wars; secondly,
to achieve *relative price stability*, ie low levels of inflation in the
economy; thirdly, to reach an acceptable level of *economic growth* in
the productive capacity of the economic system; finally, to maintain a
balance of payments equilibrium, ie where deficits are generally
balanced by surpluses on our trading and currency transactions over a
short period of years. In other words, the ideal economy is one of full
employment and low inflation coupled with balance of payments equilibrium and a gradual increase in wealth with a consequent growth in the
standard of living and welfare of the total community.

Although all governments have accepted the four objectives as targets, changing governments have often emphasised different objectives, reflecting variations in both political judgements and economic
circumstances at the time. To some extent there has always been a
degree of *conflict* between the four objectives so that to achieve one
objective has sometimes been at the expense of another. For example,
full employment and price stability were often achieved without
managing equilibrium in the balance of payments. In the 1970s the high
level of inflation meant that price stability became the prime objective
overriding all others. Nevertheless, these four policy objectives can be
regarded as the ideal targets for government policy.

In addition to these *primary objectives*, governments have often
attempted to achieve other economic objectives. These *secondary
objectives* are much more controversial in that different political
parties have had different views on both the objectives themselves and
the degrees of emphasis on each. Such secondary objectives include
changing the *balance between the private and public sectors* of the

483

economy and *redistributing the income and wealth* of the economic system. Clearly these two objectives are very much political judgements by the respective parties. *Regional policy* and *competition policy* have also been the subject of differing emphasis over the post-war period. In reality these objectives may be extended or changed depending on the circumstances of the time and the various political pressures on the government. The elected government is voted into power on the basis of a package of policies as to how the economic resources of the community are to be used and which economic policy objectives should receive priority.

Having identified the four primary policy objectives it is now possible to examine in greater detail the nature and extent of the various problems facing the UK economy. Thereafter there will be a discussion of the methods by which the government seeks to achieve the policy objectives in its management of the economy.

Policy objectives and the economic problems of the UK

Full employment

Unemployment was the major economic problem facing the UK economy between the two World Wars and reached a peak of 22% in 1932. Ths experience of massive unemployment resulted in all governments in the post-war period accepting the need to maintain full employment as the major economic policy objective. This commitment to full employment was given expression in the 1944 government White Paper on Employment Policy and Lord Beveridge's 'Full Employment in a Free Society'. Beveridge defined full employment at a target figure of 3% unemployment. In practice for much of the post-war period unemployment levels were very low making the 3% objective seem conservative in retrospect. During the 1950s and early 1960s unemployment in the UK was generally below 2% but as illustrated in Table 11.1, the level of unemployment has risen considerably since the late 1960s/early 1970s. This rise has been even more dramatic in the last few years. Unemployment on this scale is not only wasting a valuable economic resource, labour, but also creates social problems of all kinds. Moreover what the figures do not reveal is the wide variation in unemployment levels between regions of the UK. Clearly the policy objective of full employment has not been attained even by Beveredge's original target in recent years. Within the global figure of unemployment, several different types of unemployment will exist side by side. It is possible to identify the major types of unemployment as follows.

Year	* Unemployment %	Year	Unemployment %
		1970	2·6
		1971	3·4
		1972	3·7
1963	2·4	1973	2·6
1964	1·7	1974	2·6
1965	1·4	1975	3·9
1966	1·5	1976	5·3
1967	2·3	1977	5·7
1968	2·4	1978	5·7
1969	2·4	1979	5·4
		1980	6·8
		1981	10·6 (June)

Table 11.1 UK unemployment rates 1963 – 1981

Source: Economic Trends, March 1975 and August 1981
* Excluding School Leavers.

Cyclical unemployment

Ever since the nineteenth century the UK economy has followed a *cyclical pattern* alternating from boom to slump with levels of unemployment reflecting this cyclical trend. The cyclical pattern in the post-war era was less well defined with peaks of economic activity occurring in 1951, 1955–6, 1960–1, 1965, 1973–4. Cyclical unemployment is the result of an overall *lack of aggregate demand* for goods and services in the economy. It was J M Keynes' work between the wars which highlighted the causes of such cyclical unemployment. His analysis of the causes of this problem and the policies to remedy it are dealt with later in this chapter.

Frictional unemployment

This type of unemployment is a result of the frictions which prevent the perfect smoot:. working of the labour market in the economy. Even if the number of vacancies for each class of labour was exactly matched by those seeking employment some unemployment would occur for several reasons. Because of immobility of labour and natural time lags in the re-employment process, there will always be a pool of such unemployed persons.

Seasonal unemployment

Employment in some trades is especially susceptible to seasonal influences. Industries such as the building trade and hotel and catering are two where very definite seasonal patterns emerge. Although the effects of seasonal unemployment can be reduced by improving labour mobility it is impossible to eliminate altogether.

Structural unemployment

Structural unemployment is a long-term variation of frictional unemployment in that it exists mainly because of immobility in the labour market. This results from basic changes in the demand and supply for goods and services in the economy. For example, the textile industry of the UK has suffered widespread unemployment as a result of foreign competition. Much of the persistently higher regional unemployment can be explained by the decline in demand which occurred for the products of the basic industries which predominated in those areas. Such unemployment, resulting in deep structural changes in demand patterns, is often difficult to solve in the short term given the existing immobility of labour.

A form of structural unemployment which results from supply changes is *technological unemployment*. The introduction of new methods of production, eg robot machines, etc may result in a reduction in the demand for a particular type of labour in some industries. Similarly, technological advances in the printing industry have meant that the computer typesetting of newspapers is now perfectly feasible, a process resisted by the Fleet Street unions. Technological unemployment will always occur in a dynamic economy but often attitudes to change are much influenced by the general level of unemployment in the economy.

It is clear that unemployment is not the result of a single simple cause and as such there are several alternative policy actions available to the government to reduce it. These are considered later in the chapter.

Price stability

The second major policy objective of post-war governments was to achieve full employment while at the same time having relative price stability in the economy. The general level of prices can of course change in either a downward (*deflationary*) or upward (*inflationary*) direction. Deflationary trends have occurred in recent UK history when prices fell for much of the pre-war period, rising only after 1935. However the post-war period has been one of *continuous inflation*. It is possible to measure the degree of inflation by several different sets of indices, but the most usual is the *Index of Retail Prices*. The RPI records changes in the actual prices of a representative sample of goods and services bought by a typical UK household. Despite the limitations which are inherent in all statistics, it is probably the most reasonable and widely quoted measure of inflation. Although fears were expressed in 1944 that achieving full employment might cause inflationary pressures, the decades of the 1950s and early 1960s were successful not only in achieving employment targets but also in attaining low levels of inflation. Between 1952 – 5, retail prices averaged an annual rise of only 3.1% while between 1955 – 60 it was even less at 2.7%. As Table 11.2 shows the 1960s were also successful years in achieving relative price stability. Only from the late sixties did the pace of inflation quicken reaching a peak of nearly 27% in August 1975. Since this peak the trend has varied upwards and then downwards again to its level of around 10.9 (July 1981). However, inflation has been a world-wide problem in the post-war era although rates of inflation have varied widely. Clearly the late 1970s were a period of not only high unemployment but also high inflation. While the facts about inflation are relatively precise and clear, the causes of the inflationary process is much less so.

Year	% Increase	Year	% Increase
1960	1·2	1970	6·4
1961	2·7	1971	9·4
1962	3·2	1972	7·1
1963	1·7	1973	9·2
1964	3·9	1974	16·1
1965	4·7	1975	24·2
1966	3·7	1976	16·5
1967	2·4	1977	15·8
1968	4·8	1978	8·3
1969	5·2	1979	13·4
		1980	18·0
		1981	11·7 (May)

Table 11.2   UK inflation rates 1960 – 1981

Source: Economic Trends March 1975 and August 1981

The causes of inflation
The causes of inflation have been much debated in recent years, and two basic theories about inflation have emerged. These suggest *demand pull inflation* and *cost push inflation*. While these two main theories dominate economic debate there are several other less 'popular' explanations which see the causes of inflation in a much wider social and economic context. Next there is an examination of the mainstream theories and to what extent they can provide explanations of the recent inflation in the UK.

Demand pull inflation
One view of inflation widely accepted is the view originally expressed by Keynes in which changes in the price level are linked to changes in aggregate demand and supply in the economy. Aggregate demand is the total demand for goods and services while aggregate supply is the total supply of goods and services in the economy. As explained earlier, Keynes was concerned with a situation when massive cyclical unemployment existed as a result of a very low level of aggregate demand. As aggregate demand expands producers respond by increasing their production of goods and services, thereby increasing aggregate supply and reducing the level of unemployment. The general level of prices remains unchanged as output increases. However as the

economy approaches its full employment level it becomes increasingly difficult for output (*aggregate supply*) to continue to smoothly expand in response to increases in *aggregate demand*. Clearly an economy is made up of many different sectors and in some, production difficulties will be experienced before others. In the same way as explained in Chapter 1, some markets will begin to experience symptoms of excess demand and gradually more sectors will reach this situation until aggregate demand in the overall economy generally exceeds the aggregate supply capable of being produced at full employment. At this point when output cannot expand further, the effect of excess demand is to put pressure on prices.

The mechanisms by which the excess demand results in prices being increased can be briefly summarised as follows. If overall aggregate demand exceeds aggregate supply in the economy this will manifest itself in a number of ways which can be observed by the various sectors. For example, unemployment will be low with numerous job vacancies available, overtime will be worked and there will be a shortage of goods and so on. These conditions will motivate producers in two ways. Firstly, there will be a vigorous demand for labour which enables the trade unions to press for and obtain higher wages for their members. Employers concede these increases which are then passed on to consumers as higher prices. Secondly, some producers respond to market demand by directly raising their prices to what the market will bear. In these two ways prices begin to increase in the overall economy. Furthermore, once the inflationary process begins the role of *expectations* begins to reinforce price rises. In wage negotiations, unions naturally demand a higher settlement if they anticipate a rise in the level of prices in the coming year. This reinforces the increase in wages and once again prices rise. A similar effect may be found with consumers who, if they anticipate a rise in prices, will buy now. They either spend the cash they have or borrow. In either case it will simply add to overall aggregate demand in the economy.

Cost push inflation
An alternative explanation of inflation is to be found in the view that inflationary stimulus does not come from the demand side of the economy as with demand pull, but arises from the *supply side*. Inflation is caused by increases in the costs of the factors of production which in turn leads to producers passing on these cost increases as higher prices to the consumers. The original increases in costs come from either trade unions pushing up wages ahead of what is justified by productivity or independent increases in the costs of raw materials such as that caused by a falling exchange rate. This analysis of inflation is one which has the twin attractions of 'common sense' simplicity and easily identifiable 'culprits' in the inflationary process. For this and other reasons it is a view which must be carefully considered as a possible cause of the recent UK inflation.

Monetary causes of inflation

A third and most debatable cause of inflation is given in the views of the 'monetarist' economists such as Professor Milton Friedman of the University of Chicago. Monetarists see the cause of inflation as an *excessive increase in the money supply*. In doing this they are the modern exponents of earlier economists who believed in the quantity theory of money. Put simply, any increase in the quantity of money in circulation leads, after a time lag, (during which time real output may change) to increases in the level of prices and vice versa. This money supply relationship was formally expressed in *Fisher's equation*,

$$MV = PT$$

where M = the quantity of money,
       V = the velocity of circulation of money,
       P = the general level of prices,
       T = the volume of transactions or real output in the economy

By definition both sides of Fisher's equation are equal since they describe the same thing. For example, if the money supply (M) equals £100m and it circulates five times each year (V), then this £500m which is the value of the money spent on goods, must equal the value of the goods produced in that year, which is the other part of the equation (PT) eg 100 transactions at an average price level of £5 for each transaction. Each side equals £500m.

The importance of the Fisher equation lay in its highlighting of the relationships between the four variables when making certain important assumptions. Firstly, monetarists assume that the level of real output (T) is determined by many varied factors quite independent of the level of the money supply (M). They are prepared to concede that in the short run an increase in the money supply (M) might produce a transient effect upon output and employment but in the long run T is determined by non-monetary variables. Secondly, for all practical purposes the velocity of circulation (V) can be regarded as constant. If V and T are assumed to behave as outlined, then Fisher's equation becomes not a mere tautology but a statement of the behaviour of the relationship between the variables. Any increase in the quantity of money (M) will result in an equal proportional increase in the level of prices (P). For example, if M trebled to £300m (making MV = £1500m) then the average price level P must also be trebled to £15 to give PT = £1500m. This is because both V and T remain stable at 5 and 100 respectively. The real output of the economy, T, is unchanged although because of the rise in the price level, money income has increased to £1500m. The Fisher equation and its assumptions provide the theoretical framework for stating that *changes in the money supply produce changes in the level of prices — inflation*. This very crude explanation is the monetarists' theoretical view of the cause of inflation — excessive increases in the money supply beyond what is justified by the increase in real output (T). The money supply must keep pace with expansion in real output only.

To support this analysis, monetarists can produce clear (to them) empirical evidence over a long historical period and from many countries to show a cause and effect link between an increase in the money supply and a resultant increase in the level of prices.

This section began by noting that this was an area of considerable debate among economists. To a non-monetarist economist very little of the previous explanation is valid. The areas of conflict are numerous. The theoretical assumptions of a stable V and T are not accepted by such academics, so any increase in the money supply could be offset by changes in either V or T. They would accept that if V does not change, an increase in the money supply (M) can produce an increase in real output (T) but it does so by increasing the level of spending or aggregate demand. If T is at its full employment level then prices can rise once again, via the excess demand mechanism as described earlier. To these economists changes in the money supply do not necessarily always result in inflation. Moreover, controversy exists about other aspects of the monetarist views such as the exact mechanism by which an increase in M produces a rise in P, and whether the change in M is the cause of or the effect of the variation in P. Even the empirical evidence, which seems so conclusive to the monetarists, is not entirely accepted as providing practical evidence of theory. The monetarist explanation of inflation is one example of an area where economists disagree fundamentally on the causes of the inflationary disease which results inevitable in widely different prescriptions for its cure.

Causes of the recent inflation in the UK
As shown earlier the 1970s have been a decade in which inflation became a major economic and social problem in the UK. Several factors can be suggested as the possible cause(s) of this inflation. The first explanation of inflation, ie demand pull, suggests one cause. Were the 1970s an era when there was obviously excess demand in the UK economy? By all the statistical indicators of excess demand, ie unemployment, job vacancies, etc the period was one when it appears hard to find evidence of excess demand. As Table 11.1, p. 485 illustrates, unemployment levels were extremely high and rising in the 1970s compared to the earlier decade. Other indicators such as the vacancy rate give similar results. The conclusion must be that it is hard to pin the blame for inflation on excess demand. A second possible explanation lies in the increase in wage levels which occurred in the 1970s, as shown in Table 11.3.

At first sight the statistics seem to lend evidence to a *wages explosion* from 1970 onwards which results in higher prices after an appropriate time lag. Other statistics, eg industrial disputes, seem to support a more militant attitude on the part of the unions. There is no doubt that superficially at least the evidence for wage push is inviting. But on

Year	% Change	Year	% Change
1960	2·6	1970	9·9
1961	4·2	1971	12·9
1962	3·6	1972	13·8
1963	3·7	1973	13·7
1964	4·8	1974	19·8
1965	4·3	1975	29·5
1966	4·6	1976	19·3
1967	3·9	1977	6·6
1968	6·6	1978	14·1
1969	5·3	1979	14·9

Table 11.3 Percentage change in wage rates 1960 – 1979

Source: Economic Trends (Annual Supplement) 1980 and Department of Employment Gazette

closer inspection this is not so clear. For example, once inflation gets under way (may be fuelled by other factors such as import costs) it becomes difficult to determine cause and effect so clearly. Are wages merely responding to anticipated inflation rather than causing it? Furthermore, monetarists would refer back to the quantity theory, MV = PT, and say that if prices P are raised by wage push forces, a larger money stock M is required to finance the same volume of transactions or output T. (Offsetting changes in V might enable inflation to continue in the short run.) If M is not expanded, then T must fall leading to falling employment with moderating effects on wage settlements. They conclude that *monetary expansion is essential to permit wage push to continue.* But in practice, even if this is true in principle, *governments may not react in this way by allowing unemployment to rise to levels sufficient to damp down wage settlements.* In spite of these conflicting arguments, it appears that, at least in the early 1970s, some truth lies in the wage push view of inflation although after 1972, the third variable was becoming more apparent.

An alternative or complementary cost-push cause is seen by many in the rise in import prices which has occurred since the early 1970s. One major element was the rise in oil prices introduced by OPEC (Organisation of Petroleum Exporting Countries), following the 1973 Arab-Israeli war. This led to increased production costs which in turn resulted in higher prices which could have had a feedback effect in terms of stimulating wage demands thereby fuelling wage push inflation.

The final element in the inflation analysis is evidence for the monetarist view of inflation. There is no doubt that in the early 1970s there was a marked increase in the growth of the money supply as shown in Table 11.4.

Year	Percentage change
1970	9·5
1971	13·9
1972	24·5
1973	26·3
1974	10·2
1975	6·6
1976	9·5
1977	10·0
1978	15·0
1979	12·6

Table 11.4 Percentage annual change in M3, 1970 – 1979

Source: Financial Statistics, Bank of England.

The statistics provide yet more proof to the monetarists of the validity of the explanation of inflation. At this point the debate between economists sharpens. To the non monetarist any increase in M3 leads to *lower interest rates* and *credit* which is more freely available, both of which add to *spending* and boost *aggregate demand*. In other words the monetary expansion works via the excess demand process explained earlier. Lack of excess demand in the 1970s seems to rule out this cause. The evidence can thus be used to support either view of the inflationary process.

In conclusion the truth is probably that inflation is caused by many factors which also interact on each other. This complexity makes identifying the cause extremely difficult and probably gives rise to governments looking for easy obvious targets, whether these be irresponsible trade unions or excessive growth in the money supply. It is this difficulty in determining the underlying cause of inflation which results in the conflicting approaches to solutions which are discussed later in the chapter.

Economic growth

Only by achieving a satisfactory rate of growth in its productive potential can the UK economy produce more goods and services which provide its citizens with their wealth and standard of living. One of the most disturbing features of the UK post-war economic record has been the relatively low economic growth when compared to rival economies. The UKs growth rate has tended to be of the order of 2 – 3% in good years and zero or even negative in poor years. Table 11.5 illustrates varying growth rates between 1974 and 1979 for selected economies.

Japan	5·0%
USA	3·3%
France	3·0%
W Germany	2·8%
Italy	2·3%
UK	1·8%

Table 11.5 – Average % annual growth in Gross Domestic Product 1974 – 1979 (selected countries)

Source: The British Economy 1981 (Lloyds Bank)

The reasons for the UKs relatively poor performance are tied in with the reasons for economic growth itself, which is by no means a clearly understood process. Long-term growth represents an increase in *potential aggregate supply* and so initially is determined by the economic resources available to the economy together with the efficient and full utilisation of these resources. As explained in Chapter 1, capital and how it is used is probably the most decisive factor of production in determining growth rates. It has often been suggested that the UKs poor performance has been in part due to a failure to re-invest and modernise its capital stock. The use of older, less efficient machinery than our rivals has produced slower rates of growth. Why this reluctance to invest has happened is another difficult question. Answers to this question produce a very wide range of hypotheses. Some would criticise the basic capitalist structure of the economy while others argue that too much of the UKs investment spending has been wrongly directed – houses and welfare facilities instead of factories and machines. Others see the cautious investment policy and lack of lending by the banks as the root cause of the problem. The variations in political and policy targets inherent in the Labour v. Conservative syndrome is often quoted as causing a discontinuity in business planning. This has produced a lack of the confidence which is essential to industry and commerce. This vagueness in understanding what conditions are necessary for growth tends to lead to economic growth being something to be hoped for rather than a specific policy target. The announcement of a National Plan with definite growth targets is a relic of the 1960s tendency for economic planning. All that governments can hope for is that growth will be a spin off from achieving the other policy objectives of full employment and stable prices.

Balance of payments equilibrium

As seen in Chapter 9 p. 418 the UK has experienced fluctuating fortunes in its attempts to achieve balance of payments equilibrium since the Second World War. By limiting the analysis to the period of the last 20 years, a distinct pattern emerges in relation to the balance of payments. In the early 1960s, the UKs balance of trade deteriorated with the result that despite surpluses in the invisible balance, the current account moved into increasing deficit. The conclusion of this trend was seen in the devaluation of the pound in November 1967. The position changed dramatically thereafter, as the visible deficit decreased and together with the increased invisible surplus which also occurred, resulted in a current account surplus. This strong position in the UKs balance of payments did not last beyond the early 1970s however. Table 11.6 illustrates some of the key components in the balance of payments for this last decade. The major trend illustrated was the movement of the current account into massive deficit, reaching almost £3500 million in 1974. This was the result of many factors, most important of which was the price rises in primary products (especially oil) and a decline in the growth of world trade. To some extent, these deficits were alleviated by surpluses on the investment and capital flows, but still left the UK with the problem of financing an unfavourable overall deficit flow. This was achieved by relying on both overseas borrowing and drawing upon official reserves of foreign currency.

But as Table 11.6 shows the UK has achieved a turnaround in its payments position in the late 1970s. The years after 1977 showed a considerable improvement (despite temporary distortions in the 1979 figures), reaching a position in 1980 when a current account surplus of over £2500 million was recorded. An important element in this improvement has been the effects of North Sea Oil in reducing the petroleum trade deficit.

Year	Visible trade balance	Invisible trade balance	Current account balance	Investment & other capital trans-actions	Balancing item	Official financing
1970	− 32	+ 814	+ 782	+ 546	− 41	− 1420
1971	+ 190	+ 883	+ 1073	+ 1791	+ 282	− 3271
1972	− 761	+ 932	+ 162	− 683	− 744	+ 1141
1973	− 2586	+ 1498	− 1088	+ 86	+ 231	+ 771
1974	− 5350	+ 1923	− 3427	+ 1531	+ 250	+ 1646
1975	− 3333	+ 1601	− 1732	+ 126	+ 141	+ 1465
1976	− 3927	+ 2867	− 1060	− 3093	+ 525	+ 3628
1977	− 2278	+ 2072	− 206	+ 4434	+ 3134	− 7362
1978	− 1573	+ 2349	+ 776	− 3817	+ 1915	+ 1126
1979	− 3497	+ 2072	− 1425	+ 1488	+ 1647	− 1906
1980	+ 1177	+ 1586	+ 2763 (1 + 2)	− 829	− 742	− 1372

Table 11.6   UK balance of payments 1970 − 1980
(Figures in £ million)

Note: Columns 3 + 4 + 5 add up to the 'Balance for Official Financing' as explained in Chapter 9. This deficit/surplus flow is normally the opposite of the Official Financing figure in Column 6. This is not true in certain years because of the allocation of gold and SDR's.

Source: Monthly Digest of Statistics, August 1981

Overall however, the period cannot in any sense be described as one in which equilibrium in the economy has been generally achieved. This is especially true when it is considered that the recent improvements in the balance of payments have been attained against a domestic background of rising unemployment and poor economic growth.

Conclusion

Having analysed the four main causes of concern in the UK economy it is apparent that in recent years the overall performance has fallen far short of meeting the objectives identified at the beginning of the chapter.

Management of the economy

Introduction

In the previous sections the policy objectives of the government and the extent of the problems facing the UK economy were examined. In this section the way in which the government's attempts to achieve these policy objectives by active intervention in the market economy will be considered. It was J M Keynes who attempted to explain in his book *The General Theory of Employment, Interest and Money* (1936) why a market economy does not automatically produce full employment as predicted in the earlier views of the classical economists. Keynes' ideas were not accepted in time to solve the problem of massive unemployment between the two wars, but found acceptance in the 1940s and were expressed in the commitment of post-war governments to maintain full employment by a policy of *active intervention* in the market economy. This policy aimed to control the level of demand in the economy in order to achieve not only full employment but also the other three policy objectives. *Demand management* policies have been the basis of controlling the economy since 1945 under the influence of *Keynesian* Theory. To some extent Keynesian methods tended to reduce the importance of money in explaining the behaviour of income, output, employment and prices and partly as a result of this, and the problems encountered in the 1970s, there has been a revival of the *monetarist* views. This school of thought, led by Friedman and others, emphasises the importance of controlling the money supply in determining the level of demand and influencing the variables in the economy. However, the debate between Keynesians and Monetarists revolves around a common analytical framework which must first be examined. Afterwards the methods of demand management can be discussed and the problems associated with each method are considered.

It is important to realise however that this analysis is concerned with explaining short-run fluctuations in the levels of income, output and employment in the economy. As such, emphasis is placed upon *aggre-*

495

gate demand, ie total expenditure on goods and services in the economy, as being the important factor in explaining fluctuations. In the long run, as productive capacity of the economy changes, explanations of variations in output are to be found by examining changes in *aggregate supply*, ie total supply of goods and services in the economy.

The present analysis assumes that productive capacity in the economy is fixed. The starting point of the analysis is to build up a series of simple economic models which provide the basis of the explanations.

Equilibrium in the circular flow of income

Fig 11.1 illustrates an economy consisting of only two groups or sectors – *Producers* who provide all of the output in the economy by hiring the factors of production from *Consumers* who also consume all of the output produced.

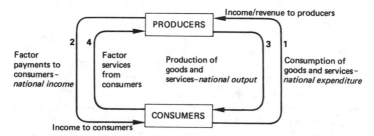

Fig 11.1   Circular flow of income in a two-sector economy

The consumers provide the factor services – in practice all the factors of land, labour and capital – to producers which enable the goods and services or national output to be produced. *National Output* represents aggregate supply. In return, the consumers are rewarded with factor payments or incomes – in practice rent, wages and interest – by the producers. This constitutes *National Income.* Consumers spend this income on the goods and services produced and this constitutes *National Expenditure* which represents Aggregate Demand. From this simple model, certain important principles emerge. First, all the four flows are inter-dependent in that flow 1 provides the money for flow 2 and flow 3 determines the size of flow 4. The critical flow 1 of aggregate demand determines the values of the other three – income, output and employment. Secondly, if the three flows are to be stable, ie the economy is in equilibrium, aggregate demand must be *stable and equal* to the value of aggregate supply. Thirdly, any variations in aggregate demand will produce variations in the other three flows and produce an unstable economy in terms of income, output and employment. The Keynesian model shows the importance of aggregate demand as the determining variable. But even if the economy is in equilibrium with stable flows, Keynes stressed that there is no reason why, in an unregulated economy, this should be at a level sufficient to ensure full employment of all the resources of land, labour and capital. The market economy experiences wide variations in aggregate demand and to explain why this occurs, it is necessary to introduce the idea of *withdrawals* and *injections* into the circular flow model.

Fig 11.2 takes account of the fact that there are both withdrawals and injections in the circular flow of income.

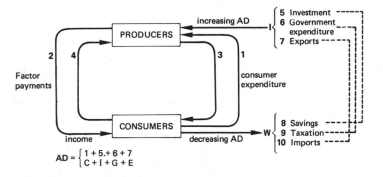

$$AD = \begin{cases} 1 + 5. + 6 + 7 \\ C + I + G + E \end{cases}$$

Fig 11.2   Circular flow of income in a two-sector economy with injections and withdrawals

When consumers receive their factor incomes from producers, not all is spent on the goods and services of flow 3. Fig 11.2 is modified to include two other groups or sectors in the economy, the *government and international sectors*, making a four sector model of the economy. The withdrawals (W) are savings, taxation and spending on imports. All three represent a withdrawal from the circular flow in the sense that they do not contribute to aggregate demand for domestic goods and services and so reduce the level of domestic income, output and employment. The injections (I) are investment expenditure, government expenditure and exports. These three contribute to aggregate demand for domestic goods and services thereby increasing domestic income, output and employment. The equilibrium condition for income can now be stated in terms of injections and withdrawals which must balance each other, W = I, or alternatively if aggregate demand (which is now flow 1 + injections 5, 6 and 7) still equals aggregate supply (flow 3). To some extent W and I are related since savings finance investment, taxation finances government spending and imports relate to exports. But the problem is that, as Keynes pointed out, there is no reason why W and I should be equal since:

a) the determinants of savings and investment are largely independent. (The classical economists did believe savings and investment were equalised via the rate of interest.);

b) governments rarely have balanced budgets where taxation equals expenditure; and

c) exports and imports are independent of each other as long as international borrowing is occurring or countries have adequate reserves to cover imbalances. To understand why fluctuations occur in the level of income, etc it is necessary to examine why variations occur in the withdrawals and injections and what happens to income when W and I are unequal.

Changes in the level of income via injections and withdrawals in a two-sector economy
As explained earlier, the level of income is only in equilibrium when W = I. If *injections exceed withdrawals* then the level of income must increase and if *withdrawals exceed injections* the level of income must decrease. Injections and withdrawals are brought into balance by changes in the level of income itself via what is called the *multiplier* process. It is this process which is now examined, but first it is necessary to make some simple assumptions about the economy in which this process operates.

Firstly, the economy has unemployed resources available so that any change in aggregate demand produces a change in real income and output and not just a change in money income, ie a change in the price level.

Secondly, it is assumed that the economy operates with a given state of technology and as a consequence, increases in aggregate demand which stimulate aggregate supply result in increases in the level of employment.

Thirdly, the analysis is a short-run theory so that at full employment level, aggregate supply productive capacity is constant.

Finally, the problem of inventories or stocks is simplified by assuming that output equals sales. To summarise, the economy is one of unemployed resources where variations in injections and withdrawals result in changes in aggregate demand thereby producing variations in the levels of real income output and employment.

The starting point of the analysis is to assume an economy in which the level of income is in equilibrium since withdrawals equal injections. Such a model is presented in Fig 11.3 and at first it is assumed that it is the original two-sector model introduced earlier. Therefore the only withdrawal is savings and the only injection investment.

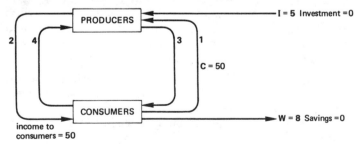

Fig 11.3   Changes in the level of income

498

At the beginning of period O, consumers receive £50m in income from producers as their contribution to production. This £50m is available either to spend on consumption (flow 1) or saving (flow 8). The question to be asked now is what will determine the levels of consumption and savings and investment?

The consumption function
At this point a fundamental concept in Keynes' analysis is introduced – the *Consumption function*. Keynes showed that the main determinant of the level of consumption (flow 1), and hence also savings, is the *level of income*. The relationship between consumption and income is called the consumption function and a hypothetical consumption function is shown in Fig 11.4. Income is measured on the horizontal axis and consumption on the vertical axis. The consumption function is a positive linear relationship of the form $C = a + bY$, where Y is the level of income. The 45° line shows the points where income and consumption are equal, i.e. there are no savings. The consumption function illustrated is of the form $C = £10m + 4/5Y$. A few important points must be considered about the consumption function before the analysis can proceed. First, when income is at zero consumption is still positive, £10m, because people or the economy as a whole are financing current consumption from past savings – they are *dis-saving*. This dissaving, shown by the distance D between the two lines on the graph continues until the level of income reaches point OY_1 where income and consumption are equal ie at OY_1, income is $OY_1 = Y_1X$. Consumption also equals Y_1X. Beyond OY_1, income always exceeds consumption therefore positive savings occur shown by the distance S between the two lines on the graph.

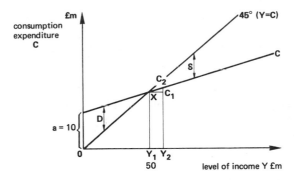

Fig 11.4   The consumption function

Second, the consumption function is shown as a simple linear relationship. Four terms are important to introduce at this point:

1 *Average Propensity to Consume* $= \dfrac{\text{Consumption}}{\text{Income}} = \dfrac{C}{Y}$

2 *Average Propensity to Save* $= \dfrac{\text{Savings}}{\text{Income}} = \dfrac{S}{Y}$

3 *Marginal Propensity to Consume* $= \dfrac{\text{Marginal Consumption}}{\text{Marginal Income}} = \dfrac{\triangle C}{\triangle Y}$

4 *Marginal Propensity to Save* $= \dfrac{\text{Marginal Savings}}{\text{Marginal Income}} = \dfrac{\triangle S}{\triangle Y}$

The marginal propensities are the more important at this point. As income increases, so the level of consumption also increases, eg an increase in income of £20m shown by Y_1Y_2 produces an increase in consumption of 4/5(20) = £16m equal to C_1C_2.

The marginal propensity to consume is $\dfrac{\triangle C}{\triangle Y} = \dfrac{C_1C_2}{Y_1Y} = \dfrac{16}{20} = \dfrac{4}{5}$.

The marginal propensity to save is $\dfrac{\triangle S}{\triangle Y} = \dfrac{4}{20} = \dfrac{1}{5}$.

Graphically the marginal propensity to consume is the *gradient* of the consumption function. It can be seen that the marginal propensities are constant in this example, whereas the average propensity to consume falls and the average propensity to save rises as income increases. A simple numerical example confirms this point. See Table 11.7.

Income £m (Y)	Consumption £m (C)	Savings £m (S)	APC $\dfrac{C}{Y}$	MPC $\dfrac{\triangle C}{\triangle Y}$	APS $\dfrac{S}{Y}$	MPS $\dfrac{\triangle S}{\triangle Y}$
0	10	− 10	−	−	−	−
				0·8		0·2*
50	50	0	1·0		0	
				0·8		0·2
100	90	10	0·9		0·1	
				0·8		0·2
150	130	20	0·87		0·13	

Table 11.7

* When Y = 0, C = 10 there is a saving of − 10. When Y increases to 50 C = 50 so savings is zero. Savings have increased from − 10 to 0 giving a mps equal to $\dfrac{10}{50} = 0·2$.

In reality, the relationship between consumption expenditure and income as expressed in the consumption schedule, is much more complicated than this simple linear function suggests. For example, although undoubtedly income level is the main influence on consumption, other factors may exert an influence especially in the short term. Consumers' expectations about future price changes may influence consumption and hence the propensities for a given income level. The availability and price of credit in purchasing consumer durables can also influence spending habits. In the longer term, such influences as changes in income distribution will also influence propensities to consume and save. In practice, Keynes' proposition of a *mpc* which was positive, fractional and reasonably stable is not altogether supported by empirical evidence. In the UK since 1945, the mpc has varied considerably, eg between 1952 and 1974 the mpc varied between 0.7 and 1.2, averaging at 0.9.

Indeed much economic research has been undertaken to discover empirical evidence for the Keynesian consumption-income relationship in the long run. It is impossible to summarise this research data here but Keynesian theory seemed to be contradicted in the long run by the empirical data which suggested a fairly constant *APC*. One approach to reconcile this evidence is to interpret the consumption functions illustrated in the figures as essentially short-term functions, in which consumers' spending habits are relatively fixed. Consumers do not dramatically change their expenditure patterns in response to short term fluctuations in disposable income. Over a longer time period as income increases so variations in expenditure occur as Consumers adjust to their higher levels of income.

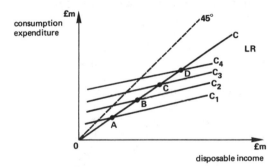

Fig 11.5   Consumption function in the long run

In Fig 11.5 points A, B, C and D are observed points of income and expenditure over four years. The schedules C_1, C_2, C_3 and C_4 are the short-term consumption functions for those years, which drift upwards over the long-run period. Joining the points A, B, C and D gives the long run consumption function C_{LR} giving a stable APC.

Several theories have been proposed to explain such long-run behaviour of the consumption function of which the most notable are Professor Milton Friedman's *Permanent Income Hypothesis* and Professor Duesenberry's *Relative Income Hypothesis*.

The investment function

Having examined the consumption function it is now necessary to briefly explain the main determinants of the level of investment. Investment is expenditure on capital goods by organisations and as such is an

501

unstable injection in the circular flow of income. Such instability means that fluctuations in the level of investment are a prime cause of changes in the level of income. There are several different explanations of what causes investment to vary, but none provides an entirely satisfactory and comprehensive theory.

Of the mainstream theories the *'accelerator principle'* is the most important. This suggests that the level of investment is influenced by changes occurring in the level of demand in the economy. The purpose of any investment project is to enable the organisation to produce goods and services in the future for sale in the market. Clearly if the economy is expanding and businesses are optimistic about future sales prospects, this will stimulate investment spending and vice-versa. The accelerator principle states that the level of investment varies directly with the rate of change in output or sales. A certain capital stock is required to produce any given output and if this output level increases then more capital will be required. At its simplest level the theory assumes that investment expenditure changes in direct proportion to the variation in the level of output at all levels of output. This amount of investment necessary to produce an extra unit of output is called the *'accelerator coefficient'* (V), ie investment in time, t, equals the change in the level of income or output, $\triangle Y$, multiplied by the investment co-efficient.

$$I_t = \triangle Y . \times V$$

It should be noted that I_t represents new or net investment in capital and not simple replacement investment for the existing capital stocks.

A simple numerical example will explain this process. It is assumed that the level of income is stable with the result that the capital stock is fully utilised and capable of producing the output required. The accelerator co-efficient is assumed to be 5. This is the position shown in period 0 of Table 11.8.

Time period	Income level Y	Change in income $\triangle$ Y	Investment I
0 – 1	100	0	0
	+ 10%	+ 10%	
1 – 2	110	+ 10	50
	+ 10%	+ 10%	+ 10%
2 – 3	121	+ 11	55
	+ 5%	+ 5%	
3 – 4	127.05	+ 6.05	30.25

Table 11.8   A numerical example of the accelerator principle

Income rises as shown in period 1 by 10% to its new level of 110. This leads to an increase in demand which can only be met by expanding output which itself requires new or net investment in the capital stock. Net investment of 50 is required in period 1, ie $I_c = \triangle Y \times V$

$$(50 = 10 \times 5)$$

502

In period 2 the income continues to increase at this 10% rate producing a change in income of 11 and resulting in net investment of 55. In the third period however, the rate of expansion in income declines to only 5% with the consequence that net investment declines to 30. The example illustrates that the level of net investment shown in the last column is determined by changes in the rate of growth in income. If net investment is to continue to grow it is not sufficient that income expands. It must grow at a constant percentage increase at the very least. Any fall in the rate of increase produces a fall in the level of investment. This is the cause of the unstable variations in the level of investment. Of course, in such a simple form, it cannot be suggested that the acceleration principle alone is an entirely satisfactory explanation. Modifications to the principle have been added to improve its sophistication, but as long as the motivations for investment are so complex economists cannot claim to have produced a satisfactory explanation of its causes.

Having examined the determinants of consumption and of savings, it is now possible to proceed with the analysis of the two-sector model.

In period O, consumers will divide their £50m of received income Y as follows: Consumption 50 and savings 0. This is income level OY_1 on the graph where income and consumption are equal with no savings, and is shown in line 0 of Tables 11.9, 11.10 and Figure 11.6.

Period	Income received by consumers at the beginning of period Y_c (Flow 2) (Y_p from previous period)	Consumption C (Flow 1) $C = 10 + 4/5Y_c$	Savings S (Flow 8)	Investment I (Flow 5)	Income received by producers at end of period Y_p (C + I)
0	50	50	0	0	50
1	50	50	0	10	60
2	60	58	2	10	68
3	68	64·4	3.6	10	74·4
4					
n	100	90	10	10	100

Table 11.9 Total changes in the level of income — caused by an increase in investment expenditure

	$\triangle Y_c$	$\triangle C$	$\triangle S$	$\triangle I$	$\triangle Y_p$
0	–	–	–	–	–
1	–	–	–	10	10
2	10	8	2	–	8
3	8	6·4	1·6	–	6·4
n	50	40	10	10	50

(total increases in periods)

Table 11.10 Marginal changes in the level of income

Since at this point investment is zero then producers receive 50 from sales which is available to pay to their factors of production thus forming consumers' income at the beginning of period 1. Line 0 represents an equilibrium situation since W (savings) = I, (investment) = 0 or alternatively Aggregate Demand (C + I = 50) is equal to Aggregate Supply (value of goods produced = 50).

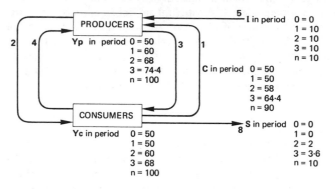

Fig 11.6   Changes in the level of income as a result of change in investment

This situation could continue indefinately. During period 1 however there is an increase in the level of investment. At this point an obvious question to ask is − what causes the level of investment to rise? A brief analysis of the investment function was given earlier but it is assumed that investment is an independent constant, unrelated to the level of income, ie it is fixed and determined by factors independent of any variable in the model. This is not to deny the importance of changes in investment, but rather to suggest at this point that unlike the role of the consumption function, the investment function does not play such a central part in the model.

Consumers receive Y_c = 50 in period 1, of which C = 50 and S = 0. But investment increases from 0 to 10 during period 1, so giving Yp = 60. Equilibrium is disturbed as investment now exceeds saving causing the level of income to rise. Producers will hire more factors from consumers in order to expand aggregate supply output (flow 3) resulting in rising employment (flow 4) and rising income (flow 2). At the beginning of period 2, Y_c = 60 of which C = 58 and S = 2 (because $\triangle Y$ = 10 and the mpc = 4/5 and mps = 1/5 therefore $\triangle C$ = 4/5 $\triangle Y$ = 8 and $\triangle S$ = 1/5 $\triangle Y$ = 2) . Investment however now remains constant at 10 for the rest of the periods. The expansionary trend will continue in subsequent periods as shown in the tables and figure. The expansion in income (and also output and employment) will end as shown in period n. In period n, consumers receive Y_c = 100 of which C = 90, S = 10, I = 10 and Y_p = 100. The economy is in equilibrium once again since S = I or AD = AS. An examination of the figures shows that the initial increase in investment $\triangle I$ of £10m has caused the level of income to increase by $\triangle Y$ =

504

50. This increase in sufficient to raise consumption by $\triangle C = 40$, but more important to raise savings by $\triangle S = 10$.

In other words, income has increased sufficiently to create extra savings equal to the extra investment. This process by which equilibrium is restored when extra savings are created to balance the extra investment is called the multiplier process. Before examining this multiplier process in more detail it can be illustrated how this rise in investment causes the level of income, output and employment to increase making use of the graph below. In the example, in period 0 the economy is in equilibrium at Y_o with $Y = 50$, $C = 50$ and $I = S = 0$. The consumption function C represents the level of aggregate demand since there is no investment. In period 1 the level of investment rise to £10m and thereafter remains constant. This results in the investment function I being added to the consumption function C to give the overall aggregate demand line $C + I$. At the end of period 1, producers receive $Y_p = 60$ shown by the distance Y_oA which is paid to consumers at the beginning of period 2, shown by the distance Y_2B. Of Y_2B (60), $C = Y_2C$ (58), $S = CB$ (2) but $I = CD$ (10) therefore $Y_p = C + I = Y_2C + CD$. Y_2D forms the income paid to consumers (68) at the beginning of period 3, shown by Y_3E and so the process continues until the economy is in equilibrium at period n with income at Y_n (100), $C = Y_nX$ (90) and $S = I = XY$ (10).

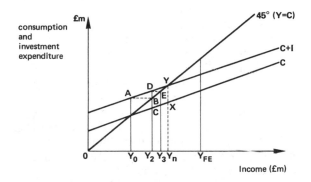

Fig 11.7   Changes in income as a result of changes in investment.

The previous example has illustrated how a change in investment, $\triangle I$, produces a multiplied change in Income, $\triangle Y$, in the same direction, ie

$$\begin{array}{ccccc} \triangle I & \times & \text{multiplier (K)} & = & \triangle Y \\ +10 & \times & 5 & = & +50 \end{array}$$

The constant K, is called the multiplier and its value depends directly upon the values of the mpc and mps. When the level of spending is raised by $\triangle I$ some of the increase in income is passed on as consumption

505

and fuels the circular flow, but some is lost to the circular flow by the withdrawal of savings. Like a water system, the greater the proportion which leaks from the circular flow (mps) in each period, the less will be final increase in income in period n. In this example, 1/5 (mps) leaks from any extra income at each stage with only 4/5 (mpc) being passed on to the next stage. Therefore the value of the mps will determine the final increase in income, ie

$$K = \frac{1}{mps} \text{ or } \frac{1}{1-mpc}$$

$$K = \frac{1}{1/5} \text{ or } \frac{1}{1-4/5} = 5$$

In this model, the value of the multiplier is 5 because the mps is 1/5. The greater the mps the less the value of the multiplier and vice-versa. The model has illustrated how a change in investment produces a change in the level of income sufficient to create additional savings to balance the original variation in investment. The multiplier process adjusts the income level until injections equal withdrawals and income is in equilibrium. It is important to realise however, that this multiplier process will result from changes in any withdrawal or injection, which has important implications when considering the role of the government in influencing the level of aggregate demand. For the present, in the two-sector model of the economy the level of income will be in equilibrium when savings equals investment. As explained earlier however, this equilibrium level may not be sufficient to ensure full employment of all resources. In Fig 11.8 income is in equilibrium at level Y_n, since savings equals investment. But full employment income is at Y_{FE}. Aggregate demand is insufficient to produce equilibrium at full employment. It requires extra expenditure equal to AB to raise the aggregate demand function to $C + I + E$. The deficiency in spending of AB is called the *deflationary gap*. In the two-sector model this could be filled by extra investment or consumption spending. Conversely if even more spending is generated as shown by $C + I + E_1$, real output cannot increase above its full employment level Y_{FE}. The only result is a rise in the level of money income not real income, ie a rise in the level of prices. The excess expenditure over that which is required to produce Y_{FE} is called the *inflationary gap* – equal to CD. In the next section there is a discussion of how governments may attempt to influence aggregate demand in order to avoid both deflationary and inflationary gaps.

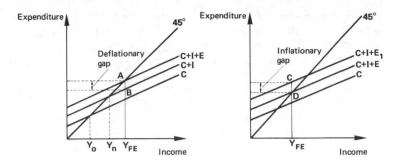

Fig 11.8   Deflationary gap   Inflationary gap

The role of the government

So far this analysis has examined how equilibrium income is established in a two-sector economy with no government activity. Now the model is expanded to a three-sector economy by looking at the role of government in influencing the level of income, output and employment. The government intervenes in the circular flow of income in order to achieve specific economic policy objectives which are regarded as desirable, ie full employment, price stability, economic growth and balance of payments equilibrium. To achieve these objectives, it makes use of various policy instruments, such as *fiscal and monetary policies.* These influence aggregate demand. Thus, the ideal target is to achieve equilibrium in the level of income at full employment level Y_{FE}, avoiding both a deflationary gap with consequent unemployed resources and an inflationary gap with consequent inflation. With this target as its aim, the government manipulates demand as part of its stabilisation policies. Before examining these methods, two warnings are required. First, although all post-war governments would accept the four targets as objectives, different governments would emphasise different targets. This is made more important by the fact that some degree of contradiction may exist between targets. For example, full employment and low inflation may be inappropriate concurrent aims. Secondly, considerable debate exists over the best instruments to use to achieve these targets, and there is even disagreement as to the very nature of the problem, eg the causes of inflation. With this warning in mind, now examine what actions the government can take in various situations. Starting from a situation where income is in equilibrium at less than full employment, Y_n in Fig 11.8, the level of aggregate demand must be raised to the level shown by the function C + I + E. To achieve this any one of the components of demand could be increased – consumption, investment or government spending. The instruments are either fiscal or monetary policy.

507

Fiscal policy measures

The activities of the government significantly influence aggregate demand and the circular flow in two ways. Firstly, by variations in the *levels of taxation* (a withdrawal from the circular flow) the government can directly influence the consumer expenditure flow and to a lesser extent the investment expenditure flow (Flows 1 and 5 in Fig 11.2). Secondly, the *government's own expenditure* (Flow 6 in Fig 11.2) can be directly varied in order to influence aggregate demand. Manipulation of taxation and government expenditure in order to influence demand is called *fiscal policy*. If the economy is in equilibrium at below full employment level Y_{FE}, then fiscal policy can be used to raise the level of aggregate demand to the required level as illustrated by function C + I + E. A number of possible different policies may be used to achieve this result. The net results must be to increase overall spending in the economy by either taxation and/or government spending policies. Now examine each in turn, looking at government spending first.

An increase in government spending G by £10m will be subject to the multiplier effect in the same way as an increase in investment or other spending. In Fig 11.9 the new aggregate demand function is shown as C + I + E. The extra £10m of government spending has created (£10m × 5) an extra £50m of income, making the new equilibrium of £150m. At £150m, C = 130, S = 20, I = 10 and G = 10. Therefore withdrawals (S = 20) equal injections (I + G = 20). Government spending can exert a powerful effect on the level of income, output and employment in the economy. The deflationary gap with consequent unemployment can be eliminated by the government *spending its way out of recession*. Alternatively, the government can eliminate the deflationary gap by reducing taxation in order to produce an increase in consumer expenditure. Suppose that the government reduced taxation in order to leave consumers with an extra £10m of disposable income available for spending on goods and services. With marginal propensities of 4/5 and 1/5 respectively, this increase in disposable income of £10m will increase consumption spending by 4/5 × £10m = £8m while the other £2m will simply be lost to the circular flow as savings. An £8m increase in consumption expenditure is multiplied five times to raise income by £40m to its new equilibrium level of £190m. The equivalent changes in G and T have different effects because any reduction in taxation increases not only consumption but also savings. The relationship between the change in taxation and the change in income is called the *tax multiplier*. It always has a value which is 1 less than the income multiplier (5 and 4 in this example).

Note: To achieve a £50m increase in the level of income will require a reduction in taxation of not £10m but £12.5m.

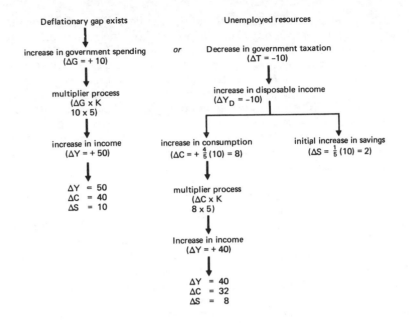

Fig 11.9   Relation using the fiscal multiplier

It is possible to illustrate this tax multiplier process by increasing the complexity of the model to allow for the withdrawal of taxation and the injection of government expenditure. For the present analysis it can simply be said that in the example described the Consumption function would move upwards in the diagram by +£8m.

Inflationary gaps may be tackled in a similar but reverse manner, either by a reduction in government spending or an increase in taxation. As previously shown however, the increase in taxation would need to be larger than the decrease in expenditure to produce a similar fall in income.

Because of the different effects of taxation and expenditure changes, *a balanced budget* will not have a neutral effect upon the economy. An increase in expenditure of £10m raises income by £50m. If taxation is increased by £10m to finance this expenditure this decreases income by £40m. The net effect of a balanced budget is expansionary, ie income increases by a net £10m. The balanced budget multiplier is equal to one. Equal increases in G and T raise the level of income by exactly the amount of the change in taxation and expenditure.

Until the Keynesian revolution changed economic thought, it was conventional good practice to always balance the government's budget whatever the economic situation – recession or boom. A balanced budget implied no active government intervention to stabilise changes in income and employment in the economy. Furthermore, in a recession such as occurred in the inter-war period, the necessity to balance the budget when income and tax revenue were falling meant having to cut government expenditures, thereby worsening the effects of the recession. Only when incomes and revenue increased could expenditure likewise be raised. Such *pro-cyclical* policies were directly opposed to Keynes' teachings which showed how *counter-cyclical* policies could be used to stablise fluctuations in the economy − boosting expenditure in recession and vice-versa.

Finally, before leaving fiscal policy, two separate groups of taxation and expenditure measures can be identified − automatic and discretionary. Automatic measures act automatically to counter the recession or boom without specific policy decisions being taken by the government. For example, in the recession, as unemployment rises, income and tax revenue fall, there will be a rise in social security payments such as unemployment, etc. This increases the injections via government expenditure into the circular flow. Similarly falling consumer income and expenditure means falling tax revenue which reduces the taxation withdrawal from the circular flow. *Automatic fiscal stabilisers* such as these help to even out the worst of the fluctuations in the economy. Despite automatic stabilisers the government will use discretionary measures which are specific policy decisions taken to counter the boom or slump, eg a planned increase or decrease in the government's capital investment programmes.

In practice fiscal policy measures are more difficult to implement and less predictive in their effects than has been assumed. Changing expenditure programmes over a short term present numerous political and economic difficulties for the government. Likewise the results of tax changes on expenditure by consumers have often been unpredictable. Despite these difficulties however, fiscal policy has been the major method of controlling the economy from the post-war period until the mid-1970s, when monetary policy began to become more accepted by governments.

Monetary policy measures
In addition to fiscal policy, the government may attempt to influence the economy by the use of monetary policy which is concerned with the *control of the supply of money* (*credit*) and *its cost* (*interest rates*). By manipulating these two variables, the government can seek to increase or decrease the level of aggregate demand to whatever it considers appropriate to achieve the policy objectives. For example, if aggregate demand is too low, resulting in unacceptable levels of unemployment, then the government might stimulate spending by increasing the money supply and making credit more easily available. An opposite '*tight*' money policy would be pursued to reduce aggregate demand. This described policy does assume of course, a particular view of the influences of changes in the supply and cost of credit upon the level of spending or aggregate demand in the economy. At one end of the academic spec-

trum is the extreme view that monetary policy is almost entirely ineffective since changes in the supply and cost of credit have no significant influence on the level of spending and aggregate demand. Only fiscal policy is of any use in regulating aggregate demand by directly changing taxation and government spending.

The opposite end of the spectrum is associated with extreme monetarist views which see money as the only important variable. Fiscal policy changes are ineffective in regulating aggregate demand. The authorities need only ensure that the growth of the money supply (M_3) keeps pace with the growth of real output (T) as explained by the quantity theory. This is the self-regulating economy as viewed by the monetarists. The practical significance of these debates is that depending on which view of the workings of the economy is taken by the government, determines which type of policy is in favour – fiscal or monetary. For much of the post-war era, the former view was dominant, leading to fiscal policy being used as the chief instrument of demand management. The late 1970s have seen the dominance of monetarist views within government circles, thereby giving monetary policy a central role in the battle against inflation and unemployment. Fiscal policy is used as a method to support monetary policies as explained later. With this debate in mind it is now feasible to briefly examine the means of monetary policy which are usually employed as part of an overall package.

In order to control the money supply the government seeks to regulate both the availability of credit that the banks are able to lend to borrowers and the cost of that credit. This can be done in several ways.

Cost of credit
The cost of borrowing is determined by the level of interest rates. In the various money markets there are in fact, several interest rates, but the most important is the *Minimum Lending Rate* (MLR). This is the rate at which the Bank of England will lend money to the *Discount Houses* when acting as lender of last resort. As explained in the chapter on capital, the discount houses play a vital role in the money market, acting as middlemen for the commercial banks and other organisations wishing to deposit funds for very short periods. They guarantee to repay these deposits at call or short notice while in turn relending these funds to borrowers who are short of money. But, if the commercial banks require their funds back immediately, then the discount houses may not be able to recall loans quickly enough. They may be forced to borrow from the Bank of England at the Minimum Lending Rate. Thus, the MLR is a reference point used by all financial institutions in establishing rates for lending and borrowing. As an insurance, the lenders must ensure that their lending rates are above MLR for if they are required to borrow themselves, they will make losses if their lending rates are below MLR. Indirectly then, MLR acts as a regulator for all market interest rates since the financial institutions are related by their borrowing and lending activities. If it is raised, then other interest rates

rise and vice-versa and in this way the authorities can influence the cost of borrowing and in so doing increase or decrease its attractiveness. Strictly speaking a change in MLR unaccompanied by other measures to influence the money supply and interest rates would be ineffectual. MLR is effective to the extent that the market is forced to borrow. Other things being equal, borrowing will usually be enforced by other measures such as *open market operations*. However changes in MLR can be used to indicate to the market the direction that the Bank wishes interest rates to move and is likely to take steps (in the open market) to ensure that they do.

For many years, it was the practice of the Bank of England to formerly announce or 'post' MLR changes which were immediately communicated to the financial markets. However as a result of discussions and the resulting Green Paper, the authorities have, as from August 1981, abandoned this practice of continuously posting an MLR. The Bank of England however, still retains the right to announce in advance a minimum rate at which it will carry out its lending activities for a short period ahead. The main purpose of this change is to allow the money markets greater freedom in determining short-term interest rates by the interaction of demand and supply in these markets. At present it appears too early to conclude whether this change will produce any significant difference in the operation of interest rates in the market. The Bank's policy is to be one of attempting to maintain short-term interest rates within a narrow range relying mainly upon open market operations to do this.

The availability of credit

The second means of controlling the money supply is by regulating the amount of credit that the banks are able to lend out. This can be done in several ways.

Open market operations

This is the process by which the Bank of England buys and sells government securities on the open market. For example, if the Bank sells securities, then the purchasers pay for these by cheques drawn on their commercial banks. The commercial banks pay the Bank of England by transferring part of their deposits held at the Bank. The government's account has been credited and the commercial bank's account debited by the same amount. This operation reduces the commercial bank's eligible liabilities to their customers, ie customer deposits at the banks, since the public are in fact holding securities in place of money. But since the commercial banks' own deposits at the Bank of England have been reduced by a similar amount, the effect is also to *reduce their ratio of eligible reserve assets to eligible liabilities*. If the commercial banks are holding no excess reserves then such a reduction will lead to a curtailing of their lending activities in some way, and the effect is to lead to a reduction in the growth of the money supply. If the commercial banks tried to call in money from the money market then the discount houses may be forced to borrow from the Bank of England at the minimum lending rate, which if it were high, would thus force up interest rates. If the Bank of England purchases securities, then the process is reversed, leading to an increase in the commercial banks reserve assets, allowing them to expand credit. To summarise, the government can, by selling its own securities in the open market, put pressure on the banks to reduce their lending acitvities. This curtails the availability of credit. This would have the tendency to reduce aggregate spending in the economy. At the same time the operations will make interest rate changes effective by forcing the Discount Houses to borrow from the Bank of England.

Changes in reserve ratios
The government, via the Bank of England, can impose conditions upon the commercial banks with respect to the amount of their total deposits (*eligible liabilities*) that they must hold in a relatively liquid form (*eligible reserve assets*). For many years, this reserve ratio (ERA to EL) was set at $12\frac{1}{2}$ % but changed to 8% in 1981. An increase in this reserve raito compels the banks, assuming that they are not holding excess reserves, to restrict their lending activities and alternatively a lowering of the ratio allows them to expand their lending. As part of the August 1981 monetary changes mentioned earlier, this requirement for the banks to hold a minimum reserve ratio has been abolished. Again, at the time of writing it appears difficult to conclude whether this change is likely to stand the test of time.

Special deposits
The Bank of England has powers to force the banks to hold a certain percentage of their eligible liabilities in the form of special deposits which are frozen but not regarded as part of the banks reserve assets. The effect on bank lending is the same as would occur in raising the reserve assets ratio. Use has also been made of requiring the banks to hold supplementary deposits which are equal to a percentage of the excess of bank lending over a selected target figure.

Other methods
Directives, in which the Bank of England instructs the banks to follow a specific lending policy in both volume and composition between borrowers, have been another instrument used in the past. Current practice does not favour such a method.

Other controls which have a long history are the restrictions placed on *consumer hire-purchase* and *credit sale transactions*. These involve specifying minimum deposits and varying the repayment period on the finance borrowed. Such controls have never been popular with those producers whose goods are purchased on HP or credit, such as cars, electrical goods, etc. Consequently, the use of such variations in hire-purchase controls have tended to lapse in recent years.

Difficulties in implementing monetary policy
It is certainly true to say that in recent years the subject of monetary policy instruments and their effectiveness has been much debated and

scrutinised. For example, the minimum reserve assets scheme was introduced in 1971, the supplementary deposits scheme in 1973 and yet discontinued in 1981 and 1980 respectively. The 1970s also saw a rapid and variable growth in the money supply (see Table 11.4 p. 499) which led to considerable doubt as to the government's ability to control it. The Green Paper on Monetary Control published in 1980 attempted to investigate the policy instruments and their respective effectiveness in some detail. The view which has emerged is that in the medium term monetary control is to be achieved via interest rate policies and especially by an appropriate fiscal policy, in which the Public Sector Borrowing Requirement is controlled and not financed via the banking sector.

Fiscal, monetary policy and the PSBR

In reality, fiscal and monetary policies are not independent means of controlling the economy, but are inter-woven. The major economic policy objective prevailing since the late 1970s has been to reduce the level of inflation. The policy adopted depends to a great extent on the government's view as to the cause of inflation. For example, if the government is committed to the monetarist diagnosis, then the obvious policy to follow is to strictly control the rate of growth in the money supply (M3). In order to achieve this the government must tackle the reasons for this excessive increase in the money supply which is at the root of inflation. One reason suggested has been that the government has financed its own borrowing – *the Public Sector Borrowing Requirement* (PSBR) – by borrowing from the banking sector, which in turn allows the banks to expand the money supply in so far as the reserve assets base is expanded.

Conclusion – monetary v. fiscal policy

As mentioned earlier, the debate as to what policy method to follow mirrors the debate between two opposing views of the economic world. One extreme regards monetary policy as ineffective in influencing expenditure and therefore output and employment. Fiscal policy alone is effective. The other extreme view discounts the effectiveness of fiscal policy in regulating spending and places reliance on the control of the money supply. The truth, as in many cases, probably contains elements of both. Recent studies in the US suggest that in the short run both fiscal and monetary measures can have considerable influence on the level of output and prices. On the other hand, it appears that in the longer term the view is supported in that changes in the money supply do not effect real output, only the price level. It appears difficult at this stage to conclude which of the two viewpoints will be seen to triumph.

Prices and income policies

Apart from fiscal and monetary policies being used to regulate the economy, successive governments have attempted the additional approach of *regulating prices and incomes* directly rather than attempting to control inflation and unemployment via aggregate demand. In practice, most post-war policies have not been complete prices and incomes policies for two reasons. Firstly, direct control of prices has often been excluded or limited and secondly, most emphasis has been placed on controlling wages rather than entire incomes such as profits, rent and interest payments. It is perhaps more accurate to describe such policies as *wages policies*. The economic justification for such policies rests in the belief that they are a way of controlling inflation caused by wage push forces. It is also a method of controlling aggregate demand through the amount of wage settlements and thereby acting as a deterrent to excess demand inflation. In both circumstances it is seen as a way of avoiding the umemployment associated with traditional deflationary fiscal and monetary policies. Such policies are broadly of two main types, voluntary or statutory in nature.

Voluntary policies
Such policies rely on the free co-operation of both unions and employers to restrict price and wage increases to some agreed level. The first post-war policy adopted by the Labour Chancellor, Sir Stafford Cripps, in 1948 was a voluntary policy with the support of the TUC. In retrospect, this appears to have been one of the more successful policies in achieving its short-term objective of limiting wage increases. Indeed, some years later in 1956, the Conservatives themselves attempted to introduce a similar voluntary policy but failed to gain the co-operation of the TUC. During the early 1960s both Conservative and Labour governments used voluntary policies. Selwyn Lloyd introduced his 'pay pause' in 1961, although it was not voluntary as far as the public sector was concerned. The pay pause was followed by the 'guiding light' which specified a norm for wage increases which remained in operation until 1964. The Labour government of 1964 produced a negotiated 'Declaration of Intent' between employers and unions, in which a $3 - 3\frac{1}{2}$ % wages norm was accepted, along with voluntary prices restraint. The Prices and Incomes Board was set up to supervise the policy. The policy was generally unsuccessful and led in July 1966 to the Labour government introducing the second type of policy — a statutory policy.

Statutory policies
A statutory policy relies upon wage controls being enforced by legislation. This type of action included Wilson's six months' pay and prices freeze under the Prices and Incomes Act 1966. Although statutory, it was voluntarily supported by the TUC, albeit narrowly. Thereafter followed a period of six months severe restraint which in turn changed into a policy which in practice was more or less voluntary.

The history since 1970 has been one of both voluntary and statutory policies being tried. The Conservative government of 1970 initially adopted a free market policy towards incomes abolishing the Prices and

Incomes Board. But by mid-1971 they had introduced a policy of reducing wage settlements in the public sector. By November 1972, after failing to secure a voluntary policy with the TUC, the Heath government turned once more to statutory controls. This policy passed through three successive stages of restraint of varying complexity until the defeat of the government in early 1974.

The Wilson government of that year rejected all statutory wage controls but not price controls. Indeed the Price Commission established by the Counter Inflation Act, 1973, remained in operation in various forms until 1980. In the Autumn 1974 the Labour government introduced a version of a voluntary policy called 'The Social Contract' which ran until the end of 1978. By this time trade union co-operation had largely disappeared as a result of increasingly long lived restrictions on free collective bargaining.

The Conservative government elected in 1979 again adopted the Heath approach of 1970, being opposed to income policies. However it might be argued that the imposition of cash limits in the public sector is a form of wages restraint.

The effectiveness of policies

Despite the use of prices and income policies over many years, economists cannot claim to have any significant proof of their effectiveness in achieving their primary objective of defeating inflation. A consensus of opinion would be that such policies can only be effective in reducing the rate of wage increases in the short term. When the policy is abandoned, as it inevitably is, there appears to be a catching up process in wage increases which negates the effectiveness of the policy. Voluntary policies often have had a limited success when supported by TUC agreement as in the Cripps policy of 1948 but inevitably result in pressure to regain lost ground in wages. Set against the apparent limited success of such policies are numerous arguments such as their distorting effect on the labour market. Perhaps more important is the fact that the incomes policies in recent years have been politically divisive causing industrial unrest and contributing to the downfall of both the Heath and Callaghan governments. A more extreme opposing case is the suggestion that incomes policies might exacerbate inflation when specific target 'norms' relating to wage increases are fixed.

Conclusion

In this chapter the economic policy objectives which UK governments have attempted to achieve over the post-war years have been considered. As the problems have changed in importance over time so has the priority of the objectives. In recent years the twin problems of inflation and unemployment have been dominant in that respective order. To some extent as one becomes less acute, eg inflation, attention is focused on the other. Also a government does not operate its economic policy in a political vacuum. Its political philosophy, electoral pressures and fashionable economic theory all contribute to moulding the way in which the government sees the policy objectives. Having set its objectives, the government has a variety of policy instruments available to use in achieving them. Once again in the'real world, the instruments used depend upon political and economic viewpoints. A cynic might say that the failure of the UK economy to solve its basic problems is proof of the ineffectiveness of all these methods. However, the economic system in reality is subject to considerably more complex pressures and changes than any economic model. The experience of the post-war period suggests that there are elements of wisdom in all the methods. In recent years to some degree there has been a polarisation of economic views and the way forward in the future may be one of a consensus approach as in earlier years rather than the conflict of the present.

Case study on government budgetary policy

Introduction

This case study attempts to analyse the Keynesian versus Monetarist debate on control of the economy by examining the measures of one specific budget and assessing their appropriateness from both a monetarist and a Keynesian standpoint. The budget which has been chosen is that which was presented to the House of Commons in March 1981 by Sir Geoffrey Howe. Normally budgets are an annual event although in recent years additional or 'minibudgets' have been used by Chancellors wishing to modify earlier policies. The form and proposals of the budget are set out in a publication called 'The Financial Statement and Budget Report (FSBR)' which consists of an account of revenue and expenditure for the previous year, an economic forecast for the year ahead and finally the government's proposals. Howe stated that his budget objectives were threefold: firstly, to press ahead with the battle against inflation by continuing the Medium Term Financial Strategy (MTFS) set out in 1980; secondly, to correct an imbalance between consumers and industry; and thirdly, to correct the imbalance between the private and public sectors of the economy. In order to understand the budget proposals it is necessary to appreciate the objectives which the proposals are designed to achieve. These objectives in turn are based upon the government's particular views of the causes of the economic problems of inflation and unemployment. It is at this point that clear divergences of opinion emerge which see the budget measures as either appropriate or disastrous. It is proposed first to examine economic policy in relation to the 1981 budget measures.

Background to the budget

The starting point of the budget measures was the view taken by the government that the cause of inflation in the UK in the 1970s and 80s was the result of excessive expansion in the money supply, M3. Throughout the post-war period until the mid-1970s, all governments, both Conservative and Labour, followed a broad Keynesian policy of demand management. Fiscal and monetary policy instruments were used to maintain a high level of demand and capacity utilisation in the economy, with subsequent high levels of employment and low inflation. From time to time balance of payments problems imposed constraints upon these objectives and both deflation and incomes policies were used to regulate the level of aggregate demand. Up until the mid 1960s this policy was generally successful. During the 1970s the UK began increasingly to experience the problems of both rising unemployment and inflation. This new situation led to a reappraisal of traditional Keynesian policies and coincided with the emergence of the Monetarist views regarding the way the economy functions. Indeed these views had already begun to appear during the Labour administration of 1974/9. The election in 1979 of a Conservative administration publicly committed to such views of the inflationary process resulted in a government which decided to fully implement a monetarist policy.

In February 1980, the Chancellor of the Exchequer, in a letter to a Select Committee, clearly stated the government's objectives. The primary objective was to reduce inflation and thereby create conditions in which a sustained growth in both output and employment could occur. As part of this policy of improving the competitiveness of the economy, there was to be reshaping of taxation in order to encourage both enterprise and hard work. Other secondary objectives included a redrawing of the balance between the private and public sectors of the economy by a process of privatisation.

Soon afterwards in the 1980 budget the Chancellor announced the Medium Term Financial Strategy (MTFS). Target growth rates were established for the M3 money supply with a projected path for the PSBR as a percentage of gross domestic product announced for four years ahead. In order to achieve such a PSBR objective it was necessary to reduce government expenditure as a percentage of GDP. This in turn could lead to the taxation reductions announced as objectives of policy. The MTFS therefore contained government objectives for achieving specified monetary targets and using fiscal measures of taxation and expenditure (and to some extent interest rates) to support such policy targets. Such was the policy followed in 1980 − 81. In practice, the growth in the money supply target of M3, of between 7 − 11%, was well in excess of this figure. This failure to achieve the target was explained in terms of the unusual conditions prevailing during 1980. Accordingly the government decided to retain M3 as the money supply policy objective for 1981 − 1982 by setting the target range at a 6 − 10% growth rate.

The budget measures

Having outlined the background to the 1981 budget, it is now possible to examine the policy measures and the reasons for them.

In order to achieve the monetary target for 1981 − 2 and later years without resorting to excessive levels of interest rates, it was necessary to reduce the level of borrowing by the government. Therefore in the government's view, the 1981 – 2 PSBR/GDP percentage was a target of about 3% which represented a PSBR of around £7500 million at current prices. However, the depth of the recession had produced a major effect upon the size of the PSBR in a number of ways. The reduced level of economic activity produces effects on both revenue and expenditure. For example, government receipts will be diminished as unemployment reduces income tax and National Insurance payments. Companies pay less corporation tax and VAT and other expenditure taxes will similarly suffer. The recession involves higher government spending on transfer payments such as unemployment and redundancy payments.

Taking this recession effect into account, the Chancellor stated that a higher PSBR figure was permissible. A projected figure of about £14 000 million for 1981 – 2 was foreseen unless specific policy measures were taken to counter it. This the government regarded as unacceptable for several reasons. Firstly, because of the implications of financing the PSBR via the banking sector and the resulting expansionary effects on the money supply and hence inflation. Secondly, such a large amount of government borrowing would push up market interest rates which in turn would have very damaging effects upon the economy. For example, as interest rates are forced up by extra government spending, this crowds out investment spending by companies. This is of course part of the overall monetarist view which claims that it is impossible for government to create extra jobs. Keynesian economists would argue strongly against this view. Indeed such government spending will encourage, or crowd in, private spending which is the whole purpose of Keynesian demand management policies. Their argument would deny any empircial evidence that the private sector has been unable to borrow funds because of government borrowing. Furthermore they could argue that such rises in the interest rates as predicted by the Chancellor could be avoided by expanding the money supply. The monetarist retort is to claim that monetary expansions will cause only inflation not create jobs. This is once again returning to the Keynesian v. Monetarist debate as outlined in Chapter 11. The major cause of inflation to Keynesians is not the money supply expansion but cost increases leading to higher prices, to which the money supply passively responds. The money supply is demand determined. It is not the purpose of this study to return to this debate, but merely to point out that the Thatcher government accepted the former monetarist views and the crowding out theory.

In the light of such views the Chancellor regarded a PSBR of about £10 500 million or 4% of GDP as being an appropriate target for 1981 – 2. The measures necessary to achieve this were, the Chancellor said, the measure of the government's determination 'to maintain the monetary and fiscal framework necessary . . . to defeat inflation. Equally, they reflect the bill that we as a nation must meet if we are to pay for the high level of public spending'.

To achieve the PSBR target required a combined policy of reducing the rate of growth in public expenditure and increasing revenue from taxation. Public expenditure plans are outlined in the government's 'White Paper on Public Expenditure', published on budget day. Although an integral part of overall strategy, it is not proposed to discuss these expenditure proposals in this study, but concentrate on the major budget proposals. The Chancellor announced new ways of financing public borrowing which he believed would not be inflationary, such as a greater contribution from National Savings, a new indexed gilt-edged security specifically for pension funds and a new BNOC oil bond. Most of the measures however were aimed at raising government revenue from taxation.

Taxation measures
In raising taxation the Chancellor was expecting to receive an extra £3611 million during 1981 – 82. In selecting taxes it was the personal sector to which the Chancellor turned rather than the business sector, although the oil and banking sector was an exception to this. Of the taxes levied on the personal sector, income tax is by far the most important. No major change was made on income tax, the tax rates being left unchanged. However, the retention of the 1980 – 81 main allowances and thresholds without adjustments for inflation, meant a 'back door' tax rise for many people as money incomes rose. Full indexation would have cost the Exchequer about £2500 million in lost tax.

This decision not to increase tax allowance was somewhat contrary to the government's election pledge to significantly reduce income taxes to promote enterprise and effort. Politically, a rise in income tax rates would have been very difficult to carry through with any credibility. But having decided against such changes meant that expenditure taxes had to bear the increases which were required. Since as shown in Table 10.1 p. 00 these are much less valuable revenue raisers than income taxes, the increases had to be significant. Excise duties bore the major impact with increases on alcohol, tobacco, petrol, diesel fuel, cigarette lighters and matches. These increases were indeed significant as shown below:

Examples of tax changes on certain product prices in 1981 budget

Taxation change		Extra Revenue Forecast for 1981 – 2 in £million
Spirits	– 60p on a bottle	60
Beer	– 4p on a pint	370
Wine	– 12p on a bottle)	67
Fortified wines	– 25p on a bottle)	
Tobacco	– 14p on 20 cigarettes	500
Petrol	– 20p on a gallon	910
Diesel	– 20p on a gallon	270
Matches	– $\frac{1}{2}$p on a box)	15
Lighters	– 35p on a lighter)	

Source: Economic Progress Report, March 1981

Further increases in taxation were obtained from raising the vehicle excise duty by about 15% together with extending the 10% car tax to motor cycles. The total increase in customs and excise revenue was expected to be around £2200 million, plus another £225 million from vehicle excise duty. The inflationary impact of these changes was predicted to be about 2%. No increases in VAT were announced by the Chancellor.

Before setting out other budget measures it is worth explaining why the Chancellor selected expenditure taxes as the main revenue raisers. Basically there were two reasons. Income tax was precluded because of the reasons previously stated, ie the government's attitude towards reducing income taxes to stimulate effort and initiative. Expenditure taxes are regarded as being a less obvious method of taxation and therefore produce less harmful effects on effort and enterprise. Another supposed advantage is that they are avoidable by consumers who decide to save rather than spend. Having selected expenditure taxes, the obvious targets were those products with relatively inelastic demand patterns. A product such as beer, which is inelastic, is ideal from the Chancellor's viewpoint (and also the sellers). The 4p extra tax on beer will result in higher prices to the consumer. How much of this extra tax the seller can pass forward to the consumer will depend upon beer's elasticity of demand. If demand is perfectly inelastic the full 4p could be passed on without having any effect upon sales whatsoever. The seller's sales revenue is constant and the Chancellor receives the full amount of the tax revenue (4p times sales). Of course most products are more likely to have a demand which is relatively inelastic rather than perfectly inelastic. In this case not all of the 4p will be passed on to the drinker by the suppliers since the price increase does decrease demand (but less proportionately than the price increase). Since sales have diminished the Chancellor's tax revenue is not as great as in the first case. This explains why the inelastic range of products are suitable tax targets for the Chancellor to select time and time again. To some extent also, the selection of tobacco and alcohol can be justified since these are products with important externalities.

Taxation is being used in its role to influence consumption patterns away from socially less desirable products. While not suggesting that this is a real motive behind the Chancellor's action, it is probably easier to justify politically than an increase in VAT. As for the company sector, the Chancellor said that he recognised the hard-pressed manufacturing industry as being unable to bear any tax increases. Those changes which were introduced were generally designed to ease some of the industry's tax burden. For example, the limit up to which the lower 40% rate of Corporation tax was payable by small companies was increased by £10 000 to £80 000. The limit for the full 52% rate was raised to £200 000. New tax incentives were to be introduced to attract individual investors to establish new businesses and a business opportunities programme was to be launched. The overall effect of these measures was aimed to correct what the Government believed was an imbalance between consumers and industry as stated in the second budgetary objective. The Chancellor said that while the incomes of most people had been rising in both money and real terms, the profits of companies had been greatly reduced, with serious implications for employment and investment.

The exceptions in the company sector were, firstly, the proposals to introduce a Supplementary Petroleum Duty (SPD) on North Sea Oil and Gas which, with changes in Petroleum Revenue Tax (PRT) reliefs, was expected to yield over £1000 million in tax. Secondly, a once and for all tax of $2\frac{1}{2}$ % on certain bank deposits was imposed and would yield £400 million. This action was taken in response to the high profit levels earned by the banks, making them an island of profit amid the general recession in industry and commerce.

Tax changes apart, the Chancellor announced various changes aimed to help specific groups. Pensions and child benefits were to be raised later in the year. Mobility allowance and other measures for the disabled were improved.

Budget measures summary

From the Chancellor's viewpoint, the budgetary proposals were expected to achieve the initial objectives stated at the beginning of this study. To continue the battle against inflation and promote growth and employment it was necessary to press ahead with the Medium Term Financial Strategy with its M3 and PSBR targets. The measures were aimed at reducing the PSBR by about £3300 million to achieve the 1981 – 2 target of some £10 500 million. To achieve this it was necessary to raise the burden of taxation so that reduced government borrowing would lead to lower interest rates which in turn would stimulate growth and employment. The second and third objectives were to be achieved within the overall strategy by shifting the tax balance towards consumers and moving the public sector/private sector balance more in favour of the latter.

The Chancellor ended by stating his belief that the future would hold out the prospect of lower inflation, lower unemployment and lower taxation burdens. When the economic recovery began, the economy would be in a much fitter state to take advantage of the upturn.

The budgetary policy – a critical analysis

Up to this point the 1980 budget and the policies underlying it have been explained in terms of the overall policy views expressed in the monetarist approach. If this economic viewpoint is accepted then the budget can be seen as a package designed to achieve its objectives. If however the alternative Keynesian approach is adopted then the budget measures are totally inappropriate from every standpoint. To conclude this summary it is proposed to examine the budget measures from such a viewpoint. Perhaps the most extraordinary thing about the budget was the way in which the PSBR was placed at the forefront of economic objectives. It was this PSBR target which had been a major influence on government policy since 1979 and continued to be despite evidence that monetarism had not worked.

Briefly, a Keynesian economist would start from the position as outlined in Chapter 11 p. 507. It is the level of demand which determines output and employment and the cause of an unacceptable level of unemployment is an obvious lack of aggregate demand in the economy. If no action is taken by government then the prospects will be for a continuing rise in unemployment levels. What is required is a policy of reflation to stimulate aggregate demand. Such stimulus could come from any component of demand, consumption, investment, exports or government spending. In such circumstances a Keynesian would argue that it is government expenditure that must lead the way. Increases in government spending programmes such as rail electrification, etc.

The CBI, as the principal representative of employers, at its 1981 conference suggested a modest reflation of about £1500 million, but many Keynesian economists would argue for a much *larger* reflation of up to £5000 million. In addition to extra government spending, consumer expenditure should be stimulated by a policy of tax reductions, not increases as in the 1981 budget. Such policies would increase the circular flow of income via the multiplier process by increasing injections (G) and reducing withdrawals (T). Output would be stimulated and unemployment fall. Monetarist critics respond to such a policy by saying that while some temporary stimulus in output might be achieved, the major result would be to cause inflation to increase, so deepening the recession. But would an expanding PSBR inevitably lead to a growth in the money supply? Most of the growth in the money supply had come not from excessive financing of the PSBR via the banks, *but* from long-term gilt-edged securities sold to the non-bank private sector. The impetus for M3 growth had been provided by private sector borrowing from the banks. The money supply is demand determined by companies requiring finance for working capital and individuals borrowing to finance expenditure. The severity of the recession forced many companies to rely on such bank finance to survive. Indeed public borrowing can slow down money growth. For instance if the government buys cars for use by public employees from a private sector organisation, such purchases may be financed by selling government securities. A private company is much more likely to finance its fleet purchase of cars by bank lending, which expands the money supply. Clearly then the money supply is difficult to control as the Thatcher government found.

Keynesians would argue that the purpose of reflation is to crowd in resources from the private sector by increasing the level of demand and encouraging investment via the accelerator principle as well as making savings available for investment as the level of income rises. The more sophisticated argument that financial crowding can occur seems equally dubious since there is no evidence to suggest that the private sector has been unable or unwilling to borrow as a direct result of government borrowing. A Keynesian conclusion is that what the economy required in 1981 was the exact opposite of the budget measures implemented. The danger of pursuing a rigid monetarist policy is that much of the manufacturing base of the economy can be destroyed. The consequence would be a massive process of de-industrialisation. In the event of an upturn occurring in the economy the danger lies in the prospect that it would be met from imports, resulting in a severe impact upon the balance of payments, exchange rate problems and a possible inflationary stimulus. As the economy expands the size of the PSBR can be reduced as tax revenue increases and the recession-linked expenditure decreases. The inflationary danger is only apparent when the economy approaches its full employment capacity. Critics of monetarism see conclusive evidence in the failure of these policies to achieve their objectives. Following the budget, inflation remained in double figures. By the summer of 1981, unemployment had reached a post-war record of nearly 3 million with its resultant social and economic consequences. Keynesian critics argued fiercely that the time for a drastic change of policy was apparent. The objects as set out by the MTFS were both unworkable and could not be achieved by the government. The budget policy measures were severely deflationary and so produced an even deeper recession.

Conclusion

This study illustrates that policy objectives and measures are very much areas of debate between economists, politicians and observers of the economic scene. The implementation of government economic policy clearly has powerful and practical effects upon everyone's lives. Keynes expressed this perfectly in the last chapter to his General Theory when he said '. . . the ideas of economists . . ., both when they are right and when they are wrong, are more powerful than is commonly understood. Indeed the world is ruled by little else. Practical men, who believe themselves to be quite exempt from any intellectual influences, are usually the slaves of some defunct economist'.

Glossary of terms

Ab initio from the beginning.

Accord and satisfaction accord is agreement. Satisfaction is consideration, eg a new agreement supported by consideration necessary to vary an existing contract.

Activity rate the proportion of the working population in paid employment.

Accelerator relationship between the variation in the rate of change of output or sales and changes in the level of investment.

Administered price pricing policies of monopolists and oligopolists, based on considerations other than marginal cost ignoring free market forces.

Administrative tribunals tribunals which exercise jurisdiction conferred on them by Parliament, outside the hierarchy of courts, eg Industrial Injuries Tribunals.

Advisory, Conciliation and Arbitration Service (ACAS) body established under Employment Protection Act 1975 to encourage the extension and development of collective bargaining.

Agency: the granting of authority to one person (the agent) to act on behalf of another (the principal), eg to enter into contracts.

Aggregate demand total effective demand or expenditure of all buyers of capital and consumer goods within a given market or the economy as a whole.

Aggregate supply total physical volume of goods and services coming on to a given market or the economy as a whole.

Anticipatory breach occurs where one party to a contract, prior to performance, declares their intention to break the contract and thus gives the other party the option to repudiate the contract at the time of the breach or the time set for performance.

Arbitration means of settling disputes by referral to an impartial person or body. Both parties should agree in advance to accept the arbitration procedure.

Articles of Association statutory regulations which govern the internal organisation and operation of a company.

Bailment the temporary transfer of the possession of property from the owner to some other person for a specific purpose, eg hiring.

Balance of payments the accounts covering all financial transactions between the UK and the rest of the world.

Balance of trade the relationship between a country's payments for visible imports and the value of its visible exports. Known as the visible balance.

Balanced budget situation where government expenditure is exactly equal to the revenue it receives.

Bankruptcy the legal process regulated by statute by which an individual or unincorporated association which has become insolvent has its assets realised to meet its liabilities.

Bills of exchange an unconditional order in writing for the making of a specific payment at an agreed date, eg used in international trade as a form of commercial IOU.

Barrister a lawyer specialising in advocacy and having the right to appear before all courts.

Binding precedent the principle of law expressed within a previous judgement of a court which will bind a subsequent court faced with a similar factual situation.

Board of directors those persons responsible for the formulation and direction of company policy appointed and removable by shareholders.

Breach of contract the failure to fulfil any obligation undertaken in a contract.

Budget line line linking together all possible combinations of expenditure within a given income.

Call a demand for the payment of an unpaid amount due on shares which are not fully paid up.

Caveat emptor let the buyer beware.

Certificate of Incorporation document creating a registered company, issued by the Registrar of Companies, when the statutory requirements in relation to formation have been complied with.

Ceteris paribus other things remaining unchanged.

Circuit judges judges appointed under the Courts Act 1971, with authority to sit in the County Court and the Crown Court.

Circular flow of income the flow of income and expenditure between the different sectors in the economy such as consumer expenditure and factor payments.

Circulating capital the stock, and cash-in-hand of any organisation, and any debts owed to it.

Civil law expression used to describe all law other than criminal law.

Class rights rights attaching to differing classes of shares.

Codes of practice rules of guidance with respect to the requirements of a statute not having statutory effect but may be used in evidence.

Collective agreement agreement reached after negotiations between trade unions and employers or their associations.

The common law all law other than that contained within statute that has been created by the operation of the doctrine of judicial precedent.

Comparative advantage the specialisation in the production of goods which can be provided most profitably to the mutual benefit of the parties concerned, eg in international trade.

Collective responsibility the principle by which individual cabinet members must abide by decisions taken by the cabinet as a whole.

Complementary product products which are normally used in conjunction with one another.

Composition an alternative to bankruptcy whereby a debtor agrees with his creditors to pay a percentage in the £ of debts owing.

Concentration ratio the percentage of value of sales/output accounted for by a specific number of organisations in an industry, eg five firm concentration ratio.

Conciliation officer a civil servant having the responsibility to attempt mediation in industrial disputes.

Condition a term that is fundamental to a contract, the breach of which will entitle the innocent party to repudiate the contract and/or recover damages.

Consideration the value transferred under a contract which may be in a tangible or intangible form, eg a money payment or the promise of a money payment.

Consolidated fund the major financial account kept at the Bank of England by the government into which receipts are paid and from which payments are made.

Constructive dismissal a form of dismissal in which the employee leaves his employer's service as a result of the conduct of the employer.

Consumer surplus the excess of the price a consumer is willing to pay for a product over the price he or she actually pays.

Consumption function function relating aggregate consumption expenditure to the level of income.

Corporation tax tax charged on the trading profits of a company.

Contract a legally enforceable agreement.

Contra proferentem rule of construction used by the courts to determine the validity of contractual terms which are ambiguous.

Contracts of adhesion a contract usually in a standard form based upon terms formulated by one of the parties.

Contracts of record contract recorded by the court, eg a judgement debt.

Contract of employment a contract under which an individual agrees to provide his or her labour in consideration of receiving payment from the employer.

Corporation an artificial body created under the law having its own legal capacity.

Cost push inflation inflation caused by increases in the costs of production.

County court an inferior Civil Court exercising a wide jurisdiction subject to financial limits.

Court of appeal part of the Supreme Court of Judicature having the jurisdiction to hear both civil and criminal appeals from first instance courts.

Criminal law the law dealing with acts that are forbidden by the state and are punished by the state.

Crown court a court established under the Courts Act 1971 having exclusive jurisdiction over all trials on indictment. It sits with a judge and jury.

Current account first part of the balance of payments account dealing with transactions in goods and services.

Cyclical unemployment unemployment linked with the downswing of the trade cycle resulting from a fall in aggregate demand.

Damages financial compensation awarded to an injured party.

Debenture a document recognising a company's indebtedness to a creditor.

Deed a formal written contract signed sealed and delivered by the party or parties to it.

Defamation a tort which consists of the publication of a statement which reduces a person's reputation or standing.

Deflation a situation where prices and money incomes are falling. Also used to describe a reduction in the rate of production of goods and services. May be government induced.

Deflationary gap amount of additional expenditure necessary to restore national income to its full employment level.

Delegated legislation legislation produced by a person or body to whom Parliament has delegated the power.

Demand management government measures aimed at regulating the level of aggregate demand.

Demand pull inflation inflation induced by excess aggregate demand in relation to aggregate supply.

Derived demand where the level of demand for one commodity or factor of production is dependent upon the level of demand for a final product or service.

Development areas economically depressed areas where the government offers special incentives to encourage the growth of industry.

Discount houses financial institutions which buy bills of exchange at less than face value and hold them until maturity.

Dividend profits of a company distributed to shareholders when declared.

Easement a right enjoyed over another's land.

Economic rent the payment over and above the essential supply price (transfer earnings) of a factor of production.

Economies of scale the reduction of costs of production per unit of output gained by the increased size of the plant, organisation or industry.

Elasticity of demand and supply
1 responsiveness of demand to changes in price/price of other goods/income, eg
% change in quantity demanded

% change in price.
2 responsiveness of supply to changes in price/price or other goods/factors of production, eg
% change in quantity supplied

% change in price.

Equality clause a term implied by statute into a contract of service aimed at preventing discrimination between the sexes.

Exchange rate the rate by which one currency can be exchanged for another.

Exclusion clauses contractual terms contractual terms designed to exclude or limit liabilities arising under the contract.

Explicit costs costs which are in the form of a payment by cash or kind.

Express terms terms in a contract that are actually agreed upon by the parties.

Factoring the activity in which a specialised company (the Factor) undertakes the debt collection of another in return for an immediate payment made to the initial holder of the debt.

Factors of production the resources which are combined in the production of goods and services. Traditionally they are land, labour and capital, with enterprise an optional fourth.

Fee simple an estate in land of uncertain duration that is associated with absolute ownership, and is more commonly referred to as a freehold estate.

Fiduciary issue the part of the banknote issue not backed by gold.

Firm the description applied to a partnership by the Partnership Act 1890.

Fiscal policy policy of using taxation and government expenditure to control the economy.

Fiscal stabilisers government tax and expenditure measures operating counter cyclically increasing government deficits during slumps and increasing government's surpluses during booms, thus stabilising the state of the economy.

Fixed factor factors of production which cannot be altered very easily in the short run, usually referring to land or capital.

Fixed charge specific assets of an organisation identified as a security for a loan preventing the owner from dealing with those assets.

Frictional unemployment unemployment resulting from lack of perfect mobility of labour in the economy.

Fraud something said, done, or omitted by a person in order to deceive another for personal gain.

Fraudulent misrepresentation a misrepresentation made knowingly without honest belief in its truth.

Frustration a change in the circumstances occurring subsequent to the contract which makes performance radically different to that envisaged by the parties when the contract was made.

Fundamental breach contractual breach going to the root of a contract which automatically brings the contract to an end.

Full line forcing refusal of an organisation to supply certain of its products unless the buyer stocks the complete range of the organisation's products.

Goodwill an intangible asset which is the benefit gained by a company through its reputation and business connections.

Gross misconduct conduct by an employee sufficient to justify a summary dismissal.

Gross national product the value of all goods and services produced in a country during one year at factor cost, including net income from abroad.

The government body of persons who are responsible for the administration of a nation's affairs.

Health and safety commission principal body set up under the Health and Safety At Work Act 1974 charged with the duty of assisting and encouraging those affected to carry out the purposes of the Act.

Health and safety executive set up under HSWA 1974 having responsibility for enforcement of the Act.

High court the term applied to the first instance civil courts of the Supreme Court of Judicature. For administrative purposes the Court comprises three divisions – Queens Bench, Chancery and Family.

Hire purchase a contract under which a person (the debtor) agrees to hire goods by installments over a period and having the right to exercise an option to purchase the goods on payment of the final instalment.

Implied terms clauses which may be implied into contracts under the common law or by statute.

Implicit/imputed cost the opportunity cost of inputs owned by the organisation which have alternative uses.

Improvement notice notice made ordering the remedy of a contravention of the Health and Safety At Work Act 1974.

Income the monetary value of goods and services accruing to an individual/organisation/economy.

Income effect the effect of a price change on purchasing power. If a price falls, a consumer can buy the same amount for less money and vice versa.

Incomes policy government policy of restraining the rise in incomes in order to prevent the inflationary effect. Can be compulsory or voluntary.

Indifference curve analysis a study of consumer demand behaviour using curves linking the points where a consumer is indifferent between one commodity and another.

Inflation a rise in the general level of prices (see Cost Push/Demand Pull inflation).

Inflationary gap the excess of aggregate demand over that which is required to produce full employment income.

Injunction an order of the court designed to prohibit conduct (prohibitory) or requiring conduct (mandatory).

Innocent misrepresentation a misrepresentation that is neither fraudulent or negligent.

Insolvency a situation where the liabilities of an organisation or individual are greater than the total value of its assets.

Integration the amalgamation of organisations vertically, horizontally or laterally in the production process.

Inter se between themselves.

Intestate property undisposed of by will.

Investment and capital account account on the balance of payments which details investment and capital flows.

Investment function relationship between the level of investment and its determinants.

Invisible trade trade involving services such as insurance, freight haulage, and expenditure by tourists.

Invitation to treat an inducement designed to encourage an offer.

Issued capital the part of authorised capital allotted in shares that are subscribed.

Judgement debt some debt which is due under a court order.

Jury a body of persons selected and sworn to give a verdict on some matter according to the evidence presented to them.

Lands tribunal a tribunal concerned with the compulsory acquisition of land, having the duty to assess compensation.

Land registry a central registry responsible for the registration of transfers of land.

Leasehold a form of landholding consisting of an estate of fixed or certain duration.

Lien the right to retain the property belonging to another until debts due from that person have been satisfied.

Limited liability the principle of law which provides that the liability of a shareholder in a company is limited to the extent of the unpaid amount on that person's shareholding.

Limited partnership a partnership created under the Limited Partnership Act 1907 in which there must be a partner whose liability is limited and a general partner having unlimited liability.

Litigation the process by which legal action is taken by one party against another.

Liquidator a person appointed to oversee the winding-up of a company.

Liquidity the extent to which an asset can be readily converted into cash.

Local commissioner for administration a person appointed under the Local Government Act 1974 to hear complaints of injustice caused by maladministration alleged against certain public bodies.

Long run the length of time necessary for all factors of production to become variable.

Loss leaders the practice of offering goods for sale at lower than normal retail price, usually loss making, in order to attract customers into a store.

Marginal propensity to consume the fraction of each extra unit of income that is spent on consumption, ie

$$\frac{\text{marginal change in consumption}}{\text{marginal change in income}}.$$

Marginal propensity to save the fraction of each extra unit of income that is saved, ie

$$\frac{\text{marginal change in saving}}{\text{marginal change in income}}.$$

Marginal utility theory theory on consumer demand behaviour based on the extra amount of satisfaction gained from a small increase in a commodity consumed.

Memorandum of association the document containing the constitution of a company which must be lodged with the Registrar of Companies prior to incorporation.

Mens rea an element found in most crimes, representing the intention necessary to constitute the offence.

Minimum lending rate (MLR) the minimum rate at which the Bank of England will discount first class bills of exchange.

Monetary policy the management of the economy via the control of the money supply, and the cost and availability of credit.

Monopoly strictly a situation where a market has only one seller of a commodity and so determines price and output (price maker). In practice, under present legislation, refers to any dominant supplier which has excess of 25% of the market share.

Monopolostic competition competition between many organisations supplying similar products which are not perfect substitutes due to product differentiation.

Monopsony situation with one buyer in a market.

The multiplier ratio showing the effect on total employment/income of a change in a component of aggregate demand.

Mutual coincidence of needs the situation in which two parties in a bartering situation each have what the other party requires.

Negligence this may be either a state of mind sufficient to constitute the mens rea of a criminal offence, or a separate tort.

Negligent misrepresentation a false statement made by a person who has no reasonable grounds to believe that the statement is true.

Nemo dat quod non habet a principle of law which states that a person cannot transfer rights of ownership that he or she does not possess.

Normal profit the amount of profit needed to keep an organisation in a certain mode of production. The level varies according to the risk and difficulty involved in the industry.

Nominal/authorised capital the amount of capital declared by a new company on registration that it is authorised to raise.

Oligopoly a highly concentrated market situation where there are only a few organisations supplying the market. Each has a significant economic influence.

Open market operations the sale or purchase of government stocks on the open market by the Bank of England. Used as part of monetary policy to control money supply.

Opportunity cost the cost of an alternative foregone; the cost of the sacrifice of alternative activities.

Optimal production the level of output at which all factors of production are combined in the most efficient way. Average costs of production will be at their lowest point.

Ordinary shares referred to as the 'equity share capital of a company' such shares usually have voting rights and entitle holders to a dividend after preference shareholders.

Paid up capital the amount of issued capital that is actually subscribed by shareholders.

Parliamentary commissioner for administration a person created under statute who investigates complaints from members of the public about maladministration of government departments and public authorities.

Passing off a tort whereby one party attempts to pass off goods as those of another party in order to deceive.

Patents the granting of exclusive rights of sale, use, or production, of a new invention. A patent holder has a legal monopoly in the patented product.

Perfect/imperfect market
1 market where the product is homogeneous and easily transferable, there are many buyers and sellers, and there is perfect information. No one buyer or seller can influence the market. Single market price determined by interaction of supply and demand;
2 market where above conditions are not satisfied.

Persuasive precedent those precedents which are not binding, such as the decisions of Commonwealth Courts.

Planned/command economy economy where all economic activity, such as production and distribution, is decided by a central planning authority, and not by market forces.

Planning permission permission to carry out development to land sought from the local planning authority.

Precedent a previous judicial decision.

Preferred debts these are the liabilities that rank highest in the order of payment of debts in the event of a settlement following a bankruptcy.

Preference shares a characteristic of such shares is that they entitle their holders to preferential dividends.

Price the value of a good or service in terms of other goods, normally expressed in terms of money.

Price leadership theory in an oligopoly market, the practice whereby one organisation assumes price leadership which is followed by the other suppliers.

Price makers market a market where one or more producer is large enough to influence the market price by their individual actions (monopoly or oligopoly).

Price takers market competitive market where no individual producer is large enough to influence the market price, and therefore accepts price determined by market forces (perfect competition).

Prima facie on the face of it; on first impression.

Private costs and benefits
Social costs and benefits
1 cost or benefits accruing to an individual or organisation as a result of their own economic activity;
2 costs or benefits to society resulting from economic activity, eg pollution or education provision.
Also referred to as externalities.

Private limited company a registered company limited shares which is not a public limited company.

Privity of contract the principle that only persons who are party to a contract can incur liabilities under that contract.

Production any activity satisfying human wants for which payment is received.

Production function the relationship between the input of factors of production and the output of actual product, per unit of time.

Prospectus document issued by a company wishing to raise capital by public issue of shares.

Public limited company a registered company limited by shares which states that it is such in its Memorandum and in its name, and has an authorised capital of at least £50 000, of which at least $\frac{1}{4}$ is paid up.

Public sector borrowing requirement (PSBR) the total amount of money which the public sector must borrow in a year.

531

Quantity theory theory relating the price level to the money supply, velocity of circulation of money, and the number of transactions, ie

$$P = \frac{MV}{T}$$

Quantum meruit literally 'how much he has deserved.' Used to claim damages by a person who has performed work under a contract which has been broken.

Quotas restrictions imposed by government on imports or exports, either in terms of quantity or time, or both.

Real property property originally protected by a real action giving a person the right to recover the thing lost. The expression applies only to freehold land.

Reciprocal trading the practice whereby trading organisations agree to purchase each other's products exclusively.

Rent a payment by one person to another in exchange for the use of an asset, eg land or buildings.

Repudiation the expression describing the action of a person who has rejected or disclaimed his contractual liabilities.

Resale price maintenance the practice whereby a supplier stipulates a retail price for his product which must be adhered to by shopkeepers and dealers.

Reserve currency foreign currency held by a country as part of its reserves, that is generally acceptable to meet international financial commitments, eg dollars, sterling.

Res ipsa loquitur 'the thing speaks for itself'. A rule of evidence applicable in determining liability in negligence.

Restraint of trade a restriction on a person's freedom to carry on his chosen business trade or profession.

Restrictive trade practices trade practices which are anti-competitive.

Revealed preference theory theory of consumer demand based on the actual choices revealed by the consumer in relation to alternative purchases.

Seasonal unemployment unemployment caused by seasonal variations in demand, eg hotel staff, building employees.

Shareholders a member of a company who has contributed capital and has been allotted shares in that company.

Short run period in which fixed factors of production cannot be varied.

Siege economy government policy imposing strict barriers such as tarrifs and quotas to isolate domestic economy from foreign competitive influences.

Simple contracts any contract not made by deed.

Sole trader business form in which ownership is by one person who is responsible for providing capital, bearing risk, and making all management decisions.

Special deposits deposits called in from the commercial banks by the Bank of England and then frozen. Used to curtail monetary expansion.

Special drawing rights (SDRs) allocations of foreign currency distributed by the IMF to its members in proportion to their quotas. They become part of that country's reserves and increases international liquidity.

Special resolution a decision passed by not less than three-quarters of the members of a company entitled to vote.

Specialty contracts contracts that are under seal.

Specific goods goods which are identified and agreed upon at the time a contract of sale is made.

Specific performance court order requiring a party to perform contractual obligations.

Standard form contract contracts which set out the terms in a standard form.

Statute an Act of Parliament.

Structural unemployment an extreme form of frictional unemployment resulting from structural changes in demand and supply. Caused by occupational immobility of labour.

Subpoena a writ which directs a person to give evidence and in some cases bring relevant documents.

Substitution effect the effect of a price change on the demand for a product in which a consumer substitutes an alternative product.

Substitute product a product which is regarded by the consumer as an identical alternative for another.

Summary dismissal instant dismissal of an employee.

Tariffs duties imposed by one country on products it imports from another country. Used to protect home industries or to reduce total import bill.

Tax multiplier relationship between changes

in the level of taxation and the level of aggregate demand.

Tender an offer to undertake some work or supply some goods at a stated price.

Tort a civil wrong which arises from breach of a duty which is imposed by law.

Transfer earnings the amount a factor of production would earn in its next best paid alternative employment.

Transfer payments payments made by public authorities to other groups in society not in respect of goods or any service rendered, eg student grants, old age pensions.

Treasury bill security issued by the Treasury to finance government short term borrowing requirements. Also used as part of monetary policy.

Uberrimae fidei of the utmost good faith. Applies to disclosure of relevant information for certain contracts, eg insurance contracts.

Ultra vires 'beyond the powers'. Applied to the actions of a corporate body which acts outside its stated powers.

Unfair dismissal dismissal of an employee which is unjustifiable by statute.

Utility the satisfaction derived from a good or service.

Variable factor a factor of production of which the supply can be altered in the short period, eg labour.

Vicarious liability substituted liability, arising, for example, under the employer/employee relationship.

Visible trade the import and export of tangible goods, as opposed to trade in services.

Wage drift the difference between nationally agreed wage increases and actual increases in earnings. Generally caused by localised bonus or overtime agreements.

Warranties terms in a contract, the breach of which gives rise to an action in damages.

Winding-up the process describing the dissolution of a company.

Wrongful dismissal dismissal of an employee in a wrongful manner.

Index

538